W9-BGT-096

The Power Law

The POWER LAW

Venture Capital and the
Making of the New Future

SEBASTIAN MALLABY

A Council on Foreign Relations Book

PENGUIN PRESS NEW YORK 2022

PENGUIN PRESS
An imprint of Penguin Random House LLC
penguinrandomhouse.com

Photo Credits:
page 1: photo courtesy of Arthur Rock & Company; page 2: courtesy of Don Valentine Family; page 3: San Francisco Chronicle/Hearst Newspapers via Getty Images; page 4, top: photo courtesy of Daniel Kaufman; page 4, bottom: Ann E. Yow-Dyson/Getty Images; page 5, top: photo courtesy of Jim Swartz; page 5, bottom, and page 7: AP Photo/Paul Sakuma; page 6, top: The Asahi Shimbun via Getty Images; page 6, bottom: James D. Wilson/Liaison Agency via Getty Images; page 8, top: photograph by Karl Chiu; page 8, bottom: Xaume Olleros/Bloomberg via Getty Images; page 9: © Robyn Twomey/Redux; page 10, top: courtesy of Sequoia Capital China; page 10, bottom: Paul McKellar; page 11: photo courtesy of Tiger Global; page 12: photo courtesy of the Breakthrough Prize; page 13: Jeffery Newbury; page 14, top: photo courtesy of Michael Moritz; page 14, bottom, and page 15, top: photo courtesy of Sequoia Capital; page 15, bottom: photo by Brian Ach/Getty Images for *TechCrunch*; page 16, top: Cole Wilson/The New York Times/Redux; page 16, center: Chris Ratcliffe/Bloomburg via Getty Images; page 16, bottom: PETER EARL MCCOLLOUGH/The New York Times/Redux

ISBN 9780593491782 (international edition)

LIBRARY OF CONGRESS CATALOGING-IN-PUBLICATION DATA
Names: Mallaby, Sebastian, author.
Title: The power law : venture capital and the making of the new future / Sebastian Mallaby.
Description: New York : Penguin Press, 2022. | "A Council on Foreign Relations Book." |
   Includes bibliographical references and index. | Identifiers: LCCN 2021038348 (print) |
   LCCN 2021038349 (ebook) | ISBN 9780525559993 (hardcover) | ISBN 9780525560005 (ebook)
Subjects: LCSH: Venture capital—California—San Francisco Bay Area. | High-technology industries—
   Finance. | New business enterprises—Finance. | Technological innovations—Economic aspects.
Classification: LCC HG4963 .M334 2022 (print) | LCC HG4963 (ebook) | DDC 332/.041540973—dc23
LC record available at https://lccn.loc.gov/2021038348
LC ebook record available at https://lccn.loc.gov/2021038349

Printed in the United States of America
10   9   8   7   6   5   4   3   2   1

Book design by Daniel Lagin

To Zanny

Most people think improbable ideas are unimportant. The only thing that's important is something that's improbable.

—Vinod Khosla

Silicon Valley is gripped by the cult of the individual. But those individuals represent the triumph of the network.

—Matt Clifford

The great challenge at venture partnerships is that the principals must refrain from killing each other.

—Michael Moritz

Spend as little as you can, because every dollar of the investor's money you get will be taken out of your ass.

—Paul Graham

John, venture capital, that's not a real job. It's like being a real estate agent.

—Intel's Andy Grove,
addressing John Doerr

Contents

The Power Law

Introduction

Unreasonable People

N ot far from the headquarters of Silicon Valley's venture-capital industry, which is clustered along Palo Alto's Sand Hill Road, Patrick Brown strode out into his yard on the Stanford University campus. Atop a little hill behind his house, Brown got down on his hands and knees, a shaggy fifty-four-year-old professor in a T-shirt, peering at the vegetation through rounded glasses. Proceeding delicately, like a detective collecting samples that might yield a vital clue, Brown began digging out the roots of some wild clover plants.[1] It might impress the ordinary gardener to know that those roots would soon yield $3 million.

Brown was one of the world's leading geneticists. In 1995, his lab had published pioneering work on DNA microarrays, which help distinguish between normal and cancerous tissue. He had been elected to the National Academy of Sciences and the National Academy of Medicine. He was the recipient of a Howard Hughes award, which guaranteed no-strings-attached research funding. But his objective on that hilltop had nothing to do with genetics. The year was 2010, and Brown was using a sabbatical to plot the downfall of the meat-industrial complex.

A friend had set him on this path by means of a stray comment. Possessed of a keen environmental conscience, Brown had been worrying that animal husbandry occupied one-third of the world's land, causing significant greenhouse gas emissions, water degradation, and a loss of biodiversity. The planet was clearly going to need a better kind of food for the growing population of the twenty-first century. Then Brown's friend mentioned that if you could make a vegetarian burger that tasted better than a beef burger, the free market would magically take care of the problem. Adventurous restaurants would serve it, and then McDonald's would serve it, and pretty soon you could eliminate meat from the food system.[2]

The more Brown pondered this, the more he grew agitated. *If* you could make a yummier vegetarian burger? *Of course* you could make a yummier vegetarian burger! Why was nobody treating this as a solvable problem? "People just figured we have this insanely destructive system and it's just never going to go away," Brown fumed. "They thought, 'Bummer, but there you are.'"

In most places and at most points in human history, Brown's epiphany would have been inconsequential. But, as Brown himself reflected later, he had "the very good fortune of living in the epicenter of venture capital."[3] Because Stanford sat at the heart of Silicon Valley, its golf course laid out along the edge of Sand Hill Road, Brown was digging up his yard with a clear purpose. Those clover roots contained heme, an iron-carrying molecule found in hemoglobin, which gives blood its red color. If Brown could show how this plant molecule could mimic the properties of bloody meat, there was a good chance that a venture capitalist would fund a plantburger company.

Brown dissected the clover roots with a razor blade and blended them up to extract and culture the juices. Pretty soon, he had what he needed to fashion a vegetarian burger that smelled and sizzled and dripped and squished like 100 percent Grade A beef. "I got to a point where, though I didn't have much data, I'd enough to go and talk to some venture-capital companies—of which there are a ridiculous number in Silicon Valley—and hit them for some money."

A scientist friend mentioned that Vinod Khosla, a venture capitalist who ran the eponymous Khosla Ventures, was interested in environmentally friendly, "cleantech" projects. What he didn't mention was that Khosla was also a preacher of the Valley's most bracing creed: the belief that most social problems can be ameliorated by technological solutions, if only inventors can be goaded to be sufficiently ambitious. "All progress depends upon the unreasonable man," the "creatively maladjusted," Khosla declared, borrowing eclectically from George Bernard Shaw and Martin Luther King Jr.[4] "Most people think improbable ideas are unimportant," he loved to add, "but the only thing that's important is something that's improbable." If you were going to pitch Khosla an invention, it had better not fall into the incremental category he called "one sheet of toilet paper, not two."[5] Khosla wanted radical dreams, the bolder and more improbable the better.

Brown rode a bicycle to Khosla's office, a sleek designer building of glass and wood. He had prepared a slide deck that he admitted "in retrospect was ridiculous."[6] The first slide laid out his goal: rendering the entire meat industry redundant. Those rounded glasses—the John Lennon, Steve Jobs, visionary look—seemed altogether appropriate.

Khosla has large eyes and chiseled features and thick, cropped gray hair. He fixed his visitor with an impish stare.

"That's impossible!" he said, delightedly.

Silently, Khosla was thinking to himself, "If there is a one-in-a-hundred chance that this works, this is a shot worth taking."[7]

Brown explained how he proposed to out-beef the beef industry. He would break the challenge down into its component parts: how to replicate the smell, the consistency, the taste, and the appearance of a real beef burger. Once you analyzed each question separately, an apparently impossible ambition became a set of soluble problems. For example, the clover-root juices would drip like blood onto hot coals; they would turn from red to brown as they sizzled on a barbecue. Dr. Frankenstein had met Ray Kroc. Nobody would eat ground cow flesh again.

Khosla ran through a test that he applied to supplicants. The onus was not on Brown to prove that his idea would definitely work. Rather, the question was whether Khosla could come up with a reason why it obviously could not work. The more Khosla listened to his visitor, the less he could rule out that he was onto something.

Next, Khosla sized up Brown as a person. He was fond of proclaiming a Yoda approach to investing: empower people who feel the force and let them work their magic.[8] Brown was evidently brilliant, as his credentials as a geneticist demonstrated. He was gate-crashing a new field, which meant he was unburdened by preconceptions about what conventional wisdom deemed possible. Moreover, Brown was clearly as determined as he was bright: he was ready to leave his academic perch—the prestige of a Stanford professorship, the blank check from the Howard Hughes foundation. All in all, Brown fitted Khosla's archetype of the ideal entrepreneur. He had the dazzling intellect, the willingness to put his own neck on the line, the glorious hubris and naïveté.[9]

There was one last test that Khosla cared about. If Brown managed to produce a yummy plantburger, would he generate profits that would be commensurately succulent? Khosla routinely put capital behind moon shots with a nine-in-ten chance of failure. But the low probability of a moon landing had to be balanced by the prospect of a large payout: if the company thrived, Khosla wanted to reap more than ten times his investment—preferably, much more than that. There was no point gambling for success unless the success was worth having.

Brown had gotten to his final slide, where he stuck all the mundane market data that failed to interest a scientist. He noted matter-of-factly that "it's a trillion-and-a-half-dollar global market being served by prehistoric technology."[10]

Khosla latched on. If plant patties could reproduce the properties of beef—the taste, the consistency, the browning, and the bleeding as you flipped the burger on the grill—the potential was cosmic.

Brown looked Khosla in the eyes. "I promise to make you even more insanely rich than you already are, if you give me this money," he told him.[11]

At that, Khosla bet $3 million on Impossible Foods, as Brown fittingly named his company.[12] Recounting this story in 2018, Khosla happily noted Impossible's progress since 2010: the company would soon have more than $100 million in annual revenues, and the Impossible Whopper would be served at Burger King. But the main message that Khosla emphasized transcended dollars and even the food system. "You can imagine, if Pat fails, the hubris of saying he could eliminate animal husbandry; he'll be mocked for that," Khosla observed. But, he continued, the mockery would be misplaced.

Which is better: to try and fail, or to fail to try?[13] Reasonable people—well-adjusted people, people without hubris or naïveté—routinely fail in life's important missions by not even attempting them; the way Khosla saw things, Brown should be hailed as a hero, whatever happened to his company. Truly consequential changes are bound to seem outrageous when they are first imagined by messianic inventors. But there is no glory in projects that will probably succeed, for these by definition won't transform the human predicament.

Khosla was himself an unreasonable man, creatively maladjusted. As a boy in his native India, he rebelled against his parents' religion, declined to follow his father into the army, and refused an arranged marriage. On his wedding day, he set his watch alarm, declaring that the religious portion of the ceremony had to be done inside thirty minutes. As soon as he earned an engineering degree, he left for the United States, where he studied more engineering at Carnegie Mellon University. After that, he set his sights on Stanford Business School; learning that he needed two years' work experience to qualify for admission, he did two jobs at once and declared after one year that he had met the requirement. In 1982, after completing his business degree, Khosla teamed up with three computer scientists to found Sun Microsystems, whose powerful workstations stamped their mark on the evolution of computing. Cocky and obnoxious, Khosla was soon fired. He became a venture capitalist.

Joining the storied venture partnership of Kleiner Perkins, Khosla discovered his true métier. His unreasonable impatience—his determination that anything might be possible and everything should work his way—made him one part tyrant, two parts visionary. In later life, he bought a village with forty-seven cottages on the California coast and fought a series of losing court cases to block public access to the beach, even though he never found time to spend the night there—not once, ever. But he channeled his contempt for conventional thinking into a series of dazzling investments, frequently losing his money and sometimes generating bonanzas. By the time he met Patrick Brown, everything about Khosla—his risk appetite, his love of hubris, his quest for improbable ideas—made him the living embodiment of the power law, the most pervasive rule in venture capital.[14]

Many phenomena in life are normally distributed: nearly all the observations in a data set cluster around the average. For example, the average height of an American man is five feet ten inches, and two-thirds of American men are within three inches of that average. When you plot height on an *x* axis and the probability that a man will have that height on a *y* axis, what you see is a bell curve: the greatest probability is that a man's height will be the average height, and the probabilities decline as you move away from that midpoint. The chances of meeting a man whose height is ten inches from the average—that is, less than five feet or more than six feet eight—are exceedingly small. Further away from the mean, the thin tails of the curve taper toward zero.

NORMAL DISTRIBUTION

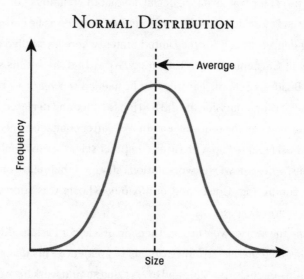

Not all phenomena follow this pattern, however. A chart showing the wealth of Americans rather than their height looks very different. People who are richer than the median are sometimes vastly richer, so the far right side of the wealth chart features an extended fat tail between the curve and the *x* axis. Because the very rich are numerous enough and wealthy enough to impact the average for the whole nation, the average is pulled to the right: unlike in a normal distribution, the mean is higher than the median. In a normal distribution, moreover, you can remove the biggest outlier from a sample without affecting the average: if a seven-foot NBA star walks out of a cinema, the average height of the remaining ninety-nine movie-watching men falls from five feet 10 inches to five feet 9.9 inches. In a non-normal, skewed distribution, in contrast, the outliers can have a dramatic effect. If Jeff Bezos walks out of the cinema, the average wealth of those who stay behind will plummet.

Power Law Distribution

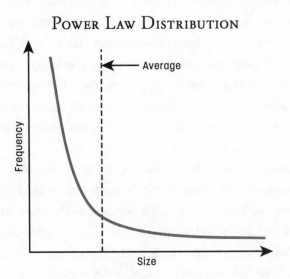

This sort of skewed distribution is sometimes referred to as the 80/20 rule: the idea that 80 percent of the wealth is held by 20 percent of the people, that 80 percent of the people live in 20 percent of the cities, or that 20 percent of all scientific papers earn 80 percent of the citations. In reality, there is nothing magical about the numbers 80 or 20: it could be that just 10 percent of the people hold 80 percent of the wealth, or perhaps 90 percent of it. But whatever the precise numbers, all these distributions are examples of the power law, so called because the winners advance at an accelerating, exponential rate, so that they explode upward far more rapidly than in a linear progression. Once Jeff Bezos achieves great riches, his opportunities for further enrichment multiply; the more a scientific paper is cited, the better known it is and the more likely it is to attract further citations. Anytime you have outliers whose success multiplies success, you switch from the domain of the normal distribution to the land ruled by the power law—from a world in which things vary slightly to one of extreme contrasts. And once you cross that perilous frontier, you better begin to think differently.

The rethinking required is especially pronounced in finance. Investors who focus on currencies, bonds, and stock markets generally assume a normal distribution of price changes: values jiggle up and down, but extreme moves are unusual. Of course, extreme moves are possible, as financial crashes show. But between 1985 and 2015, the S&P 500 stock index budged less than 3 percent from its starting point on 7,663 out of 7,817 days; in other words, for fully 98 percent of the time, the market is remarkably stable.[15] Because the distribution of price changes in these widely traded markets approaches normal, speculators concentrate on harvesting profits from the modest fluctuations that occur on most days.[16] Like the seven-foot NBA star in the cinema, unexpectedly large price jumps are rare enough and moderate enough that they do not affect the average.

Now consider the returns in venture capital. Horsley Bridge is an investment company with stakes in venture funds that backed 7,000 startups between 1985 and 2014. A small subset of these deals, accounting for just 5 percent of the total capital deployed, generated fully 60 percent of all the Horsley Bridge returns during this period.[17] (To put that in context, in 2018 the top-performing 5 percent of subindustries in the S&P 500 accounted for only 9 percent of the index's total performance.)[18] Other venture investors report even more skewed returns: Y Combinator, which backs fledgling tech startups, calculated in 2012 that three-quarters of its gains came from just 2 of the 280 outfits it had bet on.[19] "The biggest secret in venture capital is that the best investment in a successful fund equals or outperforms the entire rest of the fund," the venture capitalist Peter Thiel has written.[20] "Venture capital is not even a home-run business," Bill Gurley of Benchmark Capital once remarked. "It's a grand-slam business."[21]

What this means is that venture capitalists *need* to be ambitious. The celebrated hedge-fund stock picker Julian Robertson used to say that he looked for shares that might plausibly double in three years, an outcome he would view as "fabulous."[22] But if venture capitalists embarked on the same quest, they would almost guarantee failure, because the power law generates relatively few startups that merely double in value. Most fail completely, in which case the value of their equity rounds to zero—an unthinkable catastrophe for a stock market investor. But each year brings a handful of outliers that hit the proverbial grand slam, and the only thing that matters in venture is to own a piece of them.[23]

When today's venture capitalists back flying cars or space tourism or artificial intelligence systems that write film scripts, they are following this power-law logic. Their job is to look over the horizon, to reach for high-risk, huge-reward possibilities that most people believe to be unreachable. "We could cure cancer, dementia, and all the diseases of age and metabolic decay," Peter Thiel enthuses, dripping with disdain for incrementalism. "We can invent faster ways to travel from place to place over the surface of the planet; we can even learn how to escape it entirely and settle new frontiers."[24] Of course, investing in what is categorically impossible is a waste of resources. But the more common error, the more human one, is to invest too timidly: to back obvious ideas that others can copy and from which, consequently, it will be hard to extract profits.

Which brings us back to Vinod Khosla. In the two decades he spent at Kleiner Perkins before starting his own venture firm, he learned not to worry about the bets that went to zero. All he could lose was one times his money.[25] What Khosla cared about were the bets that did pay off, and in the mid-1990s he fastened on an especially audacious and contrarian notion: that, with the coming of the internet, consumers would not be satisfied with a mere doubling or tripling in the capacity of traditional phone lines. Rather, they would clamor for a step change in bandwidth, involving routers that handled data flows a thousand times larger. While the telecom establishment snickered at this sci-fi babble, Khosla set out to kick-start the companies that would make the step change possible.

The startups that Khosla backed are largely forgotten names: Juniper, Siara, Cerent. But they illustrate what venture capitalists do best and how they generate both wealth and progress. While incumbent telecom companies planned incremental upgrades, Khosla wagered on the idea of a big leap, even though he had no precise vision of what people would do with all the extra bandwidth. Nobody yet imagined social media or YouTube; digital photography was little more than a concept. But Khosla had witnessed what had happened with other breakout technologies. After the invention of the semiconductor, or after the invention of the Ethernet cables that hooked personal computers together, usage picked up gradually and then exploded upward in an exponential curve; this was the innovation power law that underlay the financial one observed in venture-capital portfolios. Khosla was willing to bet that the internet would follow a similar pattern: steady adoption in the first half of the 1990s, a breathtaking acceleration as the power-law curve went almost vertical.

The result was a set of Khosla companies that did more than just succeed. By inventing a new generation of bandwidth-boosting hardware and software, they captured huge chunks of an exploding market. Khosla's first jackpot, Juniper Networks, built internet routers: he invested $5 million and reaped an extraordinary $7 billion for Kleiner's fund—multiplying his initial stake by an astonishing 1,400 and generating, at the time, the greatest venture-capital bonanza ever.[26] Khosla put another few million into a network equipment company, Siara Systems, and reaped $1.5 billion.[27] In the case of Cerent, he invited the dominant router giant, Cisco, to co-invest with him: among other things, Cerent would facilitate the handling of voice data. When Cisco refused, calling Cerent too much of a long shot, Khosla went ahead alone, investing $8 million, recruiting the first engineers, serving as chief executive.[28] And then he exacted sweet revenge. As soon as Cerent's technology proved workable, Cisco made two offers for the firm: $300 million in December 1998; $700 million the following April. But Khosla, believing in the power law, knew that winners often carry on winning: he took the risk of turning Cisco down and watched Cerent's revenues take off exponentially. Four months later, in August 1999, Khosla was informed that Cisco had prepared another bid, this time for $7 billion. The news reached him when he was vacationing at Machu Picchu, twenty-five hundred meters up in the Peruvian Andes. Khosla boarded a helicopter, then a plane, and shook hands on the deal over breakfast in San Jose the next morning.

Khosla was by some calculations the top venture capitalist in the Valley, and he had no objection to vast riches.[29] He conducted a worldwide search for an architect for his home near Stanford and lavished money on the vineyard surrounding it.[30] But what really animated Khosla was the contrarianism he had exhibited in youth: Why did his parents go to the temple, why couldn't he choose where to work and whom to love, why couldn't everything be different? And, just as Patrick Brown wanted nothing less than to eliminate the entire meat industry, so Khosla made extraordinary claims for his work. Venture capital was not merely a business; it was a mindset, a philosophy, a theory of progress. Seven hundred million people enjoyed the lifestyle that seven billion wanted, he liked to say. Bold innovators goaded by even bolder venture capitalists offered the best shot at satisfying human aspirations.[31]

Venture capitalists often fail to live up to this hype, as we will see shortly. But you don't have to swallow all of Khosla's riff to agree that it's important. The venture-capital approach of high-risk, high-reward experiments does represent a distinctive way of coming at the world, one that people outside Silicon Valley might learn from. To illustrate, a huge amount of energy in government, financial houses, and corporations is spent on forecasting the future, mostly by running statistical analyses on patterns from the past; without a clear forecast, committing resources would seem irresponsible. But the way venture capitalists see things, the disciplined calibrations of conventional social scientists can be a blindfold, not a telescope. Extrapolations from past data anticipate the future only when there is not much to anticipate; if tomorrow will be a mere extension of today, why bother with forecasting? The revolutions that will matter—the big disruptions that create wealth for inventors and anxiety for workers, or that scramble the geopolitical balance and alter human relations—cannot be predicted based on extrapolations of past data, precisely because such revolutions are so thoroughly disruptive. Rather, they will emerge as a result of forces that are too complex to forecast—from the primordial soup of tinkerers and hackers and hubristic dreamers—and all you can know is that the world in ten years will be excitingly different. Mature, comfortable societies, dominated by people who analyze every probability and manage every risk, should come to terms with a tomorrow that cannot be foreseen. The future can be *discovered* by means of iterative, venture-backed experiments.[32] It cannot be *predicted*.

What type of experiment is likely to be fruitful? Here, too, people outside innovation hubs can learn something from Khosla. Most of us might assume that experts in each field will advance the frontiers of knowledge. But, as we have seen from Khosla's bet on Patrick Brown, that is much too sensible. Experts may be the most likely source of incremental advances, but radical rethinks tend to come from outsiders. "If I'm building a health-care company, I don't want a health-care CEO," Khosla says. "If I'm building a manufacturing company, I don't want a manufacturing CEO. I want somebody really smart to rethink the assumptions from the ground up." After all, he continues, retail innovation did not come from Walmart; it came from Amazon. Media innovation did not come from *Time* magazine or CBS; it came from YouTube and Twitter and Facebook. Space innovation did not come from Boeing and Lockheed; it came from Elon Musk's SpaceX. Next-generation cars did not come from GM and Volkswagen; they came from another Musk company, Tesla. "I can't think of a single, major innovation coming from experts in the last thirty, forty years," Khosla exclaims. "Think about it, isn't that stunning?"

If the future is best discovered by means of maverick moon shots, another insight follows. Thanks to the work of the Nobel laureate Ronald Coase, the economics profession has long recognized two great institutions of modern capitalism: markets, which coordinate activity via price signals and arm's-length contracts; and corporations, which do so by assembling large teams led by top-down managers. But economists have focused less on the middle ground that Khosla inhabits: the venture-capital networks that lie somewhere between markets and corporations. And yet networks of venture capitalists deserve closer attention. By means of Khosla-style maverick experiments, they have delivered more progress in applied science than any kind of rival: more than centralized corporate R&D units, more than isolated individuals tinkering in garages, and more than government attempts to pick technological winners. Because VC-backed startups have proved so fertile, they have changed how people work, socialize, shop, and entertain themselves; how they access information, manipulate it, and arrive at quiet epiphanies—how they think.

Venture capitalists have achieved this disproportionate impact because they combine the strengths of the corporation with the strengths of the market. They channel capital, talented employees, and large customers to promising startups; in this way, they replicate the team formation, resources, and strategic vision to be found in corporations.[33] But at the same time, because their network is fluid and amorphous, they have the flexibility of the market. The rainmakers of Sand Hill Road can get behind a startup with a fresh business idea or a scientific breakthrough; they can shape it, expand it, murmur its name into the right ears. But when a round of venture funding is exhausted, it is time to put the startup to a market test. If there are no enthusiastic buyers for the next tranche of the startup's equity, the price signal will do its work: the venture capitalists will close it down, avoiding the waste of resources that comes from backing speculative R&D beyond the point at which success appears impossible. Because of this periodic submission to the discipline of price signals, venture capitalists are good at recognizing failure and good at doubling down on early indicators of success. Their blend of corporate strategizing and respect for the market represents a third great institution of modern capitalism, to be added to the two that Ronald Coase emphasized.

The underappreciated significance of venture-capital networks has become especially glaring in the past few years as the industry has expanded in three dimensions. First, it has spread beyond its historical stronghold in Silicon Valley, building thriving outposts in Asia, Israel, and Europe as well as in major U.S. cities.[34] Second, the industry has spread sectorially, colonizing new industries as venture-backed technologies reach ever more widely, touching everything from cars to the hotel business. Third, venture capital is spreading beyond the startup phase of a company's existence as Silicon Valley has sprouted multibillion-dollar corporations that have delayed raising capital from public shareholders. Back in 1997, Amazon went public three years after launch, when it was worth just $438 million. As of this writing in 2020, more than 480 "unicorns" boast a valuation of more than $1 billion yet seem in little hurry to go public.[35] Many of the world's most dynamic and disruptive companies are owned—and therefore governed or misgoverned—by venture capitalists and other private technology investors.

This book has two broad purposes. The first is to explain the venture-capital mindset. There are dozens of histories of Silicon Valley focusing on the inventors and entrepreneurs; there have been fewer efforts to get under the skin of the people who finance and often shape their companies. Through careful reconstruction of celebrated transactions—from Apple and Cisco to WhatsApp and Uber—the story in these pages shows what happens when venture capitalists and startups connect, and why venture is so different from other types of finance. Most financiers allocate scarce capital based on quantitative analysis. Venture capitalists meet people, charm people, and seldom bother with spreadsheets.[36] Most financiers value companies by projecting their cash flows. Venture capitalists frequently back startups before they have cash flows to analyze. Other financiers trade millions of dollars of paper assets in the blink of an eye. Venture capitalists take relatively small stakes in real companies and hold them. Most fundamentally, other financiers extrapolate trends from the past, disregarding the risk of extreme "tail" events. Venture capitalists look for radical departures from the past. Tail events are all they care about.

This book's second purpose is to evaluate venture capital's social impact. VCs themselves frequently assert that "they are making the world a better place." This is certainly true sometimes: Impossible Foods is an example. On the other hand, video games and social media promote screen addiction and fake news, even as they entertain, inform, and allow Grandma to admire pictures of her distant grandchildren. The gap between VC rhetoric and VC practice is easily mocked. In April 2020, in the throes of the coronavirus pandemic, the venture capitalist Marc Andreessen proclaimed that it was "time to build." "Where are the high-speed trains, the soaring monorails, the hyperloops, and yes, the flying cars?" he demanded.[37] The following month Andreessen's partnership invested in Clubhouse, an invitation-only social-media app. Meanwhile, the venture industry's expansive pronouncements stand in contrast to the narrowness of its monoculture. Women are badly underrepresented: as of 2020, they account for 16 percent of investing partners. Racial diversity is even more limited: only about 3 percent of partners at venture-capital firms are Black.[38] Precisely because venture capital does so much to shape society, it must become more diverse, both in terms of the investors it hires and the startups it finances. Finally and most tellingly—since this lies at the heart of what the industry presents as its core function—venture capitalists must reckon with their record as the stewards of tech companies. VCs have a proud tradition of building fledgling startups. They are less successful at governing multibillion-dollar unicorns such as the office-rental company, WeWork, or the ride-hailing giant, Uber.

In short, venture capitalists are far from perfect. Yet even as the public mood has turned against the tech-industrial complex, the positive case for venture capital has grown more compelling. Until relatively recently, economists explained why some geographies grow wealthier than others by examining country-level differences: successful nations benefit from sound rule of law, stable prices, educated people, and so on. Lately, however, the more pressing question is why some regions within countries leave other regions so far behind as innovation hubs and generators of prosperity. It has long been obvious that one area can outperform others, as Silicon Valley has done; but the rule of law and price stability cannot explain why the Valley is more innovative than Montana or Michigan.[39] To understand the Valley's secret, we need to update Ronald Coase's framework: we must study venture-capital networks as deeply as we study markets and corporations. In a world of intensifying geoeconomic competition, the countries with the most creative innovation hubs are likely to be the most prosperous and ultimately the most powerful. In a world of intensifying income inequality, the countries that can foster greater regional diversity in the locations of those hubs will be happier and more stable. Even as they seek to regulate Big Tech, governments must do everything possible to foster technology startups—a policy challenge to which we will return presently.

For now, it is enough to say one thing about this challenge. Whatever the failings of venture capitalists, they are an essential ingredient of dynamic startup clusters. On any given day in Silicon Valley, hundreds of VCs are chasing youths in T-shirts: they are schmoozing people, connecting people, vouching for one startup as it seeks to hire a wary programmer, assuring a skeptical customer that another startup's product is reliable. It is the contention of this book that this frenzy of activity explains much of the variation in creativity across regions: by forging connections among entrepreneurs, ideas, customers, and capital, venture capitalists transform a mere agglomeration of smart people into an inventive network. The traditional accounts of economic growth need to make space for this phenomenon, which also explains China's emergence as a top-flight technology power. Indeed, if the United States risks falling behind China in today's technology race, this is precisely because Valley-inspired venture capital has kickstarted China's digital economy. Moreover, the Chinese venture industry has an advantage over its U.S. rival. It is more open to women.

But that is to jump to the end of our story. To understand venture capitalists—to grasp how they think and why they matter—we must begin at the beginning. For, without this strange tribe of financiers, the orchards of the Santa Clara valley might never have been linked to silicon, and a staggering amount of wealth might never have been created.

Chapter One

ARTHUR ROCK AND
LIBERATION CAPITAL

S uccess has many fathers, and Silicon Valley is no exception. Searching for the origins of this miraculously innovative region, some fasten on 1951, when Fred Terman, the engineering dean at Stanford, created the university's famous research park. Others begin the story five years later, when William Shockley, the father of the semiconductor, abandoned the East Coast to launch a company on Terman's campus, bringing silicon to the Valley for the first time. But the most compelling origin story—the one that aims the spotlight squarely at the force that makes the Valley so distinctive—begins in the summer of 1957, when eight of Shockley's young PhD researchers rose up in revolt and went out on their own. Shockley's seniority, his fame, and even his Nobel Prize did nothing to deter the rebels; the "Traitorous Eight" were fed up with Shockley's heavy-handed leadership and resolved to find a different home. It was that act of defection that created the magic culture of the Valley, shattering traditional assumptions about hierarchy and authority and working loyally for decades until you retired with a gold watch.

The defection of 1957 was made possible by a new form of finance, originally dubbed adventure capital. The idea was to back technologists who were too dicey and penurious to get a conventional bank loan but who promised the chance of a resounding payoff to investors with a taste for

audacious invention. The funding of the Traitorous Eight and their company, Fairchild Semiconductor, was arguably the first such adventure to
take place on the West Coast, and it changed the history of the region. After
Fairchild got its $1.4 million in financing, it became evident that any team
in the Valley possessed of grand ideas and stiff ambition could spin itself
out, start itself up, and generally invent the organizational form that best
suited its fancy. Engineers, inventors, hustlers, and artistic dreamers could
meet, combine, separate, compete, and simultaneously collaborate, all courtesy of this new finance. Adventure capital could sometimes be defection
capital, or it could be team-building capital, or almost just experimental
capital.[1] But whichever way you looked at it, talent had been liberated. A
revolution was afoot.

The invention of this new liberation capital explained more than most
people still realize. The rival theories of what established the Valley's
preeminence—that it was home to Stanford University, that it benefited
from military contracts, that it had a certain West Coast, countercultural
irreverence—have never been especially persuasive. After all, Stanford was
no more distinguished than the Massachusetts Institute of Technology,
which in turn was located a short drive from Harvard, creating a research
cluster more powerful than anything that Silicon Valley could muster in its
early days.[2] Similarly, it was true that Stanford benefited from military research dollars; that film from U-2 spy planes was processed at the nearby
NASA Ames Research Center; and that the Lockheed Missiles and Space
Division built submarine-launched weapons at its campus in the Valley.[3] But
the famous military-industrial complex of the 1950s was primarily an East
Coast alliance between the Pentagon and Cambridge, Massachusetts. The
personification of that axis, Vannevar Bush, was dean of the MIT School of
Engineering, founder of the Cambridge-based defense contractor Raytheon,
and Franklin Roosevelt's top science administrator during World War II.
Millions of dollars in federal funding flowed to the Pentagon-backed research centers around Boston, and by the end of the 1960s more than a hundred tech startups had spun out of these labs.[4] If military ties had determined
the location of applied science, in other words, Cambridge should have
been the center of the universe.[5]

If neither Stanford nor defense contracts explain Silicon Valley's rise to preeminence, what of the theory that the region was distinguished by that West Coast counterculture, which freed people to imagine technologies as yet unborn? Doug Engelbart of the Augmented Human Intellect Research Center in Palo Alto, who conceived the early versions of the computer mouse and the graphical user interface, was involved in LSD experiments and hijacked Pentagon funding to explore the personal-growth training method known as est. The young Steve Jobs was similarly enthralled by eastern mysticism; he went about barefoot, rinsed his feet in the company toilet, and maintained that his fruitarian diet rendered regular washing obsolete. "The people who invented the twenty-first century were pot-smoking, sandal-wearing hippies from the West Coast like Steve, because they saw differently," observed Bono, the rock musician and friend of Steve Jobs's; and some version of this story is widely accepted in the Valley, whose denizens like to think of themselves as cool as well as rich and powerful. The hippies' anticorporate vibe drove them to share ideas rather than run to the nearest patent lawyer, according to this narrative. Their egalitarianism ensured that they were open to any unkempt upstart who might see something, sense something—something with the potential to change everything.

You can still see traces of this counterculture in the Valley: in the sandals, even if next-gen nylon has displaced frayed leather; in the left-liberal, sometimes libertarian politics; in the conviction that your productivity can be augmented by micro-dosing LSD. But the trouble with the cultural explanation for West Coast exceptionalism is that the rest of the world has never been as buttoned up as the Valley's boosters imagine. The hacker ethic, championed by communalist nerds who obsessed over code and declined on principle to monetize it, actually originated at MIT—with the Tech Model Railroad Club, a group of MIT undergrads enthralled by the technology behind model trains before their attention was diverted to the TX-0 computer.[6] (The TX-0 was so captivating that the authorities at MIT considered getting rid of it. "People stopped washing, stopped eating, stopped their social life, and, of course, stopped studying," according to one account.)[7] Similarly, Tim Berners-Lee, the British-born and Geneva-based inventor of the World Wide Web, combined creative imagination with an antimaterialist disdain for business. "If you're interested in using the code, mail me," he wrote in a public announcement, refusing to profit from his invention. In Finland, not the sort of place where Bono played a lot of gigs, Linus Torvalds created the bare bones of the Linux operating system and gave it away freely. In short, there was no lack of inventiveness outside Silicon Valley, and no lack of countercultural antibusiness prejudice, either.

The truth is that the distinguishing genius of the Valley lies not in its capacity for invention, countercultural or otherwise.[8] The first transistor was created in 1947, not in Silicon Valley, but at Bell Labs in New Jersey. The first personal computer was the Altair, created in New Mexico. The first precursor of the worldwide web, the network-management software Gopher, was from Minnesota. The first browser was developed by Marc Andreessen at the University of Illinois. The first search engine, Archie, was invented by Alan Emtage at McGill University in Montreal. The first internet-based social-networking site was SixDegrees.com, launched by Andrew Weinreich in New York City. The first smartphone was the Simon Personal Communicator, developed by Frank Canova at IBM's lab in Boca Raton, Florida.[9] No single geography—not even Silicon Valley—dominates invention. And yet all these breakthrough products have one thing in common. When it came to turning ideas into blockbuster products, the Valley was the place where the magic happened.

What explains that magic? The title of a 1995 *Time* essay echoed Bono's answer: "We Owe It All to the Hippies."[10] But the Valley's distinguishing genius is that the patina of the counterculture combines with a frank lust for riches. The pot-smoking, sandal-wearing inventors of Bono's acquaintance have never been ashamed to earn vast fortunes, and the Valley is the place where career ladders have been scorned not just by bohemians, who disdain them as bourgeois, but even more by overachievers, who regard them as a pitifully slow way to get ahead. Steve Jobs was among the many who embodied both sides of this contradictory culture. He was too modestly egalitarian to demand a boss's reserved slot in the company parking lot but too arrogantly entitled not to steal the space designated for disabled drivers.[11] He was a communalist collaborator, sharing his intellectual property freely with ostensible rivals; he was also a capitalist competitor, paranoid and controlling. It was this combination of laid-back creativity and driving commercial ambition that truly defined Silicon Valley, making it the place where flights of imaginative fancy begat businesses that shaped societies and cultures.

Quite where this contradictory culture sprang from is naturally difficult to pinpoint. Some put it down to the frantic pioneer materialism of San Francisco's nineteenth-century gold rush, which enriched individualistic hustlers from outside the old hierarchies and spawned a burst of entrepreneurship, including the creation of the first Levi Strauss jeans. Other theories emphasize California's education and prosperity, which fostered progressive open-mindedness and workaholic focus all at once. But the tonic of liberation capital provides another explanation, one that merits more attention than it has received until now. By freeing talent to convert ideas into products, and by marrying unconventional experiments with hard commercial targets, this distinctive form of finance fostered the business culture that made the Valley so fertile. In an earlier era, J. P. Morgan's brand of finance fashioned American business into muscular oligopolies; in the 1980s, Michael Milken's junk bonds fueled a burst of corporate takeovers and slash-and-burn cost cuts. In similar fashion, venture capital has stamped its mark on an industrial culture, making Silicon Valley the most durably productive crucible of applied science anywhere, ever. Thanks to venture capital, the Traitorous Eight were able to abandon William Shockley, launch Fairchild Semiconductor, and set this miracle in motion. By 2014, an astonishing 70 percent of the publicly traded tech companies in the Valley could trace their lineage to Fairchild.[12]

In the year before they turned to liberation capital, the young researchers at Shockley Semiconductor Laboratory were discovering that their boss was at once a scientific genius and a maniacal despot. When Shockley had recruited them, they had felt honored to be chosen: getting a call from the great scientist was "like picking up the phone and talking to God."[13] Handsome, bespectacled, with a professorial receding hairline, Shockley was not only the father of semiconductors but also a fine showman: he would begin lectures by promising to get into a hot subject; then he would open up a book and smoke would burst from the pages.[14] But as soon as the young recruits entered the presence of this deity, his flaws became apparent. Shockley staged public firings, posted employee salaries on a company bulletin board, and laughed at one scientist for agreeing to work for too little.[15] He hired the smartest researchers he could find, but was quick to belittle them, sometimes taunting an employee, "Are you sure you have a PhD?" When a few members of his team ventured that they would like to publish academic papers, Shockley responded with contempt and egotism. He jotted down some notes on one of his own theories and told them, "Here, flesh this out and publish it."[16]

"I don't think 'tyrant' begins to encapsulate Shockley," one of the young researchers said later.[17]

In May 1957, fifteen months after Shockley had launched his operation, his financial backer paid him a visit. The previous year, when Shockley had wanted money, venture capital had barely existed.[18] So Shockley had turned to Arnold Beckman, founder of the eponymous Southern California company Beckman Instruments. Beckman had set Shockley up as a division of his company, hoping to see rapid and profitable progress. Now he arrived to demand more commercial output and less managerial dysfunction.

Shockley responded with defiance. "If you don't like what we're doing up here I can take this group and get support any place else," he railed.[19] Then he stormed out of the room.

Watching their boss yell at Beckman, Shockley's young researchers realized that they faced a choice. This was the 1950s, the era of big corporations, big labor, and big white-collar hierarchies; the title of a 1956 bestseller proclaimed a new kind of American, the meek "organization man." Even research and development were increasingly stultified: one chapter of *The Organization Man* was titled "The Bureaucratization of the Scientist."[20] Shockley's engineers could either submit to the zeitgeist and languish unproductively under a suffocating manager or seize the opening created by his outburst. Huddling over lunch after the confrontation, they resolved to take their grievances to Beckman and demand that he clamp down on Shockley. "Look, goddammit!" one rebel declared. "We either have to do something about this or stop talking about it!"[21]

Gordon Moore, who would later become head of research and development at Fairchild, was chosen as the group's spokesman. Balding, with bushy brows lurking behind fashion-forward 1950s glasses, Moore was at once unpretentiously quiet and unyieldingly confident. Borrowing a phone at a colleague's home after the rebels' lunch conference, he dialed Beckman.[22]

"That's not a serious threat," Moore told Beckman, referring to Shockley's outburst. "Shockley couldn't take the group with him if he wants to at this stage of the game."

"Things aren't going well up there, are they?" Beckman asked nervously.

"No, they really are not."[23]

Beckman agreed to meet Moore and his colleagues, and after a few rounds of discussion he promised to take their side against the boss. Despite his scientific talent, Shockley was stifling progress; sometimes it takes a good defenestration for capitalism to advance. Shockley would be phased out of his management responsibilities, Beckman assured the rebels. His role at the company would be restricted to an advisory function.

Within a few days, however, Beckman lost his nerve. He was running his own company, and he could make decisions as he wanted; unlike a modern venture capitalist, he had no investors holding him accountable for his return on capital.[24] He was therefore free to duck unpleasant decisions, and a call from a senior East Coast scientist, protesting that Shockley would be ruined by a demotion, might have been enough to change his mind. Shockley might be a tyrant, but he was after all a Nobel Prize–winning tyrant, Beckman now reasoned. He informed the young rebels that they would have to make their peace with the boss.

Having experienced the difficulty in changing a company from the inside, the mutineers considered their options. They were all supremely qualified and could easily get hired elsewhere, but they knew they were most likely to accomplish something if they stuck together as a team. At the same time, if keeping the team together meant suffering under Shockley, it was not a pleasant prospect. In a recent episode, the tyrant had demanded that his staff submit to a lie detector test.[25]

One evening as they pondered their predicament, the rebels hit on a possible solution. Eugene Kleiner, the only member of the band over thirty, had a connection via his father to a New York investment firm. Kleiner would write to his father's broker and request assistance. A team of Shockley engineers stood ready to quit the company, Kleiner would explain in his letter. Perhaps a well-connected finance house could identify an employer willing to hire the entire squad?

———◆———

At this stage in the story, none of the rebels had thought of starting a new enterprise. The idea had simply not occurred to them: venture-capital funds willing to back a crew of young and unknown scientists were virtually unheard of; what's more, they were contrary to the spirit of postwar finance. The 1929 crash and the ensuing Depression had destroyed investors' risk appetite for a generation; the big money-management houses had names like Fidelity and Prudential and were more interested in preserving capital than in taking chances. To the extent that financiers wanted to buy any corporate equity, they preferred safe, established companies—preferably ones sitting on enough working capital that a shareholder could count on making money *even if they went bust*. The legendary investor Benjamin Graham, assisted by a young hire named Warren Buffett, ferreted out companies that traded at least one-third below the value of their cash, inventory, and receivables so that they could be liquidated at a profit: in one coup, Buffett bought a block of Union Street Railway of New Bedford, Massachusetts, which was selling for $45 but had $120 per share of cash in the bank.[26] So long as there were bargains to be found with such huge margins of safety, risky technology ventures appeared almost disreputable. In 1952, *Fortune* observed that "it might shock the unsuspecting holder of, say, a John Hancock life-insurance policy to learn that his money was helping to finance . . . scientific gadgetry."[27]

Of course, there were exceptions to this caution, but they were scattered and obscure. In 1949 a romantic ex-Marxist named Alfred Winslow Jones had created the first "hedged fund," but until the 1960s, when a crowd of sideburned gunslingers began to emulate his methods, he operated under the radar. Three years before Jones, a pair of rich East Coast families—the Whitneys and the Rockefellers—had begun to dabble amateurishly in risky fledgling businesses, but their motives were patriotic and philanthropic rather than straightforwardly commercial. On the West Coast, a group of San Francisco brokers invited entrepreneurs to pitch startups over informal lunches, but at the time of the Shockley defections they were only just getting started. The most serious early experiment—the one with a real claim to be seen as the forerunner to modern venture capital—was American Research and Development. But ARD focused on the Boston area, and the Shockley rebels had not heard of it. Like the Whitneys and the Rockefellers, it was imbued with public-service motives. And, as we shall see presently, it did not serve as the model for later venture investors.

John Hay Whitney exemplified these early experiments in adventurous finance.[28] He was possessed, as a 1951 *New Yorker* profile put it, of a "vibrating social conscience," the result of his experiences during World War II.[29] Taken prisoner by the Germans, he had informed his captors that he was fighting for freedom; when his enemies retorted that the United States was no freer than Hitler's Germany, Whitney saw some of the captured American soldiers nodding in agreement. Appalled, he returned home after the war, withdrew his name from the Social Register, and created a foundation to address social problems. As part of his efforts, he launched a $5 million fund to safeguard the spirit of free enterprise by providing investment capital for entrepreneurs.[30] But after five years in operation, J. H. Whitney & Company had backed just eighteen ventures; his successes included an early maker of the building material perlite and Vacuum Foods, the producer of Minute Maid orange juice. In his first five years, moreover, Whitney outperformed the much safer S&P 500 by a relatively modest margin.[31] Indeed, on the risk-adjusted basis that financiers use to measure themselves, the fund could not justify its existence.[32]

Whitney's ego, not to mention that vibrating conscience, bridled at commentators who bracketed him with ordinary bankers. *The New York*

Times referred to his fund as a "New York investment banking firm," and one day the irritated patriarch challenged his colleagues to come up with a better term.

"I think we should get the connotation of risk into the description of our firm," one person responded.

"I think the most interesting aspect of our business is the adventure," said another.

"How about private venture capital investment firm?" a third offered, abbreviating the term "adventure capital," which was already used in some circles.[33]

"That's it!" Whitney concurred. The *Times* editors were duly informed of the philanthropist's desired usage, and by 1947 the paper was making occasional reference to venture capital.[34] But despite Whitney's efforts, his linguistic innovation failed to catch on widely. As late as 1962, pioneering tech investors who introduced themselves as venture capitalists were met with blank stares.[35]

In April 1946, the Rockefeller family launched a parallel effort to Whitney's, aiming to solve the generally acknowledged lack of finance for new firms. "What we want to do is the opposite of the old system of holding back capital until a field or an idea is proved completely safe," declared Laurance Rockefeller, the prime mover, adding, "We are putting money into many underdeveloped areas."[36] His fund proceeded to back a cotton mill in Africa, a South Pacific fishing company, a Pennsylvania helicopter company, and a motion picture project on Long Island. "Capital no longer is used just for profit," Rockefeller exulted. "It goes where it can do the most good."[37] Perhaps as a result, his profits were not good. In 1961, *Barron's* reported that Rockefeller Brothers had returned $40 million on the $9 million invested during fifteen years in business.[38] The S&P 500 had shot up by 600 percent over this period.[39]

The early West Coast amateurs were at least able to claim some spectacular returns. Reid Dennis, one of the half a dozen financiers who attended the investment lunches in San Francisco, won an early bet on Ampex, a pioneering maker of tape recorders. Ampex had captured the attention of the singer Bing Crosby, who preferred to play golf on Sunday afternoons rather than perform his radio show live. "I don't know anything about tape recording," Dennis later recalled thinking, "but I think that technology is going to be useful for a lot more things than just recording Bing Crosby's voice."[40] And so in 1952, fresh out of business school, Dennis wagered all his savings—a total of $15,000—on the company, telling his wife that "if she was good enough to get me, she ought to be able to get somebody else to support her if anything happened."[41] Ampex succeeded wildly, going public in 1958, and Dennis earned about $1 million—a return, as venture capitalists learned to say later, of 67x.[42] "I realized it was a pretty good way to make a living," Dennis mused fondly, "so I began looking around at other high-tech companies down here."[43]

The Ampex win earned Dennis a reputation among San Francisco brokers, which in turn led to the creation of the informal lunch club that styled itself "the Group." Starting in 1957, five or six regulars convened at Sam's or Jack's in the financial district, restaurants "where the sole was dependable and the sourdough fresh."[44] Sam's was a particular favorite because it had little plywood booths that permitted an illusion of privacy, even if the plywood was just an eighth of an inch thick.[45] The entrepreneur would tell his story, the men would munch their sourdough, and then the supplicant would be instructed to stand outside on the sidewalk while he awaited a verdict. If all had gone well, there would be a handshake and a promise of perhaps $80,000 or $100,000, with the likelihood of more capital from the Group's camp followers and hangers-on.[46] "We essentially grew up in the business, and then they changed the name of it to venture capital," Dennis remembered.[47] But even though the San Francisco lunch club boasted some successes, it financed only around two dozen deals in the late 1950s and early 1960s. Its full significance would emerge later, when it was formalized as the Western Association of Venture Capitalists.[48]

Of all the early experiments, it was, unsurprisingly, Boston's that led during the immediate postwar years. Given MIT's position at the heart of the military-industrial complex, it was natural to bet that the region's economic development could be accelerated by financing technologies from its labs. To lead such an effort, an elite band of New Englanders—among them the head of MIT and the president of the Boston Federal Reserve Bank—turned to Georges Doriot, a dapper French immigrant with a military mustache and a military bearing who taught at Harvard Business School. With the blessing of the Boston patriarchs, Doriot assumed the helm at American Research and Development in 1946.

Doriot was the ultimate embodiment of the military-industrial complex. During World War II, he had overseen technology procurement for the Pentagon's Quartermaster Corps, a position he had used to champion innovations—cold-weather shoes, water-repellent fabrics, and the lightweight plastic armor Doron, which was named after him. He was thus perfectly suited to the task of investing in high-tech firms emerging from the Pentagon-backed laboratories around Boston.[49] He badgered his investment team to visit the labs regularly, sometimes placing a subway token on a desk and admonishing the young man sitting too peacefully behind it, "MIT is only a token away."[50] An early Doriot win was High Voltage Engineering Corporation, an MIT spinout that made generators and nuclear particle accelerators, challenging incumbents such as General Electric.[51]

In 1957—the year the Group started its lunch meetings, and the year of the mutiny against Shockley—Doriot made the bet that transformed ARD's fortunes. He financed Digital Equipment Corporation, a company founded by two MIT professors who had helped to develop the TX-0 computer at the military-backed Lincoln Laboratory. The TX-0's achievement was to show how transistors could outperform vacuum tubes in equipment built for the military; Digital Equipment's premise was that transistors could also revolutionize computers made for civilians. To a modern venture capitalist, this pitch would have been instantly attractive: the founders came from a cutting-edge research lab, and they proposed to commercialize a technology that was already proven. But in the financial climate of the 1950s, even the most compelling scientists had a hard time raising money, and Doriot exploited this circumstance to the maximum, making Digital's founders an offer that by later standards would have counted as an insult. ARD would provide a $70,000 investment and a $30,000 loan in return for 70 percent of the company: it was a "take it or leave it" offer. Lacking any alternative, the MIT professors accepted; nor did they protest when Doriot managed to push his stake up to 77 percent.[52] Having seized so much of the equity,

Doriot was in a position to profit massively when the professors succeeded. By the time ARD closed in 1972, it had reaped some $380 million from its bet on Digital—or $2.3 billion in today's money.[53] It was a bonanza that accounted for perhaps 80 percent of all the gains that ARD generated over a quarter of a century.[54] It was an early demonstration of the power law.

Doriot is sometimes regarded as the father of venture capital—a case made by his biographer, Spencer Ante.[55] Like John Hay Whitney, Doriot was at pains to distinguish himself from ordinary financiers, but being a business school professor, he was more penetrating and persuasive in defining venture capital's mission. In lectures delivered in his thick French accent, he proclaimed that the greatest rewards were to be had from the most ambitious and least obvious projects; that investors would have to wait patiently for returns to mature over the long term; and that the best prospects involved advanced technology, not orange juice or fishing in Asia.[56] Anticipating later venture capitalists, he understood that his role was to provide not simply money but also managerial counsel, assistance with hiring, and tips on everything from marketing to finance. He staged technology fairs to advertise his portfolio companies' products and advised Digital Equipment to present sample circuit boards on sheets of purple velvet, in the manner of a jeweler showing off a brooch. Plugging his protégés into ARD's network was all part of Doriot's service. "Your company was on display," one founder said of ARD's well-attended annual meetings, at which entrepreneurs mingled with investors. "The networking that was created and the introductions that were possible, all of that was very important. Anything that helps you keep your confidence, when you have no reason to have confidence, is valuable."[57]

The way Doriot talked about his partnership with company founders was eerily modern. The founders were young, willful, and courageous; the venture capitalist's role was to contribute wisdom and experience. The founders were brilliant, erratic, and sometimes emotionally fragile; "the venture investor must always be on call to advise, to persuade, to dissuade, to encourage, but always to help build."[58] Like later venture capitalists, Doriot was emphatic that the company founders were the stars of the entrepreneurial drama. "Seek out creative men with the vision of things to be done," he counseled; show "loyalty to the idea and to its initiator, the creative man."[59] Needless to say, Doriot's adoring deference to "creative men with the vision" did not prevent him from pocketing 77 percent of a creator's output. In this, too, Doriot anticipated the hypocrisy that would occasionally mark the venture industry in years to come.

Yet in other ways Doriot was less a founding father than a failed prophet: a pioneer who stumbled onto the wrong territory and led his followers astray. ARD was the first venture outfit to raise capital from institutional investors, but rather than setting up ARD as a partnership, in the manner of future venture capitalists, Doriot structured it as a public company, a decision that ensnared him in a cat's cradle of regulation.[60] ARD was restricted in its ability to grant stock options to employees, in its freedom to invest fresh capital into portfolio companies, and in the way that it calculated the value of investments.[61] In 1964, the Securities and Exchange Commission raided ARD's offices, showing up at the John Hancock building in Boston without warning. "They fully expected that we were here with nothing else to do but receive them and spend the next two days with them," Doriot huffed.[62] Following the raid, the SEC claimed that Digital Equipment's valuation—at one hundred times its acquisition cost—needed restating. "Is the valuation too high? Is it too low? Just what is wrong with it?" Doriot protested furiously.[63] "I rather resent, after twenty years of experience, to have two men come here, spend two days, and tell us that we do not know what we are doing." Doriot kept files of his letters to the regulators. One folder was labeled "Not sent—on advice of counsel."

Aside from his poor choice of legal structure, Doriot damaged the appeal of his example by disdaining financial incentives. He never shed the public-service brand that came with ARD's original regional-development mission. "Capital gains are a reward, not a goal," he proclaimed loftily.[64] He refused to pay his young lieutenants generously, telling them that they were in business not to make money but to serve their country.[65] Likewise, he promised never to abandon underperforming portfolio companies, even if they hogged capital that could be more productively deployed elsewhere; it was as though pulling the plug on one of his protégés would be morally akin to abandoning a wounded comrade on the battlefield. Because Doriot refused to tie money to success and vice versa, his staff and his investors grew fed up with him: they were fine with psychic income, but they also wanted the financial sort. Charles P. Waite, an ARD employee who worked hard to take one portfolio firm public, remembered, "I had made a very substantial contribution to that company. The CEO's net worth went from 0 to $10 million and I got a $2,000 raise."[66] For their part, Wall Street investors viewed ARD as a freakish philanthropic enterprise and consistently valued its shares at a discount to the value of its portfolio companies.[67]

ARD's inability to impress Wall Street, and its consequent failure to spawn an industry of imitators, entailed a painful irony. Whatever his faults, Doriot assembled stakes in thrilling growth enterprises over his twenty-five years in business; thanks to Digital Equipment and the power law, he multiplied his original investors' stake some thirty times over, trouncing the S&P 500.[68] And yet throughout ARD's existence, its own stock mimicked one of those pitifully undervalued, stodgily mature companies beloved by Benjamin Graham and Warren Buffett. Because Wall Street disdained it, ARD would be worth more to its owners if liquidated or merged into another company. And so, in 1972, it was.

<hr>

Such was the inhospitable financial landscape in June 1957, when Shockley's young researchers plotted their revolt. ARD had not yet financed Digital Equipment; the San Francisco lunch group was just getting started; a pair of philanthropic plutocrats financed odd projects in exotic overseas locations or on the East Coast. It was hardly surprising that the Shockley rebels could not imagine raising money to start their own enterprise. Instead, Eugene Kleiner's letter to his father's broker laid out a different aspiration: the team of disaffected Shockley scientists hoped to be hired by "a company which can supply good management."[69] Kleiner's wife, Rose, typed up the letter, dated June 14, 1957. Then she mailed it to the New York firm of Hayden, Stone.

The broker who had served Kleiner's father was preparing to retire from Hayden, so he passed the letter on to a young MBA named Arthur Rock.[70] Slight, taciturn, his eyes often clouded behind large glasses, Rock was not an obvious founding father, especially not of a new kind of swash-buckling finance. Unlike the Whitneys and the Rockefellers, he had grown up poor in Rochester, New York, the child of Yiddish-speaking immigrants, and had worked as a soda jerk in his father's small grocery store. Unlike Doriot, he had no experience with military technology, and not much even with the military; during a miserable stint as an army conscript, he had bridled at reporting to superiors whom he considered "not too bright." Perhaps because of his tough childhood—he suffered from polio, performed miserably in athletics, and was brutally victimized by anti-Semitic classmates—Rock was reserved to the point of being prickly.[71] Deal-making financiers are supposed to be suave. But Rock suffered fools impatiently, and the fools always knew.

And yet, as luck would have it, Rock was the perfect person to receive Kleiner's letter. Two years previously he had assembled a funding package for General Transistor, the first independent manufacturer of germanium semiconductors, which were to be used in hearing aids. Having steeped himself in this emerging industry, Rock appreciated Shockley's divine status among scientists: the god could hire anyone, so it followed that Kleiner and his comrades must be top of their field. At the same time, the fact that Kleiner's crew was on the point of mutiny added an extra dimension: the scientists evidently had character as well as credentials.[72] The combination of an elite team and a potentially breakout technology added up to an obvious commercial opportunity. It was a prospect analogous to Digital Equipment, which Doriot would finance later that summer.

On June 20, 1957, Rock placed a long-distance call to Kleiner, assuring him of his interest. The next day he wrote Kleiner a letter, urging him to keep his team together until they could meet face-to-face.[73] The following week Rock flew to San Francisco, accompanied by a glad-handing Hayden partner named Alfred "Bud" Coyle.

Rock and Coyle met Kleiner and his comrades at a San Francisco restaurant for dinner. The visitors from Wall Street understood that the rebels wanted to operate as a team, without Shockley's suffocating oversight. They further understood that the engineers wanted to remain in the Santa Clara valley, where they all had bought homes. But they had come to propose a novel way of meeting those objectives—one that the rebels had failed to imagine.

"The way you do this is you start your own company," Rock said simply.[74] By striking out on their own, the scientists would be able to work independently in the location of their choosing. But more than that, they would be company founders. They would own the fruits of their creative wizardry. A self-made loner from outside the establishment, Rock felt strongly on this last point. A certain kind of justice would be served.[75]

Rock's proposal took some digesting. "We were blown away," a researcher named Jay Last remembered later. "Arthur pointed out to us that we could start our own company. It was completely foreign to us."[76]

Gordon Moore, the engineer who led the failed appeal to Arnold Beckman, recalled a similar reaction. Years later, when he had achieved fame as the co-founder of two iconic Valley companies, Moore was still at pains to describe himself as an "accidental entrepreneur." "I'm not the sort who can just say, 'I'm going to start a company,'" he reflected. "The accidental entrepreneur like me has to fall into the opportunity or be pushed into it."[77] At that restaurant in San Francisco in late June 1957, Rock was pushing him firmly.

Rock himself remembered something different. Thinking back on that same dinner, he recalled that his mention of company ownership had changed the researchers' bearing. "They seemed to perk up a bit," he said later.[78] Unburdened by Doriot's sense of patriotic mission, untroubled by a plutocrat's vibrating conscience, Rock celebrated silently. The way he saw things, the fact that the scientists responded to financial incentives was all to the good.[79]

The discussion moved to practicalities. The researchers said they needed $750,000 to get their business started. Rock and Coyle countered that they should have at least $1 million. The Wall Streeters were projecting more confidence than was really justified: finding north of $1 million to launch an untested collective would not be straightforward.[80] But the financiers' bravado served to win over doubters. With the promise of a seven-figure funding package, whatever resistance the researchers had been feeling began to melt away.

Next came the question of who should lead the rebels. In his letter to Hayden, Kleiner had stated openly that the band of traitors, then numbering seven, included "no person who has ambitions as a manager at the top level." That had been fine while the plan was to be managed by another company. But if the new goal was to stay independent, the scientists would need to identify a leader who could unite their group. Persuading investors to finance a loose collective with no plausible chief executive would be out of the question.

Among the young men at Shockley's laboratory, Robert Noyce stood out as the obvious leader. A charmer, a prankster, physically graceful, he was the engineer who had compared Shockley's recruitment phone call to a divine audience. But Noyce had been agonizing about whether to join the mutiny and had stayed out of the meetings so far. The son and grandson of Congregational ministers from small-town Iowa, he worried about the ethics of betraying Shockley. According to one mutineer, Noyce was asking himself, "What would God think?"[81]

Rock and Coyle persuaded the seven to get to work on Noyce. The financiers had laid out a vision of liberation. The researchers would have to reciprocate by recruiting a chief.

The plotters designated a member of their band named Sheldon Roberts to phone Noyce. The call stretched late into the night, with Noyce swinging erratically between eagerness and caution. Finally, with the carrot of the $1 million–plus funding package dangling in front of him, Noyce agreed to join the others for a meeting with Coyle and Rock.[82]

The next day Sheldon Roberts picked up Noyce in his family's station wagon. They toured their colleagues' houses, stopping in Los Altos, Palo Alto, and Mountain View, picking up a new conspirator at each stop. Then they made their way to the Clift hotel in downtown San Francisco and proceeded to the grand, art deco Redwood Room where Rock and Coyle were waiting.

When the meeting got under way, Rock understood that the deal's weakness had been fixed. This newcomer, Robert Noyce, was a natural born leader. His eyes blazed fiercely.[83] His colleagues were content to let him speak for them.[84]

There were no more reasons not to go forward. Bud Coyle pulled out ten crisp dollar bills and proposed that every man present should sign each one. The bills would be "their contracts with each other," Coyle said.[85] It was a premonition of the trust-based contracts—seemingly informal, yet founded, literally, on money—that were to mark the Valley in the years to come.

Unlike Doriot's American Research and Development, the brokers from Hayden, Stone lacked a ready pot of money to fund startups. Instead, they backed companies by assembling coalitions of willing investors on an ad hoc basis, with the Hayden partners' capital accounting for a small share of the total. Now, to raise the $1 million–plus that he had promised the eight traitors, Rock jotted down the names of around thirty-five potential backers. ARD and Rockefeller Brothers were on the list.[86] So were technology companies that might have an interest in a semiconductor investment.

Rock quickly discovered how radical his vision was. The investment groups such as ARD and Rockefeller came up with excuses. The rebels had no management experience; the idea of writing such a large check made them queasy. Meanwhile, the technology companies Rock contacted cited a different objection: they would consider putting up the capital to create a new subsidiary, much as Beckman had done for Shockley, but they were not inclined to back eight scientists without the right to control them.[87] Besides, backing the Shockley defectors and allowing them to own stakes in their new enterprise would set a disruptive precedent: What if the backer's own employees demanded company stock, too?[88] Where Rock saw justice in young scientists owning the fruits of their own enterprise, others saw trouble. The whole point of the organization man was that he was instinctively obedient. Why buy workers' loyalty with stock options when the culture of the 1950s provided it for free?

After approaching thirty-five potential investors, Rock had failed to raise a single cent. Then Bud Coyle suggested Sherman Fairchild, a playboy with an inherited fortune who was a self-described "putterer" and science enthusiast.[89] Like the Whitneys and the Rockefellers, Fairchild had enough money to yawn at the prospect of more of it. Unlike the Whitneys and the

Rockefellers, he might be tickled by the notion of a new semiconductor venture.

In late August 1957, Bob Noyce and Eugene Kleiner flew to New York. They made their way to Sherman Fairchild's Manhattan town house, which was fitted out with glass walls and whizzy blinds that opened and shut electronically.[90] After some initial pleasantries, Noyce uncorked the flair that Rock had seen in him. Fixing Fairchild with those blazing eyes, he explained that the future would be built on silicon-and-wire devices, meaning on simple sand and metal, materials that cost almost nothing. Huge profits would flow to the company that fashioned transistors from these basic elements, and Fairchild could be the visionary who backed the winner.[91] It was a version of the "call to greatness" speech that charismatic entrepreneurs would deliver repeatedly in the Valley. Fairchild was sold.

Now all that remained was to close the terms of the deal. Rock had promised the defectors the chance to own their own company, and he did his best to deliver. Each of the eight founders was invited to put up $500 in return for 100 shares in the startup. The men scraped together the money, but not without difficulty; $500 was two or three weeks' salary, and Noyce had to call his parents to ask if his grandmother could lend him the funds.[92] For its part, Hayden, Stone bought 225 shares at the same price as the founders, and 300 more shares were set aside in a kitty to help recruit senior managers; despite Noyce's charisma, Fairchild saw him as merely the interim chief. Each founder was therefore left with just under 10 percent of the company, with the prospect that this share would fall to 7.5 percent when new management materialized. Meanwhile, Fairchild's company, Fairchild Camera and Instrument, was stumping up just about all of the initial capital—some $1.4 million, dwarfing the $5,125 put up by the scientists and Hayden. But because Fairchild's money came in the form of a loan rather than equity, the founders' ownership was not being diluted.[93]

On the face of it, the eight scientific founders had landed a great deal. But, anticipating the opacity of later venture financings, some of these numbers were not what they seemed. After all, Sherman Fairchild's negotiators had a powerful hand to play: thirty-five other investors had rejected Rock outright. If Georges Doriot of ARD could seize 77 percent of Digital Equipment by risking just $100,000, Fairchild's men would have been fools to risk $1.4 million without getting something back. The result was a deal that gave the eight scientists the appearance of autonomy but not much of the substance. The Fairchild loan was actually not really a loan: it came bundled with an option to purchase all of the new company's stock for $3 million.[94] Likewise, the Shockley defectors were getting ownership that was not really ownership: Fairchild Camera and Instrument controlled the semiconductor operation via a voting trust. Rock had done his best to keep his promises, but he could not deliver miracles.

If Rock's purpose had been to liberate talent from a suffocating manager, the results soon proved to be more raucous and more glorious than he could have imagined. For the first couple of months, the eight scientists worked out of a garage; then they moved to a half-constructed building that lacked electricity. Undeterred, the freed men attached wires to a nearby electricity pole so they could rig up a power saw; it was winter, and Vic Grinich, a lanky, curly-haired tinkerer, could be seen outside battling the elements, decked out in gloves, hat, muffler, and pipe, with a heater hooked up to the power line.[95] Company strategy at Fairchild was hashed out at collaborative bull sessions; sales meetings featured brownies and whiskey; and new hires straight out of grad school were empowered to make major purchasing decisions. As the weather turned warmer, Bob Noyce, the acting chief of the collective, showed up at work in shorts.[96]

Six months after the founding, Rock went out to California to check on progress. He had multiple motives. Hayden still held shares representing just over a fifth of the new startup, not counting the Fairchild fine print, and Rock was on the hunt for more West Coast tech deals. Besides, Rock had warmed to the eight scientists personally. Aged thirty-one, he came from the same generation as they did. He bonded particularly with the bachelors who enjoyed weekend escapes to the mountains.[97] Scarred by the experience of childhood polio, Rock had turned himself into an accomplished skier and climber. The Sierras were another good reason for a trip to the West Coast.

On Wednesday, March 26, 1958, Rock had dinner with Noyce. The next day he sent Coyle an excited memo: "I got a lot of the inside poop, and apparently things are going along better than they have let anyone believe." Fairchild had made its first sale, shipping one hundred transistors to IBM for $150 a piece. Each device contained materials worth two or three cents, plus maybe a dime for the labor, so the operating margin was spectacular. In the meantime, Noyce and his colleagues were pushing the scientific frontiers at a pace that Shockley would never have permitted. The team was trying out new combinations of metals in semiconductors, and Noyce had ideas for innovative switches and a revolutionary scanner. The whole effort, moreover, was self-consciously commercial. Before Fairchild's founding, as Noyce would reflect later, researchers wore white smocks and were locked up in the laboratory. But at Fairchild they were out talking to the customers; even before developing their first transistors, they had met potential buyers in military avionics and figured out what kind of device would sell. Other corporate research teams—Bell Labs, Texas Instruments—could claim to rival Fairchild in terms of scientific excellence. But the Fairchild founders were more focused on the market. They wanted to understand what products would be useful and what would make the value of their equity go up.[98]

Fairchild had gotten off to such a good start that Noyce was feeling expansive. Rock ended his memo to Coyle jokingly: "You will be glad to learn that my arm was broken in an unsuccessful attempt to pick up the check."[99]

By the second year of its existence, Fairchild Semiconductor was doing even better. Noyce and his colleagues came up with a revolutionary process that made it possible to combine multiple transistors in one tiny integrated circuit, and in 1959 Fairchild took in orders worth some $6.5 million, thirteen times more than the previous year. The young company's after-tax earnings already came to about $2 million, and given its huge operating margins, it had every reason to expect windfall profits as its sales volumes ramped up.[100] The news was so excellent, in fact, that Fairchild Camera and Instrument decided to exercise its option, paying the agreed $3 million for all of Fairchild Semiconductor's stock.[101]

For Noyce and his co-founders, it was a bittersweet moment. The Traitorous Eight each received $300,000, fully six hundred times what they had invested two years previously; the bonanza amounted to around thirty years' salary. But at the same time, Fairchild Camera was doing even better: it was paying a price-earnings multiple of about 1.5 for a spectacular growth firm. To put that in perspective, in 1959 IBM's stock price ranged between thirty-four and fifty-one times its earnings.[102] Given that Fairchild was in the midst of an extraordinary expansion—between early 1959 and early 1960, its staff count hurtled from 180 to 1,400—a reasonable price-earnings multiple for Fairchild Semiconductor would have been at the top of IBM's range, around 50. These rough numbers imply that because earnings were running at about $2 million, Semiconductor might have been worth $100 million in an open transaction. In return for risking an initial $1.4 million, in other words, the East Coast investors had secured a memorable bonanza. Noyce and his co-founders had worked flat out and earned a combined $2.4 million. The passive financier had walked off with forty times more than that.[103]

From Arthur Rock's perspective, it was time for the next act. His firm had made the same 600x as the eight traitors, a nice profit of almost $700,000. But Rock had a feeling that there was scope to do better. He had landed the deal, but he had allowed the lion's share of the profits to flow to Fairchild. He had tried to stand up for the eight scientists, but had succeeded only partially. What he had done, however, was to demonstrate that liberation capital was about much more than keeping a team together in the place where its members happened to own houses. Liberation capital was about unlocking human talent. It was about sharpening incentives. It was about forging a new kind of applied science and a new commercial culture.

Chapter Two

FINANCE WITHOUT FINANCE

I f liberation capital launched the Traitorous Eight and Fairchild Semiconductor, the following decade brought two further advances that
forged the modern venture-capital profession. First, technology investors embraced the idea of an equity-only, time-limited fund, rejecting various rival formats. Second, technology investors devised a new kind of risk
management, suited to the peculiarities of venture portfolios. Unlike other
investors, venture capitalists could not diversify their risks across stocks
and bonds and real estate: they were bound to hold lumpy, concentrated
bets on a small number of technology startups. During the 1960s—the period, ironically, when finance professors made diversification the corner-
stone of modern portfolio theory—Arthur Rock and his imitators improvised
an entirely different approach to risk-taking, inventing what amounted to
finance without finance.

The first innovation—the creation of a new kind of financial war chest—
had preoccupied policy thinkers for several years. In 1955 the rising management guru Peter Drucker, later hailed as the most important business
thinker of the era, put his finger on a paradox of mid-century capitalism.
Burgeoning pension funds were managing the "small man's" money, increasingly assuming the effective ownership of great public corporations, but
the small man's money was not being channeled to small companies. The

sources of capital were being democratized, in other words, but access to capital wasn't, because the large pension funds that served as agents for the little guy had no practical way of scoping out startups. As a result, entrepreneurs struggled to find funding. Their likeliest source of capital came from the retained profits of established businesses—thus Beckman Instruments financed Shockley, and Fairchild Camera and Instrument financed the eight traitors. But this form of funding came with a bias. Established businesses "naturally invest in fields with which they are familiar," Drucker lamented; in consequence, "more promising areas of economic enterprise may have to go without." There were "clear signs," Drucker concluded, that the economy was "inadequately nourished with venture capital."[1]

Drucker had identified the problem, but neither he nor other policy thinkers hit on the solution. He cited what he saw as the promising example of Georges Doriot's American Research and Development. "Ultimately we might have a number of development companies, some within one region, some within one industry," he proposed. But, as we have seen, ARD's public-company structure attracted an exhausting regulatory burden, and because ARD was set up as an open-ended corporation rather than a time-limited fund, it lacked a sense of urgency. Instead of pushing successful ventures to raise additional capital from other investors in order to expand quickly, Doriot was content to let them grow by reinvesting profits. Thanks to Drucker's endorsement, ARD attracted imitators. Despite his endorsement, none performed well.

Other reformers embraced Drucker's diagnosis but favored a different solution. In 1958, spurred by the Soviet Union's launch of the first man-made satellite, Sputnik, the federal government promised subsidies for a new kind of venture vehicle, the Small Business Investment Company. The subsidies were generous, featuring cheap loans and tax concessions. But, like most venture incentives that governments across the world would later offer, they came with conditions. To qualify for maximum assistance, an SBIC's fund had to be no bigger than $450,000; this deprived SBICs of the scale necessary to retain competent professionals. SBICs could not compensate their investment staff with stock options, nor could they invest more than $60,000 into a portfolio company, making it hard to prime startups with adequate capital.[2] Even the boss of the SBIC program grew exasperated. "The rules were drawn on a legalistic basis and without too much awareness of the business effects," he grumbled.[3]

Not that this prevented aspirant investors from holding out their hats. In 1962, Bill Draper and Pitch Johnson, Harvard Business School graduates who had taken Doriot's class on management, formed the twelfth SBIC in the country and set up shop in Palo Alto. The two made an unlikely pair: Draper was tall and lean with eyebrows like caterpillars; Johnson was compact, a former college track star. But both men had the advantage of family wealth, which helped them scrape together $150,000, which in turn qualified them for a cheap loan of $300,000 from the SBIC program. Thus equipped with a fund of $450,000, the regulatory maximum, the partners rented a pair of matching Pontiacs and headed out into the plum and apricot orchards of the Santa Clara valley.[4]

There was nothing particularly sophisticated about their investment method. They trawled up and down two roads in particular: one was named Commercial and the other was called Industrial.[5] When they spied a sign for a company with "electro-" or "-onics" in the name, they would pull up in the unpaved parking lot, push open a door, and greet the lady at the front desk. Was the president around? they'd ask.

"I'll see if he's in," the receptionist would answer. "What did you say your business was again? Venture capital?"[6]

Draper and Johnson were assiduous, and both prospered as venture capitalists in the decades that followed. But their early experiment with the SBIC format was only moderately successful. Because of the restraints imposed by regulators, the partners sought out opportunities to buy the maximum possible stake in a company for the permitted investment of $60,000: their first transaction secured 25 percent of Illumitronic Systems, a maker of scales for assembly lines. But entrepreneurs who accepted such terms were unlikely to amount to much. "The company wasn't going anywhere," Draper wrote of Illumitronics later. "It was a good living for the entrepreneur, but it was a bad investment for the venture capitalists."[7] Another Draper-Johnson investment, a startup called Electroglas, further illustrated the drawbacks of the SBIC structure. When Electroglas ran into trouble, Draper and Johnson wanted to support it with a new strategy and fresh capital. But the regulatory cap on their investment limited their influence on strategy and forbade them to inject additional cash.[8] After three years of financial prospecting, Draper and Johnson dissolved their partnership, selling their portfolio for a modest profit.[9]

Most SBICs fared worse than that. More even than the restrictions on how they invested their capital, their fatal flaw turned out to be the apparently generous terms on which they raised it. A large loan from the government sounded attractive, but the loan had to be serviced. Even with a subsidized 5 percent interest rate, this obligation had a crippling consequence: it forced SBICs to invest in startups that paid dividends. This was antithetical to the whole idea of technology investing: new ventures generally required at least a year of research and development before they began selling their product, and then, if the product proved successful, they typically wanted to reinvest every dollar of income in scaling up their sales effort before a rival copied them. The SBICs' need for dividends thus put them at cross-purposes with the growth-oriented firms they should have been backing. To promote innovation, the government had come up with an investment vehicle that was unsuited to innovative companies.[10]

Because of this design flaw, most SBICs gave up trying to invest in technology ventures. By 1966, only 3.5 percent of SBIC portfolio companies were engaged in applied science, undermining the original purpose of the SBIC program.[11] And not only did the SBICs fall short as public policy; they also struggled commercially. Because they shied away from promising but risky tech ventures, their investment performance languished, and they soon found it difficult to raise capital.[12] At their peak in the early 1960s, the SBICs had accounted for over three-quarters of all venture-capital investments. By 1968, they had been eclipsed by a new rival that neither the government nor Peter Drucker had anticipated: the private limited partnership.[13]

◆

The ascent of this new rival began in 1961, when Arthur Rock quit the New York brokerage business. He had tired of dealing in the shares of public companies, not least because the bull market of the late 1950s had made it

hard to find growth stocks at attractive prices. Rock therefore resolved to
set up shop where there still might be bargains—in California, where he
proposed to seek out "the more speculative, completely unseasoned companies."[14] Arriving in San Francisco, he joined forces with Tommy Davis, a
dashing southerner and war hero who shared his enthusiasm for technology. "The fortunes of the past were made by stringing steel rails across the
country," Davis remarked. "I came to believe that the fortunes of my generation would come out of men's minds."[15]

Davis and Rock set out to change the way that technology was financed.
Before 1961, Davis had experimented with tech investing on behalf of the
Kern County Land Company, an oil, cattle, and real estate business in California's Central Valley.[16] This fitted Peter Drucker's observation that the
chief source of capital for innovation lay in the retained profits of established companies; unfortunately, just as Drucker had anticipated, Kern
County Land soon ordered Davis to steer clear of speculative electronics
that were outside its comfort zone.[17] Arthur Rock, for his part, had encountered his own challenges at Hayden, Stone. There, the procedure had been
to identify deals first, then call around haphazardly to find a willing source
of capital. Because there were almost no dedicated pools of money looking
to finance startups, such money was scarce and the bargaining power lay
with the investors. Innovators suffered, just as Drucker had promised.

To fill this gap in the capital market, Davis and Rock set themselves up
as a limited partnership, the same legal structure that had been used by a
short-lived rival called Draper, Gaither & Anderson.[18] Rather than identifying startups and then seeking out corporate investors, they began by raising a fund that would render corporate investors unnecessary. As the two
active, or "general," partners, Davis and Rock each seeded the fund with
$100,000 of their own capital. Then, ignoring the easy loans to be had from
the fashionable SBIC structure, they raised just under $3.2 million from
some thirty "limited" partners—rich individuals who served as passive investors.[19] The beauty of this size and structure was that the Davis & Rock
partnership now had a war chest seven and a half times larger than an SBIC,
and with it the ammunition to supply companies with enough capital to
grow aggressively. At the same time, by keeping the number of passive in-

vestors under the legal threshold of one hundred, the partnership flew under the regulatory radar, avoiding the restrictions that ensnared the SBICs and Doriot's ARD.[20] Sidestepping yet another weakness to be found in their competitors, Davis and Rock promised at the outset to liquidate their fund after seven years. The general partners had their own money in the fund, and thus a healthy incentive to invest with caution. At the same time, they could deploy the outside partners' capital for a limited time only. Their caution would be balanced with deliberate aggression.

Indeed, everything about the fund's design was calculated to support an intelligent but forceful growth mentality. Unlike the SBICs, Davis & Rock raised money purely in the form of equity, not debt. The equity providers— that is, the outside limited partners—knew not to expect dividends, so Davis and Rock were free to invest in ambitious startups that used every dollar of capital to expand their business.[21] As general partners, Davis and Rock were personally incentivized to prioritize expansion: they took their compensation in the form of a 20 percent share of the fund's capital appreciation. Meanwhile, Rock was at pains to extend this equity mentality to the employees of his portfolio companies. Having witnessed the effect of employee share ownership on the early culture of Fairchild, he believed in awarding managers, scientists, and salesmen with stock and stock options. In sum, everybody in the Davis & Rock orbit—the limited partners, the general partners, the entrepreneurs, their key employees—was compensated in the form of equity. It was a world away from ARD, where the investment professionals had almost no financial interest in the expansion of their portfolio companies.

Even as they forged this aggressive equity culture, Davis and Rock promoted a division of the spoils that heralded a new order. At ARD, Doriot had seized 77 percent of the stock of Digital Equipment for just $100,000 in capital, leaving a meager 23 percent for the founders. In the new order envisaged by the Davis & Rock partnership, things would be different. Allowing for some inevitable variation across companies, founders could generally expect to keep about 45 percent of their startups, with employees getting about 10 percent and the venture-capital partnership contenting itself with the remaining 45 percent.[22] That 45 percent would in turn be split between

the limited partners and the general partners. The passive providers of
capital would keep four-fifths of the venture fund's gains, equivalent to
owning 36 percent of capital gains at the portfolio companies. Davis and
Rock would share the other nine percentage points, meaning that they received about a fifth of what the founders got. In short, the capital providers
would do well, but not absurdly well. "I never wanted to be the richest corpse
in the cemetery," Rock said later.[23]

On October 10, 1961, Davis & Rock filed its Certificate of Partnership. Its
outside investors included six of the eight founders of Fairchild, some of
whom had become Rock's companions on ski trips and hiking adventures.[24]
Hayden, Stone invested, too, as did several Hayden clients whom Rock had
enriched with his technology tips. The two general partners—one shy and
laconic, the other sunny and garrulous—rented an anonymous office on the
sixteenth floor of the grand, brick-fronted Russ Building on San Francisco's
Montgomery Street. On a door at the end of a long corridor, a small sign said
only "1635." Backing low-profile startups would be a low-profile activity.

Rock and his partner articulated an approach to risk management that
would resonate with future venture capitalists. Modern portfolio theory,
the set of ideas that was coming to dominate academic finance, stressed diversification: by owning a broad mix of assets exposed to a wide variety of
uncorrelated risks, investors could reduce the overall volatility of their
holdings and improve their risk-return ratio. Davis and Rock ignored this
teaching: they promised to make concentrated bets on a dozen or so companies. Although this would entail obvious perils, these would be tolerable
for two reasons. First, by buying just under half of a firm's equity, the Davis
& Rock partnership would get a seat on the board and a say in its strategy:
in the absence of diversification, a venture capitalist could manage his risk
by exercising a measure of control over his assets. Second, Davis and Rock
insisted that they would invest only in ambitious, high-growth companies—
ones whose value might jump at least tenfold in five to seven years. To critics who called this test excessively demanding, Davis retorted that it would
be "unwise to accept a less stringent one." Venture investing was necessar-

ily speculative, he explained, and most startups would fail; therefore, the winners would have to win big enough to make a success of the portfolio.[25] "Trying to play it safe in small companies is, to my mind, self-defeating," Davis insisted.[26] Although they did not use the term, Davis and Rock were acknowledging the logic of the power law. The best way to manage risk was to embrace it fearlessly.

In the early 1960s, when the partners were laying out this vision, academia was turning finance into a quantitative science. But the way Davis and Rock saw things, the art of venture investing was necessarily subjective. Judgments about technology startups would "come from either 'the seat of the pants' or the 'top of the hat,'" as Rock once wrote to Davis.[27] Quantitative investment metrics such as the price-earnings ratio would be irrelevant, because the most promising ventures were likely to have no earnings whatever at the point when they sought capital. Likewise, they would lack the physical assets—the buildings, machines, inventory, and vehicles—that constituted "book value" at mature companies: thus another standard metric used in public markets would be meaningless. In sum, venture capitalists would have to bet on startups without the reassuring yardsticks used by other financiers. They would have no choice but to practice finance without finance.

Having discarded conventional investment metrics, the partners needed something else to go by. They found it in judgments about people, never mind that these could sound like a soft basis on which to commit capital. The central principle of the venture business, Davis once explained boldly, could be summed up in four words: "Back the Right People."[28] For his part, Rock made a habit of skipping over the financial projections in business plans and flipping to the back, where the founders' résumés were presented.[29] "The single most important factor in the long run for any company is, of course, management," Rock told the Harvard Business School Club of San Francisco in 1962. "However, I believe that in the applied science industry this is especially true." The only asset of tech startups, and the only possible reason to invest in them, was human talent, or what Rock liked to call "intellectual book value." "If you are buying intellectual book value, then you'd better place a great deal of emphasis on the people who you hope will capitalize on their intellect," Rock lectured.[30]

Unlike later venture capitalists, many of whom were engineers by back-ground, Davis and Rock lacked the training necessary to evaluate the tech-nical ideas of founders.[31] They made up for this deficiency by seeking advice from their fund's limited partners, several of whom were running scientific startups. But they also relied on emotional intelligence. Rock in particular believed that his intuitions about people gave him an edge as an investor. His shy outsider's temperament made him an expert listener, and he would meet promising company founders multiple times before committing to back them. His method was to pose open-ended questions—Whom did they ad-mire? What mistakes had they learned from?—and then wait patiently for the entrepreneurs to fill the vacuum created by his silence.[32] Self-contradiction, wishful thinking, a fondness for ingratiation at the expense of honesty: these were the clues that Rock should pass on an investment. Intelligent consistency, gritty realism, fiery determination: these were the signs that he should seize the opportunity.[33] "Do they see things the way they are and not the way they want them to be?" Rock would often ask himself.[34] "Would they drop what they're doing at a minute's notice to do something which would help the business, or would they continue their dinner?"[35] "When I talk to entrepre-neurs, I'm evaluating not only their motivation but also their character, fiber," Rock reflected.[36] "I believe so strongly in people that I think talking to the individual is much more important than finding out too much about what they want to do."

This belief in individuals—and the correspondingly low priority at-tached to the product or the market they were working on—featured dra-matically in one of the first Davis & Rock investments. Before opening for business, the two partners had agreed to steer clear of computer startups: IBM's dominance of this industry made it a kill zone. But on the day that Davis took possession of the office in the neo-Gothic Russ Building, he got a call from a consultant whom he knew from his days with Kern County Land.

The consultant was evidently excited. He was singing the praises of a mathematician named Max Palevsky, touting his new venture as "the most exciting proposition you ever saw."

Davis listened, seated on the floor of his bare office, which had yet to be furnished. He was eager to believe. Exciting calls like this one were precisely why he had cut the cord with Kern County, and here he was on his first day in his new office, listening to the sort of pitch he had dreamed of. Presently, he grew emotional. "My voice shot up in the treble clef," Davis later remembered.

Then he thought to ask a question. "Wait a minute, what's this guy going to do?"

Make computers, the consultant answered.

Conjuring this interchange years later, Davis toppled over in mock dismay. The entrepreneur sounded so wonderful. But challenging IBM was a fool's game.[37]

Out of deference to the consultant, Davis agreed to meet this mathematician anyway. As soon as he did so, it was clear that Max Palevsky was special. The son of a Yiddish-speaking Russian house painter, he had grown up in a hardscrabble section of Chicago, then vaulted to the city's famous university, where he had studied logic. This proved to be a springboard for computing, and after several successful years in the industry, Palevsky was now a bundle of late-thirties energy, brandishing a novel vision of the computer market. Thanks to the advent of the semiconductor, computers no longer needed bulky and expensive vacuum tubes; therefore, Palevsky could build machines that would outperform IBM's. But what mattered more than Palevsky's résumé and market vision was the dynamism of his presence. Davis later said that when he went to the races, he liked to back the horse that *wanted* to win. Well, Palevsky was so passionate about his proposed company that despite his fear of flying he had crisscrossed the country in search of capital, subsisting on candy and adrenaline.[38]

Davis called Rock, who had not yet even packed up his belongings to make the move from New York. He had found a wonderful investment, Davis explained breathlessly. Together, they had to back this venture: a brand-new computer company that would take on IBM.

There was a silence on the other end of the line. Finally, Rock said, "Jesus, I've gone into partnership with an idiot."[39]

Yet when Rock met Palevsky, he too was won over. What struck Rock particularly was Palevsky's warmth and informality.[40] He could joke, flatter and cajole, and generally draw the best out of others: he was an anti-Shockley.

Entrepreneurs with managerial magic can't lose, Rock reflected later. "If their strategy doesn't work, they can develop another one."[41]

Davis & Rock duly invested $257,000 in Palevsky's new company, Scientific Data Systems. The bet turned out better than they could have imagined: SDS was the fastest-growing computer maker of the 1960s. By the time Davis and Rock wound up their partnership, in 1968, their shares in SDS were worth $60 million, more than justifying the contention that one audacious bet could drive the success of an entire portfolio.[42]

Because Davis and Rock focused so intently on the quality of the founders, they exercised their power respectfully after investing. They used their board seats to protect their fund against the risk of foolish errors, refusing to let founders waste money, insisting on a sense of urgency, sometimes squelching poorly considered proposals by abruptly demanding, "What good will it do?"[43] In the case of Scientific Data Systems, Rock chaired the board and did everything he could to help, vetting most prospective hires and ensuring that the company accounts reflected the true state of the business.[44] Palevsky appreciated Rock's contribution, later describing him as "a very steady hand on the helm." The two men traveled together on a sales trip to Russia: American sons of Yiddish-speaking Russians, visiting the land of their ancestors and hating every moment. ("The best thing about going to Russia was leaving it," Rock recalled later.)[45] In 1969, when Xerox made a bid for SDS, Palevsky recognized Rock's superior grasp of the financial details and asked him to negotiate. The result was the corporate sale of the decade, with Xerox paying just under $1 billion.[46]

On June 30, 1968, Davis and Rock wound up their partnership. Thanks overwhelmingly to SDS, but also to a defense contractor called Teledyne, their initial fund of $3.4 million was now worth almost $77 million, an extraordinary return of 22.6x; it was a performance that easily eclipsed Warren Buffett in this period, as well as that of the inventor of the "hedged fund," Alfred Winslow Jones. Adding together their share of the fund's appreciation plus the gain on their personal $100,000 stakes, each partner walked off with almost $10 million—or $74 million in today's money. Letters flooded in from the limited partners. "Dear Tommy and Arthur, The absolutely phenomenal record which you established as investment managers during the seven years of Davis & Rock leaves me as a participating partner at a loss for words to express my appreciation," one said.[47]

Two years earlier, in 1966, a *Fortune* article had broadcast the mouthwatering returns of Alfred Winslow Jones, and a whole new hedge-fund industry had sprung up. Now the Davis & Rock partnership attracted similar attention, with similar effects on venture capital. An admiring *Los Angeles Times* profile featured a picture of the partners decked out in suits and ties, Davis with natty handkerchief peeking from his breast pocket.[48] Meanwhile, *Forbes* posed the existential question on the minds of many readers, "How do you get to be like Arthur Rock?"[49] In the course of answering that question, Rock laid out his theory of people-led investing, mentioning that he aimed to find a younger partner with whom to launch a new fund. Soon letters from job applicants came in from all over the country, including from a young man in Boston named Dick Kramlich, whom Rock eventually hired. Meanwhile, Davis launched his own new partnership, calling it the Mayfield Fund, and rivals started to proliferate. Two young challengers named Bill Hambrecht and George Quist launched an eponymous venture fund–cum–technology investment bank that would later play a central role in the Valley. A Texas engineer named Burt McMurtry quit the electronics industry to try his hand as a venture investor, beginning a career that would culminate in a partnership that backed Sun Microsystems and Microsoft. In New York, the Rockefeller family formalized its commitment to venture capital by creating Venrock, a dedicated fund modeled on Davis & Rock, and the big Wall Street banks showed up for the party, hiring MBAs to staff their own venture units. In San Francisco, the informal investing club known as the Group morphed into the Western Association of Venture Capitalists. In the banner year of 1969, $171 million worth of private capital flowed into the sector, the equivalent of fifty new Davis & Rock partnerships.[50]

The triumph of the Davis & Rock model was underscored by the failure of the alternative venture formats. In Boston, Georges Doriot's deputy, Bill Elfers, expressed the simmering frustration with ARD's public-company structure by defecting to found a Davis & Rock–style partnership named

Greylock; by 1972, ARD was gone. Money stopped flowing to the SBICs, and the better ones—including an outfit called Sutter Hill, which had bought out the Draper and Johnson portfolio—paid back their government loans and recruited private limited partners, embracing the equity culture of Davis & Rock. Meanwhile, Peter Drucker's observations on the pitfalls of corporate venture investing were illuminated by the fate of Fairchild Semiconductor. It was as though the gods of fate relished full-circle endings.

In a famous essay in *Esquire*, the master storyteller Tom Wolfe presents Robert Noyce, the charismatic leader of Fairchild's eight traitors, as the father of Silicon Valley.[51] Noyce came from a family of Congregational ministers in Grinnell, Iowa, the very middle of the Midwest, where the land was as flat as the social structure. When Noyce moved out to California, he brought Grinnell with him, "as though sewn into the lining of his coat." He wanted instinctively to run Fairchild without any divisions between bosses and workers. There would be no reserved parking spots for managers, no fancy executive dining rooms, and no limits on who could speak at meetings. Rather, there would be a level playing field, a ferocious work ethic, and a belief that every last employee had a stake in the firm.

In Wolfe's telling of this story, the problem with Fairchild Semiconductor's East Coast overlords was that they could never fathom this egalitarian ethic. The East Coast had a feudal approach to corporate organization: there were kings and lords, and there were vassals and soldiers, and the boundaries were established by protocol and perquisites. Whereas Noyce's West Coast semiconductor guys shuddered at social pretension, the East Coast managers had limousines and peak-capped chauffeurs. Whereas the semiconductor guys operated out of utilitarian cubicles, decorated in a style that Wolfe called "Glorified Warehouse," the East Coast managers prized their baronial offices "with carved paneling, fake fireplaces, escritoires, bergeres, leather-bound books, and dressing rooms." And beyond these colorful stylistic clashes, there was a practical conflict. The West Coast engineers believed that the men who built the business should be rewarded with stock. The East Coast overlords were too greedy and shortsighted to share the bounty.

Yet despite Wolfe's masterful storytelling, it was Arthur Rock who understood this conflict earlier and more instinctively than Noyce did, and it was Rock who ensured that West Coast egalitarianism triumphed. Ever since his first meeting with the Traitorous Eight, Rock had grasped that owning a stake in their company was powerfully motivating to the scientists: that was why he had structured Fairchild Semiconductor so that all of them got stock. After Fairchild's East Coast bosses exercised their option and assumed full ownership, Noyce continued to serve the East Coasters loyally, but Rock quickly sensed that the magic of the company had been spoiled. His favorite hiking companions, two members of the Traitorous Eight named Jay Last and Jean Hoerni, griped about the changes at Fairchild, airing their resentment at the fact that they no longer owned shares. Jay Last said he now felt like "just another employee working in a research lab for somebody else."[52]

Rock listened to his friends' grievances and urged them to take their fate into their own hands. There was no point waiting; they deserved a financial share in the fruits of their research. If Rock had liberated them once, he could easily do so a second time. He advised Last and Hoerni to talk to Teledyne, the firm that would become the second most successful investment in the Davis & Rock portfolio.

Time passed and nothing happened. Last and Hoerni seemed too timid to act. So Rock spoke with Teledyne's boss, Henry Singleton, explaining why his hiking friends would be assets to his enterprise. Then he placed a call to Fairchild midway through the company's Christmas gift exchange, which featured none other than Jay Last dressed up as Santa Claus. Now was the time to seize the moment, Rock pressed the vacillating Santa, wheeling out the man-or-mouse challenge beloved by later headhunters. Henry Singleton was by his phone, Rock urged him. He was sitting there, waiting, expecting Last's call.[53]

Last duly dialed Singleton and agreed to meet him at Teledyne's headquarters in West Los Angeles.[54] He promised to bring Hoerni along.

Hoerni hated flying, so the two researchers donned what they called their negotiating suits and drove south. After several hours of discussion, in which Last and Hoerni made sure they would get a generous slug of equity, a deal was all but concluded.[55] Elated, the two men got back into their car and drove out into the Old Woman Mountains in the eastern Mojave Desert. They retrieved some horns and noisemakers from the trunk and sat in the middle of the desert, two besuited scientists blowing on their horns, celebrating the New Year and their new prospects—prospects made possible by Arthur Rock.[56]

Now that Rock had demonstrated that scientists could be liberated from oppressive corporate overlords not once but repeatedly, the fate of Fairchild's corporate venture bet was sealed. Last and Hoerni soon persuaded two more of the Traitorous Eight, Sheldon Roberts and Eugene Kleiner, to follow them to Teledyne, where they too were rewarded with suitable grants of stock.[57] More defections followed, and at the end of 1965 a particularly spirited engineer filled out the six-page exit questionnaire at Fairchild by scrawling over it, in capitals, "I-WANT-TO-GET-RICH."[58] In the spring of 1967, no less a figure than Noyce's top lieutenant quit, luring thirty-five Fairchilders to its main competitor, National Semiconductor.[59] The demoralized rump at Fairchild gathered weekly at a local bar called Walker's Wagon Wheel. "Well, it's Friday, who did National grab this week? Son of a bitch!"[60]

Toward the end of 1967, Fairchild's East Coast bosses finally awoke from their slumber. Thanks to the cultural shift that Rock had initiated, their refusal to grant stock to talented researchers was untenable. But although Fairchild now approved an options package for employees, it was too little, too late. Hemorrhaging talent, the company was losing money, and after nine years of laboring for the East Coasters, even Noyce could see that the game was up. In April 1968, he turned to Gordon Moore, one of the two traitors who remained with him at Fairchild. "I'm thinking of leaving," he said.[61]

When Noyce had broken ranks with Shockley, it had been a fraught decision; the possibility of launching a new firm had been beyond his imagining. But now, a decade later, the West Coast had changed. There was no need

to move meekly to another company; there was no need even to take investment from a corporate overlord. Thanks to the success of the Davis & Rock
partnership, money was available to back startups with no assets or profits,
just talent and ambition. The gap in the capital market identified by Peter
Drucker had been plugged.

Noyce placed a call to Arthur Rock. There were plenty of venture investors to pick from, but Rock had financed Fairchild. His reputation had blossomed thanks to SDS and Teledyne.

Noyce explained that he was quitting Fairchild and was plotting a new
firm.

"What took you so long?" was all that Rock said.[62]

Noyce said he thought he needed $2.5 million, considerably more than
Fairchild or SDS had raised at their inception.

"You got it," Rock promised.[63]

A few weeks after that phone call, Noyce and Gordon Moore quit Fairchild. Venture capital was liberating them, again.

What came next extended the revolution in which talent was rewarded and
capital learned its place. To raise money for the new company, which Noyce
and Moore called Intel, Rock devised a business plan that inverted the Fairchild model. Rather than giving special rights to the investor—rights consisting, in Fairchild's case, of the option to buy all of the company—the Intel
financing was designed to privilege the entrepreneurs. Noyce and Moore
would each buy 245,000 shares for $245,000, with Rock himself buying a
further 10,000 shares on the same terms. The outside investors would kick
in $2.5 million, but they would do so at a different valuation—not $1 per
share, but $5—meaning that they would control the same number of shares
as the founders even though they had stumped up five times more cash. As
was by now standard with Arthur Rock's deals, another pot of shares was
set aside to reward employees, but this time the principle was pressed further. At other Rock portfolio companies, the key engineers, managers, and
salespeople had received stock and stock options. In the case of Intel, all
employees got some.

On October 16, 1968, Rock started to round up the outside money. Having recently closed down the Davis & Rock fund, he lacked an investment vehicle to provide the capital himself. But now he had no trouble finding eager backers. Of the thirty-two names on Rock's original list, only one declined to invest; the rest counted themselves lucky to receive Rock's phone call. Max Palevsky came in, as did the venture operation of the Rockefeller family, which was about to make up for its shaky debut in the industry. The six other members of the Traitorous Eight bought shares, and Robert Noyce saw to it that his small alma mater, Grinnell College, was invited to participate.[64] Meanwhile, Sherman Fairchild was struck off the list after due consideration, and a throng of frustrated would-be investors clamored for access; one especially persistent admiral telephoned Moore's wife repeatedly.[65] Now, instead of capitalists selecting companies to invest in, the entrepreneurs were choosing among capitalists. The shift inaugurated by the Davis & Rock partnership had reached its full fruition.

Quite how much credit Rock himself deserves for these developments is of course debatable. But he certainly merits more credit than he has gotten. The prevailing narrative about Silicon Valley's culture lionizes company founders, and Tom Wolfe's exquisite storytelling has played up Noyce's roots in small-town Iowa as the genesis of the egalitarian, stock-for-everyone business culture of the West Coast.[66] But, as we have seen, it was Arthur Rock who provided the impetus for Fairchild's creation and who opened the founders' eyes to the possibility of owning the fruits of their research. It was Rock who demonstrated the potential of the limited partnership that developed the Valley's equity culture, and Rock who helped to catalyze the failure of the corporate venture model at Fairchild by prying away Jean Hoerni and Jay Last. When it came to the creation of Intel's employee stock plan, moreover, it was probably Rock who proposed access for everyone, and it was certainly Rock who devised the plan's details.[67] In a letter laying out his thinking in August 1968, Rock described a way of balancing the interests of investors and workers: Intel should avoid equity grants to short-term employees but extend them to everyone who made a long-term commitment. "There are too many millionaires who did nothing for their company except leave after a short period," he observed wisely.[68] Without Rock's judicious counsel, Intel's employee stock program would not have set the standard in the Valley, because it would not have been sustainable.

Noyce was indeed the son and grandson of Congregational ministers, as Tom Wolfe correctly emphasized. But Rock hated hierarchies with at least as much passion. He was the bullied, Jewish, physically insecure boy in a small town. He was the youth who despised the ranked rigidity of the army. He was the man who liberated himself from the corporate establishment of the East Coast at the first opportunity. In his laconic, just-the-facts, plainspoken lucidity, Rock was as hostile to posturing and pretension as Noyce was. If Tom Wolfe had written an epic profile of Rock rather than Noyce, the origins of Silicon Valley's egalitarian culture might be ascribed not to the entrepreneur but to the financier. No doubt the truth lurks somewhere in the middle.

Chapter Three

SEQUOIA, KLEINER PERKINS, AND ACTIVIST CAPITAL

In the summer of 1972, a trio of West Coast engineers produced something called *Pong*, one of the world's first video games. No sober person would have called *Pong* sophisticated. Players toggled a virtual paddle up and down, trying to block a virtual ball, and when the ball collided with the paddle, some deep crevice of the lizard brain was rewarded with a pleasing, popping sound—*thonk!* There was just one rule for players to master: "Avoid missing ball for high score."[1] Even the heroically inebriated could participate, and *Pong* was soon installed in bars around the Bay Area, raking in the punters' quarters at a rate of $1,000 a week.

Within a couple of years, the team behind *Pong* attracted the interest of a venture capitalist. By this time Atari, as their company was called, had infiltrated bars all over the nation.[2] It had opened a factory in a former roller-skating rink and retained a team of bell-bottomed engineers to dream up novel games for customers. But investing in Atari would take a new kind of venture capitalist, because Atari was a new kind of tech firm. When Arthur Rock had backed Fairchild—or SDS or Teledyne or Intel—the gamble lay in the technology: Would the research and development yield products that worked? With Atari, in contrast, the technology was relatively trivial: the first *Pong* game was rigged up by an inspired tinkerer with a bachelor's degree from Berkeley. Instead of technology risk, Atari involved business risk, marketing risk, and what might be termed wild-man risk. It was not for the faint of heart.

Nolan Bushnell, Atari's twentysomething founder, had no time for the basic disciplines of business. With a six-foot four-inch frame and a shaggy head of hair, he presided over his company like a high-tech Hugh Hefner.[3] He kept an oak beer tap outside his office and liked to hold business meetings in a hot tub—either the one in his house or the new one he had installed in Atari's engineering building.[4] The hot tub meetings and hot tub parties— it could be difficult, sometimes, to be sure of the difference—were part of the Atari culture, which hinged on keeping the male game designers happy by hiring the best-looking female secretaries available.[5] Bushnell's approach to corporate strategy was to scrawl epiphanies on scraps of paper that fell out of his pockets. His employees got travel expenses paid in advance and sometimes absconded with the cash, never to be seen again. Customer orders were frequently not written down, making costly disputes commonplace. Even though *Pong* was generating revenues, money was so tight that the parking lot emptied on paydays as people raced to cash their checks before Atari's account was drained.[6] If American business had been dominated since the 1950s by the organization man, Nolan Bushnell was the disorganization man: unkempt, semi-sober, creative, and compelling.

Fortuitously, the 1970s marked the arrival of a new kind of venture investor, equipped with an expanded tool kit that transformed previously unbackable Atari-type startups into thinkable wagers. Rather than merely identifying entrepreneurs and monitoring them, as Rock had done, the new venture capitalists actively shaped them: they told company founders whom to hire, how to sell, and how to structure their research. And to ensure that their instructions were implemented, the new venture capitalists came up with a second innovation: rather than organizing one large fundraising, they doled out capital in tranches, with each cautious infusion calibrated to support the company until it reached an agreed milestone. If the 1950s had revealed the power of liberation capital, and if the 1960s had brought the equity-only, time-limited venture fund, the advances of the 1970s were twofold: hands-on activism and stage-by-stage finance.

———◆———

The chief pioneers of the new venture style were Don Valentine and Tom Perkins, the prime movers, respectively, of the great Silicon Valley rivals Sequoia Capital and Kleiner Perkins Caufield & Byers. They were equally forceful and equally suited by temperament to combative activism. Valentine is said to have remarked that underperforming company founders should be "put into a cell with Charlie Manson," and he once berated a subordinate so severely that the poor man passed out.[7] Perkins, a Ferrari-driving, yacht-owning, self-regarding dandy, loved to flout polite wisdom; in later life, when he splashed $18 million on an apartment in San Francisco, he declared defiantly, "I'm called the king of Silicon Valley. Why can't I have a penthouse?"[8]

Valentine's aggression owed something to the experiences of his youth. His father was a trucker in Yonkers, New York, and a minor functionary in the Teamsters union; he had not completed high school, and the family had never had a bank account. As a boy, Don attended a tough Catholic academy where the nuns beat their charges, especially if, like the young Valentine, they tried to write with their left hands. Arthur Rock's harsh childhood, coupled with the physical frailty he suffered after being stricken with polio, left him aloof and private. Valentine's tough upbringing, coupled with the bulk of a prize boxer, left him angry, easily offended, and spoiling for a fight.

Valentine attended the Jesuit-led Fordham University, where he hated the professors. Next came the military draft, where he bridled at the regimentation and learned that his "sense of disobedience was not totally civil."[9] Fortunately, his physique soon won him an assignment to play water polo for the navy at a base in Southern California. He loved the climate, and after his release from water polo duty he joined the semiconductor business, determined to stay on the West Coast. He rose through the ranks at Fairchild Semiconductor and later at its rival National Semiconductor, developing a sideline investing his own money, including in the Rock-Palevsky bonanza, SDS. By 1972, his reputation was such that Capital Research and

Management, a venerable Los Angeles investment firm, asked him to spearhead its new move into venture capital.[10] The culture at Capital Research was conservative; the technology investments that Valentine liked were completely unconservative. But Valentine agreed to sign on anyway. His new boss, Bob Kirby, quickly dubbed him "Rocket Man."[11]

Valentine's first challenge was to raise capital for his new fund.[12] A disciple of Ayn Rand, the fiery libertarian novelist, Valentine was not about to incorporate as a Small Business Investment Company and accept government loans.[13] He understood that debt would be a burden to growth-oriented startups, and besides he had been raised to hate it: "My father didn't believe in debt, so we always rented, and I had it drilled into my mind that debt was evil, limiting, and bad."[14] Nor would Valentine take money from pension funds, because the Department of Labor's "prudent-man rule" banned these from investing in risky assets such as venture capital. Casting about for entities that were not constrained by government, Valentine considered raising capital from rich individuals, following the Davis & Rock model. But a friend pointed out that individuals had a habit of dying or divorcing, so that their property had to be divided, which meant that it had to be priced. A venture fund that took money from individuals thus risked endless arguments about the value of fledgling portfolio companies.[15] The way Valentine saw things, the one thing worse than entanglement with government was entanglement with lawyers.

Valentine also considered raising money from Wall Street. But he lacked the polish and training that preppy New Yorkers expected. He had not attended an Ivy League college or an elite business school, and he hated conceited know-it-alls, a category that he defined to include "people with hyphenated names or roman numerals after their last name, direct descendants of immigrants who arrived on the *Mayflower*, people who had enjoyed living on the East Coast, and those who wore Hermès ties, suspenders, cuff-links, signet rings, and monogrammed shirts," as a distinguished lieutenant wrote later.[16]

On one occasion, Valentine tried to raise capital from Salomon Brothers, the New York investment bank.

"What business school did you go to?" the Salomon guys asked.

"I went to Fairchild Semiconductor Business School," Valentine growled.

"They used to look at me like I was completely nuts, not just partially nuts," Valentine recalled later, with evident delight.[17]

It took Valentine a year and a half to raise $5 million for his first fund.[18] But in the end he succeeded by tapping pools of capital that enjoyed charitable status: the universities and endowments that escaped not only regulation but also capital-gains tax. The Ford Foundation came in first, later to be joined by Yale, Vanderbilt, and eventually Harvard; ironically, the Ivy League investment bosses showed a greater open-mindedness about a gruff Fordham graduate than many alumni could muster. In so doing, the endowments set in motion one of the great virtuous cycles of the American system. Venture capitalists backed knowledge-intensive startups, and some of the profits flowed to research institutions that generated more knowledge.[19] To this day, the conference rooms at Valentine's old firm are named after their main limited partners: Harvard, MIT, Stanford, and so on.[20]

◆

In the summer of 1974, soon after he had raised his $5 million, Valentine showed up at the old roller-skating rink that was now Atari's makeshift factory. He was fit and in his early forties, but as he made his way around the factory, he appeared to be struggling. He coughed uncomfortably, then seemed to gulp and hold his breath. As he described the scene later, the building was bathed in enough marijuana smoke to "knock you to your knees."[21]

"What's the matter?" Nolan Bushnell asked him.

"I don't know what those people are smoking," Valentine answered. "But it's not my brand."[22]

Venture capitalists had visited Atari before and retreated quickly. Burt McMurtry, one of the new venture capitalists who entered the business in the wake of Rock's successes, dismissed the company as "open-loop," engineering slang for chaotic.[23] But Valentine's combative personality allowed him to take a different view. Unfazed by the prospect of having to yell at wayward founders, he felt free to back wild people if they were onto something lucrative. More than that, backing a company like Atari appealed to Valentine's idea of himself. Those precious East Coast blue bloods would not touch Atari with a ten-foot pole, which was precisely why Valentine was keen to throw his arms around it. Years later, he delighted in recounting a meeting that took place in the Atari hot tub. At Bushnell's invitation, Valentine had stripped off confidently and waded in. Meanwhile, a nervous investor from Boston had sat off to the side in a white shirt and tie and with an uncomfortable expression.[24]

If Atari's loose culture was not a deal killer for Valentine, the important question was whether the company could build on *Pong*'s early popularity. Fortunately, this involved a set of issues that played to Valentine's strengths. Unlike Arthur Rock, he was a hands-on business operator by background, and in his years as a semiconductor salesman he had learned how to translate products into profits. You had to go with the version of your invention that would earn you the fattest margin, and you had to open sales channels to as many customers as possible. In the case of Atari, this meant capitalizing on one of Bushnell's many semi-formed epiphanies: if *Pong* could be sold to families rather than bars, the market could be expanded enormously.[25] To go after that home market, Valentine figured, Atari would have to do two things. The engineers would have to modify the game for private use. And the company would have to team up with a prestigious retailer—one with the clout to thrust *Pong* into the consciousness of every American shopper.

In late 1974, a few weeks after his visit to Atari's factory, Valentine made a decision. He was not going to invest yet: Atari was too chaotic. But he was not going to walk away: the potential was too terrific. Instead, he would get involved cautiously, in stages, and he would start by rolling up his sleeves and writing an Atari business plan. If all went well—if Bushnell embraced his strategy, and if the plan attracted interest from other venture capitalists—then Valentine would invest. He would risk his money, in other words, only when Atari had been at least partially de-risked. Activism and gradualism would thus combine to make a hot tub culture backable.

◆

Valentine could afford to wade in gradually because of the market climate. The guns-and-butter expansion of the 1960s had given way to tougher times; defense cuts had eliminated thousands of jobs, and the Arab oil embargo of

1973 had entrenched a depressing mix of low growth and high inflation. The tally of initial public offerings plummeted from more than one thousand in 1969 to just fifteen in 1974, and the S&P 500 returned more or less nothing over this period.[26] The collapse all but wiped out the nascent hedge-fund business, and likewise a headline in *Forbes* wondered, "Has the bear market killed venture capital?"[27] After attracting $171 million in new funds in 1969, venture capitalists raised only $57 million in 1974 and a mere $10 million the year after.[28] A *New Yorker* cartoon showed two men chortling, "Venture capital! Remember venture capital?"[29]

But adversity brought some advantages. Valentine could stalk Atari patiently; there was no need to worry about rivals swooping in on his target. He duly set about writing a strategy for the firm, focused on the development of *Home Pong*; he was not going to leave this task to the company's leaders, who were incapable of basic bookkeeping. By the start of 1975, with Valentine pushing and prodding, Atari had created a home version of its product, code-named Darlene after one of the women at the company.[30] Now, if Atari could secure a powerful distributor, it would meet Valentine's two conditions for investing.

Atari's first attempts to land a distribution deal ended in failure. An Atari team took the *Home Pong* prototype to the New York toy fair and returned empty-handed. An approach to Toys "R" Us was rebuffed, and talks with Radio Shack faltered.[31] So Valentine rolled up his sleeves again. He talked to a portfolio manager at his parent company, Capital Research, who held a large position in Sears, one of the most formidable retailers in the country.[32] Could the portfolio manager arrange an invitation for Bushnell to visit the Sears Tower in Chicago?

Having secured the introduction, Valentine packed Bushnell off to Sears with instructions to wear one of his "nonclown suits" and avoid being too "humorous."[33] Bushnell did as he was told, and a buyer from Sears soon returned the visit.[34] By the middle of March, Sears had placed an order for seventy-five thousand *Home Pong* machines.[35] Atari now had what Valentine had been waiting for: a promising new product and a powerful distributor.

At the beginning of June 1975, Valentine duly invested. He bought 62,500 shares for $62,500, making what would now be termed a "seed investment" in Atari.[36] But it was only the start. Once the partnership with Sears had matured and the risks in Atari had gone down some more, it would be time to put together a larger round of financing. To scale up its production of *Home Pong*, Atari would need much more than $62,500.

Over the summer, Valentine watched as the Atari-Sears alliance flourished. The Sears team seconded manufacturing experts to help Atari, and both sides strove to bridge the cultural chasm that divided them. One day a dozen Sears managers in three-piece suits came out to see Atari's factory, only to be confronted with a gaggle of long-haired twentysomething engineers in jeans and T-shirts. Bushnell defused the tension by setting giant cartons on a conveyor belt and inviting the Sears men to hop aboard, and the group set off happily on a tour of the factory. At dinner that evening, the guys from Atari made amends by dressing up in suits and ties. Meanwhile, the Sears team had changed into T-shirts.[37]

By the end of August 1975, Valentine felt ready to go forward with the next investment round—the "Series A" in modern parlance. He put together a syndicate that would provide a bit over $1 million, a solid sum in a year when the fundraising of the entire venture-capital business nationwide slumped to just $10 million. Atari used the capital to mass-produce *Home Pongs*, and Sears sold them as fast as it received them. Activism and patient stage-by-stage financing were paying off nicely.

Twelve months later, in the summer of 1976, Valentine confronted his next challenge. Atari's bell-bottomed engineers had come up with a fresh idea: a console that could play not only *Pong* but multiple games of the owner's choosing. To capitalize on this breakthrough, Atari was going to need a far larger capital infusion—perhaps as much as $50 million. There was no way the venture capitalists of the era could mobilize that kind of cash, and the stock market was all but closed; in 1976 only thirty-four companies managed to go public.[38] For Atari to develop its multi-game console, Valentine would have to come up with another way of raising capital.

Valentine resolved that Atari should sell itself to a deep-pocketed parent. But for this to be an option, he would have to bust through a heavy wall: Bushnell's opposition. "It was his first company, like a child, and he didn't want to give it up," Valentine recalled later.[39]

Blessed with the personality of a steamroller, Valentine informed Bushnell that his child needed a new parent. He proposed the entertainment company Warner Communications, turning to his friends at Capital Research to organize a second introduction.[40] Pretty soon, Steve Ross, the founder and chairman of Warner, invited Bushnell to New York to discuss a deal. Valentine made sure he was invited also.

In late 1976, a Warner company jet fetched Bushnell and Valentine from California. On board, they were greeted by Clint Eastwood and his girlfriend, Sondra Locke; Eastwood graciously made Bushnell a sandwich.[41] When the plane touched down in Teterboro Airport, a limo ferried the Atari people to suites in the Waldorf Towers hotel. That evening there was a dinner at Steve Ross's palatial apartment, and the group watched an unreleased Eastwood movie together. By the end of the day, a starstruck Bushnell had agreed to sell Atari for $28 million.

For Valentine and his fledgling fund, it was a satisfying exit. Sequoia notched up a useful 3x return, demonstrating the value of the new investment methods. Thanks to Valentine's tough activism and stage-by-stage approach, an unbackable company had been turned into a winner. Meanwhile, the same formula brought other successes. By 1980, Valentine's first fund had chalked up an annual return of almost 60 percent, matching the achievement of Davis & Rock and trouncing the 9 percent return on the S&P 500.[42]

◆

Valentine's activist investing style had several echoes in the 1970s. In 1973, Bill Draper's Sutter Hill Ventures struck a landmark deal with Qume, the inventor of the electronic daisy printing wheel. What made the deal special was that Sutter Hill imposed a condition: Qume's founding engineer had to dump his underpowered chief executive and allow the venture guys to bring in a star graduate of Harvard Business School. When the company took off, the CEO's stock options generated a huge payout, and the message went out to his HBS classmates, who were earning merely decent salaries at Fortune 500 enterprises. Sutter Hill went on to repeat the Qume formula over and over, liberating up-and-coming big-company executives and distinguishing West Coast venture capital from the tamer version in the East. Boston VCs shrank from backing startups that lacked a credible chief executive. By controlling risk through activist recruitment of the CEO, West Coast VCs could afford to be bolder.[43]

The boldest of them all was Tom Perkins, the pioneering investor who, along with Don Valentine, defined the post–Arthur Rock generation of venture capitalists. A child of the Depression, Perkins had grown up on "Spam, margarine, Wonder Bread, and lime Jell-O," but he was nourished by a nerdy fascination for electronics, to the disappointment of his athletic father.[44] As a teenager, he aspired to become a TV repairman, but his physics teacher pointed him toward MIT, where he studied electronic engineering and joined the swim team and a fraternity, going "from being a nerd in a school of jocks to a jock in a school of nerds," as he later wrote in his memoir.[45] After MIT and a spell at a military contractor, Perkins enrolled at Harvard Business School, where he took Georges Doriot's classes. A few years later, in 1969, Doriot tried to persuade Perkins to give up a job at Hewlett-Packard and take the helm at ARD. Perkins declined. The compensation was inadequate.[46]

On a Friday morning in the summer of 1972, Perkins showed up for breakfast at Rickey's Hyatt House in Palo Alto, the hotel where the Traitorous Eight had toasted Shockley's Nobel Prize and later celebrated their liberation. Suitably enough, the purpose of the breakfast was to meet Eugene Kleiner, the traitor who had written the letter to Hayden, Stone, requesting liberation.[47] Having thus assisted in the birth of venture capital, Kleiner was now thinking of contributing directly. He aimed to start a venture fund, and like Doriot he wanted to recruit Perkins. After all, Perkins was by now an established figure on the West Coast. He was the general manager of HP's computer division. He had also founded a startup that had developed a new laser technology.

Kleiner and Perkins extended their breakfast conversation late into the morning. At a quarter to twelve, the staff at Rickey's kicked them out so that they could prepare the restaurant for lunch clients; the two men went over to Perkins's house to continue talking.[48] Perkins spoke grandly, spouting out ideas. Kleiner responded calmly in a rich Viennese accent. Perkins found himself imagining Sigmund Freud counseling his patients.[49]

The next day was Saturday, and the two men started to work out the mechanics of a venture fund. They resolved to put their own names on the door; after all, if they believed in their brainchild, they should not be shy to have their names on it.[50] They also determined that their fund should be time limited and that they should each commit some of their own savings; in this they followed the example of Davis & Rock, which Kleiner knew well because he had been a limited partner there. Most of all, Kleiner and Perkins agreed that they should emphasize a robustly activist approach. Both men had served as managers at storied West Coast companies, and both had started their own firms. "We distinguished ourselves right from the beginning by saying: We are not investors. We're not Wall-Street, stock-picker, investor people," Perkins later said. "We are entrepreneurs ourselves, and we will work with entrepreneurs in an entrepreneurial way. . . . We will be in it up to our elbows."[51]

Soon after Labor Day, Kleiner and Perkins set out on a road trip to raise capital. Perkins insisted on driving because Kleiner had a habit of drifting off the road when he got absorbed in conversation.[52] Their first port of call was Henry Hillman, a Pittsburgh tycoon who had been smitten by the success of Davis & Rock and who had tried unsuccessfully to get Tommy Davis to manage his money. Seeing in Kleiner and Perkins a chance to get a piece of the West Coast action, Hillman committed up to $5 million, provided that the partners could raise a matching sum from others. Kleiner and Perkins proceeded to raise $1 million from Rockefeller University, nearly that much from two insurance companies, and a bit more from wealthy individuals and trusts. By the first week of December 1972, they had put together a fund of $8.4 million, considerably more than Don Valentine would manage to come up with.

Kleiner and Perkins set up shop in a new low-slung office park at 3000 Sand Hill Road, becoming the first partnership to occupy what was to be the epicenter of the venture industry.[53] Their timing was poor: they were launching their fund on the eve of the first oil shock, and their first few investments performed as poorly as the economy. They backed a plausible semiconductor startup, but it was run into the ground by inexperienced managers. They fell for an inauspiciously named contraption called the Snow-Job, which converted motorcycles into snowmobiles; Perkins fondly imagined Hells Angels and their biker girlfriends churning up snowfields. Unfortunately, the government responded to the oil shock by outlawing the sale of gasoline for sports vehicles, dooming the Snow-Job to bankruptcy.[54] By the end of 1974, Kleiner Perkins had shelled out $2.5 million for nine investments. Although four of these ultimately did well enough to rescue the portfolio, there was no sign of this happy ending at the time. Kleiner and Perkins felt sufficiently glum to rethink their strategy.

The new Kleiner Perkins formula doubled down on activism. Rather than funding outside entrepreneurs, the partners would incubate startups in-house, kicking ideas around with junior associates. They had already hired a potential company founder, a drawling Texan with an impressive frizz of hair named Jimmy Treybig. A Hewlett-Packard manager who had worked under Perkins, Treybig dressed in a disheveled, absentminded style; once, when colleagues pointed out he had forgotten his belt, he went off to smarten himself up and returned wearing two belts.[55] But the down-home country-bumpkin patina disguised a competitive drive, and Treybig had joined Kleiner Perkins on the understanding that the partnership would fund him to start a business.[56] In the lingo that took root later, Treybig was an entrepreneur in residence.

In 1974, about a year after joining Kleiner Perkins, Treybig hit on an idea for a company. Borrowing from aircraft design, he would build a computer system with backup processors so that one engine could fail without the whole thing crashing. At Hewlett-Packard, Treybig had dealt with customers such as banks and stock markets, and he knew how valuable such a system would be. Computer crashes that destroyed data and brought business to a halt were horribly expensive. If Treybig could build a fail-safe system, he was sure he could sell it. In an inversion of Atari, the technical risks were daunting, but the market risks were negligible.

Despite that inversion, Perkins approached Treybig's idea using the same methods as Valentine. First, he rolled up his sleeves, spending long afternoons brainstorming with Treybig, debating the workability of an operating system that would switch from one processor to the next if the first one malfunctioned. "Jimmy and I made diagrams of how the logic might work, and we couldn't prove to ourselves that it couldn't be done," Perkins recalled later.[57] Then, having cleared that hurdle, Perkins invested $50,000 in the project. It was a token amount, roughly equivalent to Valentine's initial seed investment in Atari. If the project hit a wall, the Kleiner Perkins fund would lose less than 1 percent of its capital.

Perkins set out to spend the $50,000 seed money on consultants who could take his internal brainstorming to the next level. He worked his network to bring in the best experts in the Valley at the lowest price possible. He paid a computer scientist he had known at Hewlett-Packard to sketch out a workable architecture for a fail-safe computer system.[58] He roped in another HP alum to work on the hardware, and a third one to develop the software.[59] All other expenditures were pretty much ruled out. Treybig was still operating out of his office at Kleiner Perkins, at no cost to the venture. To the extent that the project needed financial advice, it was provided for free by another in-house associate, Jack Loustaunou. Brook Byers, who joined Kleiner Perkins a few years later as a young partner, reflected on the lessons that KP drew from this experience. By focusing exclusively on the "white-hot" risks in a project, you could find out whether the venture was likely to work while risking as little capital as possible.[60]

By November 1974, the consultants had grappled with the white-hot risks and emerged victorious. For the first time in the history of computing, they solved the challenge of "contention": the problem that arises when two processors within the same system request access to the communications circuits at the same moment.[61] Now, finally, Perkins gave the go-ahead for Treybig to incorporate his new company, which he called Tandem Computers. Jack Loustaunou signed on as the finance director, and Tom Perkins became the chairman of the board: three of Tandem's five founders—Treybig, Loustaunou, and Perkins—were KP insiders; the other two founders were the hardware and software consultants whom Perkins had recruited. The 1970s activist approach had been distilled to its purest essence.

Perkins's next step was to raise a Series A round for Tandem. He

coached Treybig on how to pitch. In the end, venture capitalists were trying to figure out one thing: "Why is this a big market, and how are you going
to build a really strong position in it?"[62] He took Treybig to Brooks Brothers and bought him shoes, socks, shirts, ties, jacket, and pants. "The salesman probably thought he was my boyfriend," Perkins wrote later.

Suitably dressed, the two men flew to New York. Perkins aimed to raise
money from Venrock, the Rockefeller family venture firm that had backed
Intel. His face framed by sprouts of curly hair, Treybig ambled into the Venrock conference room.

"Well, how do I look?" he asked. "Tom dressed me."[63]

Despite Treybig's disarming style, Tandem failed to raise money. Venrock passed, Arthur Rock passed, and so did other venture partnerships. It
was an illogical outcome, and it reflected poorly on the venture capitalists
who refused to get involved. After all, Perkins had eliminated most of the
technical risks; the remaining commercial risks were modest. But almost
no capital was flowing into venture partnerships, making it a terrible time
to pitch for funds. *Business Week* had just revived the old trope that no
startup could take on IBM. Such was the pessimism of the mid-1970s.[64]

At this point, Perkins might have folded. He had made only a small seed
investment in Tandem, and he could have walked away easily. But, because
he had built the company from scratch, he knew that Rock, Venrock, and
Business Week were wrong. Tandem's technology was distinctive, and it had
applied for patents on its breakthroughs; it could stand up to IBM because
it was genuinely innovative. Other venture capitalists, especially those
lacking engineering backgrounds, had failed to appreciate Tandem's scientific edge. "These were financiers," Perkins sniffed dismissively.[65]

With that, Perkins resolved to finance Tandem's Series A round without sharing the risk with other partnerships.[66] Shoveling his chips onto the
table, he invested $1 million in Tandem in early 1975, receiving 40 percent
of the equity: it was the largest bet that Kleiner Perkins made during the
1970s. As Perkins himself confessed, if Tandem had not worked out, there
might never have been a second Kleiner Perkins fund.[67]

But it did work out. Tandem spent 1975 turning its basic designs into a
full-spec blueprint, and by December it had progressed enough to justify a

Series B round of financing. Kleiner Perkins put in another $450,000, and this time other investors wanted in as well, so Tandem raised a total of $2 million. A few months later, Tandem made its first sale, and then revenues started to ramp up, multiplying fourteen-fold between 1977 and 1980.[68] Pretty soon, Tandem offered a spectacular demonstration of what became known as Perkins's law: "market risk is inversely proportional to technical risk," because if you solve a truly difficult technical problem, you will face minimal competition.[69] Thanks to the high barrier to entry, Tandem's profit margin remained juicy even as its sales soared. By 1984, Tandem had generated a bit over 100x on KP's $1.45 million investment. The $150 million profit dwarfed the combined $10 million return that KP made on all of its first nine investments.

But as Tandem was taking off, Perkins was working on another project that would be even more spectacular.

◆

To replace Jimmy Treybig at the partnership, Kleiner Perkins hired a new junior associate named Bob Swanson, a baby-faced twenty-six-year-old with a penchant for unfashionably neat clothes and a puppyish manner.[70] Swanson had arrived as an undergraduate at MIT with a fine felt hat and a suitcase grandly stenciled with his name, and he had proceeded to avoid the draft by taking a time-consuming dual degree in chemistry and business.[71] Before joining KP, he had worked in the venture-capital team at Citicorp, which trained several successful VCs of the era. But he failed to impress Kleiner and Perkins. He was soon kicked off the payroll.[72]

This forced Swanson to think afresh about his direction. He knocked on the doors of the big Silicon Valley electronics firms, but his lack of operational and engineering experience made him an unattractive prospect.[73] Yet he did have an idea. As an associate at KP, he had attended a lunch talk featuring a mention of a technology called recombinant DNA. It was a passing reference, and it failed to register with the others at the table. Now that he found himself jobless, Swanson resolved to discover more about it.[74]

For weeks, Swanson read everything he could find on this new frontier in biology. Kleiner and Perkins had allowed him to keep coming to the office, even though he was no longer being paid, and when Swanson ran into Perkins one day, he told him of his new obsession. By cutting and splicing DNA strands and recombining them to make artificial genetic material, scientists could reproduce everything from medicines to rubber—indeed anything that existed in nature. "This idea is absolutely fantastic! It is revolutionary! It will change the world! It's the most important thing I have ever heard!" he told Perkins.[75]

Perkins remained unconvinced, but Swanson put together a list of scientists with expertise in the technology. He cold-called all of them. In each conversation, he heard the same message: recombinant DNA had a commercial future, to be sure, but it was a distant one—probably decades away. Then Swanson called Herbert Boyer of the University of California, San Francisco, not fully realizing that Boyer was the co-inventor of the DNA technology. Swanson launched into his standard pitch: recombinant DNA held such promise; surely it could be commercialized in the near future! To his amazement, Boyer responded that he was probably right.[76]

Swanson immediately asked if he could come over. He wanted to meet Boyer. He wanted to discuss the possibilities.

Boyer said he was busy.

"I really need and want to talk with you!" Swanson insisted.

Boyer told him he could meet for ten minutes on Friday afternoon. Not more than that.[77]

On January 16, 1976, at around 5:00 p.m., Swanson drove over to the UCSF campus and made his way to Boyer's office. A handkerchief poked out of his suit pocket.

Dressed altogether more informally, Boyer greeted him. He had a laid-back style, shaggy curls, a thick mustache, and the build of a high school football player.

Swanson had no inkling that Boyer had been pondering the commercial applications for recombinant DNA for months, ever since he had thought his sick son might need a scarce growth hormone.[78] But to Swanson's delight, Boyer reiterated that commercial applications might be just years away—not decades. The men chatted in the laboratory—the square 1950s puppy and the shaggy 1970s cool cat—and soon Swanson's enthusiasm for the world-changing potential of recombinant DNA created an unexpected bond between them. Boyer took Swanson to a bar, and after three hours they concluded that they should work together.[79] Boyer knew science; Swanson knew business. Boyer understood the stately pace of academic lab research. Swanson wanted to put several thousand volts through it.

"You've got to write the research grants, and you've got to get the funding," Boyer explained.

"Well, what if you had the money?" Swanson objected. "What if you didn't have to write any research grant, you just have the money?"[80]

Pretty soon, Boyer found himself thinking in a different way. Unshackled by venture capital, recombinant DNA technology could be commercialized a lot faster than he had imagined.[81] Money could free scientists to do things they would not have tried before. It was a new form of liberation capital.

Boyer and Swanson formed a partnership, each pitching in $500 to cover the legal fees that came with getting started.[82] They wrote up six pages outlining an investment pitch. Then they prepared to meet Tom Perkins.

On April 1, 1976, Swanson appeared with Boyer in the Kleiner Perkins conference room.[83] Swanson sketched out the business plan. Their company, now named Genentech, needed six months to negotiate licenses governing the gene-splicing techniques, which were held by the University of California and Stanford. Then it would recruit a microbiologist and two organic chemists to embark on the research. Swanson figured it would take eighteen months and half a million dollars to get close to manufacturing the first product. The money would go to renting space, buying equipment, hiring scientists, and carrying out experiments. The time horizon was a fraction of what the biology establishment believed possible. Naturally, there could be no guarantee that the experiments would be successful.

Perkins was enthralled by the technology. Creating what he termed a "microbial Frankenstein" came perilously close to playing God.[84] He was also impressed by Boyer. Whether or not the experiments worked, at least this curls-and-mustache guy knew how to conduct them.[85] And if the experiments did work, the sky was the limit. The first product that Genentech proposed to manufacture was insulin, for which there was a huge and growing market. The existing way of harvesting insulin conjured up images of medieval witchcraft: every drop of the hormone had to be pressed from the pancreas glands of pigs and cows. Perkins figured to himself that Genentech would have a bit less than a fifty-fifty shot at creating a viable product.[86] But precisely because the technical challenges were so formidable, the barriers to entry in this business would be high, and Genentech would be able to extract fat margins if it succeeded. It was another illustration of Perkins's law.

The next day Perkins met Swanson again and laid out a suggestion. The science was captivating, but the $500,000 cost of proving it was prohibitively high, given the uncertainty. So Perkins proposed to repeat the formula he had developed for Tandem: identify the white-hot risks, then find the cheapest way of going after them. Swanson should cut the cost of his experiments by not hiring scientists or setting up a lab.[87] Instead, he should contract the early work to existing laboratories.

Perkins was suggesting what amounted to a virtual company. America's postwar economy had been dominated by big corporations and big labor unions; Genentech would mark the arrival of a new industrial form, more networked and more nimble.[88] In future, the central research departments at industrial behemoths would be displaced by venture-backed startups that brought in knowledge as they needed it. Already, Perkins had launched Tandem by recruiting short-term consultants from Hewlett-Packard. Now he was urging that Genentech do the same in the more complex field of biotechnology.

Swanson and Boyer accepted the proposal. They would use their initial budget to contract with the University of California, San Francisco, where Boyer's team had expertise in gene splicing; with a research hospital called City of Hope, which had specialists in gene synthesis; and with Caltech, which had an exceptional testing facility. In this way, they would have the benefit of the best teams in the field, and they would also slash their costs. Genentech still might fail, but it would do so cheaply.

Perkins agreed to invest the new sum that Swanson needed: a mere $100,000. It was scarcely more than the $50,000 he had advanced to hire the early Tandem consultants. In exchange for this modest commitment, representing just over 1 percent of the Kleiner Perkins fund, he acquired fully one-quarter of Genentech's stock. There was nothing unfair about this: Swanson had tried to shop the deal elsewhere and had found no takers.[89] But by buying a quarter of Genentech so cheaply, the venture capitalist had taken a position that could pay off at an extraordinarily high rate. If Perkins might have hoped for, say, a 20x return based on Swanson's proposed $500,000 investment, it followed that he now stood to make 100x on his $100,000 investment. With a 100x multiple in prospect, Perkins was getting a good deal so long as Genentech had better than a one-in-a-hundred chance of coming up with a product. Perkins's private estimate of Genentech's chances was much higher—not one in a hundred, but a bit under fifty-fifty. By coming up with a strategy to isolate and neutralize the white-hot risks, Perkins had transformed a daunting venture bet into an irresistible one.

In May 1976, a California securities regulator wrote to Kleiner Perkins, expressing concern about the riskiness of the Genentech investment.

"Kleiner & Perkins realizes that an investment in Genentech is highly speculative, but we are in the business of making highly speculative investments," Kleiner wrote back calmly.[90]

◆

As it turned out, creating a first product cost Genentech more time and capital than Swanson had predicted. To keep the company going, Perkins put together a new financing round in February 1977 and then another one in March 1978, each time attracting money from other investors by promising to reach the next research milestone. But the virtue of stage-by-stage financing became increasingly obvious. As successive risks were eliminated, each financing round valued Genentech higher than the previous one, so the founders could raise larger sums while giving away less equity. Having parted with a quarter of their company for a mere $100,000 in 1976, Boyer and Swanson sold a 26 percent stake the next year for $850,000, and in 1978 they sold just 8.9 percent for $950,000.[91] If Swanson and Boyer had insisted on raising all the capital they needed at the outset—the moment of maximum risk—they would have given more equity away and owned less of their own company.

Even as it mitigated the dilution of the founders' equity stakes, stage-by-stage financing also boosted incentives for the researchers who set to work on the DNA technology. The scientists knew that they could continue their experiments only if they hit the promised milestones before Genentech's money ran out.[92] At the same time, when they did reach their targets, they had a personal stake in the higher company valuation that resulted. Just as Arthur Rock had done at Intel, Perkins had insisted that Genentech employees, including the key contractors, get stock options.[93] At first, not all the scientists cared about the options or understood what they meant. "I had a ponytail halfway down my back. I smoked marijuana every day," said one. "I didn't give a damn about money or stock or anything." But as Genentech's valuation multiplied twenty-six-fold during its first two years, the equity culture took hold.[94] Everyone from the janitor up was rooting for the company to do well. Even that ponytailed scientist changed his tune when his stock proved to be worth more than $1 million.[95]

Perkins also contributed intangibly to Genentech's culture. He was the first venture capitalist to revel unashamedly in the role of promoter and front man, signaling to the scientists that they had left academia behind and were now part of something glamorous. He would roar up to the office in his red Ferrari and announce orders and deadlines, imbuing researchers with the sense that they were on a special mission.[96] One lovely evening in July 1978, Perkins invited Swanson to dinner with two of his key scientists and their wives. The visitors trooped up to the Perkins mansion in the hills overlooking San Francisco and the Golden Gate Bridge, and Perkins showed off his tumbling gardens and tapestries and vintage cars, and the group ate dinner served by a uniformed butler. Standing outside the mansion, Swanson waved at it excitedly and exclaimed to his researchers, "This is what we're all working for!" "It was motivating to us that he would invite two lowly scientists to his home," one of the guests recalled later.[97]

A few days later, the motivation proved its usefulness. Perkins dispatched one of his dinner guests, a young PhD named Dave Goeddel, to goad the contract researchers at the City of Hope lab to complete the last

stage of the insulin project. Summoning the full power of his gilded charisma, Perkins instructed, "Don't come back until you have got insulin done."

Goeddel sprang to attention. He was honored to be chosen for the mission and delighted to be getting the order directly from Perkins.[98] He flew
down to Los Angeles and pulled a blizzard of all-nighters. In September
1978, under the glare of television lights, a press conference announced the
production of artificial insulin to an astonished nation.

Two years later, in 1980, Genentech staged a stock market debut that
anticipated the 1990s. By conventional standards, the company was completely unready for a flotation: it spent so much on research that it was still
barely profitable. But Perkins was part of a rich venture tradition: to persuade investors to bet on the technologies of tomorrow, you must first un-
shackle them from the financial metrics of yesterday. In the early days of
venture capital, Arthur Rock had persuaded investors to back companies
that failed the standard value-investing benchmarks, inventing the idea of
"intellectual book value." Two decades later, Perkins emerged as the pitch-
man for the next logical step: not only should companies without profits attract venture financing; they should also be able to go public. To push Wall
Street across that watershed, Perkins sent Boyer out on the road to dazzle
prospective investors with science: wielding props of brightly colored
beads, the professor explained how DNA from one organism could be in-
serted into another, and his financial audiences gaped in admiration. To
underwrite Genentech's share offering, Kleiner Perkins hired Bud Coyle,
Arthur Rock's old boss at Hayden, Stone, luring him out of retirement.
Coyle was celebrated on Wall Street for his part in discovering the semiconductor business. Every investor remembered how profitable that had
been.

Genentech went public on the Nasdaq exchange on October 14, 1980.
Within a minute of the bell's ringing, its stock had jumped from the offering price of $35 to an astonishing $80, and within twenty minutes it had
risen to $89, the fastest first-day spike in Wall Street history. Perkins, who
was in New York for the occasion, phoned Swanson back in California and
roused him. "Bob," he announced to the associate he had once fired. "You're
the richest man I know."[99]

For Kleiner Perkins, the rewards were almost as impressive. When the market settled at the end of the first trading day, the shares that had cost KP an average of $1.85 were worth $71 each.[100] As the stock continued to soar, the partnership found itself sitting on a multiple of more than 200x.[101] Together with Tandem, the Genentech bonanza turned the first Kleiner Perkins fund into a legend, and a dramatic illustration of the power law. As of 1984, the fourteen investments in the first fund showed a combined profit of $208 million; of that, fully 95 percent came from Tandem and Genentech. Without those two home-run investments, the first fund would have generated a multiple of 4.5x, still comfortably outperforming the return on the S&P 500 over the eleven-year period. With the home runs, the multiple was 42x. Approaching the performance of Don Valentine and Davis & Rock, Kleiner Perkins had roughly quintupled the return on the stock market.[102]

Was this luck, or was it more than that? Proving skill is difficult in venture investing because, as we have seen, it hinges on subjective judgment calls rather than objective or quantifiable metrics. If a distressed-debt hedge fund hires analysts and lawyers to scrutinize a bankrupt firm, it can learn precisely which bond is backed by which piece of collateral, and it can foresee how the bankruptcy judge is likely to rule; its profits are not lucky. Likewise, if an algorithmic hedge fund hires astrophysicists to look for patterns in markets, it may discover statistical signals that are reliably profitable. But when Perkins backed Tandem and Genentech, or when Valentine backed Atari, they could not muster the same certainty. They were investing in human founders with human combinations of brilliance and weakness. They were dealing with products and manufacturing processes that were untested and complex; they faced competitors whose behaviors could not be forecast; they were investing over long horizons. In consequence, quantifiable risks were multiplied by unquantifiable uncertainties; there were known unknowns and unknown unknowns; the bracing unpredictability of life could not be masked by neat financial models. Of course, in this environment, luck played its part. Kleiner Perkins lost money on six of the fourteen investments in its first fund. Its methods were not as fail-safe as Tandem's computers.

But Perkins and Valentine were not merely lucky. Just as Arthur Rock

embraced methods and attitudes that put him ahead of ARD and the Small
Business Investment Companies in the 1960s, so the leading figures of the
1970s had an edge over their competitors. Perkins and Valentine had been
managers at leading Valley companies; they knew how to be hands-on; and
their contributions to the success of their portfolio companies were obvious. It was Perkins who brought in the early consultants to eliminate the
white-hot risks at Tandem, and Perkins who pressed Swanson to contract
Genentech's research out to existing laboratories. Similarly, it was Valentine who drove Atari to focus on *Home Pong* and to ally itself with Sears,
and Valentine who arranged for Warner Communications to buy the company. Early risk elimination plus stage-by-stage financing worked wonders
for all three companies. Skeptical observers have sometimes asked whether
venture capitalists create innovation or whether they merely show up for it.
In the case of Don Valentine and Tom Perkins, there was not much passive
showing up. By force of character and intellect, they stamped their will on
their portfolio companies.

Chapter Four

The Whispering of Apple

B y the late 1970s, when Kleiner Perkins backed Genentech, the West Coast venture-capital industry had developed much of its modern tool kit. The equity-only, time-limited fund had displaced the lever-aged Small Business Investment Company and the open-ended ARD model. Venture investors understood that they must swing for home runs, not singles and doubles. Activism and stage-by-stage financing had become the accepted ways to manage risky startups. Up and down Silicon Valley, venture capitalists hunted for opportunities to liberate talent and drive it to create new industries.

The next advance for venture capital was not an expansion of the tool kit. Instead, it related to the emergence of a venture network. Buoyed by the power-law returns on early VC investments, as well as by a relaxation of restrictions on pension-fund investments and a cut in the capital-gains tax, money flooded into venture funds and a scattering of pioneering investors morphed into something qualitatively different. In the place of a few smart individuals, there was now a thick web of startup connoisseurs, significant because the combined force of their actions was greater than the sum of their separate endeavors. It was like going from a system driven by genius to one driven by evolution. A brilliant person can do great things. A large group of people can try many things. Through an evolutionary process of trial, failure, and occasional breakthroughs, the group may advance faster than the individual.

The fertility of the network was illustrated by the story of Apple, founded in 1976 by Steve Jobs and Steve Wozniak. On the face of it, Apple was an obvious candidate for venture investment, because scores of insiders already understood that the personal computer would be the next big thing in technology. Xerox's Palo Alto Research Center, or PARC, had recognized the PC as "an idea whose time has arrived" and had produced a prototype complete with mouse and graphical interface. Intel and National Semiconductor had considered making a PC, and Steve Wozniak had twice offered the Apple I design to his employer, Hewlett-Packard.[1] But all four companies had decided not to build a PC, inhibited by what the business thinker Clayton Christensen termed the "innovator's dilemma." Xerox worried that a computerized paperless office would harm its core photocopying business. Intel and National Semiconductor feared that making a computer would put them in conflict with existing computer makers, which were among their top customers. HP fretted that building a cheap home computer would undercut its premium machines, which sold for around $150,000. All four companies had too much of a stake in the status quo to risk disrupting it. A startup that filled the resulting vacuum looked like an obvious bet for venture capitalists.

And yet when Apple set out to raise money, the stars in the venture-capital firmament failed to recognize the opportunity, proving that even the most brilliant VCs are capable of costly errors. Tom Perkins and Eugene Kleiner refused even to meet with Steve Jobs. Bill Draper of Sutter Hill sent an associate to visit Apple, and when the associate reported that Jobs and Wozniak had kept him waiting, Draper wrote them off as arrogant.[2] Meanwhile, Draper's old SBIC partner, Pitch Johnson, wondered, "How can you use a computer at home? Are you going to put recipes on it?"[3] Rejected repeatedly, Jobs cast his net as far as Stan Veit, the owner of New York City's first retail computer store, proposing that Veit acquire 10 percent of Apple for a mere $10,000. "Looking at this long-haired hippie and his friends, I thought, 'You would be the last person in the world I would trust with my ten grand,'" Veit recalled regretfully.[4] Jobs offered Nolan Bushnell, who had employed him at Atari, one-third of Apple for $50,000. "I was so smart, I said no," Bushnell remembered. "It's kind of fun to think about that, when I'm not crying."[5]

Fortunately for Jobs and Wozniak, the Valley's venture-capital network was already big enough in 1976 that a handful of refusals did not have to be terminal. Pretty soon, the duo found their way to Don Valentine of Sequoia.

The way this happened was a testament to the power of networks. In refusing to back Apple, Nolan Bushnell had softened the blow by introducing Jobs to the venture guy who had backed Atari—Valentine. At the same time, Jobs had approached Regis McKenna, the top marketing guru in the Valley, proposing that McKenna's company design Apple's commercials in exchange for a sizable 20 percent stake in the startup. McKenna's reaction was that 20 percent of nothing was worth approximately nothing. But, like Bushnell, McKenna softened the blow of rejection by passing Jobs along to someone else. Again, that someone was Don Valentine.

It was natural that the Valley's network should steer Jobs in Valentine's direction. Having backed Atari, Valentine had established himself as the toughest wrangler of wild young founders. As a veteran of the semiconductor industry, Valentine prided himself on investing in products that capitalized on chip technology. Finally, Valentine was the ideal investor in Apple because of his marketing background. Kleiner and Perkins had refused to meet Jobs because they preferred technical risks to business risks.[6] Having led sales at Fairchild and National Semiconductor, Valentine was a good fit for a startup whose greatest challenge would be to convince unsuspecting consumers that they wanted computers in their kitchens.[7]

Even though Valentine was perfectly suited to be Apple's first investor, his initial reaction to Jobs and Wozniak was skeptical. Jobs "was trying to be the embodiment of the counterculture," Valentine said later. "He had a wispy beard, was very thin, and looked like Ho Chi Minh."[8] Still, Bushnell and McKenna had told him that these guys were worth an audience. Because he valued his network, Valentine went through the motions of asking what Apple was up to.

"What's the market?" he asked Wozniak.

"A million," said Wozniak.

"How do you know?"

"Well, there's a million ham radio operators, and computers are more popular than ham radio."[9]

Wozniak's answer implied that Apple did not aspire to reach much beyond the finite circle of tech hobbyists. And whereas Atari games had been in multiple cities by the time Valentine had paid his visit, Apple in 1976 had barely sold anything. Valentine was looking doubtful.

"Tell me what I have to do to have you finance me," Jobs demanded.

"We have to have someone in the company who has some sense of management and marketing and channels of distribution," Valentine countered.

"Fine," said Jobs. "Send me three people."

After that encounter, Valentine berated Regis McKenna for recommending that he take the meeting. "Why'd you send me these renegades from the human race?" he protested.[10] Valentine might be the only VC in the network who was equipped to back Apple, yet even he was not ready to bet money on it. But just as Bushnell and McKenna had rebuffed Jobs but connected him with Valentine, so Valentine now followed up on Jobs's openness to hiring an outside marketing expert. It was almost a reflex. A large part of Valentine's job came down to making and accepting introductions.

Valentine went through his contacts and identified three seasoned managers who could help build Apple. Jobs vetoed one; another met Jobs and ruled out working with him. The third was an engineer and sales executive named Mike Markkula, whom Valentine had known at Fairchild. Markkula had subsequently struck it rich on Intel stock options and retired at thirty-three, planning to play tennis and build furniture.

On a Monday in the early fall of 1976, some eighteen months into his retirement, Markkula drove his gold Corvette up to Jobs's suburban garage, the modest structure that would later inspire waves of tech startups. Markkula had long sideburns and a flashy leisure suit. His first thought when he saw Jobs and Wozniak was that they needed haircuts.[11]

But then he noticed something else—something that other visitors to the garage had not appreciated. Wozniak's technology was truly impressive. The Apple II prototype lying on his workbench was free from the standard mess of circuit boards strung together with fiddly connectors. The whole machine worked on a single board, and there were slots for plugging in printers or other devices. The design also incorporated random-access memory chips; as far as Markkula knew, it was the world's first computer to do that. "This was one elegant, beautifully crafted design that Woz had done," Markkula recalled. "And I'm a circuit designer. I know."[12]

With that, Markkula decided to put his energy behind Apple. He became an adviser to the Steves, writing their business plan, serving as marketing chief and company chairman, arranging a bank credit line, and ultimately investing $91,000 of his own capital in exchange for 26 percent of the company.[13] After a circuitous and iterative process, the Silicon Valley network had finally come to the right solution. Jobs and Wozniak had been turned down repeatedly, by multiple investors. But one introduction had led to another, and Apple had eventually secured the lifeline it needed.

Markkula was not a venture capitalist. He was arguably the Valley's first "angel investor": somebody grown rich from the success of one startup who recycles his wealth and experience into more startups. But what mattered most about Markkula was his web of connections. As a veteran of Fairchild Semiconductor and Intel, Markkula was an established member of the Valley's charmed inner circle. Now that he had signed on with Jobs and Wozniak, Apple became part of it too.

Apple still needed help with its publicity, so Markkula asked Regis McKenna to give the Steves a second look. "Regis, I'll pay the bill; I want you to do this," Markkula told him.[14] Previously, not even the offer of one-fifth of the company had induced McKenna to bother with Apple. But now that someone in his network was asking a favor, McKenna was willing. His firm duly designed a rainbow-striped logo of an apple with a bite missing.[15]

Next, Markkula sought out management talent. Before, no experienced tech executive had been willing to risk working for Apple. Now Markkula persuaded Mike Scott, part of his network of Fairchild alumni, to quit a secure job to be Apple's first president. To recruit Scott and other seasoned executives, Markkula replicated Intel's stock option plan. Apple was now part of Arthur Rock's equity culture.

Markkula also got to work on the venture-capital community. Don

Valentine remained reluctant to invest, but Markkula did not have to rely on any single VC, because he had other connections. At Fairchild, he had befriended a colleague named Hank Smith, who had gone on to join Venrock, the Rockefeller family venture fund. Markkula now called Smith and planted the idea that he might want to invest in Apple. Then he prepared to go after the big prize. While at Intel, Markkula had also known Arthur Rock, Intel's chairman. Leveraging his network, he asked Rock to meet Jobs and Wozniak.

By 1977, Rock was enjoying life as the Valley's senior venture statesman. He supported the San Francisco Ballet and collected modern art. At his dinner parties he would ring a silver bell to summon his waiter.[16] Because he valued his relationship with Markkula, Rock agreed to meet Jobs. But his reaction was predictable. "Steve had just come back from India and been with his guru or whatever," Rock recalled later.[17] "I'm not sure, but it may have been a while since he had a bath."[18]

With Rock wrinkling his nose, Markkula swiveled back to his old friend Hank Smith, and Smith's firm, Venrock. In the fall of 1977, he and Jobs took the red-eye to New York, following in the footsteps of Perkins and Treybig one year earlier.[19] They made their way to 30 Rockefeller Plaza and rode the elevator to the fifty-sixth floor, where Venrock had its offices. On arrival they ducked into the men's room to change out of the clothes they had worn on the flight over.

Dressed in new blue suits, Markkula and Jobs were shown into a windowless conference room where they addressed Peter Crisp, the senior investor at Venrock, together with Hank Smith and a couple of other partners.[20] It was not entirely clear what the Venrock team was listening for. Jobs and Markkula talked about the potential size of the market for PCs; since Valentine's visit to the garage, they had refined their pitch and now talked grandly about a future in which computers graced every living room. But the partners seemed to zone this message out. "The specifics of what Steve said would not have mattered," Hank Smith recalled later. "The whole territory was so speculative you could not take that stuff literally."[21]

"We were flying blind," Peter Crisp added.[22]

After an hour and a half, the questions ran out, and Jobs and Markkula stopped talking. The Venrock partners told them to wait; then they stepped out into the hallway to make a decision. Because Hank Smith had been at Intel, the Venrock team understood that advances in semiconductors made the idea of a PC feasible. Because Smith knew and respected Markkula, they had some confidence in Apple's ability to deliver. On the other hand, like most East Coast venture capitalists, Venrock was relatively risk averse; it often refused to back early startups, preferring to invest only when they had serious revenues.[23] All in all, they could do this deal or they could walk away; who knew what was the right decision? "We went out in the hall—four or five of us—we looked at each other, and we shrugged our shoulders and said, What the hell?" Crisp recalls.[24] "People gave us too much credit later for being smart about this decision."[25]

And so, almost on a whim, Venrock committed $300,000 for 10 percent of Apple.[26] By valuing the company at $3 million, the deal implied that Apple's value had increased by around thirty times since Stan Veit had refused to pay $10,000 for a tenth of the stock, a year or so earlier.

With the Venrock offer in his pocket, Markkula returned to the West Coast to continue his networking. He quickly struck a deal with Andrew Grove, another former colleague who would soon become the president of Intel. Grove was well aware of Apple because Markkula kept trying to poach his employees. Now he agreed to buy a small stake in the new company, and Markkula added a big name to his roster of backers.

With Venrock and Grove on board, Apple acquired momentum. It became the subject of an almost audible murmur; it was as though the Valley's grapevine were whispering its name insistently.[27] The once aloof Don Valentine began to stalk Markkula, demanding a piece of the action. He showed up at Apple's offices repeatedly, without invitation; one time, spotting Markkula at a restaurant, he sent him a bottle of wine and a note: "Don't lose sight of the fact that I'm planning on investing in Apple."[28] "We didn't need his money," Markkula recalled, but he eventually let Valentine invest on the condition that he accept a directorship.[29] Having a top venture capitalist on the company's board would further add to its momentum.

Around the same time, Regis McKenna visited Arthur Rock's office.

Was Arthur hearing the whispers? The opportunity to invest in Apple was now. Some big names were on board. The train was leaving.

The image of the moving train represented a new gloss on stage-by-stage investing. In the case of Atari or Genentech, follow-on venture capitalists wrote checks once the white-hot risks had been neutralized. In the case of Apple, VCs were being told that they should invest simply because others were investing. However circular this logic, it was by no means crazy. The whispering grapevine was sending a message: Apple would be a winner. In the face of that social proof, the objective truth about the skills of Apple's managers or the quality of its products might be secondary. If Apple was attracting funding, and if its reputation was soaring thanks to well-connected backers, its chances of hiring the best people and securing the best distribution channels were improving, too. Circular logic could be sound logic.[30]

After listening to McKenna, Rock set aside his doubts about Jobs and his hygiene. It was time to invest; the question was how to do so. With Venrock in for $300,000 and Valentine waving his checkbook, Apple definitely did not need capital.

Rock turned to Dick Kramlich, the young partner who had joined him after Tommy Davis. The Rock-Kramlich VC fund had recently been dissolved, returning capital to limited partners. But the two men still worked out of the same office, and Rock asked Kramlich to call Peter Crisp at Venrock. This was another network-driven maneuver. Kramlich and Crisp knew each other from Harvard Business School.

Kramlich often resented Rock's imperious style, but he was happy to call his Harvard buddy. "Peter, can you carve us in for a little bit of this?" he asked him.[31]

Crisp was well disposed to his old friend. Besides, Arthur Rock had let Venrock into Intel when he had put together its financing in 1968, so Crisp owed him a favor. And by offering Kramlich and Rock part of Venrock's $300,000 allocation, Crisp would lay off some risk. Having the legendary Arthur Rock connected to Apple could not hurt, either.[32]

Crisp told Kramlich that he could offer $50,000 worth of Venrock's Apple allocation.

Kramlich thanked him excitedly and went to tell Rock. "Arthur! Got us

$50,000!" he announced triumphantly. Kramlich figured he would take $10,000 for himself and let Rock take the other $40,000.

Rock retired to his office, closed his door, and made a few phone calls. When he emerged, he had bad news for Kramlich. "I have a lot of favors I have to repay, so you're number eleven on my list of ten," Rock said. He was not going to let his erstwhile partner buy any of the Apple stock.

Kramlich seethed bitterly, but Rock's status in the Valley's network made resistance inadvisable.[33]

A little while later, an entertaining British friend of Kramlich's visited Silicon Valley. His name was Anthony Montagu. He had founded a London investment firm called Abingworth, and he was an outsider in the Valley.

"Richard, what's hot?" Montagu asked.[34]

Kramlich told him that Apple was hot but that there was no chance of investing. A financing round had just closed. Kramlich himself had failed to get a piece of it.

Montagu still seemed eager. He had come to California with the express purpose of checking out the nascent PC business, and he knew that Apple was a leader. So Kramlich called Apple's president, Mike Scott. Could his British friend come over and visit? he asked. Montagu was the second son of a wealthy family, so he had to work for a living, Kramlich teased.[35] Could Scott do him a favor?

Scott agreed. But he also told Kramlich firmly that there was no chance his friend could invest. Apple had no need of further money.

Montagu set off for Apple's offices. A few hours later, he called Kramlich. "Dick, I am so excited," he said. "This is really the most exciting company I've ever seen." He was going to invest in Apple, no matter what.

"You know, Mr. Scott," Montagu told his host in his impressive British accent. "I brought my overcoat with me, and I have my toothbrush, and I'll just sit in the lobby. I'm not going to leave without acquiring some stock." It was hard to tell if he was an eccentric clown or a ferociously determined pain in the neck.

Scott replied that his visitor could sit in the lobby if he liked, but the chances of acquiring stock were zero.

Montagu said he would wait. "I have my toothbrush, and I can just lie here," he repeated, as though dental hygiene were the only conceivable reason not to bed down in someone's office.

At a quarter to seven that evening, Mike Scott appeared again. "Mr. Montagu, you are really a fortunate guy," he said. Steve Wozniak had decided to buy a house. To raise the cash, he wanted to sell some of his own equity.

Montagu asked how much stock Wozniak was selling.

"Four hundred and fifty thousand dollars," came the answer. It was more stock by far than Venrock or Valentine had laid hands on.

A giddy Montagu called Kramlich again. "Dick, I wouldn't be here without you!" he said, offering to split the allocation.

Kramlich never told Rock that he had acquired a large slice of Apple through this roundabout route, and for years he kept quiet about it. He permitted himself just one discreet celebration, like a man who pumps his fist and screams a victory scream, but silently. On the front gate of Kramlich's San Francisco home, the iron handle is shaped like an apple.

———◆———

The financing of Apple showed how the network could be stronger than the individual. No venture capitalist in this story covered himself in glory. Several missed Apple completely, despite the rather obvious opportunity that the innovator's dilemma presented. Venrock invested on the basis of a shrug of the shoulders, and mostly because of a chance connection between Hank Smith and Mike Markkula. Valentine and Rock came in at the last moment and, especially in Rock's case, in modest size; Valentine went on to sell out early, in 1979, realizing a quick 13x profit that boosted his first fund but missed Apple's later expansion.[36] Two of the biggest winners in this saga were the improbable duo of Anthony Montagu and Dick Kramlich, proving that sheer luck can sometimes matter more than anything.[37]

But none of this messiness changed the outcome for Apple. The company raised capital and gathered connections, and its success testified to the power of the Valley's network. Once Venrock, Valentine, and Rock clambered aboard, it did not matter how hesitantly they had arrived; they set about working their contacts to help their new portfolio company. An introduction from Valentine led Apple to hire Gene Carter, a seasoned veteran from Fairchild. A phone call from Peter Crisp helped Apple to recruit a manufacturing boss from Hewlett-Packard.[38] Meanwhile, Arthur Rock saw to it that Apple basked in his reflected glory. On one occasion, when two big shots from Morgan Stanley came out to the West Coast, they had lunch with Rock, who duly talked up Apple. "Arthur Rock is a Legend with a capital 'L,'" the Morgan Stanley duo reported in a subsequent memo, relaying Rock's view on Apple as though it were the word of an oracle rather than a self-interested advertisement. "The people running this company . . . are very bright, very creative and very driven," Rock had assured them.[39]

In December 1980, two months after Genentech's IPO, Morgan Stanley helped Apple to go public. Of the 237 initial public offerings that year, Apple's was easily the largest, raising more money than any IPO since the Ford Motor Company made its debut twenty-four years earlier.[40] By the end of December, Apple had a market value of nearly $1.8 billion; it was now deemed to be worth more than Ford.[41] And whereas Valentine had made a quick 13x on Apple by getting out in 1979, Rock's stake had now rocketed 378x, and Rock took a seat on the Apple board, pairing it with his position as Intel's chairman. He was, more indisputably than ever, the Valley's senior statesman, and yet the Apple investment was his last home run, after which he faded. "He should have dominated; he should have been the guy that wrote every check," Bill Hambrecht reflected. "He had the standing; he had the money behind him. It should've been him by default."[42] But standing and money were not the only metrics that mattered. New technologies and industries were coming to the fore, and skills beyond financial judgment were increasingly needed. Rock was the father of West Coast venture capital. He was not the man to drive it forward.

But that barely mattered, because by now venture capital had achieved escape velocity. In 1978, Congress had slashed the capital-gains tax from 49 percent to 28 percent, greatly increasing the incentive to invest in venture funds. The following year, the government had relaxed its prudent-man rule, opening the way for pension managers to invest in high-risk assets.[43] In 1980, in a scene that might have sprung directly from a conspiratorial Hollywood drama, the venture capitalist Bill Draper sat semi-naked at the secretive power gathering in Bohemian Grove and seized the opportunity to lobby a close Reagan adviser for an additional capital-gains cut; sure enough, the rate was cut again, this time to 20 percent, soon after Reagan took office.[44] The low capital-gains tax and the change to the prudent-man rule rounded out a policy mix that was extraordinarily favorable to venture investors. Venture-backed firms could go public without showing a history of profits. Employee stock options were taxed only when they were finally exercised, not when they were initially granted. Limited partnerships were exempt from tax, and they protected investing partners from lawsuits. No other country was so friendly to the venture industry.

Powered by the mouthwatering profits generated by exits such as Genentech and Apple, capital flooded into venture funds from the late 1970s. In the five years from 1973 to 1977, the venture industry had raised an average of $42 million annually. In the next five years, it averaged more than twenty times that—fully $940 million annually.[45] With the return of the hot IPO market following Apple's debut, established VC operators began to generate extraordinary profits: annual returns of between 30 and 50 percent became commonplace.[46] And so, not surprisingly, the top VC partnerships began to raise money on an unprecedented scale. Having drummed up $5 million for his first fund, Don Valentine raised a second fund of $21 million in 1979, followed by a $44 million fund in 1981.[47] Kleiner Perkins went from $8 million to $15 million to $55 million over roughly the same period.[48] Even an upstart such as New Enterprise Associates, founded in 1977 by Dick Kramlich and two East Coast partners, was able to raise $45 million for a fund in 1981.[49] All in all, the capital managed by venture funds quadrupled from $3 billion to $12 billion between 1977 and 1983, and the number of independent venture partnerships more than doubled in this period.[50]

Arthur Rock might be fading, but his legacy was booming.

Chapter Five

Cisco, 3Com, and the Valley Ascendant

T he full significance of the late 1970s and early 1980s venture boom was not evident to everybody. Despite the logic of the innovator's dilemma—that new industries were likely to be started by new companies, and therefore that a surge in venture capital could affect the vitality of the economy writ large—most commentators assumed that established industrial champions would decide America's fortunes. In 1978, Merrill Lynch forecast confidently that "future developers of promising technologies, new products and new services are likely to be well-financed divisions of major corporations."[1] It was as though the United States were still locked in the world of IBM and Sherman Fairchild. But Silicon Valley's venture-capital machine, now equipped with a full tool kit as well as a dense network of players, was about to deliver two simultaneous lessons. First, that it could fight off the challenge of Japan, whose formidable semi-conductor manufacturers threatened the Valley's core industry. Second, that it could at last eclipse its long-standing American rival, the technology hub centered on Boston.

Silicon Valley's success could not be explained in terms of government interventions. It was not as though federal initiatives had suddenly favored California over Massachusetts. Nor was it the case that the United States, facing competition from hyperefficient Japanese chip makers, responded with some magical industrial policy. Believers in the power of state activism often cite a government-led consortium named Sematech: starting in 1987, the federal government funneled $100 million per year into this effort, improving coordination among private chip makers and driving gains in manufacturing quality. But while Sematech helped to cut defect rates and accelerate miniaturization, Japanese manufacturers retained their edge, and the United States gave up trying to compete in the market for memory devices—the segment in which manufacturing quality was the chief differentiator.[2] Instead, Silicon Valley emerged triumphant by funneling its energy into new areas: specialized microprocessor design, disks and disk drives, and networking gear that linked up all the new equipment. These new industries capitalized on breakthroughs in physics and engineering coming out of government-backed labs: in this sense, public-sector support certainly did matter. But the Valley's success in turning basic research into commercial products reflected the triumph of a less fashionable science: sociology.

AnnaLee Saxenian, the Berkeley sociologist who has written perceptively about this phase in tech history, put her finger on the key difference between the Valley and its competitors.[3] In Boston and Japan, the electronics business was dominated by large, secretive, vertically integrated corporations: Digital Equipment and Data General, Toshiba and Sony. In contrast, Silicon Valley was a bubbling cauldron of small firms, vigorous because of the ferocious competition between them, formidable because they were capable of alliances and collaborations. The special virtue of the Valley's small companies, Saxenian argued, was that boundaries between them were porous. The founder of a disk-drive company would be out talking to PC makers, looking for ways to slot his device into their production chains: information on technical standards and design was traded constantly. An engineer could ask a colleague from another startup for advice on a problem; no culture of secrecy inhibited cooperation. A sales manager could quit a startup on Friday and begin at another one on Monday; sometimes he didn't even have to change parking lots, because the two companies were in the same building. Hierarchical organizations can be good at coordinating people when the objectives are clear: think of an army. But when it comes to commercializing applied science, the Valley's culture of "coopetition" has proved more creative than the self-contained, vertically integrated corporations of Boston or Japan. Large companies bottle up ideas and often waste them. Shifting coalitions of small ones conduct myriad experiments until they find the best path forward.

Why did it take a sociologist to spot Silicon Valley's advantage? Economists have always acknowledged the vitality of industrial "clusters"—finance in New York, movies in Hollywood, tech in Silicon Valley. They observe that clusters develop deep labor markets in specialized fields, so a company needing experts in, say, a particular kind of database software can hire the precise skills that it is seeking.[4] But Saxenian was going beyond economists' focus on productive matching between workers and employers. By emphasizing the porous boundaries between Valley startups, she was probing the quality of the relationships within a cluster and suggesting why some clusters pull ahead of others. A cluster that is dominated by large, self-contained, secretive companies will be characterized by tight relationships among insiders at each firm, but few links between professionals at one firm and similar professionals at another one. In contrast, a cluster that consists of transient startups will feature fewer deep bonds among colleagues, but it will be enriched by myriad, looser external connections. Saxenian's contention was that a small number of tight relationships makes for less idea sharing and innovation than a large number of loose relationships. In this she was building on an insight from one of the most cited social science papers of all time. In a celebrated article published in 1973, the sociologist Mark Granovetter argued that a plethora of weak ties generates a greater circulation of information than a handful of strong ones.[5]

At least until recently, the economics profession has offered no equivalent insight. Paul Krugman, whose pioneering work in economic geography helped earn him the Nobel Prize, regrets that "the stuff that I stressed in the models is a less important story than the things that I left out because I couldn't model them, like spillovers of information and social networks."[6] But Saxenian and her fellow sociologists put information spillovers and social networks at the center of their accounts, and they were clearly right to do so. Without Tom Perkins's loose ties to his old friends at

Hewlett-Packard, Tandem Computer would never have been conjured into being. Without Nolan Bushnell's loose ties to Don Valentine, and without Valentine's loose ties to Mike Markkula, Apple might never have become a real business. Ideas spread like wildfire around Silicon Valley because of places like Walker's Wagon Wheel, a packed watering hole where the engineers from IBM and Xerox PARC traded gossip freely. In other industrial clusters, the same ideas might not have spread at all, because the social relationships were not wired for fast dissemination.[7]

Of course, Saxenian's thesis raises a question: If porous boundaries and an abundance of weak ties make for a productive industrial cluster, what created these conditions in the Valley? There are two familiar answers. First, California law prevents employers from tying up employees in noncompete agreements; talent is free to go where it pleases, unlike in most states, including Massachusetts. Second, Stanford has been generous in allowing professors to take sabbaticals to work on startups, and this permissiveness has fostered ties between academia and business; in contrast, MIT professors have risked losing tenure if they spent too much time on side projects. Yet although an absence of non-compete clauses and the porousness of Stanford have contributed to the creative fluidity of the Valley, they are not the whole story. For one thing, some legal scholarship has sought to qualify the significance of non-competes.[8] For another, California tech startups are far more likely to involve Stanford grad students than Stanford professors.[9] The main answer to the Saxenian question—the reason why the Valley has a plethora of weak ties—is to be found elsewhere. It lies in the fact that one tribe of professionals is relentlessly focused on cultivating such ties. This tribe is the venture capitalists.

Which brings us back to the venture boom of the late 1970s and early 1980s. It was not a coincidence that the flood of money into VC partnerships anticipated the moment when Silicon Valley outran its competitors in Japan and Boston. The surge in venture dollars meant that more eager connectors plied their trade in the Valley, listening to pitches, interviewing prospective hires, linking ideas, people, and money. For many of these venture novices, building their networks was not just one thing that they did. Rather, it was *the* thing—the key to getting established in business. Bill Younger, who joined Sutter Hill in 1981, set himself the task of taking the smartest people in his Rolodex to lunch; at the end of every meal he'd ask, "Who is the absolutely best guy you've worked with?" Younger then made it his mission to meet that best guy—it was almost never a woman—and toward the end of the meeting he would repeat the question: "Who is the absolutely best guy out there?"[10] After a year of moving from one best guy to the next one, Younger had a list of about eighty superstars, and he cultivated each of them methodically. He would send one luminary a technical article that might be relevant to his research; he would call another to mention that an old colleague was asking after him. In this way, Younger spun a web of loose connections that would form the basis for productive startups when the right opportunities beckoned. The social capital that Saxenian stressed did not arise by accident.[11]

Insiders could feel how the surge in VC networking changed the metabolism of the Valley. One Friday in 1981, Fairchild's former chief executive Wilfred Corrigan circulated a business plan for a new semiconductor company, LSI Logic. By the following Tuesday, Kleiner Perkins and two co-investors had stumped up $2.3 million; "the only reason it took so long was because Monday was a holiday," one said later.[12] In similar fashion, an engineer named William Dambrackas raised money from the first VC he talked to, even though he had neither a prototype nor financial projections. "I had heard that venture capitalists bet more on the jockey than on the horse," Dambrackas marveled. "I was amazed that someone would invest in a company that didn't yet exist."[13] VCs were siphoning talented people out of large companies so rapidly that even Valley stalwarts took umbrage: Andy Grove, the president of Intel, complained that venture investors were playing the role of Darth Vader, luring innocent young engineers and managers to the "dark side" of entrepreneurial capitalism. "You know, we don't put bags on their heads and drag them out of the companies," Don Valentine retorted.[14] The absence of enforceable non-compete agreements helped the venture capitalists in this standoff. But contract law was less a power in its own right than an amplifier of liberation capital.

The change in the Valley's metabolism discomfited old-timers. Gone were the days when venture investors could do deep due diligence before backing a startup. "It used to be that you had two or three months," Eugene Kleiner lamented. "Now it's a matter of weeks or even days, because if we don't somebody else will."[15] But whatever the risks in this frenetic scramble, the new atmosphere was a tonic. The surge of venture dollars "helped flush the capable entrepreneurs out of their safe nests in the large corporations and into the gutsy and creative new ventures," as Bill Draper of Sutter Hill put it.[16] The risk-taking and tolerance of failure, often ascribed to some sort of magical potion in the Silicon Valley water, had everything to do with this fillip. When an engineer named Chuck Geschke quit a secure job to found the software company Adobe, he declared himself untroubled by the prospect of failure. He had watched other entrepreneurs navigate the world of venture-backed startups, and he had seen that failure often meant that you raised more venture dollars the next time.[17]

With the feeling of risk drowned out by venture capital, and with so many innovative experiments being funded, some were bound to hit it big. It would take only a handful of exceptional venture-backed winners to entrench Silicon Valley as the world's dominant technology center.

No equivalent venture boom occurred in and around Boston. Starting in the mid-1960s, when Georges Doriot's ARD began to falter, a trio of Davis & Rock–style partnerships emerged from its shadow: Greylock Partners, Charles River Ventures, and later Matrix Partners. All three performed well, but they were part of a smaller, weaker network, and they were markedly less go-getting than their West Coast rivals. There was no tradition of VCs rolling up their sleeves and helping to design startups, as Tom Perkins had done with Tandem and Genentech. There was not even the habit of backing a promising technologist and then finding him a CEO, as Sutter Hill had done in its Qume deal. Instead, East Coast venture capitalists expected companies to pitch for money with their team already in place; "it was a theory of immaculate conception," a West Coast veteran remembered.[18] "There is no real venture capital in Massachusetts," a senior Boston technology manager concurred. "Unless you've proven yourself a hundred times over, you'll never get any money."[19] One Boston entrepreneur, who quit a local tech giant to set up his own firm, concluded, "People in New England would rather invest in a tennis court than high technology." He packed up and moved to Silicon Valley, where he founded a successful computer company called Convergent. "I got commitments for $2.5 million in twenty minutes from three people over lunch who saw me write the business plan on the back of a napkin," he said later.[20]

The caution of the East Coast venture tribe permeated everything it did, from the selection of which founders to back to the way it coached them after investing. Seeking to reduce risk, Boston VCs often provided what they called "developmental capital" to businesses that already had a proven product and some early sales; this was a whole lot safer than betting on fledgling startups. Howard Cox, who embarked on a career at Greylock in 1971, boasted that he lost money on only two of his forty investments. "I did not back companies where the product might fail," he said, articulating an approach that West Coast venture capitalists would have found laughably fainthearted.[21] The contracts between VCs and startups reflected the same East-West divide. East Coasters insisted upon rights to seize a startup's assets if it fared badly, much as mortgage lenders assert rights to seize homes if borrowers default. West Coasters were less hung up on such conditions because if infant startups failed, they would have few assets worth seizing. In a final mark of caution, East Coasters took risk off the table early, often preferring to sell a portfolio firm to a bigger rival once it had made 5x or so. Because they were making fewer bets that went to zero, they did not feel compelled to drive their winners to 10x or higher.

◆

The contrast between the coasts was crystallized in the story of Bob Metcalfe.[22] A self-styled "Viking-American," with grandparents from Oslo, Bergen, Leeds, and Dublin, Metcalfe sported bushy strawberry-blond hair and wing tip loafers and called himself "a right-wing hippie."[23] After studies at MIT and Harvard, he moved out west to Xerox PARC, where he seldom used an alarm clock, frequently pulled all-nighters at the lab, and invented a computer-networking technology called Ethernet. He was a ferociously competitive tennis player and a force of nature: he combined the promotional charisma of Steve Jobs with the engineering virtuosity of Steve Wozniak. But to Metcalfe's immense frustration, Xerox showed no sign of building a business out of his Ethernet invention, nor did the company appear eager to promote such a free spirit up the managerial ladder.[24] So Metcalfe quit and founded a startup called 3Com, promising that Ethernet would link up personal computers in offices and living rooms across the nation.[25]

Fifteen years earlier, an ambitious engineer like Metcalfe would have lined up a financial backer first, then summoned the courage to quit afterward. But now the ubiquity of liberation capital could be taken for granted, allowing Metcalfe to reverse the sequence. It never so much as occurred to him how miraculous this was. *Of course*, a brilliant young scientist should not languish at a bureaucracy that failed to make the most of his talents. *Of course*, if a scientist so chose, he had the option—almost the right—to found his own company. Economists often think in terms of markets and firms. But Metcalfe was betting on that intermediate institution: the network.

Metcalfe set out to raise money for 3Com in September 1980. He attracted offers in no time. The Mayfield Fund, set up by Rock's former partner Tommy Davis, proposed to value 3Com at $2 million, or $7 per share. Dick Kramlich of New Enterprise Associates, another former Rock partner, put together a syndicate willing to pay a valuation of $3.7 million, or $13 per share; this was before 3Com had done anything. But Metcalfe was determined to get more. Declaring that his company was worth $6 million and that his shares should fetch $20 a piece, he set out to beat the venture guys at their own game. "I've always resented MBAs," he confessed. "They always got paid more than I did, and I was smarter than them."[26]

Metcalfe began to take venture capitalists to lunch and solicit their guidance. "If you want money, you ask for advice. If you want advice, you ask for money," he reflected shrewdly.[27] His goal was to absorb the VCs' way of thinking, and before long he noticed a pattern. At some point in each conversation, the venture guy would launch into a lecture on the three reasons startups failed: the excessive ego of the founder, too little focus on the most promising products, and too little capital. Having recognized this mantra, Metcalfe started to preempt it. "Here are the three mistakes I am not going to make," he would announce, before the unsuspecting venture capitalist got a chance to lodge the standard caveats. "A, I have decided that it's more important that this company succeed than that I run it. Two is, even though I have this business plan that shows a million products, trust me, we're going to focus on a few of them. And three, I'm here raising money, because we're not going to be undercapitalized."[28]

Metcalfe's first promise was particularly intriguing. Precisely because he had staked his ego on getting a $20 share price, he was willing to subordinate his ego when it came to who would run the company. He had penetrated the venture capitalists' mindset well enough to understand the Qume formula: he knew that if he accepted the VCs' money, they were bound to bring in outside managers. Given this inevitability, Metcalfe figured, why not flip the sequence on its head? If he hired an outside executive before he raised capital, his company would appear stronger and his shares would sell at a higher valuation.

3Com's tiny founding team did not love this prospect. They thought they could build the company themselves, with Metcalfe as their leader. One of them gave Metcalfe a cartoon showing a king and a queen looking out over their domain.

King, appearing doubtful: "I'm not sure I can do this."

Queen, looking stern: "Shut up and rule."[29]

Despite this teasing, Metcalfe stuck with his plan to hire an outside executive. Toward the end of 1980, he used a speech at Stanford to announce a new kind of venture-capital auction: he would accept funding, he declared, from whichever investor brought him the best operational guy with grown-up management experience.[30] By demanding that the venture capitalists find him a company president *before* they invested, Metcalfe aimed to make them boost 3Com's prospects and then pay him for the value that they had created.

On the East Coast, the venture capitalists might have shrugged and walked away. Who was this crazy inventor to dictate to them? But the West Coasters were willing to work with potential home-run founders almost no matter what. With the increasing penetration of the PC, computer networking was a hot business.

Wally Davis, a senior partner at Mayfield, heard Metcalfe's speech at Stanford. He went back to the office and recounted the story. Ethernet's inventor was imposing Sutter Hill's Qume formula on himself. In order to invest, Mayfield would have to work its recruitment network and find a seasoned manager for 3Com.

"I know a guy who would be a perfect fit," a junior Mayfield partner named Gib Myers offered. Myers had previously worked at Hewlett-Packard with a manager named Bill Krause. A graduate of the Citadel, a military college in South Carolina, Krause was an orderly, process-oriented adult; in fact, he was too orderly for most people. He was in his element when composing a MOST memo—"Mission, Objectives, Strategy, and Tactics." He was precise about the distinction between a product-marketing manager and a director of product marketing. Levity was not his thing. But with the wing-tipped hippie by his side, his dogged style would generate the ideal balance.

Myers called Krause and asked him to meet Metcalfe at Mac's Tea Room in Los Altos. He explained that Metcalfe was launching a new firm. He and Krause had different styles, but maybe they could be complementary.

Krause happily accepted the proposal. He had always wanted to lead a startup. Having run HP's personal-computer division, he knew about Ethernet and felt appropriate respect for the engineer who had invented it. Besides, Krause's old Hewlett-Packard buddy Jimmy Treybig had left the stability of HP to start the venture-backed Tandem. That had worked out pretty well for him.[31]

The meeting in Los Altos went off well. Krause, like Metcalfe, was a competitive tennis player, and the two men had a meeting of the minds on the future of computing. The utility of a personal computer would rise exponentially when it was hooked up to a network, they both agreed. Indeed, this insight came to be known as Metcalfe's law: the value of a network rises with the square of the number of devices connected to it.

A few days later, Krause met Howard Charney, Metcalfe's chief lieutenant, as well as the other early employees. The more he got to know 3Com, the more he grew enthusiastic. If he quit Hewlett-Packard, he would be leaving a stable company and taking a pay cut. But it would be a chance to build something from nothing and to own a large chunk of the equity.

Krause's next move was to broach the subject with his wife, Gay. He chose a moment when they were out running together. It was a beautiful morning, and Gay loved to run, and Krause told her he might sign on with a startup. He would be leading an exciting team! He had always yearned to do something like this!

Gay kept running without saying anything. Presently, Krause looked over and saw that she was crying.

Krause called Metcalfe and asked for help. The family conversation had not gone so well. Maybe Metcalfe and Howard Charney could join Gay and him for dinner?

The Krauses duly dined with Metcalfe and Charney. Afterward Gay said, "Howard Charney's the smartest guy I ever met."

Then she added, "Bob Metcalfe's the most charismatic guy I ever met."

Then she demanded, "What the hell do they need you for?"

"Is that a yes?" Krause asked.

"Go for it," Gay responded.[32]

◆

With Krause ready to come on board, Metcalfe thought he had what he needed to press for a $20 share price.[33] But even with adult supervision in place, the venture guys were not budging. By now they had routinized the Qume formula: they would have fixed 3Com's management anyway, so the fact that Metcalfe had preempted them was not a game changer. Dick Kramlich of New Enterprise Associates was sticking with his offer of $13 per share. Jack Melchor, known for backing a successful 1970s computer maker called ROLM, was also offering $13. Mayfield had upped its number from $7, but refused to go higher than that apparently magical $13 level. Metcalfe suspected collusion. The Valley network was bountiful, but it could also feel like a cartel. It was ganging up against him.

Metcalfe resolved to cast his net wider. He was not going to pay for the privilege of raising money from a brand-name Valley venture firm. Boston financiers had money that was just as green. Capital was a commodity.

The good news for Metcalfe was that Boston venture capitalists were properly impressed by the hiring of Krause. They liked to invest in ready-made teams. 3Com now had a top-flight inventor and a top-flight manager. Pretty soon, Fidelity Ventures, the VC branch of the storied Boston money house, announced that it would finance 3Com at $21 per share. At last, Metcalfe had a valuation that exceeded his $20 target.[34]

Elated, Metcalfe called Kramlich. "Dick," he said, "we have somebody who thinks we're worth what we're worth. They just want a month to do their due diligence. So if you insist that this is the deal and you won't wait a month, we're going to walk away."[35]

Metcalfe hoped that Kramlich would now increase his price. Didn't these financiers respect auctions and price discovery? Wouldn't they cave now that their cartel had been busted?

Kramlich refused the bait. He wished Metcalfe luck, but he was not going to compete with Fidelity's $21 bid. He believed he could judge what startups were worth, even when there were few objective, quantitative metrics to anchor his judgment.

Metcalfe went back to Fidelity and announced he was ready to sign a "term sheet," a document laying out the price and conditions in a private investment. For once, it appeared, the Boston venture community was going to steal a West Coast deal from under the noses of the Sand Hill Road fraternity. But Metcalfe soon discovered what he came to call the Oh-by-the-Way Syndrome. As in, "Oh by the way, a condition of the deal is that we have some other investors."

The first time Metcalfe encountered this demand, it seemed innocent. The Boston guys wanted a co-investor, and they didn't seem to have their own network of ready suitors. Thinking nothing of this, Metcalfe went off to find another partnership ready to pay $21 per share, eventually identifying a willing New York outfit. But then he confronted a second condition. "Actually, we need a *West Coast* firm," Fidelity insisted; evidently, the Boston guys craved validation from the Valley. Metcalfe gamely hustled a bit more, eventually identifying a small West Coast VC willing to invest at the $21 level. No, the Bostonians now objected, it had to be a *major* West Coast firm. Metcalfe's candidate did not cut it.

Still determined to clear his $20-per-share hurdle, Metcalfe made the rounds again, finally coming up with a major West Coast firm willing to put in $100,000.

"What we really want is a *significant* participation of a major West Coast firm or we can't close this deal," Fidelity then informed him.

As Metcalfe jumped through one maddening hoop after another, he confronted a further problem. New terms and conditions kept appearing in the Bostonians' fine print. There was an "exploding board" clause that gave investors power to appoint all directors of the company. There was a "ratchet-down" clause, protecting them against possible dilution of their stake if 3Com later sold a tranche of equity at a lower price. Fidelity was trying to manage the intrinsic riskiness of startups by unleashing the lawyers. It did not want to recognize that startups can fail, in which case board rights and ratchets make no difference.

Eventually, after a month of frustration, Metcalfe concluded that the promised $21 investment was a mirage: it vanished every time he neared it. A startup's scarcest asset is time. Venture capitalists in Boston turned out to be champions at wasting it.

Not wanting to go back to Kramlich with his tail between his legs, Metcalfe instead went to see Jack Melchor, one of the other Valley VCs who had offered $13.

"I need this deal closed," Metcalfe told him. Without a capital infusion fast, 3Com would run out of cash to pay its people. Metcalfe was now willing to accept $13 per share to get the funding process over with.

"I have only one stipulation," Metcalfe added. Fidelity Ventures had to be cut out of the financing.[36]

With that, Silicon Valley's network delivered the deal in a matter of minutes. Melchor picked up the phone and spoke with Mayfield and Kramlich, and soon it was agreed that Melchor's fund would commit $450,000, Mayfield and Dick Kramlich would be in for $300,000 each, and another $50,000 would come from small investors with connections to 3Com. There were no futile protection clauses in the fine print, no eleventh-hour conditions, and no need for Metcalfe to hustle for dollars at the expense of time with his company. On Friday, February 27, 1981, 3Com received a check for $1.1

million in exchange for a third of its equity. If the cash had not arrived that day, 3Com would have missed payroll.[37]

Metcalfe had failed to get the $20 per share that he had wanted. But he did have the pleasure of calling his Boston tormentors one last time. They would not be investing in 3Com, he informed them.

"Why?" came the aggrieved response. "We supported you when no one else would."

"No," Metcalfe shot back. "You lied to me when no one else would."[38]

———◆———

3Com went public in 1984, generating a 15x return for its early investors. But this success was a small part of a larger phenomenon. The personal-computer revolution was gathering pace, and venture capitalists' function of connecting up networks became especially valuable. The PCs made by startups such as Apple and Compaq would only be useful if they could be linked to a host of complementary inventions: disk drives, memory disks, and software programs as well as networking technologies such as Ethernet. Each of these "peripherals" was produced by a separate company, and each had to be compatible with the PCs at the heart of the system. So venture capitalists hustled around the Valley, mingling with the engineers at bars like Walker's Wagon Wheel and listening to the technical chatter. Then, having gathered intelligence on which protocols were gaining acceptance, they backed firms that embraced them. Don Valentine of Sequoia, who made a point of dropping by the Wagon Wheel on Wednesdays and Fridays, called this the "aircraft carrier model."[39] Venture-capital dollars launched flotillas of startups to service the PCs at the center of the armada.

As they filled in the spaces around the PC, the venture guys often brokered technical alliances between companies. In one example, Sequoia invested in 3Com's second round of financing, then suggested that a collaboration between 3Com and a chip maker called Seeq could help resolve an engineering challenge. The two firms duly pooled their know-how and embarked on a win-win partnership, proving that "some secrets are more valuable when shared," as people in the Valley put it.[40] In another example,

Kleiner Perkins invested in Sun Microsystems and in an advanced chip maker called Cypress; John Doerr, the young KP point man on both deals, brought the two companies together to produce a new device known as the SPARC microprocessor, which improved the performance of Sun's workstations. Doerr, a hyperkinetic evangelist of whom we will hear much, grew so keen on such collaborations that he spoke of a "keiretsu model": mimicking Japan's formidable industrial networks, Kleiner would turn its portfolio of firms into a web of fertile associations. Hard-pressed company founders necessarily had their heads down, fixing engineering glitches and worrying about sales. But venture capitalists could see the map and the territory and tell founders how to navigate it.

Fostering collaborations among startups required some sensitivity. Silicon Valley's culture of "coopetition" involved cooperating on some days and competing on others. It was up to the venture capitalists to supervise this balance—to ensure that secrets would be shared and yet confidences not violated. In 1981, Doerr introduced a chip maker called Silicon Compilers to a networking company called Ungermann-Bass: as with the Seeq-3Com alliance, there was an opportunity for synergy. Because KP held stakes in both Silicon Compilers and Ungermann, there was a presumption of trust, and the two firms quickly pooled their know-how. "We accepted their credibility and ethics faster because of KP's imprimatur," an Ungermann-Bass engineer recalled later.[41] But after the two companies had worked together for some time, Ungermann-Bass was unimpressed. The bespoke chip that Silicon Compilers developed seemed little better than the standard and far cheaper chip available from Intel. Ungermann-Bass duly broke off the partnership and assumed that this was the end of the matter.

Then things got messy—for the companies and for Kleiner Perkins. Spurned, Silicon Compilers struck up a new relationship with Ungermann's rival, 3Com. Thanks to the fruitless collaboration initiated by Doerr, Ungermann's intellectual property now seemed likely to fall into the hands of its fiercest competitor. The Ungermann-Bass leaders called Kleiner Perkins. "You can't do that!" they protested. "We gave you everything we know!"[42]

What happened next illustrates the secret magic of the Valley. Ralph

Ungermann, the senior Ungermann-Bass founder, was summoned with his lieutenants to Kleiner's magnificent designer office high up in San Francisco's Embarcadero Center, with spectacular views over the bay. There, he was invited to lay out the full detail of his complaint in front of KP's senior rainmaker, Tom Perkins. With Doerr and the team from Silicon Compilers in attendance, Perkins presided over the hearing like a latter-day Solomon. "We just told them this is not right," one of the Ungermann lieutenants recalled later.

"Well, what do you want?" Perkins asked presently. His office was decorated with models of the supercharged Bugatti cars that he collected.

Summoning up the courage to demand what he thought to be an outrageous compensatory payment, Ralph Ungermann answered. He wanted half a million dollars.

Doerr turned white. One of the Ungermann guys thought he might faint at any moment.[43]

"Could you excuse us?" said Perkins.

Ungermann and his team walked out into the lobby. "That was pretty ballsy," one of the lieutenants said.

After a short wait they were called back in.

"Okay. We'll pay you $500,000," Perkins announced simply. It was an extraordinary concession. Ungermann would get almost half the sum that 3Com had raised in its Series A round, and he would get it without surrendering a single share of equity.

"Fine. We'll drop all claims," Ungermann responded.[44]

"VCs are always walking this fine line between competition and cooperation," one of Ungermann's colleagues later reflected. "The whole identity of a VC partnership revolves around managing the relationship between their portfolio companies—around taking advantage of that when it is appropriate and not causing a problem when it is not appropriate."[45] Kleiner Perkins's business hinged on its reputation for ensuring fair play. To preserve the deep trust on which its franchise depended, half a million dollars was a bargain.[46]

And it was also a boon for the Valley. Venture capitalists' success in managing the coopetition among small firms had everything to do with Silicon Valley's triumph in the 1980s. Reputation and trust ensured that costly litigation was rare. Dozens of new ventures could hustle for business, and yet the Valley's collaborative vibe was undiminished. In semiconductors, for example, venture-financed upstarts such as LSI Logic and Cypress Semiconductor helped to develop the market for specialty circuits, allowing the Valley to regain its crown as the world's semiconductor leader.[47] In disk drives, West Coast VCs backed more than fifty startups in the first years of the decade, and although the overcrowding resulted in dozens of failures, the survivors ensured that the Valley stole the industry away from the vertically integrated, East Coast computer behemoths.[48] All in all, Northern California's tech firms added more than sixty-five thousand net new jobs during the 1980s, more than triple the number created around Boston. By the end of the decade, the Valley was home to thirty-nine of the nation's hundred fastest-growing electronics companies. The Boston area claimed just four of them.[49]

The brightest of all the 1980s Valley stars was an unlikely outfit called Cisco. Its two prime movers were a married couple, Leonard Bosack and Sandy Lerner; they were not the sorts of people who could easily raise venture capital. Bosack was intense, hostile, and robotic in his mode of thought. "Len's kind of an alien," Lerner confessed; "he can scare people."[50] Lerner, for her part, had survived a tough childhood and developed a wild streak. She once posed for a *Forbes* photograph lying on a horse, naked.

Lerner grew up without a father and with an alcoholic mother, spending much of her time on a ranch with an aunt in California. By the time she had graduated from high school, at the age of sixteen, she had refused to pledge allegiance to the flag, been hassled by police at an antiwar protest, and built a surprising business for a future technologist—a cattle herd. After a short spell working as a junior bank clerk, she enrolled at Chico State, an outpost of California's university system distinguished mainly by its terrible fight song ("Hail to Chico State . . . where the men are square / and our fair coeds are fairer"). Lerner majored in political science, with a concentration in comparative communist theory. Her politics were so far to the left that her idea of an appropriate Pentagon budget was "enough stamps to mail out going-out-of-business messages," as a colleague put it later.[51]

Lerner completed her Chico State degree in two years and enrolled for a master's in econometrics at Claremont McKenna College. She toyed with the idea of an academic career but wanted to get rich, and her interests moved toward computing. This led to further work in computational mathematics at Stanford; she had ascended from college backwater to academic pinnacle with remarkable speed, and she was the only woman in her Stanford program. Among her fellow students was Len Bosack, who stood out because he washed. "Nerd culture at Stanford was pretty extreme," Lerner recalled.[52] Len "actually knew how to bathe and eat with silverware."[53] The two embarked on a fiber-optic-speed romance.[54] In 1980 they married.

Completing her master's degree at Stanford in 1981, Lerner took a job as the director of computer facilities at the university's business school. Bosack took on the same role at the computer science department. Their offices were separated by only five hundred yards, but their machines could not communicate. Thanks to Bob Metcalfe's Ethernet technology, the computers in Bosack's lab could talk to one another via a local area network. But Lerner's business school lab ran on a different protocol. Nobody had succeeded in constructing a bridge between the two networks.

Without seeking the blessing of the university, Lerner and Bosack set out to fix this problem; according to later Cisco lore, they wanted to send love notes to each other. First they solved the engineering problem of connecting two networks that used different protocols. Next, Bosack began to develop a more advanced device—a multi-protocol router, which could link up networks that worked on a wide variety of standards. The router also solved a headache that plagued large networks: the so-called broadcast storm, in which packets of information were rebroadcast by thousands of computers, causing the networks to choke on the overload. Incorporating the efforts of various Stanford colleagues, Bosack marshaled hardware and software to avoid these crashes, creating what he and Lerner called the Blue Box. Then they set about threading coaxial cable through manholes and sewer pipes, linking up all of the five thousand or so computers on Stanford's sprawling campus. The university had still not sanctioned their efforts.

"It was very much a guerrilla action," Lerner said later.[55] But, authorized or otherwise, the new network of networks proved robust, and Lerner recognized the opportunity. She and Bosack had something that could make them rich. Their technology could be a company.

Lerner and Bosack approached the university authorities, asking for permission to sell their inter-networking breakthrough to other universities. Despite Stanford's reputation for encouraging entrepreneurs, in this case it refused; it was less generous to its technical staff than to the tenured faculty. The couple decided that if Stanford was not going to behave reasonably, it would be reasonable to disregard its rules. "And so, with tears in our eyes, we took our $5 up to the Secretary of State's office up in San Francisco, and made Cisco Systems," Lerner recounted later.[56]

In 1986, Lerner and Bosack quit Stanford to work full time on Cisco. They were joined by three other former Stanford employees, and they began to sell homemade versions of the multi-protocol router. Money was tight, and the founders sought out venture capital, showing up at networking events and pitching dozens of investors. But their efforts came to naught. For one thing, the venture boom had cooled. A surfeit of capital had depressed returns, and the previous year private venture partnerships had raised $2.4 billion, down from a bit over $3 billion in each of the two previous years.[57] For another thing, the multi-protocol router could not be protected by patent: Stanford claimed ownership of Cisco's inter-networking breakthrough. Then there was the question of the founders themselves. Bosack was by turns silent and given to relentless logical soliloquies; Lerner developed a habit of saying "Control-D" when she tired of his algorithmic monologues. Lerner, for her part, was off-putting to venture capitalists for different reasons. Whether because of her nature, her disjointed childhood, or the prejudice visited upon a woman in an almost exclusively male field, she came across as scarily abrasive.

Spurned by investors, the Cisco team soldiered on tenaciously. They kept the lights on by maxing out credit cards and deferring salaries; Lerner took a side job to help pay the bills, and one co-founder made a personal loan to the company.[58] Bosack's ferocious work ethic kicked into overdrive. "Sincerity begins at a little over a hundred hours a week," he said. "You have to get down to eating once a day and showering every other day to really get your life organized."[59] The team's determination deepened as customers began to order its products. Brown delivery trucks started to show up regularly outside the suburban home that the couple shared with Bosack's parents.[60]

By the start of 1987, Cisco had made enough progress to recruit a couple of extra people. But without venture backing, the company could not attain escape velocity. In the absence of experienced guidance, Lerner and Bosack hired cheaply and eccentrically. A former naval officer with no startup experience arrived to serve as vice president for finance. A new chief executive took it upon himself to veto a sale of routers to a lab with military ties, explaining that if Cisco's gear malfunctioned, it might trigger World War III, which was more responsibility than he could handle.[61] (The next day the veto was revoked. "I heard that somebody had gotten a bottle and just smashed him on the head," one Cisco alumnus remembers.[62]) And while Cisco stumbled, competitors emerged. By mid-1987, Paul Severino, a Boston engineer and serial entrepreneur, had raised an impressive $6 million in funding for a rival called Wellfleet Communications. He looked set to win the race for the inter-networking market.

But then Cisco's fortunes turned—in classic Silicon Valley fashion. The antimilitary chief executive knew a lawyer, and the lawyer had a partner named Ed Leonard, and Leonard happened to work with people in the venture industry. In a different corner of the world economy, this might have been irrelevant: a lawyer like Leonard would not have bothered senior venture guys on behalf of some random half acquaintance. But Silicon Valley rainmakers were unlike rainmakers elsewhere: they positively wanted to be bothered. Making and taking introductions was their stock-in-trade. If Leonard introduced them to a long-shot entrepreneur, it could only boost his standing.

Before doing the introductions, Leonard met Bosack and Lerner to size up their potential. They were wearing T-shirts with combative slogans. Bosack picked apart the possible meanings of every word that Leonard uttered.[63]

Despite his misgivings, Leonard put a call into a friend at Sequoia, and soon he was speaking with Don Valentine. "I don't know whether I'm doing you a favor," he confessed. "But I'm about to introduce you to a company that has very, very *different* people."

As the investor who had backed Nolan Bushnell and Steve Jobs, Valentine was not going to pass on Cisco merely because its founders were unusual. The test he cared about was whether Cisco's routers did what the founders claimed for them. If they did, the sky was the limit. A technology that made possible a network of networks would be hugely valuable.

Valentine enlisted the advice of Charlie Bass, the younger of the two founders behind Ungermann-Bass, 3Com's old rival. Bass was thinking of signing on as a partner at Sequoia.[64] In the meantime, he served as a consultant on potential deals. He promised to find out if Cisco's technology worked as Bosack said it did.

Pretty soon, he had the answer. Hewlett-Packard was an early customer of Cisco's, and Bass spoke to a friend there. The friend delivered some good news and some bad. In HP's experience, Bosack's routers were more than good; they were so excellent, in fact, that HP would pay almost anything to have them. However, an investor in Cisco would have to be ready for trouble. The word among the HP engineers was that Bosack was impossible to work with.

Bass judged that the personality issue outweighed the excellence of the technology. He doubted whether Bosack was investable.[65]

Valentine listened to Bass and reached the opposite conclusion. He had already met Bosack and understood his failings: so far as he could tell, the only subject on which Bosack shed his robotic demeanor was Dr Pepper sodas, to which he was passionately devoted. Valentine had also sized up Lerner. She was smart and articulate but confrontational and loud, which was not good for her prospects as a team builder.[66] However, the way Valentine saw things, none of this mattered. Hewlett-Packard had testified that engineers were "tearing the hinges off the doors to get the products," as Valentine put it.[67] If Lerner and Bosack were difficult to work with, so what? Valentine would sit on them.

Midway through Sequoia's due diligence process, on October 19, 1987, the Dow Jones stock index collapsed by 23 percent. The following Monday, a leading technology banker visited Sequoia's offices for lunch. "Stop buying. It's over," he advised grimly.[68] But Valentine remained determined to press on. How often did a seven-person company generate sales without the benefit of a sales force?

At the end of 1987, Sequoia duly invested $2.5 million for a third of Cisco.[69] On the face of it, these terms were fairly generous: six years earlier, 3Com had sold a third of itself for just $1.1 million, although it had been at an earlier stage in its development. But Valentine had understood Cisco's weaknesses and structured the deal accordingly. Fully one-third of Cisco's stock was set aside for existing managers and future employees, enabling Valentine to recruit a clean slate of executives who would take over the leadership from the founders.[70] Lerner and Bosack retained the remaining third, but the majority of their stake was converted into nonvoting stock options, giving Valentine control of board decisions. Bosack was allowed to occupy one board seat, but Lerner was excluded, possibly because she was tougher to deal with—or possibly because of sexism. When Lerner complained, Valentine assured her that he would revisit her status, but later.[71]

Before long, Valentine did revisit Cisco's leadership structure, but with a different purpose. The CEO had lost the confidence of Lerner and Bosack, and Valentine had never liked him anyway. So he fired him and took on the role of interim chief executive. For good measure, Valentine made himself chairman of Cisco's board and installed his tough Sequoia partner, Pierre Lamond, as head of engineering. There was no question now about who was running the firm, and there was no question either about whether this was a good thing. Kirk Lougheed, one of the co-founders who had quit Stanford to build Cisco, was silently cheering Valentine's power grab. "I was hoping, here come the professionals!" he remembered. "I had put time into this, and it was about to succeed. I did not want Len and Sandy to screw it up."[72]

Tasked with building up the engineering department, Lamond worked Sequoia's network and began to hire new people. Sensing her control slipping away, Lerner pushed back furiously.

"This guy's brain-dead!" she declared after one of Lamond's new engineers showed up at Cisco.

"Brain-dead!" she repeated loudly after the arrival of the next one. Lamond soon concluded that this was Lerner's favorite expression.[73]

Meanwhile, Valentine set out to find an outsider who could serve as permanent chief executive. He asked each candidate to describe the most outrageous thing he'd done. He needed a manager who was not afraid to act crazy, because Cisco was a crazy company.

"I've never done anything outrageous," one candidate answered.

"Okay, you're dead," Valentine thought to himself.[74]

In the fall of 1988, Valentine settled on John Morgridge, a veteran executive from Honeywell who had also led an unsuccessful startup. Morgridge cheerfully confessed that Honeywell had been "a great education in how not to do things." This was music to Valentine's ears. He liked humility as much as he detested conceit. Experience of comprehensive corporate dysfunction was the perfect preparation for Cisco.[75]

Although he was bringing in an outside CEO, Valentine understood that there were risks to this strategy. It was more straightforward, obviously, to retain a gifted founder: as the owners and creators of their firms, founders had the financial and emotional incentives to go for greatness. Sutter Hill's Qume formula involved bringing in an outside CEO to pair with a technical founder. But complementing founders was not the same as displacing them.

To make a success out of Morgridge, Valentine gave him founder-type incentives. He loaded him up with stock options so that he would pocket around 6 percent of Cisco's success; this gave him more skin in the game than some CEO-founders.[76] Valentine also did his best to re-create a founder's emotional incentives. Entrepreneurs who start companies have their egos at stake; they can't just coast along and accept a good-enough outcome. Valentine made it clear to Morgridge that if he coasted, he'd be out. "I'm not very good at picking people," he growled, "but I correct my mistakes very quickly."[77]

When Lerner heard of Morgridge's hiring, she was furious. She declared him brain-dead. She confronted Valentine again, shouting at him in the office. Meanwhile, the rest of Cisco's management team fought wildly among themselves; on one occasion, a fistfight broke out between rival vice presidents. A company psychologist was summoned. "His role was not necessarily to cause us to love one another, but to avoid us taking physical action against one another," Morgridge remembered.[78]

It was easy to see why Charlie Bass had doubted whether Cisco's founders were investable. But, step-by-step, Valentine and Morgridge turned a dysfunctional collective into a serious company. They hired a new finance director, a new marketing manager, and a new corporate sales force; they built a manufacturing operation where none had previously existed.[79] They instilled a fearsome cost-control culture, and their discipline percolated through the company. On business trips, Morgridge would stay with a distant cousin to save the cost of a hotel, which gave him the moral authority to tell Cisco managers to fly coach, which he himself did, naturally. When a few dissenters objected, Morgridge responded that they could travel in "virtual first class." They should transport themselves mentally from their cramped economy seats by closing their eyes and picturing caviar.

Two years after Sequoia's investment, at the end of 1989, Cisco had become a mature firm with 174 employees.[80] As Valentine had foreseen, sales and profits were exploding.[81] Sadly, however, Lerner was exploding too. She convinced herself that all the newcomers at Cisco were contemptuous of clients. "I saw them, rightly or wrongly, as the people that I was trying to protect the customers from," she confessed later.[82] She lost her temper with increasing frequency, and her marriage with Bosack broke down. The colleagues who used to tolerate her outbursts were at the end of their tethers.

On a late summer's day in 1990, Valentine arrived at his office on Sand Hill Road to an ominous greeting from his assistant. Seven Cisco executives, led by the chief financial officer, John Bolger, were waiting in the conference room. "I just sensed that they were not there to celebrate my birthday or anything," Valentine said later.

The visitors got straight to the point. Sandy Lerner had to go. Otherwise, in an echo of the Traitorous Eight, Cisco's senior team would quit together.[83]

The meeting concluded in less than an hour. When his visitors were gone, Valentine phoned Morgridge.

"I have a rebellion on my hands here. What should I do?" he asked.

"I told them to go see you, and if you agreed, she's gone," Morgridge responded.[84]

Valentine did agree, and Morgridge duly summoned Lerner to his office. The way he tells it, he tried to explain to Lerner that she should leave for her own good. Thanks to the success of Cisco, she had no financial need to work. And judging by her behavior, she was unhappy. "I don't know if you want to live your life this way," Morgridge remembers pleading.[85] Lerner rejected his entreaties: she was not ready to retire. Then Morgridge cut to the chase. "Today was your last day," he informed her.[86]

When Bosack was told of Lerner's firing, he quit in sympathy. The two never again set foot inside the company that they had founded. Bosack, once described by Lerner as an "alien," went on to fund efforts to discover extraterrestrial intelligence.[87] Lerner channeled her energy into a successful cosmetics brand called Urban Decay, which challenged the "Barbie" aesthetic of the beauty-industrial complex. One Urban Decay product was a nail polish named Bruise. It was a fitting coda for a fighter.

◆

The firing of Cisco's founders became part of Valley mythology. It was supposedly the moment when venture capital revealed itself in all its ruthlessness. Valentine himself did much to feed this story line, cultivating the image of the tough guy who canned people. But the truth about Cisco, and about the removal of company founders elsewhere, is subtler. Venture capitalists are not always the ax wielders when founders get the chop; often it is the top managers who turn on their chief, forcing his or her departure.[88] Valentine had been the one who authorized Lerner's dismissal, but he did so to keep the rest of Cisco's team together. The truth is that Lerner's firing probably says less about VC heartlessness than about sexism at tech firms. As late as 1990, women accounted for only 9 percent of engineers in the United States and were even rarer at Valley startups.[89] It was tough to be so isolated.

The terms of Sequoia's investment are also controversial. Years later,

Lerner would accuse Valentine of exploiting her lack of financial experience.[90] The Cisco term sheet had laid down that two-thirds of the founders'
shares would vest over four years; when Lerner and Bosack left in August
1990, a third of these conditional shares, or just under a quarter of their
total equity holdings, were still unvested. A legal confrontation followed, in
which the founders, having shed their innocence, retained an aggressive
Los Angeles attorney who rolled up to meetings in a white stretch limou-
sine.[91] But although the resulting legal settlement remains murky, Lerner
and Bosack left Cisco with at least $46 million each, and probably with
more than that. Had they spurned Sequoia's investment, they would have
retained control of Cisco. But, owning a larger slice of a much smaller pie,
they would have been considerably less wealthy.[92]

But the larger lesson from Cisco relates to the rise of Silicon Valley. Naturally, most of the region's storied companies were built by strong-willed
founders, and it is not their habit to share credit with investors. When it
comes to Cisco, however, the contribution of venture capital is indisput-
able. Don Valentine took control of the company, ejecting the founders and
installing his own team; there is no doubt that the hands-on, West Coast
style of venture investing explains the success that followed. In contrast,
Cisco's East Coast rival, Wellfleet, lost its lead in networking for charac-
teristically East Coast reasons. Wellfleet had an excellent engineering
team, and its founder, Paul Severino, was a respected inventor. But precisely because Severino was an established figure, his venture backers deferred to him too much; they let him take his time perfecting his products,
so they were slow to get to market.[93] "Wellfleet debated the finer points of
the technology for days," a rueful Boston tech executive recalled. "Cisco
was out there making sales happen."[94]

The upshot for the Valley was not merely that it gained a successful
company. It acquired a whole industry. Through the 1990s and into the 2000s,
Cisco dominated the networking business, and Don Valentine, who had set
out a decade earlier to develop a flotilla of companies to service the PC,
now found that the scrappy startup he had backed became its own aircraft
carrier. A fleet of switching and routing companies sailed around Cisco, and

Valentine stood on the deck of the flagship, remaining its chairman long after an IPO had multiplied Sequoia's investment nearly forty times over. From this privileged vantage point, Valentine could see which sorts of innovative networking technology Cisco might want to acquire. As a result, Sequoia backed a series of startups that it sold profitably to the mother ship. The partnership's reputation swelled, and Silicon Valley flourished.

Chapter Six

PLANNERS AND IMPROVISERS

One day in 1987, an entrepreneur named Mitch Kapor was sitting in his private jet, flying from Boston to San Francisco. "Bear with me," he told his guest, a software engineer called Jerry Kaplan. He took out a portable Compaq 286 from his luggage. It was about the size of a small sewing machine.

"I've got to update my notes," Kapor said, peering at handfuls of yellow stickies and ripped notebook pages that he fished out of his pockets. He had rich black hair and a laid-back, beachy style. Before founding a software company, he had worked as a disc jockey, a psychiatric counselor, a stand-up comedian, and a teacher of transcendental meditation. An *Esquire* magazine profile had described him as "a cross between Rocky Balboa and a yoga master."[1]

"I wish there was some way for me to get all this stuff directly into the computer and skip the paper," Kapor continued.

Perhaps there could be such a way, Kaplan suggested. What if there were a computer so light and so small that you could take it with you everywhere?

Kaplan and Kapor debated the feasibility of this vision. A computer's disk drives weighed two pounds each; the battery added another few

pounds; the glass wrapping the display was heavy. Progress in each category could de-bulk tomorrow's computer, but the trickiest challenge was
the keyboard. Given the need for sixty-plus buttons, the keyboard could
shrink only so much. The friends ate lunch, and Kaplan closed his eyes and
napped for a bit.

When Kaplan awoke, Kapor was still typing on his Compaq. Then, unexpectedly, a post-snooze inspiration popped into Kaplan's head. "Suppose
that instead of typing in text, you write with some sort of stylus directly on
the screen," he ventured.

"A device like that would be more like a notebook or pad of paper,"
Kapor reflected.

Kaplan absorbed this simile for a moment. Could this be the next generation of computers? he wondered.

Suddenly he experienced what he later described as "the modern scientific version of religious epiphany." Kapor was evidently experiencing
the same feeling: his eyes became glazed and teary. "We were momentarily
unable to speak," Kaplan later wrote in his vivid memoir of Valley entrepreneurship.[2]

As soon as Kapor regained his composure, he resolved to turn this
pen-computer epiphany into a business. His own experience led him to
believe it could be done. When he had founded his software company in
1981, he had called it Lotus Development: the name invoked Buddhist enlightenment. Two years later, when Lotus went public, its main association was with capitalist profits. For a while, its spreadsheet program made
it the biggest software company in the world, and Kapor generated a quick
return of about 35x for his venture backers, including Kleiner Perkins.
Perhaps a pen-computer company could repeat the same trick, Kapor
thought.

After a couple of weeks noodling with the concept, Kapor put a proposal to Kaplan. "Why don't you try to do this project?" he demanded.

"I've never managed squat," Kaplan objected.

"You think I had any more experience when I founded Lotus?" Kapor
asked, chuckling. "C'mon, I'll introduce you to some VCs."

The story that ensued captured one half of the Valley's venture vibe at the end of the 1980s. The surge in venture dollars had drawn new partnerships into the game, and these tended to be self-conscious and deliberate. To fight their way into what was by now an established industry, the newcomers had to ask questions. How did the best incumbents operate? How could their methods be improved upon? The most thoughtful new entrant was Accel Capital, the first venture partnership to position itself as a specialist in particular technologies. By accumulating deep expertise in software and telecoms, Accel aimed to have the inside track on which entrepreneurs to back and how to guide them to a healthy exit. At the same time, Accel embraced an approach that it came to call "the prepared mind." Rather than looking anywhere and everywhere for the next big thing, the partnership carried out management-consultant-style studies on the technologies and business models that seemed to hold promise. But alongside this deliberative culture, there were still plenty of venture investors who led with their gut, believing that breakthrough ideas were by definition so shocking that no amount of mental preparation could anticipate them. This tension between the planners and the improvisers tested the industry's identity, as we shall see presently.

To raise money for their pen-computer plan, Kapor took Kaplan to meet John Doerr, the high priest of the Valley's improvisers. With the retirement of Eugene Kleiner and Tom Perkins, Doerr and his friend Vinod Khosla set the pace at KP, and they were out to back truly revolutionary startups that could spawn entirely new industries. Magnetic and messianic, Doerr in particular became the go-to investor for fearless founders, who loved him for championing their visions even more passionately than they did. He had "the emotional commitment of a priest and the energy of a racehorse," one entrepreneur marveled. "The number of different things about which John Doerr has said, this is the greatest thing ever, is a big number," a rival investor noted, with a mixture of respect and cynicism.[3] Rake thin, ascetic, a fizz of nervous energy, Doerr slept little, drove dangerously, and strove earnestly to be in three places at once. One Friday afternoon, Tom Perkins invited him to spend the next day on his yacht. "I'm not sure," Doerr replied. "I may have to be in Tokyo."[4]

Doerr seemed too busy to notice material possessions—an affect that appealed to Mitch Kapor's yogic sensibilities. He went about in a utilitarian van, dressed in rumpled khakis and plain button-down shirts, and was said to own a total of two neckties. Still, with the proceeds of his early windfalls, which included Compaq and Sun Microsystems as well as Lotus, Doerr bought a fine house in the Pacific Heights neighborhood of San Francisco and then bought a second house because it obstructed the view from the first one. The offending building was shortened, shorn of an obtrusive balcony, and turned into a guesthouse. Whenever he visited San Francisco from Boston, Kapor would stay there.

Given Kapor's relationship with Doerr, it was hardly a surprise that KP was his first port of call when he set out to raise money. Even so, the way the money raising happened was extraordinary. As Kaplan tells it, he and Kapor rolled up at the Kleiner office expecting an exploratory conversation; they had not prepared a business plan or financial projections. To their surprise, they were ushered into the conference room and told to pitch in front of all the partners. Figuring he had nothing to lose, Kaplan winged it with gusto, compensating for his lack of detailed preparation by playing up the grand vision. The computer of the future, he proclaimed, would be as light and sleek as a notebook. To drive home his point, he flicked his leather-bound folder into the air. It landed with a smack in front of the Kleiner Perkins partners.

A little while later, Doerr called Kaplan at his hotel. Kaplan was surprised again; he had no idea how Doerr knew how to reach him. Brushing aside Kaplan's confusion, Doerr announced that Kleiner intended to invest in his company.

Kaplan fumbled. He didn't actually have a company—not yet, at any rate. Shouldn't Kleiner at least see some financials?

"We're backing you and the idea," Doerr said firmly. Details did not matter for an inventor of Kaplan's vision.

Both men were traveling over the next days, but they juggled their schedules to arrange a layover at St. Louis airport. Doerr met Kaplan at the gate, and they hammered out a deal: together, Kleiner Perkins, Mitch Kapor, and Vinod Khosla would purchase a third of Kaplan's project for $1.5 million. Doerr would become chairman. Kapor and Khosla would serve as board directors.

What would he call his company? Doerr asked him.

"GO, all caps. As in GO forth, GO for it, GO for the gold."

"As in GO public," Doerr added.

A year after its launch, GO was going nowhere. It was one thing to sell investors a vision. It was quite another to deliver on it. Kaplan and his two co-founders had yet to build a functioning computerized notebook. They were running short of capital.

At a board meeting in 1988, Doerr reassured Kaplan that there was nothing to worry about. Sure, he needed extra cash, but raising it would not be difficult. "Everyone will want in on the deal," Doerr declared confidently.

"At the right price," cautioned Vinod Khosla. GO's first $1.5 million had been raised at forty cents per share, and the same team of investors had later kicked in an additional $500,000 at sixty cents. Kaplan worried that this was a steep price for an outfit that had yet to deliver a product, and Khosla seemed to agree. The second financing had pegged GO's value at $6 million.

Before anyone could endorse Khosla's caution, Mitch Kapor weighed in. He wanted to double GO's value. "Twelve million!" he announced ebulliently.

Kaplan looked over at Doerr, expecting him to tamp down Kapor's exuberance. The board chairman was cradling his head in his hands. "I assumed he was composing a polite way to tell Mitchell he was full of shit," Kaplan wrote later.

Doerr sat still for several seconds. He bounced his left leg on the floor and then abruptly shot upright. "I think we should ask for sixteen million," he announced.

Doerr and Kapor now engaged in a staring contest. In Doerr's recollection, he and Kapor were merely trying to do their jobs: to define a full and fair price for a difficult financing.[5] But Kaplan couldn't help feeling he was watching two poker players after one has raised the other's stake. One of Kaplan's co-founders slid lower in his chair to avoid getting between the two investors.

Khosla spoke up again. "Look, there's no harm in asking," he said, "but this is a dangerous game. Pricing of these intermediate rounds is highly unstable. If they think you're close to running out of cash, they'll wait you out. If the price starts to crack, everyone gets cold feet."

"Hey, there's no right price," Doerr retorted. "It's willing buyer meets willing seller!"

After the meeting, Kaplan huddled with his co-founders. "I guess that went well," he said nervously.

"Too well," one responded. "These sky-high valuations give me a nosebleed."

"Hey, these guys are the experts," the other retorted. "Who are we to judge? They do financings all the time."

A couple of days later, Kaplan called Doerr for advice on whom to pitch to. Doerr began shooting off names at a dizzying speed: regular venture capitalists, corporations with VC subsidiaries, some Kleiner Perkins limited partners, a few investment banks, and Steve Jobs for good measure.

Kaplan's hand was hurting from the effort of taking notes. "Enough!" he shouted. Calling in the KP partnership could be like calling the fire department, he wrote later. "They tend to show up in force and attack a project with benevolent but single-minded fury. The fire is sure to be out when they leave, but the furniture may be waterlogged and the windows broken."

Kaplan set about pitching his startup to Doerr's list of investors. One after another, they were interested but noncommittal. Frustrated, Kaplan returned to Doerr. "Look, we have about four weeks of cash and then it's the Doggy Diner," he told him. "No one buys the price."

"All right," Doerr answered. "Let's drop it to twelve and close it up. Put out the word." He was now back at the $12 million valuation that Kapor had proposed originally.

Kaplan called up twenty-one would-be investors, asking them to get back to him by Monday at 5:00 p.m. Not a single offer materialized.

The following morning Kaplan dialed Doerr again. The call went straight to voice mail. Gritting his teeth, he left a message. "John, this is your Tuesday wakeup call," he said. "No one wants to invest. We're screwed. What should we do?"

At noon, Doerr returned the call. He had spoken with a guy at Bessemer in New York who thought his partners might be interested. Kaplan should get on a plane and pitch them.

Kaplan did as he was told and was met with more humiliation. The Bessemer team seemed totally uninterested. "We have to run to the airport," they said briskly, ignoring the fact that Kaplan had run to an airport and crossed the continent to see them.

Kaplan figured that the end had come. He phoned Doerr again to tell him.

But Doerr had not given up. "You have to practice this craft with conviction," he would later say, and nobody else in Silicon Valley could sell company visions the way he could.[6] Ignoring questions about severance pay for GO employees, he asked Kaplan and his co-founders to be waiting in a Kleiner conference room at 5:00 p.m. the following Monday.

At the appointed hour, Doerr marched into the conference room without so much as a hello and set the office phone in the middle of the table.

"What did Scott Sperling say?" he asked, referring to a venture partner at the Harvard endowment.

"That was a long time ago," Kaplan answered. "I think he said he thought the price was too high."

"What price does he think *isn't* too high?"

"I'm not sure."

"Let's call him and ask." Doerr rang the number, ignoring Kaplan's protest that it was after eight o'clock in Boston. Sperling's wife picked up. In the background, they could hear baby noises.

"Hi, can I talk to Scott, please?"

"Just a minute," Sperling's wife responded. "He's got the baby on his lap."

Sperling picked up and Doerr jumped straight in. "Scott, we need to close up this financing and we don't have a lead. Where do you stand?"

"There's a big market if you can make it work," Sperling answered. "But we feel the deal is overpriced at twelve million."

"At what price would you be willing to lead?"

"Eight million."

"And how much would you be willing to commit at that level?"

"Up to two million."

Doerr pressed the mute button. "What is that per share?" he asked Kaplan, who was already pecking at his calculator.

"Looks like about seventy-five cents," Kaplan said. This was way below the numbers that Kapor and Doerr had bandied about. But Sperling was proposing a respectable markup over the $6 million valuation at the time of the second financing.

Doerr looked at the GO team. "Are you guys willing to do it?"

"OK with us," said Kaplan.

Doerr unmuted the phone. "Scott, it's a deal," he said. "Jerry'll call you in the morning to get the paperwork started."

Doerr pressed the disconnect button and turned to the GO team. "Congratulations, gentlemen, you have your lead," he said. Then he marched out of the room, a wiry fireman with angular glasses, rushing to his next emergency.

After Doerr's intervention, Kaplan was able to raise $6 million in a matter of days; it was more than the $5 million he had targeted. He soldiered on until 1993, raising money periodically with Doerr's help but failing to realize his vision of building a pen-operated computer. In the end he sold GO at a fire-sale price to a division of AT&T. His backers were left with almost nothing.

As a parable of venture capital, the GO story exposed Doerr's swashbuckling overreach. He had invested on the basis of an improvised presentation unsupported by a business plan, doing so because he believed that he could will huge technological leaps into being. By embracing maximum ambition, he had probably harmed Kaplan's prospects, steering him away from the sort of incremental advance that could have been achievable. "They should have got the thing to work in a small area like UPS delivery guys," Mitch Kapor reflected later. "GO showed me the downside for entrepreneurs of Kleiner's approach. If it couldn't be a home run, Kleiner did not care if the company struck out. It was like, go big or go home. . . . There is an arrogance to the KP approach. All that ego about changing the world."[7]

Kapor was correct that Doerr's style invited trouble. Around the same time as the GO fiasco, Doerr and Khosla launched a next-generation laptop company called Dynabook Technologies that burned through $37 million of investors' capital before closing.[8] Doerr also trumpeted a string of technological prospects that turned out to be busts: human gene screening, anti-aging drugs, designer chemicals.[9] He seemed to have forgotten the old Tom Perkins dictum: when you invest in a company facing a technical challenge, the first thing you do is take the white-hot risks off the table.

If Kleiner Perkins embodied the swashbuckling spirit of the Valley, the upstart challenger Accel was deliberately different. The two founders, Arthur Patterson and Jim Swartz, were already veterans of the business, and they were planners rather than improvisers, strategists rather than evangelists. Patterson, in particular, was self-consciously cerebral. The scion of a Wall Street rainmaker, the product of both Harvard College and Harvard Business School, he was less narrowly focused on the next technology than some of his engineer rivals, and more broadly interested in financial markets, business models, and even government policy. He read widely, theorized fluently, and wrote a series of internal papers codifying the Accel approach. It was he who had come up with the Accel watchword, "prepared mind," having borrowed it from the nineteenth-century father of microbiology, Louis Pasteur. "Chance favors only the prepared mind," Pasteur had observed sagely.

Patterson was tall, slender, and possessed of a certain patrician eccentricity. He once surprised a new Accel recruit by serving him a dinner consisting of nothing but twelve ears of grilled corn and exceptional Bordeaux from his wine cellar.[10] Jim Swartz, for his part, contrasted just as much with Kleiner Perkins, but for different reasons. Raised in small-town Pennsylvania, the son of a man who worked as a bus driver and farmhand, he believed in character and discipline.[11] The Kleiner Perkins improvisers might traffic in messianic visions, but Swartz backed solid founders, enforced financial controls, and radiated sobriety, integrity, and realism. Once, when an entrepreneur welcomed him onto his startup's board by printing him some business cards, Swartz returned the cards wrapped in a furious letter denouncing the flagrant waste of money. The founder opened the note, gasped at Swartz's aggression, and then decided he was right. He kept the letter on his desk, a daily reminder to discipline spending.[12]

Accel was founded in 1983, at the height of the surge of capital into venture funds following the cuts in the capital-gains tax and the lifting of the prudent-man rule. With unprecedented sums of money to deploy, the established partnerships hogged the good deals for themselves; gone were the days of the Intel or Apple financings, when lead investors controlled risk by bringing in co-investors. A new venture contender therefore had to earn the opportunity to invest, and one obvious way of appealing to entrepreneurs was to specialize in their technologies. Moreover, the expansion of the venture business meant that specialization was more feasible than before: you could narrow your focus and still have enough deals to choose from. Swartz, who was known for his spectacular bet on the pioneering network company Ungermann-Bass, chose telecoms as his specialty and based himself in Princeton, a short drive from the engineers at Bell Labs in Murray Hill, New Jersey. Patterson picked software as his specialty and based himself in Silicon Valley. Inevitably, the West Coast won out. As time went by, Swartz found himself visiting Northern California increasingly often, and eventually he moved there.[13]

To underscore its strategy of specialization, Accel's second fund, raised in 1985, was aimed exclusively at telecoms. The offering document proclaimed that "in an information-based economy virtually every electronic system will communicate with other systems"; the market for modems, networking, video sharing, and other telecom applications would be enormous.[14] To prove their commitment to this thesis, Patterson and Swartz recruited additional telecom experts and planted their flag on the telecom map by staging elaborate conferences at Stanford. There was an annual black-tie dinner for telecom grandees, and the next day three hundred people would show up to hear speeches from industry seers.[15] During breaks in the program, entrepreneurs brought out slide decks and pitched investors. "Our strategy," Jim Swartz said later, "was to announce a fund, get quoted on telecoms in the press, organize a conference, and generally make a noise."[16] Incumbent VC rivals were impressed. Kleiner Perkins invested $2 million in Accel Telecom.

Accel liked to say that its strategy of specialization helped it to avoid faddish distractions. Borrowing an analogy from the oil industry, its partners would not be wildcatters, drilling wells almost at random. They would be methodical explorers who studied the geological properties of the territory. Pen computing was a case in point. By the early 1990s, dozens of startups were imitating GO, and there were conferences to celebrate this gold rush. Swartz dutifully attended one of these jamborees to see what the hype was about. But when subjected to Accel-style scrutiny, neither the pen technology nor the associated business plans seemed auspicious, and Swartz refused to waste capital on them. Perhaps because of this indifference to fashion, relatively few Accel investments turned out to be busts. Around the partnership's tenth birthday, a tally showed that of the forty-five Accel investments that had experienced an exit, only seven had lost money.[17]

Specialization also helped Accel when it went on the offensive. Because the partners were experts in the sectors they invested in, they could quickly grasp the essence of an entrepreneur's pitch and come to a rapid decision. If they resolved to make the investment, the next challenge was to persuade the entrepreneur to choose Accel over rivals, and specialization helped with this step also. Starting a company is an isolating experience—founders invest life and soul into niche projects that, at least at the outset, strike most people as quixotic—so entrepreneurs can't help warming to investors who appreciate their plans: who "get it." Accel partners aimed to comprehend entrepreneurs so thoroughly that they could complete their sentences and predict the next slide in their pitches. They spoke internally of the "90 percent rule." An Accel investor should know 90 percent of what founders are going to say before they open their mouths to say it.[18]

Accel's specialist approach made it particularly adept at identifying what venture capitalists call "adjacent possibilities." By embedding them-selves in their respective sectors, sitting on boards of portfolio companies, and blending their direct observations with management-consultant-style analyses, Accel partners could anticipate the next logical advance in a tech-nology. "Every deal should lead to the next deal," was another Accel say-ing.[19] Swartz in particular liked to invest in successive iterations in a single product class. He backed a videoconferencing startup in 1986, another in 1988, and a third in 1992; on two of these three bets, he made fourteen times his money.[20] Admittedly, this incrementalism involved a potential cost. Accel shrank from KP-style paradigm breakers that were not adjacent but rather two leaps ahead: this might mean missing some gargantuan winners. Likewise, having embedded themselves among the intellectual leaders in their sectors, Accel partners tended to pass over uncredentialed challeng-ers of the sort favored by Don Valentine. Thus Accel missed the mother of all 1980s telecom deals—Cisco—despite being aware of the company and having a dedicated telecom fund. Still, Accel was making a deliberate choice. It would push the boundaries of engineering enough to create value but not so much as to be guilty of overreach. Its motto was "if you go for sin-gles, the home runs will take care of themselves." Some of those intended singles would sail off your bat more powerfully than you expected.

Accel's performance in its first few funds left no doubt that it was onto something.[21] The specialist telecom fund multiplied its capital 3.7 times, generating an annualized return that was more than twice as high as the median venture fund of its vintage.[22] Taking the first five funds together, Accel generated an even better performance: the average multiple was eight times capital. And yet the striking thing about Accel was that despite the partners' firm intention not to chase hubristic grand slams, it was grand slams that dominated performance. Accel Telecom more than conformed to the so-called 80/20 rule: a whopping 95 percent of its profits came from the top 20 percent of its investments.[23] Other early Accel funds exhibited similar power-law effects. In the firm's first five funds, the top 20 percent of the investments accounted for never less than 85 percent of the profits, and the average was 92 percent.

In short, the power law was inexorable. Even a methodical, anti-Kleiner, prepared-mind partnership could not escape it.

◆

The dominance of the power law was illustrated by UUNET, one of several unforeseen grand slams in Accel's first dozen years in business. Now a forgotten company, subsumed into Verizon's vast telecom empire, UUNET, pronounced "you-you-net," sounds like a throwback to a different age: this strange non-acronym, vaguely inspired by software protocols loved only by engineers, is a world away from the brand-conscious zippiness of later startup names—think Zoom or Snap or Stripe or Spotify.[24] Yet UUNET is worth recalling because, in addition to illustrating the power law, it illuminates two features of venture investing. First, it showcases the distinct roles of government-backed science and VC-backed entrepreneurs in driving technological progress. Second, it demonstrates a paradox at the heart of venture capital's impact on society. VCs *as individuals* can stumble sideways into lucky fortunes: chance and serendipity and the mere fact of being in the venture game can matter more than diligence or foresight. At the same time, venture capital *as a system* is a formidable engine of progress—more so than is frequently acknowledged.

UUNET began life in 1987 as an obscure Northern Virginia nonprofit. Its mission was to address the central limitation of the internet as it existed then: only around 100,000 computers were connected to it.[25] Having started out as a military communications system funded by the Pentagon, the internet had become an email, bulletin board, and file-sharing platform for scientists at government labs, including government-backed ones at universities. Private companies and individuals were barred from the network, and commercial activity was prohibited. But by the late 1980s, a growing community of nongovernment scientists wanted a similar utility. Armed with a $250,000 loan guarantee from a loose association of programmers, UUNET set out to be their internet service provider.[26]

UUNET's founder was Rick Adams, a genial thirtysomething engineer who worked for the government's Center for Seismic Studies. He had floppy brown hair and a full beard and wore white jeans and polo shirts. Still holding down his government job, Adams worked part time on the rudiments of a parallel internet for private-sector scientists who were excluded from the main one.[27] Typically, major private corporations had linked up their employees via local area networks, but sending messages from one corporation to another was horribly expensive. Adams combined Cisco routers and networking software to build cheaper connections. He charged for the service, but only enough to recover costs. It was a long way away from the Sand Hill Road mentality.

At first, almost nobody noticed. The internet had always been a government project.[28] Most people assumed that if anyone was going to bring online connections to the masses, it would be the government, again, and in July 1990 a young Tennessee senator named Al Gore laid out a public-sector vision for an "information superhighway." Rather than operating on existing telephone lines, as the internet did, Gore's superhighway envisioned brand-new fiber-optic pipes that would turn household TVs into interactive terminals. The jump to fiber optics would allow information and entertainment to reach American households in dazzling Technicolor, replacing the internet's drab bulletin boards.

Initially, the flashy superhighway plan generated broad excitement. In 1991, Gore championed a $1.75 billion government spending package to support his vision. In 1992 his profile rose when Bill Clinton picked him as his vice presidential running mate. By 1993, a posse of muscular tech companies were positioning themselves to win government backing to build the superhighway's infrastructure.[29] But as all this was happening, something else was stirring under the radar. Scientists at corporate labs began flocking to UUNET, which, finding itself awash with revenue, gave up its non-profit status. Then, acknowledging the progress of UUNET and one or two smaller rivals, the National Science Foundation announced a policy reversal. Rather than trying to keep private users off the government network, it would invite private internet service providers into the tent; in fact, it would let them take over its management.[30] The government had invented the internet, to be sure. But as far as the National Science Foundation was concerned, the

job of turning the internet into a mass medium that democratized information and changed lives was best entrusted to the private sector.

At this stage in the story, none other than Mitch Kapor made an en-
trance. While his pen-computing venture struggled to raise capital, Kapor
experienced another one of his epiphanies. Gore's government-led fiber-
optic superhighway was still dominating the headlines. But the way Kapor
saw things, it would be prohibitively disruptive and expensive. Rather than
ripping up the ground to lay fiber-optic cable, it would be cheaper by far to
build out the copper-wire-based internet. Responding to insatiable customer demand, not political edict, UUNET was already grafting routers and
servers onto the existing phone networks, turning voice lines into data
lines, and now the NSF's privatization announcement opened the way to
even faster progress.[31] As a way of getting millions of users online, this
market-led movement would eclipse Gore's grandiose project.

"Okay, so this is going to happen," Kapor told himself. "I want to have
some skin in the game."[32]

In August 1992, Kapor visited Washington and arranged to meet Rick
Adams. "There's a poker game going on and I don't have any chips in the
game. I need to invest," he explained frankly. If Adams let him buy a modest stake in UUNET, he would act as a bridge to venture investors who could
pump in real capital.

Adams was of two minds. On the one hand, he was generally suspicious
of financiers, and he had no wish to answer to venture-capital overseers.
He cared about the mission of promoting open communication online. He
did not want to compromise his purity of purpose. On the other hand, however, Adams needed capital; in fact, he needed a ton of it. The more UUNET
expanded, the quicker demand grew, because growing usage made the network more attractive to the next wave of potential users. "The project was
swallowing cash by the trash-can full," recalled UUNET's chief scientist,
Mike O'Dell. "We had to put hardware everywhere. There were these big-
boy pants that we had to grow into real quick."[33]

Kapor scraped away at Adams's misgivings about venture capital, using
his own history as a chisel.[34] He too had gone through a phase of disliking

VCs. As a young product manager, he had worked for a company that was backed by Arthur Rock. Sitting in on a board meeting one day, Kapor had watched as Rock had "basically issued an execution order on somebody or some project as casually as I'd flick a flea off my arm. . . . It was like a 'Godfather' kind of moment."[35] As a result, when it came time to raise capital for Lotus Development, Kapor had been prickly, warning prospective investors that he would put humanity before profits.[36] But then he had relaxed. So long as a startup flourishes, he realized, venture investors will defer to the founder. "You don't have to get steamrolled by the VCs," Kapor urged Adams.[37]

Adams wrestled with his dual instincts. If Kapor had been a standard investor, he would have turned him away. But, in his idealism and political outlook, Kapor felt like a kindred spirit.[38] After some further thought, Adams accepted Kapor's offer.[39]

Having secured his skin in the game, Kapor proceeded quickly. UUNET had to grow into those big-boy pants before competitors muscled in on its market. Whatever Adams's misgivings about investors, this accidental East Coast startup needed to raise serious West Coast venture capital.

Kapor's first stop was John Doerr at Kleiner Perkins. Never mind the excitement about the information superhighway, Kapor urged. Over the next handful of years, the internet would leave Gore's vision in the dust.

Unlike in the case of GO, Doerr was unpersuaded. UUNET was not the sort of company that Kleiner Perkins liked to back. It owned no intellectual property, so was defenseless against larger competitors.[40] It required bucket loads of capital, so Kleiner would be unlikely to generate a home-run multiple.[41] Doerr refused even to meet Adams.

Spurned by Kleiner Perkins, Kapor took the project to Accel. The choice of whom to go to was almost random and had nothing to do with Accel's status as a specialist in telecoms. Serendipitously, Kapor had recently invested in an Accel fund. He called up his contact there and made his pitch. The internet was about to go big, he urged. There was a chance "to make this into a thing where everyone talks to each other."[42]

If Kapor's call was a stroke of luck, Accel's deliberative, prepared-mind process was grinding along in the background. At the firm's Princeton office, a telecom researcher named Don Gooding had begun to track the internet. Meanwhile, on the West Coast, another Accel telecom specialist named Jim McLean understood that things were stirring. Visiting the office that ran the NSF internet infrastructure in Mountain View, McLean had been amazed to see racks of expensive servers and routers.

How could a government outfit afford this fancy equipment? McLean asked innocently.

"We get it all for free," the engineers told him. The router manufacturers were bartering their hardware for illegal access to the supposedly government-only NSF network. They were so hungry for connections that they would break the law to get them.[43]

By now Accel had gotten wind of the internet's potential through three different channels. Kapor had called; Gooding was following the scent; McLean had caught a glimpse of the voracious demand for online connections. The question was whether Accel would convert these hints into an investment.

At first, nothing happened. Juggling dozens of investment leads, the Accel team lost interest. At the end of January 1993, Kapor tried to get UUNET back on Accel's radar by visiting its San Francisco office. To his disappointment, none of the investing partners showed up for the meeting. Accel "didn't give off the body language that they were close to a positive decision," Kapor confessed to Adams.[44]

Below the top partner level, however, Jim McLean remained enthusiastic. When he heard about the NSF plan to privatize the internet, he hunted for outfits that might seize the opportunity. His search led him to UUNET, which looked to be the likely winner from the coming gold rush.

When the opportunity came to pitch Accel's investment team, McLean laid out half a dozen business cards collected from his recent meetings.

"What's new about these cards?" McLean demanded.

He was met with blank stares. Nobody said anything.

"They all have email addresses," McLean pointed out. What better evidence could the partners want? The internet was spreading fast. Now was the time to invest in it.

The partners pushed back. People did not need UUNET in order to use email. They could sign up for CompuServe or Prodigy, services that between them allowed three million subscribers to email other account holders.[45] Luck and a good telecom team had put the opportunity of UUNET clearly in view. But Accel was still not seeing it.

As often happens in the venture world, it took a nudge from a competitor to change Accel's attitude. In February 1993, a telecom company called Metropolitan Fiber Systems made a play for UUNET.

Adams turned to Kapor for advice. Maybe a corporate investor such as Metropolitan Fiber would be better than a venture capitalist?

Kapor fastened on a different point. Corporate capitalist, venture capitalist—who cared? The main thing was to have two investors competing for your attention. Kapor made sure the Accel partners knew about the Metropolitan Fiber bid. That would get them "heated up," he assured Adams.[46]

Adams met with a Metropolitan Fiber representative at the Ritz-Carlton hotel near the UUNET office. The guy wrote some numbers on a Ritz-Carlton notepad. Then he detached the page theatrically, turned it facedown, and slid it over to Adams. Metropolitan Fiber was ready to invest $500,000 at an $8 million valuation.[47]

Adams's next stop was Accel's West Coast office. At last, he had been awarded a forty-five-minute slot in which to pitch to the investment committee. After he presented, the Accel partners kept him talking for a further three hours. Just as Kapor had predicted, the temperature shift was miraculous.

But Accel had not named a price yet. To match the $8 million valuation that Metropolitan Fiber had proposed, it would have to believe that UUNET might hit it big; otherwise the risk would not be worth it. "They are currently waffling around deciding the size of the market," Adams wrote to Kapor. "They are convinced that UUNET can become a $30 million company but aren't (yet . . .) sure it has the potential for $100 million."[48]

On top of doubts about the size of the market, there was a question about Adams's managerial ability. If UUNET was going to grow, it would need experienced operational leaders, and the VCs would have to identify them, woo them, and support their efforts once they came on board. There was a risk that Adams might resist. His ego would have to be managed, and UUNET's location in Northern Virginia would make this babysitting difficult.

As Accel's senior software investor, Arthur Patterson resolved that he would do the deal if he could find the right partner to share it with. In an inspired act of networking, he placed a call to New Enterprise Associates, one of the venture shops that had backed 3Com. NEA had an office in Baltimore, not far from the UUNET premises in Virginia. What's more, an executive named Peter Barris had just joined NEA's Baltimore team. A few years earlier, Patterson had flown to Texas specifically to meet Barris; at the time, Barris was an up-and-coming software executive, the number two at a Dallas firm, and Patterson had made it his business to know him.[49] Now that trip to Texas was about to pay off. Patterson urged Barris to take a look at UUNET.

A few days after Patterson's call, Barris visited Adams. The two made an unlikely pair. Adams was bearlike and casual. Barris was trim and preppy. But just as Patterson had expected, Barris's experience made him the perfect partner for Adams. He had spent part of his career at the information services division of General Electric, which sold digital business tools to corporate customers.

Barris told Adams about the software that GE provided: financial ledgers, customer-tracking programs, human-resource systems, and so on. Would it be possible, Barris wondered, to deliver those same services over the internet?

Adams assured him that it would. In fact, the internet could deliver those programs far more cheaply than GE, which relied on expensive mainframe computers accessed via costly dial-up connections.

Barris realized he was onto something. Because of his GE background, he knew what sorts of online services big customers would pay for. Because of his internet background, Adams knew how to provide them efficiently. By combining their knowledge, the pair of them could mint money.[50]

In July 1993, Accel and NEA joined forces in presenting Adams with a four-page term sheet. It had been more than six months since the first contact between Kapor and Accel; after almost missing out, the firm was meandering toward the right decision. But the process was not done. The Accel-NEA term sheet proposed to value UUNET at just $6 million—$2 million less than Metropolitan Fiber. Adams was indignant.[51]

Again, competitive pressure shifted the investors in Adams's direction. This time the nudge came from a Silicon Valley partnership named Menlo Ventures, which had heard of UUNET through another serendipitous connection. UUNET's chief scientist, Mike O'Dell, had previously worked for a Menlo-backed company.

A new partner at Menlo, an engineer named John Jarve, used the O'Dell connection to get a meeting with Adams. The two got along: they had engineering in common.

Adams told Jarve he planned to reject the $6 million valuation and challenged him to go higher.

"Let me write a term sheet because you guys are worth a lot more," Jarve responded eagerly.[52]

Jarve duly produced a term sheet valuing UUNET at just over $8 million, beating out both the Accel-NEA and the Metropolitan Fiber offers. At NEA, Barris was by now keen to work with Adams, so he quickly agreed to match Jarve's higher valuation. Delighted, Adams told Barris that he would do the deal exclusively with NEA; after all, Barris was the investor best positioned to help UUNET. But, in an example of VCs acting to protect their reputations and networks, Barris declined the opportunity to squeeze his rivals out. He had been brought to the dance by Arthur Patterson, and he refused to double-cross him. Eventually Accel agreed to the new price. In October 1993, the three partnerships stumped up a total of $1.5 million.[53]

◆

The venture-capital process can feel like a relay. Kapor, the first investor to back UUNET, had passed the baton to Arthur Patterson at Accel. In turn, Patterson had passed it to Peter Barris, who, because of his East Coast base, would be the most hands-on of the three venture backers. Next, Barris set out to recruit effective managers for UUNET so that he too could fade into the background.

Barris called Joe Squarzini, a veteran from GE Information Services.

At fifty-two, Squarzini didn't look to be a natural fit with the youthful engineers at UUNET.

When Squarzini showed up for his job interview, Adams told him straight that he didn't want a guy who was going to import the GE culture.

Squarzini protested. He might look like a cookie-cutter GE stiff, but he was also a ham radio operator.

Adams wasn't convinced.

"I can out-solder any person in this company," Squarzini persisted. The candidate was ready to connect electrical wires with a hot iron to establish his credentials.

Now Adams was impressed. "I couldn't solder worth a damn anymore," he said later. "So we hired him."[54]

Assigned the rank of vice president, Squarzini set to work imposing some structure on UUNET's freewheeling operation. Pretty soon, the urgency of this mission became apparent. In the course of straightening out UUNET's accounting, a bookkeeper came across a box of unpaid invoices. UUNET had lost track of debts for routers and other gear that amounted to a horrifying $750,000. The sum canceled out half of the capital that UUNET had just raised. Weeks after its $1.5 million Series A, the company was almost out of money.

Somebody would have to break this news to UUNET's investors. They had committed their capital on the basis of financial statements that now turned out to be false; they were not going to be happy. After all, if UUNET had been a public company, the dramatic restatement of its cash balance would have punished its share price. Likewise, if UUNET had borrowed from a bank, it could not have expected a fresh loan after this sort of embarrassment. UUNET's prospects now hinged on its venture backers responding in a different way. They would have to take the hit calmly and cough up fresh funds. Otherwise UUNET would run out of working capital.

Years later, Barris reflected that if Adams had broken the news of the $750,000 screwup, UUNET's future might have been precarious. The VCs already doubted Adams's managerial capacity; the misplacing of three-quarters of a million dollars might have driven them to cut their losses. But because of the hands-on way that venture capitalists operate, there was no need for Adams to deliver the message. Barris had already installed Squarzini at the firm, and Squarzini was a grown-up with the confidence of the investors. By volunteering to explain the blunder to the board, old Joe could save the young company.

On the day of the board meeting, Squarzini wore a GE suit and GE shirt and what he called his "armor-plated wing tips." Never mind what Adams had told him at his interview; now was the time to come across as stiff and starched as possible. When Squarzini leveled with the investors, he looked them in the eyes and swore that this bungling would cease. New financial controls were already in place. Amateur hour was over.

For Barris and Jarve especially, it was a dreadful moment. They were both new to the venture game; they had won the approval of their senior partners for the UUNET bet, but it had not been easy. Jarve remembered only too clearly how the founder of Menlo Ventures, DuBose Montgomery, had put his arm around his shoulder and said, "John, this better work out." Now it was not working out, and Jarve worried for his job security. Barris, for his part, recalls listening to Squarzini and experiencing "a very empty feeling." His NEA partners had not been jazzed about UUNET's prospects; now there would be an I-told-you-so moment. On the drive back to his office in Baltimore, a loop kept playing in Barris's head. How would he break the news to his partners? What words were there to say it?

The truth was that word choice didn't matter. What mattered was that venture capitalists are not like banks or stock market investors. They spend their lives dealing with startups that crash from one crisis to the next; they know better than to cut and run at the first sign of adversity. Years later, Patterson did not even recall UUNET's setback; as the most seasoned investor of the three, he had experienced dozens of similar accidents. And even as Barris worried about his partners' reactions, he remembers thinking pragmatically about the next step. "The money's been wired. We're here. What do we do about it?"[55]

Rather than pulling the plug on UUNET, the VCs extracted compensation. They promised to inject another $1 million into the company's kitty, but demanded in return a generous slug of equity. "I feel as if I've got a gun to my head," Adams wrote to Kapor in an email with the subject line "hard ball VCs." This was the flip side of the Kapor dictum: if a startup is not going well, the VCs will punish you.[56]

Still, as Adams reluctantly acknowledged, punishment was preferable to bankruptcy. In December 1993, he accepted the venture capitalists' lifeline.

◆

As it turned out, the $750,000 shock coincided with a portent of UUNET's eventual triumph. That December, the front of the *New York Times* business section featured a story on a revolutionary web browser called Mosaic, "a map to the buried treasures of the Information Age," as the article described it.[57] Almost a year earlier, the same author, John Markoff, had captured the excitement about Al Gore's vision for an information superhighway. Now the new buzz was about its dowdier rival, rendered suddenly sexy by Mosaic's point-and-click navigation. Before, finding information on the internet had required typing commands like "Telnet 192.100.81.100." Now users could simply click on words or images to summon web pages. Mitch Kapor's epiphany was proving right. The UUNET version of the information future trumped that of the U.S. vice president.

For the investors in UUNET, there remained only one task: to make doubly sure that Adams and his team capitalized on the opportunity. In the first weeks of 1994, Peter Barris met Adams for breakfast regularly, stopping off at the Pooks Hill Marriott on his way from his Northern Virginia home to the NEA office in Baltimore. Over coffee and a plate of eggs, Barris and Adams would discuss personnel and strategy, including the delicate question of bringing in an outside chief executive. Barris spent his days scouring his network for a star CEO candidate, and by the spring he had made double progress. Adams now trusted him enough to give an outside CEO a chance. And Barris had found someone.

The question was whether he could persuade this someone to join UUNET. The candidate was another GE Information Services veteran named John Sidgmore, whom Barris remembered for his streak of "entrepreneurial chutzpah." Back in his GE days, Sidgmore's phone was always ringing off the hook and people would be stopping by; with a cigarette in

his mouth and a coffee in his hand, Sidgmore would hold court with an as-
suredness that Barris could only marvel at. The trouble, a decade or so later,
was that Sidgmore had already committed himself to running another company, pocketing a $450,000 signing bonus. When Barris urged Sidgmore to
rip up his commitment in favor of UUNET, he got the predictable brush-off.
"Why in the world would I want to go to this little company, YoYo Net,
WeWe Net, or whatever you call it?"[58]

Barris explained the revelation he had felt when he had first encountered Adams. The GE programs that he and Sidgmore had sold to corporate
customers could be delivered over the internet at a fraction of the cost.
"Think of the margins, and what those margins are going to do to the value
of your personal equity," Barris said, seductively. UUNET represented an
opportunity for Sidgmore to modernize and cannibalize the entire GE Information Services playbook.[59] YoYo Net, WeWe Net: this was not just any
little company.

Barris's pitch hit home, and soon it was just a question of how much equity Sidgmore demanded. In June 1994, he signed on for 6 percent of the
company. It was roughly the same stake that John Morgridge had received
upon joining Cisco. It was more or less what each of UUNET's venture backers had received for kicking in $500,000.

After he brought Sidgmore on board, Barris's job was mostly over. With
a star CEO in the driver's seat, UUNET quickly raised three further venture
rounds, scaling up at breakneck speed and acting on the lessons from GE
that Barris had understood from the outset. In January 1995, UUNET secured the contract to build the network infrastructure that supported Windows 95, Microsoft's first operating system designed around the internet.
The next month Sidgmore pulled off the extraordinary coup of landing a
similar deal with Microsoft's chief rival in online services, AOL. Having
done the equivalent of securing both Coke and Pepsi as clients, UUNET
took off exponentially. Three months later, in May 1995, the company went
public.

Back in 1993, a coin toss might have decided who backed UUNET: the
corporate capitalists at Metropolitan Fiber or Accel's venture capitalists.
Now Accel stood to be fabulously rewarded. UUNET's flotation gave the

company a valuation of $900 million, and then, in a wonderful full-circle ending, Metropolitan Fiber made its second appearance, buying control of UUNET at a valuation of $2 billion. Through luck more than brilliance, Accel found itself pocketing fifty-four times its original stake, a profit of $188 million. Menlo received a similar return. NEA made even more because it held on to its position longer.[60] Venture capitalists as individuals had made plenty of errors. But venture capital as a system helped UUNET to spread the internet to millions.

Despite all his misgivings about investors, Rick Adams felt properly rewarded.

"I'd like to thank you again for nudging me in the right direction all those years ago," he wrote to Mitch Kapor after the flotation.

"I've got $138 million. Pretty surreal," he added.[61]

There was a coda to the UUNET story, and it reinforced the lessons about venture capital. The magical Mosaic web browser, announced by *The New York Times* in December 1993, had come out of a taxpayer-backed lab at the University of Illinois: it was another instance of government science kick-starting the online revolution. But the lead inventor of the browser, Marc Andreessen, did not stay in Illinois for long. The government was good at basic science. It was not good at turning breakthroughs into products that changed society.

The university's mistake was to take talent for granted. Andreessen had developed the browser as a temporary employee of the university's National Center for Supercomputing Applications, earning $6.85 an hour.[62] After Mosaic made him a geek celebrity, the center offered him a permanent position, but only on condition that he give up his involvement with the browser. It was a classically bureaucratic maneuver: the center wanted to make sure that it, and not its young prodigy, took credit for a successful project.[63] Andreessen responded by quitting the public sector and moving to the Valley. He teamed up with an inventor named Jim Clark who knew what talent could be worth and how to get the most out of it.

The University of Illinois had released Mosaic for general use and was trying to make a business out of it. Andreessen was convinced that this would fail and that a superior iteration of the browser could capture what was sure to be a giant market. Together with Clark and Clark's checkbook, he returned to his old campus at Urbana-Champaign: the pair interviewed seven of Andreessen's original collaborators on the Mosaic project. Clark met with each of them individually in his hotel suite—it was, Clark later wrote, "a standard-issue, chocolates-on-the-pillow overnighter"—and offered these astonished $6.85-an-hour employees a $65,000 annual salary plus 100,000 shares of stock. "I am pretty sure that your holdings will be worth more than a million dollars," he told them, "but within five years, if things go the way I hope they will, it is my objective that you make over ten million."[64] Unsurprisingly, all seven engineers jumped at the chance. Counting Andreessen, Clark had liberated eight traitors.

Clark initially bankrolled his venture with the proceeds from his previous company, Silicon Graphics, which pioneered the market for high-performance computers that could handle 3-D images. He took a dim view of venture capitalists, who had treated him shoddily—or so he thought—by taking nearly all the equity in that startup, leaving him with a measly stake of 3 percent or so.[65] At Silicon Graphics board meetings Clark would turn red in the face and scream furiously at Glenn Mueller, the investor from the Mayfield Fund who had been the first to back him. Mueller would sit quietly and take it.[66]

When Clark recruited his eight traitors in 1994, the venture capitalists he had abused were keen to back his new enterprise. It was the inverse of the syndrome at the University of Illinois: rather than disdaining talent and allowing it to walk away, VCs would wade through swamps to get their arms around it. NEA's Dick Kramlich, who had invested in Silicon Graphics, assigned a young associate to follow Clark around; whatever Clark did, Kramlich wanted a piece of it. Glenn Mueller, for his part, was equally eager. When he got wind that Clark was building a new web browser, he phoned repeatedly, begging for the opportunity to invest. Clark rebuffed him.

Mueller placed yet another call from his car. When Clark refused his entreaties, he said, "Jim, if you don't let us invest, my partners are going to kill me."

A week later, on April 4, 1994, Clark officially founded Mosaic Communications. His wife called with some news. Glenn Mueller, on his boat in Cabo San Lucas off the coast of Mexico, had put a shotgun in his mouth and pulled the trigger.[67]

Clark put the tragedy behind him and focused on building his company. He arranged for Mosaic Communications to issue $3 million worth of shares in its Series A round, then bought the entire amount himself, seizing half the total equity.[68] (When Mosaic Communications, by then renamed Netscape, went public the following year, the young Marc Andreessen owned just 3 percent—the same share that Clark had owned in Silicon Graphics.)[69] But however much Clark despised venture capitalists, he needed their support. His company wanted to expand. It was not as though a bank would back him.

In the fall of 1994, Clark invited venture capitalists to invest, but at a valuation that was three times higher than what he himself had paid just a couple of months earlier. Nothing much had happened to justify that jump. A sober venture capitalist, who kept price discipline in mind, would regard Clark's valuation as extraordinary. No venture-backed startup had ever secured a valuation of $18 million before shipping a product.

Clark first approached Mayfield, Glenn Mueller's fund. Perhaps not surprisingly, Mayfield had no stomach for Clark by this point. Next, Clark turned to Dick Kramlich, his other Silicon Graphics connection. Kramlich and his partners balked at the tripled valuation. Clark then looked around for a venture investor with the vision, or perhaps the craziness, to rise above small-minded sticker shock. Naturally, he found his way to John Doerr at Kleiner Perkins.

It quickly became clear that Clark had chosen the right target. Doerr's change-the-world improvisation had gotten him into trouble at GO and Dynabook. But that same excitable ambition was a perfect fit for Mosaic—and, more important, for this moment in history. Previously, when Doerr had boasted that he aimed to create new industries rather than just companies, he had been guilty of hype. But Mosaic really was a revolutionary product. Its browser would change the way that people accessed information, communicated with one another, and collaborated.

Mosaic also marked a new stage in the evolution of the power law. Venture-capital returns are dominated by grand slams partly because of the dynamics of startups: most young businesses fail, but the ones that gain traction can grow exponentially. This is true of fashion brands or hotel chains as well as technology companies. But tech-focused venture portfolios are dominated by the power law for an additional reason: tech startups are founded upon technologies that may themselves progress exponentially. Because of his experience and temperament, Doerr was especially attuned to this phenomenon. As a young engineer at Intel, he had seen how Moore's law transformed the value of companies that used semiconductors: the power of chips was doubling every two years, so startups that put them to good use could make better, cheaper products. For any given modem, digital watch, or personal computer, the cost of the semiconductors inside the engine would fall by 50 percent in two years, 75 percent in four years, and 87.5 percent in eight. With that sort of wind at a tech startup's back, no wonder profits could grow exponentially.

Mosaic, and the internet more generally, turbocharged this phenomenon. Again, Doerr grasped this better than most others. As well as working at Intel, he had known Bob Metcalfe, so he understood that Metcalfe's law was even more explosive than Moore's law. Rather than merely doubling in power every two years, as semiconductors did, the value of a network would rise as the square of the number of users.[70] Progress would thus be quadratic rather than merely exponential; something that keeps on squaring will soon grow a lot faster than something that keeps on doubling. Moreover, progress would not be tethered to the passage of time; it would be a function of the number of users. At the moment when Doerr met Clark, the number of internet users was about to triple over the next two years, meaning that the value of the network would jump ninefold, an effect massively more powerful than the mere doubling in the power of semiconductors over that same period. What's more, Metcalfe's law was not supplanting Moore's law, which would have been dramatic enough. Rather, it was compounding it. The explosion of internet traffic would be fueled both by its rapid growth in usefulness (Metcalfe's law) and by the falling cost of modems and computers (Moore's law).[71]

After listening to Clark's pitch, Doerr was determined to invest. A magical browser that attracted millions to the internet had almost limitless potential. The price Doerr had to pay was secondary.

Doerr called his partner, Vinod Khosla, right after the meeting. He urged him to meet Clark and Andreessen the next day, a Saturday. NEA and Mayfield had turned Mosaic down, but Doerr was convinced that even a steep valuation was worth paying.

Khosla duly visited the founders at their office on the corner of El Camino and Castro in Mountain View. He liked to think of venture bets as financial options. You could never lose more than your initial stake, but the upside was unbounded. Given what the power law meant for startups, what Moore's law meant for computing power, and what Metcalfe's law meant for networks—and given how each law compounded the effect of the others—Mosaic Communications was one of those options you just had to have. After the meeting, Khosla called Doerr. "We should just do it," he told him.[72]

A few days later, Clark and Andreessen returned to pitch to the full Kleiner Perkins investment committee. There had been no Accel-style prepared-mind planning, but that did not matter: it took the Kleiner Perkins partners all of forty-five minutes to approve the investment. "We knew it was a high price," said one partner, "especially with what seemed like a twelve-year-old as the technology guru behind it."[73] But everybody around the table remembered another one of Tom Perkins's dictums: you succeed in venture capital by backing the right deals, not by haggling over valuations.

In August 1995, Mosaic (now named Netscape) went public. At the close of the first trading day, Kleiner's original $5 million stake was worth $293 million.[74] As Netscape's stock climbed further, Kleiner soon found itself sitting on a profit of $500 million: it had achieved a multiple of 100x, or roughly twice as much as Accel's multiple on UUNET. In the face of this sort of bonanza, it really didn't matter how many Kleiner bets went to zero. In the internet age, it was worth paying whatever it might take for stakes in turbo-power-law companies.

Chapter Seven

BENCHMARK, SOFTBANK, AND "EVERYONE NEEDS $100 MILLION"

At the start of 1995, somebody mentioned a strange name at a UUNET board meeting. Don Gooding, the telecom analyst at Accel, had been building a company website—the first internet presence established by a venture firm. As he had spent time on the web, Gooding kept returning to a handy guide to its best offerings. The guide was called Yahoo.

Yahoo? The people around the table laughed. This couldn't be a serious outfit.

Gooding, who had been gearing himself up to propose Yahoo as an Accel investment, got cold feet. There was no point pitching an idea that would be met with giggles.[1]

A few weeks later, in that familiar pattern, the error of one group of VCs was corrected by others. The Silicon Valley veteran Bill Draper tracked down Yahoo's creators, who were operating from a modest trailer on the Stanford University campus.

Draper stooped to duck into the trailer. He maneuvered his tall frame around a bicycle and over some skis and approached a computer known as Konishiki. The computer's owner, a quiet graduate student named David Filo, was fond of goofy names. Konishiki was his favorite sumo wrestler.

Filo invited Draper to suggest a question that he would like to have answered.

Draper asked to be told the cost of tuition at Yale, where he served as a trustee.

Filo typed some keywords, and an image of a few fat books appeared on Konishiki's screen; this was Yale's earliest home page. After more keystrokes, up popped the answer: Yale's $21,000-per-year tuition.

Draper was astonished. The new Netscape browser helped to navigate the web, but it did not offer a directory or search service. The idea that you could look up almost anything online felt like digital magic. Draper resolved to encourage his son, Tim, who ran the Draper family office, to make an investment in Yahoo.[2]

Around the same time, a dapper, bespectacled figure also made his way to the trailer. Whereas Draper was Silicon Valley royalty—he could remember a time when Sand Hill Road was a dirt track where Tim rode a chopper with ape-hanger handlebars—the dapper visitor was a parvenu, a Welshman named Michael Moritz. He had come to the United States as a graduate student and covered Silicon Valley for *Time*, using the magazine as a calling card to get to know technology celebrities. In the mid-1980s, Moritz had worked briefly on his own startup, a venture that offered tech newsletters and conferences. Then, in 1986, in an improbable career switch, he had landed a job at Sequoia.

Moritz entered the trailer and recoiled at the ferocious heat thrown off by the computer gear. The floor was strewn with unwashed clothes and pizza cartons, and the shades were drawn to keep the glare off the screens. Some golf clubs had been propped up against a wall.[3] Given the state of the trailer, the inmates presumably needed to escape to the fairways.

Like Gooding and Draper, Moritz understood that Yahoo was compelling. The web was rapidly opening up to millions of users. Yahoo might become the internet equivalent of *TV Guide*: the service that directed consumers to the information that they wanted on this new medium. The question was how an internet guide would make money.

"So, how much are you going to charge subscribers?" Moritz asked Filo and his comrade, Jerry Yang.[4]

Filo and Yang exchanged glances. Each knew what the other was thinking. This guy doesn't get it.[5]

Yahoo was free, they informed Moritz. They had begun assembling their directory as a distraction from their PhD theses: it was a hobby, like joining a Frisbee club or indulging in horror-movie marathons. Their goal was to be playful, not boringly obsessed with revenues. They listed offbeat sites that caught their fancy—Brian's Lava Lamp, Quadralay's Armadillo Home Page.[6] Their penchant for wacky nomenclature should have clued Moritz in to what they were about. Konishiki's companion workstation was called Akebono. Yahoo stood for "Yet Another Hierarchical Officious Oracle." Charging customers would be contrary to the quirky spirit of their enterprise.

When Moritz had first arrived at Sequoia, some of his colleagues had been skeptical. He was an Oxford history graduate, a magazine journalist, the author of two business books. He had no engineering or managerial background. "This guy doesn't know anything!" one Sequoia partner exclaimed after Moritz showed up for his job interview. Don Valentine had overruled these objections because he had seen in Moritz a versatile learner, and he preferred to hire a hungry upstart than someone who was coasting on experience.[7] Now, serendipitously, Moritz's unconventional background was about to prove its value.

Moritz could not recall a precedent for what Yahoo was intending: to raise money from venture capitalists while giving its product away for free.[8] But a few seconds of lateral thinking told him that Yahoo's scheme could work. The media industry that Moritz himself came from featured grown-up corporations that did precisely what Yahoo proposed: radio stations and TV networks broadcast news and shows for free, then raked in profits by charging for advertising. What's more, the media guys served up whimsical plotlines with cheeky names. There was no contradiction between irreverence and profits. Equipped with this analogy, Moritz grasped the case for Yahoo more firmly than Draper had. He was not merely impressed by the product. He understood the future business model.

Moritz kept chatting with Yang and Filo, but now he switched subtly from cross-examiner to courtier. He knew he would face competition to get into this deal: Yahoo was also weighing acquisition offers from two larger internet firms, AOL and Netscape. To muscle out these rivals, Moritz asked sensitive questions, listened intently to the answers, and climbed inside the young grad students' heads. Years later, asked why he had picked Moritz over other suitors, Yang replied enigmatically that Moritz had "soul."[9] Despite his unpromising opening gambit, Moritz had connected with him.

At a telling point in their courtship, Yang asked Moritz if the company should change its name, maybe to something more serious. Moritz retorted that if Yang did that, Sequoia would not back him.[10] Moreover, Moritz had a rationale for his retort—one that Yang himself had never thought of. In his years as a journalist, Moritz had written a perceptive book about Steve Jobs. Now he insisted that Yahoo was that precious thing, an inspired and memorable company name. Like Apple.[11]

Whether by instinct or cunning, Moritz had given the perfect clincher of an answer. Because he understood Jobs as well as anybody in the Valley, he had the credibility to imply a connection between two unknown grad students and a storied Silicon Valley legend. Like all great venture capitalists, he knew how to amplify the sense of destiny of even the most confident founders. It was the ultimate seduction.

In April 1995, Sequoia duly invested $975,000 in Yahoo, taking 32 percent of its equity. Filo and Yang each retained 25 percent of the venture, and the balance of the shares was reserved for Yahoo staff, including a new outside chief executive whom Moritz recruited. Bill Draper's son, Tim, asked to be let in on the deal: he had been slower than Moritz to pounce, and now he had the zeal of the converted. But Sequoia resolutely froze him out. It wanted as much skin in this game as possible.

◆

Sequoia's investment in Yahoo set the stage for the second half of the 1990s, the period of the exuberant internet build-out that culminated in the bursting of the tech bubble. The innovation of backing companies that charged little or nothing for products spread through the venture-capital business like wildfire. Startups came to be assessed not according to this year's revenues or even next year's, but rather according to their momentum, traction, audience, or brand—things that could, in theory at least, be monetized in the future.

To build Yahoo's momentum, Moritz helped to position Yang as the face of the Valley—a sort of second coming of Steve Jobs, even though Yang himself resisted the comparison.[12] As a tribune of the 1970s counterculture, the barefooted Jobs had kick-started the PC business. At a time when immigrants, and especially Asian immigrants, were starting to make their mark on the Valley, the Taiwanese American Yang emerged as the evangelist for a new style of startup. His picture appeared frequently in magazines: a broad, toothy grin, thick black hair, collegiate chinos. He held forth at tech conferences on Yahoo's strategy for building an audience online; he was part geek, part marketing guru. After Yang wowed one gathering in June 1995, no less a figure than Bob Metcalfe turned to his neighbor. "This is going to be the first great Internet brand," he pronounced confidently.[13]

The dirty secret was that Yahoo had no choice but to build a brand, because it was not much of a technology company. It boasted no patents and not much of an engineering edge: its directory was put together by surfing the web and classifying sites, and much of the work was done manually. As a result, it presented a negative illustration of Tom Perkins's dictum: because Yahoo entailed no technological risk, it involved a huge amount of market risk, because no technological moat protected it from competitors. What's more, competition was bound to be especially ferocious because of the winner-takes-all logic of Yahoo's business. Internet users were likely to gravitate to a single way of searching for information on the web. The winner would capture the lion's share of online ad dollars. The also-rans would collect pennies.

Confronting this extreme version of the power law, Yahoo did not have the option of behaving like traditional tech companies. It could not simply invent a product, market it, and count on technological novelty to bring in sales and profits. Rather, it had to remain buzzier than its rivals, which meant that it had to project an aura of momentum. Anticipating the dynamics of future internet companies, a precarious circular logic took hold: the key to Yahoo's growth was that it had to keep growing. As a result, Yahoo's early success in generating revenues did not translate into profits. Every dollar of advertising income had to be plowed back into marketing expenditures to keep expanding the business.[14] Indeed, recycling advertising income soon proved not to be enough. Eight months after securing $1 million from Sequoia, Yahoo set out to raise another round of capital.

Traditional venture capitalists, observing a cash-burning business with no technological moat and nothing more substantial than a brand, might have refused Yahoo the lifeline that it needed. But by late 1995, tradition was passé. Netscape's flotation in the summer had shown how the coming of the internet had changed the game: given the astronomical returns to be had from turbo-power-law companies, it was crazy not to gamble on them. What's more, jackpots like Netscape and UUNET had been noticed by university endowments and pension funds, which responded by pouring extra capital into venture. In 1995, U.S. venture partnerships raised $10 billion, up from $3 billion five years before.[15] There was so much money in the Valley, and so much faith in the logic of the power law, that Yahoo was almost bound to be funded.

The funder who appeared was ideally suited to the moment. He was a short, slight entrepreneur named Masayoshi Son, and he had earned a reputation as the Bill Gates of Japan by hitting it big with a software distributor called SoftBank. Unlike Gates, who came from a privileged background, Son was an extreme example of a self-made man. His family was part of Japan's marginalized Korean minority, and his childhood home was a squatter's shack near a railroad that he shared with six siblings. But although Son's impoverished beginnings contributed to his legend, they were also a burden. Son's father attempted to disguise the shame of his ethnicity by adopting the Japanese family name of Yasumoto, and the humiliation drove Son to leave home at sixteen and make his way to California. "I will own my name to prove all human beings are the same," he vowed as he was leaving.[16] Years later, Son's ingrained outsider complex was cited by a colleague as the key to his extraordinary investment style. He gambled like a desperado with nothing to lose, even when his fortune was worth billions.

By the fall of 1995, Son was engaged in a second California odyssey.

After the first one, he had returned to Japan with an economics degree from Berkeley and had made his fortune with SoftBank. Now, having got wind of the internet gold rush, he was shifting his business from Japan to America. It was an extraordinarily bold jump for an Asian entrepreneur: Silicon Valley's dense networks could be hard to penetrate for an unconnected outsider. But Son bought control of an American technology publisher and the leading U.S. organizer of computer conferences, acquiring information flow and connections that might help him spot the next exciting frontier.

In November 1995, Son visited Yahoo at its new office in Mountain View, a few miles down the valley from the Stanford campus. Yang and Filo had spackled the walls with paint, and Filo's work space was littered with Rollerblades, CD cases, crumpled soda cans, old copies of the *Micro Times*, and a blue-plaid polyester blanket. It was ironic that Filo's professional mission was to bring order to cyberspace.[17]

Embarrassed by the state of their office, Yang and Filo offered to take their visitor out to a French restaurant. Son waved the idea away. He wanted to get down to business.

In his later career, Son acquired a reputation for raising and committing funds extraordinarily quickly. In 2016, when he was plotting an investment vehicle called the Vision Fund, he talked $45 billion out of Saudi Arabia's crown prince in the space of forty-five minutes.[18] Now, as he encountered Yahoo, his approach was similarly direct. He wanted a piece of Yahoo. His hosts wanted his capital. There was no need to complicate the conversation.

Son invited Filo and Yang to say what they thought Yahoo might be worth.

The founders tentatively suggested a valuation of $40 million, up from just $3 million when Sequoia had invested eight months earlier.

Son said yes immediately, without hesitating. He was even readier to pay up than John Doerr at Kleiner Perkins.

"Shit, I should have been higher!" Yang thought to himself.[19]

Son duly led Yahoo's Series B financing, providing more than half of the $5 million that the company raised, with Sequoia and the news agency

Reuters kicking in smaller amounts.[20] But Son was just getting started. In March 1996, he returned to Yahoo's office.

The passage of four months had done nothing to cure Yahoo's addiction to burning money. The company's rivals, notably two search engines called Excite and Lycos, were also trying to build their brands, and Yahoo had to stay ahead of them. Consequently, Filo and Yang had spent a good chunk of the $5 million Series B capital on marketing. Just recently, moreover, Excite and Lycos had doubled down: to fortify their marketing war chests, they had announced plans to go public. Desperate not to lose its front-runner position, Yahoo had turned to Goldman Sachs to arrange its own public offering.

Son arrived at Yahoo's office looking as slight and uncommanding as ever. But he brought a bazooka. In a bid without precedent in the history of the Valley, he proposed to invest fully $100 million in Yahoo. In return he wanted an additional 30 percent of the company.

Son's bid implied that Yahoo's value had shot up eight times since his investment four months earlier. But the astonishing thing about his offer was the size of his proposed check: Silicon Valley had never seen a venture stake of such proportions.[21] The typical fund raised by a top-flight venture partnership weighed in at around $250 million, and there was no way it would put 40 percent of its resources into a single $100 million wager.[22] Private-equity investors and corporate acquirers sometimes made investments in the $100 million range, but in return they expected to take full control of companies.[23] Son, in contrast, would be a minority investor and on an unheralded scale. Because he had SoftBank's corporate balance sheet behind him, he could pump in fully one hundred times more capital than Sequoia had provided when Yahoo got started.

After Son dropped his bombshell, Yang, Filo, and Moritz sat in silence. Disconcerted, Yang said he was flattered but didn't need the capital.[24]

"Jerry, everyone needs $100 million," Son retorted.[25]

There was little doubt that Son was right—at least in the new era of online brands fighting for attention. Yahoo was preparing to go public precisely because it did need capital.

"How much do you have to pay Netscape to feature you?" Son continued. He was referring to the fact that Netscape, as the leading web browser, was auctioning off the right to be the featured search engine on its site. If Excite or Lycos had deeper pockets than Yahoo, one of them would seize the advantage.

Yang admitted that Netscape charged a lot. It followed, as he also admitted, that $100 million would actually be useful. In the new world of winner-takes-all brand competition, Yahoo's future growth depended on its immediate growth. Therefore it needed growth capital.

The question was who would provide it. The normal way for a young company to raise tens of millions was to go public, which was just what Yahoo was planning. But now here came Son, this Korean Japanese outsider, who appeared to have some kind of magic coolant in his veins. Politely, without swagger, he was offering the scale of money that usually came from public markets, coupled with the simplicity of a private deal. He was ready to shake hands on his audacious bid immediately.

It took Moritz and the Yahoo founders some time to formulate an answer. The certainty of Son's offer was seductive: there was always a risk that an IPO might flop. On the other hand, Goldman Sachs was suggesting a listing price that would value Yahoo at fully twice as much as Son was proposing. If Goldman could deliver on this, a successful IPO would leave Sequoia, Yang, and Filo a lot richer.

Before the Yahoo team arrived at a decision, Son made a second move that defied all convention. He asked Moritz and the founders to name Yahoo's main competitors.

"Excite and Lycos," they answered.

Son turned to one of his lieutenants. "Write those names down," he commanded.

Then he turned back to Moritz and the founders. "If I don't invest in Yahoo, I'll invest in Excite and I'll kill you," he informed them.

For Yang and Filo, and particularly for Moritz, Son's threat was a revelation. There would be only one victor in the race to be the go-to internet guide, so the investor who could write a $100 million check could choose who won the competition. Like a digital Don Corleone, Son had made Moritz an offer that he could not refuse. Moritz later resolved never to be in this position again.[26]

Asking Son to excuse them, the Yahoo team went off to speak privately among themselves. When they were alone, Moritz counseled the two founders that Son's threat to back a rival had to be taken seriously. No Silicon Valley veteran would turn against a startup in which he had already invested: venture capital was a repeat game, and in order to earn trust, you had to honor your relationships. But Son was an interloper, ignorant of the unwritten rules. Silicon Valley convention was not going to constrain him.[27]

After half an hour, the three returned with a decision. They would take Son's money. But they would proceed with the IPO anyway.

After a bit more negotiation, Son ultimately invested just over $100 million in Yahoo.[28] Adding in the shares that he had purchased in the Series B financing, Son now held 41 percent of the company. Sequoia's ownership had been diluted down to 19 percent. Filo and Yang retained 17 percent each.

On April 12, 1996, Yahoo went public. The shares took off on a wild ride, closing the first day at fully two and a half times what Son had paid for them.[29] It was a breathtaking bonanza: Son had made an instant profit of more than $150 million. Years later, Moritz recalled the psychological impact of this spectacle. Until the Yahoo flotation, no single deal had earned Sequoia more than $100 million, the record set by Don Valentine's bet on Cisco. "How are we ever in a month of Sundays, years of Sundays, decades of Sundays, ever, ever going to be able to beat $100 million from one investment?" he remembered thinking.[30] But by buying into Yahoo on the eve of its flotation, Son had blown past the $100 million mark in a matter of weeks, and without any of the heartache of building a management team from nothing. The business of venture capital was forever altered.

———◆———

The alteration took two forms, the first flashy and obvious, the second slow-burning and subtle. The obvious transformation was in Son himself: he was famous now not just in Japan but everywhere. Leveraging his new reputation as a digital Midas, he followed the Yahoo bonanza with a dizzying investment blitz, barely pausing to sort gems from rubbish. To borrow the language of hedge funds, he didn't care about alpha—the reward a skilled investor earns by selecting the right stock. He cared only about beta—the profits to be had by just being in the market. One young investor who managed Son's funds recalls betting on at least 250 internet startups between 1996 and 2000, meaning that he had kept up an insane rate of around one per week, ten or maybe even twenty times as many as a normal venture operator.[31] Meanwhile, that same cowboy sat on more than thirty boards. "I did not have the experience to know it was crazy," one Son lieutenant recalled later.[32]

Repeating the Yahoo playbook, Son also made large bets on later-stage companies. At the end of 1997, he used the balance sheets of SoftBank and Yahoo to pump $100 million into the pioneer web-hosting company Geo-Cities, doubling his money when the company went public the following August and ultimately realizing an astronomical gain of well over $1 billion. In 1998, in a variant on his formula, Son bought 27 percent of the online financial-services company E*Trade after it had already gone public. He paid $400 million for the stake; a year later it was worth $2.4 billion. To reduce his reliance on SoftBank's balance sheet, Son raised a new kind of venture fund: a $1 billion war chest exclusively for late-stage stakes, or what became known as "growth investing."[33] Meanwhile, Son used his Japanese connections to launch subsidiaries of American champions: Yahoo Japan, E*Trade Japan, and so on.[34] There was almost no arena in which Son did not play. He launched venture funds in South Korea, Japan, and Hong Kong. He partnered with Rupert Murdoch's News Corp to invest in Australia, New Zealand, and India. In Europe, he linked up with the French media conglomerate Vivendi. In Latin America, he maintained venture offices in Mexico City, São Paulo, and Buenos Aires.

With this hurricane of activity, Son anticipated changes in the venture industry that emerged more obviously a decade later. As we shall see presently, growth investing became a Silicon Valley staple from around 2009, and venture partnerships transformed themselves from hyper-local businesses to more globally minded operations. It all followed logically from the shift that Yahoo marked. Branded internet companies faced an imperative to grow, creating an opportunity for investors to provide growth capital. Branded internet companies were not built on cutting-edge technology, so they could flourish far away from the tech hub in Silicon Valley. As often happens in finance, the player who first sees a shift in the landscape, and who has the ready capital to match the novel need, can make bumper profits before competitors wake up. By one reckoning, Son expanded his personal fortune by $15 billion between 1996 and 2000.[35] This was at a time when no other venture capitalist even appeared on the *Forbes* billionaires' list: not John Doerr, not Don Valentine, not anyone.

<hr/>

The second, subtler transformation took place within Sequoia. After Yahoo's dramatic stock market debut, Don Valentine and his colleagues grew agitated. Yahoo's valuation had gone from nothing to $600 million in the space of a year, and the older partners wanted to lock in the winnings. "Every single week everybody is vibrating about where the Yahoo stock price is and how ridiculous it is, and how preposterous, and what's going to happen if the thing melts down," Moritz recalled later.[36] But Moritz himself took the opposite view. Having seen how much Son had profited, partly at Sequoia's expense, he was determined to hold on to the remaining Yahoo stake: there was so much upside to be had from riding winners. It was all very well celebrating the fact that, taken together, Sequoia's Series A and Series B stakes in Yahoo were up about 60x after the first day of trading. But you can't fatten your bank account with multiples. In dollar terms—the terms that actually counted—Sequoia had made less from Yahoo than Son had.

Moritz came to see the Yahoo experience as a tipping point for Sequoia. It coincided with Don Valentine's retirement and Moritz's emergence, together with a hard-charging contemporary named Doug Leone, as the leader of the partnership. The old guard had been born into the Depression and had grown up during the world war; their families had lived in fear of losing everything. "If you are afraid of losing everything, you tend to take your chips off the table too early," Moritz reflected.[37] In the case of Apple, for example, Valentine had sold out before the IPO, realizing a quick profit but depriving his limited partners of the bounty from Apple's flotation. Moritz, in contrast, was a child of the postwar boom and had experienced little but success in his own life: he had risen from Wales, to Oxford, to Wharton, to Sequoia; and now, a short time after his fortieth birthday, he had made his golden bet on Yahoo. He and his contemporaries were far less inclined than the older generation to worry about stuff that could go wrong. "I think one of the huge changes at Sequoia is that we've been trying, without getting giddy about it, trying to imagine with some of these companies, what can happen if everything goes right?" Moritz reflected.[38]

The Yahoo investment crystallized this culture clash within Sequoia, pitting the cautious old guard against its optimistic successors. Moritz seized the moment to make his case for the long game, pressing his partners to distribute the Yahoo stock only gradually. In the case of Cisco, he reminded them, the biggest gains had come after a few years: at its flotation in 1990, Cisco had been worth $224 million; by 1994, it had shot up to $10 billion. By winning this argument and cementing his authority within the firm, Moritz saw to it that the last distribution of Yahoo was put off until November 1999, when the company was trading at $182 per share, fully fourteen times more than the price at the flotation. Thanks to masterful procrastination, Yahoo generated more gains for Sequoia than all its prior investments, *combined*, and more than ten times as much as Sequoia had earned from Cisco. The secret, Moritz said laconically, "was just learning to be a little patient."[39]

But the true secret went deeper. Thanks to the Yahoo experience and Son's example, Moritz came to see that a venture partnership must adapt constantly. He learned that huge, growth-capital checks conferred king-maker powers and that it paid to think bigger than just the Valley. Later, Sequoia would apply these lessons with clinical efficiency, achieving a position of unrivaled strength in the business of financing technology.

◆

While Son was making his mark in the Valley, a contrasting contender arrived on the scene: a venture partnership called Benchmark. Three of Benchmark's founders—Bruce Dunlevie, Bob Kagle, and Andrew Rachleff—had served at other Valley venture shops; the fourth, Kevin Harvey, had founded a Valley software firm and sold it to Lotus Development. With its professional capital so geographically concentrated, Benchmark's strength was local rather than global: it was the anti-Softbank.[40] Further, the Benchmark model was about being nimble rather than large: the partnership made a virtue of the deliberately small size of its first fund, which weighed in at $85 million, or less than a single check that Son might write to one company. "God is not on the side of the big arsenals, but on the side of those who shoot best," Benchmark's prospectus insisted.[41]

Benchmark's founding partners believed that by staying lean and focused, they had developed a "fundamentally better architecture." The small fund size meant that they would carefully evaluate each deal: they aimed for alpha, not beta. Small would also ensure that each partner sat on just a handful of boards, and so added value to each portfolio company. Small would promote camaraderie among the four partners: the venture industry was masculine and monocultural, but the Benchmark team exhibited an especially intense case of jocular male uniformity. Finally, small was emphatically not a sign of weakness. Benchmark could have raised more capital if it had wanted to, and to underscore their strength, the Benchmark guys announced that they would keep an aggressive share of their fund's profits, more than the 20 percent industry standard.[42] Benchmark also charged a relatively low management fee on the capital in its care. The partners wanted to be paid for results, not merely for amassing money.

Some venture firms believed that selecting the right deal was nine-tenths of the job; coaching entrepreneurs was an afterthought. Benchmark partners tended toward a more fifty-fifty attitude. Knowing with confidence which deal to do was generally impossible; it was in the nature of the venture game that many bets went to zero.[43] Therefore, to be sure of creating alpha, Benchmark had to descend into the trenches with the entrepreneurs; "I'm so far down, I can't see much sky," one Benchmark partner said with a chuckle.[44] Skeptics might counter that the best entrepreneurs, the ones who generated the home runs that drove a fund's performance, needed little input from investors and that lavishing time on lesser founders would never move the needle on a portfolio. But Benchmark rejected this defeatism. Apparent laggards could turn into winners if you dug in and helped them. "Sometimes magic happens," a Benchmark partner insisted.[45] Moreover, if you acquired a reputation for sticking by your hard cases, your loyalty would be repaid. Word would get around, and entrepreneurs would flock to you.

Getting down into the trenches was an exercise in empathy. You had to give advice while knowing that you might be wrong, and you had to communicate it tactfully.[46] Picking the right moment was part of the technique: there was no point offering counsel when it would fall on unreceptive ears, so you had to seize the openings when guidance was really wanted. "What's venture capital?" Benchmark's co-founder Bruce Dunlevie mused. "It's sitting at your desk on Friday at 6:15 p.m., packing up to go home when the phone rings, and the CEO says, 'Do you have a minute? My VP of HR is dating the secretary. The VP of engineering wants to quit and move back to North Carolina because his spouse doesn't like living here. I've got to fire the sales guy who's been misreporting revenues. I've just been to the doctor and I'm having health problems. And I think I need to do a product recall.' And you, as the venture capitalist, you say, 'Do you want me to come down now or get together for breakfast in the morning?'"[47]

Benchmark's trademark likability was illustrated by Bob Kagle, who had grown up in Flint, Michigan, and attended the General Motors Institute, which offered a college education consisting of alternating six-week stints in the classroom and at a GM plant. Kagle studied engineering, then won admission to Stanford's business school, arriving in a gold Pontiac Trans Am with an American eagle emblazoned on the elongated hood. His straight eyebrows, trimmed mustache, and stubbly goatee formed three parallel lines. He had an infectious, empathetic laugh. He loved to work with entrepreneurs on deals that "brought out the humanity."[48]

Despite his engineering training and midwestern automotive roots, Kagle was happy to back companies that had no connection to either. Before co-founding Benchmark, he had tried to persuade his previous partnership to invest in a Seattle-based coffee chain called Starbucks. On another occasion, he had seen a long line outside a joint called Jamba Juice and had canceled that morning's appointments to interview the staff and customers.[49] After the launch of Benchmark, Kagle oscillated between technology bets and consumer ventures. Unlike Accel-type specialists, he refused to stay in a single industry lane; if there was a theme to his approach, it was that thing about *humanity*. In 1997, Kagle chanced upon a hybrid that combined all his interests. It was a technology firm that was simultaneously a consumer firm. It involved the human element, big-time. It was also the first illustration of what VCs would later call *ownable* network effects.

The creator of this hybrid was a software engineer named Pierre Omidyar. Born in Paris of Iranian parents, Omidyar was another immigrant who would make his mark in the Valley; by now, immigrants accounted for about a third of the scientific and engineering workforce in the region.[50] He was steeped in the antihierarchical communities of the early internet; he had a ponytail, a Vandyke beard, and glasses.[51] Somewhat to his chagrin, Omidyar had previously worked at a startup that helped established corporations to expand online sales; it entrenched power rather than democratizing it. And so, to balance out his social impact, Omidyar had devised an online auction tool for buyers and sellers of secondhand stuff. The tool was free to anyone to use. It was a form of atonement.

True to his roots in the early internet, Omidyar liked to think of his buyers and sellers as a community, not just as a bunch of self-interested dealers. He built a feedback system to allow auction users to rate one another, figuring that this would encourage considerate behavior. He added a bulletin board for sharing tips on stuff like how to upload pictures. New members of the community posted their queries. Experienced ones volunteered their time to answer. In February 1996, when the traffic on his auction site breached the limit on his internet account, Omidyar appealed to the community to help pay for an upgraded subscription. The appeal assumed goodwill: sellers were asked to send Omidyar a small cut of their earnings, but there was no thought of forcing them to do so. Pretty soon Omidyar's sunny view of human nature was vindicated. Checks arrived in a trickle, then a flood. By the end of the year, Omidyar was taking in more than $400,000 monthly.

Omidyar quit his day job and hired two people to help him. He cleared extraneous stuff from his website and named his auction platform eBay. Growth was running at 40 percent per month, but what was more impressive was the motor that was driving it. Unlike Yahoo, which was pouring money into marketing, eBay's marketing budget was zero. Its hectic expansion was instead propelled by Metcalfe's law: as the size of its auction network grew, its value rose exponentially. The more sellers listed stuff on eBay, the more bargain hunters were drawn to the site; the more buyers there were, the more sellers turned to it. Moreover, unlike telecommunications networks, which were stitched together with routers and switches made by a variety of firms, eBay captured 100 percent of the commissions generated by its auctions. It was profiting from a network effect. What's more, it owned the network.

Thanks to this self-reinforcing growth, eBay had no financial need for venture capital. It was accumulating its own capital internally: every month, roughly half of its revenues fell to the bottom line as profits. Yet it was out of its depth. Omidyar and his two friends were not equipped to pilot a business that accelerated this fast entirely of its own volition. Seeking managerial guidance, Omidyar turned to the counselor who had helped make a success of his online sales startup: Benchmark's co-founder Bruce Dunlevie.

Physically imposing but approachable in manner, Dunlevie was a walking vindication of the Benchmark thesis that helping struggling founders would pay off in the future. He took hands-on counseling so seriously that he compared going on a board to having a child: for the next several years, your life would be different. One time, coaxed to tell a story that he might like to be remembered by, Dunlevie spoke of a chief executive whom he had felt obliged to fire because the firm had outgrown him. Several years later, that same CEO readily accepted an invitation to run another Benchmark startup, saying he had always appreciated Dunlevie for treating him fairly.[52] Omidyar, whose company had been through a dark tunnel before Dunlevie helped it out into the light, had even more positive feelings. He checked in with Dunlevie regularly.

"I've got this e-commerce site called eBay. It's gathering steam," Omidyar reported.

"It sounds great. Why don't you send me a business plan?" Dunlevie answered.

Omidyar didn't have a business plan, but a few months later, in early 1997, he checked in again.

"Why don't you—" Dunlevie began. But this time Omidyar interrupted him.

"Why don't we get together? Old times' sake."

Dunlevie agreed and put him on the calendar.[53]

When the meeting rolled around, Dunlevie persuaded Bob Kagle to tag along, figuring that Kagle was the Benchmark guy who liked retail investments. Omidyar arrived without a slide deck, planning instead to demonstrate his auction site; after all, the site was that rare thing, an internet property that made money. But, creaking under the burden of exploding traffic, eBay's servers had crashed. Seeking to rescue Omidyar from his embarrassment, Dunlevie assured him, "Our internet connection is flaky—I apologize."[54]

Kagle left the meeting feeling skeptical. Later, he checked out the eBay website and found it surprisingly crude: Courier typeface, no color, just lines of drab listings. But when Kagle looked a little closer, his opinion changed. He was a collector of hand-carved fishing lures, and the site had plenty of fine pieces on offer, including one by a carver from his hometown in Michigan. Fascinated, Kagle placed a bid and lost. But he recognized that feeling when a product connects with something in your brain. The lure had hooked him.

Kagle went to meet Omidyar again, outside Benchmark's office. The writer Randall E. Stross, who reconstructed Benchmark's early story in masterful detail, captured how Kagle latched onto Omidyar's focus on community: every other sentence, Omidyar spoke about the eBay community, building the community, learning from the community, protecting the community. Other venture capitalists, hearing this same riff, were quickly turned off. "He pitched the idea of an online community. I thought, community of what?" one of them remembered.[55] Still others ridiculed the idea of a business built on flea market auctions of $10 trophies: a Beanie Baby trading site, some called it.[56] But Kagle, with his penchant for deals that "brought out the humanity," had the opposite reaction. "This guy is good people," he kept thinking.[57] Besides, as a VC who had backed both retail guys and software guys, Kagle had an edge. Retail businesses were all about connecting with customers, and treating the customers as a community was a fine way to go about this. Software businesses had long understood the power of network effects, and Omidyar's "community" was maybe just a cozy term for what a software guy would call a "network." Network effects explained why Netscape had minted money for John Doerr. They explained why eBay was exploding.

eBay's growth rate also impressed the other Benchmark partners. "When companies grow exponentially, they don't suddenly stop," Andy Rachleff observed later, adding that it is the "second derivative"—the changes in the rate of growth of a company's sales—that really tell a venture investor whether to back it.[58] And so, with the support of his colleagues, Kagle offered to invest $6.7 million in eBay, valuing the company at about $20 million.

If Omidyar's goal had been solely to get rich, he might have rejected Kagle. He had received a rival offer from a newspaper chain that proposed to buy him out for $50 million. But Omidyar had come to like Kagle as much as he had liked Dunlevie, and, rather like the Yahoo founders, he went with the venture guy who seemed to understand him. When the investment was concluded and Benchmark wired over the funds, Omidyar left them in the bank untouched. He wanted Kagle's connections and counsel. He didn't need his capital.

◆

Kagle's first move was to find an outside CEO for eBay. He consulted Benchmark's recently recruited fifth partner, David Beirne, who had previously co-founded an executive search firm; increasingly, recruitment was recognized as a core skill for VCs, just a little way behind a business or engineering degree. Beirne spoke highly of Meg Whitman, a general manager at the toy company Hasbro, and, by a coincidence, Kagle also had a friend from business school who recommended her. The more Kagle learned about this toy executive, the more he came to think that she would be perfect for the role. Whitman understood how to get the most out of a retail brand. She had a gut sense for "the emotional component of the customer experience," as Kagle put it.[59]

Much as with Barris's hiring of Sidgmore, the question was how to persuade a fancy exec to make the leap to an obscure startup. Before Benchmark's investment, Omidyar had tried to attract high-powered outside managers to eBay, but none had been willing to take a risk on a flea market. Now, however, Omidyar had the imprimatur of Benchmark, and Benchmark in turn had retained the services of Dave Beirne's old executive search firm, Ramsey Beirne. The combined prestige of the two induced Whitman to agree to a meeting. She might need the relationship with the search guys if she wanted a new job in the future.

Whitman flew out west for a day and met Kagle and Omidyar. She was intrigued: as Kagle emphasized, eBay's growth was truly exponential. Returning for a second visit, she noticed something else. Unlike other retailers, eBay did not hold inventory. It had no carrying costs, no shipping costs, no hassles with storage. As a result, its profit margins were formidable.

Whitman flew back for a third visit, this time with her family. To help coax her on board, Kagle invited Whitman to dinner at his house, along with her family. Whitman's husband, an accomplished surgeon, had doubts about eBay's prospects. Kagle did his best to reassure him. The couple had two sons, so Kagle had swag bags delivered to them at their hotel, ensuring there was a Stanford cap for each of them. The Whitmans wondered what life would be like on the West Coast, so Kagle sent them off with a realtor to look at some attractive neighborhoods. At the next meeting of the Benchmark partners, Kagle reported on his efforts and added an auspicious twist. According to Whitman, one of her sons had thought Kagle's thirteen-year-old daughter was cute.

"I'm feeling pretty good," Kagle confided to his colleagues.[60]

A little while later, Whitman decided that eBay amounted to an opportunity that she might never again encounter. Against the advice of her colleagues and bosses, she moved her family out west to join a company that nobody in her circle had heard of.[61]

With the hiring of a skilled CEO, eBay was on the path to an initial public offering. The company sold its millionth item, a Big Bird jack-in-the-box toy, and the business kept growing. Kagle remained as engaged as ever, but he stayed in the background. So long as Whitman and Omidyar were working well together, he did not want to complicate things.

In September 1998, eBay duly went public, pricing its shares at $18. At the close of the first day of trading, they hit $47. Then, after some unnerving bumps, they hit $73 in late October. It was a more dramatic upward spiral even than Yahoo's. But unlike at Sequoia, where vast unrealized profits opened up a deep generational split, the reactions at Benchmark were initially jocular.

"Holy Christ," said Beirne.

"It goes up from there," predicted Dunlevie.

"Can we sell now?" asked Beirne.

"If you want to leave most of the money on the table, you can," said Dunlevie.

"Yeah, I'm a pussy," Beirne said, chuckling.

Someone called out that Kagle would never sell a share of eBay until it was valued like GM. There was laughter around the table.[62]

The stock continued to imitate a rocket. On November 9, it closed at $103. The next day it hit $131. Financial commentators struggled to respond. "It's like watching every mesmerizing, discombobulated absurdity you can possibly think of, all rolled into one colossal Ur-event—like watching Mark McGwire step up to the plate blindfolded and hit 400 home runs in a row," one wrote. The bankers who had arranged the public listing at $18 and then followed later with bullish analysts' reports were engaging in "full-frontal, right-in-your-face stock hyping," the commentator continued. How else could they say, only six weeks earlier, that eBay "was worth $18 a share, and now say, Oops, we made a mistake, it's really worth $130."[63]

Hype or not, Benchmark was making venture history. As far as anybody knew, Sequoia's Yahoo deal and Kleiner's investment in a cable startup called @Home were the biggest venture home runs to date, each delivering a profit for the VCs of between $600 million and $700 million.[64] But Benchmark was on track to make well over $1 billion from eBay, depending on where its stock price settled. By the end of November it had soared to $200.

Now even the Benchmark partners felt vertigo. "This is mania. This is nuts," groaned Kagle. Unlike other internet darlings, such as the e-tailer Amazon.com, eBay could at least claim to be profitable. But as a multiple on its earnings, eBay's stock price was fantastical.

Kagle conferred with Howard Schultz, the founder of Starbucks, whom he had recruited to the eBay board. The stock price spelled trouble, the two of them agreed. It was bound to crash, leaving recently recruited eBay employees with stock options that would be worthless—how was eBay going to retain people?[65] But the market did not care about eBay's staff morale. By April 1999, the stock had soared above $600.[66]

Later that month, Benchmark finally distributed part of its winnings. eBay's share price gave it a market value of $21 billion; Benchmark's stake was worth an astonishing $5.1 billion. This bonanza not only dwarfed the records at Sequoia and Kleiner; it far exceeded even Son's biggest wins, and it had been achieved by risking a mere $6.7 million worth of capital. Benchmark's cottage-industry style of venture capital suddenly looked inspired. Who needed to write outsized growth-capital checks? Who wanted to bother with an Asia strategy?

The remarkable thing was, eBay was not an isolated victory. There was a software distributor called Red Hat that generated well over $500 million for Benchmark. There was an online office-supply company called Ariba, which generated more than $1 billion. By mid-1999, Benchmark had raised and invested three funds, deploying a cumulative $267 million of capital. But after that summer's crop of IPOs, the value of the portfolio surpassed $6 billion, implying a multiple of about twenty-five times capital.[67] The back-to-basics vision of venture capital was evidently thriving, whatever the message from Masayoshi Son's example.

The contest between these two models would persist into the future. The Benchmark partners practiced venture capital the way that traditionalists loved, intelligently assessing startups, empathizing with founders, and serving as enlightened counselors. Son stood for a less elegant but still formidable approach. He shot from the hip, seemed indifferent to risk, and delegated the detailed work of monitoring companies to others.[68] Yet while Benchmark deployed capital more carefully, it generated less wealth, and even though Son's portfolio collapsed spectacularly when the tech bubble burst in 2000, the setback proved temporary.[69] Moreover, Son's methods had a way of forcing others to follow. As Moritz realized, you had to match Son's techniques or he would pull a Corleone on you.

Even the Benchmark partners could feel the pull of Son's example. After raising three deliberately small funds—the biggest had weighed in at $175 million—the partners found themselves contemplating a radical break with their tradition.

In the summer of 1999, Dave Beirne broached the issue at a partners' meeting. "I think we should raise a billion dollars. Seriously."

Rachleff sympathized. "SoftBank is raising more money," he noted. "If we're not prepared to fight, we're going to get our clocks cleaned."

"You don't go on the lacrosse field without a fuckin' stick," Beirne carried on. "You'll get killed."

Kagle wasn't sure. A big fund could cause trouble: if you gave founders too much money, they would lose focus, attempt too many things, and the resources would be wasted. "We might overcapitalize companies," he said. "I don't want to follow everyone else into big-check-dom."

"We need money to play," reiterated Rachleff. SoftBank and the bull market more generally were pushing up the quantity of capital that startups expected to raise. "Every one of my telecom deals is ten million. Table stakes."[70]

Dunlevie pointed out that if the price of individual deals went up, a small fund would be able to afford positions in just a handful of companies.

The loss of diversification would be dangerous. He leaned in favor of a billion-dollar fund because even though "we know size doesn't matter, there are some who will regard it as leadership."[71]

In the end, Benchmark went ahead and raised $1 billion for its 1999 fund, more than ten times as much as it had accepted for its first fund four years earlier. The partnership also experimented unsuccessfully with offices in London and Israel, and attempted a Son-style pre-IPO bet of $19 million on an e-tailer called 1-800-Flowers.com, quickly losing money.[72] But while Benchmark could close its foreign satellites and give up on pre-IPO wagers, the dilemma about sizing persisted. In the years that followed, Benchmark repeatedly found that reckless later-stage investors seized effective control of its portfolio companies by stumping up tens of millions of dollars. Unable to muster equivalent sums, Benchmark lacked the muscle to protect startups from the hubris that came with so much capital. In two notorious cases—the ride-hailing company Uber and the office-rental giant WeWork—Benchmark lived through the painful spectacle of its wards going off the rails.[73] Such was the limitation of the cottage-industry model.

Chapter Eight

MONEY FOR GOOGLE, KIND OF FOR NOTHING

One day in August 1998, two Stanford PhD students sat on a porch in Palo Alto. They were looking to raise money for a new way to navigate the web: it felt like a repeat of Yahoo three years earlier. But whereas Yahoo's founders had raised $1 million from Sequoia, surrendering a third of their company in the process, what happened next could not have been more different.

The two PhD students were named Sergey Brin and Larry Page, and their fledgling company was called Google. It was, on the face of it, an unpromising venture: there were already seventeen other firms offering internet search services. But, not suffering from humility, Brin and Page were confident that their technology would blow others away. Hence their presence on that porch, where they awaited a storied Valley engineer called Andy Bechtolsheim.

Presently, Bechtolsheim arrived in a silver Porsche, a handsome, floppy-haired presence with a light German accent. After Brin and Page demonstrated their search engine, Bechtolsheim grew keenly interested. Google generated search results that were far more relevant than those of its rivals, thanks to a system for ranking websites according to how many other sites had linked to them. Bechtolsheim immediately saw the analogy with academia, where reputation was based on numbers of citations.[1]

Bechtolsheim was not a venture capitalist, but he had created two companies and had money to play with. Back in 1982, he had co-founded the hugely successful Sun Microsystems. His next venture, a networking company called Granite Systems in which Bechtolsheim himself was the principal shareholder, had been snapped up by Cisco for $220 million. Bechtolsheim liked to use his riches to back fellow engineers. A few hundred grand sprayed here or there would not affect his bank balance.

One time in the late 1980s, an early internet entrepreneur named John Little had swung by Bechtolsheim's office. Little was a fellow computer scientist. The two men knew each other from Sun Microsystems beer bashes.

How's it going? Bechtolsheim asked.

Not so great, Little responded. The co-founder of his startup was quitting, and it was going to take some cash to buy him out. Little didn't have the money.

How much do you need? Bechtolsheim prompted.

"I don't know," Little said. "Maybe $90,000."

Bechtolsheim got out a checkbook and signed over $90,000. He did it so fast that Little hardly realized what was happening. "I did not know what he was going to do when he pulled the checkbook out. I had never been in a situation when somebody had given me money like that, kind of for nothing," Little said later. Bechtolsheim gave no indication of what share of Little's company he wanted for his money. "Andy did not care too much," Little recalled. "Afterwards, maybe once a year, we would run into each other at a barbecue or something, and one of us would say to the other, we should do the paperwork on that investment. But we were always busy."[2]

Eventually, in 1996, Little raised almost $6 million from a professional venture capitalist, Arthur Patterson of Accel, and the question of who owned what had to be formalized. Bechtolsheim's impulsive act of generosity got him 1 percent of Little's company. During the internet boom the company, Portal Software, did so astoundingly well that Bechtolsheim probably made more on his $90,000 check than he had done by co-founding Sun Microsystems.[3]

Now, sitting on that porch in Palo Alto and chatting with the Google founders, Bechtolsheim rolled out the same tactic. He could see the Googlers had no business plan: they had ruled out banner ads or pop-up ads, the standard ways in which websites earned money. But having watched Brin and Page demonstrate their search engine, he understood they had a software edge; besides, he kind of liked them. They were curious, stubborn, self-possessed—not so very different from how Bechtolsheim himself had been as a young computer scientist at Stanford.

Bechtolsheim ran to his Porsche and returned carrying something. "We could discuss a number of issues. Why don't I just write you a check?" he said ebulliently.[4] With that, he presented Brin and Page with $100,000, payable to "Google Inc."[5]

Brin and Page explained that Google hadn't been incorporated yet. It didn't have a bank account to deposit the check into.[6]

"Well when you do, stick it in there," Bechtolsheim said cheerfully.[7] Then he disappeared in his Porsche without saying what share of Google he imagined he had bought. "I was so excited I just wanted to be part of it," he said later.[8]

⬧

Bechtolsheim's impromptu investment signaled the coming of a new kind of technology finance, as significant as Masayoshi Son's $100 million check two years earlier. Before the mid-1990s, semiretired technology executives had sometimes turned their hands to investing: Mike Markkula had backed and shepherded the fledgling Apple; Mitch Kapor had financed and counseled GO and UUNET.[9] But it took the booming tech market of the middle and late 1990s to turn this "angel investing" into a serious force. Thanks to the IPO bonanza, multimillionaires sprouted all around the Valley, and angel investing became the new elite pastime, like cosmetic surgery in Hollywood. In 1998, the year that Bechtolsheim backed Google, a prolific angel named Ron Conway went so far as to raise a $30 million fund to amplify his personal investing, and the "institutional angel," or "super angel," became the newest cylinder in the Valley's startup engine.[10] All of a sudden company founders had an alternative to traditional VCs, much as Son's growth-capital checks offered a partial alternative to going public.[11] To raise a first round of capital, aspiring entrepreneurs just needed a few introductions to established ones. Bechtolsheim's extraordinary investment style was becoming almost ordinary.

Brin and Page were particularly adept at working this new system. They began by courting an Indian-born technology executive named Ram Shriram who would soon strike it rich with the sale of his startup to Amazon. At first Shriram provided introductions to established search companies that might buy Google's technology. Then, when no decent offer materialized, Shriram offered to back the two grad students if they could find other angels to come in with him. Pretty soon, Brin and Page recruited Bechtolsheim and his co-founder at Granite Systems, a Stanford professor named David Cheriton. A few months later, Amazon's founder, Jeff Bezos, visited the Bay Area for a camping trip and met Brin and Page at Shriram's house. After that, he wanted in. "I just fell in love with Larry and Sergey," he said later.[12]

By the end of 1998, Brin and Page had raised a bit over $1 million from the four angels—more than Yahoo had raised from Sequoia.[13] But they had done so without speaking with a venture capitalist, without giving away more than a tenth of their equity, and without signing up for the performance targets and oversight on which venture capitalists insisted.[14] Angel investors like Bezos and Bechtolsheim were too focused on their own companies to worry about how Brin and Page were getting on. And so, in John Little's formulation, the Google guys were able to raise "money like that, kind of for nothing." The old idea of liberation capital had been taken to the next level. Never in the history of human endeavor had young inventors been so privileged.

◆

While the Googlers avoided the VCs, the venture business was booming. In 1998 venture capitalists raised the record sum of $30 billion, triple the commitments they received in 1995, the year that Son met Yahoo. In 1999, the boom turned wild: venture partnerships filled their war chests with $56 billion.[15] The number of venture partnerships in the United States hit 750, up from 400 a decade earlier.[16] The Valley seemed to hum with the adrenaline of fortunes being made, not least by venture capitalists.

To traditional venture investors, the boom was disconcerting. "It was evident that we were in a bubble," an old-timer recalled. "All of the things you think about as creating fundamental value were getting punished. And all of the things you think about as bad behavior were being rewarded." The trend that had started with Yahoo—the financing of early movers because of their momentum—could obviously be pushed too far: in many cases, the finance itself was creating the momentum, and many dot-coms would never actually earn profits. But however high the market spiraled, the boom was impossible for the old hands to resist. Unlike hedge funds, which can bet against a bubble by using derivatives or other tricks, venture capitalists can only bet on values going up. They have one simple business, which is to buy equity in startups, and they have no choice but to pay the going price for it. Moreover, this mechanical difference between hedge funds and venture capital is compounded by a psychological one. Hedge funders tend by nature to be self-contained. When the trader Louis Bacon bought a private island in the 1990s, people joked that it made no difference: he was already an Oz-like figure hidden behind a bank of screens, as insular as he could be. But venture capitalists inhabit the opposite extreme. They maintain offices near each other. They sit on startup boards with each other. They negotiate follow-on financings with each other. Geographically and mentally, they cluster. Because they are first and foremost networkers, it is costly for venture capitalists to even speak of a bubble. An investor who publicly questions a mania is spoiling the party for others.

In ordinary times, the bubbly bias of the venture crowd is balanced by the stock market. VCs know that when startups seek to go public, they will face a tougher audience, less willing to pay up for dreams, freer to denounce a company or bet that its stock will tumble. This prospect disciplines venture behavior: it deters VCs from bidding private valuations up so high that public exits won't be profitable. But in the late 1990s, the stock market stopped performing this disciplinary function. A new breed of amateur trader loaded up on internet stocks, goaded on by the financial hype on TV channels such as CNBC, which tripled its viewership during the second half of the 1990s. Sophisticated hedge funders who bet against the mania suffered excruciating losses until they flipped position, whereupon they added to the market's upward momentum.[17] Seeking to explain the public's bottomless appetite for tech stocks, Wall Streeters pointed to the spread of power-law thinking. "There has been a fundamental shift in American capitalism," marveled Joseph Perella, the chief investment banker at Morgan Stanley. "Basically, the public is saying, 'I want to own every one of these companies. If I'm wrong on nineteen and the twentieth one is Yahoo it doesn't matter.'"[18]

Once the stock market embraced the logic of the power law, nothing checked the venture capitalists. Private financing deals were done at ever higher valuations, and startups raised capital in ever greater quantities. In 1997 an online grocer called Webvan landed $7 million from Benchmark and Sequoia, even though it was less a company than a concept. In 1998, Webvan raised a further $35 million, this time from SoftBank, to finance the building of its first distribution center. In 1999, with the distribution center still barely up and running, investors were persuaded to part with an astonishing $348 million. By this point, venture speculators had assigned Webvan a paper value of more than $4 billion, even though it was losing money. In sum, Webvan looked like GO on steroids, a fantastical venture-capital ego trip. And yet, given the euphoric stock market, the VCs were not the only culprits in this tale. Webvan staged a successful IPO in the fall of 1999, and its value shot up to $11 billion. With public-market investors prepared to value companies this way, the venture-capital frenzy was at least partly rational.

Given the boom in venture finance, Google was almost bound to come to it for money. The $1 million from the angel investors would last only a few months, especially because Brin and Page were more interested in building an audience than in generating income. In early 1999, Ram Shriram, the most engaged of the angels, made so bold as to tell the Googlers that they needed a clear story about how they'd eventually earn profits. It was time to write a business plan.

"What's a business plan?" Brin responded.[19]

Shriram persevered, assigning the job of drafting a plan to a Stanford student who kept dropping by the Google office. Then he reached into his network and produced a grown-up executive willing to work for the company.[20] Shriram was serving the same role that Mitch Kapor had played in preparing UUNET to pitch investors.

In May 1999, the Googlers duly set out to meet the venture capitalists. But, having raised money on such favorable terms from the angels, Brin and Page were determined to maintain the upper hand in the next round of financing. Given the flush state of the venture funds, it was a good time to test their limits. Capital, being plentiful, would logically be cheap. A pair of unusually confident founders had an opportunity to show how far the capitalists could be forced into concessions.

The first task was to choose the most desirable investors. Sequoia was a natural candidate; after all, it had backed Yahoo. But Page and Brin were also eager to meet John Doerr, the fizzing coil of energy at Kleiner Perkins. His setback with GO now firmly behind him, Doerr had emerged as the internet's most impassioned promoter, and nobody was more effective than he was at attracting talent to portfolio companies. After investing in Netscape, Doerr had somehow managed to sign up an established telephony executive—a sober southerner named Jim Barksdale—to join this flighty, fledgling firm. "Bark was just infatuated with the whole aura of John Doerr," an insider explained later.[21] Doerr had then turned Netscape into a springboard for a series of ventures aimed at building out the web: there was @Home, his audacious project to deliver high-speed internet connections over cable broadband; drugstore.com, an attempt to sell pharmaceuticals online; and even a project to turn Martha Stewart, doyenne of domesticity, into an internet franchise. All over the Valley, entrepreneurs vied to join Team Doerr. "There's this notion that if you get John and Kleiner Perkins as an investor you can practically buy your Ferrari now," one admirer told *The New Yorker*.[22]

The greatest mark of Doerr's prowess was his investment in Amazon. In 1996, Doerr had snagged 13 percent of Bezos's startup for $8 million; by the spring of 1999, Amazon was a public company with a valuation of more than $20 billion. But what was most remarkable was the way that this had come about and what it said about Doerr's stature. Founded in 1994, Amazon was already going gangbusters by the time it sought venture funding.

Would-be investors were calling so often that the company joked about re-setting its voice mail: "If you're a customer, press 'one.' If you're a VC, press 'two.'"[23] General Atlantic, a respected technology investment house in New York, pursued Amazon especially assiduously, presenting Bezos with a for-mal term sheet. But far from chasing after Amazon, Doerr himself became the object of a chase: his reputation was such that Amazon came after him. At first, Doerr was too busy to notice; the pager and the cell phone on his belt buzzed constantly. Eventually, after a CEO at a Kleiner portfolio com-pany persuaded him to have dinner with Amazon's marketing chief, the penny dropped: Doerr flew to Seattle, bonded instantly with Jeff Bezos, and stole the deal from under General Atlantic's nose, even while offering a less generous valuation. Asked why he had accepted the lower bid, Bezos ex-plained, "Kleiner and John are the gravitational center of a huge piece of the Internet world. Being with them is like being on prime real estate."[24]

Given Doerr's investment in Amazon, and Bezos's investment in Google, it was only a matter of time before Brin and Page landed a meeting with Kleiner's celebrity rainmaker. They took this coup almost for granted. Other entrepreneurs, visualizing their Ferraris, might have stayed up all night pre-paring their pitch decks. But the Googlers did not strain themselves too hard: they showed up to see Doerr with a PowerPoint presentation consist-ing of just seventeen slides, three of which displayed cartoons and only two of which had actual numbers.[25] Yet what they lacked in presentational for-mality they made up for in sheer poise. Primed by Shriram, they had boiled their mission statement down to just eight words: "We deliver the world's information in one click."

Doerr loved nothing more than a bold, high-concept presentation. He was an engineer by background; he was a dreamer by vocation. Besides, Google had used the time afforded by the angel financing to develop trac-tion: it was now handling half a million searches daily. Doerr privately cal-culated that if Google muscled its way into the top tier of search firms, it could attain a market capitalization of as much as $1 billion.

Seeking to gauge the founders' ambition, Doerr asked, "How big do you think this could be?"

"Ten billion," Page answered.

"You mean market cap, right?"

"No, I don't mean market cap. I mean revenue," Page declared confidently. He pulled out a laptop and demonstrated how much faster and more relevant Google's search results were compared with those of its rivals.

Doerr was flabbergasted and delighted. Revenue of $10 billion implied a market capitalization of at least $100 billion. This was fully one hundred times more than Doerr's estimate of Google's potential; it implied a company as big as Microsoft and much bigger than Amazon. Whether or not this goal was plausible, it certainly telegraphed audacity. Doerr seldom met entrepreneurs who dreamed bigger than he did.

As they courted Doerr, the Googlers went after their second quarry. They had recently met the "super angel" Ron Conway and proposed a deal: Conway could invest in Google if he helped get them to Sequoia. Conway had happily accepted. Even by the exalted standards of the Valley, he was a grand master of networking.

Conway was especially close to Doug Leone, the gruff partner who managed Sequoia together with Michael Moritz. Where Moritz was ferociously competitive and made enemies as well as friends, Leone was at heart a gregarious Italian.[26]

Leone took a call from Conway after lunch on a Friday. He had never heard of Google, but he dialed Brin and Page immediately. By 4:00 p.m. he was sitting in front of the founders, marveling as they demonstrated their search engine. The results from a Google search were by a large margin more useful than results from Yahoo.[27]

As soon as Leone got out of the meeting, he called Moritz and asked him to come over. Moritz showed up at 6:00 p.m., and the Googlers made their second Sequoia presentation. Although they didn't know it, they were pushing on an open door. Moritz had already heard good things about their technology from Jerry Yang, Yahoo's co-founder. Yahoo was thinking of using Google to power the search box on its website.[28]

By now, Moritz and Doerr were both hooked on the idea of investing in Google. But their logic was subtly distinct. In the unscientific world of venture, when two investors share an enthusiasm for the same deal, it's not necessarily for the same reasons.

For Doerr, an engineer who backed engineers, Google's technical edge was the main attraction. Plenty of skeptics argued that with eighteen rivals jostling for position, search would be a low-margin commodity business. But Doerr had enough faith in technological advance to believe that a late-comer with a better algorithm could stand out from its competitors. His partner, Vinod Khosla, explained the point this way: If you thought exist-ing search technology was 90 percent as good as the best possible version, then pushing performance up to 95 percent was not going to win you cus-tomers. But if you thought there was more headroom—that existing search technology represented only 20 percent of the potential—then Google might be three or four times as good as its rivals, in which case its margin of en-gineering excellence would attract a flood of users.[29] Khosla himself had made a fortune in the 1990s by investing in successive generations of inter-net routers, each radically better than the previous one. The lesson was that engineering products could improve more than non-engineers imagined.

For Moritz, the ex-journalist, the case for Google was different. Of course, he could see that Google's search engine was superior. But he did not quite imagine that the superiority would be transformative. This was partly because of his vision of the internet's future. Given his experience with Yahoo, and given the way the internet was developing in 1999, Moritz expected it would be dominated by brands.[30] Technical features such as search engines would exist as lowly plug-ins on popular websites that com-manded consumer loyalty. Already, *The Washington Post* was paying Google to power the search box on its home page, and Page and Brin would soon strike a similar deal with Netscape. The idea of a tie-up with Yahoo fitted this pattern: Google might have a solid future as the unassuming provider of search on Yahoo's popular portal.[31] Moritz's misapprehension stood as a testimony to the sheer unpredictability of technological advance. In 1999, the idea that Google would eclipse Yahoo, or that Amazon would eclipse every other e-commerce contender, was by no means obvious.

Having separately wooed Kleiner and Sequoia, Page and Brin consid-ered their options. Other venture partnerships such as Benchmark and Accel were offering a lower valuation. A New York bank was ready to pay a higher price, but Shriram counseled the founders to stick with West Coast venture firms that understood how to build companies.[32] That left the Googlers with a choice between Sequoia and Kleiner. Determined as ever to do things their own way, they resolved to go with both of them.

Bechtolsheim objected that there was "zero chance" of these proud firms agreeing to co-invest: they were used to leading deals, not splitting them. But Brin and Page were undeterred. In the go-go atmosphere of 1999, the impossible would be possible.

Using their angel investors as intermediaries, they let it be known that they would sell 12.5 percent of their equity to Kleiner and the same amount to Sequoia. If the VCs refused, Google would sell nothing to either of them. Kleiner and Sequoia huffed and puffed: neither Amazon nor Yahoo had treated them like this. But amid the euphoria of the bull market, it was evident that if they declined to come to terms, somebody else would provide Google with the capital it needed.

Sensing the strength of their negotiating hand, the Googlers stood firm, dispatching Conway to reiterate their ultimatum to Sequoia and telling Shriram to do the same with Kleiner.[33]

A few days later, Conway was sitting in a Starbucks parking lot when he got a call from Shriram.

"The fight is over," Shriram said. "They're both going to invest, and it's going to be fifty-fifty."

On June 7, 1999, the three parties signed a deal. For Doerr, the $12 million investment was the biggest bet of his career. "I have never paid more money for so little a stake in a startup," he said wryly.[34] Thanks to the emergence of angel investors, and thanks to the sheer amount of money that had flooded into the business, the balance of power between entrepreneurs and VCs had shifted.

◆

Whatever Shriram said, the fight between Google's founders and their investors was not actually over. The VCs had submitted to nearly all the Googlers' conditions, but they were determined that the company should have an outside chief executive. The status quo was almost comical: Page styled himself CEO and chief financial officer of Google; Brin had arrogated unto himself the titles of president and chairman. Their abundance of managerial designations was matched only by their lack of managerial experience. To build a company that rivaled Microsoft, they would need a seasoned chief executive.

At the time of the venture financing, Brin and Page had agreed that a new CEO should be hired at an unspecified time in the future.[35] A few months later, they informed Doerr, "We've changed our minds. You know, we actually think we can run the company between the two of us."[36] From 1973, when Sutter Hill invented the Qume formula, to the mid-1990s, when startups such as Yahoo and eBay embraced outside chief executives with open arms, it was almost a given that VCs would bring in a new leader. But now the Googlers cited the handful of successful founders who had retained management control—Michael Dell, Bill Gates, and their own angel investor Jeff Bezos. "What they didn't see were all the others who had failed. That wasn't in their data set," one Doerr lieutenant observed tartly.[37]

Moritz and Doerr took the rebellion badly. "If Larry and Sergey were given instructions by a divine presence, they would still have questions," Moritz sniped later.[38] In the course of one especially heated argument, the two VCs insisted that the Googlers were harming their company's prospects and that, if Page and Brin refused to make space for an outside CEO, they would pull their investment. "I rattled my saber loudly," Moritz said later.[39]

The venture capitalists' mood was not helped by the financial climate. In the spring of 2000, the long boom in tech stocks ended abruptly; go-go was gone, and over the next year bubbly companies like Webvan went bankrupt. Before, venture capitalists had spent their time arranging public offerings and tallying their winnings. Now, with the IPO window virtually closed, they found themselves closing down portfolio companies. Naturally, their performance took a dive. The median venture fund launched in 1996 or 1997 had achieved an annual return of more than 40 percent, trouncing the return on public stocks. In contrast, the median fund launched in 1999 or 2000 lagged the public market and actually lost money.[40] The normally unflappable Doug Leone recalls the shock. "I woke up one day in 2000, and everything had changed. I was on twelve boards. One company more troubled than the other. Oh my God, what do I do now?'"[41] Jim Swartz of Accel had similarly visceral memories of the collapse. "For the first time in my career, I had to walk into a board meeting and say, 'Look, guys, we got X kajillion dollars in the bank but this model is not going to work in the new world. Let's just liquidate the company.'"[42] "It was so depressing that it was hard to feel good even about the new deals that got pitched to you," another VC remembered.[43]

The bust hit Doerr as hard as anyone. His Martha Stewart venture lost 60 percent of its value in the first four months of 2000. His cable company, @Home, had boasted a market capitalization of $35 billion in early 1999; in 2001 it filed for bankruptcy. Even Amazon's stock price collapsed, and a prominent analyst at the Wall Street firm Lehman Brothers warned it might default to bondholders. Doerr phoned Lehman's boss, Dick Fuld, insisted that the analyst's numbers were wrong, and managed to get Lehman's next critical broadside delayed and diluted. "Dick appreciated the call," Doerr said later.[44]

Battling these tides, Doerr channeled his irritation with the Googlers into a novel strategy. In the summer of 2000, he made Brin and Page an offer that appealed to their vanity. He and Moritz would introduce the Googlers to celebrated founders they admired, then leave it up to them to discuss the value of a seasoned outside manager. If Brin and Page refused to listen to their VC backers about the need for imported talent, maybe they would listen to fellow entrepreneurs, Doerr hoped. Recognizing that power had shifted in favor of company founders, he was mimicking the light-touch manner of angel investors.

"If you think we should do a search, we will," Doerr told Brin and Page, describing what might happen after the two guys had talked to other founders.

"And if you don't want to, then I'll make a decision about that," Doerr added.[45]

Over the next weeks, Brin and Page duly consulted a string of Valley oracles: Apple's Steve Jobs; Intel's Andy Grove; the Sun Microsystems CEO, Scott McNealy; and of course Jeff Bezos of Amazon.[46] Doerr followed up discreetly after each meeting, asking the senior statesmen what they

thought of the Googlers and their determination to run their company un-
aided. "Hey, some people just want to paddle across the Atlantic Ocean in
a rubber raft," Doerr recalled Bezos saying. "That's fine for them. The question is whether you want to put up with it."[47]

At the end of the summer, Brin and Page paddled their way back to
Doerr. "This may surprise you," they told him, "but we agree with you."[48]
They now wanted an outside chief executive, and they even had identified
their man. There was one person, and one alone, who met their standards.

"We like Steve Jobs!" Brin and Page reported.[49]

Jobs not being available, Doerr hustled for an alternative. He sometimes described himself as a "glorified recruiter." "We're not investing in
business plans, we're not investing in discounted cash flows, it's the people," he insisted, revealing how the essence of the venture craft remained
unchanged since the days of Arthur Rock and Tommy Davis.[50] Doerr duly
worked his network to identify an executive with a computer science background, but his first choice refused to see a future in the umpteenth search
engine. Then, in October 2000, Doerr fastened on another computer scientist turned manager. His name was Eric Schmidt, and he was running a
software company called Novell.[51]

Spotting Schmidt at a political fundraiser at the home of Cisco's CEO,
Doerr went up to speak with him. The two had been friendly since the 1980s,
when they had both been involved with Sun Microsystems. Schmidt had
risen through the ranks at Sun and had shown a talent for humoring bois-
terous engineers. One year his team had disassembled a Volkswagen Bee-
tle and rebuilt it, fully functioning, in his office. A video shows a surprised
young Schmidt enjoying the prank as much as anyone.[52]

Doerr knew that Schmidt was angling to sell Novell and would soon be
ready for a new job.[53] Summoning his most urgent tone, he told Schmidt
that his next move should be to Google.

"I can't imagine that Google would be worth that much," Schmidt answered dismissively. "Nobody really gives a shit about search," he added.

"I think you should have a talk with Larry and Sergey," Doerr reiterated. Google was "a little jewel that needs help in scaling."[54]

Schmidt trusted Doerr too much to brush off his entreaties. "John knew me well. He knew what I cared about. And if someone I trusted asked me to do something, I would do it," he said later.[55]

Schmidt duly visited Google, which was coincidentally housed in Sun's old building. Schmidt thought he recognized the same lava lamps that had been there in the 1980s. He noticed that his bio was stuck up on the wall. "Really odd," he told himself.

Brin and Page set about grilling Schmidt on his performance at Novell. The firm's efforts to speed up internet response times using a method called proxy caches were mistaken, according to the Googlers. For the next hour and a half, Schmidt engaged in what he later recalled as a thoroughly stimulating argument; he was at heart an intellectual, an engineer's engineer, not just a business guy determined to hit commercial targets.[56] But however much Schmidt enjoyed the sparring, the warning was obvious. An incoming CEO would have his work cut out to manage these young guys, especially because revenues at their outfit remained an afterthought.[57] Because Brin and Page had sold the venture capitalists only a quarter of their shares, they retained ultimate control. If they hired a CEO and then regretted it, they would have the power to fire him.

Schmidt felt simultaneously excited about the prospect of joining Google and anxious about entrusting his future to two mercurial twenty-somethings. In the end, the balance was tipped by the trusted guardians of the Valley's networks. "I had the surety that the venture guys would be kind to me if Larry and Sergey bounced me out," Schmidt said.[58] If Google did not work out, Doerr and Moritz would slot him into an equally good job elsewhere. With the venture capitalists' safety net stretched out beneath him, Schmidt took the leap. At last, Google had the experienced direction it needed to become a global company.

<hr />

With the recruitment of Schmidt in 2001, the Googlers taught the venture-capital tribe the second of three lessons. The first had concerned the pricing of the deal: as Doerr had said, it was the most Kleiner had ever paid for a modest share in a startup. The second concerned the revolt against the Qume model: Schmidt was hired only after a long period of foot-dragging, and even then he functioned as just one voice in the triumvirate that led the company. The third lesson came in 2004, as Google prepared to go public. Defying Valley tradition, and ignoring protests from Doerr and Moritz, Brin and Page insisted on maintaining their power even after they sold shares to the public. Following a precedent set mainly by family-owned media firms, they decreed that Google would issue two classes of shares. The first, to be held by the founders and the early investors, conferred ten votes on big company decisions. The second, to be held by outside stock market investors, conferred only one vote. Collectively, outside investors would receive shares bestowing only a fifth of all votes. Insiders, chief among them Brin and Page, would retain control over the company.[59]

When the Googlers proposed this share structure, Doerr and Moritz raised two objections. First, outside investors might recoil at the prospect of second-class citizenship. Consequently, some might refuse to buy the stock, resulting in a lower share price and a less profitable VC exit. Second, enshrining founder control indefinitely seemed ill-advised. Brin and Page were young; they were likely to change; and so indeed was their company. As Google grew, it would be harder to manage. What if the founders decided to enjoy their wealth on Caribbean islands?[60]

In response, the Googlers made two counterarguments. The first stressed Google's public mission. Newspaper groups such as the Washington Post Company and the New York Times Company believed that journalists could report honestly on events only if shielded from profit-hungry public shareholders. An enlightened newspaper family, imbued with a sense of civic duty, would pursue the truth without fear or favor. Public shareholders, whose reputations were not bound up with the quality of the reporting, were more likely to flinch at the prospect of alienating powerful governments or advertisers. Brin and Page saw Google in a similar light. Their IPO prospectus invoked the company's "responsibility to the world"—the responsibility to deliver free, abundant, and unbiased information. A dozen years later, when tech behemoths were denounced for hoarding customer data and blurring the distinction between real and fake news, the alleged link between founder empowerment and the common good would come to seem dubious. But in 2004, the Googlers insisted that young founders would be better guardians of the public interest than public shareholders. Shareholder democracy would harm political democracy.

The Googlers' second counterargument stressed long-term profits. Echoing a familiar critique of shareholder capitalism, they asserted that stock market investors were too shortsighted to back managers who compromised today's profits to invest in tomorrow's expansion. By implication, stock market investors should be disenfranchised for their own sakes: their interests would be best served if their influence was minimized. Of course, the analogous argument about political democracy—that the masses should be denied votes for their own good—would be met with derision. Nor is it obvious that stock market investors are incapable of understanding their own long-term interests; to the contrary, they frequently bid up the price of investment-intensive companies such as Amazon, Netflix, and Tesla precisely because they do value the future.[61] But the Googlers invoked the tendentious thesis of stock market short-termism with gusto. Their IPO message to prospective investors defiantly declared, "We will not shy away from high-risk, high-reward projects because of short-term earnings pressure."[62]

On August 19, 2004, Google duly went public. Much of the attention focused on the mechanism used to allocate the shares: in another of their revolts against the financial establishment, the Googlers had refused to pay investment bankers their traditional fee for placing stock, preferring instead to sell shares via an auction. But whereas Google's experimental pricing mechanism did not become the model for later Valley IPOs, the dual-class, ten-votes-versus-one share structure was copied by companies such as Facebook.[63] Google's extraordinary growth after its flotation—over the next three years, the stock price quintupled—made the VCs' objections to the dual-class structure look irrelevant. Evidently, investors were only too delighted to buy so-called second-class stock. And the idea that the founders enjoyed too much power was belied by the success with which they steered the company.

As the most celebrated Valley star of the era, Google had a profound influence on the way startups raised money. Other entrepreneurs increasingly turned to angels for their early capital. They forced Series A investors to pay through the nose. They rejected the Qume model in favor of running their own show. They dispensed with shareholder democracy. In sum, entrepreneurs used every trick at their disposal to secure more of the wealth and—crucially—power. Venture capital confronted a new challenge.

In the first years of the twenty-first century, Google's significance was not yet obvious. The venture community was fixated instead on the ruin of its investment performance. As of 2003, Sequoia was struggling to prop up a venture fund that had lost around 50 percent of its value; the partners felt honor-bound to plow their fees back into the pot to eke out a return of 1.3x.[64] The equivalent Kleiner Perkins fund performed even worse, never making it into the black. Masayoshi Son, who had briefly become the richest person in the world, lost more than 90 percent of his fortune. Having loaded up with capital during the boom years, many venture partnerships saw no way of deploying the money. Some returned uninvested dollars to outside partners, others stopped raising fresh funds, and the few that tried to raise money were rebuffed by their backers.[65] At the peak in 2000, new capital commitments to VC firms had hit $104 billion. By 2002, they were down to around $9 billion.[66]

Without the fillip of abundant venture capital, entrepreneurship itself appeared to shrivel. "Money like that, kind of for nothing," was replaced by a freeze on risky new projects. Startups became less common than shutdowns, and few had the stomach to slog away at a young firm, working every waking hour with almost no prospect of a financial payout. Silicon Valley lost 200,000 jobs between 2001 and early 2004; highway billboards were bereft of ads, and physics PhDs were waiting tables. To be in the Valley was to realize that "only the cockroaches survive, and you're one of the cockroaches," as one entrepreneur put it.[67]

Google's public offering in the summer of 2004 marked the end of this dark period. It proved that software companies could flourish even against the background of the dot-com bust. It showed that digital progress could continue at a dazzling pace, even as the rest of the country was reeling from the shock of the 2001 terrorist attacks and an accompanying recession.

Around the time of Google's stock market debut, another software star called Salesforce went public, and in 2005 the internet-phone startup Skype made its venture backers rich when eBay bought it for $3.1 billion. But as animal spirits roared back to life, the venture industry woke up to the echoes and extensions of the Brin-Page challenge. Young entrepreneurs no longer deferred to experienced investors. In fact, they often regarded them contemptuously.

The change in mood was crystallized by Paul Graham, a self-described hacker who became an influential guru among young startup founders. In 1995, together with a fellow Harvard grad student, Graham had founded a software company called Viaweb, selling it in 1998 to Yahoo for $45 million worth of stock: it was a classic hacker-makes-good story. Then Graham had turned his hand to writing, expounding on everything from the virtues of the programming language Lisp, to popularity in high school, to the challenges of entrepreneurship. His essays, which celebrated coders and disparaged business types, appeared first on his blog and then, in 2004, as a book. The fact that Graham hailed from Cambridge, Massachusetts, underscored the significance of his teachings. The rebelliousness of the Google founders was part of a nationwide phenomenon.

Graham's first advice to younger hackers was to be wary of venture capitalists. "Spend as little as you can, because every dollar of the investor's money you get will be taken out of your ass," he told his readers. At Graham's own company, one of the angel investors had been a fearsome metals trader who "seemed like the kind of guy who would wake up in the morning and eat rocks for breakfast." When Graham's startup had hit a bump, another of his investors had tried to seize his equity. As a result of such experiences, Graham had figured out how to stand up to rich guys. "You're doing them a favor by letting them invest," Graham told his disciples. Thanks to the Brin-Page example, the moneybags would always be thinking, "Are these guys the next Google?"[68]

Graham also echoed the Googlers' opinion of seasoned executives. "People who are mature and experienced, with a business background, may be overrated," he declared flatly. "We used to call these guys 'newscasters,'" he went on; "they had neat hair and spoke in deep, confident voices, and

generally didn't know much more than they read on the teleprompter."
When he was running his startup, Graham had resisted the rock eater's
pressure to bring in an experienced CEO, instead hiring a humbler manager
who was happy for hackers to control the company. "What I discovered was
that business was no great mystery," Graham wrote. "Build something users
love, and spend less than you make. How hard is that?" he demanded.

Perhaps most significantly, Graham put his finger on the way that software was changing the venture business. Like Yahoo, eBay, and indeed Graham's own Viaweb, Google signaled an important shift. With the coming of
the internet, the hottest kind of company produced little more than code: it
had no need for large amounts of capital with which to build manufacturing operations. Meanwhile, the open-source movement made chunks of
software available for free, and the internet itself slashed the cost of marketing and distributing new products.[69] For all these reasons, the new generation of startups required relatively little cash, but venture capitalists
were out of step with this development.[70] Thanks to the bubble of the late
1990s, they had grown used to managing big funds and collecting correspondingly big fees. As a result, they force-fed startups with more capital
than was good for them, like farmers stuffing geese to make foie gras.

The way Graham saw things, force-feeding by VCs created at least
three problems. First, big investments meant big valuations for startups,
which narrowed the odds of a profitable exit. Many founders might be
happy to sell their company for, say, $15 million, but VCs who had already
marked up the valuation to $7 million or $8 million would not be satisfied
with a mere 2x multiple. Second, big investments meant that VCs took "ag-
onizingly long to make up their minds," and their dithering distracted
founders from their highest calling, which was to write code and create
products. Finally, big investments meant that nervous VCs were quick to
eliminate the wondrous and weird features of startups. They installed hu-
morless MBAs to oversee quirky coders, much as the Bolsheviks foisted political commissars on Red Army units.

Sweeping these criticisms together, Graham propounded what he
called "a unified theory of VC suckage." "Add up all the evidence of VCs' behavior and the resulting personality is not attractive," he concluded. "In

fact, it's the classic villain: alternatively cowardly, greedy, sneaky, and over-bearing."[71] But, Graham continued, the villains were about to be humbled. "When startups need less money, investors have less power.... The VCs will have to be dragged kicking and screaming down this road, but like many things people have to be dragged kicking and screaming toward, it may actually be good for them."[72]

Graham's prediction proved more prescient than even he imagined. The youth revolt among software founders—heralded by the Googlers, articulated by Graham—would soon test venture investors in new ways. And, much to his own surprise, Graham himself would play a star role in that testing.

Chapter Nine

PETER THIEL, Y COMBINATOR, AND THE VALLEY'S YOUTH REVOLT

Toward the end of 2004, Sequoia's investment team assembled for an intriguing meeting. Roelof Botha, a thirty-one-year-old partner, had arranged for a visit from an even younger entrepreneur, a Harvard sophomore named Mark Zuckerberg. These days, Sequoia realized, startup founders could be *very* young; this Zuckerberg was only twenty. In the new era of software ventures, entrepreneurs just needed a mastery of code, an idea for a product, and a maniacal focus.

The meeting was set for 8:00 a.m. At 8:05 a.m., Zuckerberg had not shown up. Such were the hazards that VCs faced when wealth creators were practically adolescents. Botha got on the phone to check that the guest of honor was still coming.

Presently, Zuckerberg and his buddy Andrew McCollum appeared at the Sequoia headquarters. They were not merely late. They were dressed in pajama bottoms and T-shirts.

Don Valentine, by now retired, had come into the office that day and spied the boys in the lobby. Remembering the 1970s, when he had dealt with wayward characters such as Nolan Bushnell of Atari, Valentine got the message. The pajamas were a provocation, a challenge. To have a chance of investing in Zuckerberg's company, Sequoia would have to do the 2004 equivalent of what Valentine had done with Bushnell. Stay calm. Strip off. Get into the hot tub.

Valentine hurried to the boardroom to prepare his colleagues for the visual shock. "Do not notice what he's wearing. It's a test. Don't ask him why he's wearing pajamas," he barked fiercely. Then he made himself scarce, knowing that a septuagenarian retiree was not going to lubricate the conversation.[1]

Arriving at the conference room, Zuckerberg and McCollum claimed to have overslept—hence the pajamas. The message was: "Sequoia? Who cares?" A meeting with this celebrated firm was no reason to set an alarm clock.

Not everyone believed the oversleeping story. Zuckerberg appeared fresh from a shower; his hair had not dried yet.[2] But the alternative explanation for the late arrival was hardly more encouraging. Zuckerberg had risen, washed, and then *decided* to dress up in pajamas and show up insolently late. A deliberate snub was worse than an unintended one.

Zuckerberg sat down at the Sequoia conference table and produced a slide deck. His presentation made no mention of Thefacebook, his social-networking website that was spreading like wildfire on college campuses. Instead, Zuckerberg pitched an unproven file-sharing idea called Wirehog. Accustomed to having the pick of Valley deals, Sequoia would have to listen to a spiel about a side project.

The title of Zuckerberg's deck was even more insulting. "The Top Ten Reasons You Should Not Invest in Wirehog," it proclaimed mockingly.

"The Number 10 reason not to invest in Wirehog: We have no revenue," the deck began.

"Number 9: We will probably get sued by the music industry."

A bit later, "Number 3: We showed up at your office late in our pajamas."

"Number 2: Because Sean Parker is involved."

"Number 1: We're only here because Roelof told us to come."

The Sequoia partners were used to working with tricky founders, and they aspired to be more disciplined than other venture outfits. Their pride and their prejudices were under control. Fortified by Valentine's heads-up, they were not going to rise to a pajama provocation. But however much they attempted to connect with Zuckerberg, the partners could not get through to him. The young visitor evidently admired Roelof Botha; later, he tried to recruit him to Facebook. But he would not allow himself to be charmed by the partnership at large, and especially not by its leader Michael Moritz. It was as though Zuckerberg were acting out some kind of sophomoric fantasy: interview for a job that you don't want, then relish the pleasure of ridiculing your elders.

Zuckerberg's pajama prank marked a watershed for venture capital. By the time of his stunt, in late 2004, Google had gone public, and other young entrepreneurs were playing hard to get, following the Brin-Page playbook. But it was one thing for entrepreneurs to drive tough bargains with VCs and then take their money anyway, as the Google founders had done. It was quite another to adopt Zuckerberg's stance. He genuinely did not want Sequoia to back him.

◆

In the immediate aftermath of the Wirehog pitch, the Sequoia partners did not quite grasp that Zuckerberg would never accept capital from them. But the penultimate slide—the one mentioning the name of Sean Parker—should have clued them into the reality. Notorious already at the age of twenty-five, Parker was a prime example of the Valley's increasingly rebellious youth culture. As a sixteen-year-old coder, he had been busted by the FBI for hacking into corporate and government computer networks and had been made to perform community service.[3] At twenty, Parker had fallen afoul of the law again, this time for his role in the music-piracy website Napster. Then, for his third act, Parker had launched a software startup called Plaxo. It was at once a triumph and a humiliation.

Plaxo automatically updated online address books. When you installed the program, it mined your contacts and emailed every one of them with a message: "Hi, I'm updating my address book. Please take a moment to update me with your latest contact info."[4] If recipients did so, the software would blitz every name in their address books with similar emails, and new users would be recruited. Within a short time, millions of email accounts had been hit with Plaxo pitches, and Parker had created a playbook for the viral online marketing that drove the growth of later tech behemoths.[5] Critics complained that Plaxo was the most insufferable service on the web: innocent bystanders were being spammed multiple times daily. But Parker was unabashed. "Plaxo is like the indie band that the public doesn't know but was really influential with other musicians," he boasted.[6]

By the start of 2004, Plaxo had attracted almost two million users. It had also accepted two rounds of investment led by Michael Moritz at Sequoia. But then, as usually happened with Parker, he snatched defeat from the jaws of victory. Sometimes he didn't show up for work.[7] When he did appear, he was not always constructive; "he's bringing a bunch of girls back to the office because he can show them he's a startup founder," one of his two co-founders grumbled.[8] In April 2004, Sequoia and the other Plaxo investors weighed in. To the relief of the co-founders, they fired Parker from his own company.[9]

After Sequoia wielded the ax, Parker embarked on his fourth act: he was nothing if not resilient. Hearing of Facebook's conquest of the campuses, he emailed Mark Zuckerberg with an offer to introduce him to investors. The pair had dinner in New York and found they had plenty in common: two ambitious young founders who had launched experiments in online social networking. When Zuckerberg moved out to Palo Alto in June 2004 with a few friends, the guys rented a ranch-style house a block from where Parker was living.

One evening, Parker met up with Zuckerberg and his Facebook buddies for dinner. Midway through the meal, he got a call from his lawyer. The board of Plaxo, which had already given him the boot, had now decided not to allow about half of his remaining shares to vest. As Parker flew into a rage, the Facebook team looked on in awe. "VCs sound scary," Zuckerberg thought to himself.[10]

Zuckerberg invited Parker to move in to his house. There was nothing apart from a mattress on Parker's floor, but he managed to hold on to a white BMW from richer times, which the Facebook guys now shared with him. They began to work together, too. Parker hired his Plaxo lawyer to help incorporate Facebook. He found an operations manager for the company. He managed relations with investors. Google wanted to buy shares. Benchmark Capital came calling.

By September 2004, Zuckerberg was referring to Parker as Facebook's president, and Parker was steering Zuckerberg away from conventional venture capitalists. He told Benchmark and Google to back off, preferring to take a leaf out of Google's own book; he wanted to raise capital from angels. His first port of call was an entrepreneur named Reid Hoffman, who had coached him through the Plaxo denouement. Hoffman declined to lead an investment in Facebook; he had himself founded a social network called LinkedIn, and there might be some rivalry. So Hoffman put Parker in touch with a Stanford friend named Peter Thiel, the co-founder of an online payments company called PayPal. Pretty soon, Thiel agreed to kick in $500,000 in exchange for 10.2 percent of the firm, with Hoffman providing a further $38,000.[11] A third social-networking entrepreneur named Mark Pincus also wrote a check for $38,000.

Somewhere below the venture capitalists' radar, a revolt was stirring. Like Google, Facebook had raised a round of angel financing. Unlike in the case of Google, the financiers were all entrepreneurs who focused on Facebook's business niche of online social networking.[12] They formed a tight-knit group, united by the shared experience of founding a particular kind of software startup in a particular moment. Recalling the atmosphere of this period, Mark Pincus remarked, "There were about six people that I knew who were interested in doing anything in the consumer internet, and we all kind of went to the same two coffee shops."[13]

Given the currents of the times, this new cluster of entrepreneur-angels was naturally skeptical of the traditional venture community. The Googlers had shown how to stand up to VCs, and Paul Graham had emphasized the tensions between ever larger venture funds and the limited need for capital at software startups. There was a generational factor at work, too. The extraordinary VC profits of the 1990s had encouraged senior venture partners to stay on, and because the boom made everyone look good, nobody was forced into retirement. As the average age of VC partners drifted up, the average age of company founders was falling: small wonder that a cultural gap was opening. Google's angel backers, notably Ram Shriram and Ron Conway, had served to connect the startup to venture investors. But the new cohort of entrepreneur-angels had no equivalent bonds with traditional VCs. They were more likely to spout some variation on Paul Graham's unified theory of VC suckage.

Partly by coincidence, and partly because success comes at a price, this general hostility to venture capital was concentrated on Sequoia. Sean Parker, as we have seen, had a particular resentment of Michael Moritz: Zuckerberg's strange pajama act was Parker's elaborate way of getting even after Plaxo. But Parker was not alone. Peter Thiel, the angel who had backed Zuckerberg, also held a grudge against Moritz.

◆

A lawyer, a philosopher, a hedge-fund trader, Thiel was in many ways a Silicon Valley maverick. Although he had two degrees from Stanford, and so fitted the standard Valley mold, he had studied neither engineering nor business. Instead, he had immersed himself in libertarian thinking, excelled at law school, and abandoned California for New York. There, he practiced securities law, traded derivatives at a bank, and grew disillusioned with the corporate treadmill. In 1995 he quit his trading job and returned to the West Coast, but not to get involved in the tech boom. Instead, he published a polemical book attacking campus multiculturalism and founded a small hedge fund, an almost countercultural act in Northern California. Fashioning himself as a younger, right-wing version of the philosopher-speculator George Soros, he combined high-stakes trading with ambitious abstractions. He contributed to the libertarian *Stanford Review*, which he had co-founded as a student.

In mid-1998, around the time when the Googlers met Bechtolsheim, Thiel went to Stanford to deliver a lecture on currency trading. The university auditorium offered a pleasant air-conditioned refuge from the raging heat of the high summer. At the end of his talk, an intense young figure with a faint eastern European accent introduced himself.

"Hey, I'm Max. I'm a friend of Luke Nosek's."

"Oh, you know Luke. Great."[14]

Thiel remembered the connection. Luke Nosek was a high-octane computer scientist who had arrived in the Valley after studying at the University of Illinois a bit after Marc Andreessen. This Max—his full name was
Max Levchin—was a product of the same computer science course. They
were all libertarians.

Levchin told Thiel he had an idea for a security company. It would be
based on his academic work in cryptography.

Thiel liked smart people, and Levchin's project intrigued him. In high
school, Thiel had been a math prodigy, coming in first in a California-wide
contest; he could appreciate the elegance of cryptographic puzzles. Besides, it was hard to be a financial risk-taker in Silicon Valley and *not* want
to speculate on startups. Thiel had already made an unsuccessful $100,000
bet on a company started by Levchin's friend Nosek.

"What are you doing tomorrow morning?" Thiel asked.

"I'm doing nothing," Levchin responded.

"Great, how about we meet for breakfast?"

The pair met at Hobee's, a breakfast joint near the Stanford campus.
Levchin misjudged the distance from his apartment and arrived, flustered
and panting, fifteen minutes late. Thiel had already drained a red, white,
and blue smoothie.

"You're here," Thiel said, sounding pleased. He ordered another
smoothie. Levchin chose egg whites.

Levchin stumbled through an explanation of his notional new company. Using the techniques of elliptical curve cryptography, he would turn
the PalmPilot, a popular handheld device of the late 1990s, into a digital
safe box for business information. Companies would purchase the encryption tool for employees because they wouldn't want their corporate secrets
to be stolen.

Thiel took a second and a half to respond. Though only thirty years old,
he had a grave, deliberate manner. "Well, I'd like to invest," he said finally.

Thiel promised Levchin $300,000—three times more than Bechtol-
sheim had risked on the Googlers. Then he told Levchin to find more capital elsewhere to launch his new company.

Even though this was the height of the late-1990s boom, finding the next financing proved difficult. Levchin had impeccable coding credentials; he was less persuasive on the business vision. Not everybody agreed that corporations would pay to encrypt data; what if they saw no need for digital security? To compensate for Levchin's weak suit, Thiel began to join in on his pitches, posing as the startup's business chief even though he was simultaneously engaged in hedge-fund trading. At the same time, Thiel helped Levchin to rethink his plan. If corporations had yet to wake up to the need for encryption, what about encrypting something else—something where the security need was obvious? Thiel suggested cash payments. If Levchin applied his coding wizardry to this field, people could safely email money to each other.

Having executed this pivot, Thiel and Levchin called their payments service PayPal and their company Confinity. They set out again to raise capital and met with a fresh round of rejections. Just about every brand-name venture shop said no, until eventually, in mid-1999, they managed to land $4.5 million from the new venture arm of the Finnish phone company Nokia. The snubs from the venture-capital A list left Thiel nursing a grudge. The fact that the PayPal service immediately took off raised further questions in his mind about the wisdom of the venture establishment.

If Thiel and Levchin had sailed onward to success, the history of Silicon Valley might have been different. Confinity would have staged a triumphant IPO, and its founders would have joined the ranks of Valley royalty, forgetting their earlier resentment of the VC princes. But at the end of 1999, Confinity found itself battling a rival called X.com, led by an entrepreneur named Elon Musk. The two companies were close equivalents in many ways. Both had around fifty employees and 300,000 users. Both were growing fast, and for a while both had offices in the same building on University Avenue in Palo Alto. But X.com had one distinguishing advantage. Whereas Confinity had secured capital from Nokia, a marginal Silicon Valley player, X.com had been anointed by Sequoia. None other than Michael Moritz had pumped $25 million into X.com, five times more than Confinity had raised. Moritz had also fortified X by recruiting a seasoned chief executive named Bill Harris.

Confinity and X.com went head to head, offering discounts to attract customers and accepting heavy losses. Pretty soon, both sides understood that they could either fight to the death or end the bloodshed by merging.

Moritz told his partners at Sequoia that merging was the better option. The two sides were like feuding families in a medieval Italian town, firing arrows across the street at each other. A merger would mean that Sequoia's share in the resulting company would shrink. But it would be worth it.[15]

Thiel and Levchin met Elon Musk and Bill Harris at Evvia, a Greek restaurant in Palo Alto, to discuss Moritz's proposal. Musk was all for bringing the two companies together, but because he had Sequoia at his back, he presumed he was by far the senior partner. X.com had more money in the bank, and having a brand-name venture investor ensured that it could raise further cash if needed. By some reckonings, Confinity had the better engineering team.[16] But in any drawn-out fight, it would be the first to run out of capital.[17]

Musk informed the Confinity founders over dinner that if a merger were to go ahead, X.com's shareholders should own fully 92 percent of the resulting company.[18]

That's great, Levchin growled to himself. *We'll see you at the barricades.*

Thiel was less hotheaded than Levchin. "We'll give it some thought," he told Musk and Harris evenly.

Over the next days, Thiel began to haggle. He pushed Musk until he agreed to cut the X shareholders' share of the merged firm from 92 percent to 60 percent. On these terms, Thiel was tempted to settle. He could get rich, get out, and get back to his hedge fund.

To Thiel's frustration, Levchin wasn't satisfied with this negotiating achievement. As the guy who led the coding team, Levchin wanted everyone to recognize that his creation was at least as good as his rival's. It was a matter of honor. "I just can't do this at sixty-forty," Levchin insisted.[19]

Thiel reluctantly agreed that the deal should be called off. Cooperation was out. Bloody competition would continue.

At this point in the story, Moritz stepped out from behind the curtain. Venture capitalists had managed the balance between competition and cooperation in the Valley since the 1980s, when Tom Perkins had presided, Solomon-like, over the dispute between two Kleiner Perkins portfolio companies, Ungermann-Bass and Silicon Compilers. In this instance, twenty years later, Moritz was determined that cooperation should prevail. Sequoia would be better off owning a small share of a grand-slam company than a large share of a failure, as he had put it to his partners.

On a weekend in February 2000, Moritz showed up at the Palo Alto block where X and Confinity had offices. Finding Levchin, Moritz sat down in front of him. He leaned forward, placed his elbows on his knees, threaded his fingers together, and rested his chin on top of them. Years later, Levchin vividly remembered that Moritz had not removed his theatrical dark coat. Their faces were barely a meter from each other.[20]

Moritz told Levchin, "If you go forward with this merger, I'll never sell a single share"—the implication being that a merged company would grow and grow forever. It was one of those classic VC call-to-greatness challenges. The senior venture statesman was asking the young entrepreneur, do you want to forge a major company that will be remembered years from now? Or do you lack the character to make your mark on the universe?

Levchin was suitably impressed. He dropped his objections to a sixty-forty deal, subordinating his coding pride to Moritz's grand vision. The path to a merger was now clear. The bloodshed would be over.

A day or so later, Levchin saw Musk. "This sixty-forty is too good for you," Musk taunted him. "Just so you know, you're getting a great deal. This merger of unequals is a steal for you guys."

Levchin withdrew with a pale smile, then called Thiel and vented. "It's off. I'm not doing this deal. This is insulting. I can't handle it," he told him. He marched out of the office and home to his apartment.

Bill Harris heard that Levchin had stormed out. Having been installed at X.com by Moritz and Sequoia, Harris was particularly sensitive to the shareholders' preference for cooperation over competition. He hurried out of the office and went to find Levchin.

Levchin had taken refuge in the laundry room of his apartment building. There were old washing machines made by a company called WEB, which Levchin found amusing. You had to feed the weary beasts with quarters.

Harris helped Levchin fold clothes and reconsider his decision. Ignore

Musk's sixty-forty insult, Harris pleaded; he and the X board had nothing but respect for Levchin. Indeed, to show it was sincere, X was prepared to sweeten its offer. It would do the deal at fifty-fifty.

At last, Levchin swallowed his objections and the merger went forward. Musk's gratuitous taunting of his adversary had cost him serious money.

◆

With the merger in place, Thiel might have felt a grudging gratitude to Moritz. The VC had pushed Levchin toward the merger that Thiel himself had favored, and he was surely behind the surprise fifty-fifty clincher that had made Thiel richer than the sixty-forty deal that he had himself negotiated. But what happened next buried any sense of gratitude. The merged company, which kept the name X.com, descended into an internal war. In the skirmishes that ensued, Thiel butted heads repeatedly with Moritz.

The first clash hinged on who would run the merged entity. Not without reason, Moritz regarded Thiel as a sharp intellect but not a manager. He was a hedge-fund trader, after all; he had no experience in scaling up a company.[21] As a result, Moritz saw to it that Bill Harris was picked to serve as CEO, and when Harris was removed, Musk was chosen to succeed him. Passed over for the top slot, Thiel quit his job as X.com's vice president for finance, though he remained a big shareholder and continued to serve part time as chairman.

A few months later, in September 2000, Musk went to Australia on a honeymoon. His senior lieutenants, many of whom came from the Confinity side of the merger, seized the opportunity for a rebellion. Musk had mismanaged the integration of the two companies, insisting that Levchin's software be rewritten and failing to clamp down on the fraud that plagued the PayPal service. And so, in an echo of the uprising that had removed Sandy Lerner from Cisco, the X.com vice presidents showed up at Sequoia's office and threatened to resign if Musk was not ousted.

"Palace coup!" Moritz said to himself. He remembered the Cisco saga well, and he knew how it had ended. No venture capitalist could protect a chief executive who had lost the backing of his team. "We have seen this before," he told himself silently.[22]

Moritz understood that Musk would have to go, but he wasn't ready to accept the rebels' second demand: that Thiel should take over. Contrary to Moritz's suspicions, Thiel evidently commanded the loyalty of his peers. He was more of a natural leader than he appeared to be.

Moritz was in no mood to reflect on this signal. He was in the middle of the fight to get the Googlers to accept an outside CEO. He did not like to be pushed around by uppity young managers. Venture investors had a right—in fact, a duty—to oversee a startup's management and choose the top executive: there was a principle to defend here. Besides, Sequoia's performance had been hit by the tech crash. Even after the vice presidents' show of faith in Thiel, Moritz did not feel like entrusting one of his few promising bets to an unconventional manager who was simultaneously focused on his hedge fund.

The six members of X.com's board—three founders and three investors—convened for a contentious meeting. Ironically, two of the founders, Thiel and Levchin, dialed in from Thiel's hedge fund, where Levchin had doctored a fax machine so that it functioned as a speakerphone. The two could count on the support of a third director, John Malloy, the VC at Nokia who had originally backed them. They had no hope of winning over Moritz or Musk. The outcome hinged on the sixth board member, an investor from a later venture round.[23]

Eventually, the directors agreed to replace Musk with Thiel as chief executive. But Moritz saw to it that Thiel's triumph was incomplete. The CEO appointment was on an interim basis, and a search firm was retained to identify an outsider who would serve as the permanent replacement. Even though the search firm ultimately found nobody and Thiel kept the top job, his resentment of Moritz intensified. Thiel wore the armor of Germanic earnestness, whereas Moritz flashed his wit like a saber. "Peter felt abused by Moritz, very keenly, very personally," one of Thiel's allies remembered.[24]

Five months later, in February 2001, the bitterness deepened. Despite the disastrous tech market—the Nasdaq stock index was down by about half from its peak the previous year—X.com managed to raise a $90 million Series D round. Believing that the economy was soft and that the market would decline further, Thiel proposed that X.com protect itself by entrusting some of its newly raised capital to his hedge fund. By placing bets that would pay out if the Nasdaq lost value, the hedge fund could ensure X.com against a prolonged market slump, which might endanger its future ability to raise capital.[25] But while Thiel was correct about the market's direction, and logical in his desire to hedge X.com's risk, his proposal smacked of self-dealing. He would be using his position at one company to enlarge the capital pool of the other. Moritz rounded on Thiel, denouncing his tin ear for corporate governance and stinging him with condescending ridicule. "It was high theater," one board member remembered.[26]

Over the next year and a half, the relationship grew even more contentious. Moritz and Thiel clashed on whether to sell out to a suitor; at one point, eBay offered $300 million for the company. Having learned his lesson with Yahoo, Moritz opposed a premature exit; in his view, the magic of paying other people by email would ultimately make for a much higher valuation. Thiel, on the other hand, never shed the mentality of a trader; there was always a price that he would sell for. "He was the hedge-fund guy. Wanted to take all his money out. I mean, goodness gracious," Moritz said later.[27]

At one point, Moritz went to work on Levchin, seeking to stiffen his opposition to a sale, just as he had earlier opened his eyes to the merits of a merger. PayPal was doing better and better, so why would Levchin sell? How would he find a higher use for his talents?

"Max, what else would you do?" Moritz asked him.

"I'd start another company like PayPal," Levchin answered.

"Max," Moritz countered, summoning the weight and experience of fifteen years in the business. "You have no idea how rarely these opportunities come around. Even if you live to be 150, you will never have another opportunity as big and as unbounded as PayPal."[28]

At this, Levchin took Moritz's side and the $300 million offer was rebuffed. But in July 2002, eBay came back with another bid for the company, which had by now gone public under the name PayPal. This time the offer was for $1.5 billion. Moritz's doctrine of patience had increased Levchin's wealth by a factor of around five, and the same was true for Thiel's fortune.

Looking back on these events, it was hard to say where Moritz blew it in the eyes of the younger generation. He had fired Sean Parker from Plaxo, but with the support of Parker's co-founders and in the company's best interest. He had clashed with Thiel repeatedly, but he had been reasonable, at least initially, in suspecting that Thiel was not a natural startup CEO, reasonable in slapping down Thiel's self-dealing hedge-fund idea, and dramatically correct in rejecting eBay's early lowball offer.[29] Meanwhile, Moritz had also played his part in steering Confinity and X toward a merger, without which PayPal might have come to nothing. A decade later, when Thiel reflected on the startup lessons he had learned in the Valley, avoidance of competition was a key one.[30] "All failed companies are the same," he reflected. "They failed to escape competition."[31]

Yet the fact was that Moritz had alienated Parker and Thiel, and the price became clear with Zuckerberg's pajama put-down.[32] Facebook, the hottest startup of the time, featured a board that consisted of Zuckerberg plus two Moritz enemies: Sequoia stood no chance of investing. Moreover, the penalty for Sequoia threatened to extend beyond one deal, for the full scope of the youth revolt was wider. Within a few months of the Wirehog episode, two upstart venture operations made their debut. Each set out to challenge the traditional venture business.

The first of the two challengers was launched by Thiel, and it happened in a sideways, almost ad hoc way that echoed the founding of Confinity. Much as Thiel had met Levchin by coincidence, then invested, then been drawn in as chief executive because there was an evident vacuum, so Thiel advanced crabwise into starting his own venture fund.

When eBay bought PayPal in 2002, Thiel negotiated secret terms that allowed him to leave the company. The conditions of the acquisition required others on his management team to stay at their posts, but Thiel sprang himself loose and cashed out to the tune of $55 million.[33] Now in his mid-thirties, he quit Palo Alto and set himself up in San Francisco, financing an ostentatiously lavish nightclub and buying a silver Ferrari. He relaunched and rechristened his hedge fund, calling it Clarium Capital, bulking it up with $10 million of his own wealth, and pursuing the thesis that a global scarcity of oil would drive energy prices higher.[34] Meanwhile, he hatched a series of projects that built on the relationships he had forged at Stanford and PayPal. In 2004 he recruited a PayPal engineer to develop national-intelligence software, and he brought in a Stanford Law School friend to lead the resulting company, Palantir. Thanks to Reid Hoffman, another Stanford friend who had also worked at PayPal, Thiel made the angel investment in Facebook, also putting money into Hoffman's social-networking startup, LinkedIn. Any of these initiatives would have been enough to multiply Thiel's fortune. At its zenith, Thiel's hedge fund was managing assets of about $7 billion, though the fund later suffered losses and a wave of investor redemptions. LinkedIn and Palantir went on to achieve valuations of more than $20 billion; Facebook grew to be worth hundreds of billions. But meanwhile, and almost as an afterthought, Thiel got talking with another Stanford-and-PayPal graduate named Ken Howery about setting up a venture firm.

Launched in 2005, Thiel's new outfit was called Founders Fund. The name signaled the ethos: founders who had created companies like PayPal were out to back the next entrepreneurial cohort, and they promised to treat this new generation with the respect that they themselves had wished for. Luke Nosek, Max Levchin's old friend and another PayPal alum, was a founding partner; soon, none other than Sean Parker joined them. "Largely because we were all founders ourselves, we're inherently more interested in helping new entrepreneurs develop into successful leaders than we are in getting rich," Parker asserted.[35]

Naturally, given the fights that Thiel and Parker had been through with Moritz, Founders Fund explicitly ruled out the Qume formula of bringing in an outside CEO. Entrepreneurs should control their own companies, period. The Googlers had pioneered this path, accepting Eric Schmidt as one member of a triumvirate rather than as the outright boss. Facebook had gone further: Zuckerberg reigned unchallenged. Now Founders Fund set out to spread this kingly model to every startup that it backed. Thiel felt that all great startups had a "monarchy aspect," as one of his lieutenants put it. "It's not the libertarian part of Peter that made Founders Fund. It's the monarchist part."

For some Founders Fund partners, enthroning entrepreneurs was an ethical imperative. Nosek, who came up with the Founders Fund name, had worked up a passionate dislike of Moritz during his time at PayPal and viewed traditional venture capital as "disgusting."[36] "These people would destroy the creations of the most valuable inventors in the world," he exclaimed furiously.[37] For other Founders Fund partners, there was an element of brand: a newcomer to the venture industry had to differentiate itself from the established giants, a fact that Howery confronted when he failed to raise capital for Founders Fund from U.S. institutional investors.[38] But the way Thiel himself saw things, the case for corporate monarchism was subtler. It connected to an unusually clear view of how venture capital functioned.

Thiel was the first VC to speak explicitly about the power law. Past venture investors, going back to Arthur Rock, had understood full well that a handful of winners would dominate their performance. But Thiel went further in recognizing this as part of a broader phenomenon. Citing Vilfredo Pareto, the father of the "Pareto principle"—or 80/20 rule—he observed that radically unequal outcomes were common in the natural and social world. At the start of the twentieth century, when Pareto was writing, 20 percent of the people owned 80 percent of Italy's land, much as 20 percent of the peapods in Pareto's garden produced 80 percent of the peas. Likewise, Thiel continued, the most destructive earthquakes are many times more powerful than all smaller earthquakes combined, and big cities dwarf all mere towns put together. It was therefore not just a curiosity that a single venture-capital bet could dominate a whole portfolio. It was a sort of natural law; indeed, it was *the* law to which venture capitalists were subject. In the past, the present, and surely the future, a startup that monopolized a worthwhile niche would capture more value than millions of undifferentiated competitors.[39]

Thiel was methodical in thinking through the implications of this insight. Past venture investors had seen the home-run nature of their business as a justification for risk: their limited partners should forgive the many instances in which they backed failures, because it took only one or two big hits for a fund to generate a profit. But Thiel saw in the power law an additional lesson. He argued, iconoclastically, that venture capitalists should stop mentoring founders. Venture investors from Rock onward had taken great pride in coaching and advising startups; for a firm like Benchmark, this was the bread and butter of the business. One survey in 2000 found that coaching and advising were growing more important, not less so: a venture partnership called Mohr Davidow retained five operating partners whose full-time job was to parachute into portfolio companies to provide managerial support, and Charles River Ventures in Boston retained no fewer than a dozen staff to help startups with executive search, equipment leasing, contract law, and other functions. Paul Gompers of the Harvard Business School described these developments as progress. "It's the evolution of venture capital from an art into a business," he suggested.[40]

The way Thiel saw things, this evolution was misguided. The power law dictated that the companies that mattered would have to be exceptional outliers: in all of Silicon Valley in any given year, there were just a handful of ventures that were truly worth backing.[41] The founders of these outstanding startups were necessarily so gifted that a bit of VC coaching would barely change their performance.[42] "When you look at the strongest performers in our portfolio, they are, generally speaking, the companies that we have the least amount of engagement with," one Founders Fund partner observed bluntly.[43] It might flatter venture investors' egos to offer sage advice. But the art of venture capital was to find rough diamonds, not to spend time polishing them.[44]

As if this were not sufficiently provocative, Thiel went further. To the extent that VC coaching did make a difference, he contended, it might well be negative. When venture capitalists imposed their methods on founders, they were implicitly betting that tried-and-tested formulas trumped outside-the-box experiments. To use the old distinction between Accel and Kleiner Perkins, they were saying that the prepared mind was better than the open one. But if the power law dictated that only a handful of truly original and contrarian startups were destined to succeed, it made no sense to suppress idiosyncrasies. To the contrary, venture capitalists should embrace contrarian and singular founders, the wackier the better. Entrepreneurs who weren't oddballs would create businesses that were simply too normal. They would come up with a sensible plan, which, being sensible, would have occurred to others. Consequently, they would find themselves in a niche that was too crowded and competitive to allow for big profits.[45]

It was surely no coincidence, Thiel continued, that the best startup founders were often arrogant, misanthropic, or borderline crazy. Four of the six early PayPal employees had built bombs in high school.[46] Elon Musk spent half the earnings from his first startup on a race car; when he crashed it with Thiel in the passenger seat, all he could do was laugh about the fact that he had failed to insure it. Such extremes and eccentricities were actually good signs, Thiel contended; VCs should celebrate misfits, not coach them into conformity. A few years into its existence, Founders Fund made an expensive error by refusing to invest in the ride-hailing startup Uber; its bratty founder, Travis Kalanick, had alienated both Howery and Nosek. "We should be more tolerant of founders who seem strange or extreme," Thiel wrote, when Uber had emerged as a grand slam.[47] "Maybe we need to give assholes a second and third chance," Nosek conceded contritely.[48]

If Thiel opposed VC mentoring of founders lest it suppress quirky genius, he also disliked it for another reason. From the investor's point of view, there was a hefty opportunity cost. Venture capitalists who spent their days mentoring portfolio companies would not be seeking out the next batch of investment opportunities. At one point, Luke Nosek allowed himself to be sucked into the troubles at a portfolio company called Powerset: the CEO had left, and the company was desperate to sell itself to an acquirer. "I put tons of effort into this and I made like $100,000," Nosek remembered ruefully. And because he was preoccupied with Powerset, Nosek failed to pursue opportunities elsewhere, including in Facebook and Twitter. "I was just too busy, and I never ended up meeting with the people."[49]

With his grave and almost ponderous manner, Thiel could come across as a detached armchair philosopher. He was given to breathtakingly sweeping statements, delivered in a tone of deadpan certitude that made few allowances for the messiness of reality. He liked to dabble philanthropically in eccentric causes: "seasteading"—the idea of building a floating libertarian utopia beyond the reach of governments—as well as projects to defeat aging or to encourage gifted kids to drop out of college. But, like George Soros, Thiel had the courage to connect his philosophical convictions to his investment practices. As a student at the London School of Economics, Soros had absorbed the notion that limits to human cognition prevent people from stably apprehending truth; it followed that Soros should speculate aggressively on the self-reinforcing booms and busts that imperfect cognition generated.[50] Likewise, having absorbed the implications of the power law, Thiel imprinted them methodically on his venture firm. Founders Fund resolved that it would never eject founders from their startups, no matter how strangely they behaved; fifteen years later, it had stuck faithfully to this principle.[51] Indeed, Founders Fund never once sided against a founder in a board vote, and was generally content to do without a board seat. It was a bold reversal of the hands-on tradition established by Don Valentine and Tom Perkins.

Thiel acted on his faith in mavericks by recruiting investing partners who themselves tested convention. His first-ever conversation with Luke Nosek had been about how Nosek wanted to be frozen upon death in hope of medical resurrection. This did not stop Thiel from welcoming Nosek into his partnership. Likewise, Sean Parker had been in trouble with the law, not to mention with power brokers such as Moritz; Thiel nonetheless embraced him. To banish consensual thinking, Founders Fund broke with the industry practice of Monday partnership meetings, replacing the Sand Hill Road tradition of collective responsibility with radical decentralization. Founders Fund investors sourced deals independently, even writing some small checks without consulting one another. Bigger bets required consultation—the bigger the check, the more partners had to assent—but even the biggest investments did not require a majority to vote in favor. "It usually takes one person with a lot of conviction banging their fist and saying, 'This needs to be done,'" one partner explained, by way of summary.[52]

Like Soros's, Thiel's philosophical interests convinced him of the case for unusually aggressive risk-taking. Soros's longtime partner and alter ego

Stanley Druckenmiller observed that huge and well-timed gambles were the essence of Soros's genius. Soros was right about the market's direction no more often than other traders. What distinguished him was that when he felt a truly strong conviction, he acted on it more courageously.[53] Likewise, Thiel had the guts to act on his understanding of the power law by betting big at the right moments. Because only a handful of startups would grow exponentially, there was no point getting excited about opportunities that seemed merely solid; in venture, the median investment was a failure. But when he encountered a potential grand slam, Thiel was ready to pile his chips onto the table. In 1998, his $300,000 bet on Max Levchin had been three times bigger than Andy Bechtolsheim's bet on Brin and Page, even though at that time Bechtolsheim had more money to play with. In 2004, Thiel's angel check to Facebook was thirteen times larger than the checks written by Hoffman and Pincus. Other investors, seeking to manage risk through diversification, lacked the stomach for such concentrated wagers. But in a field ruled by the power law, Thiel was certain that a small number of huge, high-conviction bets was better than a large spread of half-hearted ones.[54]

Thiel liked to tell a story about Andreessen Horowitz, another upstart venture shop of which we shall hear more later. In 2010, Andreessen Horowitz invested $250,000 in the social-networking app Instagram. It was by some metrics a spectacular home run: two years later, Facebook paid $1 billion for Instagram, and Andreessen netted $78 million—a 312x return on its investment. And yet by other measures this was a debacle. Andreessen Horowitz made the Instagram investment out of a $1.5 billion fund, so it needed fully nineteen $78 million payouts merely to break even. To have backed a winning company was nice for the ego. But the brutal truth was that Instagram had been a wasted opportunity. In contrast, when Founders Fund got excited about a follow-on opportunity to invest in Facebook in 2007, Nosek went all in. He called up the Founders Fund limited partners and persuaded them to plow extra capital into a Facebook-only special purpose vehicle. Then he invested his parents' entire retirement fund in the company.[55]

As time went by, Thiel embraced an extra source of risk. As well as writing big checks, he backed increasingly audacious projects. A couple of years after launching his venture fund, he explained that he intended to go after the "somewhat riskier, more out-of-the-box companies that really have the potential to change the world."[56] Rather than confining himself to fashionable software, he would underwrite moon shots in less obvious fields that might be more important and lucrative. In 2008, Thiel hit upon an opportunity to make good on his promise.

Attending the wedding of a friend, Thiel ran into Elon Musk, his old rival from PayPal. Given that Thiel's allies had ousted Musk from PayPal, relations between the two had not always been cordial. But Musk had picked himself up from that episode, investing his share of the PayPal proceeds in two new startups: Tesla, which made electric cars, and SpaceX, which boasted the modest ambition of cutting the cost of space transportation so radically that colonizing Mars might become possible. Now, at the wedding, Musk told Thiel that he was open to an investment in SpaceX.

"Sure," Thiel said. "Let's bury the hatchet."[57]

Thiel emailed his partners, suggesting a relatively modest investment of $5 million. Sean Parker responded by washing his hands of the idea: space travel was too far out for him. But Nosek had the opposite reaction. If Founders Fund was in the business of backing moon shots, a Mars shot was surely irresistible.

Nosek began to conduct due diligence on SpaceX. "It wasn't clear to anyone that this was going to work," Ken Howery recalled. "Every rocket had blown up," he added.[58] While Nosek was investigating, another potential SpaceX backer pulled out, and a third inadvertently copied Founders Fund on an email saying that Thiel and his partners had taken leave of their senses.[59] But Nosek was determined to believe. Space travel was one of those technologies that had racked up progress in the 1960s and then more or less flatlined: the cost of launching one kilogram of mass into space was the same in 2000 as it had been in 1970. Surely SpaceX could harness scientific progress to unblock this frontier? Besides, Musk's rockets had blown up, but Musk's engineers understood why they had blown up: failure was a bonus if you learned from it. Finally, Musk himself was the quintessential arrogant genius. If Founders Fund believed its own theories, the fact that he had laughed about crashing his uninsured race car was reason enough to back him.

In July 2008, right after SpaceX's third attempted rocket launch had failed, Nosek persuaded Thiel to bet fully $20 million on Musk, receiving in exchange about 4 percent of his company. One decade later, SpaceX had achieved a heady valuation of $26 billion. Through this and other high-risk wagers, Founders Fund established itself as a top-performing venture shop, a vindication of its hands-off, high-risk, radically contrarian approach to startup investing.[60] For the traditional VC industry, the warning was clear. The youth revolt—started by the Googlers, dramatized by Zuckerberg's pajama prank—was now being institutionalized by Thiel and his fund. And the Thiel effect was compounded by a second venture upstart, launched almost simultaneously by another cultish critic of the venture establishment.

This second upstart was Paul Graham, the hacker and blogger who had propounded his "unified theory of VC suckage." Like Thiel, Graham had strong convictions about what venture capitalists were doing wrong. Even more than Thiel, he set about correcting their errors almost as an afterthought.

A few months after the pajama prank, in March 2005, Graham showed up at 305 Emerson Hall on the Harvard campus to speak to the university computer society. The title of his lecture was "How to Start a Startup," and the auditorium was packed beyond capacity; a hundred or so students had read Graham's musings on coding and living, and wanted to found companies, as he had.[61] Not a whisper could be heard as Graham arranged his notes on sheets of lined yellow paper.[62]

Graham proceeded to lay out his favorite themes. Any hacker with a good idea was qualified to launch a business. No hacker should defer to venture investors. Founders needed only small amounts of cash to cover rent and groceries. Ideally, Graham added, this cash should come from an angel investor who had experience launching a startup—someone who could provide counsel and comradeship.

Someone like you, the audience must have thought, because Graham suddenly had that prickly feeling that everyone was staring at him. "I had this horrifying vision of them all e-mailing me their business plans," he re-called later. Shuddering at the legal and administrative hassles of investing, Graham cut the audience off right there. "Not me. No," he insisted; he rev-eled in the way that young computer scientists looked up to him, but he had no plans to become a venture capitalist.[63] "The rumble of one hundred si-multaneously disappointed nerds echoed through the room," a student in the audience wrote later.[64]

At the end of the talk, Graham found himself surrounded by admirers. Two University of Virginia students had traveled fourteen hours by train to listen to him. The first, a thin blond young man with oval glasses, asked for Graham's autograph but seemed too awed to say much. The second, loom-ing and lanky, produced one of Graham's books on the Lisp computer lan-guage. Please would the author sign it?

Graham chuckled. This was not the first time that he had been asked to sign one of his works on programming.

The tall youth had one more request. Could he and his friend buy Dr. Graham a drink and talk about their idea for a startup?

Flattered, and momentarily forgetting his resolve on the stage, Graham agreed to meet that night. "I guess since you came all the way from Virginia I can't say no," he said.[65]

Graham arrived a little late in a loose polo and khaki shorts. The group got a table at a place called Café Algiers, and as the hummus arrived, the tall youth began speaking. He introduced himself as Alexis Ohanian, and his friend was Steve Huffman. Their mission was to change the way that res-taurants worked. They would write a program that allowed people to order food by text message.

Five minutes into Ohanian's spiel, Graham interrupted. "This will be the end of lines," he exclaimed, seizing on the big idea in the small project. "No one will ever have to wait in line again!" All of a sudden Graham was connecting restaurant orders to the history of developments in mobile communications and urging the undergraduates to think on a grand scale. It was a thrill to share his knowledge.

Four days later, Graham and his girlfriend, Jessica Livingston, were walking home after a Friday evening dinner in Harvard Square. Although it was almost spring, the temperature in Cambridge hovered just above freezing. The usual chatter ensued. Livingston had applied for a marketing position at a venture firm and was waiting to hear back. For his part, Graham was fresh from the encounter at Café Algiers and was feeling the pull of angel investing. Despite his reservations about becoming a venture capitalist, mentoring young founders would be a way of giving back. "I always thought, people who start startups feel like they should do at least a little bit of angel investing," he reflected later. "Because if no one had invested in them, how would they have gotten started, right?"[66]

An idea gelled as the couple walked along the spotted brick sidewalks. They'd start a little angel investment firm together. Livingston could work there instead of at the venture fund that was taking forever to answer. She could take on the administrative and legal stuff that Graham found so unappealing. Graham, for his part, would draw on his experience as a founder to pick the next generation of winners. It would be the perfect partnership.[67]

Over the next couple of days, the pair came up with a plan for a novel form of seed investing. It would plug the gap that Graham saw in mainstream venture capital: the new breed of software founders just needed enough cash to buy groceries, plus occasional guidance and camaraderie to relieve the solitude of coding. The Graham-Livingston plan would also be more structured than the ad hoc impulses of scattered angels: it would involve an office and employees and standardized procedures. Graham put up $100,000 of his own money, and two co-founders of his old software startup, Viaweb, promised $50,000 each. Then he announced the plan in no-frills 10-point Verdana on his blog. The red bold title announced, "Summer Founders Program."

Graham billed the program as an experimental replacement for conventional college summer jobs. Instead of a salary, participants would get $6,000 each to sustain them through three months of programming. They would also receive practical and emotional help. Y Combinator, as the Graham-Livingston operation was called, would incorporate the participants' startups, open company bank accounts, and advise about patents. Graham and a few of his smart friends would provide feedback on the young hackers' projects, and there would be a dinner once a week so that the summer schoolers got to know each other. In return, Y Combinator would take equity—usually 6 percent of the shares—in each micro-company that it incorporated.[68]

At first Graham thought of the summer program as a temporary expedient. Y Combinator would invest in several teams at once so it could learn what worked and what didn't. But soon he realized that batch processing was marvelously efficient.[69] The batch members would provide support for one another, relieving the burden on himself and Livingston. And YC could help the startups as a group. It could invite a speaker to a dinner and have all its protégés listen. It could organize a single demo day at which all its founders would pitch to follow-on investors. No one had previously thought to structure angel investments in this fashion.[70]

In April 2005, Livingston, Graham, and the two Viaweb co-founders convened in a former candy factory that Graham had recently purchased. There were five skylights, bright white walls, and some sparse midcentury modern furnishings. The front door was painted persimmon.

Graham and his gang set about conducting interviews. Twenty teams had been culled from 227 applications. In successive forty-five-minute sessions, the visitors parried questions, with the Viaweb co-founder Robert Morris playing the curmudgeon. Graham doodled a caricature of Morris's face on a whiteboard, complete with furrowed eyebrows and a protruding lower lip. "It will never work," ran the accompanying caption. Yet some pitches actually seemed quite likely to work. There was a poised nineteen-year-old from Stanford who appeared wise beyond his years; this was Sam Altman, who went on to succeed Graham as Y Combinator's guiding spirit. And there were Huffman and Ohanian, the pair from Virginia, who later ditched their restaurant-booking scheme in favor of a news site called Reddit, which provided YC with its first profitable exit. Altogether, eight teams made the cut. Y Combinator's acceptance rate was 3.5 percent, comparable to that of Harvard Medical School.

With enough money for rent and pizza and not much else, the chosen worked maniacally, replicating the round-the-clock programming lifestyle that Graham had embraced when building Viaweb. Relief came on Tuesday evenings, when the coders assembled for dinner. Graham would man the kitchen in the converted toy factory, emptying cans into Crock-Pots and stirring up what was affectionately known as "glop." The summer schoolers milled about, comparing progress on their coding projects, sometimes drinking the lemonade and mint iced tea that was a Livingston specialty.[71] Presently, they took their seats on unstable benches laid out on either side of a long formica table under the skylights.[72] They filled themselves gratefully with glop and listened to an outside speaker whom Graham had invited. Not surprisingly, the speakers often amplified Graham's own views. One visitor presented a slide with a discussion question for the group: "VCs: soulless agents of Satan, or just clumsy rapists?"[73]

A couple of years later, when Y Combinator had established itself in Palo Alto, Graham invited none other than Mark Zuckerberg to speak at an event at Stanford. The veteran of the Wirehog presentation stood up and voiced the shared conviction of the rising generation: "Young people are just smarter."[74]

Coming on the heels of Masayoshi Son's growth checks, the spread of Bechtolsheim-type angels, and Peter Thiel's hands-off investing, Y Combinator represented yet another challenge to traditional venture capital. Having diagnosed the shortcomings of the venture incumbents, Graham was offering micro-investments on the theory that large checks were toxic for fledgling software startups. He had come up with the batch-processing idea and had invented a folksy, unsatanic way of turning hackers into founders. The way Graham saw things, his new investment formula was fundamentally different from conventional VC. He was not just meeting entrepreneurs and piggybacking on their talent. He was recruiting teenage coders and *creating* entrepreneurship.

Graham described this alchemy in programming lingo: it was a hack on the world economy. Like a hacker who sees an inspired shortcut in a stretch of code, he had studied human society and realized that with a modest tweak it could be made to run more efficiently. "There are thousands of smart people who could start companies and don't, and with a relatively small amount of force applied at just the right place, we can spring on the

world a stream of new startups," he wrote in 2006, a year after Y Combinator's founding. A new stream of startups would be desirable not just because they would create extra wealth, but because they would signal a fuller
freedom for young hackers. "When I graduated from college in 1986, there
were essentially two options: get a job or go to grad school. Now there's a
third: start your own company," Graham wrote. "That kind of change, from
two paths to three, is the sort of big social shift that only happens once every
few generations. It's hard to predict how big a deal it will be. As big a deal
as the Industrial Revolution?"[75]

Of course, this idea of freedom for hackers was not entirely novel.
Rather, it extended the original promise of venture capital. Arthur Rock
had liberated talent that would otherwise have suffocated inside hierarchical corporations. Graham was saying you could liberate yourself before you
even joined a company. He distilled his message into a few stirring phrases.
Work for yourself. Capture the value of your own ideas. Rather than climbing a ladder, grow a ladder underneath you. "The monolithic, hierarchical
companies of the mid 20th century are being replaced by networks of
smaller companies," Graham cheered, celebrating the startup clusters
whose innovative edge had been identified by AnnaLee Saxenian.[76] Except
that now, as Graham realized, the rise and rise of software meant there
would be more small companies than ever before. Located somewhere between the corporation and the market, networks of startups would constitute a third category of capitalist organization. Perhaps this really was a
change on the scale of the Industrial Revolution.

Graham's expansive views were matched by the expansion of his investment model. After the success of their first summer school, Graham
and Livingston took their format to the West Coast. They increased the
number of teams they accepted, and added new experiments: extra capital
to fuel their protégés, startup assistance for nonprofits, conferences at
Stanford. As word spread of their programs, dozens of imitators sprang up,
sometimes adding clever tweaks to Graham's model. In 2006, a rival named
Techstars got going in Boulder, Colorado, and within a few years it had
spread to Boston, Seattle, and New York City. The following year, Seed-
camp, a European incarnation of Graham's idea, started up in London. In

2018, Daniel Gross, a YC graduate who later returned as a YC partner, launched an online startup accelerator called Pioneer, which aimed to spread something like the YC experience to entrepreneurs in developing countries, who lived far from any tech hub. Meanwhile, believing that one barrier to entrepreneurship is that isolated programmers have trouble finding like-minded partners, an outfit called Entrepreneur First provided a sort of dating service. It recruited individual coders rather than established founding teams, enrolled them into YC-style programs, and encouraged them to couple up together. Led by Alice Bentinck and Matt Clifford, two charismatic young Britons, Entrepreneur First quickly sprouted offices in London, Berlin, Paris, Singapore, Hong Kong, and Bangalore.

In sum, Y Combinator's example and the wider youth revolt signaled a new phase for venture capital. An industry that had initially consisted of generalist investors, and that later featured Accel-style specialists, was now dividing into seed investors, early-stage investors, and growth investors. Meanwhile, the capitalists were learning to defer to the founders; VC became less about Valentine-Perkins hands-on investing and more about Rock-style liberation. But there was a limit to the new ideas. Peter Thiel's power-law-driven theories could be pushed too far. From Genentech to Cisco and onward, there had been plenty of cases in which hands-on venture capital had fueled the success of portfolio companies. Likewise, Paul Graham's critique of overbearing, big-check venture capitalists was justified when he was talking about investments in small software concerns, which were simple to manage and required little capital. But companies that grew larger would still need guidance and money.

Over the next years, this last caveat turned out to be especially significant. Some Silicon Valley companies would grow *much* larger. They would consume billions of dollars, serve tens of millions of consumers, and frequently require tough investor oversight. Thanks partly to the cultural shift wrought by the youth revolt, they would not always get it.

Chapter Ten

To China, and Stir

I n late 2004, when Mark Zuckerberg and Sean Parker were taunting Sequoia, a burly venture capitalist named Gary Rieschel visited a Shanghai office tower on the banks of the Huangpu River. More than most American technologists, Rieschel had an international outlook, and he knew what booms smelled like. He had worked in Japan during the go-go 1980s. He had run Masayoshi Son's Silicon Valley venture fund in the frenetic 1990s. He had shifted his focus back to high-growth Asia when the Valley's boom had turned to bust. Now, as he gazed out from the forty-seventh floor of this palatial office, his breath stopped for a moment. All he could see were construction cranes; for miles and miles across Shanghai, steel and glass towers were sprouting like bamboo. In all his travels, Rieschel had never witnessed such activity. Suddenly he found himself imagining the Huangpu River as a flow of molten money, irrigating the city with wealth.[1]

Rieschel had moved to Shanghai for a six-month family adventure, but he soon decided he should stay. He rented an office in that tower by the Huangpu, approving the lease with an unauthorized Chinese-character signature block he had bought from a street vendor. He rekindled old connections, including with a Stanford-trained engineer named Duane Kuang, whom he had known when they had worked together at Cisco. Kuang had since returned to his native China and run an investment fund for Intel, and now he agreed to join Rieschel in launching a new China-focused venture firm, which they called Qiming. Toward the end of 2005 they went out to raise capital from American limited partners.

In standard Silicon Valley style, Rieschel seized every opportunity to befriend people in the local technology community. He was a gregarious and jovial presence, and he knew his place in Asia. He would never develop the feel of a local, but as a veteran technologist approaching his fiftieth birthday, he had experience to contribute.[2] Startup founders in Shanghai proved eager to learn from him, and their energy was astonishing. Frequently, Rieschel's phone would ring in the evening, after he had finished dinner. Someone somewhere in the teeming city would be demanding a meeting.

"When?" Rieschel would ask the caller.

"Now!" came the response, as though the answer were obvious.

Rieschel would climb into his car and drive past endless construction teams, at work on the next skyscraper or subway extension. His meeting might get going at around ten in the evening and could carry on until one the next morning. There were hardware startups, software startups, medical startups, and all manner of e-commerce. With China's economy growing at 10 percent per year, and with internet usage expanding roughly twice that quickly, the opportunities were everywhere.[3] Ordinary Chinese had computers, modems, cell phones, and more disposable income than their parents could have fathomed. "All you had to do," Rieschel said later, "was sprinkle capital on that and stir."[4]

It was an extraordinary moment, and all the more extraordinary in light of the mixed performance of technology clusters elsewhere. Since the 1980s, when Silicon Valley had eclipsed its rivals in Japan and Boston, there had been countless attempts to imitate it, most of them sponsored by local or national governments. By the late 1990s, the United States alone featured Silicon Desert (Phoenix), Silicon Alley (New York), Silicon Hills (Austin), and Silicon Forest (in both Seattle and Portland, Oregon). Israel, Taiwan, India, and Britain launched similar efforts, and Egypt boasted the Pyramid Technology Park.[5] But even the most successful silicon wannabes came nowhere near to rivaling the original. Thanks to a tradition of engineering excellence and clever government support for venture funds, Israel became the standout innovation center outside the United States, with break-throughs ranging from instant messaging to car-navigation software. But because of the small size of Israel's economy, the country's startup cluster was more of an adjunct to Silicon Valley than a competitor. When their inventions showed promise, Israeli entrepreneurs' first move was to seek U.S. venture backing and to target the U.S. market. In the process, many shifted their business headquarters to the West Coast. Far from challenging the Valley's dominance, they reinforced it.

The boom that Rieschel sensed in China was of a different magnitude. In 2005, the year that he and Kuang hatched the idea of Qiming, venture funds aimed at China raised $4 billion, a fraction of the $24 billion raised in the United States. One decade later, the gap would have vanished.[6] By then, Qiming would have made around $1 billion in venture bets, ultimately returning $4 billion to investors, and Chinese venture investors would appear alongside American luminaries at the top of the *Forbes* Midas List of global VC stars.[7] U.S. technology giants such as Google, Amazon, Facebook, and Apple would face off against Chinese rivals such as Baidu, Alibaba, Tencent, and Xiaomi, the latter being China's leading smartphone maker and one of the many Qiming-backed triumphs. For the first time since the Japanese challenge of the 1980s, startups fueled by U.S. venture capital could no longer be certain that they dominated the world.[8]

Except, in a way, they could be. For, as Rieschel's presence hinted, China's technology boom was forged to a remarkable extent by American investors, and the Chinese VCs who emerged alongside them were themselves quasi-American—in their education, professional formation, and approach to venture capital. They had studied at top U.S. colleges, worked at U.S. companies, and carefully absorbed the U.S. venture playbook: equity-only funds, stage-by-stage financing, sleeves-rolled-up involvement, and stock options for startup employees. Neil Shen, whom *Forbes* ranked for three years as the top venture capitalist not just in China but globally, was in no sense a challenger to the U.S. way of fostering innovation, nor to Silicon Valley partnerships such as Sequoia.[9] To the contrary, he had attended Columbia University and Yale University, worked at both Lehman Brothers and Citibank, and eventually became the head of Sequoia's China operation. JP Gan and Hans Tung, two other China-linked VCs who featured among *Forbes*'s global top ten, underscored the point. Both had been educated at U.S. colleges. Both had gone on to work at U.S. financial firms. Both had emerged as stars when working with Rieschel at Qiming. Among the top Chinese VCs, only one stood out as a partial exception. Raised and educated on the mainland, Kathy Xu had been exposed to western financial practices in her mid-twenties, when she had joined a British accounting firm in Hong Kong.

Because of the might of China's Communist Party, both Chinese and foreign observers tend to ascribe the nation's technology success to the country's supposedly farseeing political leaders. But the truth is more surprising. Far from vindicating the industrial strategy of the Communist Party, China's tech success was a triumph for the financial model created by Arthur Rock.

◆

China's first magical venture deal, the rough equivalent to Rock's financing of Fairchild's eight traitors, took place in 1999, five years before Rieschel's arrival in Shanghai. Just as Rock had gone from Harvard to the Wall Street brokerage Hayden, Stone, so his spiritual successor, a fast-talking prodigy named Syaru Shirley Lin, had progressed from Harvard to Morgan Stanley and then Goldman Sachs. Rock had parted with Hayden, knowing that it lacked the appetite to focus on startups. Likewise, Lin would fight battles with her ambivalent Wall Street employer, culminating in one of the more embarrassing misjudgments in Goldman Sachs's history.

A Taiwanese American who gained admittance to Harvard at sixteen and skipped her freshman year, Lin was a kinetic go-getter. She became the youngest woman ever to make partner at Goldman, and her energy and charm made her a natural deal maker. Bicultural and bilingual, she was also a bridge between two worlds. After Goldman hired her away from Morgan Stanley in the early 1990s, Lin arranged for the bank to take a stake in a Chinese diesel company and advised the Chinese government on restructuring and privatizing its airlines. After that, Goldman parachuted her into Asia's largest privatization ever, of Singapore Telecom. The fact that she was a woman did not hold her back. Relative to Silicon Valley, China's fast-developing business culture was flexible, fluid, and somewhat less of a boys' club.[10]

In 1999, Lin used her status as a rising star at Goldman to set out in a new direction. Intoxicated by Silicon Valley's IPO euphoria, Chinese engineers emerging from U.S. graduate programs were itching to launch technology startups. They had business ideas, technical training, and relentless ambition. But, like the Traitorous Eight in California half a century earlier, they lacked an obvious source of capital. They were not going to get it from a Chinese bank, because Chinese lenders viewed startups as too risky.[11] They were not going to get it from a partnership on Sand Hill Road, because most American VCs regarded China as too risky. Seeing an opportunity, Lin set about building a China-focused venture shop.[12] Soon, business plans began to arrive by the crate load at the Goldman Sachs office in Hong Kong.

Lin began to look for deals that blended the advantages of the United States and China. They would be structured in the U.S. way, with Silicon Valley lawyers drafting all the documents. But they would involve startups founded by American-trained Chinese and would sell into China's vast market. Sina, an early Chinese internet portal, was a case in point: it targeted Chinese consumers, but its board meetings were held in the Valley. Lin also backed Sohu and NetEase, two other promising portals.

One day Lin heard about a startup founded by an English teacher named Jack Ma, located in the provincial capital of Hangzhou. The referral came from another Taiwanese American, Joe Tsai, who had studied at Yale and then Yale Law School while Lin had been at Harvard. The two had met as students on a flight to their respective summer jobs in Taipei; Tsai spent most of the journey reading a textbook on U.S. constitutional law while Lin was buried in *The Wall Street Journal*.[13] Later, both had worked at prestigious New York firms; while Lin had gone into investment banking, Tsai had worked for the white-shoe law firm Sullivan & Cromwell. Then, in the mid-1990s, Tsai had followed Lin's example and taken an investment job in Hong

Kong. Now he had resolved to back this startup in Hangzhou. He wanted Lin to co-invest with him.

At first, Lin was doubtful. "Absolutely not!" she said, laughing dismissively.[14] The pitches flooding her office were from graduates of famous U.S. colleges. What could be so special about a provincial English teacher? Moreover, the business that this Jack Ma was pursuing—a website to help western companies source goods cheaply from China—sounded rather similar to pitches she had seen before. And even if it was marginally different, so what? Lin had discovered that the wannapreneurs who approached her were willing to amend their business plans at the drop of a hat. Lin could get any of them to implement Ma's concept.

"The aspiring CEOs would come to me and say, which sector do you want me to be in?" Lin recalled. "And if I said I wanted a content person, they said they would do content."

"But you don't know anything about content," Lin would retort.

"Wait!" came the answer. A few days later, the supplicant would return with a team of ten content people, all of whom had been to Stanford.[15]

Soon after she rebuffed Tsai, Lin heard of a pitch from a successful company named Asian Sources. It was a so-called yellow pages business: big U.S. retailers used Asian Sources to procure goods from China. The company now proposed to launch an online version of its formula, and even before the first employee had been hired, it was brazenly demanding a valuation of $1.7 billion for the project. Despite the astronomical price, Goldman was thinking of backing it.

A light went on in Lin's head. This was the same vision that Tsai's Hangzhou guy was pitching. Lin knew that when brick-and-mortar outfits tried to cannibalize their own business by taking it online, the vested interests of the company's old guard often frustrated progress. Maybe it would be better to back the greenfield version, and at a fraction of the price? The next time Tsai pleaded with Lin to visit his project in Hangzhou, she agreed to go with him.

A few days later, the pair of Ivy Leaguers showed up at Jack Ma's apartment. A dozen employees, including Ma's wife, were working there together day and night, subsisting on pot noodles. Ma and his team were evidently too obsessive to worry about hygiene: the apartment smelled pungently. But with a wide smile and elfin features, Ma exuded a cute charm, and he made an engaging change from the eager pleasers who pitched Lin incessantly. The Stanford crowd would do just about anything to win funding from a prestigious firm like Goldman Sachs. Ma, in contrast, was fervently committed to his business plan. He was not going to change it at the suggestion of a financier. Besides, if Ma lacked the polish of the U.S.-educated Chinese, Lin could look to her co-investor to compensate. Joe Tsai was not only determined to back Ma's project. He was ready to help out actively.

Over tea with Ma, Lin announced that Goldman Sachs was ready to invest, but only if the bank got more than half the equity.

Ma protested. The company was his baby.

The meeting wrapped up with Lin leaving Ma to consider her offer. She figured that her leverage would grow as the startup's cash needs mounted. Sure enough, Ma began phoning her on a regular basis. He still wanted to keep most of his shares, but he needed capital urgently.

One weekend, when Lin was swimming with her family on the south side of Hong Kong Island, Ma called her again. "This is my life!" he pleaded. Couldn't Goldman allow him to retain the majority of his equity?[16]

"What do you mean, this is your life? You've only just started!" Lin said firmly. She reiterated that Goldman needed to own more than half of Ma's company.

Ma hung up. Then he called right back again. He was beside himself with anxiety.

Lin pressed her advantage. "After this weekend, I'm not going to think about this anymore," she said, menacingly. "This is a waste of my time. I'm going to look at other teams." Lin had stacks of business plans that amounted to "I'll do anything you like!" If Goldman saw promise in China sourcing as an idea, it could find plenty of credentialed stars who were eager to go after it.

Ma's tone softened. He suggested a compromise: fifty-fifty ownership.

Eventually, the two settled on the even split, a rough echo of the terms that Arthur Rock offered founders in the 1960s. Goldman would pay $5 million for its half of the company, which Ma called Alibaba. After all the sparring about ownership, the size of Goldman's check was oddly uncontentious. "I pulled out a random number," Lin said later.

Before there was time to discuss further details, Lin's red Nokia cell phone slipped from her hand and fell into the sea. The conversation ended.

The following Tuesday, Lin dialed into the Goldman Sachs investment committee in New York. She explained her proposal.

The response was icy. "They said, 'Five million dollars for this nothing?'" Lin paraphrased later.

"Okay, but we run the company," Lin countered.

The New Yorkers refused to approve Lin's deal unless she off-loaded one-third of the stake. "Get rid of $1.7 million tomorrow," they ordered.[17]

Rather like Venrock, which landed the Series A deal with the pungent Steve Jobs and then gave away a chunk of the equity to Arthur Rock, Goldman duly gave up 17 percent of Alibaba, parceling it out among four other investment companies. Fifteen years later, Goldman could see what it had given up. Alibaba staged a triumphant IPO. That $1.7 million stake would have been worth an astonishing $4.5 billion.

Two months later, in December 1999, Ma and his team were desperate for more capital. Facing unaccustomed scrutiny since going public back in May, Goldman was loath to pump more money into the obscure Chinese startup. The New York bosses instructed Lin to find another investor. If somebody could be persuaded to come in at a premium to the valuation that Goldman had paid, the new round would boost the paper value of the bank's stake. "Why don't you try to mark it up?" New York suggested.

"First you want me to get rid of $1.7 million; then you want me to mark it up?" Lin huffed. "Every day they want me to perform magic!" she told herself bitterly.[18]

In January 2000, Lin spoke to Mark Schwartz, Goldman's Asia Pacific chairman. Schwartz was close to Masayoshi Son and on the board of SoftBank. Lin explained her dilemma: she had a portfolio of China startups, but New York didn't like them. "I've got seven companies. Maybe your friend Masa could invest in all of them?" she asked hopefully.

"Which one is most desperate?" Schwartz asked her.

"Alibaba is very, very desperate," Lin answered.[19]

Schwartz talked to Son. The China market was hot. Goldman had a portfolio of startups that could use some extra capital.

Pretty soon, SoftBank arranged for Son to meet several Chinese tech entrepreneurs in Beijing. They lined up to meet him, one after another, providing Son with a day of investment speed dating. Ma was on the roster, and Son liked his manner; "his eyes were very strong, shining eyes," Son said later.[20] The two shook hands on an investment, with Son advising Ma to spend the money fast and expand his business rapidly.[21]

To finalize the deal, Son and Ma met again, this time at Son's office in Tokyo. There was a traditional tatami floor, rice-paper walls, and samurai swords by way of decoration. As the principal incumbent shareholder, Lin joined the meeting too. Her original deal with Alibaba gave her an effective veto right on new capital raisings, so Son had to negotiate with her.

Lin proposed that SoftBank invest $20 million in Alibaba in exchange for a fifth of the company. The implied valuation of $100 million was ten times what Lin and her co-investors had paid three months earlier.

Just as he had done with Yahoo, half a decade before, Son said yes immediately, without hesitating.

"He just accepted the number I said," Lin marveled later. "I was thinking, 'He is crazy!' It was like when somebody says yes to you in the most improbable way. You feel that total excitement."[22]

In quick succession, Son invested in several of Lin's China startups. But there was more method to Son's madness than Lin recognized. Although Son appeared to commit to Alibaba almost casually, on the strength of a self-interested tip from Goldman and two meetings with Ma, there was a reason for his conviction. Because of his position on the board of Cisco, he knew that router sales to China had begun to take off. Internet usage was about to explode, so it made sense to sprinkle capital on anything that stood to benefit.[23] Lin's startups were a convenient way for Son to get some skin in the game, and $20 million was pocket change to him.[24] With the Nasdaq's fall two months away, he was by his own reckoning one of the richest men on the planet.[25]

In time, Son's willingness to bet fast would rebuild the fortune he would lose during the Nasdaq's implosion. When Alibaba went public in 2014, Son's stake was worth $58 billion.[26] It was the single most successful bet in venture history.[27]

◆

At this stage in the story, two points are worth noting. First, the Chinese government had played no direct role in launching Alibaba, a company that would become a pillar of the nation's digital economy. Second, and contrastingly, U.S. finance had made all the difference. But the U.S. influence on Ma and Alibaba extended beyond the capital that they received. Arthur Rock's intellectual heirs conspired with Ma to deploy stock options as a magic weapon.

Implanting Silicon Valley's equity culture in China involved some heroic maneuvers. The whole idea of tradable equity was novel to the mainland; its two clunky stock exchanges, in Shanghai and Shenzhen, had opened as recently as 1990. Employee stock options were not recognized in Chinese law, nor were the various sorts of "preferred" stock that Silicon Valley investors use to solidify their rights in startups.[28] In a further complication, the Chinese government forbade foreign ownership of a broad swath of Chinese businesses, including ones that ran websites. This meant that U.S. venture investments into companies like Alibaba were on their face illegal, as was the listing of Chinese internet stocks on America's Nasdaq market. Because China's immature stock markets were not set up to deal with listings by young tech companies, this legal blockage could have killed China's digital economy in its cradle. Far from promoting the development of the tech sector, Chinese policy threatened to smother it.

To breathe life into China tech, the U.S. VCs and their lawyers came up with a series of workarounds.[29] To begin with, the Chinese internet companies they backed were incorporated in the Cayman Islands. Cayman law allowed for every variety of stock: common shares for the startup founders, share options for employees, preferred shares for the investors. Further, a Cayman outfit could accept investment capital from a non-Chinese VC: Goldman Sachs was forbidden to invest in an internet startup in Hangzhou, but it could buy shares in its Cayman parent. Finally, the Cayman shell could easily be listed on a non-Chinese stock exchange such as the Nasdaq, providing a way around the blockage of China's primitive markets.

Once the Cayman company had been established, the next task was to use its venture dollars to build a business in China. To get around the prohibition on foreigners owning equity in a Chinese internet venture, the Cayman dollars were pumped into a parallel Chinese-owned operating company in the form of a loan.[30] Then, to give foreign investors the sorts of rights that they expected from venture deals, Silicon Valley's lawyers invented what amounted to synthetic equity. They executed a series of side contracts between a China-based subsidiary of the Cayman company and the Chinese-owned internet operator. The Chinese internet company granted control rights to its foreign creditors, simulating the influence that comes with an equity stake. The Chinese company also agreed to pay interest on its foreign loan in amounts that varied according to the success of the business: in effect if not in law, the foreigners received dividends. Finally, to cap off these arrangements, all parties agreed that disputes would be resolved under New York law. Chinese officials refused to bless this Silicon Valley confection. But, to be fair, they tolerated it.[31]

Having grafted in the U.S. equity culture and its legal props, China's internet startups enjoyed opportunities that Chinese law denied them.[32] They could raise money from U.S. venture investors. They could aspire to go public on the Nasdaq. And they could recruit star employees by offering them stock options. This was all so novel that in the first part of 1999 Chinese American entrepreneurs were struggling to translate "stock option" into Chinese and to understand how these things functioned.[33] On a trip to Silicon Valley shortly before Goldman's investment, Jack Ma dined with John Wu, a Chinese-born, American-trained coder who was the lead engineer at Yahoo. Wu remembers Ma grilling him about how Silicon Valley startups recruited staff, prompting Wu to deliver a tutorial on the mechanics of stock-based compensation.[34]

Once he took Goldman's money and acquired the Cayman structure, Ma was in a position to put this tutorial into practice. His first coup was to hire Joe Tsai, his ex-Yale, ex–Sullivan & Cromwell investor, who waved goodbye to the $700,000 salary that went with his Hong Kong finance job. Because Ma's small company had big prospects, Tsai accepted cash wages of just $600 per year, figuring that the accompanying options would more than compensate. Next, Ma set out to upgrade his engineering team, targeting none other than John Wu of Yahoo. Initially, Wu dismissed Ma's advances—why would he leave his position at one of the Valley's hottest companies? But Ma countered with a generous package of options, plus a twist. He told Wu he could remain in California, build his own team, and use an additional pool of employee stock options to attract great people. Wu duly accepted, creating a thirty-strong Alibaba outpost in Fremont, across the bay from Palo Alto. The style of the Fremont operation, Wu said later, was "totally American." "I would not have left without the options," he added.[35]

Thanks to world-class recruits like Tsai and Wu, Ma built Alibaba into a world-class company. It became what Fairchild had been for the Valley— not just a formidable enterprise in its own right, but a training ground for go-getters who spun out and created their own startups. And Alibaba was not the only pillar of China's digital economy created with U.S. input. Tencent, Alibaba's future rival, also got its start in 1998, backed by a $1.1 million investment from a U.S. venture shop called IDG. Baidu, at times China's third-largest internet giant, received capital from a fund led by the Silicon Valley investor Tim Draper. The three early Chinese internet portals—Sina, Sohu, and NetEase—all took foreign capital. So did Ctrip and EachNet, pioneers, respectively, in online travel bookings and online auctions. In 2004, in an echo of Alibaba's recruitment of Joe Tsai, Tencent used equity-based compensation to lure away a Goldman banker, Martin Lau, to become one of its top executives.[36] In short, U.S. capital, legal structures, and talent were central to the development of China's digital economy. Without this American input, companies like Alibaba could not have gotten off the ground, and today's Chinese dominance of technologies such as mobile payments would not have been likely either.

Looking back on her experiences two decades later, Shirley Lin's only regret was that her firm never embraced her China internet portfolio. Not being a proper venture-capital shop, Goldman Sachs was leery of investment specialties whose rules were imprecise. It preferred to back companies whose competitive edge was obvious: an established business with demonstrated pricing power, or a younger firm with a proprietary technology. "I could not fit in, because you could not formally describe my method as a VC," Lin remembered. One time, Lin visited a senior Goldman partner, a woman who had worked on the technology sector in Israel. The partner inspected Lin's stack of one-pagers on her startups and poured scorn on the entire bunch: lacking a technological edge, they would never amount to anything. To make sure she got her message across, she flung Lin's stack of papers on the floor. "So dramatic!" Lin recalled. "Like I'm in a TV show."[37]

Soon after that incident, in 2001, Goldman encouraged Lin to give up her position as a director of Alibaba. The internet bubble had burst, and Goldman wanted its partners to spend time on big-ticket investments, not scruffy long-shot ventures. Lin resisted fiercely, but her place at Alibaba was assigned to one of her deputies, Allen Chu, whose mandate was to implement the view from New York: that Goldman should never have invested. At one point, Chu suggested winding up the company and taking out the cash: for a proud firm like Goldman, Alibaba was just not worth the energy.[38] Lin eventually left the firm, and Goldman went on to sell its Alibaba stake for a forgettable profit of 6.8x on her original position.[39]

Goldman's fit of impatience resulted in one of venture history's worst-timed exits. Gary Rieschel would soon be arriving in Shanghai, and the second China internet wave was about to get started.

———◆———

Whereas the first wave of China venture deals had been led by a surprising mix of investors, many of them offshore, the second wave featured mainstream venture capitalists, mostly based in China. Rieschel's commitment to build a U.S.-style venture partnership headquartered in Shanghai was one sign of this shift, but Qiming was part of a broader phenomenon. Starting in the mid-2000s, several big U.S. venture shops jetted into China to recruit local teams; in fact, talented Chinese investors were in such demand that they frequently hopped from one U.S. partnership to another. Meanwhile, Chinese investors who had worked at western outfits began to set up on their own. The goal was to combine U.S. venture methodology with Chinese implementation.

The first notable spinout was Kathy Xu, another woman who managed to flourish in China's venture industry. Rather than studying in the United States, Xu had experienced U.S. instruction at Nanjing University, where she had majored in English. One teacher, an impressive African American woman named Donda West, instilled in her pupils an American ethos. "You are unique, you are a marvel. There has been no person like you in the last 500 years and there will be no person like you in the next 500 years," she lectured. This paean to individualism was, as Xu recalled vividly, an eye-opening experience for a Chinese teenager from Sichuan.[40] Donda West also stuck in Xu's memory because of her son, who was often seen performing acrobatic tricks on campus. Years later, Xu was intrigued to discover that the boy, named Kanye, had become famous.

Xu progressed from Nanjing University to a job as a clerk at the state-owned Bank of China. She earned 78 renminbi per month, the equivalent of about 10 U.S. dollars. Enthusiastic and diligent, she became a leader of the Communist Youth League and spent her tea breaks helping co-workers learn English. For her efforts she was awarded the title of "Woman Banner Holder," an honor that came with a certificate and a bedsheet.[41] In 1992, the year of her twenty-fifth birthday, Xu applied for a coveted audit position at Price Waterhouse in British-ruled Hong Kong, and by cramming an accounting textbook over the course of several nights, she landed it. For the next dozen years, she absorbed Hong Kong's version of Anglo-American finance, moving from Price Waterhouse to an investment bank and then to a private-equity partnership.[42] Along the way, she invested in Chinese internet startups, including the early portal NetEase and an online jobs agency called ChinaHR. The experiences taught her how to bond with young founders, hire and fire chief executives, and help to build teams. When ChinaHR was eventually acquired by its American competitor, the English major from Sichuan earned $50 million.

In 2005, Xu quit Hong Kong to establish Capital Today, her own

Shanghai-based venture fund. She raised $280 million and went out to hunt for startups. Her plan was to make just a handful of investments, as few as five or six per year, and ride the winners for as long as possible. "There are not many great companies in the world," she reflected, sounding like a Chinese version of Peter Thiel, who launched Founders Fund in the same year. "If you're lucky enough to find one, hold on. That's how you make money."[43]

Toward the end of 2006, Xu showed up for a meeting at the Shangri-La Hotel in Beijing. It was ten in the evening—a normal time for a venture pitch in China's frenetic business culture. Xu was to meet Richard Liu, the young founder of an e-commerce site that he would later call JD.com.[44]

Even by Chinese standards, the young man seemed driven. His coding was self-taught. He held management meetings on Saturday mornings. He watched his website like a hawk, responding to user comments every two minutes. By dint of aggressive discounting and speedy delivery, Liu quickly dominated every product segment he tackled. Sales at JD.com were growing by 10 percent per month. At this rate, in three years, JD's size would have grown almost thirty-fold.

Around two in the morning at the Shangri-La Hotel, Xu resolved that she would not miss this investment. She asked Liu how much capital he needed.

"Two million dollars," Liu answered.

"Not enough," Xu countered. To sustain his exponential growth, Liu surely needed more than that. The world's largest online retail market beckoned. JD had to grab it fast, before competitors muscled in on the territory.

"I'll give you $10 million," Xu said.[45]

Liu seemed excited, perhaps even overwhelmed, which was exactly what Xu wanted. In the United States, the youth revolt had brought a backlash against venture capitalists who doled out too much cash. But China's startup founders confronted a vast market opportunity and relatively scarce finance.

To make sure she sealed the deal, Xu informed Liu that they must fly to her office in Shanghai to finalize the term sheet. She bought tickets for the flight leaving at 9:00 a.m., in just a few hours; that way, "he had no time to meet anyone else," as she explained later.[46] After a moment's hesitation, she booked herself an unaccustomed seat in economy class. She wanted to sit next to Liu, and she also wanted him to stay frugal.

Xu's company, Capital Today, duly invested $10 million in exchange for 40 percent of JD.com. Liu quickly expanded his range of products and up-graded JD's distribution. For her part, Xu coached Liu on the case for hir-ing top-class talent: as JD grew, the founder would have to delegate. At first, Liu objected that new hires could not on any account be paid more than early ones: the long marchers had to be respected. But Xu coaxed him into accepting a finance chief who breached the pay ceiling, and Liu quickly came around. "This 20,000-renminbi guy is much better than the 5,000-renminbi guys!" he marveled. "Can you hire more for me?"[47] Xu duly came up with a new head of retail and a new head of logistics. Pretty soon, JD began recruiting on China's elite college campuses.

Just as Arthur Rock had done at Intel, Xu designed JD's employee stock-option plan. She adopted the standard vesting period of four years, condi-tional upon JD.com hitting its business goals. After just two years, however, the company had blown past its targets, and Xu happily released the pay-out early. Liu assembled his employees to announce the good news. His goal, he informed them, was to make everybody rich. He aimed to have a hundred employees worth more than 100 million renminbi (about $15 mil-lion) and a thousand employees worth more than 10 million ($1.5 million). He sounded like Jim Clark of Netscape, liberating Marc Andreessen's cod-ing friends from the University of Illinois.

Of course, the riches also flowed to Xu, whose firm had laid its hands on fully two-fifths of JD's equity. Thanks to this and other hits, Capital To-day's first fund racked up a remarkable return of 40 percent per year after subtracting fees; for every dollar invested, her backers got a payout of more than $10. Not surprisingly, given this springboard, Xu raised a larger fund of $400 million in 2010 and then an even larger long-term fund of $750 mil-lion. Chinese venture capital was gathering momentum.

In that pivotal year of 2005—the launch year for Founders Fund, Y Combi-nator, Qiming, and Capital Today—a wiry entrepreneur named Neil Shen flew to Laguna Beach in California. He had grown up in China, attended graduate school in the United States, and worked as an investment banker. Now he was in California to tell a financial conference about one of the two startups he had co-founded: the Nasdaq-listed online travel company Ctrip. While he was at the conference, he got a message from a friend. Sequoia's leaders, Michael Moritz and Doug Leone, wanted to meet him.[48]

Shen could guess the reason. With his fluency in two cultures, his background in investment banking, and his entrepreneurial success, Shen was ideally positioned to join China's venture gold rush. Already, three China-based VCs had tried to recruit him. Sequoia was a natural sequel.

Shen agreed to extend his California stay to make a stop in San Francisco. He met Moritz and Leone at the Four Seasons Hotel on Market Street, which was emerging as a tech cluster as Silicon Valley's tentacles spread northward. Sequoia had also invited a China-based VC named Zhang Fan, who was ready to jump ship from his current fund. Like Shen, Zhang had the perfect binational profile. He was an alumnus of Goldman Sachs, Stanford, and Beijing's prestigious Tsinghua University.[49]

The four men talked together for an hour and a half. They made for a surprising group: the British American Moritz, slim and dapper; the Italian American Leone, with a chest like a barrel; and the two hard-charging prospective partners, American by training and Chinese by passport.

As the conversation developed, the Sequoia duo warmed to the visitors. Leone, who had made seven or eight trips to China to identify a local team, could see that Shen and Zhang were stronger than the other candidates he had encountered.[50] Both had quit the security of investment banking to get involved in venture and startups: they understood entrepreneurial risk-taking. As well as co-founding the Nasdaq-quoted Ctrip, Shen had helped to start a budget hotel company, Home Inns & Hotels Management, which was also heading for a U.S. listing. Meanwhile, Zhang could boast a role in the early backing of Baidu, the Chinese equivalent to Google.

Shen and Zhang were likewise impressed by the Sequoia partners. As an entrepreneur, Shen had seen his peers grow frustrated with China-based investors who reported to distant U.S.-based investment committees that knew nothing of the Chinese context. But before Shen could even state his objections to long-distance meddling, Moritz and Leone announced emphatically that their China partners would make independent decisions. They had already established a Sequoia team in Israel and had met with mediocre results. The chief lesson they had learned was that there should be no California committee micromanaging far-off judgments. "Think global, act local," was how Moritz put it. Staffing and investment choices should be made by the people on the ground. "The joke was, 'Unless you want to call yourself Neil Shen & Associates, why would you say no to this proposal?'" Shen remembered later.[51]

Toward the end of 2005, Shen and Zhang signed on as co-leaders of Sequoia China. Leone paraded them in front of some Sequoia limited partners, and they raised a fund of $180 million—smaller than the war chest raised by Kathy Xu, because Sequoia was not going to risk its reputation by going big immediately.[52] Shen then chose a correspondingly modest office in Hong Kong, in the same block where Ctrip was located. Sequoia China was itself a scruffy startup, after all. It would not mimic the flashy quarters of the U.S. investment banks and private-equity shops on the island.[53]

Despite their promises of autonomy for the Chinese team, Moritz and Leone approached Shen and Zhang like other Sequoia-backed founders. They respected them, to be sure. But they were also determined to be mentors and guides, whatever the challenges of culture and distance. This meant steering a course between excessive meddling and the disengagement that doomed foreign satellites at other venture partnerships. For example, Benchmark's partners had set up a London operation in 2000 and left the locals to make their own way; they had not logged enough air miles to integrate the satellite into the mother ship. The upshot was that in 2007 the London team formalized its de facto independence, stopped sharing profits with the California gang, and left Benchmark without a European presence. Meanwhile, Kleiner Perkins suffered a similar setback in China. In 2007, John Doerr helped to recruit four Chinese investors, but he made the fatal error of delegating most of the managerial follow-up to lieutenants who lacked the standing to build the culture of the new shop. "When John came, he helped because he has the character, the stature," one of the KP China team recalled. "But when you have someone more junior coming in . . . Frankly, do they really know what they are doing?"[54] In less than a year, Kleiner's China shop disintegrated and had to be built back again.[55]

In their approach to Shen and Zhang, Moritz and Leone were more consistent and determined. Far from delegating China challenges, they took the burden on themselves, cycling in and out of the country every couple of months.[56] "We were not franchising our name; we were operating Sequoia," Moritz said later.[57] The China partners made reverse trips to California to observe best practices: how to run a Monday investment meeting, what to listen for in company pitches, how to conduct due diligence on prospective investments. Shen in particular was eager to learn. "I had never been a venture capitalist before," he acknowledged.[58]

Transferring best practices from Silicon Valley to China proved less than straightforward. It was one thing to borrow U.S. legal structures that operated offshore, thereby enabling the use of stock options for employees. It was another to graft U.S. investment methodology, and indeed ethics, onto the practice of venture capital in China's Wild West economy. The mainland's commercial culture was notoriously cutthroat. Entrepreneurs were sometimes known to use political contacts to have rivals harassed or arrested. U.S.-backed Chinese venture capitalists therefore found themselves straddling two worlds. As veterans of China's business battles, their instinct was to fight their corner. But as bearers of a Silicon Valley brand, they would get in trouble if they cut corners.

Sure enough, in late 2008, Shen found himself facing an embarrassing lawsuit. The private-equity shop Carlyle sued him for $206 million, claiming that he had cheated it out of an investment in a Chinese medical research company. According to the complaint, Carlyle had signed an exclusive term sheet with the firm, but Shen had elbowed it aside by fraudulently backdating a rival bid so that it appeared to preexist the Carlyle one.[59] The case was settled privately, without Shen admitting fault. Meanwhile, Shen also clashed with a rival firm called Hillhouse, which had spun out of the Yale endowment. "The Sequoia guys in California could have panicked and said, 'I am not going to deal with this,'" one of those involved said later. Instead, Moritz and Leone stood by their man. Like any venture bet, Sequoia China was risky. But Moritz and Leone were practiced risk-takers.

Around the same time as the lawsuit, Sequoia faced an even greater test of its resolve. One Saturday evening, when Moritz was north of San Francisco enjoying the peace of his weekend home, he took a call from China.

On the other end of the line, Moritz could hear the opposite of peace: Shen and Zhang were arguing. One was demanding that a team member be fired. The other was adamant that he not be.

Moritz listened to the tension between the two men. If this was just the tip of the iceberg, Sequoia's China team was about to unravel. The next morning Moritz cut short his weekend and headed to the airport.

Landing in Hong Kong, Moritz spent time talking to the team at the Sequoia office. He soon picked up that Zhang's first investments didn't appear to be going anywhere.[60] Meanwhile, Shen had backed at least two startups that were showing promise. If the two founders were at odds, Moritz knew which one to bet on.

By the end of 2008, Zhang had resigned from the firm and the tension had ended. Sequoia was ready to push forward with its China investment.

Like many founders whom Sequoia backed, it took Shen five years to demonstrate progress. But in 2010, four Sequoia China companies went public on the New York Stock Exchange, and Sequoia Capital hosted its biennial investors' conference in Beijing, the first time it had convened its limited partners outside U.S. borders.[61] The heating and air-conditioning in the Beijing Hyatt malfunctioned, subjecting the assembled crowd to strange changes in temperature. But Sequoia had made the leap from a Valley firm to a global one.

By now, the broader China technology scene was also maturing. In 2010, China-focused venture capitalists raised $11.2 billion, an almost threefold increase in five years, and U.S.-headquartered venture firms completed more than one hundred investments in China for the first time ever.[62] With capital easily available, China's entrepreneurs began to dream bigger. Pioneers such as Alibaba had shown the heights that could be scaled, and upstart imitators could see that the fastest-growing economy in the world offered unbounded opportunity. As the network of VCs and founders grew denser, China's innovation system approached its next significant inflection point—the watershed that Silicon Valley had reached around 1980.

Silicon Valley's early development could be divided into three phases. At first, capital was scarce, investors few, and entrepreneurs had trouble raising money: this described China in the late 1990s, at the time of Lin's Alibaba investment. Next, money flowed in, the tally of venture capitalists shot up, and startups multiplied both in numbers and in ambition: this was analogous to China around 2010. Finally, as competition among startups became hectic and costly, the Valley's venture capitalists performed a co-ordinating function. They brokered takeovers, encouraged mergers, and steered entrepreneurs into areas that were not already swamped; as the super-connectors in the network, they shaped a decentralized production system. This was the final threshold that China had to cross. By 2015, it would have done so.

China's progress from phase two to phase three was crystallized in the story of Wang Xing, the founder of a stupendously successful Chinese food-delivery empire named Meituan. Introverted, analytical, certain of his own judgment, Wang was in many ways a Chinese version of Mark Zuckerberg. After graduating from Tsinghua University, he pursued a PhD in computer engineering in the United States, but he soon decided to drop out, deter-mined to make his fortune with a startup. In quick succession, he pursued a string of copycat ventures, churning out a Chinese version of the early social-networking website Friendster, then mimicking Facebook and Twit-ter. In 2010, noticing the explosive growth of the U.S. discount-booking website Groupon, he pivoted again. His new company would bulk buy res-taurant tables, cinema seats, and retail goods at a discount, then sell them on to bargain hunters. This was the venture he called Meituan.

Wang was not the only entrepreneur to go after the group-buying op-portunity. A polished showman named Wu Bo had launched a similar ven-ture, and a rush of other Groupon clones seemed likely. But with three previous startups behind him, Wang had graduated summa cum laude from the school of hard knocks, and he had a firm sense of what it took to at-tract users cost effectively. When Sequoia China considered which horse it

Arthur Rock kick-started the modern venture-capital industry, backing
early hits such as Fairchild Semiconductor and Intel, and improvising an
investment style that ignored the standard rules of finance. In 1968, *Forbes*
posed the burning question on the minds of its readers, "How do you get
to be like Arthur Rock?"

Don Valentine founded Sequoia Capital in 1972, adding a muscular, hands-on activism to the venture-capital playbook. He backed entrepreneurs who were brilliant but wayward: the early video-game impresario Nolan Bushnell held board meetings in his hot tub.

Kleiner Perkins Caufield & Byers was founded the same year as its archrival, Sequoia. Tom Perkins, the flamboyant force behind Kleiner's early triumphs, is pictured second from the left. On the far left is his young partner, John Doerr. Frank Caufield, far right, called Doerr "a little Mozart."

Mitch Kapor (left) a former teacher of transcendental meditation, founded the software pioneer Lotus Development, generating a big win for Kleiner Perkins and John Doerr (below) when Lotus went public. Later, Doerr and Kapor collaborated on a disastrous tablet-computer project called GO, proving that being early can be the same as being wrong in venture capital. By the 1990s, Doerr was said to have "the emotional commitment of a priest and the energy of a racehorse."

Jim Swartz (left) and Arthur Patterson (right), the cofounders of Accel Capital, developed an investment style that contrasted with Doerr's swashbuckling moon shots. Patterson advocated a deliberative, "prepared-mind" approach, and Accel became the first partnership to position itself as a specialist in particular technologies.

David Filo (left) and Jerry Yang (right) founded Yahoo, the first deliberately zany internet brand. Yahoo's mission was to bring order to cyberspace, but Filo's office was often littered with Rollerblades, CD cases, crumpled soda cans, old copies of the *Micro Times*, and a blue-plaid polyester blanket.

Masayoshi Son persuaded Yahoo's founders to accept an unprecedented
$100 million investment, telling them that if they turned him down, he would
put capital behind their rivals. Son's willingness to up the stakes with enormous
checks caused rivals to compare him variously to a reckless poker player and
to North Korea's dictator.

Pierre Omidyar (left) turned eBay into a hit with the help of Benchmark Capital.
The venture team persuaded Meg Whitman (right) to quit a safe corporate job
and make the leap to run an obscure startup. Derided by some as a Beanie Baby
trading site, eBay generated a $5 billion profit for Benchmark.

Prodded by Sequoia, Peter Thiel (left) and Elon Musk (right) merged their startups to create PayPal, the precursor to today's fintech companies. Later, Thiel's loyalists ousted Musk while he was abroad on honeymoon. Thiel went on to back a string of hit ventures, including Facebook and Musk's company, SpaceX. He went further than other VCs in expounding on the significance of the power law.

The youngest woman to make partner at Goldman Sachs, Shirley Lin brought the U.S. venture playbook to China, backing a slew of internet startups, including Alibaba. Goldman later sold the Alibaba position prematurely, forgoing billions in profits.

Kathy Xu spent four hours with the entrepreneur Richard Liu, offered $10 million for 40 percent of his startup, and escorted him to her office to sign the deal before he could meet other investors. With her help, Liu built JD.com into a top e-commerce player and a member of the Fortune Global 500. Born and educated in China, Xu's success signaled the indigenization of Chinese venture capital.

PayPal alumni grew so powerful that they came to be known as the PayPal Mafia. In this mock-mobster photo, from left to right, top to bottom: Jawed Karim, cofounder of YouTube; Jeremy Stoppelman, cofounder of Yelp; Andrew McCormack, a member of the founding team at Thiel's hedge fund, Clarium Capital; Premal Shah, cofounder of Kiva; Luke Nosek and Ken Howery, early partners at Thiel's venture firm, Founders Fund; David Sacks, founder of Yammer; Thiel; Keith Rabois, a senior executive at LinkedIn and Square and later a venture capitalist; Reid Hoffman, cofounder of LinkedIn; Max Levchin, cofounder of Affirm; Roelof Botha, a top investor at Sequoia; and Russel Simmons, Stoppelman's cofounder at Yelp. Musk is conspicuous by his absence.

For all the winning bets it made on Silicon Valley startups, Sequoia's most successful play was to recruit Neil Shen, who established Sequoia China as the dominant venture firm in the country. For three straight years, Shen was the world's top venture capitalist.

Paul Graham (right) and Jessica Livingston (center) founded Y Combinator, revolutionizing the business of angel investing. A cult figure among coders, Graham showed that software startups could get going with minimal capital and just the right amount of camaraderie. On Tuesday evenings, he cooked "glop" for his protégés at the Y Combinator office, while Livingston served her trademark lemonade and mint iced tea. Ev Williams, cofounder of Twitter, is on the left.

Chase Coleman (right) and Scott Shleifer (left) applied hedge-fund and private-equity thinking to tech firms in emerging markets. They scoured the world for "the this of the that": the Amazon of China, the Google of Russia, and so on. By placing large bets on companies entering their take-off phase, Coleman and Shleifer built their firm Tiger Global into one of the world's most lucrative technology-investment franchises.

Yuri Milner (right) brought the Tiger Global model to the United States. A Russian who had never set foot in Silicon Valley, he talked his way into the office of Mark Zuckerberg (left) on the strength of his analysis of the global social-media business. The resulting $300 million investment in Facebook made Milner a Valley celebrity and quickly inspired imitators.

Marc Andreessen (left) and Ben Horowitz (right) launched a new venture partnership in 2009, immediately vaulting into the top tier. Big characters with big reputations as coders and entrepreneurs, they rode the boom in cloud software and claimed to reinvent the venture business. They also learned from Milner's example, writing big "growth" checks to companies as they emerged from their startup phase.

Sequoia's leaders, Michael Moritz (above, left) and Doug Leone (below), were a study in contrasts. Moritz, a Brit who took Italian lessons, was a wiry endurance cyclist. Leone, an Italian who joked that working with Moritz was like taking English lessons, was a committed weight lifter. Despite their differences, Moritz and Leone pulled off the most successful buddy act in venture history. Moritz is pictured here, in blue, with fellow Welshman and Tour de France victor Geraint Thomas.

Jim Goetz (above, right) and Roelof Botha (below) helped to lead Sequoia after Moritz retired from management. Goetz introduced Accel's "prepared-mind" thinking to the partnership and backed WhatsApp, one of Sequoia's most lucrative investments. Botha, a member of the PayPal Mafia, applied lessons from behavioral science to Sequoia's decision process. Goetz is pictured here with the WhatsApp founders Jan Koum (center) and Brian Acton (left) in front of the welfare office where Koum had once stood in line to receive food stamps.

As tech firms delayed IPOs, they achieved "unicorn" status: their valuations shot past the $1 billion mark, even as they remained private. WeWork's Adam Neumann (right) and Uber's Travis Kalanick (middle) became the poster children for the risks in this state of affairs: as passive growth investors showered them with capital, unicorn founders could be disciplined neither by their venture backers nor by the stock market. Bill Gurley of Benchmark (bottom), the lead venture capitalist behind Uber, found himself unable to talk restraint into Kalanick as the founder veered from scandal to scandal. Eventually, Gurley ousted him.

should back, Wang emerged as the first choice. Shen's most trusted lieutenant, a quiet partner called Glen Sun, took on the task of courting him.[63]

Sun soon found that the new generation of entrepreneurs could be challenging to deal with; in this, too, Wang resembled Zuckerberg. Four years earlier, Xu had met JD's founder and deftly shepherded him to her office in Shanghai. Wang was harder to corral. It was hard even to meet him.

Sun had a JD from Harvard and a track record at the U.S. private-equity company General Atlantic. It was not the sort of pedigree that encourages humility. But now Sun embraced the role of supplicant, hanging around the run-down coffee shop next to Meituan's office in Beijing, hoping for an audience with a thirty-one-year-old. If he spotted Wang, he would sidle up and talk, often to be rewarded with no more than a few syllables. Undaunted, Sun tried to get to Wang by speaking to his wife, who ran Meituan's finances. He befriended Wang's co-founders and asked them to put in a good word for him. The chase presented a subtle psychological challenge. "You had to sort of figure out what he's thinking about and then make him interested in talking to you," Sun recalled. "We tried to talk about things that he's not very familiar with, so we could add value."[64] Annoyingly, Wang had educated himself on an encyclopedia of subjects. It was hard to find a worthwhile topic that he hadn't mastered already.[65]

"We're very interested in your company. We can sign anytime. We can wire money," Sun entreated Wang's wife.

"We are good people," he pleaded.[66]

Eventually, Wang relented, signing an agreement to part with a quarter of Meituan in exchange for a $3 million investment. But during the three months or so it took to prepare the Cayman legal structure, Meituan experienced a growth spurt. Ignoring his written agreement, Wang now demanded a fourfold jump in valuation. For a quarter of his company, Sequoia would have to pay $12 million.

At this, a western venture capitalist might have walked away. But during his time at Ctrip, Shen had pulled a similar trick on an investor.[67] Comfortable in China's ruthless culture, he and Sun accepted Wang's new terms, and the deal was completed.

Having paid top dollar for its stake, Sequoia found itself caught up in an extreme version of the fight between X and PayPal. In 2011, an extraordinary five thousand group-buying websites sprouted in China; sometimes copious venture capital could liberate too many founders. What became known as "the war of a thousand Groupons" ensued, with combatants splurging money on ever deeper discounts in order to attract users. Chinese consumers seized the moment and ate out in droves. As the investor and author Kai-Fu Lee would comment, it was as though the venture-capital community were treating the whole nation to dinner.[68]

Meituan survived the first phase of the war easily. Most of the contenders were underfunded and naive; they were killed off quickly. By 2013, Meituan's chief remaining rival was Dianping, the creation of a Wharton-educated founder named Zhang Tao who had also raised capital from Sequoia China. Dianping had started out as a clone of the online review site Yelp. But it had pivoted into group discounts, putting Sequoia in the uncomfortable position of backing two sworn enemies.

With the field much narrowed but competition still fierce, the natural way forward for Sequoia was to merge its two portfolio companies. But China's ruthless business culture was wired to compete. The idea of a merger was an alien U.S. stratagem.

Knowing he needed to tread delicately, Shen suggested to Wang that he speak to his Dianping counterpart, Zhang Tao. It would make sense to end the bloodshed with a merger.

Wang agreed to try, but his idea of a good merger was one that gave him control of the combined company. Zhang was older and mellower. But he was not ready to play second fiddle.

At the start of 2015, the two sides resumed open warfare. Meituan returned to its investors and raised $700 million, hoping to administer a deathblow to its rival. Dianping counterpunched, assembling its own war chest of $850 million. A blitz of competitive spending ensued. By the summer, exhausted and running low on cash, both companies returned to their backers for yet more ammunition.

This time, however, the investors balked. There were only so many restaurant meals they were prepared to subsidize. Moreover, while the Groupon clones were slugging it out, the changes stirring inside China's venture system were advancing.

—◆—

In the five years since Sequoia's triumphant Beijing conference and Wang Xing's founding of Meituan, venture fundraising in China had tripled again, hitting $32 billion.[69] As the industry expanded, clear leaders emerged, with Neil Shen foremost among them.[70] The best-connected Chinese investors, moreover, had come to know each other well. They provided the follow-on financings for each other's companies. They thought in the same terms. They had developed a professional code that made trust and coordination possible.[71] In February 2015, this maturation found expression in the first high-profile tech merger. Two ride-hailing companies, Didi and Kuaidi, ended their blood feud and joined forces.

In the summer of 2015, after Meituan and Dianping failed to raise further capital to continue their war, two things happened almost simultaneously. On the Meituan side, Wang Xing visited Neil Shen and asked him to reactivate the merger talks. On the Dianping side, the VC backers conspired to ensure that the founder was receptive to Wang's overture.

One of the investors in Dianping was Kathy Xu. When venture funding for the warring Groupon clones dried up, her supposed adversaries at Meituan contacted her, asking for capital.

"Really?" Xu exclaimed, astonished. "I'm the investor in your competitor!"

Xu put down the phone and pondered what had happened. Why had Meituan called? The company must be desperate.

Xu called Martin Lau, the ex-Goldman banker who had traded his job for Tencent's options package. Lau was now in charge of Tencent's extensive startup portfolio, which included a 20 percent stake in Dianping.

"You've got to play the white knight," Xu urged Lau on the phone. "I think they probably cannot raise money. And we cannot raise money.... It's either merge or die."[72]

Lau needed no persuading. In fact, he had already been thinking along these lines. As a former Goldman banker, he had grown up on the idea that mergers could be good for business. To make sure that Dianping warmed to the idea, Lau promised that Tencent would invest $1 billion into the business on the condition that it merged with Meituan.

With investors refusing to finance competition but pledging to finance its absence, the scene was set for a merger. VCs in China were now playing the coordinating role that they had long performed in the Valley.[73]

On September 19, 2015, Neil Shen and Martin Lau hosted Wang Xing and Zhang Tao at the discreet W hotel, located across a causeway from Hong Kong Island. The protagonists arrived separately so as not to attract attention. During the meal, which lasted two and a half hours, the conversation covered every conceivable topic except the question of the merger. Wang wore a light gray sweatshirt and faded jeans. Zhang sported a striped red and blue T-shirt.[74]

After lunch, the group moved upstairs to a suite that Shen had booked for the negotiations. Shen and Lau gave opening speeches, emphasizing the logic of the merger and the synergy between the two firms. Stitching the two together would involve painful decisions, but Shen and Lau assured the assembled company that the pain would be worthwhile. As the trusted senior statesmen of China's digital economy, they pledged to do their part to make the merger fair to both parties.

Having set the direction, the statesmen stepped aside and let the entrepreneurs discuss the details. Each point of progress was written out on a whiteboard: corporate structure, brand name, who would call what shots in the merged company. But with the prestige of Tencent and Sequoia weighing on the proceedings, the outcome was not in doubt. At 7:07 p.m., the two sides shook hands on a rough framework for the merger.

As soon as he could extricate himself, Shen left hurriedly for a pizza restaurant in the Landmark shopping mall, across the causeway in the business district. His wife was out of town, and he was late for dinner with his two daughters.

"This is business, unfortunately," he apologized when he got there.[75]

A week or so later, Shen flew to Hayman Island, a lavish resort off the coast of Australia. He was there for a celebrity wedding: Richard Liu, the JD founder, was marrying a much younger bride, famous on Chinese social media for her innocent beauty. In its splashy extravagance, the celebration signaled that Chinese tech had arrived: the country's newly minted billionaires could live as opulently as American ones. But it signaled China's arrival in another way as well. The guest list was thick with names from China's digital-cum-financial elite. As in Silicon Valley, China's innovation engine had become a social cluster.

Shen attended the ceremony, elegant in black tie, and left swiftly afterward. On the day of the merger negotiations at the W hotel, he had rushed from a business engagement to a social one. Now it was the opposite.

Leaving the wedding party, Shen found Martin Lau and Bao Fan, a former Morgan Stanley banker who had been hired to turn the Meituan-Dianping framework into a completed merger.

Still wearing their bow ties, the three disappeared into a room and got down to business. The negotiators from Meituan and Dianping were proceeding at a crawl; driving them across the finishing line was going to require the coordinating force of their investors. Both Meituan and Dianping employed teams of executives running duplicative business lines: each had a food take-out service, a restaurant-booking service, and so on. Competition had involved one kind of intolerable bloodbath. Now it felt as though consolidation might involve another.

Shen and his fellow wedding goers went through the list of sticking points, checking each one off. All three shared an interest in getting the deal done. If Meituan and Dianping could not figure out the needed compromise, the men from the wedding would guide them to the answers.

Eventually, after more long-distance direction dispensed from Australian beaches, Shen got what he wanted. On October 11, Meituan and Dianping announced their merger, creating a giant provider of take-out deliveries, movie tickets, and other local services. Just as Shen and Lau had prophesied, the combined company was far more valuable than the two had been as cash-burning rivals, and when Meituan-Dianping raised its next round of capital in January 2016, the sheer size of the bonanza became evident. Together, the companies were worth an astonishing $5 billion more than they had been as competitors.[76] The process begun at the W hotel had conjured a jackpot that even Sand Hill Road might envy.

—◆—

With that, China's venture-capital industry had completed its journey. An entirely Chinese network of investors, entrepreneurs, and bankers had pulled off a spectacular merger, creating a company ten times larger than PayPal had been at the point when it was sold to eBay. Neil Shen was entering the period when he would be crowned the number one venture capitalist in the world, not just once, but for three years consecutively. Wang Xing, for his part, progressed from billionaire to deca-billionaire, and his company became Sequoia Capital's most lucrative investment ever, surpassing even Google.[77] By 2019, admittedly, Meituan-Dianping had been eclipsed. But Sequoia's new gold medalist was another Chinese venture, ByteDance, operator of a wildly popular short-form video app named TikTok.

In the summer of 2016, Gary Rieschel packed his suitcases in Shanghai. He had known when to arrive, and now he knew when it was time to leave. An American outsider could no longer add much to China's venture industry.

Chapter Eleven

ACCEL, FACEBOOK, AND THE
DECLINE OF KLEINER PERKINS

I n the early years of the twenty-first century, in the shadow of the tech
bust, an entrepreneur named Kevin Efrusy joined Accel. It seemed a
crazy moment to be signing on: the venture industry was struggling,
and Accel was no exception. But the firm's senior partners made a persuasive pitch. Efrusy had engineering and business degrees from Stanford; he
had founded a startup and built up another one. But to become an established venture capitalist, Efrusy would need five years. If he began his training now, he would hit his stride as the tech market recovered.

Efrusy bought the argument. "In a way I had no choice," he said later.
"I was thirty; my wife was pregnant."[1] And although Accel was in the dol-
drums, he was soon pleasantly surprised. The firm's leaders, including the
gray-haired founders, Arthur Patterson and Jim Swartz, were serious about
investing for the long term, and this went for their young hires just as it did
for their portfolio companies. The way they saw things, Efrusy's primary
responsibility was not to serve in a support role for the senior investors. It
was to develop his own capacity to risk millions on startups.

From the day he attended his first Accel meeting, Efrusy was expected
to participate in the decisions. He could propose an investment to the
partnership, and if he convinced colleagues of his case, the investment
would go forward. He could vote against proposals from others; even if

the project was not in his wheelhouse, he was supposed to have a view on it. Nor was it enough to comment usefully; he was required to express a verdict, yes or no, and take responsibility for it. "There is a saying in our business, 'If you are treated like an analyst, you are going to act like an analyst,'" Efrusy explained later.[2] An analyst could point out the arguments on both sides of an issue, but that was different from taking a stand, and this difference defined the psychological gulf between being a venture capitalist and not being one. In the end, venture investing came down to that scary jump from messy information to a binary yes-or-no call. It came down to living with the reality that you would frequently be wrong. It was about showing up at the next partners' meeting, rising above your wounded pride, and mustering the optimism to make fresh bets on a bewildering future.

A few months into Efrusy's tenure, in October 2003, Accel conducted one of its "prepared mind" exercises. The investment team gathered at the Casa Madrona, an upscale place across the Golden Gate Bridge from San Francisco, in the pretty town of Sausalito. There was mountain biking in the afternoon, and a room was arranged to house the bikes of the two keenest young cyclists.[3] But the serious reason for the meeting was that Accel had closed only four deals so far that year, fewer than most of its rivals. A series of slides listed sixty-two software or internet investments done by other top firms; next to some there were notes saying, "Aware—lost?" or "Aware—didn't evaluate," signifying that Accel had failed to invest despite knowing of the opportunity. The slides also noted the particular promise of a new kind of online business. If Internet 1.0 had been about selling stuff (Amazon, eBay), Internet 2.0 was about using the web as a communications medium. "'2.0' frenzy around social networking; Accel may have missed the boat," one slide read.[4]

Having recognized Internet 2.0 as a hot field, the partnership's leaders encouraged Efrusy and other junior members of the team to go after it. The way Accel's founders saw things, there was a link between deliberately choosing a promising investment space, thereby reducing risk, and empowering the novices, thereby embracing risk. "It is a lot easier to turn young investors loose if you know they are working fertile ground," Jim Swartz said later.[5] With his mandate thus clarified, Efrusy began to look around. The first prospect to excite him was the internet telephony startup Skype. Here was a product that slashed the cost of long-distance calls, saving people real money.

Accel's London office was also tracking Skype, and Efrusy set up a video call to introduce the startup's Swedish creators to a London-based partner named Bruce Golden. For reasons of geographic proximity, Golden now became Accel's point man in pursuing the possibility of an investment. Efrusy remained in the loop, rooting for the deal from California. Jim Swartz, who had assumed responsibility for the cultural fit between Accel's California and London teams, helped to keep everybody on the same page. He shuttled back and forth each month, prompting and nudging to ensure that the two offices collaborated productively.

Golden was impressed by Skype's innovation and its exploding popularity. But he soon understood that Skype would be a challenging investment; there was more "hair on the deal" than he had ever seen before, as he wrote in his investment note.[6] Accel was accustomed to backing solid, straight-arrow entrepreneurs, but Skype's founders had been sued by the entertainment industry over online music theft. Accel favored startups that developed intellectual property that entrenched their market leadership; worryingly, Skype licensed its IP from a separate company and did not actually own it. Finally, Skype's founders were ruthless and inconstant in the negotiations over the term sheet. "I felt I was being jerked around," Golden said later. "The commitment that they had expressed to work with us seemed to mean little to them."[7] In the end, "Skype looked too weird to us," Efrusy recalled. "We decided not to do it. And then it proceeded to take off, up, up, up every month."[8]

As Skype's value soared, the Accel partners recognized the magnitude of their error. In venture, backing a project that goes to zero costs you one times your money. Missing a project that returns 100x is massively more painful. "There were some colleagues who said we should have locked the Skype guys in a room and not let them out until they signed," Golden remembered, perhaps with Efrusy in mind. "There was a lot of frustration

within the partnership."[9] But the good news was that Accel's distinctive culture gave it a way of processing its miss. It could build on the prepared-
mind exercise begun in Sausalito.

The building began with a reckoning about what it would take to land
deals in the Internet 2.0 arena. Skype was not the partnership's only painful social-media miss. Accel had also offered term sheets to a quiz company
called Tickle and a photo-sharing site called Flickr. Just as with Skype,
Accel had felt concerns about both firms and lost out to rival bidders.[10] Now,
as they extended the prepared-mind exercise, Efrusy and his colleagues
turned these experiences into a pair of lessons. First, Accel must reach beyond the reassuring engineers whom it was used to backing. Experience
showed that consumer internet companies were often founded by unorthodox characters: Yahoo and eBay had been founded by hobbyists. Second,
the good news about consumer internet companies was that you could
judge their prospects in a different way: you could look past the founders
and analyze the data on their progress. The next time Accel came across an
internet property that customers turned to multiple times per day, it should
seal the deal no matter what. In a world of power-law returns, the costs of
missing out were higher by far than the risk of losing one times your money.[11]

As one of the keenest proponents of the Skype deal, Efrusy could see
that the partnership's mindset had evolved. Accel would not be weirded out
by the next Skype-type opportunity. "When I first arrived at Accel, I thought
prepared mind was bullshit," Efrusy recalled later. "It isn't."[12]

◆

In the summer of 2004, Efrusy spent the July 4 holiday with his wife's family in Chicago. While he was there, a friend called him about a startup called
Myspace. It was a new kind of communications platform, a so-called social
network, and it was competing with the pioneer in the field, a startup called
Friendster that was backed by Kleiner Perkins and Benchmark. What
piqued Efrusy's interest was the difference between the two competitors.
Myspace had escaped the problem that bedevils most popular clubs: as
more people join, the original vibe gets watered down, and the early loyalists grow disaffected. Friendster in particular had developed a reputation

for being popular with Asian sex workers. Its original customers were drifting away, in some cases because they were tired of lurid solicitations.

"Check out Myspace," Efrusy's friend said. "It's Friendster with fewer prostitutes."

Efrusy opened his laptop and began counting the suggestive posts on the two websites. While he was still busy, another phone call interrupted him.

Efrusy's stepmother-in-law came by and saw his open laptop. Anxious, she told her stepdaughter, who in turn asked her husband to explain himself. Why was he trawling the internet for sex workers?

Strictly work, Efrusy assured her.

Indeed, it was work, and it was useful. Just as the prepared-mind exercise had primed Accel to jump on viral internet startups, so Efrusy's laptop research alerted him to a more specific opportunity. So long as Friendster had been the leading example of a social network, its troubles had suggested that the concept faced limits: as with nightclubs, you couldn't expand the service without tarnishing it. "Myspace told me, wait, there might be something here," Efrusy said later.[13]

In December 2004, Efrusy checked in with Chi-Hua Chien, a Stanford graduate student. Chien had a part-time gig that involved alerting Accel to startups that were popular on campus. He mentioned one called Thefacebook.

Efrusy dug out a Stanford alumnus email address, which allowed him to gain access to this thing that Chien had mentioned. The mere fact that he had to do this was a hopeful sign. By restricting admission to users with Stanford emails, Thefacebook was managing the Friendster problem of unwanted guests. It had put up the equivalent of a velvet rope outside a nightclub.

Once he had logged on, Efrusy was impressed to see that the site was labeled "Facebook Stanford." It was not just Facebook, or Facebook Worldwide; it promised a customized community. Stanford kids would get the feeling that they were joining their own crowd. This was the club that they belonged to.[14]

Efrusy resolved to meet the team behind this clever business. But the timing was bad: Thefacebook's leaders, Mark Zuckerberg and Sean Parker, had just made a mockery of Sequoia. As the Wirehog presentation showed, Zuckerberg and Parker liked nothing better than to snub prestigious venture partnerships.

Efrusy pulled all the standard tricks to get around this obstacle. Through a friend who had interviewed for a job with Thefacebook, he got an appointment to talk by phone with Parker. Then Parker canceled on him. Next, Efrusy discovered that another friend, Matt Cohler, had recently begun working for Parker. He called and asked for a second introduction. Sorry, Cohler said. Parker wasn't interested.

In early 2005, Efrusy heard from a colleague that Thefacebook had begun talking to other investors. He took a deep breath and emailed his contacts again. When nobody answered, Efrusy resorted to that old technology: the phone. Parker refused to return his voice messages.

Efrusy now opened up a third channel. He learned that Reid Hoffman, the founder of LinkedIn, had invested in Thefacebook. An Accel partner named Peter Fenton was close to Hoffman. Efrusy asked Fenton to help him.

Fenton called Hoffman and hit the same wall: Thefacebook wasn't open to a meeting. This time, however, the rejection was paired with a reason. As Hoffman explained it, Parker and Zuckerberg believed that venture capitalists would never understand their firm. They would not pay fair value for it.

Hoffman also mentioned that Thefacebook had an offer at a high valuation from a corporate investor. "You're not going to pay as much. This isn't worth your time," he said, as though not meeting Thefacebook might be in Accel's best interest.

Fenton relayed the message to Efrusy.

"It is worth my time!" Efrusy insisted. "I don't value my time as much as you value yours."

Fenton called Hoffman again. "It's worth our time," he told him.[15]

Having given a reason for the rejection, Hoffman felt obliged to help when that reason was invalidated. If Accel promised to take Thefacebook seriously—if it promised not to make an insulting lowball offer—then Hoffman would arrange a meeting with Parker.

Even after this, no meeting transpired. Hoffman did his best. But Parker was in hiding.

On April Fools' Day 2005, Efrusy grew tired of waiting. Emails had not worked. Telephoning had not worked. He had deployed three different intermediaries. There was one last maneuver he could try. He resolved to show up at Thefacebook in person, with or without an appointment.

It was a Friday afternoon, and Efrusy asked another thirtysomething colleague if he would accompany him. A visit from two Accel investors would make a stronger impression than a visit from one. And if Efrusy was going to sell the deal to his colleagues, he could always use an ally.

Efrusy's young colleague was busy.[16] But, in a testament to Accel's collaborative culture, Efrusy felt able to rope in the other investor who happened to be in the building: Arthur Patterson, the firm's co-founder.

Efrusy and Patterson walked four blocks down Palo Alto's University Avenue. Efrusy was big, balding, and thirty-three years old, with full cheeks and a strong build. Patterson was slender and sixty, his steely hair brushed into a clean part.

Arriving at Thefacebook office on Emerson Street, the pair ascended a long stairway, freshly spray-painted with graffiti. At the top was a giant image of a woman riding a big dog. The Ikea furniture in the loft space was only semi-assembled, like an outsized puzzle that had exhausted its owners. Half-empty booze bottles were strewn about the floor, a testament to Cohler's recent twenty-eighth birthday.[17]

Cohler himself was not at his best. In his struggle with the furniture, he had torn his jeans. His left pant leg was hanging open and his boxer shorts were visible.

"Hey Kevin," Cohler called out to Efrusy.

Efrusy had been hoping to see Sean Parker and Mark Zuckerberg. Both were said to be unavailable, or sick. So Efrusy and Patterson sat down with the disheveled Cohler.

Even with his underwear showing, Cohler was impressive. He rattled off statistics about Thefacebook's growth, the number of daily active users on the site, and the time they spent there. In his early days as an investor, Patterson had looked at media firms. Relative to the traditional user benchmarks he remembered from those days, the engagement that Thefacebook claimed was astonishing. Moreover, everything about this meeting followed the script laid out in the prepared-mind exercises of the past two years. Thefacebook's founders were unorthodox and elusive, and their office mural was an invitation to a sexual harassment suit. But if you ignored their conduct and focused instead on their data, Thefacebook was a can't-miss opportunity.[18]

Presently, Parker and Zuckerberg appeared at the top of the stairs. They were not sick after all. They were eating burritos.

Knowing the founders' impatience with questions from VCs, Efrusy avoided asking any. "I get how valuable this could be," he assured Parker and Zuckerberg, preempting what he knew to be their doubt. "Come to our partnership meeting on Monday, and I promise I'll either give you a term sheet by the end of the day Monday, or you'll never hear from me again."

Parker agreed to meet Efrusy for a beer the next evening. But before Efrusy and Patterson left, he wanted to show them the mural in the women's bathroom. It depicted one naked woman embracing the legs of another.

On the walk back to the Accel office, Patterson slapped Efrusy on the back. The prepared-mind exercise had done its work. "We have to do this," he exulted.[19]

***

Around lunchtime the next day, Efrusy headed over to the Stanford campus. He stopped students at random to ask if they knew of Thefacebook.

"I don't study. I'm addicted," one replied.

"The hub of my life," said another.[20]

Efrusy had an introduction to a sophomore at Duquesne University in Pittsburgh. He called her.

"Oh yeah, Thefacebook. It came here on October 23," the student told him.

"You know the exact date?" Efrusy asked.

"Of course," came the reply. Duquesne had been looking forward to its Facebook rollout for months. Her friends could hardly wait to try it.

Efrusy talked to his wife. He had never seen so much pent-up demand. "I've got to invest in this company," he told her.

That evening, Efrusy met Sean Parker for the promised beer at a scruffy student dive near Stanford. Parker reiterated his conviction that Thefacebook was so valuable that Accel would not offer enough for it. Did he still really believe this, or was he simply trying to push up Accel's bid? Either way, he was doubtless enjoying the opportunity to taunt a venture capitalist.

Efrusy begged to be given a chance to show what he could pay. All Parker had to do was come with Zuckerberg to the Monday partners' meeting.

On Monday morning, the Accel team assembled in its conference room. "Are they gonna show up?" one team member remembers wondering.[21] At 10:00 a.m., they did show up.

If Accel had still been wedded to its traditional instincts, the meeting would have been a failure. The most important visitor, Mark Zuckerberg, arrived in shorts and Adidas flip-flops. He presented his hosts with a business card that gave his job title as "I'm CEO . . . bitch!"[22] Throughout the presentation Zuckerberg said almost nothing. When coaxed to speak about his background and his vision for the firm, he confined his answer to two minutes.[23] Accel's partners were being asked to invest in a twenty-year-old who barely deigned to talk to them. But thanks to the prepared-mind exercise, the team was not deterred. "We had already decided that an unorthodox character like Zuck was not an unlikely profile," Efrusy reflected later. "It was actually the likely one."[24]

Dressed more professionally, with T-shirts under sports jackets, Sean Parker and Matt Cohler laid out the story that erased the doubts about Zuckerberg's demeanor. They described how Thefacebook had captured the nation's campuses, one by one, displaying almost military efficiency. Multiple colleges had asked for the service; to get to the front of the line, they were required to provide student emails, information about sports teams and clubs, class lists, and other information. That way, Thefacebook could sign up a high fraction of the students on each campus as soon as it launched, achieving critical mass immediately. Moreover, as it added more students to its community, Thefacebook was experiencing the opposite of the Friendster conundrum. Most college kids had high school buddies at other universities, so when those universities joined, the early loyalists grew even more engrossed in the platform. Thefacebook confronted no trade-off between expanding user numbers and diminishing user engagement.

When the meeting was done, Accel's verdict was unanimous. Nobody minded about Zuckerberg's mute style. Nobody brought up the alarming sexual imagery at the Facebook office. Nor did anybody worry about the fact that Sequoia's leaders, Michael Moritz and Doug Leone, had warned Accel to be wary of Parker. The only thing that mattered was the exploding popularity of the product. The fact that Zuckerberg was too young to buy a beer merely added to his authenticity.[25]

The question was how to get Thefacebook to accept Accel's capital. The partnership knew it was up against a corporate investor, probably a big media firm, and Parker had revealed the terms that the rival was offering: a pre-money valuation—that is, the value without counting the new capital going in—of $60 million. After some deliberation, Accel sent Thefacebook a term sheet valuing it at the same $60 million price, but with an offer to inject more money than the other bidder.

That night, Cohler sent an email back: thank you but no thank you. Evidently, the rival bid was real. By now, Accel's well-connected managing partner, Jim Breyer, had figured out that it was almost certainly from the Washington Post Company.[26]

The next day the Accel team regrouped to consider how much to increase its offer. That afternoon, Efrusy and two colleagues marched down University Avenue, catching Thefacebook gang midway through a meeting. He slapped down a new offer. Accel was now valuing Thefacebook at fully $70 million before any new capital went in. It proposed to invest $10 million in the firm, taking the post-money valuation to $80 million.

For once, Parker was impressed. "Okay, this is worth considering," he conceded.

Accel had now outbid its rival. But it still faced a hurdle. Zuckerberg had come to an oral agreement with the Washington Post Company, and he trusted its CEO, Don Graham, not to interfere with his leadership at Thefacebook. Parker had taught him to believe that Valley venture capitalists were bad guys. Maybe he would be better off sticking with the Post and accepting a lower valuation.

That evening, Accel laid on a small dinner for Zuckerberg and his lieutenants at the Village Pub, a Michelin-starred restaurant whose name was a study in false modesty. The group discussed Thefacebook's growth strategy, and the two Accel hosts—Efrusy and the managing partner, Jim Breyer—tried to coax Zuckerberg into the conversation. Breyer in particular was making headway. He had opened up a private channel to Zuckerberg after the Monday pitch, and the young founder appeared to be impressed by his golden Rolodex and silky confidence. But just as Breyer seemed to be connecting, Zuckerberg tuned out; he fell silent and turned in on himself, as though absorbed in an internal dialogue. Presently, he got up and went to the bathroom. For a long time, there was no sign of him.

Matt Cohler left the table to go check on the boss. He found him on the men's room floor, sitting cross-legged, crying.

"I can't do this. I gave my word!" Zuckerberg sobbed. He liked Jim Breyer, but he felt terrible about taking his money. Stiffing Don Graham of the Post was more than he could stomach.

"Why don't you just call Don up and ask him what he thinks?" Cohler suggested.[27]

Zuckerberg composed himself and returned to the table. The following morning, he got in touch with Graham to break the news that he had a higher offer. Although he respected Graham, he was conscious that Breyer had more experience in guiding startups to stardom. And although he had absorbed Parker's hostility to VCs, he appreciated Accel because it backed its convictions with big money.

Graham was not prepared to get into a bidding war. His friend and mentor Warren Buffett had schooled him in the discipline of value investing, and he regarded Silicon Valley's power-law mentality with suspicion. Rather than promising Zuckerberg a better financial deal, he pitched a better psychological one.

"You know that taking their money will be different from taking our money, don't you?" Graham asked. "We're not going to tell you how to run the company."[28]

Given the context of the youth revolt, Graham's appeal might have succeeded. Just one month earlier, Paul Graham, the YC founder, had propounded his "unified theory of VC suckage," denouncing venture capitalists for force-feeding young entrepreneurs with too much capital. Peter Thiel, who had backed Thefacebook as an angel investor and sat on its board, was emphasizing that founders should retain control of their own companies, not share governance with venture investors. But even in this climate, Graham's bid failed. Never mind the Wirehog presentation, the in-your-face business card, and the Adidas flip-flops. Zuckerberg had thought through the consequences of dealing with a venture firm and was happy to embrace them.

At this, Don Graham graciously released Zuckerberg from his moral dilemma.[29] He wished him the best of luck with Accel. Thefacebook's path had been decided.

For Sean Parker, the Accel-Facebook deal brought two kinds of reckoning. On the positive side, it cemented his reputation as a master negotiator. He played the venture suitors skillfully, securing a string of additional victories in the last phase of the talks, leaving Zuckerberg with more wealth and control over his company. But a few months later, there was a sting in the tail. In September 2005, soon after Thefacebook became plain Facebook, Accel ousted Parker from the company. In a reprise of his conduct at Plaxo, Parker had resumed his erratic behavior: he was arrested (but never charged) for possession of cocaine at a beach house where he was partying with several friends, including an underage woman who was his assistant at Facebook.[30] Having earlier ignored the lurid murals at the Facebook headquarters, Accel now decided that Parker had crossed the line. Jim Breyer, the Accel managing partner who had taken a seat on Facebook's board, seized on the incident to demand Parker's ouster. Despite Zuckerberg's desire to forgive his friend, Breyer got his way, doing Facebook the service of eliminating a corrosive force within the company. In an echo of the Plaxo finale, Parker was forced to forfeit half of his options. Five years later, those options would have been worth about $500 million.[31]

For the venture-capital industry, the Facebook deal showed how a traditional partnership could navigate the youth revolt. It could gather intelligence from a Stanford grad student. It could train and empower an investor in his early thirties. It could deploy the worldliness and connections of the forty-something managing partner. It could even draw on the investment judgment of its sixty-year-old founder. When Facebook went public in 2012, Accel reaped an astonishing profit of more than $12 billion.[32] For shrugging off the slings and arrows of arrogant youth, the partnership had been amply rewarded.

But the Facebook episode also demonstrated that, at least for the moment, there were limits to investors' forbearance. Confronted with a toxic rebel who painted VCs as villains while himself getting into trouble with the cops, the venture guys were capable of asserting their authority: they had defenestrated Parker. A decade later, this capacity for discipline would fade, as we shall see presently.

◆

If Accel had what it took to succeed into the twenty-first century, the story of Kleiner Perkins shows that success was not inevitable. Through the 1980s and 1990s, Kleiner had been the leading venture firm, its portfolio companies said to account for as much as a third of the market value created from the internet.[33] By around 2015, after a series of mediocre funds, Kleiner had disappeared from the top table.[34]

Kleiner's descent was especially striking because of the path dependency in venture performance. VCs who back winning startups acquire a reputation for success, which in turn gives them the first shot at the next cohort of potential winners. Sometimes they get to buy in at a discount, because entrepreneurs value the imprimatur of renowned investors. This self-reinforcing advantage—prestige boosts performance, and performance boosts prestige—raises a delicate question. Is there really skill in venture capital, or are the top performers merely coasting on their reputations? The story of Kleiner Perkins illustrates what academic study has confirmed.[35] Reputation matters, but it cannot guarantee outcomes. Success has to be earned afresh by each successive generation.

Kleiner's fall from grace is commonly ascribed to a spectacularly bad investment call. Starting in 2004, the firm pursued so-called cleantech startups—bets on technologies that help fight climate change, from solar power to biofuels to electric vehicles. In 2008, Kleiner doubled down, devoting a new $1 billion growth fund exclusively to this sector. The commitment reflected a mixture of idealism and wishful thinking. John Doerr, Kleiner's dominant partner, was unabashedly emotional in his public promises to help save the planet. He liked to quote Mary, his teenage daughter: "Dad, your generation created this problem; you'd better fix it."[36] At the same time, Doerr insisted on the financial case for going green, reminding audiences that energy was a $6 trillion business. "You remember that Internet?" he asked rhetorically in 2007. "Well, I'll tell you what. Green technologies— going green—is bigger than the Internet."[37]

Whatever its existential importance, cleantech was a tough field for venture investors, and Doerr should not have suggested that large markets were the same as profitable ones. Startups working on wind power, biofuels, or solar panels were capital intensive, heightening the risk of losing large sums; their projects took years to mature, depressing annual returns on the few that succeeded. To compensate for the large capital requirements and long time frames, cleantech investors could in theory have invested at lower valuations and demanded additional equity for their money. But because of the fashion for "founder-friendliness" entrenched by the youth revolt, Doerr didn't want to go there. Compounding this error, Doerr's early cleantech forays focused on businesses that lacked an obvious "moat": solar and biofuel projects involve producing energy, an undifferentiated commodity whose price is wildly cyclical. When oil prices collapsed in the summer of 2008, Doerr's alt-energy bets foundered. After that, a flood of subsidized solar panels from China and the advent of fracking dragged energy prices down further. Meanwhile, this run of market setbacks came on top of a political error. Doerr overestimated the federal government's willingness to deliver on its promises to tax or regulate carbon.[38]

For Kleiner's limited partners, the upshot was painful. The first wave of green investments did particularly poorly, and the venture funds raised in 2004, 2006, and 2008 suffered accordingly. A dozen years after investing in the 2006 fund, one limited partner complained that he had lost almost half his capital.[39] Kleiner's second cleantech wave, starting with the green growth fund raised in 2008, did better. The partnership homed in on businesses that did have a moat, and produced a few dramatic hits: as of 2021, the plant-based meat company Beyond Meat had generated 107x, the battery maker QuantumScape had made 65x, and the "smart solar" company Enphase had produced 25x. This was enough to generate at least one venture fund that ranked in the industry's top quartile.[40] But Kleiner's overall performance remained dull.[41] Back in its heyday, in 2001, Vinod Khosla and John Doerr had ranked first and third, respectively, on the *Forbes* Midas List. In 2021 Doerr came seventy-seventh, and no other Kleiner figure featured in the top hundred.[42]

When the run of bad news began, most Kleiner limited partners stuck with the firm, proving the power of path dependency. At first, they hoped that the old magic would return. After all, Doerr's hits with Google and Amazon made him one of the most successful venture capitalists of all time, and he remained personally magnetic. Later, some limited partners carried on investing for a different reason: they valued the association with a famous Silicon Valley name, even when insiders understood that the name in question was tarnished. For example, one fund-of-funds confided that its own backers—small, unsophisticated pension funds—were impressed to hear that their capital was being managed by the storied Kleiner Perkins: this was the sort of privileged access that they could not dream of securing without a fund-of-funds intermediary. But by 2016, even these brand-conscious investors began to drift away. The Kleiner name had no cachet anymore, and a much diminished Doerr stepped down from his perch as an investing partner.

This standard cleantech explanation for Kleiner's troubles is partly correct. Astonishingly, the firm that had minted money during the first internet wave, preaching the power of Moore's law and Metcalfe's law, rushed into a sector that lacked these magical advantages. And yet there is another side to the story—one that reveals a subtler truth about the venture business. As Accel's Facebook deal suggested, and as many other case studies confirm, venture capital is a team sport: it often takes multiple partners to land a home-run deal, and the investors who lead the chase are not always the same as the stewards who guide the portfolio companies after the deals have been completed. For a venture team to work productively, the culture of the partnership has to be right. This is what Kleiner Perkins mismanaged spectacularly.[43]

◆

In the early years of Kleiner Perkins Caufield & Byers, the partnership had appeared lopsided. Tom Perkins was the flamboyant and domineering rainmaker, the creative genius behind Tandem and Genentech, and he overshadowed the other three named partners. But if you looked under the hood, the other partners did matter—not necessarily because of their investments, but because of their effect on Perkins. When the big man's ideas were crazy, they talked him down. When his temper threatened to blow up a deal, they knew how to smooth things over.

On one such occasion in 1983, Mitch Kapor showed up at the Kleiner office to pitch Lotus Development. For no evident reason, Perkins flew into a fury. "I don't see why I should waste my time listening to some company that we are obviously not going to invest in," he barked, storming off to his office.[44] John Doerr, then three years into his career at Kleiner, looked like an inflatable balloon figure that had sprung a leak. He had worked hard with Kapor to prepare the pitch; now the pitch seemed dead before delivery. But at this point in the story, the value of teamwork came into play. Frank Caufield, one of the partnership's unsung investors, assured Doerr that he would talk sense into Perkins; he knew how to make him laugh and bring him down from his high pedestal. With Doerr sufficiently reflated, the Lotus pitch went ahead, and everyone ignored the brooding figure of Perkins, visible through the glass wall of the conference room. Thanks to Caufield's intervention, the tantrum did not matter and the deal was done. Perkins's volatility, which could have cost the partnership millions, had been elegantly managed.

From the late 1980s through the early 2000s, Kleiner attained an equilibrium that was even more successful. John Doerr and Vinod Khosla emerged as the two successors to Perkins: they were both domineering, difficult, and wildly successful. Having two superstars at the table was much better than one: each could be a healthy intellectual check on the other. But, as in Kleiner's early period, there were also less celebrated partners who were essential to the team. One named Doug Mackenzie was known for asking hard questions: in venture investing, the optimists get the glory, but the pessimists keep people grounded.[45] Another partner named Kevin Compton was the keeper of Kleiner's ethical flame. "Kevin was the moral compass," a younger Kleiner investor remembered. "I adored him. Low ego. A great mentor," said another.[46]

In the first decade of the twenty-first century, however, Kleiner Perkins lost this equilibrium. Part of the problem was that the firm grew. Whereas traditional partnerships such as Benchmark still had only half a dozen general partners, Kleiner now had about ten—plus various senior advisers and junior investors. In 2004, Vinod Khosla tired of this unwieldy structure and quit to set up his own shop, leaving Doerr without an intellectual counterweight. That same year, Mackenzie and Compton followed, creating a firm called Radar Partners. Doerr replaced these seasoned colleagues with a string of famous names. In 2000 he had hired Ray Lane, the Valley's top software sales guru, who had driven the success of Oracle. In 2005 he followed up with Bill Joy, a cofounder of Sun Microsystems, and the former secretary of state Colin Powell, who signed on as a strategic adviser. In 2007, Doerr rounded out his team by adding the former vice president Al Gore as a sort of adjunct senior partner. The newcomers had no investment experience and were in their fifties or sixties. Kleiner had effectively embraced the opposite of the philosophy at Accel, which believed in recruiting hungry up-and-comers and training them.[47]

This change in Kleiner's culture set the stage for the cleantech fiasco. When Doerr decided to bet the franchise on a challenging sector, nobody was there to check him. Compton and Mackenzie were especially missed: they were openly skeptical of cleantech, regarding it as too capital intensive, too slow to mature, and too hostage to the whims of government regulation.

With the benefit of hindsight, Compton even argued that the cleantech error violated the lessons handed down by Tom Perkins himself. Far from going all in on high-stakes bets, Perkins had used small amounts of capital to eliminate the main risks in a venture—the "white-hot risks," as he called them. Moreover, far from swooning over new technologies, Perkins often cautioned that for an innovation to matter, it had to be radically better than what came before. "If it's not 10x different, it's not different," went his mantra.[48] If Kleiner had not suffered a brain drain, Compton and Mackenzie would have been on hand to make these arguments. But without the old gang at the table, "John became impossible to challenge," an insider recalled, probably exaggerating only slightly. Tom Perkins's firm went from being a white-hot-risk eliminator to a Hail Mary risk-taker.

Looking back on this period, Doerr disputes that he was dominant. "We've never had a controlling managing partner or CEO. I never played that role," he says. "Just because John Doerr wanted to invest, doesn't mean we invested."[49] But most of his former colleagues differ with this account, and Doerr's whirlwind charisma, coupled with his outsized stature in the venture world, raise doubts about his story. Moreover, because Kleiner's underlying problem was cultural, stemming from the lopsided power structure within the firm, it affected everything, including initiatives that might have offset the cleantech losses. Kleiner's move into China, as we have seen, ran into trouble. Doerr was not enough of a manager to make sure that the local team gelled; his U.S. partners lacked the stature to compensate for his deficiencies. Likewise, Kleiner failed to make up for the cleantech losses with traditional IT venture bets. Perhaps because it was too heavy with mature stars who lacked the hustle to connect with young founders, its venture team missed the home runs of the era: Uber, Dropbox, LinkedIn, WhatsApp, Stripe, and so on. The one standout Kleiner success in this period involved the hiring of Mary Meeker, the former Morgan Stanley analyst who had pioneered the evaluation of digital businesses. Unlike the other established fifty-somethings who arrived at the partnership around this time, Meeker had grown up in the investment world. She proceeded to run a series of growth funds, profiting from late-stage bets on companies that the venture team had missed and partially redeeming Kleiner's performance.

———◆———

Kleiner's most painful failure in these years underscored its tragic mix of idealism and mismanagement. Starting at the end of the 1990s, Doerr embarked on another noble crusade: he began to chip away at the gender imbalance in the venture industry. More than most West Coast engineers of his generation, he believed in smart women; his wife had been an engineer at Intel, and he doted on his two daughters. By the late 1990s, moreover, it was clear that change was overdue. The paucity of senior women in technology had been embarrassing in the 1970s, but back then women had been scarce in nearly every industry. As women progressed in other professions, their absence in the tech sector became glaring. At the end of the 1990s, the proportion of women in investment banking and management consulting was five to seven times as high as in venture capital. Women accounted for only 9 percent of new recruits at venture partnerships, and their absence was self-perpetuating. Accomplished women choosing a career were apt to strike venture off the list; it seemed like a bizarre relic from a former age, like a men's-only dining club.[50] Emerging from MIT's Sloan School of Management in this period, a young Asian American banker named Aileen Lee dismissed the industry as the province of white guys who "grew up in Connecticut with a businessman father."[51]

In 1999, after a spell at Morgan Stanley and a second business degree from Harvard, Lee got a call from a woman who introduced herself as a recruiter.

Would Lee consider a job working for John Doerr at Kleiner?

"It's all men," Lee said. "I'm going to have no friends."

The recruiter pushed back. "The world is never going to change if you don't go do this interview," she admonished. "No man would say what you just said to me."

"She really knew how to push my buttons," Lee said later, chuckling.[52]

Lee went to meet Doerr and decided to test him. She told him she had planned her life: marry at twenty-eight, first child at thirty, second at thirty-two. Because she was already pushing thirty, she was falling behind schedule. "I want you to know that my plan is to catch up on my plan," she said, wondering if she would be confirmed in her fear that venture capital was the wrong place for her.

"All good with me," Doerr answered.[53]

Lee took the job, still feeling nervous. She was the youngest professional on Kleiner's investment team as well as the only woman. She often felt that she was being judged, even after she had been there for years—in fact, even after she became one of the few Kleiner associates to make the jump to partner and then senior partner. Looking for ways to explain this nagging feeling of hostility, Lee came to the view that when a man joined Kleiner, he became part of a club. If he said something dumb, he'd get a slap on the back; it would be funny, not embarrassing. But a woman, not being a club member, could never depend on camaraderie and indulgence. If she said something dumb, it would affect her standing.

Lee managed this problem by being careful about what she said.

"Why don't you speak up more?" her colleagues wondered.

Lee absorbed this feedback, and spoke up more.

"Don't be too assertive," the same colleagues warned her.

Lee went on maternity leave; she was catching up with her plan. While she was away, a partner took one of her board seats. Astonishingly, no one told her.

"That makes you feel like they don't even remember you exist," Lee said later.[54]

Why did Kleiner Perkins lead the way in promoting a woman yet fail to create an environment in which she could flourish? Looking back as a successful venture capitalist, by now the head of her own firm, Lee blamed poor management rather than ill will or bias. Inevitably, bringing women into the partnership would require an effort, a conscious resetting of some practices and rules, just as establishing a China team required a plan to manage relations between satellite and mother ship. But Doerr was too distracted to implement this sort of organizational revamp, and others at the firm lacked the authority to do it for him. "Nobody was minding the shop," Lee said later.[55]

———

Lee was not the only woman to experience the good and the bad sides of Doerr's leadership. In 2000, a Stanford MBA student named Trae Vassallo went to hear Doerr deliver one of his inspiring speeches on campus. She walked up to him afterward and asked for some advice; before studying business, she had done two engineering degrees, and she had thirteen patents on her résumé. Recognizing Vassallo's ability and leaping at the chance to help, Doerr introduced her to a startup that invited her in as a co-founder. "It would not have happened without John. He thought it was important to have diversity around the table," Vassallo said later. "He actively sought chances to make sure that young women had opportunities."[56]

A year or so later, when Vassallo left the startup, she continued to benefit from Doerr's mentorship. At his invitation, she joined Kleiner as an unpaid entrepreneur in residence. In 2002, when she needed an income because she had a nine-month-old baby and her husband was at business school, Doerr gave her a paid job as an associate. In 2006, she made her first investment. "I really feel like John cared about my career," Vassallo reiterated.[57]

But as Vassallo spent longer at Kleiner, the frustrations began mounting. Doerr had by now hired multiple women. They were all smart and accomplished: Doerr knew how to spot talent. But with a couple of exceptions, they were not being promoted. Worse, they were not even getting the chance to build their credentials, because the older people at the firm did not want to make space for them. In 2008 one of Vassallo's young colleagues, an investor named Ellen Pao, worked on a deal with a startup named RPX, but after the deal was concluded, a senior Kleiner partner named Randy Komisar took the RPX board seat. In 2010, Vassallo herself helped to land a deal with a startup called Nest Labs, a maker of IT-enabled thermostats and smoke detectors. Komisar took that board seat too, reaping most of the credit when Nest was sold to Google in 2014 for a gratifying 22x multiple.

At the time, neither Pao nor Vassallo complained about these decisions: Komisar was a tech veteran, and he had a strong personal relationship with Nest's founder.[58] But Vassallo did feel that as a matter of good management Kleiner had an interest in following the Accel model of developing the younger members of the team. Nobody should be condemned to a Catch-22: to go on boards, you must have been on boards.[59]

In May 2012, the firm's simmering tensions came to a head with the filing of a gender discrimination lawsuit. The plaintiff was Ellen Pao, the investor who had worked on the RPX deal; she was a graduate of Princeton and Harvard Law School. Like Lee and Vassallo, Pao owed her position directly to Doerr. He had brought her in as his chief of staff in 2005, stressing that Kleiner was one of the few Silicon Valley partnerships that cared about advancing women. But, also like Lee and Vassallo, Pao came to believe that Doerr's decency was unsupported by the culture of the firm he led. As she put it, Kleiner was suffused with "the California art of superficial collegiality, where everything seems tan and shiny on the outside but inside, behind closed doors, people would trash your investment, block it or send you on 'rock fetches'—time-consuming, unproductive tasks to stall you until you gave up."[60]

The merits of Pao's lawsuit remain somewhat murky. She alleged, among other things, that she had been denied promotion because of gender discrimination. In response, Kleiner presented evidence that Pao had been a difficult colleague and that she had been denied promotion because her performance had not warranted it. Kleiner supported this contention by producing Pao's performance reviews, and the jury found Kleiner not guilty on all counts, but Pao's allegations cast a shadow over Kleiner's reputation. She alleged that a partner named Ajit Nazre had harassed her and obstructed her work over the course of five years, although at one point she had consented to a brief affair with him. (For his part, Nazre issued a statement saying that he was not a defendant in the case and that Kleiner had denied Pao's allegations about him.)[61] Pao also claimed that a more senior partner had presented her with a sexually suggestive gift and invited her to a Saturday dinner, mentioning that his wife would be out of town that evening. She asserted that repeated complaints to the partnership's leaders had failed to elicit steps to improve the environment for women.[62] Meanwhile, Trae Vassallo testified at the trial that Nazre had once asked her to come to a business dinner in New York. When the two got to the city, there was no business dinner on the agenda, and Vassallo allegedly had to push Nazre to stop him from entering her hotel room. The worst part came when Vassallo reported the incident to one of the general partners at Kleiner. "You should be flattered," he told her.[63] Only after that was Nazre ejected from the partnership.

Kleiner was not alone in mismanaging gender issues. The fact that Accel had not flinched at Facebook's murals told you that misogyny was accepted as normal in the tech community. After the Pao trial, Vassallo helped to conduct a survey of more than two hundred women in the Valley. Three in five reported unwanted sexual advances, with one-third being afraid for their safety. Three in five were also dissatisfied with the way that complaints of harassment were handled.[64] Meanwhile, research led by Paul Gompers of Harvard showed how male venture capitalists failed to collaborate productively with female colleagues. Male venture capitalists generated better investment performance if their partners had strong records, demonstrating the advantages of teamwork. Female venture capitalists enjoyed no such boost, presumably because male partners didn't share their networks or ideas with them. Tellingly, this female disadvantage was absent at firms that had multiple female partners and formal human-resource systems. As Lee, Vassallo, and Pao suspected, partnerships that relied on clubby informality were bad for women.[65]

John Doerr's idealism was sincere and mostly admirable. He believed passionately that VC-fueled innovation was a force for good, which made cleantech irresistible. He was right that the Valley's near exclusion of women represented wasted talent and was socially untenable. By throwing his energy behind cleantech and female advancement, he shoved history forward. A few cleantech investments worked out—Nest's smart thermostats, for example—and the early failures helped to clear the way for the more successful second wave. Likewise, Doerr's hiring of women ultimately worked out for the women, even if Kleiner failed to capture the results of their talent: by 2020, four ex-Kleiner women were running their own venture firms, and three were ranked among the top hundred VCs globally.[66] But by embracing change without slogging through the detailed work of implementing it, Doerr almost destroyed his firm. Venture capital is a team sport, and a dysfunctional team loses.[67]

Accel, for its part, continued to flourish in the years after the Facebook deal. In a testament to the power of teamwork, it generated a series of grand slams without depending on the genius of one or two investors. Its top seven investments, each generating a profit of more than $500 million, were led by seven different partners—or actually eight, because one was a two-person effort.[68] Relative to Kleiner, Accel hired fewer women, but it was more successful at empowering them: two rose to the very top of the partnership.[69] Accel's culture of training and trusting young investors seemed to hold the secret of success. "I am prouder of that culture transfer and the individuals that have grown up in the firm than I am of Facebook or any other investment," Jim Swartz reflected.[70]

———◆———

Accel's triumph and Kleiner's failure illustrated the tumult in the venture industry. The tech bust, the youth revolt, the rise of mobile internet platforms, the false siren of cleantech, the fraught gender dynamics in the industry, the promise and perils of China: all served to separate the strong partnerships from the weak ones, ensuring that path dependency alone was not enough to guarantee performance.[71] Famous venture firms faced challenges from upstarts like Founders Fund; fittingly, a business that specialized in financing disruption could itself be disrupted. Meanwhile, in 2008, as the venture industry was still grappling with these shocks, the world's financial system succumbed to its biggest meltdown since the 1930s. Venture capital would change again, but not in the way that people expected.

Chapter Twelve

A Russian, a Tiger, and the Rise of Growth Equity

———▼———

At the start of 2009, Gideon Yu, the chief financial officer at Facebook, took a call from Moscow. A soft Russian voice announced that it wanted to invest in his company. Facebook had raised money from Peter Thiel, Accel, and most recently Microsoft; it did not accept capital from just anyone. Yu told the Russian not to waste his time. "How do I know you are serious?" he asked him.

The caller persisted. He had a gentle but insistent style. He wanted to meet in person.

"Don't come all the way here just to see me," Yu replied bluntly.[1]

On the other side of the world, the caller put down the phone and looked out of his floor-to-ceiling windows. He had a slight build, a nose bent to his right, and an oval face crowned by a smooth dome. His name was Yuri Milner, and he had never been to Silicon Valley.

This was about to change, however. Ignoring Yu's warning, Milner booked a plane ticket and flew to San Francisco.

Landing in California, Milner phoned Yu again. He was not in Moscow anymore. Now would Yu see him?

Surprised, curious, even a little bit impressed, Yu suggested a meeting at the Starbucks in Palo Alto. It was his job to raise capital for Facebook, after all, and these days even implausible investors were worth seeing. In the wake of the financial crisis triggered by the collapse of Lehman Brothers, U.S. pension funds and endowments were scared. The VCs who invested their money were holding back from new commitments.

Yu arrived at the Starbucks and found Milner already there, together with a business partner who had flown in from London.[2] The Russian ordered black tea and proceeded to lay out his proposal. He had heard from a Goldman Sachs banker that Facebook might have to raise capital at a discount to the $15 billion valuation in its previous round, but he was willing to bid hard. His starting offer was $5 billion.

The bid was sufficiently strong to command Yu's attention. But the logic behind the number was even more compelling. Facebook had recently passed the mark of 100 million users, and many Valley investors assumed that it was approaching saturation point. But Milner took a different view and had the evidence to back it. His team had compiled a voluminous spreadsheet on consumer-internet businesses in multiple countries, with cells tracking daily users, monthly users, the amount of time spent on the site, and so on.[3] Milner himself had invested in VKontakte, the leading Facebook clone in Russia, and had witnessed its growth from the inside. All the international experience told him that the saturation thesis was plain wrong. Facebook was still not among the top five websites in the United States, whereas in other countries the leading social-media firm was generally in the top three. If America followed the typical pattern, much of Facebook's growth still lay ahead of it.

Moreover, Milner continued, Facebook lagged foreign social-media sites in converting users into revenues. By virtue of being in Silicon Valley, Zuckerberg had found it easy to raise money from investors, so he had faced limited pressure to squeeze money out of customers. In contrast, foreign social-media businesses had been forced to maximize revenue from the get-go. Again, the multi-country spreadsheet tabulated this phenomenon, allowing Milner to point out to Yu that Facebook was an outlier. In China, most social-media revenues came from selling virtual gifts, an option that Facebook had not even tried. In Russia, VKontakte's revenues per user were fully five times Facebook's.[4] International experience demonstrated that Zuckerberg had enormous room to monetize mindshare. Thanks to his

global perspective, the Russian who had never set foot in the Valley understood Facebook better than the Palo Alto mafia.[5]

Yu was hooked. He invited Milner to meet Zuckerberg.

Milner arrived in Zuckerberg's conference room in a crisp white shirt
that peeked through his dark sweater. The plain clothes, the quiet voice, the
smooth domed head: there was no bluster about him. He proceeded simply
to repeat his pitch, noting that many Facebook users were outside the
United States. He had experience with social media all over the world. He
knew the map and the territory.[6]

Over the next weeks, Milner sweetened his bid with two innovations.
He knew that Zuckerberg jealously protected his control over Facebook, recently spurning an advance from an investor who had demanded two board
votes.[7] So he declared he would not take a board seat—not even one—and
Zuckerberg would get the right to vote Milner's shares as he wanted. In one
stroke, the entrepreneur's chief qualm about raising money was erased.
Rather than diluting the founder's control over his company, a capital injec-
tion from Milner would concentrate it.

With his second innovation, Milner assuaged another of the founder's
worries. In August 2008, Zuckerberg had confronted the problem that
besets successful startups that delay going public. Facebook's early employees had become stock-option millionaires, but they had no way of converting paper wealth into a car or an apartment. To deal with this morale
issue, Zuckerberg had promised to let his lieutenants sell about a fifth of
their vested stock, figuring that the investor that led Facebook's next financing would be happy to buy these additional shares from employees.
But the onset of the global financial crisis had upended Zuckerberg's plan.
There would be no new financing for the time being—and no new cars or
apartments.

Milner promised to fix this problem. He would happily buy employee
stock in addition to shares freshly issued by the company. What's more, he
proposed a clever twist: he would pay one price for the company-issued (or
"primary") stock and a different, lower price for the secondary stock sold
by Facebook workers. Up to a point, it was obvious that the primary stock
should be worth more: it was "preferred," meaning that it came with some

protections against losses. But Milner used the two-tier pricing to add a secret weapon to his negotiating arsenal. He could offer Zuckerberg a satisfying valuation for Facebook's primary stock while holding down the cost
of acquisition by lowballing his offer to employees.

As Milner and Facebook negotiated during the first months of 2009,
this two-tier price trick proved useful. Emboldened by a recovering stock
market, rival suitors approached Zuckerberg, but Milner was able to outbid
them. For one thing, his multi-country spreadsheet gave him the confidence
to pay more. For another, the two-tier pricing enabled him to up his headline bid while controlling his blended cost of acquisition.

Marc Andreessen, the 1990s software prodigy who had co-founded
Netscape, had a ringside seat during these bidding wars: he was a Facebook
board member. He watched U.S. tech investors come in with offers that they
believed were good: $5 billion, $6 billion, even $8 billion. But by this point
Zuckerberg had set his sights on a $10 billion valuation. Only Milner would
pay that.

Andreessen called the U.S. suitors to warn them. "You guys are missing the boat. Yuri is bidding ten. You are going to lose this."

The same response came back each time. "Crazy Russian. Dumb
money . . . this is insane."[8]

Andreessen knew otherwise. Milner was neither crazy nor dumb, nor
was he even impetuous in the way that Masayoshi Son was. To the contrary,
what distinguished Milner was his data-driven approach. He had meticu-
lously compiled the key metrics on the world's social-media firms, and his
revenue projections told him that a $10 billion valuation was reasonable.

At the end of May 2009, while Neil Shen was cementing his leadership
over Sequoia China and Kleiner Perkins was grappling with its struggling
cleantech bets, Milner and Zuckerberg concluded their negotiations. Milner's investment company, DST, bought $200 million worth of company-
issued primary stock in exchange for a 1.96 percent stake, giving Zuckerberg
the $10 billion pre-money valuation that he wanted. At the same time, DST
arranged to purchase secondary employee stock at a lower valuation of $6.5
billion. The employees' desire for cash outweighed any misgivings they felt

about the price Milner offered. So DST ended up buying well over $100 million of the cheaper shares, pushing the blended valuation to $8.6 billion.[9]

Needless to say, Milner reaped a bonanza. Facebook's audience and revenues exploded, just as he had predicted. Eighteen months later, in late 2010, the company was valued at $50 billion. DST was sitting on a profit of more than $1.5 billion, and Facebook continued to head skyward.[10]

For Silicon Valley, it was a watershed. Thirteen years earlier, Masayoshi Son had shocked the traditional venture shops by foisting $100 million on Yahoo. In contrast, Milner had initially bought more than $300 million worth of Facebook.[11] Equally, Son had provided what amounted to a sort of bridge financing ahead of Yahoo's stock market debut. Milner was injecting so much capital that he actually put off the need for Zuckerberg to go for an initial public offering. DST's money satisfied both Facebook's requirement for growth capital and its employees' requirement for liquidity. It signaled that private tech companies could delay going public for perhaps an additional three years.[12] As a result, enormous amounts of wealth would be created away from the public stock markets and for the exclusive benefit of private investors.

At the same time, Milner's Facebook investment heralded the next stage of entrepreneur empowerment. Peter Thiel had marketed his venture outfit as the founder-friendly alternative to Sand Hill Road, but Milner pushed this concept to a whole new level. He was investing at a later stage and injecting far more capital; it was remarkable that he was willing to put hundreds of millions of dollars at risk while forgoing any say over the company. And whereas Thiel's deference to founders was grounded in his understanding of the power law, Milner framed his concession more simply. He was investing in a company whose size and sophistication qualified it to go public. Therefore he would behave like a public stock market investor: passively.[13]

In 1995, the flotation of Netscape had proved that a red-hot internet startup did not have to be profitable to go public, a revelation that unleashed the dot-com boom of the second half of the decade.[14] In 2009, Milner's financing of Facebook imparted the opposite message: that a mature and profitable company had the option of staying private.[15] By accepting money from Milner, tech founders could escape the normal oversight exercised by traditional private investors, who typically demanded board seats. At the same time, tech founders could avoid the disciplines of a public listing: quarterly calls with Wall Street analysts, regulatory disclosures, hedge-fund traders looking to bet against their stock. Precisely at the point when tech companies achieved escape velocity and founders were apt to feel too sure of themselves, the usual forms of private or public governance would thus be suspended. In the 1970s, hands-on venture investors had invented the idea of building governance around a startup founder. Now Milner was inverting the model. He was protecting founders from governance.

Like Netscape's flotation, Milner's investment unleashed a boom that would ultimately be pushed too far. Instead of a 1990s-style bubble in over-heated IPOs, there would be a bubble in the hubris of tech founders.

———◆———

The road to Milner's Facebook coup began in an office in midtown Manhattan, home to a small hedge fund called Tiger Global. Chase Coleman, the fund's young founder, had worked at one of Wall Street's legendary shops, Julian Robertson's Tiger Management. Then he had set up on his own with Robertson's backing. At the time Coleman went independent, in 2001, Milner's appearance in the Valley was still eight years off. But a curious series of events would connect his fledgling fund to the soft-spoken Russian.

Coleman was still in his mid-twenties when he set up his firm, and felt daunted by the idea of managing older subordinates.[16] So he looked around for talent that was even greener than he was. After a bit of searching, he alighted on an analyst named Scott Shleifer, a loud, laughing, vigorous presence who had just completed three years of eighty-hour weeks at the private-equity firm Blackstone. Remarkably, Shleifer was still laughing.

In the summer of 2002, a few months after Shleifer signed on, a friend called. How was he doing?

"My work is going very poorly," Shleifer answered sardonically.[17] His mission was to scope out investments in semiconductors and hardware. In the wake of the Nasdaq technology bust, he could find nothing exciting.

Shleifer's friend was in worse shape. His tech-focused investment fund had collapsed around him. But he agreed to help Shleifer by sending him a list of companies he followed.

An email arrived, and Shleifer clicked on the promised spreadsheet. There were tabs for internet infrastructure, dot-com consumer companies, and companies that provided online services such as search engines or job postings.

Shleifer homed in on the part of his friend's spreadsheet listing the Chinese web portals that had gone public just before the bubble burst: Sina, Sohu, and NetEase. All three had taken off with the help of venture capitalists like Shirley Lin and Kathy Xu, who had bet on the character of the founders and the potential of their markets. But now Shleifer would apply a different kind of investment skill. The three portals had matured to the point where they had customers, revenues, and costs. An analyst with twelve hundred hours of training at Blackstone could model their fair value.

Shleifer began by applying a technique that was standard at Blackstone but foreign to most Valley investors. Rather than looking at profit margins— that is, the share of revenues remaining after costs are deducted—he looked at *incremental* margins, meaning the share of revenue *growth* that falls to the bottom line as profits. Any amateur could see that the three Chinese portals all had negative margins; put simply, they were losing money. But a pro would know to focus on the incremental picture, and this looked spectacularly positive. As revenues grew, costs grew much less, so most of the additional income showed up as profits. It followed that growth would soon drive the three portals into the black. By thinking incrementally, Shleifer could see into the future.

Encouraged, Shleifer set out to discover more about the companies. This was a challenge. After the tech crash, the Wall Street investment houses had ceased to write reports on the portals; often they would not even release their old reports, because they were mired in post-crash lawsuits. But fortunately for Shleifer, the CEOs and finance chiefs of his three Chinese investment targets were all comfortable in English. He set up a string of phone appointments, then stayed in the office overnight to make the calls during Chinese work hours.

On each call, Shleifer mentioned breezily that the portals' rapid growth should be expected to slow. He was inviting his interlocutors to confess weakness.

No, came the reply. The growth of China's online ads was only just getting started.

"What about costs?" Shleifer probed. If revenues grew, wouldn't costs grow also?

Sure, costs would grow, the answer came. But much more slowly than revenues.

Shleifer registered this good news: incremental margins were going to remain juicy. But he also fixed on something unexpected. One after another, the voices on the phone declared that he was the first western financier they had spoken to in ages.

In Silicon Valley, investors pursue deals because other investors are pursuing them. There is a logic to this pack mentality, as we have seen: when multiple prestigious venture capitalists chase after a startup, the buzz is likely to attract talented employees and important customers. But Shleifer's East Coast training had taught him the opposite instinct. Recently, he had read an investment bible by the Fidelity fund manager Peter Lynch that described how to identify potential 10x bets. "Stalking the Tenbagger," Lynch called this process.[18] The way Lynch explained things, if you liked a stock but other professional investors did not own it, this was a good sign; when the others woke up, their enthusiasm would drive your stock higher. By the same logic, if you liked a stock and Wall Street analysts did not cover it, this too was a good sign: shares were most likely to be mispriced when nobody was scrutinizing them. Finally, in an uncanny premonition of Shleifer's China calls, Lynch listed a third important buy signal. When chief financial officers tell you that they haven't talked to an investor in ages, you really may be onto something.

Feeling his excitement build, Shleifer took his notes from the phone calls and fed them into his earnings model. For now, of course, the portals were losing money. But because revenues were growing much faster than costs, profits in 2003 were set to surge: they would come in at around one-third of the companies' market capitalization. In 2004, Shleifer calculated, the profits might equal two-thirds of market cap, and for 2005 he penciled in a one-for-one ratio. Said differently, an investor could buy these portals almost for free. If Tiger Global put in, say, $10 million, it would acquire a claim on $3.3 million of profits the first year and $6.7 million the second year, so it would have earned its cost of acquisition back. In the third year it would have a claim on another $10 million in earnings, with the out-years promising exponential bonanzas.

After staying up all night, Shleifer walked into Coleman's office.

"Okay, Sina, Sohu, and NetEase," he announced.

"Let's dance," he added.

Quieter and less impulsive, Coleman was the perfect check on Shleifer's rational exuberance. But in this case Shleifer took him through the numbers and quickly won him over. The fact that Shleifer was proposing to place bets in a country he hadn't visited did not bother Coleman in the least. Julian Robertson, the founder of Tiger Management, taught that the best investments were often to be found abroad, where Wall Streeters were thin on the ground and local investors were unsophisticated. "Why would I sit here and try to hit major-league pitching, if I can go to Japan or Korea and hit minor-league pitching?" Coleman remembered Robertson saying.[19] It was the inverse of the traditionally parochial outlook of Silicon Valley investors.

During September and October 2002, Tiger Global duly bought $20 million worth of Sina, Sohu, and NetEase, committing a bit under a tenth of the fund's $250 million portfolio. A tiny team of New Yorkers became the largest public shareholder in China's digital economy.

———◆———

By the summer of 2003, Tiger Global's China positions were up between 5x and 10x.[20] In less than a year, a $250 million hedge fund had become a $350 million one. Coleman elevated Shleifer to partner and moved him from his cubicle into an office. Together, the two were advancing down the path that would lead to Yuri Milner.

Shleifer decided it was time for some fresh thinking on China. Unlike venture capitalists, who have no choice but to stick with illiquid positions, a hedge fund is free to sell at any time. The portals had gone up so much it was not clear that Tiger should still hold them.

"We've got to dig deeper," Shleifer remembers thinking. "How durable is the growth? Investments require that you ask different questions at different prices."[21]

Shleifer now acted on another Julian Robertson dictum: to assess the outlook of a company, you talk to its customers. He found out who was buying ads on the Chinese portals, contacted the purchasers, and probed them on whether they were likely to spend more. The good news, Shleifer discovered, was that the e-commerce players that accounted for most of the ad buying were extremely satisfied with the results: more ads meant more sales for them. What's more, their own businesses were booming, meaning that they would surely buy even more ads in the future; therefore, the stocks of Sina, Sohu, and NetEase were still worth holding. But the booming growth of the e-commerce companies also meant that they needed to raise capital. Sensing another round of ten-baggers, Shleifer resolved to take a trip to China.

Shleifer's mother was not happy to hear of her son's plans. China was in the grip of a SARS epidemic. In deference to her worries, and possibly his own, Shleifer packed some face masks before heading off to Asia.

In June 2003, Shleifer landed in Beijing, donned his mask, and got a cab to the Grand Hyatt. The vast hotel was virtually deserted, and Shleifer was treated to the empty presidential suite at a gratifying discount. Evidently, other westerners had less faith in three-ply fiber than he did.

The next day, still wearing his mask, Shleifer headed off to his first meeting. It was with the founder of eLong, the number two player in online travel.

"It's great that you are here," the founder said. "Now take off that mask if you want to do business in China."

Shleifer heard his mom's voice in one ear. "Stay safe. Keep the mask on."

In the other ear, he heard a different voice. "Do the deal! This is the opportunity of a lifetime!"

"I was like, all right, fuck it, life is risk. I took off the mask and didn't wear it again for the whole trip," Shleifer said later, chuckling.[22]

After two weeks in China, Shleifer had found five companies to invest in. Thanks to SARS, he negotiated term sheets that secured bargain prices on each of them. But there was a snag: the companies were private, so Tiger would be locked into illiquid positions. For a hedge fund, this would be difficult to manage. Limited partners had the right to withdraw their capital at one or two months' notice. Illiquid assets that had to be held for the long term combined with liquid funding that might flee in the short term amounted to an unstable mix. If the limited partners decided to recall their capital, Tiger would be in trouble.

For most traditional hedge funds, the illiquidity of Shleifer's proposed China bets would have made them a nonstarter. The freedom to dump positions at a moment's notice was central to the hedge-fund style: George Soros was famous for responding to stray comments at meetings by springing out of his chair to reverse one of his wagers. The ability to go "short" as well as "long"—that is, to bet on the decline of stocks as well as their advance—was another prized hedge-fund freedom; if Tiger moved into private assets, there would be no way to short them. But fortunately for Shleifer, his boss, Chase Coleman, was ready to rethink the standard formula. When he had worked for Julian Robertson, Coleman's job had been to look for short and long ideas amid the dot-com bubble of the late 1990s, and he had discovered firsthand why long bets are superior. A great short position could make you a maximum of 100 percent, if the company went to zero. A great long position could make you five or ten times capital. "Why do twice as much work to make half the profit?" Coleman ended up thinking. Besides, the synergies from investing in both public and private companies would be a boon. Understanding public companies would help Tiger to identify good private companies, as Shleifer was demonstrating in China.

The more he considered Shleifer's proposed bets, the more Coleman wanted to do them. But he still had to manage the liquidity risk—the danger of holding unsellable positions using capital that could be withdrawn at short notice. In July 2003 he came up with a fix: he would set up a separate pool of capital to make private investments. The analytical techniques of hedge-fund investing would be married to the structure of a venture-style fund, with the limited partners locked in for long periods. True to the hedge-fund tradition, Tiger Global would rely on its facility with earnings models; it would not make subjective VC-style bets on an entrepreneur's character or vision. True to that same hedge-fund tradition, Tiger would also take a global view; it had no interest in embedding itself in a dense local network, the way that VCs did. But borrowing from the venture-capital tradition, Tiger would use locked-in long-term funding to invest in private tech. It would just sit out the first stages of a startup's life, allowing it to see which entrepreneurs were really good rather than which talked a good game at pitch meetings.

Coleman drafted a letter to Tiger's investors, announcing his new Private Investment Partners fund. He described how he and Shleifer divided the digital world into segments. There were internet portals, online travel, and e-commerce sites, and the trick was to go country by country, identifying the firms that were emerging as the winners in each category. Unlike venture capitalists, Tiger was not looking to bet on original ideas. To the contrary, it liked companies that implemented a proven business model in a particular market. The goal was to invest in the eBay of South Korea or the Expedia of China. "The this of the that," Coleman and Shleifer called it.

Coleman went on to explain that Tiger's top-down analysis had singled out China as the world's most promising digital market. The share of Chinese citizens who had internet connections was set to triple in the next five years, and other forces would compound this leap. Improving bandwidth would increase time spent online; China's economic growth was stunning. Already, Coleman told the investors, Tiger had visited China and identified five promising bets: the country's top two online travel sites, its top two e-commerce sites, and a business marketplace called Alibaba.

Coleman hoped to raise $75 million for Tiger's new private fund, but he met with resistance. "Twentysomething white guys talking about the really interesting investments they had found in China . . . we sounded completely nuts," Coleman said later.[23] Everyone had war stories about Americans who went to China and got fleeced. Many were still scarred by the tech bust and leery of dot-com investing. But despite this skeptical reception, Coleman managed to raise $50 million. It was enough to close a few investments.

It was not enough to close all five Chinese prospects, however. In a testament to the difference between venture thinking and the hedge-fund mindset, the one that Tiger chose to drop was Alibaba. Shleifer had negotiated a term sheet to buy 6.7 percent of the company for $20 million; it was a bet that could have earned the partners billions. But Tiger was put off by the fact that Jack Ma was difficult to pigeonhole: he had a site that helped western businesses find Chinese suppliers, but he was planning to pivot to the different field of eBay-style auctions. An investment in Alibaba was not simply a bet on "the this of the that"; it was a bet on an entrepreneur who proposed to conquer a new market. By gauging Ma's character and the quality of his team, a venture investor might have gotten comfortable with this gamble. But Tiger's method, which in many instances brought glory, led it astray this time. Its focus on metrics such as incremental margins could not capture the value of entrepreneurial genius.[24]

There was another China bet that nearly got away, and the fact that it did not revealed the stronger side of Tiger. During his time at the Grand Hyatt, Shleifer had discussed an investment with Neil Shen, the future Sequoia China boss who was then the finance chief at the online travel company Ctrip. The two had agreed on a valuation, and while Shen said later that the agreement was provisional, Shleifer had mentally banked it.[25] A few weeks after he had left China, Shen called him in New York. SARS had ended, Ctrip's revenues had jumped, and Shen was now demanding a 50 percent increase in Ctrip's valuation.

From his desk in Manhattan, Shleifer unleashed a torrent of expletives down the phone, causing heads to turn in the office. He was furious to lose the SARS discount he had counted on, and even more furious because of the embarrassment it would cause Tiger. In the course of raising money for their private fund, Coleman had told limited partners the prices Shleifer had negotiated for the proposed China deals. The LPs had committed their money on the basis of a promise that now proved hollow.

Shleifer put down the phone and started thinking. A venture investor in his position might have canceled the deal. Because personal chemistry matters so much with early-stage bets, a perceived violation of trust before the moment when the money is wired can be fatal—hence the breakdown of Accel's Skype negotiations. (Of course, after the money has been wired, the VCs are locked in and have to be supportive—hence Accel's willingness to stick by UUNET after its accounts were exposed as inaccurate.) Shleifer's focus, however, was not on personal chemistry but on cash flows. Once he had calmed down, he recognized that, however infuriating, Shen was correct. The end of SARS would indeed boost Ctrip's revenues.

Shleifer walked over to Coleman's office to announce the upshot of his phone outburst. Tiger should swallow its pride and focus on Ctrip's numbers. A higher valuation matched by higher revenues left the price-earnings ratio unchanged. "Let's dance," Shleifer concluded.

Seventy-one days after this hiccup, Ctrip went public, and Tiger found itself sitting on a profit of $40 million. Raised in modest circumstances, Shleifer could not relate this story sixteen years later without choking up. "My dad sells couches for a living, and we were up $40 million," he said, his voice thickening.[26]

The creation of Tiger's private fund marked the arrival of a new kind of technology investment vehicle. Like many innovations, it was improvised rather than planned. "There was no whiteboard discussion about 'Hey, let's be private-equity investors,'" Coleman said later.[27] But by moving sideways from hedge-fund stock picking into private technology bets, Tiger had created the template for Milner's later Facebook investment. The Tiger tool kit featured the global tabulation of tech business segments, the modeling of earnings and fair value, and rapid intercontinental opportunism in response to a shock—in Tiger's case, SARS; in Milner's case, the collapse of Lehman Brothers. Yet in order for Milner to learn from Tiger's template, he had to know of its existence.

At the end of 2003, around the time that Ctrip went public, Shleifer flew to Moscow. He was looking, again, for "the this of the that": he had heard that Russia had two Yahoos and a Google. His first meeting took place at a bar on the roof of a hotel. His host had a quiet, unassuming style. His name was Yuri Milner.

To Shleifer's amazement, Milner thought the way he did. The son of a Soviet management professor who specialized in American business, he had been the first Russian to study at Wharton, and he was romantically pro-capitalist. The 1980s takeover artists—Henry Kravis, Ronald Perelman, Michael Milken—were among his heroes.[28] After returning to Russia and losing his banking job in the financial crisis of 1998, Milner had read a pile of investment bank studies, seeking career inspiration. Among them was an internet report by Mary Meeker, then Morgan Stanley's star tech analyst. At the time, nobody in Russia was talking about the internet, and Milner himself did not even use email. But Meeker laid out how internet penetration was spreading everywhere and how certain online business models would catch the wave, like exquisitely designed surfboards. As Milner said later, this was "a revelation."

Meeker's favorite companies were Amazon, Yahoo, and eBay, so Milner resolved to choose one of them and launch a Russian clone. Then he decided, "You know what, what the heck? Let's start all three!"[29]

At the time he met Shleifer, in 2003, Milner had abandoned his attempt at cloning Amazon, and his eBay project had gone sideways. But his version of Yahoo, called Mail, was thriving, and he had assembled a variety of investment stakes in other internet properties. Now he gave Shleifer the lay of the land. Based on analysis of how Yahoo clones had generated revenues elsewhere, Mail would soon be worth $1 billion. A rival named Rambler would be worth another $1 billion. The Russian Google, called Yandex, would be worth $2 billion.

Over the first half of 2004, Tiger duly invested in Mail, Rambler, and Yandex. The following year, even as Shleifer began chasing "the this of the that" in Latin America, the relationship with Milner deepened. Tiger became the first institutional backer of Milner's investment vehicle, Digital Sky Technologies. Through Milner, Tiger gained exposure to other Russian internet stocks, including VKontakte, the clone of Facebook.[30] Through Tiger, conversely, Milner's eyes were opened to the possibility of investing globally. "All of a sudden this whole world opened to me," Milner said later. "Tiger was an inspiration."[31]

When U.S. venture capital kick-started China's internet sector, there was a simple one-way flow of influence from the United States to Asia. With the kick-starting of "late-stage" or "growth" investing, the influence flows were more complex. In 1996, a maverick Korean Japanese outsider had demonstrated the king-making power of a $100 million investment. A few fast learners such as Sequoia had picked up on this example and started growth funds, but the 2000 Nasdaq crash took the wind out of this movement.[32] Then, in 2003, the lure of Chinese e-commerce prompted a New York hedge fund to move into private investing, and in 2004 and 2005 the New Yorkers went into partnership with a Russian, sharing their top-down, comparative approach—what they called "global arbitrage." In 2009, borrowing the New Yorkers' tool kit, the Russian wowed a Korean American chief financial officer at the Palo Alto Starbucks. An idea had spun around the world. Tech investing would henceforth be different.

———◆———

Milner's 2009 Facebook coup immediately attracted imitators, and the fastest out of the gate was Tiger. Briefly annoyed that its Russian ally had invaded its home turf, Tiger began to pursue growth investments of its own in Silicon Valley. A few months after Milner, Coleman and his team made their first bet on a U.S. firm, staking $200 million on Facebook. Their investment logic was the same as Milner's, which is to say that it came down to "the this of the that," except now the experiences of technology businesses abroad were used to illuminate the future in the United States, not vice versa. Relative to projected earnings, and when cross-checked against the value of foreign internet companies such as China's Tencent, Facebook was a clear bargain, even if Tiger had to pay a higher valuation than Milner had.[33] "We could buy Facebook, which was dominant in basically the entire world excluding China, for a lower valuation than what Tencent was available for in the public market," Coleman recalled later, as though describing the discovery of a winning lottery ticket on a sidewalk. "It was dominant in countries with a combined GDP eleven times China's, and the users were three times as engaged."[34] After buying into Facebook, Tiger followed up with bets on the social network LinkedIn and on the gaming company Zynga.

Milner did more than set an example. He identified deals and invited others into them. When Tiger bought into Zynga, for example, it was joining an investment round led by Milner's DST. Milner had already backed four gaming companies abroad; it was natural for others to fall in line behind his view of Zynga's future. In April 2010 and January 2011, Milner led two more investment rounds on behalf of the discount website Groupon. Traditional fund-management firms such as T. Rowe Price, Fidelity, and Capital Group joined his syndicate. So did the private-equity group Silver Lake, a hedge fund named Maverick Capital, and Morgan Stanley. Silicon Valley venture firms such as Kleiner Perkins joined too; Kleiner had recently signaled its enthusiasm for growth deals by hiring Mary Meeker. In June 2011, shortly after posing for the cover of the annual *Forbes* edition listing the world's billionaires, Milner led a round for the music-streaming service Spotify. This time Accel, which was just closing an $875 million growth fund, was among the firms that invested with him.[35]

In a remarkably short time, Milner lent shape and momentum to a new form of technology investing. Much as the idea of tech incubators took off after Y Combinator's founding in 2005, so growth investing blossomed after Milner showed how to deliver capital to precocious breakout firms, seducing founders by allowing them to vote his shares and providing employees with a way to sell some equity. In 2009, the year of the Facebook deal, the total amount of capital invested in private U.S. tech companies had been $11 billion. By 2015 the total had jumped to $75 billion, and most of the increase took the form of late-stage growth investments.[36] Aileen Lee, the pioneering woman venture capitalist who had by now left Kleiner to set up her own shop, identified a group of fifty-one companies that had raised six or more private investment rounds, pulling in an average of $516 million per firm.[37] Floating on this wave of capital, private technology companies frequently achieved valuations of $1 billion or more. Lee dubbed these companies "unicorns."

Flushed with success, Milner moved his family, including his mother and father, to a mansion in the hills above Palo Alto. It was a world away from the Soviet Union of his youth, and yet it was a natural place for him. As a boy growing up in Russia, Milner had been entranced by the United States; he had smelled it before he had seen it. The scent had drifted through the doorway of his family's Moscow apartment, and moments later his business professor father had appeared in the living room and cracked opened his suitcase. Bars of pristinely wrapped soap spilled onto the floor, mementos of hotel rooms in New York, Boston, and Philadelphia. "It was the scent of a new world," Milner would say, in a commencement speech at Wharton. "Suddenly there in our small apartment was America."[38] Now, half a century later, Milner owned a palatial California home, with as much soap as he could wish for. He had become one of those swashbuckling capitalists he had admired in his youth, as American in spirit as a Kravis or a Vanderbilt.

◆

The most striking sign of Milner's influence came from a surprising quarter. In early 2009, Marc Andreessen, the Netscape founder and Facebook board member, launched a venture firm together with a fellow Netscapee, Ben Horowitz. Like other splashy new entrants—Accel in the 1980s, Benchmark in the 1990s, Founders Fund in 2005—the new Andreessen Horowitz sought to differentiate itself: to claim it had invented a new kind of venture capital. Although the marketing spiel made no mention of Milner, the Milner effect was palpable.

The Andreessen Horowitz public-relations pitch was an extension of the youth revolt. As the young CEO of Loudcloud, a startup he had launched with Andreessen after leaving Netscape, Horowitz had been incensed by a Benchmark partner. When was he going to replace himself with a "real CEO" the Benchmark guy had demanded. Horowitz responded with defiance. Echoing Google's Sergey Brin and Larry Page, he insisted that the most successful tech companies were run by their original founders.[39] Sutter Hill's Qume model—which involved subjugating inventors to outside chief executives—had gotten things backward. Rather than replacing technical founders with "real CEOs," venture capitalists should coach the technical guys to mature as managers.

Other venture partnerships that began during the youth revolt tended to gloss over this need for coaching. Peter Thiel believed that superstar founders came to entrepreneurship with their superpowers already fully formed, as though some magical spider had bitten them. For his part, Paul

Graham of Y Combinator preached that there was nothing much to learn. "Build something users love, and spend less than you make. How hard is that?" he demanded. But Horowitz was acknowledging that even talented founders would have to suffer through a grueling learning period. He had discovered this himself when leading Loudcloud through the wreckage of the post-2000 tech recession. The title of his compelling memoir—*The Hard Thing About Hard Things*—captured the trauma of entrepreneurship.

After the successful sale of his company, by now named Opsware, in 2007, Horowitz teamed up with Andreessen to make angel investments. The friends assembled a portfolio of thirty-six small bets, and the logical next step was to get into venture capital. Conscious that top entrepreneurs tend only to deal with top venture firms, Andreessen and Horowitz had to figure out a way to vault straight into the first tier. To be merely average would be to fail, because most profits in venture are generated by a handful of elite partnerships.[40]

To mark themselves out, Andreessen and Horowitz proposed a fresh approach to technical founders. They promised not to displace them, as traditional VCs had often done. But they also promised not to abandon them, as newer VCs might do. Rather, they would coach technical founders as the tough questions arose: how to motivate executives, how to rally sales teams, how to sideline a loyal friend who has poured all his energy into your company. At the same time, Andreessen and Horowitz would supply technical founders with the sort of Rolodex that a seasoned CEO would have— connections to customers, suppliers, investors, and the media. Accel had differentiated itself by specializing in certain fields; Benchmark had pitched its "better architecture" of high fees and small funds; Founders Fund had pledged to back the most original and contrarian companies. For their part, Andreessen and Horowitz promised to smooth the learning curve for scientists who wanted to be chief executives.

As Andreessen and Horowitz cheerfully admitted, brazen PR was a large part of their strategy. Horowitz was something of a Paul Graham figure, but on a grander scale: a computer scientist turned entrepreneur who wrote a blog on business and life that attracted a cult following. Andreessen, for his part, had an even stronger brand, and he and Horowitz were keen to exploit it. Known as the genius behind Netscape, memorable for his six-foot-five-inch frame and towering bald skull, Andreessen juggled ideas at intoxicating speed, nailing his conclusions with a rat-a-tat-tat of stories, facts, and numbers. Around the launch of his new venture firm, Andreessen appeared on the cover of *Fortune* and sat for an hourlong television interview. "Our claim to fame is 'by entrepreneurs for entrepreneurs,'" he declared confidently.[41]

Of course, Andreessen's pitch was less original than he pretended. Many venture capitalists—nearly all the early Kleiner Perkins partners, not to mention Thiel, Graham, Milner, and others—had entrepreneurial experience. The idea of coaching founders was not original, either. When Michael Moritz helped to turn Jerry Yang into a celebrity, or when he persuaded Max Levchin of PayPal not to sell his firm prematurely to eBay, he was coaching technical founders to be business leaders. Nor was it even clear that entrepreneurship was the best background for a venture capitalist. An entrepreneur typically had worked at just one or two outfits, whereas VCs who had joined the investment business young had been in a position to see under the hood of dozens of startups. A couple of years earlier, in 2007, no less a figure than Andreessen himself had mused, "There's probably still no substitute for the VC who has been a VC for twenty years and has seen more strange startup situations up close and personal than you can imagine."[42]

In June 2009, the month after Milner closed his Facebook deal, Andreessen Horowitz announced it had raised $300 million from investors. To make good on the promise of coaching founders, the partnership promised to recruit a much larger head count than other VC outfits. In the past, other VCs had hired "operating partners" who focused on helping portfolio companies rather than making investments, but Andreessen Horowitz aimed to build an extensive consultancy under its roof. There would be a team to help startups find office space, another to advise on publicity, and yet others to source key recruits or provide introductions to potential customers.

Up to a point, this promise of coaching corresponded to the reality. Andreessen Horowitz—its name frequently abbreviated to a16z—backed a string of technical founders and helped them to learn the rules of business. Often, the key interventions came not from the elaborately staffed consulting service but from Andreessen and Horowitz themselves. In the case of a next-generation networking startup called Nicira, for example, Horowitz saved the company from two extremely costly errors.

The first came before a16z was founded, when Horowitz was still an angel investor. He had backed Nicira's founder, a newly minted Stanford computer science PhD named Martin Casado, and one day he visited the team at its repurposed dental office in Palo Alto. It was a dump of a site behind a dive bar called Antonio's Nut House.

Casado raised the question of how to price his networking software. He was so focused on the technical challenge of building it—the plan was to replace physical routers with software-only substitutes that operated in the cloud—that he dismissed the price point as a trivial matter. He would pick a number almost at random. If it turned out to be wrong, he could change it.

Horowitz steepled his fingers. Whereas Andreessen sprayed ideas around effortlessly, Horowitz took time to formulate his words; he had a heavy, deliberate manner, as though the exhausting years of startup trench warfare still weighed on him. Casado waited while Horowitz gazed out of the window. "He had that look he has when great thoughts are forming," Casado said later.[43]

"Martin, there is no single decision you will make that will impact your company value more than the pricing," Horowitz declared, with oracular finality. When a software company markets a new product—something original that nobody has seen before—it has one chance to set the price. Whatever point it chooses will stick in customers' minds, making it hard to raise prices later. Moreover, any given price difference will generate a bigger difference in a company's profit margin. If a salesperson earns a $200,000 salary and signs up six corporate customers per year, pricing the product at $50,000 yields revenues of $300,000 and a margin after deducting the salary of $100,000. But if the price is set at double that level, at $100,000, the margin will *quadruple* to $400,000. To an extent that first-time entrepreneurs seldom realize, this sort of margin difference can transform the value of their company.

"Without Ben, I would have thought to myself I can set the price low and then generate more profits later by inventing something new," Casado acknowledged. "This is the bias of the technical founder."[44]

In January 2010, a16z led Nicira's Series A round. Horowitz joined the board, and together with the a16z machine he helped the company expand its operations. Around twenty of Nicira's engineers were recruited from a16z's network, and Nicira's first customers—major companies such as AT&T—resulted from a16z introductions. The startup's promise of cloud-based network infrastructure was winning converts. Henceforth, networks would consist purely of software, much as alarm clocks had come to consist of strings of code, operated via smartphones.

In the summer of 2011, Nicira's success generated an astonishing offer. Cisco proposed to buy the company for $600 million, fully three hundred times earnings. Casado wanted to seize the offer with both hands, but now Horowitz made his second intervention. The shockingly rich bid revealed that Casado was in a much stronger position than he recognized. "I had seen this at my startup," Horowitz said later. "The high offer is a signal that something in the environment has changed. A high offer from an acquirer means you should not take it!"

"Martin, the reason Cisco is offering this price is because their customers are telling them that you are the most amazing thing going on in networking," Horowitz counseled. When powerful customers started spreading that kind of message, other acquirers would soon appear at Nicira's door. "Don't just sell to Cisco. Run a process," Horowitz said firmly.[45]

Andreessen reinforced the message in his own voluble way. "Don't sell, don't sell, don't sell," he told Casado. "This thing is just getting into position."[46]

When Horowitz indicated that he would use his board seat to oppose a sale, Casado refused to speak to him. But after a couple of weeks of fury, Casado managed to cool down. Horowitz was right: there was no need to settle for the first offer that came to him. Nicira duly retained an investment banker to solicit multiple bids. The upshot was that Nicira was sold to a Cisco rival not for $600 million but for $1.26 billion.

"I doubled the value of the company!" Horowitz said, without exaggeration.[47]

There was certainly no doubt that Horowitz was an effective board member. In February 2010, soon after the Nicira Series A, he led another a16z cloud software investment in a startup called Okta. Where Nicira made networking function in the cloud, Okta would build an interface between a company's cloud-based software tools and its employees. The idea was that a single gateway, protected by a secure sign-in, would safeguard company data. But by the fall of 2011, Okta was flailing. It had missed its sales targets and was running low on cash. A talented engineer announced he was quitting.

Horowitz sat down with the engineer to understand why he was leaving. The whole engineering team was demoralized, he discovered. Todd McKinnon, Okta's CEO, was blaming them for the bad sales performance.

Horowitz tracked down McKinnon. "Stop holding the engineers accountable," he told him.

"What do you mean, not hold people accountable?"

Too much of a tough attitude would cause further defections, Horowitz answered. The priority for now was to keep the engineers in place while Okta fixed its real problem: its sales strategy. The startup had been trying to sell its secure dashboard to small companies. But small companies generally don't care about network security.

Following Horowitz's advice, Okta revamped its sales team. A search was conducted for a new marketing chief—someone with the Rolodex and poise to land big corporate customers. When the interviews were done, McKinnon called Horowitz to discuss his selection.

When the call came through, Horowitz was driving to a meeting at another startup. Rain blurred the view through his windshield. He listened as McKinnon started to tell him which candidate he had chosen.

Horowitz pulled over and stopped his car. As far as he was concerned, McKinnon was choosing the wrong person. This call was going to take all of his concentration.

When McKinnon stopped talking, Horowitz hit him with a verbal punch. "This is the last hire you are going to make if you get it wrong," he said bluntly.[48]

Having gotten McKinnon's attention, Horowitz explained his reasoning.

The a16z recruitment machine had identified another candidate whom Horowitz knew well. There was no doubt that he could do the job. To take a chance on someone else would be irresponsible, however much McKinnon had liked that other someone at the interview. Startups and venture capital are all about embracing risk. But when you are already in a precarious state, you don't compound your risks unnecessarily.[49]

Horowitz's rebuke revealed a distinguishing strength of Andreessen Horowitz. Even though it was a product of the youth revolt, a16z was not necessarily founder-friendly. It aimed to help technical founders succeed, but if they were set on doing the wrong thing, it had no problem confronting them.[50] Peter Thiel's fund had never opposed a founder in a board vote, and Milner did not even take board seats. But Horowitz was more hands-on: he combined the faith in scientific founders of Paul Graham with the toughness of Don Valentine. Now, on the question of Okta's marketing chief, Horowitz prevailed over McKinnon. The safe candidate was hired, and the company's fortunes turned around. By 2015 it was a unicorn.

Yet however effective Horowitz could be, his hands-on contributions were neither a novelty in the history of venture nor a full explanation for a16z's standout performance. Help with hiring, customer recruitment, strategy, and morale were standard types of venture input; besides, they probably counted for less than a16z's skill in selecting investments. In the case of both Nicira and Okta, only venture capitalists with a sophisticated grip on the trends in cloud computing could see the opportunities; arguably, the key differentiator for Andreessen and Horowitz was not their entrepreneurial experience but their computer science training.[51] Likewise, a16z's success had much to do with its fortuitous timing. The firm launched at the start of a decade-long boom in equities, and especially in software firms; the advent of smartphones, cloud computing, and ubiquitous broadband ushered in a golden age for coders. Two strong partners with computer science backgrounds were ideally placed to capitalize on this moment, and they happily announced this fact. "Software is eating the world," Andreessen proclaimed in a *Wall Street Journal* essay. The phrase brilliantly summed up the times. It surely explained more of a16z's success than the public-relations hype about a new approach to technical founders.

But the early years of a16z did feature a stealth innovation—one that was largely left out of the PR blitz. Unlike the ambitious venture firms of the past, Andreessen Horowitz combined classic early-stage bets with Milner-style growth investments.

Soon after it got going, in September 2009, Andreessen Horowitz plunked down $50 million for a stake in the breakout telephony company Skype, which by now was owned by eBay. The bet amounted to fully one-sixth of a16z's first fund, yet it had little to do with its promise to coach green technical founders. After all, Skype was already six years old; it had no shortage of sophistication. Instead, the Skype deal had everything to do with Andreessen's recent exposure to Milner and to his privileged position at the heart of the Valley network.

The starting point for a16z's Skype bet was Andreessen's presence on the board of eBay. Having bought Skype four years earlier, in 2005, the auction giant was struggling to incorporate telephony into its business. It had fired Skype's Swedish creators amid a series of management battles, and the Swedes had responded by suing eBay over the ownership of Skype's core technology. When a private-equity group, Silver Lake, offered to take Skype off eBay's hands, the Skype founders sued Silver Lake for good measure.

As an eBay board member, Andreessen had a front-row seat at each stage of this drama. Being familiar with Milner's Facebook coup, he saw an opportunity. Playing on his reputation as a software guru, he made contact with the Skype founders. He understood their vision and their technical prowess; in fact, Skype was exactly the type of product that a16z believed in—software that promised to displace hardware. Stressing his faith in their ability to move their product to the cloud, Andreessen proposed a deal to bring the founders back into their firm. The Silver Lake consortium would buy a bit more than half of Skype's stock. The Skype founders would get 14 percent in return for dropping their lawsuits. For his part, Andreessen would get the right to invest $50 million.

The deal went ahead, and Andreessen helped the new ownership team fix Skype's managerial dysfunction. Fully twenty-nine of the top thirty managers were replaced, and then Andreessen used his boardroom connections again, helping to broker an alliance between Skype and Facebook: henceforth, Facebook users would be able to chat with one another over Skype's video connections. Just as a16z had predicted, Skype's technical team proved strong enough to manage the transition to the cloud; Skype's user numbers took off, leaping from 400 million before the deal to 600 million the following year. As smartphones became ubiquitous, dialing over the internet became almost as simple as dialing over traditional phone lines; Skype suddenly resembled one of Mary Meeker's metaphorical surfboards, a platform exquisitely designed to catch the latest tech wave. Recognizing Skype's promise, Microsoft swooped in to buy the firm for $8.5 billion, three times more than the valuation that the Silver Lake consortium had paid. In just eighteen months, Andreessen Horowitz had bagged a profit of $100 million.

Andreessen's Skype coup was followed by other Milner-style growth deals. Using the capital in its first fund, a16z also invested alongside DST in the gaming company Zynga and staked $20 million on the mobile app Foursquare.[52] Its second fund, a war chest of $650 million, made a pair of $80 million bets on Facebook and Twitter; a $40 million bet on Groupon; and a pair of $30 million bets on the picture-sharing app Pinterest and the real estate rental platform Airbnb. For a venture partnership that had advertised itself as an early-stage startup doctor, committing more than a third of a fund's capital to growth deals was off brand. But this surprising pivot was a testimony to the influence of one man. "We made a bet that this expansion-stage opportunity had arisen," Andreessen said later. "A lot of this had to do with Yuri Milner."[53]

Andreessen and Horowitz achieved what they set out to do: they broke into the top tier of the venture industry. Their first fund ranked in the top 5 percent of venture funds launched in 2009, generating a return of 44 percent per year, net of fees—three times higher than the S&P 500 over the same period.[54] Thanks in particular to the Milner-inspired Skype deal, which allowed a16z to demonstrate early success, the partners went on to raise large follow-on funds, recruit additional investing partners, and expand their internal consulting operation. As Kleiner Perkins vacated its slot among the Valley's top investment firms, a16z filled it.

At first, a16z's accomplishment was greeted as a vindication for its supposedly disruptive model. Other partnerships began to lay on coaching and support services for their portfolio companies and to adopt the "by entrepreneurs, for entrepreneurs" patter. But then a funny thing happened. According to an assessment in late 2018, the next two a16z funds were struggling to outperform the S&P 500, registering provisional paper gains that placed them in the third and second quartiles among VC firms, respectively.[55] In quick succession, Andreessen Horowitz appeared to have defied the rule of path dependency not once but twice. First, the firm had busted into the top tier. Then it had fallen to somewhere around the middle of the league table.

What happened? The most obvious explanation is that as Andreessen and Horowitz expanded their business, they diluted their own talent. They thought that "by entrepreneurs, for entrepreneurs" and coaching technical founders amounted to a new approach to venture capital, one that would succeed at scale. What they discovered was that success had less to do with this vision than with their own status in the Valley. As a16z hired additional investing partners, following its proud rule that all must have an entrepreneurial background, it found that some did not work out: being a founder is not the same as being able to pick which founders to invest in. In 2018, a16z elevated a non-entrepreneur to the rank of general partner for the first time. "It's a kind of a big thing for especially me to eat crow on," Horowitz admitted to *Forbes*. "It took probably longer than it should've to change it, but we changed it."[56]

The VC firms that launch with a splash tend to have two things in common. They have a story about their special approach, and they have recognizable partners with strong networks. In a few exceptional instances, the special approach is powerful enough to explain most of the success. Such was the case with Yuri Milner, who arrived in the Valley with no connections and vaulted straight to the top. Such was the case with Tiger Global, which improvised the hedge fund/venture hybrid model. And such was more or less the case with Y Combinator, whose batch-based seed investing was genuinely novel. But in the large majority of examples, new venture firms succeed because of the founders' experience and status, not because of the claimed originality of their methods. Academic research confirms what is intuitively obvious: success in venture capital owes much to connections.[57] "Silicon Valley is gripped by the cult of the individual," the British venture capitalist Matt Clifford once remarked. "But those individuals represent the triumph of the network."

Chapter Thirteen

SEQUOIA'S STRENGTH IN NUMBERS

In the summer of 2010, a year after Andreessen Horowitz got started, a Kleiner Perkins partner named Joe Lacob made an unconventional investment. Over the course of twenty-three years at Kleiner, he had backed some seventy ventures—life-science companies, energy companies, e-commerce outfits. But this bet would be different. Founded sixty-four years earlier, it was not exactly a startup. With a demoralized team, it was not exactly innovative. Yet Lacob spotted potential. Together with a few allies, he paid $450 million for Northern California's dilapidated basketball franchise, the Golden State Warriors.

What happened next became a symbol of the wider boom that gripped Silicon Valley. Lacob brought with him a creative network of tech people and Hollywood types, and the Warriors took off on a wild streak, like a hot social-media platform. Having lost two-thirds of their games the year before Lacob's purchase, they made the NBA final in 2015 and again in each of the next four years, winning the title three times and setting an all-time record for games won in a single season. They became famous for a data-driven playing style, predicated on long-distance, three-point shots, and the innovation soon attracted imitators. Every seat in the stadium sold out. Ticket prices rocketed. Lacob moved the team from its run-down premises in East Oakland to a luxury coliseum in San Francisco. By the end of the decade, the Golden State franchise was said to be worth $3.5 billion, almost eight times more than Lacob and his syndicate had paid. It was a venture return from a basketball team.[1]

The great basketball franchises have famous superfans whom the cameras seek out before the games: Jack Nicholson for the Los Angeles Lakers, Spike Lee for the New York Knicks. Naturally, the Golden team boasted a roster of Midas investors. Its ownership group featured Bob Kagle, the Benchmark partner who had invested in eBay, and Mark Stevens, a longtime stalwart at Sequoia. Its regular fans included Ben Horowitz, cofounder of a16z, and Ron Conway, the super-angel who had backed Google. And this fusing of sports and technology finance operated in two ways: the venture capitalists rooted for the Warriors, and the Warriors became venture capitalists. Kevin Durant, the team's star forward, assembled a portfolio of some forty startups, ranging from the bike-sharing enterprise LimeBike to the food-delivery app Postmates. Andre Iguodala, the six-foot-six defensive specialist, built a similar empire, while a retired Warrior, David Lee, was recruited by a VC partnership. Steph Curry, the Golden State's transcendent talent, owned a piece of the picture-sharing app Pinterest. Together with Iguodala, Curry fronted an event to bring other athletes into this new game: the Players Technology Summit.

And indeed, why not? In the years after 2010, almost everybody in the Valley seemed touched by the tech frenzy. The small tongue of land running from San Jose to San Francisco was home to three of the world's five most valuable companies: Apple, Google, and Facebook. It boasted some of the most exciting trailblazers: Airbnb, Tesla, and Uber. It was routinely compared to Florence during the Renaissance: a money magnet, to be sure, but also a multinational melting pot and a hub of ingenuity.[2] The cloud software giant Salesforce erected a cloud-scraping glass tower in downtown San Francisco, and real estate prices soared so much that startups could barely afford the proverbial garage. The resulting inequality was staggering, and the traffic recalled Bangkok, thanks not least to the hulking double-decker buses ferrying coders from the city to the tech campuses near Palo Alto. When China's president, Xi Jinping, visited the United States in 2015, he ratified the status of this new Florence. His first meeting was with the tech executives of Silicon Valley and Seattle, not with the politicians and bankers of Washington, D.C., and New York City.[3]

Just as in previous booms, venture capital was at the center of the action. In the decade after the financial crisis, running from 2009 to 2019, the tally of U.S. venture investors more than doubled, and so did the number of startups that they funded.[4] Now more than ever, the industry's lineup was complete, offering tailored investments for any size or sort of startup. There were avuncular angels, factory-batch incubators, entrepreneur-centric early-stage sponsors, and data-driven growth investors. There were venture capitalists who specialized in everything from artificial intelligence to biotech to cryptocurrencies, not to mention agtech, big data, and cloud software. While Wall Street recovered painfully from the crisis of 2008, its wings clipped by regulators aiming to forestall a repeat taxpayer bailout, the West Coast variety of finance expanded energetically along three axes: into new industries, into new geographies, and along the life cycle of startups. In 2013, when Aileen Lee coined the term "unicorn," she counted just thirty-nine of these magical creatures. Less than two years later there were eighty-four of them.

The venture partnership that best embodied this boom was Sequoia Capital. Through the 1980s and 1990s, Sequoia and Kleiner had been the top two Valley firms, and in some ways they were similar: partnerships with a focus on networking, software, and the internet, with turbo-power-law rainmakers. Early in the first decade of the twenty-first century, when John Doerr was at the peak of his celebrity and Sequoia was on the wrong side of the youth revolt, Kleiner appeared stronger. But around the middle of the decade, the tables turned, and Kleiner and Sequoia began to look like opposites. Where Kleiner charged into cleantech, Sequoia approached cautiously. Where Kleiner led on recruiting women, Sequoia followed woefully late but then implemented the shift less clumsily.[5] Where Doerr parted with Vinod Khosla and other members of his team, Michael Moritz remained bonded to Doug Leone, who provided the engineering savvy and ability to read people that complemented Moritz's grand strategy. And where Doerr hired established, fifty-something celebrities, Sequoia had no interest in recruiting comfortable executives who, as Moritz put it, "had been too successful, had lost some spring in their step, were not hungry enough, had too many outside commitments and, most of all, were not prepared to become rookies again."[6]

The contrast in approach generated an astonishing contrast in performance. In 2021, when Kleiner partners had all but disappeared from the *Forbes* Midas list, Sequoia occupied the number one and number two slots, and three of the top ten, making it by far and away the top firm in the industry. It dominated the business in both the United States and China. It backed unicorns from Airbnb and WhatsApp to ByteDance and Meituan. It seemed to succeed at everything it touched, from venture investing to growth funds and even to an experimental hedge fund. Up and down the Valley, rivals swapped theories about what made Sequoia win. No other team had sustained performance at this level.

Sequoia's secret sauce began with the union between Moritz and Leone, the most successful buddy act in the history of venture capital. Moritz was strategic, and Leone was operational. Moritz enforced discipline, and Leone enjoyed conversations at the watercooler. Moritz was a Brit who had taken Italian lessons. Leone was an Italian who joked that working with Moritz was like taking English lessons. There were tensions under the surface: Moritz was torn between wanting the alliance with Leone and wanting to be recognized as the top dog, and Leone bristled occasionally. But they had each others' backs. From the mid-1990s, when Don Valentine retired, the two were joined at the hip on every major decision about the direction of Sequoia. They created the most tightly disciplined culture on Sand Hill Road, but also the most experimental one.

Sequoia's ferocious discipline illustrated how Leone and Moritz were at once different and united. For Leone, the tough Italian immigrant who had fought his way up, hard work came instinctively. His own life was about business, family, and staying in shape. He had no time for partners who wanted to hobnob with celebrities, join flashy philanthropic boards, or waste time holding forth at conferences. Once, to test his courage, Leone had his tooth drilled without painkillers. He was not going to tolerate colleagues who were only semi-committed. For Moritz, the Oxford-educated writer, the competitive determination took a different form, but it was no less insistent. Since his early life as a business journalist, Moritz had admired "the purposeful cadence of a relentless, disciplined march"—the stamina and willpower that patiently built success, one advance upon another.[7] To rise above mediocrity, Moritz intimated, was an almost spiritual task. You had to be obsessed—obsessed like Steve Jobs, for whom perfectionism was not a choice, or obsessed like Alex Ferguson, the legendary British soccer coach whom Moritz chose as his collaborator and muse when he wrote a book on leadership. Jason Calacanis, an entrepreneur who saw the inside of many venture shops, recalled how Moritz and Leone instilled a culture that made the partnership stand out. "I would show up at Sequoia at 8:30am for an appointment and see the top partners in conference rooms, meeting with startups. I would swing by Sequoia for coffee at 4pm and see the same partners still there, still meeting with startups."[8]

Stamina was just the start of the Sequoia formula. Moritz and Leone focused uncompromisingly on the culture of the firm: external investment hits would flow from an internal quest for excellence. Moritz once enumerated the challenges that this entailed: "recruitment, team building, setting of standards, questions of inspiration and motivation, avoiding complacency, the arrival of new competitors and the continual need to refresh ourselves and purge under-performers."[9] From this long list, team building and the development of young talent were particular priorities. Sequoia believed in "nurturing the unknown, the homegrown, and what becomes the next generation," as Moritz put it. Of course, this was a fair description of what Accel had done by training Kevin Efrusy. But Sequoia nurtured new recruits even more purposefully.

The story of Roelof Botha illustrated the Moritz-Leone approach to talent development. Sequoia hired Botha from his position as PayPal's chief financial officer in 2003; it was a canny way of forging links with a go-getting cohort of PayPal alums, who were not otherwise well-disposed toward the partnership. Beyond his PayPal connections, the South African–born Botha was a natural Sequoia hire: he had been top of his class at Stanford Business School and had the drive of an immigrant. But he was not yet thirty and had no experience as an investor, so the firm's senior partners made it their mission to develop him. Of course, if he foundered, they would push him out as clinically as they closed a weak startup, sending him on his way with an airtight nondisclosure agreement. But their vehement intention was to help him put points on the board: to make him a Sequoia warrior.

Like all recruits to Sequoia, Botha began by shadowing his experienced colleagues. He sat in on board meetings with different senior partners and at different types of companies, absorbing a range of contrasting startup cultures. He soaked up tips from old-timers: Don Valentine told him right away that the best founders are the ones who are the most difficult. After a few months at the office, Botha brought in one of his first investments, a remittances company called Xoom, and an older partner proposed a win-win arrangement. To begin with, the senior partner would go on Xoom's board, bringing Botha to the meetings as an observer. Then, if Xoom succeeded, the two would switch roles, so that Botha would gain professional standing as a director of a buzzy startup. "Look, if the company doesn't work out, the stain is on my name, not yours," the senior partner said. Botha agreed, Xoom ultimately flourished, and Botha duly completed his apprenticeship and stepped up to be a board member.[10] It was the inverse of the experience at Kleiner, where senior partners grabbed the best opportunities off the plates of younger investors. It was superior even to Accel, where the managing partner, Jim Breyer, had occupied the Facebook board seat.

It took several years before Xoom turned good, and in the meantime Botha's partners helped him through the inevitable dark periods. Unsuccessful startups generally fail faster than good ones succeed, so demoralizing losses materialize before the winners. The first time Botha had to report that one of his companies was a zero, he teared up at the partners' meeting: normally, he was composed and certain of his judgment; failure was acutely painful. Then, three years into his tenure, Botha shifted from anguish to elation. In 2005 he led Sequoia's Series A investment in the video platform YouTube, and in 2006—after a freakishly brief gestation—the company was snapped up by Google, delivering a return of around 45x on Sequoia's investment. Another three years later, Botha was in the dumps again. He began torturing himself not about the investments that went wrong but about the great ones that escaped him. He had passed on Twitter when it had been a crude messaging technology. He had gone after Facebook, only to suffer through that strange pajama performance. Even the YouTube triumph turned sour in Botha's mouth: in retrospect, Sequoia had sold out too early. For any venture investor, these swings of fortune can play havoc with judgment. A dark period lumbers you with excess caution as you size up the next deal; inversely, joy can lead to hubris. Looking back on this period, Botha credits his partners with keeping him centered. When he was down, they encouraged him to take the shot. When he was up, they saved him from getting starry-eyed about a startup's prospects.[11]

Despite Sequoia's cerebral and disciplined culture, the firm's team-building efforts included a surprisingly soft side. Partnership off-sites began with something called "check-ins": colleagues opened up to one another about marital tensions, insecurities at work, or a sickness in the family. "If you're willing to expose yourself and nobody takes advantage of it, it creates a trusting atmosphere," Doug Leone reflected.[12] The off-sites also featured poker tournaments: Partners competed for the "Don Valentine tartan," a monstrously garish red, yellow, and black jacket. At one retreat, during an intensely muddy game of flag football, Botha allowed his South African childhood to seize control of his instincts. He barreled toward a muscular opponent and felled him with a rugby-style tackle. "It was one of the moments that unlatched our friendship," Botha remembered later.[13]

The team building extended to the way that Sequoia celebrated its successes. When a portfolio company achieved a profitable exit, the newspapers would profile the named partner on the board, as though venture were a lone-wolf business. Sequoia itself went out of its way to ascribe the triumph to the group; successful investments were nearly always a collective effort. For example, when Sequoia toasted the second-biggest windfall thus far in its history, the sale of the messaging service WhatsApp, the partnership's internal "milestone memo" began by saluting Jim Goetz, the partner who had led the deal and who had been Botha's flag-football victim. But the memo pivoted quickly to a different message: WhatsApp had been a "classic Sequoia gang tackle." More than a dozen partners had contributed to this win: Sequoia's in-house talent scouts had helped WhatsApp quintuple the size of its engineering team; Botha and Moritz had advised the company on its distribution and global strategy; Sequoia's teams in India, Singapore, and China had provided on-the-ground intelligence; the partnership's communications chief had prepared Jan Koum, WhatsApp's introverted CEO, to be a public figure. The milestone memo gave a special shout-out to an office assistant called Tanya Schillage. At 3:00 the previous morning, Koum's car had broken down en route to finalizing the sale documents, and Schillage had sprung into action and found Koum a new ride. Somehow, in a flourish of nocturnal overachievement, she had managed to supply Koum with nearly the same model of Porsche that he'd been driving.[14]

◆

To deepen the teamwork, and to promote the self-renewal that Moritz emphasized, Sequoia was quick to give rising partners at the firm management responsibility. So it was that, in 2009, the partnership underwent a quiet shift in leadership.[15] Moritz and Leone remained in charge, bearing the title of "stewards." But front-line management of U.S. venture investments passed informally to Jim Goetz and Roelof Botha. The emergence of this younger duo brought in a fresh wave of ideas, tightening the rigor of Sequoia's investment processes.

The main innovation pushed by Jim Goetz was an emphasis on proactive thinking. He had begun his investing career at Accel, where he had absorbed the idea of the "prepared mind," and he saw that this top-down, anticipatory approach could be especially useful at Sequoia. Because of Sequoia's status as the Valley's leading venture firm, most startup founders were eager to pitch to it; by the partnership's own reckoning, it was invited to consider around two-thirds of the deals that ended up getting funded by the top two dozen venture shops. But this privileged deal flow was both a blessing and a curse. The partners' days were crammed with meetings organized at the visitors' request. It was easy to become reactive.[16]

To manage this danger, Goetz brought Accel's prepared-mind approach to Sequoia, leading the partners in mapping out tech trends and anticipating which sorts of startups would prosper from them. He was early to sketch out a detailed picture of the mobile internet landscape, laying out the base stations that phone carriers would have to build, the chips that would go into the handsets, and the software that would run on them. Another prepared-mind "landscape" showed the shift of data from customer devices to the cloud, anticipating the new hardware configurations, software business models, and security vulnerabilities that would flow from it. Yet a third landscape focused on "the rise of the developer." Worldwide, a mere twenty-five million coders—one-third of 1 percent of the global population—were writing all the software that was transforming modern life. Anything that boosted the productivity of this small tribe would be immensely valuable. Predating Marc Andreessen's declaration that "software is eating the world," this last prepared-mind exercise became the springboard for a raft of Sequoia investments: Unity, a software development platform for 3-D movies and games; MongoDB, a database company; and GitHub, the leading repository for open-source code. By late 2020, Sequoia's stakes in these three firms were worth a combined $9 billion.

While Goetz led on the prepared mind, Botha pioneered the application of behavioral science to venture capital. This was a radical idea, and Botha's colleagues came to regard it as transformative for Sequoia.[17] At other venture partnerships, investors often boasted about relying on instinct. They claimed to have "pattern recognition," an investment sixth sense; "I've had this my entire career, and I do not know why," one successful VC said happily.[18] But Botha pointed out that in well-known experiments stretching back to the 1970s, psychologists had shown how human reflexes distort rational decisions, and he set out to apply the resulting insights to Sequoia's Monday partners' meetings. The goal, at a minimum, was to make the investment process consistent from one week to the next. "Sometimes we felt that if a particular company had been there the previous Monday, or the subsequent Monday, our decision would have been different," Botha explained. "That didn't feel like a recipe for sustainable success."[19]

Botha's focus on behavioral science grew partly out of the premature sale of YouTube. In accepting Google's acquisition offer, the founders had behaved precisely as behavioral experiments predict: people are often willing to gamble in order to avoid a loss, but they are irrationally risk averse when it comes to reaching for the upside. Examining the pattern of Sequoia's exits, Botha determined that premature profit-taking occurred repeatedly at the firm, despite Moritz's earlier efforts to extend the partnership's holding periods. The behavioral literature also drew attention to another tendency that Botha observed: VCs suffered from "confirmation bias," the practice of filtering out information that challenges a position you have taken. At Sequoia, the partners sometimes missed attractive Series B deals because they wanted to make themselves feel good. They hated to admit they had been wrong in saying no to the same startup at the Series A stage.[20]

The first step toward overcoming cognitive bias is to recognize it. Botha arranged for outside psychologists to present to the partnership. He led his colleagues through painful postmortems of past decisions, homing in on times when they had weighed evidence irrationally. Previously, the partners had tried to extract lessons from portfolio companies that had failed. Now Botha was equally focused on the times when Sequoia had declined to invest in a startup that subsequently succeeded. To enable scientific postmortems, the partners kept a record of all votes at investment meetings. "It's not about scapegoating," Botha explained. "It's just 'What did we learn as a team?' If we can get better at decisions, that is a source of advantage."[21]

As well as running postmortems, Botha began to build new habits into real-time decision making. To overcome the risk-aversion identified by decision science, the partners included a "pre-parade" section in each investment memo—a description of how the company would turn out assuming everything went perfectly. By building this exercise into their process, the partners gave themselves permission to voice their excitement about a deal, and to do so with a fullness that would otherwise have been uncomfortable. "We all suffer from the desire not to be embarrassed," Jim Goetz reflected. "But we're in the business of being embarrassed, and we need to be comfortable enough to say out loud what might be possible."[22]

Sequoia also began to design around the problem of "anchoring"—that is, basing a judgment on other people's views rather than wrestling with the evidence and taking an independent position. At most venture firms, partners chat with one another about the startups they are sizing up, partly to solicit advice and partly to recruit allies ahead of the vote at the Monday meeting. At Sequoia, the partners resolved that to arrive at the most ratio-nal decision possible, this vote canvassing should stop. Ahead of a decision, each of them would read the investment memo with an unpolluted mind; they should do their utmost to avoid groupthink. Then they would come to the Monday meeting prepared to take a stand. "We don't want passive 'do it if you want,'" Leone said. "The sponsor needs help. It's a very lonely place to be the lead on an investment."[23]

In 2010, acting on an idea from Moritz, Botha began to build Sequoia's "scouts program," an inspired variation on the idea of angel investing. The insight was that most angel investors were yesterday's leaders. They had cashed out from their startups; they had money to play with; but their un-derstanding of the business landscape was dated. Meanwhile, active entre-preneurs had their wealth tied up in their firms, so they lacked the ready cash to make angel investments. With the advent of growth investing, this was becoming more of a problem, because entrepreneurs were delaying the moment when they took their gains out of their companies. "You're Drew Houston in 2012 and you're worth $100 million but you can't make rent, never mind have the luxury of investing in other companies," Botha ex-plained, using the example of one of Dropbox's two founders. So Botha and his partners came up with a fix. "We give you $100,000 to invest. We take half of the gains, but you as the scout get to keep the rest."[24] Of course, the effect of this arrangement was to generate investment leads for Sequoia. Today's top entrepreneurs were identifying the brightest stars in the next cohort.

Much as they came up with their own variant on angel investing, so the partners reacted to the launch of Andreessen Horowitz. After a16z trum-peted its company-building assistance to startups, Sequoia expanded its team of in-house "operational partners" whose job was to counsel portfo-lio companies. Toward the end of the 2010s, Sequoia began to lay on work-shops for entrepreneurs: an event called Base Camp gathered founders for weekends in the mountains, featuring campfires, wigwam tents, and speak-ers on everything from technology to architecture. Another offering called the Company Design Program featured courses taught by the firm's part-ners. Amid the coronavirus pandemic of 2020, the partnership launched a

founders' app called Ampersand. Sequoia-backed entrepreneurs used it to
stay in touch with one another and test management ideas. Should they ad-
just compensation when workers went remote? How to help team members
whose mental health deteriorated?[25]

Three years after Goetz and Botha had been informally promoted, at
the start of 2012, Leone got a strange message from Moritz. His partner
wanted to visit him at home the following Saturday. When Moritz came
over, he announced that an era was ending: they had worked together tire-
lessly for sixteen years, but now a health issue that Moritz would not name
required him to give up his position as a "steward."[26] Moritz had been the
dominant figure in the partnership, chairing the key meetings and setting
the direction of the firm. Now Leone would have to fill a gaping hole in Team
Sequoia's lineup.

Leadership handovers are perilous for partnerships, especially when
money has been made and the partners have the means to head off into the
sunset. Leone managed the transition by borrowing the slogan that appeared on Warriors T-shirts: "strength in numbers." Rather than replacing
Moritz with an individual, he doubled down on Sequoia's team culture. He
flew to Hong Kong, asked Neil Shen to serve as a steward, and immediately
flew home again. He asked Jim Goetz to serve as a steward, too, creating a
leadership troika with himself at the apex. To ensure his teammates had
strong incentives, he cut his own salary by a third, signed away a large piece
of his guaranteed future compensation, and shared out the proceeds. It was
a frictionless changeover, and five years later Sequoia repeated the same
feat. In 2017, aged only fifty-one, Goetz decided to step down because the
forty-three-year-old Botha was ready to step up to be a steward, and the
shuffle created space for talent further down the ladder.[27] A forty-four-
year-old star named Alfred Lin became a co-lead of the U.S. venture team.
Strength in numbers thus combined with faith in rejuvenation.[28]

Sequoia's tight team and loose experiments illuminated the enigmatic skill
in venture capital. Taken individually, the story of every venture bet can
seem to hinge on serendipity. Investor receives random referral. Investor

meets inspired young misfit. Investor manages to connect with youth by means of an opaque alchemy. Explaining this bonding process, Yahoo's Jerry Yang had remarked mysteriously that Michael Moritz "had soul," while Tony Zingale, another Sequoia-backed entrepreneur, stated that he got along with Doug Leone because "he's another fiery Italian."[29] But despite these trivializing explanations, Sequoia illustrates the method behind the seeming arbitrariness and chance. The best venture capitalists consciously create their luck. They work systematically to boost the odds that serendipity will strike repeatedly.

Most of the modern Sequoia's venture triumphs can be traced to this sort of systematic work, put in place in the first years of the new century. By recruiting the young Roelof Botha and deliberately building his credentials, Sequoia laid the groundwork for billions of dollars of profits. After his wins in YouTube and Xoom, Botha followed up with a string of grand slams: the fintech company Square, the genetics testing outfits Natera and 23andMe, the social-media hit Instagram, and the database innovator MongoDB. When *Forbes* published its Midas List in April 2020, Botha ranked third. Five months later, he celebrated the stock market debut of the 3-D software platform Unity and a gain for Sequoia of more than $6 billion.

A skeptic might object that this story sounds too simple. Did Sequoia's coaching of Botha really generate those outsized wins, or was Botha himself unusually talented—or lucky? If Botha's story is taken in isolation, it might be hard to say. But if you consider Sequoia's efforts to cultivate each one of its recruits, the role of systematic groundwork becomes obvious. It was not just Botha who got an early chance to sit on the board of a successful startup: this was common practice at Sequoia.[30] It was not just Botha who was paired with an experienced mentor: this too was standard. In a mark of the priority assigned to training, Doug Leone made a point of meeting new recruits for one-on-ones. What had the novice taken away from the most recent partners' meeting, he'd ask, and what had been the subtexts?[31] Sameer Gandhi, a junior partner at Sequoia before moving to Accel, remembers Moritz taking the trouble to coach him on time management. "Let's look at your calendar for the last year, let me see where you're going," Moritz said. "Where did you spend time? Well, did you have to do that? Was that useful?"[32] In sum, the success of Roelof Botha no doubt reflected his talent and fortune. But he worked in a culture that pumped up talent and manufactured extra luck. Small wonder that so many of his teammates flourished.

In the first half of the 2010s, Sequoia's most successful U.S. bet was WhatsApp, the messaging service later sold to Facebook. Most accounts of this investment emphasize the hustle that Goetz showed. Jan Koum, the WhatsApp founder, was hiding in a building in Mountain View with no sign on the door and initially refused to answer Goetz's emails. When Goetz finally landed a meeting, he was greeted by an unsmiling figure in a beanie and a fearsome stare. "I'm definitely in trouble," Goetz remembered thinking.[33] It took two months for Goetz to talk Koum into visiting Sequoia, and even then he trod with care. Rather than asking the introverted Koum to stand up and present to the full firm, he led him through a casual Q&A with a subset of the partnership. In the end, Goetz overcame Koum's shyness and earned his trust. It was the perfect venture-capital fairy tale.

Yet behind this fable of the hunt and the seduction, there was another story. As part of his focus on proactivity, Goetz had conceived a system he called "early bird": seeing in the advent of the Apple App Store a trove of useful investment leads, Sequoia had written code that tracked downloads by consumers in sixty different countries. It was this exercise in digital sleuthing that alerted Goetz to WhatsApp: the messaging service was the first or second most downloaded application in around thirty-five of the sixty markets. Even though the service was not yet famous in the United States, it seemed only a matter of time before that changed, so Goetz made it his business to get to WhatsApp before his rivals spotted it. Of course, this early-bird system was not directly the cause of Goetz's investment, but it boosted the chances of its happening. If you ballparked that boost in probability at, say, 10 percent, the value of creating the web crawler ran into the hundreds of millions, because Sequoia's bet on WhatsApp generated $3.5 billion for the partnership.[34] Thanks to this coup and several others, Goetz occupied the top slot on the Midas List for four years in a row, until, in 2018, his Sequoia China teammate Neil Shen took over.

The same double story—serendipity on the surface, systematic effort deeper down—could be told of other Sequoia winners. In the spring of 2009, for example, a Sequoia partner named Greg McAdoo dropped by the Y Combinator building and struck up a conversation with Paul Graham. What type of startup might survive the post-financial-crisis slowdown? he wondered. Graham said something about startups with "intellectual toughness" and nodded toward a team of youths huddled over a laptop on one of YC's long tables. McAdoo duly approached them and wowed them with his understanding of their business model, and the result was an investment in the real estate rental platform Airbnb, which ultimately generated a multibillion-dollar jackpot for Sequoia.[35] Told like this, the Airbnb story makes the venture business sound absurdly casual, with the payoff wildly disproportionate to skill. But the deeper truth is that McAdoo's visit to the YC building was not at all casual. He was there because Sequoia had deliberately made itself the incubator's primary ally, investing in multiple YC graduates and providing capital for YC's own seed fund. McAdoo was able to wow the Airbnb founders because he had foreseen that the rental business was ripe for digital disruption, and he had spent time studying the ways in which incumbents could be challenged. Other VCs looked at Airbnb, then looked away: the idea that homeowners would take in strangers seemed wacky.[36] The Sequoia investor arrived with a prepared mind. The habits encouraged by Goetz were paying dividends.

Sequoia also backed the file-sharing company Dropbox, another YC protégé, and here the tales of serendipity and skill were even more intriguing. Sequoia's luck began when the startup's founders, Drew Houston and Arash Ferdowsi, pitched their business at a Y Combinator demo day, watched by a roomful of investors. After they wrapped up, they found themselves cornered by a cheerful man with salt-and-pepper hair who introduced himself as Pejman Nozad. Their new friend seemed to home in on them for the most arbitrary of reasons: he was an immigrant from Iran, just like Ferdowsi's parents. Nozad played the diaspora card, addressing Ferdowsi in Farsi, and then he promised to help Dropbox raise money. Inviting the founders to his premises, he mentioned the address. It was a shop selling Persian carpets.

Ferdowsi and Houston accepted—they had little to lose—but Houston felt a creeping sense of foolishness when he arrived at the carpet store. Here was this rug dealer regaling them with Persian music, serving glass cups of tea, and politely passing sugar cubes: it was a scene worthy of a Hollywood comedy. As Nozad quizzed Ferdowsi about his parents' hometown and his favorite Persian dishes, Houston even wondered if the whole thing was a setup. Perhaps he would appear as the butt of a joke on some vindictive reality TV show.

But despite all appearances, Nozad was fully serious. As well as being a rug dealer, he was an informal scout for Sequoia. One year earlier, Doug Leone had given a talk for entrepreneurs at Nozad's carpet store and had encouraged Nozad to look out for deals that might be interesting.[37] After that encounter, Nozad had become Sequoia's ambassador to the Iranian diaspora in the Valley, a group that included Pierre Omidyar, the founder of eBay, and Dara Khosrowshahi, later the boss of Uber.[38] Sequoia valued Nozad's connections because of its belief in immigrant grit: Moritz, Leone, and Botha were born in Wales, Italy, and South Africa, respectively, and three in five Sequoia-backed successes had at least one immigrant founder.[39] What seemed like serendipity, in other words, was actually the opposite. Nozad was part of Sequoia's strategy to ensure the best possible deal flow.

Three years after Nozad flagged Dropbox, Sequoia's formal scouts program got off the ground, and stories of this sort became more common. Angel investing, at times a counterweight to the power of VCs, was now transformed into a mechanism that enriched Sequoia's links to the next generation of founders. In one example, a scout investment in a cancer-test startup, Guardant Health, led Sequoia to follow up with a Series A investment, resulting in a gain for the partnership of more than half a billion dollars. In another case, the scouts program led Sequoia to a successful bet on Thumbtack, an app to connect consumers to neighborhood services such as plumbers or tutors.[40] But by far the greatest triumph of the scouts program was Sequoia's investment in the payments startup Stripe. Here was the ultimate example of Sequoia deliberately creating the circumstances in which fortune might strike. If "manufactured serendipity" could be said to exist, Sequoia was the master of it.

Stripe's founders, Irish brothers named Patrick and John Collison, were startlingly young, even by the Valley's standards. Patrick, wiry and red-headed and marginally older, had won a national science prize in Ireland at the age of sixteen; he had created a variant of Lisp, the computer language beloved by Paul Graham of Y Combinator. After that, Patrick had compressed his last two years of high school into a few months, run a marathon to celebrate, and proceeded to MIT on a scholarship.[41] John, the dark-haired younger brother, was not far behind. In 2007, aged sixteen, he left his family's village in the west of Ireland and joined Patrick in the United States, where the two worked together on their first software startup. The following year they sold the venture and became millionaires. Patrick returned to MIT. John enrolled at Harvard.

In 2009, now aged twenty and eighteen, Patrick and John spent the summer in Palo Alto. They had been noodling a new business idea, a company that would transform the experience of e-commerce sites that needed to take payments. As a side project at MIT, Patrick had built a download-able version of Wikipedia and had discovered how hard it was to collect money for it. Processing credit card transfers was expensive and frustrating; despite the earlier promise of PayPal, online payments remained in the dark ages. The Collisons set out to solve this pain point by setting up the accounting platforms to manage cash flows, verify payers' identity, and catch fraud. E-commerce merchants would be able to connect to the Collisons' service simply by pasting a few lines of code into the software powering their websites.

For almost any venture financier, this Collison idea would be intriguing. The brothers had already launched and sold a company, and they had spotted a strategic niche in the digital economy. Once online businesses incorporated the Collisons' code into their websites, agreeing to give up a small percentage of each payment they received, the Collisons would effectively own a share of the world's exploding e-commerce. And once the Collisons' code became ubiquitous, it would be hard to dislodge. A payments platform connects thousands of suppliers to millions of consumers; it's not something you switch out easily. In short, the Collisons' project had everything venture capitalists look for: a lucrative target market, a natural moat against competitors, and a team with a track record. The question was which investor would win the race to connect with the two prodigies.[42]

When he arrived in Palo Alto, the first person Patrick called was Paul Graham of Y Combinator. It was a testament to what made Graham special. By now, four years into YC's existence, Graham had parlayed his cult standing among young hackers into a formidable network. He had first gotten to know the Collisons because, as a high-schooler in Ireland, Patrick had emailed him with coding questions—"I had no idea he was a high-school kid, because his questions were so sophisticated," Graham recalled later. When Patrick had come to the United States to interview at colleges, he had stayed at Graham's house; and Graham had gone on to introduce him to a pair of YC founders, sparking the formation of the Collisons' first startup.[43] Graham had also introduced Patrick to other young members of the YC community. Among them was Sam Altman, a graduate of YC's first batch who would go on to lead the incubator after Graham's retirement.[44]

Already, even before hearing of the Collison brothers, Sequoia had an edge in the coming race to meet them. For one thing, the partnership had close ties to Y Combinator and Paul Graham. For another, these ties included a Sequoia investment in Altman's first startup. What's more, as a Sequoia-backed founder, Altman would soon become one of Sequoia's first scouts.

Graham invited Patrick Collison over for a kitchen meeting. He invited Altman too, and when the three got together, Patrick was still playing with ideas: part of him wanted to start a digital bank, which seemed a step too far to Altman. "I didn't think it was the greatest idea at the time, but I thought Patrick was incredible," Altman recalled later.[45] And so, at the kitchen table, Graham and Altman wrote angel checks for Collison's yet-to-be venture. Each signed over $15,000 for 2 percent of the company.[46]

The following summer, the Collison brothers quit college and moved to Palo Alto permanently. They had made progress with their payments idea and were ready to raise more capital. Graham duly emailed his contacts at Sequoia, Michael Moritz and Greg McAdoo. Meanwhile, Altman, who was by now a Sequoia scout, alerted Roelof Botha. The Collisons were firmly on the radar of the Valley's most relentless talent collectors.[47]

What followed next were charming tales about Sequoia's apparently serendipitous bonding with the two founders. Years later, John Collison recalled the summer day in 2010 when a black car pulled up outside the cramped Palo Alto apartment that he shared with Patrick and two friends. "This august, highly credentialed billionaire gets out and walks into the apartment and kind of sniffs the air," he remembered. The billionaire was Moritz.

"Would you like something to drink?" John offered.

"Sounds great," Moritz answered. "What do you have?"

"Oh. Water or milk," John answered.

"I'm not quite sure what he saw at the very early stage," John said, laughing modestly. "We were just squirrels in a trench coat, masquerading as a company." Then he said, perceptively, "I think Mike has a pattern he likes. Young immigrant founders with pluck, basically."[48]

At another point in the courtship, Patrick visited Moritz and Botha at Sequoia's office on Sand Hill Road. He went there the same way that he went everywhere, his stringy frame looped over a sleek Cervélo road bike, gunmetal gray with a red stripe on the fat down tube. Moritz quizzed Patrick on his life story: How had a boy raised in the emerald countryside of County Tipperary wound up pitching Sequoia in Palo Alto? Patrick described Dromineer, the village of his upbringing: two pubs, a few shops, an eleventh-century castle—but also two parents who had trained as scientists. Moritz asked about the future: If everything went right, what did Patrick imagine his company might look like? The two bonded some more, and then Moritz walked Collison out to the lobby. They stood chatting on the threshold.

Looking out toward the road, Moritz saw something that wasn't there usually: Patrick's Cervélo bike, tethered to the fence on the perimeter of the Sequoia lot. Instantly, he latched on. Did Patrick cycle everywhere? Was he a racer? And what was his best time on the Old La Honda climb, a famously grueling stretch running from the stone bridge in Portola Valley to Skyline Boulevard? When Patrick said he climbed the Old La Honda in less than twenty minutes, he felt he might have passed a test. The fact that he was competitive at a gritty sport said something about his aptitude for entrepreneurship.[49]

Of course, there were multiple reasons why Sequoia became the lead investor in Stripe, as the Collisons soon named their company. Moritz was an astute judge of character, and his questions to Patrick were designed to detect resilience and ambition. He understood the promise of digital payments; after all, he had backed PayPal. And he had faith in the prospects of challenger firms: having seen Google eclipse Yahoo, he was willing to wager that Stripe would eclipse PayPal. But on top of these advantages, Sequoia was assisted by that early tip-off from its scout network and its relationship with Y Combinator, and the combined result of all these factors was that, among Stripe's early backers, the investor with by far the most conviction was Moritz.[50] Sequoia was the biggest player in Stripe's seed round and provided nearly all the money in the Series A; alone among the investors, Moritz took a Stripe board seat. By 2021, Stripe was valued at $95 billion, and Sequoia's stake was worth $15 billion and rising.

Thanks to the Stripe bet and many others, Sequoia dominated the venture business even as the field became more crowded. Taking all its U.S. venture investments between 2000 and 2014, the partnership generated an extraordinary multiple of 11.5x "net"—that is, after subtracting management fees and its share of the investment profits. In contrast, the weighted average for venture funds in this period was less than 2x net.[51] Nor was Sequoia's achievement driven by a couple of outlandish flukes: if you took the top three performers out of the sample, Sequoia's U.S. venture multiple still weighed in at a formidable 6.1x net. Deploying the capital it raised in 2003, 2007, and 2010, Sequoia placed a grand total of 155 U.S. venture bets. Of these, a remarkable 20 generated a net multiple of more than 10x and a profit of at least $100 million.[52] The consistency across time, sectors, and investing partners was striking. "We've hired more than 200 outside money managers since I came here in 1989," marveled the investment chief at a major university endowment. "Sequoia has been our number one performer by far."[53]

Impressive though this U.S. venture record was, Sequoia's greatest achievement was to move beyond its comfort zone. In 2005 the partnership had moved into China, exhibiting the appetite for experiment that was central to the Moritz-Leone formula. The next year Sequoia expanded into India, and meanwhile the firm pushed into new kinds of investing. Sequoia operated growth funds, a hedge fund, and an endowment-style fund called Heritage. "Can you imagine, I joined Sequoia when we just had a $45 million venture fund, and now we've just raised a global growth fund worth $8 billion," Moritz marveled.[54]

Sequoia's wins were all the more remarkable because they did not come easily. In India, for example, Sequoia told itself it would repeat the China formula of trusting local partners: Moritz and Leone duly raised $700 million in dedicated India/Southeast Asia funds and handed the keys to a team of four Indians hired from an outfit called WestBridge Capital.[55] But after five years the relationship broke down. Deciding that India was unripe for early-stage venture, the WestBridge quartet proposed to pivot into public equities. When Sequoia objected, the WestBridgers responded by spinning themselves out with the help of one of Sequoia's limited partners. After this setback, in 2011, Sequoia might have chosen to abandon South Asia; indeed, some partners wanted to do that. But Moritz and Leone rebooted the operation by elevating a youngish member of what remained of the India team; they were backing the "unknown, the homegrown," to use Moritz's language. Sequoia India's new leader, a gregarious Harvard Business School graduate named Shailendra Singh, had spent much of the past five years operating out of the partnership's California headquarters. He had internalized the culture.

Singh set out to rescue Sequoia's experimental Asia bet with further sub-experiments. Acknowledging that there was little tradition of entrepreneurship in the region, he recognized that startup founders needed extra help. Following the a16z model, he hired operational consultants to advise startups on sales, marketing, and recruitment, gradually building a team of more than thirty people; given that Sequoia Capital's Sand Hill Road headquarters had an investment staff of around two dozen and a total head count of seventy-five, this was a sizable expansion. In 2019, adapting the Y Combinator model, Singh came up with what he called the Surge program, which coupled seed investments with intensive classes in entrepreneurship. The training required total immersion for five sessions lasting a week each; it was deliberately more intensive than YC's easygoing Tuesday dinners. By treating the Surge founders to dozens of encounters with accomplished startup veterans, Singh aimed to give them the confidence that YC founders acquired almost automotically, simply by virtue of being in the Valley. "When a young entrepreneur is exposed to enough successful people, he or she realizes that they are flesh and blood," Singh said. "And then the young founders say, hey, I can do this."[56]

It took all of Singh's ebullience to kick-start the Indian market. The founders he encountered barely understood what they were doing, and Singh had to educate them. Early on, for example, he began to track a prospect called Freecharge, a platform that Indians used to top up the credit on their cell phones. The thirtysomething founder, Kunal Shah, would have given other investors pause. He was not a graduate of the celebrated Indian Institutes of Technology. He had not completed business school. Instead, he had studied philosophy in college. But, resisting prejudice, Singh messaged Shah via LinkedIn. Here was the famed Sequoia, reaching out to a humble founder in a backwater of the digital economy.

Singh hit send on his message. What he got back was a resounding silence.

"Who is this guy bothering me?" Shah remembered thinking.[57] He had never heard of Sequoia. He had never heard of venture capital.

Singh broke through Shah's indifference by getting a mutual acquaintance to call him.

"These are the guys who funded Apple and Google!" the acquaintance explained, helpfully.

A little while later, Shah duly showed up at Sequoia's Mumbai office. He was not especially prepared. He had not assembled a slide deck and he was baffled by some of Singh's questions.

"What is your CAC?" Singh wondered.

Shah tried to guess what "CAC" stood for. But after offering several answers that failed to meet the mark, he gave up pretending.

"What's CAC?" he asked finally.

"Customer acquisition cost," came back the answer. Your marketing budget divided by the number of new users who show up on your website.

Shah thought for a moment. His marketing budget was zero. Therefore, his CAC was also zero. Why would he focus on an acronym that was irrelevant to his business?

"What are your user numbers?" Singh prodded.

"Fifteen thousand transactions per day," Shah answered.

"Per month?" Singh said, as though kindly correcting Shah's slip of the tongue. India's internet market was tiny. Freecharge had only a handful of employees. Fifteen thousand transactions per day was implausible.

Shah thought he must indeed have got the number wrong. He checked his notes. Then he looked up. "No, per day," he reported.

Singh could scarcely believe what he had heard. "I want to invest!" he said delightedly.

But Sequoia's challenges were only just beginning. As part of the due diligence, Singh wanted to understand Freecharge's user retention. Shah had never calculated that, so Singh's team had to do it for him. After Sequoia went ahead with a seed investment, Freecharge needed to scale up its infrastructure to cope with rising traffic. As a nontechnical founder, Shah was unsure how to begin, so Singh's recruiters hired a team of coders for him. A little while later, Sequoia hired an ex-Googler to run the engineering side as chief executive, while Shah led the other parts of the business with the title of chairman. Everything about this journey took longer than expected. But whenever Shah's spirits flagged, Singh would prop him up. "I'll get you another million bucks," he would promise. "We'll fix this."

One time, in a particularly dark period, Shah's courage failed. The latest user metrics were terrible, and Freecharge was running out of money. But, as usual, Singh seemed unperturbed. The product fitted the market, and Freecharge would succeed. Raising fresh capital was not going to be a problem.

"What's wrong with you?" Shah demanded of his venture backer. "Why are you in this crazy happy mood?"

"Don't worry about the fuel," Singh answered jovially. "Just focus on getting the plane off the ground."

Before meeting Sequoia, Shah had dreamed vaguely of building a company worth a few million dollars. In the end, Freecharge was sold in 2015 for $440 million. It was the highest acquisition price in the brief history of Indian tech startups. "They had to teach me everything," Shah said later.

Sequoia's returns in India and Southeast Asia lagged those in Silicon Valley or China. But by 2020 they were heading in the right direction. Singh's funds had backed twelve unicorns, ranging from the Indian edtech pioneer BYJU's, to Southeast Asia's ride-hailing giant Gojek, to the e-commerce marketplace Tokopedia. Singh himself was the only venture capitalist in his region to appear on the *Forbes* Midas List. In the summer of 2020, Sequoia raised its eighth and ninth India and Southeast Asia war chests, raking in $1.35 billion; it was more than twice as much as Accel India, its nearest rival in the region.[58] Meanwhile, Kunal Shah was hard at work on his next startup, a clever cross between e-commerce and credit scoring, called CRED. He had Sequoia's backing, of course. But this time he knew what he was doing.

◆

At home in its traditional market, Sequoia experimented with new kinds of investments. Ever since the Yahoo experience with Masayoshi Son, Moritz and Leone had eyed the growth-equity business, determined to avoid being outmuscled by kingmakers with larger checkbooks. In 1999 they duly raised a war chest of $350 million and made a series of big bets on the internet darlings of the era. In 2000 the Nasdaq crashed and Sequoia's fund was down $80 million that year and $65 million the next, at one point losing as much as two-thirds of its value.[59] The disaster was compounded by Sequoia's inexperience in evaluating growth deals. Incumbent venture partners managed the fund; there had been no thought of hiring a dedicated team of growth specialists. In the end, Sequoia hauled the performance back into black by reinvesting the partners' share of the proceeds from the handful of successful bets.[60] As with the India fund, Sequoia's experiment had begun painfully.

In 2005, Moritz and Leone doggedly raised another growth fund. This time they refined the strategy, hiring five investors from established growth firms.[61] The newcomers, most of whom came from a respected Boston shop called Summit Partners, had a style that differed markedly from that of Yuri Milner or Masayoshi Son. They had been trained to invest in obscure companies that had never taken venture capital—that had "bootstrapped." Most of these bootstrappers were located outside Silicon Valley, and some had no connection to technology; Summit stayed away from flashy deals, preferring unappreciated bargains. The way the Summit people sourced investments spoke volumes about their mechanical style. They sat in the office cold-calling companies that fitted their spec. Then they extrapolated revenues and costs to arrive at a forecast of earnings, finally applying a standard multiple to figure out the companies' fair value. Before going ahead with an investment, the Summit people demanded a good price. Their return target for each position was 3x. Overpaying could turn a solid bet into a pointless one.

For their first couple of years at Sequoia, the newcomers were like strangers at a tribal gathering. They imported the Summit methodology wholesale, while their Sequoia-trained colleagues continued to apply the venture mindset to growth deals. The Summit investors sat at desks under the stairs, making cold calls and plugging numbers into spreadsheets: they were reckoning with reality. The Sequoia folks sat one story above, under a pyramid-shaped ceiling with a bright skylight: they were contemplating potential. "It was pretty bumpy," one of the Summiteers recalled. "We were figuring out what it meant to be at Sequoia, and the Sequoia folks were figuring out what it meant to be growth investors." The two groups selected completely different types of firms. "We would come up with investments that were clearly working but just not that exciting," the Summit recruit said. "The Sequoia venture-trained team would come up with investments that were super exciting, but maybe not working."[62] Summit-style underreach plus venture-style overreach produced mediocre performance, and Sequoia's limited partners started to grow restive. As a condition of continued access to Sequoia's flagship venture fund, the limited partners had been strong-armed into backing the growth team and the overseas experiments; some referred to Sequoia India as the "punishment fund" because of its initially poor record. Because of their size, Sequoia's lackluster growth bets weighed especially heavily on the partnership's blended performance.

Investment innovations often result from fusing two types of traditions: think of Tiger Global mixing the hedge-fund mindset with the venture one.[63] Sure enough, around 2009, Sequoia's warring growth styles came together and performance turned a corner. The people from Summit learned how to dream, and the venture types from Sequoia internalized Summit's discipline. It was a convergence that took place gradually, through testing debates about multiple investments. But one particular episode served as the crucible of Sequoia's approach to the growth business.

The episode began with a young man named Pat Grady. He had joined Sequoia two years earlier at the age of twenty-four, having previously emerged as a star cold caller at Summit. Anyone could see he had extraordinary drive. "He has holes in his hands from working out," Doug Leone said approvingly.[64] But, unsurprisingly for a young newcomer, Grady could also be nervous. In fact, he was so anxious at partners' meetings that he could hardly talk; at one point, thinking there might be an issue with his vocal cords, Roelof Botha took him aside to suggest a speech coach. When Grady did offer an opinion, it reflected Summit's tradition of caution: Dr. No became his nickname. But, slowly and then quickly, Grady changed. Jim Goetz helped him to overcome his stage fright by making him present a prepared-mind landscape to colleagues. "I'm not ready," Grady said. "Yes you are," Goetz insisted. Meanwhile, Botha challenged Grady to be less negative about prospective deals. "Look, any smart person can come up with all the reasons to pass on an investment, but our job is to make investments," Botha reminded him.[65]

In July 2009, Grady's cold-calling generated a lead in San Diego. It was an outfit called ServiceNow, a cloud software developer that helped companies manage their workflows. Fortuitously, the migration of programs to the cloud was the subject of the prepared-mind landscape that Grady had recently presented: companies that captured this market would generate around $1 trillion in market cap, Grady had argued. ServiceNow looked set to be a winner in this game. The founder, Fred Luddy, was a coding veteran with the standing to assemble a robust team. His software was so good that he already had corporate customers.

Grady flew to San Diego, accompanied by Doug Leone. The novice and the veteran frequently teamed up together. When they returned, they put a proposal to the partnership. Sequoia could invest $52 million for a fifth of Luddy's firm, implying a post-money valuation of $260 million.

One of Grady's ex-Summit colleagues pushed back hard, calling the price "crazy." Publicly traded software companies were generally worth around three times revenues, but Grady and Leone were proposing to pay ten times. Did they really believe that ServiceNow's value could climb higher from this lofty base? ServiceNow would have to triple revenues just to get to the same multiple as normal software firms. Then it would have to triple revenues again to deliver the 3x that growth funds want from their investments.[66]

Leone and Grady stood firm. Grady had identified this opportunity in the Summit way, by cold-calling the prospect. But now it was time to evaluate this opportunity in the Sequoia way and to recognize its promise. ServiceNow combined a strong founder, a proven product, and a booming industry segment: it would triple its revenues once, twice, and then some. Besides, the skeptical case against a ServiceNow investment underestimated the value of Sequoia's activist input. Luddy and his team had built excellent software, but other parts of the business lagged. If Leone and Grady could fix functions such as finance and sales, the company's potential would be unbounded. Grady felt so confident about ServiceNow's prospects that he had almost dispensed with the hallowed Summit procedure of modeling ServiceNow's earnings. Late in the investment process, he had cobbled together a spreadsheet. But it was almost an afterthought.[67]

In November 2009, Sequoia duly invested. With Grady as his understudy and ally, Leone took a board seat. After biding his time for the first couple of meetings, he began to encourage Luddy to recruit new staff, working his network to bring in good candidates. In less than a year, he was ready for his masterstroke.

Getting into a car with Leone and Grady in the fall of 2010, Luddy admitted, "Hey, I don't know if I want to be CEO."[68]

The two investors had been preparing for this. Luddy was evidently happiest when he just focused on coding. The more ServiceNow expanded, the more complex the CEO role became, and the less Luddy was suited to it.

"We'll help you figure it out," Leone and Grady said. "Why don't we just take you around to meet some people." It was an echo of the approach that John Doerr had used on Google's young founders.

On October 7, 2010, Luddy had a packed day in the Valley. He breakfasted with a CEO who had taken a company public, and sat through six meetings with an all-star team of Sequoia connections. Each host had grappled with the management intricacies that Luddy dreaded. What's more, they seemed to relish it.

That night, Luddy dined with Leone and Grady at Evvia, the Greek restaurant in Palo Alto where the leaders of X and PayPal had once tried to hash out a merger. Luddy's face was glowing.

"That was awesome," he declared. "Now I know what I want to do. Let's go find a CEO."

Leone duly helped Luddy recruit an outside chief executive, and ServiceNow's progress accelerated. The company morphed from an overgrown startup into a well-oiled corporate machine, and Fortune 500 companies lined up to be its customers. Acquisition offers started to come in: $400 million, $1.5 billion, and eventually $2.5 billion; evidently, the Valley's faith in the superiority of founder-CEOs was not always justified. When that last offer materialized, at the end of 2011, Luddy was elated. But, equipped with Grady's analysis of the value of cloud software, Leone felt certain that even $2.5 billion was too low. Now was the time to act upon that lesson from decision science. Control the natural instinct to cash in. Lean in, hold tight, and capture all the upside.

The question was how to persuade ServiceNow's board to reject the

$2.5 billion. The majority wanted to grab the offer with both hands, and Sequoia lacked the power to stop them. So, in another hands-on maneuver that would have been inconceivable at Summit, Leone came up with a legal tactic. ServiceNow, like most American companies, was registered in Delaware. Under Delaware law, Leone contended, a board could not go forward with an acquisition without soliciting bids from others. Ambushing his colleagues on a ServiceNow board call, he declared that a hasty sale would be illegal.

Leone had taken advice from Steve Bochner, the CEO of the Valley law firm Wilson Sonsini. But his assertion contradicted the common understanding in the Valley, and ServiceNow's general counsel overruled him. The requirement to solicit rival bids applied only to public companies, the counsel insisted.[69]

It was the Christmas vacation, and Leone was with his family in Hawaii. Most of his clan was in the pool, but Leone was glued to the telephone. Certain that hundreds of millions of dollars of upside hung in the balance, he placed another call to Bochner at Wilson Sonsini.

"Steve, I've been told that it's only for public companies," Leone reported.

"Doug," Bochner answered. "We just hired the Honorable Bill Chandler, former chancellor of the Delaware Court of Chancery. He's the one that wrote the law. Private companies have to be shopped around too."

Leone digested this bolt from the heavens. Wilson Sonsini had the exact lawyer he needed.

"Can we get Mr. Chandler on the phone?" Leone asked.

"Yes," Bochner answered.

Leone talked to Chandler, confirmed his opinion, and asked him to stand by the next day. Then he worked the phone, speaking to each ServiceNow board member and pushing for another conference call. From their chairs around the swimming pool, his family watched Leone's face redden.

The next day the ServiceNow board duly convened again. Leone reiterated his case. Under the law, there was no choice. The board of ServiceNow was required to run an auction.

"No. That's only for public companies," the general counsel repeated.

"Well, I just happen to have on standby the Honorable Bill Chandler," Leone announced theatrically. "He wrote the law. I'm getting him on the phone."

There was a stunned silence on the board call. For a moment, a scene from *Annie Hall* flashed in front of Leone's eyes—the one in which Woody Allen settles an argument about the philosophy of Marshall McLuhan by summoning the philosopher from behind a billboard.

Leone dialed Chandler, who explained to the ServiceNow directors precisely what his law said. The general counsel backed down meekly. Because nobody at the company wanted to run an auction—an undesirable acquirer might materialize—the idea of a sale had to be shelved. Leone had successfully protected his shot at securing ServiceNow's upside.[70]

Six months later, in June 2012, ServiceNow went public, ending its first day with a valuation of $3 billion. As Leone and Grady had promised, it had grown 3x and then 3x and then some. As the shares continued to head upward, ServiceNow delivered the first ever $1 billion gain on a Sequoia growth position.

For the young Pat Grady, it was a vindication. In 2015 he would become co-lead of Sequoia's growth business; in that familiar pattern, the unknown and homegrown had been promoted. For the rest of the ex-Summit crowd, it was the reverse. As Moritz had put it, one of the tasks of venture leaders is to purge underperformers: one by one, the other ex-Summiteers left the partnership. Meanwhile for Sequoia, the ServiceNow experience proved that it had finally succeeded in forging a distinctive growth style, fusing the quantitative methods of the Summit tradition with the risk appetite and activism that came naturally to venture capitalists. As of early 2021, Sequoia's growth funds raised in 2009, 2011, and 2014 were showing returns of around 30 percent per year, comfortably beating the returns on public tech stocks, and the fund raised in 2016 had an extraordinary annual return of 70 percent, driven by grand-slam bets on the food-delivery company DoorDash, the videoconferencing provider Zoom, and the cloud software platform Snowflake.[71] Even more than with its India business, Sequoia's perseverance had been amply rewarded.

In 2008, Sequoia performed a reverse-Tiger shift: having focused throughout its history on private investments, it advanced into the hedge-fund arena. The idea came from Jim Goetz, and the plan was to extend the firm's bets on the best tech startups beyond their IPOs: Why let other investors capture the gains from the mature phase of these companies? After all, tech-focused hedge funds were increasingly sidling up to Sequoia for advice; evidently, Sequoia's insights could be translated into public-market profits.[72] Moreover, by setting up a hedge fund, Sequoia would acquire an additional tool. Rather than just backing the winners from digital disruption, it could profit by "shorting" the losers—that is, by betting on falls in their stock prices. For example, the advent of the iPhone spelled the eclipse of the predecessor device the BlackBerry. Sequoia would therefore short BlackBerry's creator, Research in Motion, as well as being long the companies that stood to profit from the coming mobile internet.

As with Sequoia's other experiments, breaking into the hedge-fund business proved challenging. The financial crisis of 2008 made raising funds impossible. Sequoia's limited partners had already backed the China, India, and growth funds, none of which had hit their stride, and now Sequoia Capital Global Equities, as the hedge fund was called, experienced a 100 percent rejection rate from fifty external investors. On top of that, one of Sequoia's hedge-fund hires quickly defected.

Gritting their teeth, the partners launched the fund in 2009 with $50 million of their own personal savings, most of which came from Moritz and Leone. But the trouble kept coming. Rather like the Summit recruits, the outside stock pickers brought into Sequoia had difficulty fitting in: they bought shares in relatively mature firms, including some with no connection to technology. As a result, they failed to capitalize on Sequoia's natural strength. In 2016, after seven years of indifferent performance, three younger members of the hedge-fund team announced they were quitting.

The news of the departures hit Sequoia at a tough moment. The firm was simultaneously reeling from a lurid and public humiliation. A lawsuit filed by an exotic dancer accused a Sequoia partner named Michael

Goguen of violence and abuse (which he vigorously denied). The partnership quickly decided to cut ties with Goguen, and he resigned. Four years
later Goguen won the case against his accuser, but it was a dreadful moment for Sequoia.[73]

As with China, India, or growth, the partners could have responded to
adversity at the hedge fund by shuttering the project. Several wanted to do
just that: the lackluster fund detracted from the Sequoia brand and created
a management headache. But the negative mood was broken by an intervention from Moritz. Although he had given up his responsibilities as a
Sequoia steward, Moritz continued to flourish as a backer of breakout companies such as Stripe. Because he was the largest individual investor in the
hedge fund, he had the standing to make the case for perseverance.

Acknowledging the double blow of the three hedge-fund resignations
and the Goguen scandal, Moritz conceded that Sequoia was "at the jagged
end of a draining and emotional period." "The easiest and most expedient
choice is to close the business," he added.[74] But he insisted that the original
premise for the hedge fund remained sound. Sequoia had a privileged
window on digital disruption; a better team of managers would have an excellent chance of building an outstanding business. Moritz particularly
commended the performance of an investor named Jeff Wang who ran the
short side of the hedge fund. The unknown and homegrown should be
allowed a shot at greatness.

Sequoia took Moritz's advice, and the perseverance paid off—
spectacularly. The partners fired the incumbent hedge-fund chief and promoted Wang, who proceeded to deliver on the original vision. Sequoia
turned its understanding of technological tumult into an investment edge:
the hedge fund became an edge fund. For example, Sequoia's venture team
had backed the skin-care and makeup startups Glossier and Charlotte Til-
bury, noticing that these upstart brands had figured out a way to reach customers directly via digital platforms. Now the hedge fund examined the
tools that these firms used: Facebook or Instagram for customer acquisition, Stripe for payments, Shopify as a digital storefront. The venture team
had already invested in Instagram and Stripe, which conferred an advantage in understanding the landscape. But Sequoia had not backed Shopify,

which enabled merchants to operate online with the minimum of hassles. The hedge fund duly built a large position in Shopify stock. By 2020 it had earned an astonishing 35x on its investment.[75]

At any given time, Wang and his team focused on about five "themes"— waves of innovation that would shuffle the deck, creating winners and losers. The boom in cloud software was a fruitful example. In 2018, nine years after Pat Grady had first addressed his partners on the shift of software to the cloud, the hedge funders noticed something strange: most types of code had completed the predicted migration, but communications software was lagging. This anomaly seemed bound to end. The increasing acceptance of remote working would make video calls and messaging systems part of everyday life. The recent bankruptcy of a hardware-based communications software company, Avaya, suggested that the cloud's moment was arriving. The hedge funders duly made three cloud-communications bets: Twilio, RingCentral, and the videoconferencing company Zoom. The first two generated 4x and 5x over the next two years. Assisted by the coronavirus pandemic, Zoom emerged as one of the breakout tech companies of 2020, generating 9x. Meanwhile, Sequoia's hedge fund was short legacy telecom companies that would lose out from the transition to the cloud. One thematic insight had generated multiple winning positions.

By the beginning of 2021, Sequoia Capital Global Equities had $10 billion under management. It was an extraordinary rise: in just over a decade, it had grown its assets two-hundred-fold. In the four years since the change of leadership, the fund's returns had averaged 34.5 percent per year, double the performance of the S&P 500 and among the best in the hedge-fund industry.[76] The experiment was so successful that Sequoia China launched its own hedge fund. Looking back on this saga, Moritz sighed in mock despair: "You can't raise money, your initial pick goes belly flop, but you persevere anyway."[77]

◆

As if launching Asian funds, growth funds, and a hedge fund were not adventurous enough, Sequoia created what it called its Heritage business. The idea was first to manage the wealth of the Sequoia partners and second to turn this necessity into a business by managing the wealth of Sequoia-backed company founders. In 2008, to set this experiment in motion, Sequoia hired two investors from the Stanford endowment. Ever since Don Valentine had first raised money from university investment offices, these institutions had been at the forefront of wealth management. The Yale endowment in particular had performed so well that private fortunes everywhere sought to emulate the "Yale model." Naturally, Moritz and Leone wanted their considerable means to be managed the same way, but better.

The key Stanford recruit was a thirty-one-year-old named Keith Johnson. He was the sort of outside-the-box thinker who fitted naturally at Sequoia. Indeed, he spent his first months at the partnership rebelling against the boxy thinking that he had learned at Stanford. The practice at university endowments was to divide investments into silos—stocks, bonds, real estate, commodities, hedge funds, and so forth—and to put a specialist in charge of each category. The way Johnson saw things, this made no sense.[78] The theory behind the silos was that their returns would fluctuate in an uncorrelated way, thus smoothing the performance of the overall portfolio. In reality, Johnson declared firmly, there was scant statistical evidence for this low-correlation claim. Nor was this surprising, because the investments in each silo blurred into one another. If you invested in Japan's public stock market index, for example, you would own a chunk of SoftBank, which in turn represented a bet on global tech that was neither Japanese nor public. Moreover, in chasing the mirage of safe diversification, the university endowments were paying a high price: by dividing the investment world into separate boxes, they were killing the culture of debate within their organizations. When the specialist in charge of commodity investments proposed a bet on nickel, for example, the other specialists were not equipped to push back. They focused only on their own boxes.

Having resolved to abolish the traditional silos, Johnson confronted an intellectually terrifying blank slate. It would no longer be enough to decide on an allocation to, say, real estate and then pick some deals to fill that quota. Henceforth, his team would simply look for great investments, and these could come from anywhere: the scope of the challenge was infinite. The Heritage fund would have to decide whether this was the time to buy

Brazilian land, or Chinese tech, or stakes in hedge funds engaged in litigation in Argentina. Every potential investment would have to be evaluated relative to all others, so Johnson would have to recruit exceptionally versatile colleagues—"a team capable of comparing, in a very thoughtful and debate-oriented way, apples versus oranges." In place of the old specialists, Sequoia would need investors with an appetite for learning everything. Or, as Johnson put it, "You bring in people who speak one of eight languages, and you ask them to master the other seven."[79]

Johnson went to Moritz and explained his vision. He had been hired to implement the university endowment model. Now he was announcing that the model needed radical updating. It took three or four weeks of conversations for Moritz to digest this news. But eventually he looked at Johnson and declared, "I have no interest in being second best at anything."[80]

Moritz and Leone pledged $150 million each to Johnson's plan, and together they set out to raise more from outside investors. But, much as with the hedge fund, Sequoia suffered rejection. After visiting potential investors all over the world, the team returned home with far less than it had hoped: about $250 million of external capital.[81]

In 2010, Heritage began to make investments. It chose areas as obvious as private equity and hedge funds, but also niches as esoteric as a direct stake in a chain of emergency veterinary clinics. Because it believed in actively choosing investments rather than spreading capital among silos, it made far more concentrated bets than other endowments, retaining only one-third as many outside managers. Likewise, because it had abolished silos, Heritage could move capital between strategies nimbly; there was no quota that had to be deployed in commodities or Asia or some other bucket. Between 2013 and 2015, much of the fund's gains came from public markets and real estate. Then, for the next three years, the big contributors were energy and hedge funds. Next, from 2018, late-stage technology bets drove the performance. By 2020, Heritage's assets under management had shot up to around $8 billion, and it boasted a better one-, three-, and five-year record than any U.S. endowment.

"When in doubt, take the shot," Doug Leone summarized, reflecting on this period.

"Look, I think about our business versus Amazon," he continued. "If you are Amazon, you have customers, warehouses, infrastructure, a whole bunch of things. If you are Sequoia, you have a few investors; you have nothing.

"So you better take the shot. The only way to stay alive in my opinion is to risk the franchise continuously."[82]

Moritz had another riff that he liked to share with interviewers. He would wait for the moment when the inevitable question came: What is your favorite investment? Then he would pounce: instead of mentioning Yahoo, Google, PayPal, or Stripe, he would say simply, "Sequoia." "When people write about the venture business, they're always writing about the startups we back," he would explain. "They never write about the most important investment that we make, which is in the business." Without the inward focus on decision science or the mentoring of young recruits—without the creation of the early-bird system, the relationship with Y Combinator, and the network of scouts—the partnership's parade of 10x-plus bets would not have happened. Without the perseverance in China and India—without the grit Sequoia demonstrated in pursuing growth funds, its hedge fund, and then Heritage—Sequoia would have been excellent but not extraordinary.

◆

Sequoia's success was emblematic of a wider shift in finance in this period: from the East Coast to the West Coast, from public capital markets to private ones, from financial engineering to technology. In the wake of the 2008 financial crisis, regulators forced the famous banks on Wall Street to take less risk; their lucrative proprietary trading desks were more or less shuttered. The Fed's policy of quantitative easing added to the banks' woes: their core business of borrowing cheap short-term money and lending it out long term ceased to earn much of a "spread," because long-term interest rates were held down by central bankers. Other East Coast money shops were similarly constrained. Hedge funds that had thrived on assessing financial risks entered a dull stretch: risk was being dampened by the central bank, so risk analysis ceased to be as profitable. The entire industry of credit funds, which built towers of strange derivatives atop mountains of debt, was shamed and constrained, and sometimes the only flourishing profession on Wall Street seemed to be that of compliance officer. Taking this together, the traditional financial sector was no longer where the action was. In the decade to January 1, 2020, Morgan Stanley and Goldman Sachs saw their stock prices rise 77 percent and 36 percent, respectively. Meanwhile, the S&P 500 index rose by 189 percent, and technology giants soared. Apple was up 928 percent.

Sequoia and other venture boutiques were the winners from this shake-up. During the first decade of the twentieth-first century, investors had responded to low interest rates by reaching for yield the Wall Street way: they had loaded up on subprime mortgage debt, which paid a few percentage points above the normal interest rate. When this strategy ended in disaster in 2007–2008, investors reached for yield the Valley way: they bet on private tech companies. As with the subprime wagers, the idea was to take extra risk for extra reward. But unlike the subprime wagers, tech bets had a chance of generating durable profits. Fortuitously, the financial crisis coincided with the advent of smartphones, cloud computing, and the mobile internet, setting up an opportunity to build brilliant businesses atop the new platforms: it was the perfect moment to switch capital from financial engineering to technology. The *average* venture fund launched in 2011 outperformed the S&P 500 index by 7 percent per year, and, as we have seen with Sequoia, the top venture funds outperformed by much more than that.[83] The longer the Fed persisted with its policy of low interest rates, the more the search for technology-driven yield gathered momentum. Seizing on Yuri Milner's coattails, banks, private-equity firms, and hedge funds crowded into the game. By 2020, Tiger Global was managing an astonishing $40 billion worth of assets, and Lone Pine and Coatue, two other offshoots of Julian Robertson's Tiger Management, vied to compete with it.

For Sequoia, the shift in favor of technology posed a strategic question. The partnership stood athwart the section of the investment landscape promising by far the best rewards: it could raise almost any amount of capital. With a franchise that stretched across three continents—in 2020, Sequoia opened a Europe office in London—it was poised to become global. In 1972, the year of Sequoia's founding, venture capital had been a niche business because information technology was itself a niche affair. But by the twenty-first century, technology was the main driver of economic growth, and Sequoia was the master of the type of finance that could unlock it. As the partnership approached its fiftieth birthday, it had an opportunity to challenge Wall Street, if it so chose. Given the firm's restless culture, it seemed unlikely to sit on its laurels.[84]

Meanwhile, for the rest of the venture industry, there was a darker question. The more the Fed's easy money drove inexperienced capital into the Valley, the more old-timers worried about a bubble. There was too much money chasing a finite number of great firms. One day, when the music stopped, the Valley would face a reckoning.

Chapter Fourteen

UNICORN POKER

In the summer of 2014, *Fortune* announced the arrival of a new tech star: a thirty-year-old college dropout turned self-made billionaire; a visionary who would improve the human lot; and, refreshingly, a woman. Her face appeared on the magazine's cover: black mascara surrounding strong blue eyes, a black turtleneck that invoked Steve Jobs, blond hair, and bright lipstick. The accompanying article described a unicorn startup that would revolutionize health care, courtesy of a new blood-testing technology. *Time* soon listed the young founder among the world's most influential people. Harvard Medical School invited her to join its exalted board of fellows. President Obama appointed her as an ambassador for entrepreneurship.[1]

Just over a year later, in October 2015, the story grew darker. An investigation in *The Wall Street Journal*, the first of several, revealed that the unicorn, called Theranos, was fraudulent. Its supposedly revolutionary blood-testing machines were a con. Its promise of cheap and accurate results served only to mislead patients. As more revelations followed, Theranos was beset by lawsuits, and its value crumpled from $9 billion to zero. Elizabeth Holmes, the Theranos founder, awaited trial. The icon who had invited comparisons with Jobs faced the prospect of prison.

The downfall of Theranos and Holmes was inevitably seen as an indictment of Silicon Valley. The cult, not just the priestess, had been discredited.

Holmes had started out as an undergraduate at Stanford, the Valley's ground zero, and had persuaded no less a figure than the dean of the engineering school to vouch for her. She had recruited a string of elder statesmen from Stanford's Hoover Institution to serve as Theranos directors, lending an aura of authority to her Potemkin company. Exploiting the precedents set by Google and Facebook, she had pushed founder-friendliness to the max: the shares she held in Theranos gave her one hundred votes each, erasing all checks on her behavior. Even Holmes's dishonesty reflected the culture of Silicon Valley. Since the fiasco of GO computer and before, entrepreneurs had brushed over the challenges of making their technology function: they had faked it until they could make it. Holmes apparently believed that her blood-testing equipment would do everything she claimed for it—one day. She was not so much lying as telling a "premature truth," as the Valley parlance had it.

In the popular imagination, Holmes's fall from grace fed into a broader critique of the new Florence. Hitherto, the usual resentment of plutocrats had stopped short of the friendly geeks who created search engines and iPhones. But precisely because Silicon Valley was booming, its excesses were bound to cause umbrage. The region seemed full of absurdly young people who lucked into equally absurd fortunes, meanwhile showing scant concern for the citizens whom they might harm: those whose privacy might be violated, now that digital information was the new oil; those whose wages might suffer, now that software could do their jobs; those who had relied on Theranos to diagnose their illnesses. This Florence was less a center of enlightenment than a sinister cabal: a tiny elite that presumed to shape society, even as its vision for society involved creation and destruction at a speed that many found intolerable.[2] Whatever the merits of this charge sheet, the Theranos shock inevitably sent a shiver through the Valley's venture tribe. For one thing, it showed how the nation's enthusiasm for tech entrepreneurship could turn on a dime. For another, it flagged a subtle, two-sided message about the venture industry itself. It contained both a vindication and a warning.

Theranos was a vindication for VCs because almost none of the money that Holmes raised came from Sand Hill Road practitioners. She had pitched a venture partnership named MedVenture, which specialized in medical devices. The meeting had ended with Holmes leaving abruptly, unable to answer the investors' questions.[3] Holmes also approached Tim Draper, the venture capitalist who had tried and failed to get into Yahoo. Draper made an angel bet because of a family connection, but it was modest. Tiring of skeptical professionals, Holmes raised the vast bulk of the capital from billionaire Valley outsiders. The Walton family of Walmart fame invested $150 million. The media baron Rupert Murdoch invested $121 million. The DeVos family (retail) and the Cox family (media) ventured $100 million each. Mexico's Carlos Slim, the Greek American heir Andreas Dracopoulos, and South Africa's Oppenheimer family kicked in $85 million between them. None of these venture tourists was inclined to cross-examine Holmes or demand evidence that her blood tests actually worked. The comforting lesson, from Sand Hill Road's perspective, was that amateurs had failed. The pros had stayed out of it.

But Theranos also signaled a warning. Although the venture industry had dodged this particular bullet, the scandal had shown how unicorns could run amok, causing billions in paper wealth to evaporate. Seasoned venture capitalists might hope to avoid similar disasters, but they could hardly count on doing so. In 2014, Andreessen Horowitz had led two investment rounds in an online insurance startup called Zenefits. The company had become one of a16z's largest positions, and the partnership had agitated for growth: later, the founder recalled his a16z board member barking, "You guys gotta get your heads out of your asses, start focusing on going big here."[4] Goaded to expand by all means possible, Zenefits attained a valuation of $4.5 billion in the extraordinarily short period of just over a year. But by 2016 the company was careening off track, missing revenue targets by a mile and reportedly violating insurance laws in at least seven states.[5] Amid embarrassment and scandal, the firm's valuation was slashed by more than half, from $4.5 billion to $2 billion.

The Zenefits story did have one redeeming feature. Andreessen Horowitz, being a real venture firm, quickly ejected the Zenefits founder when the legal problems surfaced. A new chief executive was installed, and the corporate motto changed from "ready, fire, aim" to "operate with integrity."[6]

But it was easy to imagine a hybrid of the Zenefits and Theranos cases in which a hands-on venture shop invested alongside passive financiers. The passive financiers might be amateurish outsiders, as in the Theranos example. Or they might be professionals who believed in deferring to founders. Either way, the activist venture partnership might invest in a company, discover it was going off the rails, but find that the passive investors lacked the stomach to help fix it. The early-stage investment might be intelligent and well judged, but the late-stage outcome could be a mess because latecomer investors were too hands-off to oversee the company responsibly.

The following year, this danger turned out to be more than just theoretical.

Around the time that Theranos and Zenefits went awry, Bruce Dunlevie of Benchmark was preoccupied with a unicorn called WeWork. Benchmark had first invested in WeWork in 2012, mainly because of its mesmerizing co-founder Adam Neumann, a six-foot-five-inch former Israeli naval officer with hair like Tarzan. WeWork's rather humdrum business was to rent out short-term office space, enlivened with perks such as fruit water, free espresso, and the occasional ice-cream party. But Neumann had a way of elevating his mission. He claimed to be selling "the future of work," or possibly a "capitalist kibbutz," or maybe a "physical social network." At the time of Benchmark's investment, Neumann's inspired marketing was filling his glassed-off cubicles with a buzzy clientele, and his grandiloquent ambition was catnip to power-law investors.

At one point during his negotiations with Benchmark, Neumann asked for a preposterously high valuation.

"You only have three buildings," Dunlevie objected.

"What do you mean?" Neumann shot back. "I have hundreds of buildings. They're just not built yet."[7]

The Benchmark partners loved Neumann's premature truths, and their bet on him was soon vindicated.[8] They invested $17 million in 2012 at a valuation of just under $100 million; less than a year later, the valuation hit $440 million. The next three funding rounds, culminating in the summer of 2015, transformed WeWork into a unicorn and then a deca-unicorn: its valuation leaped from $1.5 billion to $5 billion to $10 billion. Neumann's exposed-brick urban temples seem to have tapped into something powerful in the zeitgeist: the aesthetic of a rising generation of workers— entrepreneurial, hip, creative, and transient. By the time Theranos and Zenefits were imploding, in 2016, Benchmark's WeWork stake had generated hundreds of millions of dollars in paper profits.

Along the way, however, something fundamental had been changing. After Benchmark led WeWork's Series A and a partnership called DAG Ventures led the Series B, the next three funding rounds brought in mutual-fund houses and investment banks. The bankers in particular were in tension with the VCs. Their goal was not just to make investments that increased in value but to establish lucrative relationships. Jamie Dimon, the boss of JPMorgan Chase, likened his technology investors to Navy SEALs. Their job was to forge a connection with an entrepreneur, establishing the financial equivalent of a beachhead. Once that was accomplished, JPMorgan would send in its battalions to supply bank accounts, wealth-management services, and advice on going public. Underwriting an IPO would be the ultimate prize, because it would generate vast fees for the lucky bank that won the mandate.[9]

JPMorgan's relationship with WeWork illustrated Dimon's strategy. The bank participated in Neumann's funding round at the end of 2013. Then, in 2015, it arranged a $650 million line of credit for the company. In 2016, it followed up with a personal loan of $11.6 million for Neumann to buy a sixty-acre estate near New York City. In 2017 it lent Neumann a further $21 million to buy Manhattan property and arranged a loan syndicate that financed WeWork's purchase of the Lord & Taylor flagship store in Manhattan.[10] Thanks to this splurge of lending, JPMorgan was in pole position to underwrite WeWork's inevitable IPO. Cultivating the relationship became such a priority that when Neumann complained about the handling of his personal bank account, no less a figure than Morgan's vice-chairman ensured that the matter was smoothed over.[11]

The tension between the venture capitalists and the relationship bankers surfaced in October 2014, when WeWork raised one of its funding rounds. On the board call to approve the financing, WeWork's existing investors were informed that as part of the deal Neumann's shares in the company would acquire super-voting rights: each founder share would now confer the right to ten votes, giving Neumann the power to outmuscle the investors who were supposedly overseeing him. As a responsible venture capitalist, Bruce Dunlevie opposed this move: if the founder veered off track, Benchmark would need the votes to force a change—just as a16z had done with Zenefits. At the same time, however, Dunlevie didn't want to block the financing: WeWork needed the capital. Balancing these considerations, Dunlevie registered his opposition politely, arguing that super-voting rights were a mistake not only for investors but for Neumann himself. "Absolute power corrupts absolutely," he reminded his fellow board directors.[12]

Nobody on the call spoke up in support of Dunlevie's misgivings. With banks, hedge funds, and private-equity investors seeking yield from hot private firms, entrepreneurs had the power to demand what they liked; for a startup as dynamic as WeWork, super-voting rights had become normal.[13] Moreover, banks like JPMorgan seemed to regard governance as a side issue; they were happy to grant the founder super-voting rights because they wanted to be on super terms with him.[14] After less than ten minutes of conversation, the board dismissed Dunlevie's qualms. Neumann was granted absolute power over his company.

As Dunlevie had feared, corruption followed quickly. The year before the governance change, in 2013, Neumann had planned to buy a 5 percent stake in a Chicago building that was negotiating a lease with WeWork. This was an obvious case of self-dealing: by purchasing a stake in the building, Neumann would have set himself up to profit personally from his company's lease payments.[15] Playing its proper role as overseer, WeWork's board blocked Neumann's proposed purchase. But after the governance change empowered Neumann to overrule his board, he revived the Chicago scheme elsewhere, and now nobody stopped him.[16] He amassed personal interests in five buildings in which WeWork leased space, sometimes paying for these stakes by selling a sliver of his WeWork ownership.[17] With each of these transactions, Neumann was effectively decoupling his personal fortune from his company's profits, linking it instead to his company's lease costs. A gap between Neumann's interests and his shareholders' interests was opening.

Perhaps not surprisingly, WeWork's finances deteriorated in parallel to its governance. At the time of Benchmark's initial investment, the startup had a plausible business model. It took out cheap long-term leases and rented out the space for short periods, at a markup; in 2012 it turned a profit. But to justify the extravagant valuations affixed to it by the banks and mutual funds that invested later, WeWork had to grow at a blistering pace, and to do that, it cut the rents it charged to tenants. The result was the opposite of the strong incremental margins that Tiger Global prized: with each additional $1 million in revenues, WeWork's losses grew by more than $1 million. In 2015, for example, the company more than doubled its sales. Meanwhile, its losses tripled.[18]

To maintain investors' faith in him, Neumann generated a formidable stream of Silicon Valley clichés. WeWork was not a company but a "platform." WeWork would benefit from "network effects." WeWork was a "first mover," a "thriving ecosystem," "digitally enhanced," and "scalable."[19] To observers who were not inclined to think too critically, perhaps this sounded persuasive: after all, Silicon Valley behemoths from Google to Facebook had pumped themselves up to a commanding size before they had worried about profits. But the truth was that there was nothing particularly digital about an office-rental company, and the alleged network effects were weak, at best.[20] Adding WeWork tenants on New York's Park Avenue would not improve the experience of WeWork tenants on nearby Fifth Avenue.

By the start of 2016, Benchmark confronted a conundrum. It had made a savvy startup bet on a charismatic founder who was turning a profit. WeWork's valuation had duly shot up 100x, from $100 million to $10 billion. But because of the arrival of heedless late-stage investors, the founder was now losing money and piling up conflicts of interest, and the only consolation was a stream of faux-tech blather. The risk that WeWork's exalted valuation would collapse toward its actual value was evident not just to

Benchmark but to the fund-management house T. Rowe Price, which had invested in 2014. "We saw the valuation rise and the corporate governance erode," a T. Rowe Price executive recalled.[21] Millions of dollars in paper profits threatened to evaporate.

A decade or so earlier, an investor facing this danger would have had an obvious remedy. If the overvalued company was public, the investor would simply sell. If the overvalued company was private, the investor would use its clout to force a change so that the business strategy caught up with the valuation. But now, because abundant growth capital allowed unicorns to stay private, neither remedy was available. WeWork was not a public company, so its shares were hard to sell. WeWork's founder had been granted super-voting rights, so shareholders lacked the clout to demand a change of direction. In late 2015, Neumann demonstrated his regard for his financiers by letting off a fire extinguisher and spraying a prospective investor with white foam. Like a puppy who wags its tail eagerly even after being kicked, the investor proceeded to pour capital into WeWork the following year, driving its valuation to $16 billion.[22]

Facing a widening chasm between WeWork's alleged value and its founder's reckless conduct, Benchmark tried forlornly to change Neumann's attitude. In 2017, a delegation of five partners flew to Manhattan to visit local portfolio firms; in the meeting with Neumann, the team harrumphed about the company's losses and the founder's personal stock sales. But the partners knew they were playing a weak hand. Given the bubbly financial climate of the moment, Neumann could raise pliant capital from others; he had no obligation to listen to VCs who tried to hold him to high standards. Indeed, far from kowtowing to Benchmark, Neumann was about to link arms with the ultimate enabler.

The enabler was Masayoshi Son, now busy with his second charge into a U.S. technology bull market. In 2016, in a burst of inspired salesmanship, Son had talked $60 billion out of Saudi Arabia and Abu Dhabi; the following year he launched what he called his Vision Fund and went out to hunt for unicorns. Son's war chest, which ultimately weighed in at $98.6 billion, was more than thirty times larger than the biggest venture fund to date, and Son calculated that its sheer size would give him an edge.[23] Back in the 1990s, the ability to write a $100 million check had allowed him to muscle Yahoo. These days, his checks had to be bigger to shock and awe rivals, but the principle was unaltered. Besides, so long as the bull market continued, Son would earn more money than the venture old guard simply by deploying capital faster. He could spray capital at the unicorns without worrying about his aim. It was the old script all over again, except now he had a fatter hose to play with.

The news of Son's gargantuan fund sent shock waves through the venture business. At Sequoia, Michael Moritz intervened forcefully in the firm's strategy for the second time since his retirement from the helm in 2012. Having earlier insisted that Sequoia persevere with its hedge fund, he now urged his partners to raise a supersized growth fund: the firm had to fortify itself against the SoftBank bullying tactics that Moritz had experienced at Yahoo. "There is at least one difference between Kim Jong-Un and Masayoshi Son," Moritz wrote to his top colleagues, referring to North Korea's missile-wielding dictator. "The former has ICBMs that he lobs in the air while the latter doesn't hesitate to use his new arsenal to obliterate the hard-earned returns of venture and growth-equity firms." Armed with almost $100 billion, Son would distort the market for technology investments, driving up the value of some companies to the point that they might later crash, destroying the value of others that were forced to compete against his capital. Sequoia had to change its plan of action because Son was doing violence to the rules. "As Mike Tyson once said, 'Everyone has a plan until they get punched in the face,'" Moritz wrote. "It's time to bite some ears," he added.[24]

Prompted by Moritz, Sequoia proceeded to raise an $8 billion growth fund. If its Series A companies grew to the point where they needed gobs of capital, Sequoia could write the checks rather than letting its wards fall into the arms of SoftBank. But other traditional venture shops were not in a position to match Moritz's move. They had steered clear of the growth business and stuck faithfully to their cottage-industry roots: they lacked the standing to ask limited partners for multibillion-dollar war chests. As the most prominent proponent of the small-is-beautiful style of venture capital, Benchmark was a case in point. Its approach was about to be tested.

In 2017, Son visited Adam Neumann in one of his Manhattan buildings. He arrived an hour and a half late, glanced at his watch, and informed Neumann he could spend a maximum of twelve minutes with him. The two embarked on a whistle-stop tour of WeWork's premises; Neumann was keen to show off what he called his R&D center, featuring touch screens wired to lamps and doors, and a smart desk that adjusted to the user's height at the swipe of an ID.[25] The utility of these gadgets was not quite clear. But Son was impressed enough to invite Neumann to join him in his car when his twelve free minutes were exhausted.

The two climbed into the back of a limo, and Son began to peck at his iPad. Presently, he handed Neumann the result: a proposal for a SoftBank investment in WeWork of $4.4 billion. It was an astonishing amount, more than Benchmark had raised in its entire twenty-two-year history.

Neumann signed his name in blue ink next to Son's red signature. Half an hour later, Son emailed him a photo of the term sheet. Based on an interaction that had lasted twenty-eight minutes, SoftBank was valuing WeWork at $20 billion.[26] Like many innovations in finance, Yuri Milner's growth-investing formula was being stretched to dangerous extremes. Yet if Son's instinct on WeWork was right, he stood to repeat his Yahoo coup on a scale many times larger.

For early investors, Son's investment clarified the WeWork conundrum. Now more than ever, there was no hope of reining in the founder: Son's capital came with explicit instructions to Neumann to double down on his megalomania. "He's not told, 'I need you to be the most careful steward of this capital,'" a WeWork executive marveled. "It's like, 'I need you to go crazier, faster, bigger.'"[27] Neumann duly embarked on a wild global expansion, becoming the biggest renter in New York, splurging $63 million on a corporate jet, and promising WeLive apartment buildings, WeGrow schools, WeBanks, WeSail, and WeSleep (an airline). But even as Son closed off the possibility of disciplining Neumann, he opened a window on the other potential shareholder escape: selling WeWork equity. In 2017 and in a later round, Son was happy to buy out part of the earlier investors' holdings, rendering illiquid stakes liquid. T. Rowe Price leaped at the chance. "We sold as much as we possibly could," an executive remembered.[28] For its part, Benchmark off-loaded about a fifth of its WeWork stock. The proceeds locked in a 15x return on the partnership's original investment, according to insiders.

It was only a partial exit; Benchmark still held around 80 percent of its WeWork equity. But it was welcome insurance: thanks to Son's provision of liquidity, Benchmark knew it would get out with a good multiple, at the minimum.[29] The question for all the watching venture capitalists was whether this escape would be the norm. What if they backed a promising Series A company, celebrated its takeoff, and then watched as its governance was destroyed by late-stage investors? Would they manage to cash out before the reckoning?

◆

In February 2011, a year before investing in WeWork, Benchmark led the Series A for a ride-hailing startup called Uber. Unlike in the case of Theranos, its magic was authentic: push a button and a car came, no trickery necessary. Unlike WeWork, Uber was smack in the center of Benchmark's sweet spot: a West Coast startup headed by a battle-hardened entrepreneur, with technology at the core of its promise. WeWork was blowing smoke when it claimed to be a "platform" with "network effects," but Uber was the real thing. As Uber grew, there would be more cars, shorter waiting times, and the convenience of hailing Ubers in multiple cities.

The prime mover behind Benchmark's Uber bet was Bill Gurley, who had joined the partnership in 1998, three years after it got started. He certainly fitted the culture: In hiring Gurley, the incumbent Benchmarkers were picking someone who resembled them, just more so. The original Benchmarkers were all more than six feet tall. Gurley stood high as a door frame, six feet nine inches. The original Benchmarkers thought of themselves as the Chicago Bulls. Gurley had won a Division I basketball scholarship. The original Benchmarkers were competitive, intellectually and physically, and when they discussed Gurley before inviting him to join, they

saw those same qualities. "Lots of mindshare," one said. "Intellectually curious," echoed another. "We could go to a basketball game with him," a third
suggested.[30] Some time later, one of Benchmark's partners took Gurley on a
hunting trip, and Gurley chased a wild boar down a steep incline. "He is kind
of an animal," the partner reported. "I love that," another said, reverently.[31]

Gurley's investment in Uber was the perfect model of an intelligent Series A bet. Before joining Benchmark, he had been struck by the writings of
Brian Arthur, a Stanford professor who studied network businesses. Companies that enjoyed network effects inverted a basic microeconomic law:
rather than facing diminishing marginal returns, they faced increasing
ones. In most normal sectors, producers that supplied more of something
would see prices fall: abundance meant cheapness. In network businesses,
contrariwise, the consumer experience improved as the network expanded,
so producers could charge extra for their products. Moreover, the improving consumer experience was matched by falling production costs because
of the economies of scale in building a network.[32] As Benchmark had discovered when it had backed eBay, the rewards could be enormous.

After signing on with Benchmark, Gurley extended the eBay concept
from products to services. His first hit was a startup called OpenTable,
which connected diners to restaurants. Like eBay, OpenTable improved the
match between buyers and sellers: it allowed diners to browse restaurants
by price, location, and food type, vastly improving the experience of making a reservation. What excited Gurley about OpenTable was that the network effects proved every bit as powerful as theory predicted: as more
restaurants signed on, more diners visited the site, which in turn attracted
more restaurants. One day, during a review of OpenTable's progress, Gurley noticed that an outlier sales rep was signing up an extraordinary number of new dining spots. The reason was that this rep covered San Francisco,
where OpenTable already had a strong network. "Oh my God, this is working," Gurley remembers thinking.[33]

After OpenTable succeeded, Gurley began looking for businesses that
would do the same in other sectors. "We started discussing this internally,"
he recalled. "Which other industries would be transformed if you could put
perfect information on top of them?" With OpenTable, the diner could

search for Asian food in south San Francisco next Monday at 7:00 p.m., specifying the price range. That power was new; before, you'd have spent an hour calling around to get the answer. As Gurley and his partners pondered other sectors that might be ripe for similar treatment, they alighted on taxi and black-car services. There was so much inefficiency in pairing riders with drivers; surely better matching should be possible? Gurley had memories of emerging from a board meeting in a skyscraper in Seattle and not finding the driver he had booked. "I'm late for the airport. I'm running around the block. And of course, a block in Seattle can be kind of tilted."[34]

By following this train of thought, Gurley imagined a new startup—an OpenTable for car services. The next step was to find the entrepreneur who would turn concept into reality, and Gurley executed this stage of the process with equal diligence. Hearing of a startup in Virginia called Taxi Magic, he crossed the continent several times to discuss a possible investment. But he had thought through the business so carefully that he knew exactly how it ought to be approached, and the Taxi Magic formula was different. The founders had launched an app that allowed riders to summon a yellow taxi and pay for it via their phones. But the way Gurley saw things, this was a dead end, because taxi fares were regulated. To get the network flywheel started, a new entrant would need to cut prices and build scale. Wedded to the regulated taxi business, this East Coast outfit was blind to the network factor that made transportation worth thinking about in the first place. After months of meetings, Gurley gave up on the Virginians.

In 2009, Gurley heard of Uber, which was looking for angel backers. To his delight, Uber's strategy was to target unregulated black cars. "We've got to meet with these people immediately," Gurley recalls thinking.[35] But again he showed the discipline to control his excitement. When he met Uber's founders, Garrett Camp and Travis Kalanick, he was not impressed to learn that neither of them would commit full time to the business. Instead, they had recruited a young CEO named Ryan Graves who lacked the maturity to build a business. However much Gurley yearned to see network thinking applied to transport, he passed. He was not going to risk money on a B player.

Just over a year later, Uber reappeared on Gurley's radar. This time the company was looking for a Series A investor, and it had undergone a change: the young Ryan Graves had shifted to a lesser job, and Travis Kalanick had become the full-time chief executive. This put Uber in an entirely new light. Kalanick had two previous startups under his belt, and he had a furiously combative, take-no-prisoners style that flattened the most daunting obstacles. If anybody had the guts to shake up urban transport, confronting big-city regulators and incumbent limo fleets, Kalanick did.

Gurley also felt the chemistry was right with Kalanick. For one thing, the founder was not so full of himself that he couldn't take a joke. On the day when Kalanick was due to pitch at Benchmark's office, one partner opened the Uber app and saw that a black car was waiting outside Sequoia's nearby headquarters. In those early days at Uber, black cars were scarce, and the partner guessed that this one had taken Kalanick to pitch at Sequoia and that Kalanick was planning to take the same car again from Sequoia to Benchmark. Deciding a prank was in order, and wanting to show Kalanick that he understood his product, the partner tapped on his smartphone and summoned a car, and soon his screen showed a tiny black icon pulling out of the Sequoia parking lot. Sure enough, Kalanick arrived on foot at Benchmark's office, sweating and late. That night Benchmark sent him a gift: a pair of running shoes.

Late one Sunday night during the courtship, Kalanick called Gurley and asked to meet him at a hotel bar in San Francisco. It was a thirty-mile drive from Gurley's home in Woodside, but this was the sort of call that venture capitalists live for. As his family slept, Gurley drove north and talked with Kalanick until the early morning hours. At last, the stars he had been chasing were falling into line. He had found a startup that would attack the opportunity he had imagined—one that would do it the right way and with the right sort of chief executive.

The next day Benchmark presented a term sheet to Kalanick, and after a bit of back-and-forth the partners led Uber's Series A round, paying $12 million for one-fifth of the equity.[36] Gurley had landed his OpenTable for black cars. His ambition for the startup was that it might match OpenTable in its results, going public in due course at a valuation of perhaps $2 billion.[37]

At this point in the story, nothing about Uber anticipated trouble. Unlike Elizabeth Holmes, Kalanick was a battle-tested adult, and Gurley had carefully checked him out by calling a friend who had backed one of Kalanick's earlier companies.[38] Unlike WeWork, which Benchmark had bet on despite the partners' skepticism of real estate, Uber was the type of marketplace business that Gurley understood deeply. What's more, as Kalanick went into action with Benchmark's capital behind him, he more than lived up to Gurley's expectations. The VC watched as Kalanick pushed his way through the thicket of restrictive rules guarding the black-car market in New York. Kalanick did not quite break the law, but he ruthlessly avoided it until he managed to convince the mayor that Uber deserved a license. Meanwhile, Gurley applauded as Kalanick implemented an elegant but unpopular idea: dynamic pricing. Rather than charging a flat and predictable rate, Uber varied prices according to customer demand: when this spiked during peak hours, Uber raised fares to attract extra drivers onto the streets and forestall shortages. Critics complained of price gouging. But Kalanick stuck with the policy.

"Travis is a real entrepreneur," Amazon's Jeff Bezos remarked approvingly to Gurley.

"Why do you say that?" Gurley asked.

"Because he didn't cave on this."[39]

By late 2011, Kalanick was ready for a Series B fundraising. With Bezos praising his tenacity, he had no shortage of suitors. Bezos himself pledged to invest $3 million, and Goldman Sachs promised to come in also. As he cast around for a venture partnership to lead the round, Kalanick's first choice was Andreessen Horowitz. He particularly respected an a16z partner named Jeff Jordan, the former CEO of OpenTable and a director of another digital marketplace, Airbnb. Jordan understood the marriage between old products and new information, and as a onetime president of PayPal he knew how to scale startups. If Uber could have both Jordan and Gurley on its side, it would have the best VC advice in the Valley.

While he negotiated with a16z, Kalanick saw no harm in entertaining other suitors. The most insistent was Shervin Pishevar, a new recruit at Menlo Ventures, one of the partnerships that had backed UUNET. Pishevar was not in the same league as Jordan or Gurley. A bulky backslapper with a gift for self-promotion, he had attracted attention three years earlier for a bizarre essay, lauded as a "rambling, jetlagged, semi-lucid and beautiful email on entrepreneurism."[40] "Those inside of Facebook must know and be driven by a higher mission and cause," Pishevar wrote in one passage. "They are and should be on a mission to innovate around and extend Zuckerberg's genius and make it ever more elegant, relevant, personal and inspiring."[41] The titans on the receiving end of this obsequious nonsense tended to view Pishevar as perceptive, even wise, and Kalanick was among those who enjoyed basking in his flattery. But soon Marc Andreessen signaled that a16z might be ready to value Uber at somewhere around $300 million. It was five times more than Benchmark had paid, less than a year earlier.[42]

Satisfied with a16z's proposed valuation, Kalanick called Pishevar to say that he would not be taking Menlo's money.

"Hey, homie," Pishevar recalls Kalanick saying. "Hey, I really wanna do this deal with you, but I have to go with this other firm, for the benefit of the company."

"I remember that moment," Pishevar said later. "I could react emotionally, like, 'Don't please!'" Instead, Pishevar chose a different tone. "Listen, congratulations," he told Kalanick, manfully. "Absolutely move forward. If anything goes wrong in the diligence process, just know I'm a hundred thousand percent behind you. So negotiate with strength, because you have a backup."

"I really appreciate that," Kalanick responded.[43]

By going with a16z, Kalanick was traveling the familiar road of other Valley success stories. Having raised a Series A from one forceful investor, he was set to raise a Series B from a similarly strong one. If he continued in this vein, the governance vacuum that would later harm WeWork would not bedevil Uber.

But then history swerved in an unexpected direction. Andreessen backed off the $300 million valuation that Kalanick thought he had promised. Over dinner with Kalanick, the VC declared that Uber's customer numbers and revenues made the valuation too rich. He cut his offer by a quarter.

Kalanick tried to persuade Andreessen to meet him halfway. Andreessen wasn't budging.

A few days later, Kalanick accepted the reduced price and left for a tech conference in Ireland. The valuation still bothered him. He emailed Andreessen again, asking for a better deal, something between the original $300 million and the $220 million that a16z was now offering. But Andreessen refused to shift position.

Kalanick fumed. Then he phoned Pishevar.

The call reached Pishevar in Algeria, where he was attending a conference. He glanced at his screen. Annoyingly, being in Algeria appeared to mean that caller ID wasn't working.

After hesitating for a moment, Pishevar decided to take the call anyway.

"Hey, homie," said a familiar voice.

Pishevar felt a small surge of adrenaline. "What's up?" he responded.

"Hey, remember what you said to me, is that still on?"

"Abso-fucking-lutely."

"Can you meet me in Dublin?" Kalanick asked.

"I'm taking the next flight," Pishevar promised.[44]

Pishevar flew north across Europe and found Kalanick in the Irish capital. The two walked the cobblestoned streets and stopped in a pub to order pints of Guinness. Kalanick dialed up the charisma, riffing on Uber's unlimited potential. "That was the time when I really got it," Pishevar said later. "He's talking about trillions of dollars!"[45]

When he got back to his hotel, Pishevar sent Kalanick a text, valuing Uber at $290 million. It was almost 30 percent more than a16z's reduced offer.

Pishevar waited for Kalanick to respond. Then he got nervous. He had bonded with this guy before, only to find that he had shopped the deal to a more prestigious partnership.

But this time Kalanick was not speaking with another VC. Instead, he was speaking *about* VCs: he was on the phone to an old friend, explaining his dilemma. He and his company faced a tricky choice: a generous deal from a little-known investor, or a miserly deal from a famous one. Which should he go for? Menlo's Shervin Pishevar or a16z's Jeff Jordan? The high valuation or the high-value counsel?

"You don't need validation from a famous venture capitalist," the friend said. "You are past that." The way Kalanick's friend saw things, Uber would need enormous amounts of money to roll out its service nationwide. "It's about getting the cheapest capital you can. Capital is power. The more capital you have, the more options you have," his friend urged him.[46]

Growing anxious as he waited, Pishevar texted Kalanick again, increasing his offer to $295 million.

This time Kalanick got back to him immediately. The $290 million offer had been fine; he was happy to take it. "Done. Bring it in," Kalanick instructed.[47]

Pishevar printed out a term sheet and took it to Kalanick's hotel room, where the two men signed it. When the due diligence was done, Menlo Ventures duly invested $25 million at the $290 million valuation, taking 8 percent of the company. Bezos, Goldman, and a few other investors kicked in a further $12 million.

With the unfair benefit of hindsight, the Pishevar investment was a premonition of the troubles in Uber's future. Kalanick had decided that money was power and that expert venture-capital guidance was dispensable. Fittingly, despite the substantial size of his investment, Pishevar became a nonvoting board observer rather than a full Uber director: he had not been chosen for his ability to provide oversight, so observer status seemed appropriate. Rather, Pishevar's chief function at Uber would be to serve as cheerleader. He shaved the company logo into his hair. He arranged for the rapper Jay-Z to invest. He threw a party featuring a musician who became Kalanick's girlfriend. Thanks to Google, Facebook and the youth revolt, a patina of founder-friendliness had become almost mandatory for

VCs, but Pishevar pushed this fashion to the max, serving as buddy and valet. Once, when Kalanick flew into Los Angeles, Pishevar sent a car to meet him at the airport. In the back was a fresh suit for Kalanick to change into.[48]

It was not just the founder flattery that reflected the zeitgeist. Kalanick's decision to prioritize cheap capital was also a sign of the times, because it signaled the more problematic side of network businesses. The exciting thing about networks is that the winners win big. The downside is that also-rans may reap almost nothing. Moreover, the winner in a network industry is not necessarily the one that builds the best product. It may instead be the one that achieves scale first, setting the network flywheel in motion. To get to scale before rivals challenged it, Uber would have to splurge on subsidizing rides; it would have to "blitzscale," to use a term that swept the Valley a bit later. Back in 2005, Paul Graham had complained that VCs stuffed startups with too much money, like farmers stuffing geese to make foie gras. But in network businesses, capital really could amount to power. PayPal versus X.com; Meituan versus Dianping: technology wars are viciously expensive because the prize is so enormous.

Sure enough, a year after the Series B two competitors emerged to challenge Uber. Toward the end of 2012, an Accel-backed service named Hailo launched a taxi-hailing app in Boston and Chicago, threatening to steal a march in a part of the market that was much larger than the expensive black-car segment. Determined not to let Hailo get ahead, Uber rolled out its own taxi service. Next, a startup called Zimride began experimenting with a cut-price service called Lyft, which allowed nonprofessional drivers to pick up passengers. At first, Kalanick expected the regulators to ban Lyft; surely uncertified amateur drivers, with no commercial insurance, would fall short of public-safety standards? Setting aside its normal practice of avoiding regulators, Uber lobbied the California Public Utilities Commission to shut down its rival, pointing out that its own professional black-car drivers were properly licensed.[49] But when the California regulators gave Lyft the green light, Kalanick did not wait. He counterpunched with UberX, his own amateur-driver service.

Inevitably, the competition on the streets became a competition for dollars. In the first half of 2013, Hailo raised a Series B of $31 million and prepared to launch in New York City.[50] For its part, Lyft raised a $15 million round led by Peter Thiel's Founders Fund and then a $60 million round led by a16z, which by now regretted missing out on Uber. But the good news, from Benchmark's perspective, was that Uber remained comfortably ahead; if this was a winner-takes-all competition, bring it on, because Uber was the likely winner. In August 2013, Kalanick trumpeted his dominance by raising a crushing $258 million Series C round, which was led by the prestigious venture arm of Google. As if to emphasize his front-runner status, Kalanick also arranged for the private-equity giant TPG to come in on the deal. A clause in the closing documents gave TPG an option to invest an additional $88 million at some point in the next six months. It was a warning to rivals: Uber could out-blitzscale anyone.

By now Gurley was coming to see Uber as much more than OpenTable for black cars. The affordable UberX service signaled that the company could capture a far larger market, stealing customers away from subways and buses and even challenging private car ownership. Besides, any concerns that Gurley might have felt about Uber's governance after Pishevar's investment had been assuaged. Google Ventures was a respected player, and Gurley had enormous regard for David Bonderman, the TPG founding partner who was set to join Uber's board.[51] Gurley and his partners felt so optimistic about Uber that they made a follow-on investment of $15 million in the Series C round. This was a significant commitment for Benchmark given its modest $450 million fund. It was a conscious statement that even starting from Uber's exalted new valuation of $3.5 billion, the company had the scope to generate the 10x-plus multiple that Benchmark always targeted.[52]

Over the next eighteen months, Gurley remained buoyant. The challenge from Hailo fizzled out as the firm failed to get the network flywheel started. Another challenger called Sidecar came to nothing. Only Lyft was putting up a fight, and Uber remained comfortably dominant. In the spring of 2014, Lyft raised a Series C of $250 million. Weeks later, Kalanick countered with a Series D that brought in a thumping $1.2 billion. Both Lyft and Uber spent the proceeds on subsidizing riders, but Gurley was unfazed.

With capital from all manner of investors flooding into the Valley, Benchmark faced similar fundraising contests across its portfolio. "The burn rates went through the moon," Gurley recalled. "It wasn't like it was just ride hailing. The earth started moving all over the place."[53]

Besides, whatever Uber's burn rate, the company was creating astonishing amounts of shareholder value. In June 2014, shortly after a Series D round valued Uber at $17 billion, a New York University professor named Aswath Damodaran wrote a critical piece, arguing that Uber's true worth was far below that.[54] He estimated the size of the global taxi market to be around $100 billion and concluded that fair value for Uber might be $5.9 billion—less than half the Series D price tag. Gurley hit back with an essay on his blog, arguing that the taxi market would expand thanks to Uber's low prices. "It's not about the market that exists, it's about the market we're creating," Gurley quoted Kalanick as saying. But wherever you came down on these arguments, the striking fact was that even Uber's leading critic put the company's value at a whopping $5.9 billion. That was fully $2.4 billion more than the value established by the Series C, less than one year earlier.

Yet even as its value boomed, Uber was charting its version of the worrying shift that occurred simultaneously at WeWork. Slowly and steadily, Kalanick was consolidating his power at the expense of his investors. In addition to denying Pishevar a voting directorship, he had used his Series B round to take board rights away from an angel backer who had crossed him.[55] In the Series C round in 2013, Kalanick had followed up by arranging super-voting power for himself, his cofounders, and his early investors, with the result that the large amounts of capital provided by Series C and D backers did not translate into large leverage. As a matter of principle, Benchmark hadn't liked this, just as it didn't like WeWork's embrace of super-voting rights a year later. But Benchmark itself got super-voting rights on its Series A shares, and with Uber poised to be the biggest win in the partnership's history, Gurley was not going to rock the boat on behalf of the later investors. Besides, Gurley remained on good terms with Kalanick, and his counsel seemed to count. He had a key card that let him into

Uber's headquarters on San Francisco's Market Street. He felt he could influence the firm, whatever his formal voting rights.

Toward the end of 2014, however, Gurley began to sense his influence fading. With hundreds of millions of dollars flooding into Uber, Kalanick was becoming a celebrity; Benchmark's importance as the prestigious Series A investor was inevitably diluted. Worse, Kalanick no longer seemed interested in Gurley's advice, especially when it conflicted with Kalanick's determination to maintain Uber's scrappy startup culture. Gurley wanted Kalanick to hire a senior chief financial officer who could establish adequate controls for what was now a large operation. Gurley pressed Kalanick to find a stronger legal counsel, too, especially after Uber's leaders behaved in a way that fell short of the standards expected from a major company. In October 2014 a Valley commentator named Sarah Lacy called Kalanick out for promoting a misogynistic "bro" culture: the founder had joked that his company should be called "Boober" because it boosted his success with women.[56] Soon after Lacy's damaging broadside, Kalanick's deputy dug the hole deeper, suggesting a plan to intimidate Lacy by digging up dirt on her personal life.[57] Gurley loved Kalanick's entrepreneurial aggression, but there were lines you couldn't cross, and Uber didn't have the systems in place to tell the difference. Yet whenever Gurley made this point to Kalanick, the founder brushed him off. Kalanick came up with a nickname for the towering VC: Chicken Little.[58]

Gurley was starting to feel trapped, much as Dunlevie was finding himself trapped at WeWork. He had conceived a smart investment, waited patiently for the right jockey to appear, and earned well over $1 billion for his partners. But all of that profit existed only on paper. Uber was not public, so Gurley could not sell his stock. Uber had granted Kalanick super-voting power, so Gurley could not force him to listen.[59] If Uber had gone with a strong Series B investor, Gurley might have had a like-minded ally, but Kalanick had chosen a cheerleader. The main Series C investor was little help: Kalanick sidelined his Google board member because of Google's plans to develop driverless cars that might compete with Uber. That left TPG's David Bonderman as Gurley's main support. But two votes were not enough to sway the board. There was no effective check on the chief executive.

◆

At the start of 2015, Gurley began to air his frustrations. In a long and carefully crafted essay on his blog, he laid out the problems with unicorns that put off the day when they went public. Although Gurley did not mention Uber by name, his readers understood that Uber was his subject.[60]

Gurley's essay pointed out three problems. First, unicorns were overvalued, and unlike other Valley investors Gurley was prepared to say so. Late-stage tech investment rounds had become "the most competitive, the most crowded, and the frothiest," he announced bluntly.[61] The new money pressing into the Valley explained why this was so. The assorted tech novices—banks, mutual-fund houses, PE firms, and hedge funds—had little interest in allocating $10 million to a startup. Rather, they wanted to write $100 million checks that might move the needle on their multibillion-dollar portfolios. Inexperienced money therefore crowded into big-ticket late-stage rounds, driving valuations skyward.

The second problem had to do with financial engineering. The non-Valley investors frequently insisted on protection clauses, which further distorted unicorns' headline valuations. For example, the investors might demand a "liquidation preference": in the event of the company's liquidation, they would be entitled to a specified payoff before other shareholders got anything. Obviously, investors who received this assurance would pay extra for their shares, and that premium would drive up the company's apparent valuation. Since the earlier investors did not get liquidation preferences, their shares were logically worth less: the fact that a late-stage fund invested at a valuation of, say, $10 billion did not mean that a startup fund would value the unicorn as highly. In fact, a unicorn share might be worth one amount to a Series A investor, who had super-voting rights; a lower amount to a Series C investor, who had less voice; and a higher amount to a Series E investor, who had negotiated liquidation preferences. Amid all this complexity, a unicorn's true value was almost impossible to determine.

The third unicorn problem resulted from the first two. The unjustified inflation of headline late-stage valuations fed the hubris of tech founders, which was already threatening to spin out of control thanks to super-voting shares and the cult of founder-friendliness. As a result, entrepreneurs increasingly behaved as though they could get away with anything. They disclosed little about the true state of their business and often misled investors willfully. Bizarre accounting tricks were rife.[62] With inexperienced investors flooding into the Valley, it was just too easy to blow smoke in their eyes. Unicorn governance was broken.

At the time he published this essay, Gurley's chief worry with Uber concerned China. Determined to succeed where Amazon, Google, and nearly every other U.S. tech giant had failed, Kalanick had set his heart on cracking the Chinese market. Starting in 2014, he had poured millions into a long-shot contest against the country's domestic ride-hailing champion, Didi Kuaidi (later Didi Chuxing). This audacious gamble was only possible because Uber could raise hundreds of millions of dollars at a bubbly valuation and because Kalanick's pliant board was not going to stop him. All Gurley could do was fume. As he told Kalanick repeatedly, pouring capital into China was fundamentally different from pouring capital into the battle against Lyft. In network industries, expensive competition is justified if you are likely to win. If you are not, then it is foolhardy.

Backed by David Bonderman, Gurley pressed Kalanick to consider a merger between Uber China and Didi; it was the classic VC response to a ruinous price war.[63] In January 2015, Kalanick agreed to open talks with Didi's leaders, offering to cede the Chinese market in exchange for a slug of Didi's equity. But the price he wanted was impossibly high: Kalanick demanded fully 40 percent of his Chinese rival. Didi responded by scorning Kalanick's advances and going on the offensive not just in China but worldwide. It pumped $100 million into Uber's rival Lyft. It announced technology-sharing alliances with Uber's adversaries in other regions, including India and Southeast Asia. The blitzscaling wars had gone global.

Gurley and David Bonderman were furious. Kalanick's job was to cement his supremacy in his core markets, not burn capital in hostile territory. The CEO's Napoleonic China adventure was exactly the sort of overreach that boards would traditionally have blocked, but Uber's board had been neutered. As Gurley had foreseen in his essay, Uber was operating in such bountiful financial conditions that its value kept on rising even as Kalanick poured capital into a fight he would not win. At the end of 2015, Uber raised a Series G round at an extraordinary valuation of $62.5 billion—almost eighteen times higher than its value in the Series C, when Benchmark had doubled down on the company.

In April 2016, Gurley published a second blockbuster critique of unicorns. This time he homed in on a particular threat: because of those liquidation preferences, late-stage unicorn investors had destructive incentives.[64] With their downside protected, they had no reason not to press unicorns to grow recklessly. Faced with a choice about splurging in China, for example, late-stage investors might encourage a unicorn to take the shot: thanks to liquidation preferences, they would get their capital back no matter what, so they had every reason to gamble for the upside. Borrowing an analogy from a game that he enjoyed, Gurley summed up the danger. The typical late-stage investor was "acting like a loose-aggressive player at a poker table."[65]

The following month, Kalanick fulfilled Gurley's worst nightmares. He dispatched a fundraising lieutenant to pitch one of the loosest players of them all: Saudi Arabia's $300 billion sovereign wealth fund. All Gurley could do was groan. A big capital raise from the Saudis would serve only to dilute Benchmark's stake, and the money would disappear into the contest with Didi.[66] Now more than ever, fighting Didi seemed like a bad bet. By May 2016, the Chinese firm had a wide lead in its home market, and meanwhile it waltzed into Silicon Valley and raised $1 billion from Apple. Uber, for its part, was spending drunkenly on subsidy wars everywhere from New York to Mumbai. What it needed was not capital but sobriety.

Even Gurley's gloomy expectations failed to prepare him for what came next. Saudi Arabia's Public Investment Fund offered to invest a hefty $3.5 billion in Uber. And as part of the deal, the Saudis demanded an expansion of the board from eight seats to eleven, with the right to designate the three extra directors to be awarded to Kalanick. The originator of this demand was, presumably, Kalanick and his team. They were evidently out to destroy what little leverage Gurley still had over the company.

Like Dunlevie at WeWork, Gurley now confronted an impossible dilemma. He could not object to Kalanick's additional board seats without jeopardizing the $3.5 billion capital injection. And although he doubted that the $3.5 billion would be used wisely, of course there was a chance that he was wrong. This humongous new war chest would empower Uber to buy more market share, and in a global blitzscaling war the biggest spender stood to win a prize of unimaginable value. Weighing his belief in corporate governance against his respect for network effects, Gurley wavered— perhaps Kalanick was right to call him Chicken Little? "We all believe in network effects, but has anyone been willing to lose $2 billion to $3 billion to stay at the table?" Gurley mused. "You could have invited Warren Buffett and Jack Welch and whoever else to join the Uber board, and they wouldn't have known what to do."[67]

Deciding there was no way to derail Kalanick, Gurley assented to the Saudi investment, swallowing the poison pill of the three extra board seats. But when he looked back on the Uber saga, he confessed that he regretted his decision. "In retrospect, it probably would be one of the top things I'd play differently," he said. "I could have opposed the deal. Told them they needed to change it."[68]

One good thing happened that summer. Seeing the writing on the wall, Kalanick sued for peace in China. In August 2016, two months after the Saudi infusion, he ceded the Chinese market to Didi, accepting an 18 percent stake in his rival as a payoff. Relative to the 40 percent Kalanick had demanded eighteen months earlier, it was a modest settlement, and in the meantime Uber had incurred some $2 billion of losses in China. Still, 18 percent of Didi was worth close to $6 billion.[69] The success in negotiating a profitable exit owed much to the implied threat of Uber's Saudi money cannon.

Despite this relief, Gurley still felt trapped in a company whose shares he could not sell and whose founder seldom listened to him.[70] All he could do was to go through the motions of pressing Kalanick to mature, and particularly to shed the scrappy startup culture. In some bits of the business, Gurley urged Kalanick, dull was desirable. "You're not gonna win by having a more innovative finance program, you're not gonna win by having a more innovative legal program, you're not gonna win by reinventing H.R. They're areas where experience carries a lot of weight," Gurley remembered saying.[71] When Kalanick refused to pay attention, Gurley accepted invitations to speak to MBA classes, using these occasions to generate debate on his predicament. If the bright-eyed business students found themselves on the board of a recalcitrant unicorn, what would they do? Gurley discovered that none of them could say. "The only answer we could think of was that the public markets would do a better job of holding companies accountable," he lamented.[72]

In February 2017, the cost of Kalanick's behavior burst out into the open. An ex-employee named Susan Fowler detailed repeated instances of sexual harassment at Uber, and her complaints went viral. Kalanick attempted to apologize and regroup, hiring a pair of prestigious law firms to investigate. But before the month was over, two new crises blew up. Furious that Uber had poached one of its key scientists, Google sued the firm for stealing its driverless-car technology. Then a damning video of Kalanick surfaced, apparently confirming what many suspected: the CEO was a jerk, and Uber was a jerk company.

The video, recorded by a camera on an Uber car's dashboard, showed Kalanick in the backseat, squirming awkwardly to music and flanked by two women.

Recognizing his passenger, the driver starts to complain about Uber's tendency to cut fares in order to boost ridership.

"I've lost $97,000 because of you," the driver says. "I'm bankrupt because of you."

"Bullshit," Kalanick retorts. "You know what? Some people don't like to take responsibility for their own shit. They blame everything in their life on somebody else."

Coming on top of the sexual harassment allegations, the video of Kalanick sent Uber's reputation into a tailspin. Google, Airbnb, Facebook, and even Lyft began luring away its demoralized workforce, and in March 2017 the bad news continued. *The New York Times* broke a story about a hyperaggressive antiregulatory tactic called Greyball. In cities where ride hailing wasn't authorized, Uber engineers secretly built a shadow version of the

app and pushed it to law-enforcement officials. Then, when the law enforc-
ers tried to hail and impound an Uber car, no car arrived to meet them.[73]
Meanwhile, a Silicon Valley news site called *The Information* broke a story
about a trip that Kalanick had taken to South Korea. Kalanick and several
South Korean Uber managers had visited an escort bar, and although Kalanick had not picked up an escort, some of his colleagues had. Amid these
distasteful revelations, Gurley learned of huge financial losses in Uber's
vehicle-leasing division. As he had said repeatedly, Uber's lack of financial
controls was a disaster.

Gurley found no comfort in the fact that he had seen much of this coming. "Being right and ineffective in venture is not worth very much," he said
later.[74] Instead, the stress began to take its toll: the animal who had chased
a wild boar down a slope was overweight, unhappy, and unable to sleep
properly. As he lay awake in the small hours, he felt the burden of responsibility for one of the largest unrealized bonanzas in the history of venture:
a 13 percent stake in Uber that was now worth $8.5 billion. The gap between
this paper gain and what might be the actual gain was eating him alive:
What if Uber went the way of Zenefits or Theranos? Many of Benchmark's
limited partners had already booked profits from his presumed grand slam:
endowment investment officers had taken bonuses and bought cars and
homes; they had distributed proceeds to their universities and foundations.
If Gurley's Uber triumph morphed into a failure, the consequences would
ripple back to the lecture halls and laboratories that relied on Benchmark's
performance. What would people say of Gurley then? That he had indulged
Kalanick's aggression. That he had failed to fight the creeping governance
changes. That he had permitted a perfect investment to spiral into a
catastrophe.

It took a final Uber shock to provide Gurley with an escape hatch. In
June 2017 the two law firms wrapped up their investigation into Uber's toxic
culture. The findings were even worse than the board had imagined: hundreds of pages detailing incidents including sexual assault and other violence. The law firms recommended that a key Kalanick lieutenant be sacked.
They proposed that an independent director be added to the board. They
said that Kalanick should be required to take a leave of absence.

Gurley and his ally David Bonderman saw they had an opening. Until this moment, Kalanick had been too powerful to push around. Now the law firms' report transformed their leverage. Kalanick could be made to go on leave. With luck, he would never return from it.

"Travis, frankly, I cannot imagine this company without you, and I cannot imagine this company *with* you," Bonderman told Kalanick.[75]

Seeing retreat as the best preparation for advance, Kalanick agreed to the law firms' recommended leave of absence. He presented his departure as a respite he had voluntarily chosen: his mother had died recently in a boating accident, and he needed to get away for a bit. In the meantime, as he wrote to his employees, he would still be available for "the most strategic decisions." "See you soon," he bade them cheerily.

Gurley got the message. Kalanick would be back at Uber soon unless Gurley did something to block him. When the law firms' recommendations were unveiled at an all-hands staff meeting, Gurley rose to address the audience.

"This company is undoubtedly the most successful startup in the history of Silicon Valley," he began warmly. But then he pivoted to the challenges ahead—challenges that could only be addressed without the problematic chief who had become synonymous with Uber's dark side. "We are considered one of the largest, most important companies in the world," Gurley lectured. "Our behavior, our corporate behavior, has to begin to equal and parallel that expectation or we're going to continue to have problems.

"We're in a reputational deficit," he insisted. "You can read something and say that's not fair, but that's not going to matter."[76]

With his cheery "see you soon," Kalanick had signaled that he did not plan to quit the helm. With his lecture on Uber's reputational crisis, Gurley was signaling that he was preparing for a showdown.

◆

Gurley's advance on Kalanick involved three stratagems. Each was remarkable in its own right. Collectively, the drama was astonishing. A generation earlier, ejecting the founders of a company like Cisco had been controversial. Now Gurley was confronting a Valley cult: the cult of the founder.

Gurley began by assembling his allies. Two of Uber's angel backers had come to believe that Kalanick threatened the value of their stock; they were willing to join Gurley in blocking his return from exile. Menlo Ventures joined Team Gurley, too; by now, Shervin Pishevar had moved on, and his place had been taken by a less obsequious investor. Next, Gurley recruited experts to his team. He brainstormed with professors who specialized in corporate governance and white-collar crime. He hired lawyers and retained a crisis public-relations firm.

Pretty soon, Gurley had a game plan. His shareholder coalition lacked the votes to force Kalanick's permanent resignation. But it would present Kalanick with a demand, coupling it with a threat to leak the ultimatum to the press if Kalanick refused to go quietly. Most venture partnerships are obsessive about keeping ugly personnel battles out of the public eye. Benchmark would threaten to broadcast this showdown, calculating that a press leak would swing additional Uber investors against Kalanick.

Even as he violated Valley norms, Gurley rallied his teammates. "I think we're on the right side of history here," he told them.

On June 20, 2017, Gurley launched his attack. Two of his partners flew to Chicago, where Kalanick was preparing to interview a candidate to be his second-in-command when he returned to Uber. Meanwhile, Gurley installed himself in the Benchmark conference room and assembled his allies via conference call. This time, rather than anticipating history's verdict, he invoked Hollywood.

"Did you ever see the movie *Life?*" Gurley asked his allies, according to the masterful account by the *New York Times* writer Mike Isaac. "The one with Ryan Reynolds in space, with that black goo alien they captured?

"The alien escapes. It gets out of the box somehow, and ends up killing everyone on the spaceship. It heads to earth to kill everyone there, too. All because it got out."

A few chuckles came through the phone speaker.

"Well, Travis is exactly like that alien," Gurley said. "If we let him out of the box—at any point during the day—he'll destroy the entire world."[77]

In Chicago, Gurley's partners, Matt Cohler and Peter Fenton, stepped into a gold elevator at the Ritz-Carlton hotel. At the top of the tower, Kalanick awaited.

Cohler and Fenton lost no time in delivering their message. They told Kalanick they wanted him to go, and they handed him a letter from Team Gurley.

The letter cited the disasters of that woeful year: the harassment investigation, the lawsuit with Google, the Greyball deception. "The public perception is that Uber fundamentally lacks ethical and moral values," the letter said. The company had to "change at its core." To this end, it required a change of chief executive.

Kalanick began to pace the room. "If this is the path you want to go down, things are gonna get ugly for you," he shouted at his visitors.

Cohler and Fenton informed Kalanick he had until 6:00 p.m. to reach a decision. After that, they would go public. The story would land on the front page of *The New York Times*. Other investors would join Benchmark's side. Kalanick could leave with dignity or he could leave without it.

Kalanick asked to be alone. Fenton and Cohler left and reported back to Gurley. From Benchmark's headquarters, Gurley texted his allies. "He's stalling."

Kalanick began to dial board members and investors, hoping to break off bits of Gurley's coalition. The signatories on Gurley's letter represented about 40 percent of Uber's voting shares. If Kalanick could flip one or two of them and prevent further slippage, he could hold on to his company.

"I can't believe it's come to this!" Kalanick pleaded desperately with one investor. "I can change! Please let me change!"

The appeals fell on deaf ears. Uber's governance had fallen so low that at least a chunk of the board regretted its hands-off passivity. That evening Kalanick gave up and signed a resignation letter.

The first of Gurley's three stratagems had played out perfectly.

◆

The drama wasn't done, because Kalanick was not gone completely. He was still a board member and a major shareholder, with 16 percent of the votes;

like Steve Jobs after his ejection from Apple, he might plot a return to his company. Indeed, after allowing himself a brief vacation, Kalanick began contacting Uber officials as though he had never left. Uber's fourteen-member leadership committee threatened to quit in unison if Kalanick was allowed back. Gurley had to stop him.

In July 2017, Benchmark began to prepare a second stratagem. A few months earlier, Masayoshi Son had backed Benchmark's other troubled unicorn, WeWork. Now the partners figured that Son might provide his special brand of assistance to Uber. He was a loose cannon, to be sure, but at We-Work he had helped Benchmark by buying some of its stake; perhaps a Son investment in Uber could be turned into an opportunity for a governance reset. Usually, Son and other late-stage players were famous for their founder-friendly terms. But in Uber's case, the founder had been kicked out; Son might instead be friendly to his successor. Matt Cohler and Peter Fenton flew to Sun Valley, Idaho, to test the idea on Son. They emerged feeling optimistic.[78]

The next month Benchmark unveiled its third and most aggressive gamble. Throwing all remnants of founder deference to the winds, the partnership sued Kalanick, aiming to break his hold on Uber's board structure. According to the lawsuit, Benchmark would not have assented to Kalanick's right to name three board directors if it had known of abuses such as the theft of trade secrets from Google. Therefore Kalanick had obtained those three board seats deceitfully.[79] The suit aimed to cancel the board seats and bar Kalanick from serving as a director.[80]

Over the next weeks, Benchmark pursued the Son gambit and the lawsuit in parallel. Son seemed amenable to buying existing shareholder stock at a valuation of between $40 billion and $45 billion—a discount of roughly a third from the last price, but still a welcome escape route. In a Yuri Milner–style move, Son also offered to save the company's face by investing a smaller amount at Uber's most recent valuation of $68 billion. Meanwhile, Benchmark persisted with its lawsuit, even though it was decried by Uber's top managers and board. From Benchmark's perspective, the suit was a hammer. It served to frighten Kalanick.

In late September, Dara Khosrowshahi, Kalanick's newly installed successor as chief executive, embraced the idea of a Son investment. Just as Benchmark had envisaged, this was less about raising fresh capital than about rejigging governance. As part of the deal, super-voting powers would be eliminated, reducing Kalanick's share of the vote from 16 percent to 10 percent. Khosrowshahi would get the right to appoint new board directors, offsetting Kalanick's influence. Effectively, Khosrowshahi and Benchmark were using Son to reverse what Kalanick had done to Benchmark at the time of the Saudi investment.[81]

Kalanick did his best to resist. Canceling the super-voting powers involved an untested legal mechanism, and Kalanick tried to fight it.[82] But Benchmark's two-track strategy had him cornered. The carrot of liquidity from Son brought more shareholders to Gurley's side. The stick of the lawsuit gave Kalanick an incentive to make peace with his opponents. In the end, Kalanick assented to Son's investment and the governance change on condition that Benchmark abandon its legal offensive. In January 2018, the Son deal duly closed. Kalanick lost his purchase on the board, and Benchmark dropped its lawsuit.

For Bill Gurley and Benchmark, it had been a harrowing experience. They had ejected Kalanick and salvaged the firm, but only by shredding the normal VC rule book. The Chicago ultimatum, the use of Masayoshi Son as a battering ram, the lawsuit: all these maneuvers had been improvised, because in the pre-unicorn era none of them would have been needed.

Looking back on the excesses of WeWork and Uber, it was tempting to paint VCs as the chief culprits. "How Venture Capitalists Are Deforming Capitalism," ran the title of a retrospective in *The New Yorker*.[83] But, just as with the backlash following the Theranos scandal, the critique was too sweeping: it glossed over the different types of technology investors. WeWork's capital had come overwhelmingly from nonstandard players: banks, mutual funds, and then Masayoshi Son, acting as a conduit for Arab Gulf money.[84] The one recognizable VC in the WeWork story, Bruce Dunlevie of Benchmark, had provided only about 1 percent of the $1.7 billion raised before Son wrote his monster check in 2017: it was a stretch to present him as a significant enabler. Further, to the extent that Dunlevie had influence, he had used it to oppose Neumann's demand for super-voting rights, warning that absolute power corrupts absolutely. In the case of Uber, likewise, Benchmark had provided only about one-third of 1 percent of the money raised before the huge Saudi investment of 2016, and Gurley had alienated Kalanick precisely because he had tried to curb at least some of his excesses. The cheerleaders who invested after Gurley included one obsequious VC. But Uber's most significant enablers came from outside the Valley.

The truth is that standard venture capitalists were not the main villains: not at WeWork, not at Uber, and not at overmighty unicorns more generally. Between 2014 and 2016, more than three-quarters of late-stage venture funding in the United States came from nontraditional investors such as mutual funds, hedge funds, and sovereign wealth funds.[85] But that didn't change the fact that the venture industry confronted a challenge: unicorn governance was broken. In his anguished essay of 2015, Gurley had pointed to the clearest fix: that unicorns should go public. A public listing would get rid of those distortive liquidation preferences that encouraged unicorn recklessness. It would force hubristic founders to listen to auditors, bankers, regulators, and lawyers, compensating for the fact that they refused to listen to their venture backers.

In 2019, confirming the argument in Gurley's essay, the IPO preparations for Uber and WeWork brought about a healthy reckoning. At Uber, Dara Khosrowshahi embraced the controls that Gurley had urged: the position of chief financial officer was filled, and a new chief legal officer signaled that Uber would take ethics seriously. Thanks to this cleanup, Uber's IPO went relatively well: the company ended its first day of trading in May 2019 with a valuation of $69 billion. It was less than its peak private valuation of $76 billion, but it was still a formidable sum—one that allowed Benchmark to celebrate a 270x return on its investment.[86]

At WeWork, in contrast, the megalomaniacal Adam Neumann disdained Khosrowshahi-style reforms, so the IPO process punished him appropriately. Required to publish its financials in the run-up to its road show, WeWork produced a document that telegraphed its uncanny resemblance to a cult. "Adam is a unique leader who has proven he can simultaneously wear the hats of visionary, operator and innovator, while thriving as a community and culture creator," it incanted. As a celebrity entrepreneur in the private capital market, with an audience consisting of late-stage sycophants desperate to be let into his next funding round, Neumann could get away with this vainglorious nonsense. But now that he aspired to sell equity to public investors, he faced an altogether tougher crowd. Financial journalists ridiculed WeWork's disclosures, equity analysts poked holes in his numbers, and the Harvard Business School professor Nori Gerardo Lietz denounced WeWork's "byzantine corporate structure, the continuing projected losses, the plethora of conflicts, the complete absence of any substantive corporate governance, and the uncommon 'New Age' parlance." With public-market investors refusing to buy WeWork stock, the board canceled the IPO and belatedly fired Neumann.

Gurley had been right. The IPO process did what broken private governance had failed to do: administer the cold shower that both unicorns needed. But the question was whether larger lessons would be learned and whether the tech world would turn a corner. In the wake of the WeWork humiliation, Masayoshi Son, the single greatest corrupter of unicorn governance, confessed the error of his ways. "My investment judgment was poor," he offered.[87] By way of atonement, Son promised to push companies to generate profits rather than to be "crazier, faster, bigger." He pledged that founders would henceforth not be permitted to hold shares with those nefarious super-voting rights; that they would not be allowed to control a majority of board votes; and that SoftBank itself would give up its passive practice of not taking a board seat.[88] Meanwhile, in a sign that Gurley's critique might have gained broader acceptance, unicorns that had long delayed a public listing emerged from the shadows. In 2020, venture-backed IPOs raised $38 billion, by far the largest amount ever.[89]

But these were merely hints of change, and the Theranos-Zenefits risk still haunted the venture industry. Whether Son would stick with his new standards was anybody's guess, and other growth-stage specialists, including Yuri Milner's DST, still refused to take board seats. The rush of IPOs was an encouraging sign, but it was marred by the emergence of a device called a SPAC—a form of public listing that sidestepped the scrutiny and disclosure involved in a traditional IPO process. Meanwhile, the financial climate promoted irresponsibility: so long as the Fed kept interest rates low, the abundance of cheap capital would cause capital to be used carelessly. Too much money was chasing too few deals, and the money providers were almost obliged to throw oversight to the winds in order to get into the hot companies. Venture capital had established itself as the best form of finance for innovative young firms. But the industry could not prevent reckless late-stage investors from playing poker with unicorns.

Conclusion

LUCK, SKILL, AND THE
COMPETITION AMONG NATIONS

For anyone who has created a film, a book, a podcast, or a song, the documentary *Searching for Sugar Man* is haunting. It's about Sixto Rodriguez, a talented singer-songwriter from Detroit who invites comparisons with Bob Dylan and Cat Stevens. As a young artist in the early 1970s, Rodriguez released two albums, and they sank without a trace. Sales were miserable. The record label dropped him. He was reduced to working demolition jobs, destroying, not creating. For the next three decades, Rodriguez grew old in a derelict house that he bought for $50 in a government auction.

Meanwhile, on the other side of the world, something magnificent happened. Australians and South Africans discovered his albums and went crazy for them. An Australian label produced a compilation of his songs, and a bootlegged version went platinum in South Africa. One of his tracks became an antiapartheid anthem, but Rodriguez himself had no inkling of his stardom. When I first watched *Searching for Sugar Man*, which documents the singer's simultaneous obscurity and fame, I called a South African friend to ask if he had heard of Rodriguez. Of course, came the reply. He knew all the words in all the songs. They were his coming-of-age soundtrack.

As a doctoral student at Columbia University in 2005, a sociologist named Matthew Salganik took a closer look at the *Sugar Man* phenomenon. After all, versions of the Rodriguez story crop up repeatedly in the creative fields: *Harry Potter* became a blockbuster despite initial rejection by publishers. Many books, songs, and movies are good enough to have a shot at fame, yet a tiny number reap the majority of the spoils, and Salganik wanted to understand what determines these skewed outcomes. So, together with some collaborators, he designed an experiment. His results are a good starting point for a verdict on venture capital.

Salganik created a website where people could listen to songs by unknown artists, then choose which to download to their library. Participants were randomly assigned to different virtual rooms—parallel worlds, like the United States and South Africa in the 1970s. Not surprisingly, the participants were more likely to choose songs that others had already downloaded: they responded to social influence. As initial popularity snowballed, each virtual world created its own megahit, a song so much more popular than the rest that its triumph looked inevitable. But this appearance of natural superiority was misleading. In Salganik's different experimental worlds, different songs came out on top. For example, a track called "Lockdown" came first in one world and fortieth out of forty-eight in another, even though it was exactly the same song competing against exactly the same list of rivals. To a surprising degree, Salganik concluded, blockbusters are random.[1]

For star venture capitalists, of course, this verdict encourages humility. Because of the feedback effects in a power-law business, some venture capitalists will dominate the sector, raising the lion's share of the dollars, getting the best access to the hot deals, and generating the best performance. The rest of the industry will struggle: counting venture funds raised between 1979 and 2018, the median fund narrowly underperformed the stock market index, whereas the top 5 percent of funds trounced it.[2] But, at least theoretically, the winners in this contest may merely be lucky: an initial run of success, possibly random, could set the network flywheel in motion. If we could mimic Salganik's experiment by replaying history a few times, perhaps *Harry Potter* would have languished in obscurity in some versions of the past, perhaps Kleiner Perkins would have invested in Facebook rather than Friendster, and perhaps Goldman Sachs's bosses would have held on to their Alibaba stake, depriving Masayoshi Son of the springboard for his second coming. In any version of history, the power law would ensure that a few winners become outsized stars. But there's an element of luck in who the stars are.[3]

In 2018, a working paper published by the National Bureau of Economic Research tested this logic directly on the venture industry.[4] Sure enough, the authors confirmed the existence of feedback effects. Early hits for venture firms boost the odds of later hits: each additional IPO among a VC firm's first ten investments predicts a 1.6 percentage point higher IPO rate for subsequent investments. After testing various hypotheses, the authors conclude that success leads to success because of reputational effects. Thanks to one or two initial hits, a VC's brand becomes strong enough to win access to attractive deals, particularly late-stage ones, where a startup is already doing well and the investment is less risky, according to the authors. Moreover, those one or two initial hits seem not to reflect skill. Rather, they result from "being in the right place at the right time"—in other words, from good fortune. Much as in Salganik's experiment with songs, luck and path dependency appear to explain who wins in venture capital.

This book has pushed back against the randomness thesis, emphasizing instead the skill in venture capital. It has done so for four reasons. First, the existence of path dependency does not actually prove that skill is absent. Venture capitalists need skill to enter the game: as the authors of the NBER paper say, path dependency can only influence which among the many skilled players gets to be the winner. Nor is it clear that path dependency explains why some skilled operators beat other ones. The finding that a partnership's future IPO rate rises by 1.6 percentage points is not particularly strong, and the history recounted in these pages shows that path dependency is frequently disrupted.[5] Despite his powerful reputation, Arthur Rock was unsuccessful after his Apple investment. Mayfield was a leading force during the 1980s; it too faded. Kleiner Perkins proves that you can dominate the Valley for a quarter of a century and then decline precipitously. Accel succeeded early, hit a rough patch, and then built itself back. In an effort to maintain its sense of paranoia and vigilance, Sequoia once produced a slide listing numerous venture partnerships that flourished and then failed. "The Departed," it called them.

The second reason to believe in skill lies in the origin story of some partnerships. Occasionally a newcomer breaks into the venture elite in such a way that skill obviously does matter. Kleiner Perkins became a leader in the business because of Tandem and Genentech. Both companies were hatched from within the KP office and actively shaped by Tom Perkins; there was nothing lucky about this. Tiger Global and Yuri Milner invented the art of late-stage venture capital. They had a genuinely novel approach to tech investing; they offered much more than the equivalent of another catchy tune competing against others. Paul Graham's batch-processing method at Y Combinator offered an equally original approach to seed-stage investing. A clever innovation, not random fortune, explains Graham's place in venture history.

Third, the idea that venture capitalists get into deals on the strength of their brands can be exaggerated. A deal seen by a partner at Sequoia will also be seen by rivals at other firms: in a fragmented cottage industry, there is no lack of competition. Often, winning the deal depends on skill as much as brand: it's about understanding the business model well enough to impress the entrepreneur; it's about judging what valuation might be reasonable. One careful tally concluded that new or emerging venture partnerships capture around half the gains in the top deals, and there are myriad examples of famous VCs having a chance to invest and then flubbing it.[6] Andreessen Horowitz passed on Uber. Its brand could not save it. Peter Thiel was an early investor in Stripe. He lacked the conviction to invest as much as Sequoia. As to the idea that branded venture partnerships have the "privilege" of participating in supposedly less risky late-stage investment rounds, this depends from deal to deal. A unicorn's momentum usually translates into an extremely high price for its shares. In the cases of Uber and especially WeWork, some late-stage investors lost millions.

Fourth, the anti-skill thesis underplays venture capitalists' contributions to portfolio companies. Admittedly, these contributions can be difficult to pin down. Starting with Arthur Rock, who chaired the board of Intel for thirty-three years, most venture capitalists have avoided the limelight.

They are the coaches, not the athletes. But this book has excavated multiple cases in which VC coaching made all the difference. Don Valentine rescued Atari and then Cisco from chaos. Peter Barris of NEA saw how UUNET could become the new GE Information Services. John Doerr persuaded the Googlers to work with Eric Schmidt. Ben Horowitz steered Nicira and Okta through their formative moments. To be sure, stories of venture capitalists guiding portfolio companies may exaggerate VCs' importance: in at least some of these cases, the founders might have solved their own problems without advice from their investors. But quantitative research suggests that venture capitalists do make a positive impact: studies repeatedly find that startups backed by high-quality VCs are more likely to succeed than others.[7] A quirky contribution to this literature looks at what happens when airline routes make it easier for a venture capitalist to visit a startup. When the trip becomes simpler, the startup performs better.[8]

As the story of Sixto Rodriguez tells us, early luck and path dependency are at play in power-law businesses. Of course, venture capital is no exception, and sometimes it is better to be lucky than smart: think of Anthony Montagu, the toothbrush-wielding Briton who snagged a slice of Apple. But smartness is still a major driver of results, as are other qualities that VCs bring to the job: hustle, for getting to standoffish founders first; fortitude, for riding through the inevitable dark periods when your investment goes to zero; emotional intelligence, for encouraging and guiding talented but unruly founders. Great venture capitalists can turn themselves into instruments for modulating entrepreneurial mood swings. When things go well at a portfolio company, they ask the searching questions that keep complacency from setting in. When things go wrong, they rally the team and refresh its commitment to the mission.

——◆——

This book has also made a second argument. Whatever the skills of particular venture partnerships or individual VCs, venture capitalists *as a group* have a positive effect on economies and societies. The financing of Apple, for example, is clearly not a case study in VC skill: several venture capitalists refused to invest, even though the moment was ripe for a stand-alone

PC maker. But whatever the errors of individuals, venture capitalists as a group ultimately funded Steve Jobs. The result was a company that delighted countless consumers, creating jobs for employees and wealth for investors.

As with this book's claim about individual VC skill, there are legitimate objections to the claim about VCs' collective impact. The doubts can be grouped under three headings. The VC industry is better at enriching itself than at developing socially useful businesses. The VC industry is dominated by a narrow club of white men. The VC industry encourages out-of-control disrupters with no regard for those who get disrupted.

The least persuasive of these complaints is that venture-backed businesses are not socially useful. Of course, Big Tech has a dark side. Companies as huge as Amazon, Apple, Facebook, and Google have all kinds of social impacts, some good and some not, and governments are right to clamp down on the bad stuff. Violations of privacy, the propagation of fake news, and the sheer power of private actors to determine who gets to communicate when and to whom: these are legitimate targets for regulators. But this is not an indictment of venture capital. When VCs originally backed the tech giants, they were helping to create products that were good for consumers; nobody wants to return to a world without e-commerce, personal computers, social media, or web search. If the giants have since become threatening, this is because they have become so large: the VC/startup stage in their trajectory is long behind them. Nor can it be argued that VCs somehow programmed irresponsibility into these companies when they were in their cradles. If anything, the opposite is true: the majority of VCs tend to push founders to be more careful about legal and societal constraints, not less so. At Facebook, Accel ejected Sean Parker in an attempt to cleanse the culture of the firm. At Uber, Benchmark ultimately defenestrated Kalanick. Meanwhile, venture capitalists have backed dozens of technologies that are obvious boons: digital maps, online education, biotechnology, and so forth. The companies that VCs create are much more a force for progress than a source of regression.

Venture capital is also attacked for the businesses it has failed to create—for errors of omission. The most common form of this complaint is that venture capital has flowed more copiously to frivolous apps than to socially useful projects, notably the vital area of technologies to fight climate change. But this is not for lack of VC enthusiasm, as we have seen. Between 2006 and 2008, venture capitalists pumped billions into wind power, solar panels, and biofuels, tripling the flow of capital into cleantech. The poor performance of these green funds underscores the environmental passion of the VCs: arguably, they elevated their sense of social mission above their responsibility to their limited partners, many of which, incidentally, are universities and philanthropies. Since 2018, moreover, venture capitalists have demonstrated their enthusiasm for cleantech all over again, pouring money into electric-car projects, technologies that promote crop sustainability, and software that drives energy efficiencies in everything from recycling to shipping.

Perhaps venture investors have their hearts in the right place, but their style of finance is unsuited to capital-intensive areas such as cleantech? This suspicion is partly correct but at the same time exaggerated. It is true that technologies with high R&D costs saddle VCs with extra risk, and products that take years to develop will reduce the annualized return on VC capital. According to one study, VC investments in cleantech deals between 1991 and 2019 yielded a paltry 2 percent per year, compared with 24 percent per year for software investments.[9] But the verdict that green projects are "not venture backable" is too sweeping. For one thing, some require neither large amounts of capital nor long time horizons: software that decides when domestic appliances draw electricity from the grid, for example. For another, the pre-2010 cleantech flop was as much a government failure as a venture-capital one. Politicians had dialed up the rhetoric about pricing or regulating carbon, and VCs acted on these signals; when the politicians failed to deliver, the VCs unsurprisingly took losses. Post-2010, there has been no equivalent policy shock, and cleantech has done better. Between 2014 and 2018, green VC investments earned gross annual returns of just over 21 percent, with smart-grid and energy-storage startups generating around 30 percent.[10] Finally, the idea that venture capitalists can't manage some amount of capital intensity is unsupported by history. The early stories in this book show how venture capitalists have succeeded with expensive hardware projects in the past: recall Fairchild Semiconductor, Intel, Tandem, 3Com, Cisco, and UUNET.

In the first decades of the industry, VCs financed capital-intensive projects by writing appropriate term sheets. For their patience and ample cash, they demanded a large share of portfolio companies. In the 1960s, Davis & Rock expected to own around 45 percent of any startup it backed. In the 1970s and 1980s, Series A investors typically expected around a third of the equity. Then, in the late 1990s, the share fell further: Sequoia and Kleiner Perkins pumped a large sum into Google but took only a quarter of the company between them. Finally, at the nadir, Accel got just an eighth of Facebook when it backed Zuckerberg in 2005, a share that Arthur Rock would have found derisory.[11] This shift to ever smaller stakes followed from the assertiveness of young startup founders, as we have seen. But it also reflected the fact that software startups like Google and Facebook required limited capital and promised quick and astronomical rewards: no wonder venture capitalists were content to own a modest share of them. Today, if VCs are to finance capital-intensive projects, they need to recall their past. They can supply large sums of capital if they are allowed to own a large share of the resulting company.[12]

The extraordinary spread of the internet, smartphones, and cloud computing over the past twenty-five years has created a myth that venture capital is only about software. The myth is all the stronger because many of the resulting businesses are household names, looming so large in the public consciousness that humbler technologies become invisible. But the implication that VCs can "only" back software is doubly wrong. For one thing, software touches just about every industry; even if the software-only myth were accurate, it would hardly prove that venture capital is restricted to a narrow area. But the larger point is that, contrary to common perception, the pre-internet tradition of capital-intensive projects remains viable.

In 2007 a partnership called Lux Capital raised its first fund with an explicit mandate to avoid the obvious stuff. "No internet, social media, mobile, video games—things that everybody will keep doing," as its co-founder Josh Wolfe explained it.[13] Instead, Lux invested in areas such as medical robotics, satellites, and nuclear-waste treatment, and the results serve to prove that these capital-intensive challenges are not beyond the reach of venture capital. As of 2020, Lux boasted strong returns and managed $2.5 billion of investments.[14] In the first half of 2021, nine Lux portfolio companies staged successful exits, and the partnership raised an additional $1.5 billion.

For another illustration of how capital-intensive technologies can be venture-backable, consider Flagship Pioneering. A Boston-based venture operation focusing on ambitious medical breakthroughs, Flagship proved the point that high-risk, high-cost moon shots can pay off if the VC owns enough of the upside. Echoing what Kleiner Perkins did with Genentech, Flagship incubated startups internally and eliminated the white-hot risks before seeking capital from other firms. As a result, Flagship usually retained around half of the equity when its successful projects went public, with the result that the firm's limited partners reaped exceptional profits.[15] One Flagship startup, the biotech company Moderna, invented a vaccine for COVID-19. There could scarcely be a stronger proof of venture capital's utility.

Venture capital is of course guilty of errors of omission: no financial specialty has the answer to everything. When it comes to fundamental science, government-backed labs will always be essential. When it comes to firms with a valuation of more than about $5 billion, the stock market may deliver superior corporate governance. When it comes to highly capital-intensive investments—a state-of-the-art semiconductor factory, to cite an extreme example—deep-pocketed corporations will be more suitable. But what is far more striking is venture capital's broad reach: counting in seed and growth investing, it is the go-to source of finance for innovative and ambitious startups worth anything from a few million to a few billion dollars. So long as the startup is targeting a lucrative market and has a shot at delivering 10x-plus to its investors, it really doesn't matter what sector it is in. It could be inventing a new kind of burger (Impossible Foods), a new way of selling eyeglasses (Warby Parker), a fashion concept (Stitch Fix, Rent the Runway), a virtual-reality headset (Oculus), a fitness tracker (Fitbit), an affordable smartphone (Xiaomi), a scooter- and bike-rental service (Lime), a genetics-testing service (23andMe), medical robots (Auris Health), a mental wellness service (Lyra Health), a payments service for merchants (Stripe,

Square), or a consumer bank (Revolut, Monzo). Inevitably, there will always be critics who object that venture capitalists could allocate society's resources in some better way. But these critics' subjective priorities could be interrogated, too, and it is not as though all non-venture-backed businesses are virtuous. In putting capital behind products that they can sell at a profit, VCs are at least respecting the choices of millions of consumers.

◆

What of the second broad area of complaint: that venture capital is dominated by white men drawn from a narrow collection of elite colleges? This is far more persuasive. As of February 2020, women accounted for a shockingly low 16 percent of investment partners at VC firms, up from 11 percent in 2016.[16] In contrast, 38 percent of lawyers and 35 percent of doctors are women.[17] Admittedly, the venture industry is trying to improve. During 2019, 42 percent of the new partners appointed at U.S. venture firms were women, and the sexism in the industry showed some signs of abating.[18] Several venture capitalists known for sexual harassment have been disgraced, and men are more likely to be called out for obnoxious comments. In a 2020 paper, researchers report testing for misogyny by sending out eighty thousand pitch emails introducing promising but fictitious startups to twenty-eight thousand venture investors. The pitches ostensibly sent by female entrepreneurs received 9 percent more interested replies than identical pitches from male ones.[19] But this hopeful shift in attitudes is having a disappointingly modest impact on where money ultimately goes. In 2020 only 6.5 percent of venture deals featured startups with female-only founders. A slightly larger share of deals, 17.3 percent, went to startups with at least one female founder.[20]

On the issue of race, progress has been even slower. To be fair, the venture business is open to investors of Asian origin: about 15 percent of VC partners are ethnically Asian, more than double their share of the labor force.[21] However, on the negative side, only 3 percent of venture-capital partners are Black, even though Black Americans account for 13 percent of the labor force, and Black entrepreneurs raise less than 1 percent of venture dollars.[22] This Black underrepresentation reflects the pattern across other elite professions, but it is worse: to cite one plausible benchmark, Black representation among financial managers stands at 8.5 percent, nearly three times higher than the share in venture capital.[23] Meanwhile, Hispanic Americans are even less represented. They make up 4 percent of venture partners, even though they account for 17 percent of the workforce and 11.4 percent of financial managers.[24] Not only is this inequitable; it constrains economic progress. Talented people are being denied an opportunity to contribute to innovation. On one reckoning, U.S. GDP would be more than 2 percent higher if this failing were addressed.[25]

In the wake of the Black Lives Matter protests of 2020, a few venture leaders promised to do better. Andreessen Horowitz set up a program to train and fund a small number of founders from atypical backgrounds. "Being equal before the law, but unequal before law enforcement, is atrocious," the partnership said firmly.[26] First Round Capital, one of the seed investors that backed Uber, declared that its next partner should be Black. Google Ventures announced the appointment of a Black partner, Terri Burns, who had previously worked at Twitter. But these initiatives amount to no more than a start, and for now the industry stands guilty as charged. It is too much the province of white men, drawn from a few elite colleges: among VCs with MBAs, a third attended either Stanford or Harvard.[27] The venture industry is a meritocracy, up to a point. It is also what its critics call a "mirror-tocracy."

◆

Finally, there is the third broad area of complaint: that venture capital encourages out-of-control disrupters. This line of criticism is often a reaction against "blitzscaling" at companies such as Uber. Coined by Reid Hoffman, a venture capitalist at Greylock and before that the founder of LinkedIn, the term referred originally to an obligation more than a choice: in network industries, winner-takes-all logic obliges startups to race for scale before competitors achieve it.[28] But, in the hands of less thoughtful investors, "blitzscaling" has come to mean little more than "get rich quick," a phrase to be filed alongside other notorious war cries, from Masayoshi Son's injunction to be "crazier, faster, bigger" to Mark Zuckerberg's call to "move fast and break things." Even the recipients of blitzscaling war chests have started to call foul. In 2019, the entrepreneur Jason Fried declared that venture capital "kills more businesses than it helps," because large VC war chests create pressure to spend before managers know how to spend wisely. "You plant a seed, it needs some water, but if you just pour a whole fucking bucket of water on it's going to kill it," Fried said bluntly.[29] Noting the multitude of VC-backed companies that fail, the entrepreneur Tim O'Reilly offers a provocative idea. "Blitzscaling isn't really a recipe for success but rather survivorship bias masquerading as a strategy."[30]

Yet the O'Reilly critique is less an indictment of VCs than a warning to founders. If the objective of entrepreneurship is personal autonomy, founders must understand that venture capital comes with conditions. If entrepreneurs want to grow their companies at a measured pace, venture capital may well create unwanted pressures. But while inexperienced founders may need to be told of these realities, venture capitalists understand them all too well: they are the first to proclaim that cautious founders should raise money elsewhere. "The vast majority of entrepreneurs should NOT take venture capital," Bill Gurley tweeted in January 2019. "I sell jet fuel," Josh Kopelman of First Round Capital agreed; "some people don't want to build a jet."[31] As these comments indicate, VCs may be capable of backing companies in a broad swath of sectors, but in another sense their competence is narrow. Venture capital is suitable only for the ambitious minority that wants to take the risk of growing fast, and VCs of all people have an interest in being open about this. If they force-feed capital to unsuitable firms, they will lose it.

In a subtle way, however, the O'Reilly critique does raise a tricky question about venture capital. It's not about the founders who attempt to grow quickly and then fail: they accepted venture dollars voluntarily, presumably knowing the perils. Rather, it's about the founders who grow quickly and succeed, because these founders will upend the lives of people at incumbent companies. Of course, dislocation is usually a fair price to pay for technological advance: destruction can be creative. But if dislocation stems not from technology but rather from technology finance, the judgment may be different. When venture capitalists pour money into blitzscaling, the result is a pack of unicorns that can sell their products below cost, disrupting incumbents not necessarily because they are technologically superior but rather because they are subsidized by venture dollars. In ride hailing, for example, venture capitalists paid for artificially cheap fares for passengers, forcing incumbent taxi operators to compete on a distorted playing field. The moral and political justification for tough market competition is that it should be fair. If the market is rigged, it loses legitimacy.

No economic system is perfectly free from distortions, so the question is whether blitzscaling rises to the level where the distortions are pernicious. If it could be shown that subsidized unicorns are elbowing aside more efficient incumbents, then blitzscaling might be harming the overall efficiency of the economy. At the height of the blitzscaling frenzy in 2018, two academics tried to make this claim. "Money-losing firms can continue operating and undercutting incumbents for far longer than previously," they wrote. "Arguably, these firms are destroying economic value."[32] But while this contention may be right at some times and in some industries, it is almost certainly wrong in the vast majority of cases.

The reasons begin with the nature of market competition. To repeat: no economic system is perfectly free from distortions, and incumbent businesses generally have powerful advantages. They enjoy economies of scale, strong brands, government regulations that they have helped to shape, and established relationships with distributors and suppliers. Given these incumbent advantages, blitzscaling that helps insurgents may be a leveler, not a distorter. In ride hailing, for example, the incumbent taxi operators often had municipal regulators in their pockets. Cheap venture dollars served to balance that unfair advantage.[33] "You can make the case that if Uber and Lyft and Airbnb hadn't blitzscaled, they would have been tied up in bureaucratic red tape, and the future they are trying to build wouldn't just have happened more slowly. It would never have happened," O'Reilly himself comments. Theoretically, a really huge amount of venture dollars might represent an overcorrection: when buccaneers like Masayoshi Son are setting the pace, the anti-blitzscaling critique may have merit. But buccaneer blitzscaling is not the fault of venture capital as it is usually practiced: recall that Bill Gurley was horrified by Uber's burn rate. After the humiliation of WeWork, even Son claimed to be chastened.

One last point about blitzscaling is worth noting. The goal of the blitz-scaler is to establish market power—something approaching monopoly. This can harm society in three ways: overmighty companies may underpay suppliers and workers, overcharge consumers, and stifle innovation. But the right answer to this problem is to regulate monopolies when they arise, not punish venture capital. After all, venture capital is all about disrupting entrenched corporate power: it is the enemy of monopoly. The challenge to Amazon comes from younger VC-backed firms: upstart consumer brands such as Glossier that collect payments with the help of other upstarts such as Stripe. Similarly, the challenge to Facebook comes from the next generation of social-media platforms: the Sequoia-backed TikTok or the a16z protégé Clubhouse. Nor does the fact that Facebook has swallowed two prominent past challengers, Instagram and WhatsApp, undermine this point. For one thing, competition authorities, responding to the increasing skepticism of Big Tech, may block Facebook's acquisition of future challengers. For another, the high prices that Facebook paid for Instagram and WhatsApp have created powerful incentives for VCs to fund the next round of contenders.

Any clique that becomes as rich and powerful as the denizens of Sand Hill Road deserves critical scrutiny. But of the three complaints considered here, only one has merit. The venture-capital industry is indeed a clique: too white, too male, too Harvard/Stanford. A sector with so much influence on the shape of the future should take diversity more seriously. But it really isn't true that venture capital is unsuited to socially useful industries such as cleantech. Nor is the "go big or go home" blitzscaling mentality generally extreme enough to harm the efficiency of the economy. As technology permeates every corner of life, democratic societies are right to worry about its downsides, from the emergence of monopolies to the propagation of fake news to the compromising of privacy. But these threats come from the mature technology giants. Far from entrenching these platforms, venture capital may well disrupt them.

Meanwhile, on the other side of the ledger, an assessment of venture capitalists as a group must acknowledge the strong points in their favor.

Business schools and finance faculties have conclusively shown that VC-backed companies have a disproportionate impact on wealth creation and innovation. Only a fraction of 1 percent of firms in the United States receive venture backing.[34] But in a study covering the quarter century from 1995 to 2019, Josh Lerner and Ramana Nanda find that VC-backed companies accounted for fully 47 percent of U.S. nonfinancial IPOs; in other words, a VC-backed firm was orders of magnitude more likely to make it to the stock market than a non-VC-backed one. Moreover, the VC-backed companies that went public tended to do better than their non-VC-backed peers and to generate far more innovation. Thus, even though VC-backed firms accounted for 47 percent of IPOs, they accounted for 76 percent of the market value at the end of the study. They also accounted for fully 89 percent of R&D spending.[35] Other research confirms that more venture investment leads to more patent filings, and further that VC-funded patents are more significant than average: 22 percent of VC-backed patents are in the top 10 percent of the most cited patents.[36] These intellectual achievements generate productive spillovers for the rest of the economy. A technology created at one company can be useful to other companies. Innovative products can boost the efficiency of individuals and firms globally.

The undoubted success of VC-backed companies is often qualified with a question: Did the VCs create the success, or did they merely show up for it? But, as we have seen already, another line of research shows how start-ups that have the benefit of venture guidance fare better than their peers, and this book has related multiple cases of VCs positively impacting portfolio companies. Besides, even if it were the case that VC skill lay entirely in deal selection, and not in mentoring startups, that skill would still be valuable. Intelligent deal selection increases the chances that the most deserving startups will get the capital they need. It ensures that society's savings are allocated productively.

Moreover, this finance-centric case for VCs should be supplemented by a sociological one. Thanks to the work of AnnaLee Saxenian, it's been understood since the 1990s that Silicon Valley overtook Boston as an innovation hub because of the quality of its network: talent and ideas flowed more freely among the small startups of California than among the hermetic corporations of Massachusetts. This book has stressed a further point: that the fertile networks emphasized by Saxenian are nurtured above all by venture capitalists. In getting California's innovation flywheel started, Arthur Rock mattered as much as the presence of Stanford or the flow of defense contracts. In overtaking Boston, the Valley relied on VCs like the team behind 3Com, the Ethernet company that sought East Coast financing but ended up deciding that there was no substitute for West Coast venture capital. Remarkably, the rise of the Valley's main challenger—China—can be traced to venture capital as well. In a replay of the Valley's own development, China's internet companies got started thanks to American or American-trained venture investors. Again, venture capital's contribution to the commercialization of applied science is unmistakable.

This contribution has grown, and will continue to do so. Between 1980 and 2000, VC-backed companies accounted for an already substantial 35 percent of U.S. IPOs. In the ensuing two decades, the share jumped to 49 percent.[37] Looking to the future, venture capital will advance even more because of a fundamental shift in the economy. In the past, most corporate investment was *tangible*: capital was used to purchase physical goods, machines, buildings, tools, and so forth. Now much corporate investment is *intangible*: capital goes into R&D, design, market research, business processes, and software.[38] The new intangible investments fall squarely in the sweet spot of VCs: in explaining venture capital back in 1962, Rock said he was financing "intellectual book value." In contrast, intangible assets pose challenges to other sorts of financiers. Banks and bond investors try to protect themselves from losses by securing "collateral"—claims on a borrower's assets that can be seized and sold if the borrower defaults. But intangible assets exhibit *sunkenness*: once the investment is made, there is no physical object that can be hawked to recoup capital.[39] Likewise, traditional equity investors evaluate companies partly by tallying their physical assets, which are clearly reported in financial statements. But intangible assets are harder to measure. They elude standard accounting rules and their value is opaque: to evaluate a software development project, for example, you have to be close to the technology. Hands-on venture capitalists are better equipped to allocate capital in this bewildering world: a world in which tangibles are displaced by intangibles.

Because venture capital is particularly well suited to financing intangible assets, it is no surprise that it has spread geographically. Silicon Valley is still the center of the industry: Within the United States, the Valley is home to two-thirds of U.S. venture partners, and California's share of U.S. venture fundraising jumped from 44 percent to 62 percent between 2004 and 2019.[40] At the same time, however, California-based investors are increasingly willing to back companies in other states, and the explosion of flows into VC funds has left plenty of money to find its way to partnerships outside the Valley. The biggest beneficiaries have been the traditional financial centers, Boston and New York. But money has also flowed to strong industrial cities, such as Los Angeles and Seattle, and even to more surprising locations: Drive Capital, led by two Sequoia alumni, manages venture funds worth $1.2 billion from its base in Ohio. With the advent of remote working during the coronavirus pandemic of 2020–2021, a parade of tech royalty has abandoned the traffic jams of Silicon Valley in search of lower taxes and rents, with Austin, Texas, and Miami, Florida, emerging as two buzzy destinations. Joe Lonsdale, the leader of a partnership called 8VC, cast his move to Austin as a wager that innovation could take place anywhere. "Talented people are building top technology firms all over the country," he wrote. "We're betting that the future of America is going to be built in the middle of the country, in places with good government and a reasonable cost of living."[41]

Underscoring venture capital's advantage in financing the industries of tomorrow, venture hubs have grown outside the United States. Between 2009 and 2018, four of the top ten cities for VC investment were elsewhere: Beijing, Shanghai, Shenzhen, and London.[42] Promising VC clusters have emerged in Israel, Southeast Asia, and India. Even Europe, generally a digital laggard, saw venture investments double in the five years to 2019.[43] In 2021, three Latin Americans appeared on the *Forbes* Midas list, the first time anyone from the region had made the ranks. All in all, the U.S. share of worldwide venture financing has fallen from about 80 percent in 2006–2007 to under 50 percent in 2016–2019.[44] A generation ago, scientists and engineers saw the United States as the only place to found a company. Today, they see opportunities everywhere.

The global embrace of venture capital confirms what has been argued here: the attractions of the industry far outweigh its alleged shortcomings. As individuals, VCs do exhibit skill. As a group, they finance the most dynamic companies, generate disproportionate wealth and R&D, and knit together the fertile networks that drive the knowledge economy. In the future, as intangible assets increasingly eclipse tangible ones, venture capitalists' hands-on style will contribute even more to our prosperity. Of course, there are myriad social problems that the venture industry won't fix, and some it may exacerbate—inequality, for example.[45] But the right response to inequality is not to doubt venture capital's importance or throw sand in its gears. It is to tax the lucky people who have prospered fabulously over the past generation—including those who made fortunes as venture capitalists.

And yet, by a paradox, the success of venture capital sets the industry up for a new challenge. As it spreads around the world, it will increasingly be caught up in great-power rivalry.

◆

The geopolitics of venture capital has passed through two phases. In phase one, running roughly from the financing of Fairchild Semiconductor to the financing of Alibaba, there was barely any venture capital outside the United States, so the question of national competition was irrelevant. In phase two, starting around the turn of the century, venture capital began to spread, but like most aspects of globalization this was generally assumed to be a win-win process. When U.S. venture capitalists midwifed China's digital economy, China was a winner but so apparently was the United States, which reaped exceptional returns on its Chinese investments. Only a minority of observers worried that China's increasing technological sophistication might threaten U.S. interests. After all, Silicon Valley had such an enormous lead that a little Chinese catch-up would hardly change the picture.

Around 2017, the geopolitics of venture capital entered a third phase. In the United States and China alike, leaders were less inclined to see globalization as win-win and more inclined to view the world in terms of competition. Meanwhile, as great-power rivalry intensified, the U.S. lead in the digital economy evaporated. China boasted as many unicorns as the United States, and in some technologies it was ahead: drones, mobile payments, next-generation 5G networking equipment. Chinese consumers' habit of conducting every aspect of life via smartphones generated an extraordinary density of data, and low-cost Chinese labor allowed for the data's laborious tagging; combined, these two factors gave China an advantage in the race to train artificial intelligence systems. In 2017, much of Silicon Valley was consumed with excitement about cryptocurrency, despite its unproven utility. Meanwhile, Chinese startups rushed ahead in AI, developing applications from instant loans delivered via smartphones to recommendation algorithms to facial recognition.[46] That same year, China overtook the United States as the top source of venture returns.[47] It did not feel like a coincidence.

With the United States and China in a competitive mood, and with the technology gap narrowing, the old win-win assumptions demand reexamination. Because of its disproportionate contribution to economic growth and innovation, venture capital has become a pillar of national power; it cannot be left out of geopolitical calculations. Looking back with the benefit of hindsight, U.S. venture capitalists' role in building China's technology sector benefited China more than the United States: the U.S. investors earned money, but China gained strategic industries. This China advantage is clearest where U.S. venture capital helped to develop Chinese technologies with military potential. The world's leading commercial drone manufacturer is the Shenzhen-based DJI Technology, which counts Accel and Sequoia China among its backers.[48] The U.S. Army has banned the internal use of DJI hardware for security reasons, and in 2020 the U.S. Department of Justice prohibited the use of federal funds to purchase DJI products. Similarly, one of the world's top AI companies is SenseTime, which raised funds from Tiger Global. SenseTime is on the list of companies sanctioned by the U.S. Department of Commerce because of its work with China's surveillance agencies, notably in the Muslim-majority province of Xinjiang.

These American contributions to China's technological prowess are all the more significant because of the coming shift in warfare. Until recently, the U.S. military edge was assured by its superiority in areas such as stealth aircraft, aircraft carriers, and precision munitions. But China's military leaders aim to leapfrog those technologies by establishing a lead in AI weaponry: swarms of cheap, expendable, autonomous drones could make aircraft carriers obsolete.[49] U.S. commanders understand AI's potential equally well, but they seem locked into the weapons-purchasing habits that brought them dominance in the past—a sort of military version of the innovator's dilemma. Sometime in the 2030s, the U.S. Navy plans to start building its next carrier-based fighter jet, the F/A-XX: it will have a human pilot. Meanwhile, the battlefield of the future will be dominated by intelligent unmanned craft. Software will eat warfare.

To win the race for AI weaponry, China's Ministry of National Defense has assembled a cluster of more than two hundred AI researchers at the National University of Defense Technology, creating the world's largest government AI effort. But this Manhattan Project is not the core of China's strategy. Having experienced the power of U.S.-style VC in creating world-class companies such as Alibaba and Tencent, China understands that the way to establish dominance in AI weapons is to dominate civilian AI businesses. Artificial intelligence, remember, is a contest of scale: you need big data, big computing power, and big investments in the scientific teams that perfect the algorithms. Only a thriving global business is likely to achieve this trifecta. Already, SenseTime employs three times more AI researchers than the National University of Defense Technology and has built computing infrastructure whose power exceeds that of the world's top-ranked supercomputer at the Oak Ridge National Laboratory in Tennessee. SenseTime scientists have deep ties with AI researchers in the West: as of 2018, the MIT-SenseTime Alliance on Artificial Intelligence was funding twenty-seven projects across multiple MIT departments.[50] For now, AI teams at U.S. companies such as Google are even larger. But Google takes a skeptical view of U.S. power, so it is harder to turn the company's technological strength into military dominance. In 2018, facing pressure from its liberal and multinational faculty of scientists, Google ceased participation in Project Maven, a Pentagon AI initiative. Meanwhile, the traditional U.S. defense majors—Boeing, Raytheon Technologies, Lockheed Martin—have puny research budgets relative to the software giants.[51] They are not in a position to deliver breakthrough AI weaponry.

In sum, SenseTime, DJI, and other products of China's venture ecosystem present the United States with a challenge. Venture capital is changing the balance of power, both commercial and military. The question is what governments should do in the face of this shift. How can they maximize their chances of having a thriving entrepreneurial sector, with all the geopolitical benefit this brings? And how should the United States respond to China, in particular?

———◆———

Government efforts to promote VC-backed innovation tend to generate debate that is unhelpfully polarized. On the one hand, technology libertarians are wrong to pretend that state interventions have contributed nothing. As we have seen, the internet began as a Pentagon project, and Marc Andreessen built the first web browser when working at a government-backed university laboratory. Two government policy changes—the lifting of restrictions on pension-fund investments in VC and the reductions in the capital-gains tax—contributed powerfully to the flow of dollars into U.S. venture funds around 1980. On the other hand, believers in government industrial policy are equally wrong to gloss over the repeated failures of state interventions. In the 1960s, the U.S. government's support for Small Business Investment Companies was largely a waste; the SBICs turned out to be much less effective than private venture partnerships. In the 1980s, taxpayer subsidies for the U.S. semiconductor industry were tangential to its recovery; the private-sector shift from chip manufacturing to innovative chip design was more significant. In China, similarly, the state's investment in scientific education and research has contributed to the country's success. But other government interventions have failed. Since 2014, when China's president, Xi Jinping, called upon his country's technologists to "strive to overtake," China has poured money into a dizzying array of government "guidance funds"; in 2016 alone, 566 were created. Much of this money seems likely to be wasted.[52]

Other countries drive home the point that government action is not automatically good or bad: it depends on the design details. In 1993, Israel's leaders launched one of the most successful venture interventions of all time: a $100 million government fund called the Yozma Group. The money was used to subsidize foreign venture firms willing to set up in Israel: private investors committed around $12 million to a fund, and Yozma kicked in a further $8 million on generous terms, sharing the up-front investment risk and capping its claim on future profits. This concessional capital was coupled with regulatory fixes: the foreign investors were permitted to use the familiar U.S.-style limited-partnership structure, maximizing their freedom and minimizing their taxes. By "crowding in" skilled venture operators, most of whom were American, Israel turned its deep reservoir of scientific talent into a thriving startup scene. Before the launch of Yozma, there had been only one active venture fund in Israel. A decade later, the government had stopped subsidizing the sector, and sixty private groups managed about $10 billion in assets. By 2007, the ratio of venture capital to GDP was higher in Israel than in any other country.[53]

For a study in contrast, consider the European Union's venture interventions. In 2001, the European Commission allocated more than €2 billion ($1.9 billion) for venture subsidies. But it failed to pair this capital with the design features underpinning Israel's success. Europe did not recognize limited partnerships. It did not address burdensome labor-market regulations. It failed to build startup-friendly stock markets to facilitate VC exits. As a result, rather than crowding in private venture operators, the European initiative crowded them out: given the limited entrepreneurial opportunities in Europe, commercial VC partnerships were not interested in competing with subsidized public investors.[54] Worse, because government-sponsored investors were less skilled and motivated than private ones, this displacement reduced the quality of European VC: deal selection and post-investment coaching deteriorated. From the beginning of the industry through the end of 2007, the average European venture fund generated a return of minus 4 percent.[55]

Taken together, this mosaic of policy experiments suggests one warning and four lessons about promoting venture capital. The warning is that

Israel is unusual; Singapore and New Zealand are among the few that have managed to emulate it. In most cases, unfortunately, pumping taxpayer money into venture funds has proved ineffective, particularly when public capital swamps private venture operators.[56] In principle, the idea of boosting entrepreneurship by subsidizing the cost of capital makes sense: it allows governments to help entrepreneurs while recognizing that private investors are better at selecting startups and, importantly, shuttering them. But when governments subsidize venture operations, these operations often take on aspects of the government: the bureaucracy, the bad incentives, the cronyism. In 2009, Josh Lerner of Harvard Business School published an authoritative account of government attempts to promote venture capital. *Boulevard of Broken Dreams*, he called it.[57]

On the encouraging side, the first lesson about promoting VC is that tax breaks work better than subsidies. By inviting venture investors to speculate with government funds, subsidies encourage sloppy bets, because losses will be partly borne by taxpayers. In contrast, tax breaks achieve the same goal of reducing the cost of capital for startups, but they create healthier incentives. Investors have to reach into their own pockets for every dollar initially wagered: they have reason to incur risk thoughtfully. At the same time, the tax breaks ensure that if the bets go well, venture capitalists will keep more of the upside. This reinforces VC incentives to make the smartest possible investments and go the extra mile to help portfolio companies.

The most successful mechanism for delivering VC tax breaks is the limited partnership. Among other advantages, this structure avoids the double taxation levied on corporations. Profits at ordinary companies are taxed first at the corporate level and then, once the profits are paid out as dividends, at the shareholder level. In contrast, limited partnerships are classed as "pass-through entities": they pass on the proceeds from successful investments tax-free; the partners then pay tax just once when they receive the distributions. Limited partnerships have dominated American venturing since the days of Davis & Rock, and other jurisdictions—Britain, China, and Israel—have subsequently embraced them. Yet some countries refuse to permit pass-through partnerships because they don't want rich investors to escape tax. This is understandable, but it is also a mistake: there are ways to make the rich pay their fair share without harming entrepreneurial incentives. For example, tax concessions for venture capital can be coupled with a higher inheritance tax.

The second policy lesson is that tax breaks for venture investors should be coupled with incentives for the employees of startups. Working for a startup can be brutal: one study finds that almost three-quarters of venture-backed entrepreneurs receive no money at all when they wind up their companies.[58] The gifted people who pour their energy into these ventures have other options: they could take salaried positions at big companies. To lure talent away from comfortable safety, the prize has to be large, and societies should want it to be large, because of the positive spillovers that flow from vibrant startups. Governments should therefore go out of their way to encourage employee stock options, which have emerged as the best device for cash-poor startups to attract world-class go-getters. Yet while countries such as Britain, Canada, China, Israel, and the Baltic States have embraced the legal and tax rules that make employee options work, others have resisted. In some European countries, stock grants that do not confer voting rights are not recognized in law; as a result, they are impossible to use without turning your startup into a governance nightmare. In other places, taxes are levied on stock options at the time they are granted; for example, Belgium hits employees with an 18 percent levy the moment they accept an options grant, even though the options might turn out to be worthless. In 2020, France belatedly fixed its rules to make employee options viable, and Germany's finance minister promised to follow. But the region has a lot of catching up to do. Relative to their European peers, employees at U.S. startups own twice as much of the companies they work for.[59]

Beyond facilitating a low cost of capital and stock options for employees, governments can encourage tech startups by priming the pump of invention. Hence the third policy lesson: governments must invest in science—both the training of young scientists and the fundamental research that is too far removed from commercialization to attract VC funding. Investments in university laboratories must be coupled with legal provisions that allow the resulting discoveries to be commercialized. In the United States, the Bayh-Dole Act of 1980 allows universities to patent inventions made with the help of federal research grants and to license these patents to startups. As a result, many American universities have established sophisticated technology transfer offices that connect inventors to venture capitalists. Just as industrial clusters depend on rapid circulation of capital and people, so intellectual property must be freed to seek its most productive uses.

The last broad policy lesson is that governments should think globally. They must compete to attract foreign scientists and entrepreneurs by handing out visas liberally. They should embrace internationally accepted tax provisions and legal forms with which foreign venture capitalists feel comfortable. They should encourage young companies to list on foreign stock markets if domestic ones are underdeveloped. They should not privilege their own firms at the expense of open global competition. The more a country can link itself to other economies, the greater the incentive for venture capitalists to scout out startups: a larger potential consumer market makes for a larger investment opportunity. Israel has flourished partly because its startups aim from their inception to make something that Americans will buy. Europe's standout successes such as Skype and Spotify have made it big by taking capital from U.S. VCs and selling to U.S. consumers.

For politicians who worry about technology's geopolitical impact, it's tempting to get the government directly involved in subsidizing venture capital. But this is a mistake. In most cases, four simple steps will pay off more. Encourage limited partnerships. Encourage stock options. Invest in scientific education and research. Think globally.

◆

How should the United States respond to the China challenge in particular? Here, there are three policy levers to consider. The United States could curb further U.S. technology investments in China. It could obstruct Chinese investments from coming into the United States. It could seek to protect its intellectual property by restricting the inward flow of Chinese scientists, who may be susceptible to pressure from Chinese government agents engaged in industrial espionage. All three measures would fly in the face of America's traditional economic and intellectual openness and compromise the "think globally" injunction just mentioned. Still, given the magnitude of the China challenge, each should be considered seriously.

Curbing U.S. venture investments in China is the least attractive of these options. Even though the early wave of U.S. outward investment played to China's advantage, the calculus has since shifted. China's venture industry has indigenized. Partnerships such as Qiming have little left to learn from Silicon Valley's financiers. Therefore, there is equally little strategic advantage in keeping these financiers out of China. In future, the know-how that American VCs bring to China will be more or less balanced by the profits they make and the insights that they glean. Paradoxically, the win-win story about this aspect of globalization has become true just when most observers disbelieve it.

Restricting Chinese venture investment into the United States makes more sense from a U.S. perspective. These flows have become significant: in the three years from 2017 to 2019, they amounted to $9.2 billion.[60] But the United States gains little from the presence of Chinese capital in its technology sector: it needs neither the money nor the business acumen that might come with it. The normal point in favor of a foreign venture backer does not generally apply in the case of a Chinese one: the Chinese market is effectively closed to a broad swath of U.S. technology firms, so a Chinese VC's connections at home may well be useless. Meanwhile, this limited advantage in allowing inward venture investment from China must be set against the risk: allowing Chinese investors into the venture-capital tent means that they will gain intelligence on emerging technologies. To be sure, many U.S. startups have no national-security dimension, and here Chinese involvement might seem harmless. But, as we have seen with SenseTime, tech is often dual use. What seems like a civilian technology can morph into a military one.

What about the third anti-China policy lever, obstructing Chinese scientists who want to work at U.S. universities or companies? This presents the sharpest dilemma. For the United States, the advantage of openness to Chinese immigrants is real: the United States benefits far more from Chinese scientists than from Chinese venture capital. However, the risks of openness are real, too. China's wide-ranging program of commercial espionage includes systematic attempts to recruit Chinese scientists in the United States as informers. To balance these competing arguments for openness and restrictiveness, the United States must hedge: it should remain generally open to Chinese scientific talent while fighting Chinese commercial espionage with vigorous counterespionage. If U.S.-based scientists pass secrets to foreign powers, they should be arrested and punished. The intelligence community must have adequate resources to catch them.

China is a military competitor bent on siphoning intellectual property out of other advanced economies. The United States has no choice but to defend its commercial and strategic interests: restricting inbound Chinese VC and vigorously protecting U.S. intellectual property are legitimate ways to go about this. But as well as trying to slow China down, the United States must try harder to outpace it.[61] The government should invest significantly more in scientific education and research, seeding the ground for venture-backed innovation. It should resist populist pressure to burden venture partnerships with higher taxes. It should build better collaboration between the Valley and the Pentagon so that venture-backed firms win major defense contracts. These measures cannot guarantee that the United States retains technological supremacy, because innovation races are determined by outliers; today, U.S. power would look different if Amazon or Intel did not exist, just as Chinese power would look different without the networking giant Huawei. But if the United States continues to protect and celebrate its venture-capital system, the odds are in its favor.

This claim rests on the judgment that China's heavy-handed state is less a strength than a weakness. There are strengths, to be sure: China has shown an admirable commitment to science, increasing R&D expenditure as a share of its fast-growing GDP from 0.9 percent to 2.1 percent between 2000 and 2018. In contrast, the United States has allowed national R&D expenditure to hover between 2.5 and 2.8 percent of GDP.[62] But on the negative side, China's authoritarian political culture is ultimately at odds with freethinking entrepreneurship: a government with a vested interest in the status quo won't risk upsetting the apple cart by unleashing disruptive innovation. A vivid illustration of this tension surfaced in the fall of 2020. In September, Alibaba signaled China's remarkable technological progress by unveiling the Hanguang 800, a machine-learning chip that outclassed western competitors. Given that semiconductor design had hitherto been a Chinese weak spot, the announcement was a wake-up call to U.S. chip makers. But even at this moment of triumph, Alibaba's founder, Jack Ma, found himself on the wrong side of the Chinese state. After Ma criticized the country's financial regulation, the government blocked the IPO of his payments company, Ant Group. It launched an antitrust case against Alibaba, resulting in a fine of $2.8 billion. Amid this politically inspired clampdown, Ma himself disappeared from public view for several months, and Alibaba's stock price fell by a quarter. The following spring, apparently fearing that he might soon become the next target, the billionaire founder of the rival e-emporium Pinduoduo stepped down. "It is not safe to be at the top," an associate explained grimly.[63] By the summer of 2021, this comment seemed prescient. Tencent, Didi, and the entire education-technology industry became the objects of a political crackdown, with the Communist Party's regulatory apparatus serving as prosecutor, judge, and jury.

For all the faults of the American system, it does not treat entrepreneurs this harshly. The closest Jack Ma parallel might be Amazon's Jeff Bezos, who incurred the wrath of Donald Trump because he owns the fiercely critical *Washington Post*. But this parallel serves to underscore the difference, not the similarity, between the two nations: in China, the idea that an internet tycoon could publish a daily diet of critical antigovernment reporting is unthinkable. Spend time with venture investors in China, and you sense the pressure that they feel. Gone are the days when Shirley Lin could finance Alibaba without attracting political attention; now that digital technology is power, venture capitalists are expected to serve on government committees and invest with an awareness of government priorities. On a trip to China in 2019, I interviewed a Beijing-based VC who spoke politely of the government's constructive leadership; then, when the interview was over and I switched my recorder off, the same VC denounced state interference bitterly. Although it is hard to be certain, the escalating clampdown since then seems likely to drive talent out of China. Meanwhile, half a century after Arthur Rock's heyday, Silicon Valley's freethinking and freewheeling entrepreneurial spirit remains staggering.

To savor this spirit, and to appreciate its geopolitical meaning, recall Peter Thiel's Founders Fund. Thiel is known primarily as the founder of PayPal, as the seed investor in Facebook, and as a donor to conservative causes, including the presidential candidacy of Donald Trump—the latter being enough to make him a villain in the Valley. But whatever one thinks of this trifecta, Thiel's most unexpected achievement lies elsewhere. His Founders Fund has backed both of the major defense contractors created since the cold war: SpaceX, which launches satellites for the Pentagon; and Palantir, which supplies a variety of software, including battlefield intelligence systems. By itself, this would be remarkable. Building companies with the scale and credibility to impress the military establishment is no mean feat; in fact, it is the sort of capital-intensive, long-duration challenge of which VCs are said to be incapable. But in 2017, unwilling to rest on its laurels, Founders Fund designated a partner named Trae Stephens to identify a third defense startup that might break into the major league. When Stephens scoured the Valley and came up with nothing, his comrades responded with a simple prompt. If no such company exists, start one.[64]

Four years later, the resulting unicorn, Anduril, is building a suite of next-generation defense systems. Its Lattice platform combines computer vision, machine learning, and mesh networking to create a picture of a battlefield. Its Ghost 4 sUAS is a military reconnaissance drone. Its solar-powered Sentry Towers have been deployed on the U.S.-Mexico border. In an age when artificial intelligence will overwhelm the war machines of yesteryear, Anduril's aspiration is to combine the coding virtuosity of a Google with the national-security focus of a Lockheed Martin.

For U.S. national security, Anduril could be transformative. But the company also stands as a reminder of something even more significant. It embodies the audacity of the Valley and the special way of coming at the world that animates venture capital. If others are daunted by a problem, go there. Try and fail, don't fail to try. Remember, above everything, the logic of the power law: the rewards for success will be massively greater than the costs of honorable setbacks. This invigorating set of axioms has turned America's venture-capital machine into an enduring pillar of national power. Six decades after the formation of Davis & Rock, it remains unwise to bet against it.

Acknowledgments

My greatest debt, as with past books, is to the Council on Foreign Relations, my professional home for more than a decade. Thanks to the Council's president, Richard Haass, and to James Lindsay and Shannon O'Neil, the leaders of the studies program, I have been able to devote four years to this project, a privilege that has allowed me to conduct some three hundred interviews and to assimilate sources ranging from oral histories and email troves to YouTube clips and financial filings. Richard, Jim, and Shannon were early readers of the manuscript, as were three excellent but anonymous CFR-appointed reviewers. Their tough-minded comments pushed me through the familiar stages of the second-draft struggle: anger, exhaustion, gratitude.

Like venture capitalists, nonfiction writers need networks. Council members Nick Beim, Steve Denning, and Auren Hoffman helped with early Silicon Valley introductions. Beyond the Council circle, my friend Steve Drobny, founder of Clocktower Group, connected me with VCs both in the Valley and in China. My interviews in Beijing and Shanghai were facilitated by Clocktower's Kaiwen Wang, whose translation skills and analytical advice were invaluable. In Hong Kong, Charlie Shi opened the doors to his circle of savvy China watchers. Ben Savage, the manager of Clocktower Technology Ventures, gave me a chance to glimpse the venture process from the inside by inviting me to join his fund's advisory board. Needless to say, neither Clocktower nor any of its portfolio companies feature in this book. Still, the opportunity to sit in on Clocktower pitch meetings with entrepreneurs as well as portfolio reviews with limited partners has deepened my feel for the business.

Several academic experts have been generous with their advice. Steven Kaplan of the University of Chicago helped me to navigate the murky nuances of performance data in VC, at one point explaining that the way a prominent partnership presented its returns was nothing less than "outrageous." Josh Lerner of Harvard Business School and Leslie Berlin of Stanford University provided wonderful comments on several chapters. Peter Conti-Brown of Wharton first opened my eyes to the relevance of network theory to my subject, and Niall Ferguson of Stanford's Hoover Institution showed how networks can inform historical analysis. Marguerite Gong Hancock of the Computer History Museum in Mountain View organized an expert study group that reviewed my first chapters. Laura Linard and her colleagues at Harvard Business School's Baker Library helped me to navigate the papers of early East Coast venture capitalists. I am also grateful to Council members Joe Hurd and Steve Tananbaum, and to my friends Mala Gaonkar and Erik Serrano Berntsen, who reacted thoughtfully to my manuscript. Meanwhile scores of venture investors, entrepreneurs, tech executives, startup lawyers, and endowment officers sat for multiple extended interviews. They granted access to internal correspondence, investment memos, and performance data; they held forth on cycle rides, hikes, and, in one case, while piloting an aircraft. Where possible, I have identified these sources in my notes. Inevitably some have preferred to remain anonymous.

My closest collaborators these past four years have been the talented research associates who worked with me at the Council on Foreign Relations. Maiya Moncino helped to figure out the shape of the story and spent two years assimilating sources on the early history of venture, from the financing of Fairchild to the IPO of Apple. Cybèle Greenberg helped me to understand the rise of China's digital economy, devouring all there was to read about Silicon Valley's interactions with Chinese entrepreneurs and the surprisingly American origins of China's tech industry. Ismael Farooqui covered the Valley in the later period, delving especially deeply into the story of Y Combinator, the financing of UUNET, and the governance traumas of the unicorns. A succession of wonderful interns and freelancers filled in numerous gaps: James Goebel, Alan Liu, Aaron Pezzullo, Sabriyya Pate, Zaib Rasool, Jenny Samuels, Ezra Schwarzbaum, Jo Stavdal, Robert Wickers, and Alex Yergin. Arriving at the tail end of the project, Arif Harianawala helped to put together the charts in the appendix. I should also like to thank Toby Greenberg for her work on the picture insert; Mia Council of Penguin Press, who shepherded the manuscript through the production process; and Penguin's copyediting wizards, who have the eyes of many eagles.

Of course, I have saved some of the best until the very last. My huge appreciation and thanks go to my agent, Chris Parris-Lamb, and to my Penguin editors, Scott Moyers in New York and Laura Stickney in London. It was Scott's idea that I should tackle venture capital. In fact, though I perhaps should not admit it, Scott has suggested the subjects of three of my five books, failing to spark the other two only because at the time we hadn't met each other. With an eye for promising projects and a sixth sense for keeping them on track, he is the publishing equivalent of the best sort of venture capitalist. Meanwhile Chris was the first to see that the idea of the power law could be central to my project, thereby providing me with both a title and an organizing concept. Laura, for her part, has a magical eye for the deft cut. Time and again, she saved me from stepping on my lines. I count myself lucky to have worked with this dream team.

Appendix

CHARTS

WINNER TAKES MOST
U.S. Venture Performance, 95th, 75th, 50th, and 25th Percentile

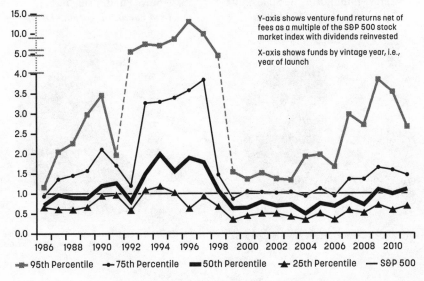

Y-axis shows venture fund returns net of fees as a multiple of the S&P 500 stock market index with dividends reinvested

X-axis shows funds by vintage year, i.e., year of launch

●—■— 95th Percentile   —●— 75th Percentile   ■■■ 50th Percentile   —▲— 25th Percentile   —— S&P 500

Source: Steven N. Kaplan; Burgiss data.

Vintages after 2011 have been excluded because funds have not yet matured.

VC WINNERS WIN BIGGER
Internal Rate of Return for investment strategies, 2004–2016 vintage years

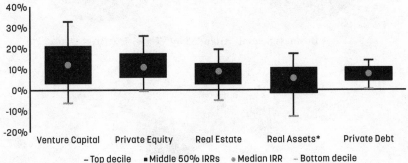

− Top decile   ■ Middle 50% IRRs   ● Median IRR   − Bottom decile

Source: PitchBook.

*Real Assets include natural resources, infrastructure, timber, metals, etc.

California Ascendant

U.S. Venture Fundraising by State, 2004
Total Fundraising: $17.0 billion

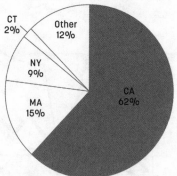

PA 3%
DC 3%
TX 5%
CT 11%
WA 4%
NY 5%
MA 14%
Other 11%
CA 44%

Source: NVCA Yearbook; Data Provided by PitchBook.

U.S. Venture Fundraising by State, 2019
Total Fundraising: $50.5 billion

CT 2%
Other 12%
NY 9%
MA 15%
CA 62%

State is determined by location of the VC fund or VC partnership.

The Diversity Deficit

VC Investment Partners, by Race

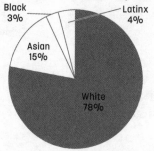

Black 3%
Latinx 4%
Asian 15%
White 78%

VC Investment Partners, by Gender

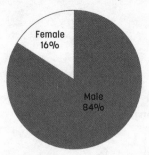

Female 16%
Male 84%

Business Schools Attended by VCs with MBAs

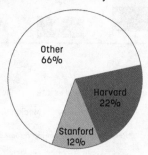

Other 66%
Harvard 22%
Stanford 12%

Sources: VC Human Capital Survey, Deloitte, NVCA, Venture Forward, 2021; Gompers and Wang, "Diversity in Innovation," 2017.

Changing Fortunes

Top Venture Partnerships, by Period

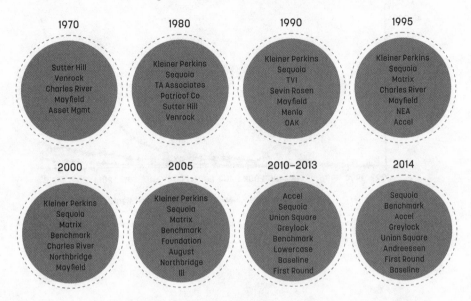

1970
Sutter Hill
Venrock
Charles River
Mayfield
Asset Mgmt

1980
Kleiner Perkins
Sequoia
TA Associates
Patricof Co
Sutter Hill
Venrock

1990
Kleiner Perkins
Sequoia
TVI
Sevin Rosen
Mayfield
Menlo
OAK

1995
Kleiner Perkins
Sequoia
Matrix
Charles River
Mayfield
NEA
Accel

2000
Kleiner Perkins
Sequoia
Matrix
Benchmark
Charles River
Northbridge
Mayfield

2005
Kleiner Perkins
Sequoia
Matrix
Benchmark
Foundation
August
Northbridge
III

2010–2013
Accel
Sequoia
Union Square
Greylock
Benchmark
Lowercase
Baseline
First Round

2014
Sequoia
Benchmark
Accel
Greylock
Union Square
Andreessen
First Round
Baseline

Source: Joe Dowling, Brown University Investment Office; Trusted Insight.

China's Rise

**Venture Fundraising
by Region, 2006–2009**
*Total Fundraising 2006–2009:
$166.7 billion*

**Venture Fundraising
by Region, 2016–2019**
*Total Fundraising 2016–2019:
$430.6 billion*

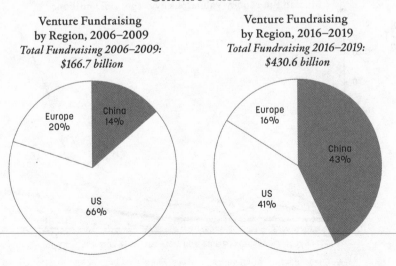

Europe 20%
China 14%
US 66%

Europe 16%
China 43%
US 41%

Source: U.S.—NVCA, Statista; China—Zero2IPO;
Europe—PitchBook.

European data converted to USD using annual rates.

SOFTWARE EATS VC
Value of venture-backed companies

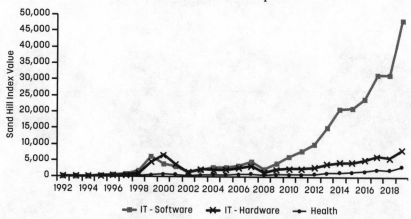

Source: Sand Hill Econometrics.

Index values are calculated from funding rounds for 33,000 venture-backed companies.

THE UNICORN BUBBLE
Median Pre-Money Valuations by Stage, USD millions

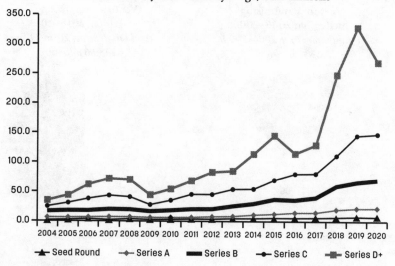

Source: Cambridge Associates; PitchBook Data.

Notes

INTRODUCTION: UNREASONABLE PEOPLE

1. Patrick Brown, interview by the author, Feb. 15, 2019.
2. Nick Rufford and Jeremy Clarkson, "Can the Impossible Burger Save the World?," *Sunday Times* (London), April 16, 2017.
3. Rufford and Clarkson, "Can the Impossible Burger Save the World?"
4. Vinod Khosla, "The Innovator's Ecosystem," Khosla Ventures, Dec. 1, 2011, khoslaventures.com/wp-content/uploads/The-Innovator%E2%80%99s-Ecosystem.pdf.
5. This chapter draws on multiple conversations with Khosla, notably two long interviews on July 31, 2017, and July 30, 2018.
6. Patrick Brown, "Food Fight to Turn Back Climate Change," interview by Tina Seelig, Stanford eCorner, Dec. 6, 2017, YouTube, youtu.be/cDiNC89Tqbg.
7. Khosla, author interviews.
8. Khosla, "Innovator's Ecosystem."
9. "Arrogance, hubris, all are just a necessary part of imagining a future that's very different." Khosla, author interviews.
10. Patrick Brown, "Impossible Foods CEO Pat Brown Speaks to Harvard Students," Green Harvard, Nov. 14, 2017, YouTube, www.youtube.com/watch?v=Fi1GMTwSZns.
11. Brown, "Food Fight to Turn Back Climate Change."
12. The amount of the investment has been reported as $7 million and $9 million, but records at Khosla Ventures show that the initial investment was $3 million.
13. Khosla, author interviews.
14. Asked how conscious he is of the power law, Khosla responded, "I think about it all the time." He added that he had taken a sabbatical at the Santa Fe Institute in order to study complex systems with power-law outcomes. Khosla, author interviews.
15. A further gauge of the stability of the S&P 500 is that between 1985 and 2015 the index moved more than 6 percent on only 19 out of 7,817 days.
16. Carry trades, volatility selling, and momentum following are examples of popular trading strategies that discount the possibility of extreme events. Although they risk large losses when extreme events happen, they are popular because the distribution of price changes is much closer to a normal one than a power-law one.
17. Benedict Evans, "In Praise of Failure," Aug. 10, 2016, ben-evans.com/benedictevans/2016/4/28/winning-and-losing.
18. Calculation based on Bloomberg data. A "subindustry group" in the S&P 500 usually comprises between five and ten companies.

19. Tren Griffin, *A Dozen Lessons for Entrepreneurs* (New York: Columbia University Press, 2017), 125.

20. Peter Thiel, *Zero to One: Notes on Startups, or How to Build the Future*, with Blake Masters (London: Virgin Books, 2014), 86. Thiel adds, with some hyperbole, "The power law . . . is the law of the universe." Ibid., 83.

21. Griffin, *Dozen Lessons for Entrepreneurs*, 146.

22. Sebastian Mallaby, *More Money Than God: Hedge Funds and the Making of a New Elite* (New York: Penguin Press, 2010), 119.

23. Andy Rachleff, formerly a venture partner at Benchmark, estimates, based on research in the late 1990s, that in the United States each year there are only around fifteen startups, plus or minus three, that will someday hit $100 million or more in revenue. Usually, these companies tend to grow far beyond $100 million and return multiples of 40x or higher. Andy Rachleff, "Demystifying Venture Capital Economics, Part 1," *Wealthfront* (blog), June 19, 2014, blog.wealthfront.com/venture-capital-economics.

24. Thiel, *Zero to One*, 102.

25. The Horsley Bridge data indicate that VC funds with the highest incidence of zeros nonetheless rack up the best overall performance. Evans, "In Praise of Failure."

26. Khosla, author interviews. The Kleiner profit reached this extraordinary size thanks to the post-IPO performance of the stock. For a list of the largest VC jackpots, with Juniper as the largest of all, see Rolfe Winkler, "Bet on Snap Shows Luck's Role in Venture Business," *Wall Street Journal*, March 2, 2017.

27. The rival was Redback Networks. The sale was for $4.3 billion. Khosla, author interviews.

28. Scott Thurm, "A Quiet Man Puts Some Sizzle in Latest Deal Involving Cisco," *Wall Street Journal*, Aug. 27, 1999.

29. In the early years of the twenty-first century, a leading university endowment calculated which venture capitalists had generated the largest cumulative profits. It considered vintage year funds 1994 through 1998 and assumed that the endowment liquidated distributed shares in a short period, as is normal practice. On this measure, Khosla came out on top. The second most prodigious profit maker was John Doerr, also of Kleiner Perkins.

30. Laura M. Holson, "A Capitalist Venturing in the Worlds of Computers and Religion," *New York Times*, Jan. 3, 2000.

31. Vinod Khosla, "Black Swan Thesis of Energy Transformation," Khosla Ventures, Aug. 28, 2011, khoslaventures.com/black-swans-thesis-of-energy-transformation.

32. "I always tell our CEOs, don't plan. Keep testing the assumptions and iterating." Khosla, author interviews.

33. Paul Graham, the cofounder of Y Combinator, was conscious of how he was replicating the strengths of corporations when he backed entrepreneurs. "When we first started YC, I thought of it explicitly as a distributed corporation. Another thing YC in particular reproduces from corporations is colleagues, except they're fellow founders instead of coworkers." Graham, email to the author, May 31, 2021.

34. The top four first-time venture funds raised in 2017 were all based in China.

35. See CB Insights, "The Global Unicorn Club." As of August 2020, the club boasted 483 members.

36. Academic survey work confirms that one in five venture capitalists do not even attempt to forecast cash flows when making an investment decision. See Paul A. Gompers et al., "How Do Venture Capitalists Make Decisions?," *Journal of Financial Economics* 135, no. 1 (Jan. 2020): 169–90.

37. Marc Andreessen, "It's Time to Build," Andreessen Horowitz website, April 18, 2020, a16z.com/2020/04/18/its-time-to-build.

38. NVCA-Deloitte Human Capital Survey, 3rd ed., March 2021, figs. 1 and 2.

39. The updating of growth theory is being spearheaded by economists such as Philippe Aghion of the College de France.

CHAPTER ONE: ARTHUR ROCK AND LIBERATION CAPITAL

1. The term "defection capital" was coined by Tom Wolfe in his classic essay "The Tinkerings of Robert Noyce," *Esquire*, Dec. 1983, web.stanford.edu/class/e145/2007_fall/materials/noyce.html.

2. The presence of an excellent research university is clearly an inadequate explanation of regional growth. Pittsburgh did not emerge as a tech hub, despite the engineering excellence of Carnegie Mellon. Similarly, the presence of a research park explains little. Modern experience with such parks suggests that they have no measurable impact on high-tech job creation. See Josh Lerner, *Boulevard of Broken Dreams: Why Public Efforts to Boost Entrepreneurship and Venture*

Capital Have Failed—and What to Do About It (Princeton, N.J.: Princeton University Press, 2009), 115.

3. Walter Isaacson, *The Innovators: How a Group of Hackers, Geniuses, and Geeks Created the Digital Revolution* (New York: Simon & Schuster, 2014), 155.

4. Margaret O'Mara, *The Code: Silicon Valley and the Remaking of America* (New York: Penguin Press, 2019), 110.

5. Observing the rapid increase in defense spending in Northern California during the 1950s, commentators forget that this increase occurred elsewhere as well. According to one study, California's share of prime military contracts had risen to 26 percent of the national total by the end of the Korean War. But three-quarters of the money went to other states, and within California the bulk went to aerospace contractors in Los Angeles and San Diego. See Stuart W. Leslie, "How the West Was Won: The Military and the Making of Silicon Valley," in *Technological Competitiveness: Contemporary and Historical Perspectives on Electrical, Electronics, and Computer Industries*, ed. William Aspray (Piscataway, N.J.: IEEE Press, 1993), 78. As of the mid-1950s, MIT attracted more federal funding than any other university, and Harvard came second. See O'Mara, *Code*, 38. In sum, it is true that military dollars supported both university research and, via procurement spending, the growth of private businesses, but it is not clear that this factor explains why Silicon Valley emerged as America's leading innovation hub. Indeed, Silicon Valley only overtook the Boston area in the late 1970s and 1980s—precisely when federal funding and military procurement became less important.

6. Steven Levy, *Hackers: Heroes of the Computer Revolution* (Sebastopol, Calif.: O'Reilly Media, 2010), 14.

7. Spencer E. Ante, *Creative Capital: Georges Doriot and the Birth of Venture Capital* (Boston: Harvard Business Press, 2008), 167.

8. Another unpersuasive theory about Silicon Valley's advantage emphasizes the weather. Aside from the fact that the weather isn't bad in Santa Barbara and Los Angeles, two university towns that were among the four original hubs for the Pentagon's ARPANET, it isn't quite clear that weather attracted engineering talent. In his classic history of early programmers, Steven Levy reports that luring engineers from MIT to San Francisco was "no small feat, since hackers were generally opposed to the requirements of California life, particularly driving and recreational exposure to the sun." Levy, *Hackers*, 134.

9. To be sure, some inventions did originate in the Valley: the microprocessor (Intel); the computer mouse (Xerox PARC); and so on. But the point is that Northern California's dominance of technology entrepreneurship is far more pronounced than its dominance of tech invention. Chong-Moon Lee et al., eds., *The Silicon Valley Edge: A Habit for Innovation and Entrepreneurship* (Stanford, Calif.: Stanford University Press), 3.

10. "We Owe It All to the Hippies," *Time*, March 1, 1995.

11. Walter Isaacson, *Steve Jobs* (New York: Simon & Schuster, 2011), 364.

12. David Laws, "Fairchild, Fairchildren, and the Family Tree of Silicon Valley," *CHM Blog*, Computer History Museum, Dec. 20, 2016, computerhistory.org/blog/fairchild-and-the-fairchildren.

13. The quotation is from Robert Noyce, later the Traitorous Eight's leader. See T. R. Reid, *The Chip: How Two Americans Invented the Microchip and Launched a Revolution* (New York: Random House Trade Paperbacks, 2001), 87.

14. Wolfe's description of Shockley as having a "roundish" face is belied by photographs. Wolfe, "Tinkerings of Robert Noyce."

15. Leslie Berlin, *The Man Behind the Microchip: Robert Noyce and the Invention of Silicon Valley* (New York: Oxford University Press, 2006), 69–70. See also Wolfe, "Tinkerings of Robert Noyce."

16. Joel N. Shurkin, *Broken Genius: The Rise and Fall of William Shockley, Creator of the Electronic Age* (New York: Palgrave Macmillan, 2006), 174–75.

17. Isaacson, *Innovators*, 164.

18. AnnaLee Saxenian, *Regional Advantage: Culture and Competition in Silicon Valley and Route 128* (Cambridge, Mass.: Harvard University Press, 1996), 79.

19. Shurkin, *Broken Genius*, 177.

20. William H. Whyte, *The Organization Man* (New York: Simon & Schuster, 1956), 217.

21. The engineer was Victor Grinich. Berlin, *Man Behind the Microchip*, 74.

22. Jerry Borrell, "They Would Be Gods," *Upside*, Oct. 2001.

23. Shurkin, *Broken Genius*, 177.

24. Beckman's company was public, but he owned 40 percent of the shares himself, affording de facto autonomy. Robert E. Bedingfield, "Along the Highways and Byways of Finance," *New York Times*, Nov. 27, 1955.

25. Gordon E. Moore, interview by Rob Walker, *Silicon Genesis: Oral Histories of Semiconductor Industry Pioneers*, March 3, 1995, landley.net/history/mirror/interviews/Moore.html.

26. Roger Lowenstein, *Buffett: The Making of an American Capitalist* (New York: Random House, 2008), 53–54.

27. Francis Bello, "The Prudent Boston Gamble," *Fortune*, Nov. 1952. In another reflection of the investment climate of the 1950s, the tech investment banker Bill Hambrecht recalls, "If you went into the business in the late '50s, as I did, you were strongly influenced by Graham and Dodd. I mean, that was kind of the bible. And you bumped into it all the time. Every time you'd go and talk to an investor." Hambrecht, interview by the author, Feb. 7, 2018.

28. The phrase "venture capital" had also cropped up in 1938, when Lammot du Pont, the president of E. I. du Pont de Nemours & Company, spoke before the U.S. Senate Committee to Investigate Unemployment and Relief. "By 'venture capital' I mean that capital which will go into an enterprise and not expect an immediate return, but will take its chances on getting an ultimate return," du Pont clarified. See Hearings Before a Special Committee to Investigate Unemployment and Relief (Washington, D.C.: U.S. Government Printing Office, 1938). Likewise, Jean Witter, of the San Francisco investment bank Dean Witter & Company, used the term "venture capital" in his 1939 address to the Investment Bankers Association of America. See Martha L. Reiner, "Innovation and the Creation of Venture Capital Organizations," *Business and Economic History* 20, no. 2 (1991). However, this phrasemaking failed to stick, and the term "venture capital" was not widely recognized until at least the 1960s.

29. Martha Louise Reiner, "The Transformation of Venture Capital: A History of Venture Capital Organizations in the United States" (PhD diss., University of California, Berkeley, 1989), 141–42.

30. Udayan Gupta, ed., *Done Deals: Venture Capitalists Tell Their Stories* (Boston: Harvard Business School Press, 2000), 96.

31. Whitney's fund reportedly doubled its value between February 1946 and August 1951. Inflation in this period came to a cumulative total of 43 percent, and the S&P 500 returned a total of 75 percent to investors who reinvested dividends.

32. Whitney's fund recognized its poor performance and shifted toward safer, more mature investments. Tom Nicholas, *VC: An American History* (Cambridge, Mass.: Harvard University Press, 2019), 308.

33. The third voice was that of Benno Schmidt. See Gupta, *Done Deals*, 98. As noted earlier, the term "venture capital" had been used by others, undermining Whitney's claim to be the father of the sector.

34. "Made General Partner in J. H. Whitney & Co.," *New York Times*, Oct. 3, 1947, nytimes.com/1947/10/13/archives/made-general-partner-in-jh-whitney-co.html.

35. Pitch Johnson recalled visiting companies in the Santa Clara valley after forming a venture partnership in 1962. "We'd tell them that we were venture capitalists. They had no idea what that meant." Likewise, Johnson's business partner, William Draper, remembered, "My wife used to tell her friends I was in private banking because no one knew what venture capital was." See "Franklin P. 'Pitch' Johnson Jr., MBA 1952—Alumni—Harvard Business School," Harvard University (website), alumni.hbs.edu/stories/Pages/story-bulletin.aspx?num=11. See also John Sterlicchi, "Six Pioneers in Venture Capital Mix Sound Advice and a Few Reminiscences," *Upside*, 2001, ivp.com/Articles/dennis_up_2_2001.htm.

36. John W. Wilson, *The New Venturers: Inside the High-Stakes World of Venture Capital* (Reading, Mass.: Addison-Wesley, 1985), 15. See also George Tucker, "A Great Many Irons in Rockefeller Fire," *Washington Post*, Jan. 2, 1949.

37. Tucker, "Great Many Irons in Rockefeller Fire." Rockefeller also said, "I like doing constructive things with my money rather than just trying to make more." Nicholas, *VC*, 309.

38. Wilson, *New Venturers*, 17.

39. The return is calculated from January 1946 to January 1961, with dividends reinvested.

40. Reid Dennis, "Reid Dennis: Early Bay Area Venture Capitalists: Shaping the Economic and Business Landscape," interview by Sally Smith Hughes, Regional Oral History Office, Bancroft Library, University of California, Berkeley, 2009, 13, digitalassets.lib.berkeley.edu/roho/ucb/text/dennis_reid.pdf.

41. Reid Dennis, email to the author, March 8, 2018. See also Reid Dennis, "Institutional Venture Partners," in Gupta, *Done Deals*, 181.

42. Timothy Hay, "Five Questions with Reid Dennis, a VC Investor Since 1952," *WSJ* (blog), June 24, 2009,blogs.wsj.com/venturecapital/2009/06/24/five-questions-with-reid-dennis-a-vc-investor-since-1952.

43. Dennis, "Institutional Venture Partners," 181.

44. Wilson, *New Venturers*, 49.
45. The Group could generally raise an additional $200,000 to $300,000 from its contacts in the financial community. Dennis, "Reid Dennis: Early Bay Area Venture Capitalists."
46. Dennis, email to the author, March 6, 2018. See also Dennis, "Reid Dennis: Early Bay Area Venture Capitalists."
47. Dennis, "Institutional Venture Partners," 183.
48. According to Dennis, the Group financed about five or six deals per year and between twenty-two and twenty-four in total. Dennis, email to the author, March 6, 2018. The Group was formalized as the Western Association of Small Business Investment Corporations in 1962, and the Western Association of Venture Capitalists in 1969. The Group was also part of the launchpad for Dennis to found Institutional Venture Associates in 1974.
49. Ante, *Creative Capital*, xv–xvi.
50. "Venture Capital, American Research Development Corporation, 1946 | The MIT 150 Exhibition," accessed Oct. 13, 2017, museum.mit.edu/150/78.
51. MIT's role in establishing American Research and Development underscores the fact that Stanford was not exceptional in encouraging private technology ventures. However, it should be added that ARD suffered a setback in the mid-1950s when MIT, whose president, Karl Compton, had been instrumental in its founding, underwent a change of heart. In 1953, the university demanded that its name be expunged from all ARD reports and publications, a U-turn that seems to have been behind Doriot's lament, written for ARD's November 1953 annual meeting, that "venture capital is not fashionable anymore." The following year, Compton died, depriving Doriot of an ally and leaving MIT's stance on ARD to be determined by its treasurer, Horace Ford, with whom Doriot did not get along. In 1955, MIT completed this process of estrangement, selling all of its ARD stock. Investing in startups was not consistent with how "men of prudence, discretion, and intelligence manage their own affairs," the university had concluded. Still, none of this prevented ARD from backing firms such as Digital Equipment Corporation that were founded by MIT faculty members. See Ante, *Creative Capital*, 138. See also Saxenian, *Regional Advantage*, 15.
52. ARD acquired additional shares that had been set aside to reward a new manager who never materialized. Ante, *Creative Capital*, 151.
53. ARD reaped $26.4 million from sale of Digital Equipment stock in 1968. In addition, it held Digital stock worth $355 million when it closed its books at the end of 1971, ahead of its sale to Textron in 1972. See Patrick Liles, "Sustaining the Venture Capital Firm" (PhD diss., Harvard Business School, 1977), 83. Based on the initial equity investment of $70,000, this would imply a return of 5,442x. However, sources differ on the amount of equity that ARD ultimately injected into Digital; some suggest the total rose to $200,000, implying that ARD's investment in Digital was a 1,907x. See Tom Nicholas and David Chen, "Georges Doriot and American Venture Capital Case Study," Harvard Business School Case 812-110, Jan. 2012 (revised Aug. 2015). Meanwhile, Ante writes that ARD's investment in Digital was a 700x. See Ante, *Creative Capital*, xviii. This dismaying range of estimates illustrates the opacity of even a well-studied venture firm.
54. ARD realized just over $20 million from exits of companies other than Digital Equipment. In addition, it had unrealized gains of $77 million when it closed its books at the end of 1971. See Liles, "Sustaining the Venture Capital Firm," 83.
55. Agreeing with Ante, Nicholas notes, "ARD is widely recognized as a key entity in the evolution of the modern venture capital industry." Nicholas, *VC*, 108.
56. Ante, *Creative Capital*, 172–73.
57. Ante, *Creative Capital*, 133.
58. Ante, *Creative Capital*, 172–73.
59. Doriot, *ARD Annual Report*, 1971, George F. Doriot papers, Baker Library, Harvard Business School.
60. Ante, *Creative Capital*, xix.
61. The public-company structure was also less tax efficient than the partnership structure. In cases where ARD owned more than 10 percent of a company, it paid capital gains on its holding; then, when the proceeds were paid out as dividends, ARD's investors would face a second round of taxation. In contrast, partnerships are pass-through entities, meaning that gains are taxed only once. See Nicholas, *VC*, 120.
62. Ante, *Creative Capital*, 185.
63. Ante, *Creative Capital*, 191–92.
64. Wilson, *New Venturers*, 20.
65. Ante, *Creative Capital*, 167.

66. Ante, *Creative Capital*, 201. Doriot's instincts were reinforced by the regulatory ban on issuing stock or stock options to ARD employees. Nicholas, *VC*, 131.

67. For example, in 1955 ARD's shares traded at just 65 percent of their net asset value. Nicholas, *VC*, 126. See also Ante, *Creative Capital*, 137.

68. ARD's net asset value per share rose from $2.01 in 1946 to $69.67 in 1971, a return of almost 35x. Over this period the market price of an ARD share rose from $2.08 to $54.88, suggesting a return of just over 26x. (ARD paid modest dividends, so these barely affect the calculation.) Between February 1947 and December 1971, the years of ARD's operation, the S&P 500 rose a bit under 18x if dividends were reinvested. ARD data from Georges Doriot to stockholders, Feb. 4, 1972. See also Liles, "Sustaining the Venture Capital Firm," 83.

69. Peter Meyer, "Eugene Kleiner: Engineer, Venture Capitalist, Founding Father of Silicon Valley," Office of University Relations, Polytechnic University, Brooklyn, Feb. 2006, 17, engineering.nyu .edu/news/_doc/article_69/giantsofpoly-kleiner.pdf.

70. The author is grateful to Arthur Rock for multiple conversations in 2017 and 2018 and for repeated access to his personal archive, facilitated by Wendy Downing.

71. Rock was once so violently attacked that his parents brought suit against the bully. Rock recalled his childhood in several conversations with the author.

72. "To leave a company with all the backing in the world from Beckman and all the prestige of Shockley's Nobel Prize, because he was not behaving right. Well, that showed character." Rock, interview by the author, Feb. 7, 2018.

73. Rock to Kleiner, June 21, 1957, Arthur Rock personal archive.

74. Jay Last, interview by the author, Sept. 20, 2017. See also Michael Malone, *The Intel Trinity: How Robert Noyce, Gordon Moore, and Andy Grove Built the World's Most Important Company* (New York: HarperBusiness, 2014), 14. Other sources have variations on this interchange. See, for example, Gordon Moore, "The Accidental Entrepreneur," *Engineering and Science* (Summer 1994): 24, calteches.library.caltech.edu/3777/1/Moore.pdf.

75. Karl Marx famously predicted that employees would be exploited by company proprietors and would suffer a form of demoralization he called "alienation." Ironically, it took a hypercapitalist— a venture capitalist—to liberate the eight demoralized employees at Shockley Semiconductor.

76. Last, author interview; "Fairchild 50th Anniversary Panel," silicongenesis.stanford.edu /transcripts/Fairchild%2050th.htm.

77. Arnold Thackray, David Brock, and Rachel Jones, *Moore's Law: The Life of Gordon Moore, Silicon Valley's Quiet Revolutionary* (New York: Basic Books, 2015).

78. Rock, interview by the author, Feb. 7, 2018.

79. Rock, interview by the author, Feb. 7, 2018.

80. The typical Hayden deal involved raising capital for a business that had already gotten started; drumming up money for a nonexistent venture would constitute a radical departure. Besides, the $1 million–plus target was almost without precedent. In 1956, General Transistor's initial public offering had netted just $300,000; similarly, in 1957, ARD got Digital Equipment going for only $100,000.

81. Berlin, *Man Behind the Microchip*, 78.

82. Berlin, *Man Behind the Microchip*, 81.

83. In his classic essay on the Traitorous Eight, Tom Wolfe wrote of Noyce's "100 ampere eyes." Wolfe, "Tinkerings of Robert Noyce."

84. Rock, author interviews. See also Berlin, *Man Behind the Microchip*, 81.

85. Berlin, *Man Behind the Microchip*, 81.

86. Michael S. Malone, *The Big Score: The Billion-Dollar Story of Silicon Valley* (Garden City, N.Y.: Doubleday, 1985), 70.

87. Wilson, *New Venturers*, 33. See also Arthur Rock, "Arthur Rock: Early Bay Area Venture Capitalists: Shaping the Economic and Business Landscape," interview by Sally Smith Hughes, 2008, Regional Oral History Office, Bancroft Library, University of California, Berkeley, 2009, 21, digitalassets.lib.berkeley.edu/roho/ucb/text/rock_arthur.pdf.

88. Felda Hardymon, Tom Nicholas, and Liz Kind, "Arthur Rock Case Study," Harvard Business School, Jan. 18, 2013, 3.

89. A meticulous man in his sixties, Fairchild was a bon vivant who frequented New York's posh 21 Club and wore "a fresh pretty girl every few days like a new boutonniere," according to *Fortune*. See "Multifarious Sherman Fairchild," *Fortune*, May 1960, 170. See also "Sherman Fairchild— Man of Few Miscalculations," *Electronic News*, Sept. 13, 1965. Fairchild had inherited a fortune from his father, one of the original investors in IBM.

90. Berlin, *Man Behind the Microchip*, 85.

91. Malone, *Intel Trinity*, 14–15.
92. At Shockley, the Traitorous Eight had each earned between $8,100 and $12,000. Berlin, *Man Behind the Microchip*, 86.
93. Fairchild Camera and Instrument is often said to have provided $1.5 million. See Rock, "Arthur Rock: Early Bay Area Venture Capitalists," 25. However, Berlin reports that Fairchild lent $1.38 million, also providing an allowance of $3,000 per month for almost eighteen months. See Berlin, "Robert Noyce and Fairchild Semiconductor," 76. Fairchild Semiconductor's founding documents appear to corroborate Berlin's numbers. See Bo Lojek, *History of Semiconductor Engineering* (New York: Springer, 2007), 105.
94. Fairchild Camera's option expired once Fairchild Semiconductor had three successive years of net earnings greater than $300,000 per year. After that, there was an additional period in which Fairchild Camera could buy Fairchild Semiconductor for $5 million. Berlin, *Man Behind the Microchip*, 89.
95. Malone, *Big Score*, 89.
96. Wolfe, "Tinkerings of Robert Noyce"; Meyer, "Eugene Kleiner," 18; Berlin, "Robert Noyce and Fairchild Semiconductor, 1957–1968."
97. Jay Last and Jean Hoerni were Rock's frequent climbing partners.
98. Wilson, *New Venturers*, 34. See also Christophe Lécuyer, "Fairchild Semiconductor and Its Influence," in Lee et al., *Silicon Valley Edge*, 167.
99. Memorandum from Rock to Coyle, March 27, 1958, Rock personal archive. The operating margin comes from a separate memo written by Rock around this time and contained in his archive.
100. This number for earnings is the author's estimate and is only approximate. In 1959, Fairchild Semiconductor employed about 40 scientists earning about $12,000 on average, meaning a salary bill of around $480,000. There were 140 other employees, with average salaries of perhaps half that, implying a total salary bill of about $1.3 million. (The staff head count in 1959 and 1960 is reported in Lécuyer, *Fairchild Semiconductor and Its Influence*, 180.) Costs of facilities, machinery, and raw materials might have added perhaps $1 million. This implies pretax earnings of $4.2 million. The corporate tax rate was 52 percent, so post-tax earnings would have been about $2 million. I am grateful to Arthur Rock for advising on this estimation.
101. Berlin, "Robert Noyce and Fairchild Semiconductor, 1957–1968," 81.
102. Eastman Kodak's price-earnings multiple was lower than IBM's, ranging between twenty-one and thirty-five times earnings in 1959. Because Fairchild was growing fast, it seems fair to take the higher end of IBM's 1959 multiple as the benchmark. See "Changing Times," *Kiplinger Magazine*, Nov. 1967, 23.
103. As noted above, ARD's return on Digital Equipment was larger. But that return materialized over fourteen years, not two years.

CHAPTER TWO: FINANCE WITHOUT FINANCE

1. Peter F. Drucker, "The New Tycoons: America's Next Twenty Years, Part III," *Harper's Magazine*, May 1955, harpers.org/archive/1955/05/americas-next-twenty-years-3.
2. Charles M. Noone and Stanley M. Rubel, *SBICs: Pioneers in Organized Venture Capital* (Chicago: Capital, 1970), 30.
3. The boss was Richard E. Kelley, who took over management of the SBIC program in 1963. Leonard Sloane, "U.S. Is Changing S.B.I.C. Approach: Regulatory Stand Shifted on Investment Units," *New York Times*, Aug. 1, 1965.
4. "Franklin P. 'Pitch' Johnson Jr., MBA 1952—Alumni—Harvard Business School," Harvard Business School (website), alumni.hbs.edu/stories/Pages/story-bulletin.aspx?num=11.
5. Pitch Johnson and Frank Caufield, interview by the author, April 26, 2017.
6. William H. Draper III, *The Startup Game: Inside the Partnership Between Venture Capitalists and Entrepreneurs* (New York: Palgrave Macmillan, 2011), 31–32.
7. Draper, *Startup Game*, 33.
8. William H. Draper III, "William H. Draper III: Early Bay Area Venture Capitalists: Shaping the Economic and Business Landscape," interview by Sally Smith Hughes, 2008, Regional Oral History Office, University of California, Berkeley, 2009, 86, digitalassets.lib.berkeley.edu/roho/ucb/text/draper_william.pdf.
9. In a conversation on May 15, 2018, Draper and Johnson recalled that they got $200,000 each when the business was sold, a return of 2.7x on the $75,000 that each had put in at the outset. Over the same three years, the S&P 500 had returned about 1.7x.
10. In a variant on the SBICs' need for dividends, American Research and Development charged management fees to portfolio companies rather than extracting fees from investors, and it

financed its companies partly with convertible debt or preferred stock on which it collected interest. Again, the perverse effect was to drain capital from portfolio companies that needed capital to grow. Tom Nicholas, *VC: An American History* (Cambridge, Mass.: Harvard University Press, 2019), 125.

11. In a further sign of the SBIC program's shortcomings, nine out of ten SBICs were so frustrated by the regulations that they were circumventing them. See Martha Louise Reiner, "The Transformation of Venture Capital: A History of Venture Capital Organizations in the United States" (PhD diss., University of California, Berkeley, 1989), 282. See also Josh Lerner, *Boulevard of Broken Dreams: Why Public Efforts to Boost Entrepreneurship and Venture Capital Have Failed—and What to Do About It* (repr., Princeton, N.J.: Princeton University Press, 2012), 38. Lerner notes that the most useful result of the SBIC program was indirect: it encouraged the development of other institutions to support startups, such as specialized lawyers and data services. Equally, the SBIC program helped to train a number of investors who later thrived at private VC partnerships. See Nicholas, *VC*, 109, 141. Still, it is revealing that the three most influential venture investors of the 1960s and 1970s—Arthur Rock, Tom Perkins, and Don Valentine—had nothing to do with the SBIC format.

12. Between 1961 and 1969, SBICs generated an average return of 5 percent per year, less than the 8 percent an investor could have had from the Dow Jones stock index. Noone and Rubel, *SBICs*, 108.

13. William D. Bygrave and Jeffry A. Timmons, *Venture Capital at the Crossroads* (Boston: Harvard Business School Press, 1992), 22. See also Paul Gompers, "The Rise and Fall of Venture Capital," *Business and Economic History* 23, no. 2 (Winter 1994): 7–8.

14. Rock laid out his disaffection with the brokerage business and his reason to move west in a speech delivered to the Harvard Business School Club of San Francisco on January 31, 1962. Arthur Rock personal archive. Copy also available at the Baker Library, Harvard Business School.

15. Thomas P. Murphy, "What Makes Tommy Davis Run?," *Forbes*, April 25, 1983.

16. Arthur Rock, "Arthur Rock & Co," in *Done Deals: Venture Capitalists Tell Their Stories*, ed. Udayan Gupta (Boston: Harvard Business School Press, 2000), 142.

17. John W. Wilson, *The New Venturers: Inside the High-Stakes World of Venture Capital* (Reading, Mass.: Addison-Wesley, 1985), 15.

18. In 1959, General William Draper, father of the SBIC pioneer, had helped to found the first venture-capital limited partnership, Draper, Gaither & Anderson. But the second named partner, Rowan Gaither, was soon diagnosed with terminal cancer, and DG&A foundered. Key limited partners withdrew; Anderson's health declined; and Draper left. It fell to Davis and Rock to prove the strengths of the DG&A format. Whether Davis & Rock consciously copied the DG&A structure is unclear. Rock says he was unaware of the DG&A precedent but that Davis might have known of it. See Leslie Berlin, "The First Venture Capital Firm in Silicon Valley: Draper, Gaither & Anderson," in *Making the American Century: Essays on the Political Culture of Twentieth Century America*, ed. Bruce J. Schulman (Oxford: Oxford University Press, 2014), 158. See also Nicholas, *VC*, 158–59.

19. Rock has said in interviews that the partnership secured $5 million in callable commitments but that it did not call all the capital, because it became too preoccupied with existing portfolio companies to consider additional investments. However, the Certificate of Partnership reports total capital of $3,390,000. Upon having this pointed out, Rock conceded cheerfully that "my memory of fifty-nine years is trumped by the facts." Rock, email to the author, March 4, 2019. Rock to the Limited Partners, 1961, and Certificate of Partnership, Oct. 10, 1961, Rock personal archive. The number of limited partners is given in Rock to Jeffrey O. Henley, Feb. 7, 1967, Rock personal archive.

20. By having fewer than a hundred "accredited investors," a partnership could avoid being regulated under the Investment Company Act of 1940, which would have required it to disclose details of its portfolio. The act also banned general partners from sitting on a startup's board and capped investments at a 10 percent stake in any individual venture. Paul A. Gompers and Joshua Lerner, *The Money of Invention: How Venture Capital Creates New Wealth* (Boston: Harvard Business School Press, 2001), 89, 97.

21. Rock not only frowned on debt payments; he opposed dividend payments equally fiercely. Once, when Pete Bancroft of Bessemer confessed at the top of a ski run to having pressed a portfolio company to pay out some cash to shareholders, Rock announced that was the dumbest thing he ever heard and disappeared at top speed down the mountain. Bancroft, interview by the author, Nov. 18, 2017.

22. The rule of thumb was a fifty-fifty ownership split between entrepreneur and the venture fund, with stock for employees being taken out of both sides' allocation. (Rock, interview with the author, Nov. 16, 2017.) Although the employee allocation varied from case to case, 10 percent was typical. See Rock to Davis, Dec. 30, 1960, Rock personal archive.

23. Rock, interview by the author, Jan. 30, 2018.

24. Of the Traitorous Eight who founded Fairchild, only Robert Noyce and Gordon Moore did not invest. As the two most senior executives at Fairchild, they were barred from placing money with a venture fund that might back Fairchild competitors. Rock personal archive. See also Leslie Berlin, *The Man Behind the Microchip: Robert Noyce and the Invention of Silicon Valley* (New York: Oxford University Press, 2006), 123.

25. Rock made the same point as Davis, saying that the portfolio needed one or two grand slams so as to "average out the goofs and still make a decent return." Speech delivered to Harvard Business School Club of San Francisco, Jan. 31, 1962.

26. The Davis quotations in this paragraph and Davis & Rock's target return come from Thomas J. Davis Jr., "How to Pick a Winner in the Electronics Industry" (speech to the Western Electronic Manufacturers' Association, Palo Alto, Sept. 19, 1966), Baker Library Special Collections, Harvard Business School.

27. Rock to Davis, Dec. 30, 1960, Rock personal archive.

28. Davis, "How to Pick a Winner in the Electronics Industry."

29. Arthur Rock, "Strategy vs. Tactics from a Venture Capitalist," *Harvard Business Review*, Nov.–Dec. 1987, 63.

30. Rock, speech to Harvard Business School Club of San Francisco, Jan. 31, 1962.

31. Rock confessed, "I am not equipped to go into the laboratory and decide whether the work being done is liable to give forth with profitable sales." Rock, speech to Harvard Business School Club of San Francisco, Jan. 31, 1962.

32. Rock, "Strategy vs. Tactics." See also Rock, interview by Amy Blitz, March 2001, 9, hbs.edu/entrepreneurs/pdf/arthurrock.pdf.

33. Wilson, *New Venturers*, 36.

34. John Markoff, "An Evening with Legendary Venture Capitalist Arthur Rock in Conversation with John Markoff," Computer History Museum, May 1, 2007, 16, archive.computerhistory.org/resources/access/text/2012/05/102658253-05-01-acc.pdf.

35. Rock, interview with the author, Feb. 7, 2017.

36. Rock, "Strategy vs. Tactics," 64. Max Palevsky agreed that Rock had "an ability to listen, not so much to what people say, because that may be technical, but to what people are expressing about themselves. He has a great deal of intuition." Quoted in Felda Hardymon, Tom Nicholas, and Liz Kind, "Arthur Rock," Harvard Business School Case Study, 9-813-138, Jan. 18, 2013.

37. The interchange between Davis and Palevsky is taken mainly from Wilson, *New Venturers*, 36.

38. James Detar, "A Chip Charger to the Max; Persevere: Max Palevsky Rose from Poverty to Help Spark the Computer/Space Age," *Investor's Business Daily*, Aug. 19, 2010. The duration of the marathon conversation between Davis and Palevsky comes from Wilson, *New Venturers*, 36.

39. Wilson, *New Venturers*, 36.

40. Rock, "Strategy vs. Tactics," 66.

41. Rock, "Strategy vs. Tactics," 67.

42. The size of the initial investment is taken from Rock's archive. Regarding the multiple, Wilson reports the gain from SDS at $60 million. See Wilson, *New Venturers*, 37. Meanwhile, in several conversations, Rock put it at $100 million. It seems likely that Wilson's number reflects the value of SDS when the Davis & Rock partnership was closed, whereas Rock's number reflects its value when it was sold to Xerox in 1969. If all Davis & Rock partners had held on to the stock until the sale to Xerox, the multiple on the SDS investment would have been 389x.

43. Michael Moritz, "Arthur Rock: The Best Long-Ball Hitter Around," *Time*, Jan. 23, 1984, 64.

44. Rock's greatest contribution to SDS came when he persuaded Palevsky's sales team to sell the first SDS computer, built at a cost of $18,000, for an aggressive $100,000. Having seen Fairchild sell its semiconductors at a vast margin, Rock understood that SDS's technology was sufficiently innovative that it could command a premium and that this premium would allow it to invest in more research, further entrenching its power to price aggressively. Wilson, *New Venturers*, 39. In his speech to the HBS alumni in 1962, Rock commented, "One of the biggest mistakes companies make is pricing their product too low."

45. Rock, interview by the author, Feb. 8, 2018.

46. Wilson, *New Venturers*, 39. To put SDS's valuation in perspective, the minicomputer maker Wang Laboratories was valued at $70 million when the market closed on the day of its IPO, in

1967. Wang's valuation had been considered remarkable, but it was less than one-tenth of SDS's. Margaret O'Mara, *The Code: Silicon Valley and the Remaking of America* (New York: Penguin Press, 2019), 86.

47. Foster Parker (a limited partner in Houston) to Rock and Davis, Aug. 23, 1968, Rock personal archive.

48. Richard L. Vanderveld, "S.F. Investor Team Bankrolls High-Flying Firms of Future," *Los Angeles Times*, Aug. 28, 1967.

49. "The Money Men," *Forbes*, Nov. 1, 1968, 74.

50. Data from Venture Economics Inc.

51. Tom Wolfe, "The Tinkerings of Robert Noyce," *Esquire*, Dec. 1983, web.stanford.edu/class/e145 /2007_fall/materials/noyce.html.

52. Berlin, *Man Behind the Microchip*, 120. Before Fairchild Semiconductor, West Coast technology firms such as Varian Associates had granted stock to engineers. Nicholas, *VC*, 192.

53. Last, interview by the author, Sept. 20, 2017.

54. Berlin, *Man Behind the Microchip*, 123.

55. Rock, interview by the author, Nov. 8, 2017.

56. George A Roberts, *Distant Force: A Memoir of the Teledyne Corporation and the Man Who Created It* (Teledyne Corporation, 2007), 14. A slight variant on this account is given by Berlin, *Man Behind the Microchip*, 123.

57. "Companies | The Silicon Engine | Computer History Museum," website, accessed Sept. 13, 2017, www.computerhistory.org/siliconengine/companies.

58. The chip designer was Bob Widlar. Michael Malone, *The Intel Trinity: How Robert Noyce, Gordon Moore, and Andy Grove Built the World's Most Important Company* (New York: HarperBusiness, 2014), 31.

59. Berlin, *Man Behind the Microchip*, 150.

60. Malone, *Intel Trinity*, 34.

61. Berlin, *Man Behind the Microchip*, 151.

62. Walter Isaacson, *The Innovators: How a Group of Hackers, Geniuses, and Geeks Created the Digital Revolution* (New York: Simon & Schuster, 2014), 185.

63. Arthur Rock, "Early Bay Area Venture Capitalists: Shaping the Economic and Business Landscape," interview by Sally Smith Hughes, Regional Oral History Office, Bancroft Library, University of California, Berkeley, 2009, 47.

64. Rock himself put up $300,000 at the $5-per-share rate. The $10,000 he had been permitted to invest at the $1 rate represented his reward for arranging the financing. Rock, interview by the author, Jan. 30, 2018.

65. John Hollar and Douglas Fairbairn, "Gordon Moore and Arthur Rock Oral History Panel," Computer History Museum, July 9, 2014, 23, archive.computerhistory.org/resources/access/text /2015/09/102739934-05-01-acc.pdf.

66. Wolfe, "Tinkerings of Robert Noyce."

67. Rock recalls, "Almost all employees accepted lower wages than they could get from established companies. So I felt they should be rewarded if the company (Intel) was successful." (Rock, email to the author, March 1, 2019.) In an earlier conversation, Rock explained, "Noyce and Moore and me were the executive committee. We decided we should give options, and the question was to whom. I suggested we give it to all employees. And the question was at what stage in their employment. We decided that it would be after one year of joining. I had been on the board of other companies that granted options, so I knew how it worked." Rock, interview by the author, Nov. 8, 2017. The caveat is that in other interviews Rock has been less explicit in saying that it was his idea rather than Noyce's to give stock options to everyone, although he has never suggested the opposite.

68. Berlin, *Man Behind the Microchip*, 165.

CHAPTER THREE: SEQUOIA, KLEINER PERKINS, AND ACTIVIST CAPITAL

1. Walter Isaacson, *The Innovators: How a Group of Inventors, Hackers, Geniuses, and Geeks Created the Digital Revolution* (New York: Simon & Schuster, 2014), 212.

2. Leslie Berlin, *Troublemakers: Silicon Valley's Coming of Age* (New York: Simon & Schuster, 2017), 120.

3. Steve Coll, "When the Magic Goes," *Inc.*, Oct. 1, 1984.

4. Berlin, *Troublemakers*, 123.

5. Luke Dormehl, *The Apple Revolution: The Real Story of How Steve Jobs and the Crazy Ones Took Over the World* (London: Virgin Books, 2013), 56.

6. Berlin, *Troublemakers*, 124.

7. See Randall E. Stross, *eBoys: The First Inside Account of Venture Capitalists at Work* (New York: Ballantine Books, 2001); "Peaks and Valleys," *Inc.*, May 1, 1985, inc.com/magazine/19850501 /7289.html.

8. Nancy Keates, "A Penthouse Fit for a King," *Wall Street Journal*, July 27, 2012, www.wsj.com /news/articles/SB10000872396390444025204577545980352957576. Perkins also turned down an invitation to speak at Harvard, saying, "Sorry, but I will be in Tahiti, leaving this weekend and not returning until late April. I am going to try to capture video of big sharks at depth using my submarine. I was the first to do this with Humpback whales in Tonga in September." Tom Nicholas, *VC: An American History* (Cambridge, Mass.: Harvard University Press, 2019), 222.

9. Donald T. Valentine, "Donald T. Valentine: Early Bay Area Venture Capitalists: Shaping the Economic and Business Landscape," interview by Sally Smith Hughes, 2009, Regional Oral History Office, Bancroft Library, University of California, Berkeley, 2010, 8, digitalassets.lib.berkeley .edu/roho/ucb/text/valentine_donald.pdf.

10. Capital Research and Management still exists and is now known as the Capital Group. Valentine, "Donald T. Valentine: Early Bay Area Venture Capitalists," 22.

11. Berlin, *Troublemakers*, 127.

12. According to Gordon Crawford, a veteran portfolio manager at Capital Research, Valentine set up the Capital Management Fund to invest money from outside clients whom he himself recruited; skeptics within the Capital Group leadership had blocked the idea that Valentine should invest capital from Group clients. Meanwhile, Valentine also ran a separate vehicle called the Sequoia fund, which invested on behalf of Capital Management employees. Senior executives at Capital could invest in the Sequoia fund without paying the usual VC fees. In return, Valentine could use the health-care and pension benefits that Capital offered and could consult Capital's analysts. Crawford, interview by the author, May 15, 2018.

13. Valentine gave his daughter the middle name Ayn. He expressed his opinion of the federal government by telling his protégé Michael Moritz, "It would be easy to be optimistic if we could manage to have an earthquake on a couple of the main streets of Washington DC." Michael Moritz, *DTV* (self-published, 2020), 31.

14. Valentine, interview by the author, April 7, 2018.

15. Valentine, author interview.

16. Moritz, *DTV*, 36.

17. Valentine, author interview.

18. The size of Sequoia's first fund is sometimes given as $7 million, but sources at Sequoia confirmed $5 million to be the correct number.

19. Over the next decade, the Harvard endowment invested or committed more than $130 million to venture capital. John W. Wilson, *The New Venturers: Inside the High-Stakes World of Venture Capital* (Reading, Mass.: Addison-Wesley, 1985), 29.

20. In 1990, Yale made the first university investment in a hedge fund, Farallon Capital, extending the role of college endowments in nurturing cutting-edge investment methods.

21. Valentine, "Donald T. Valentine: Early Bay Area Venture Capitalists," 33.

22. Daniel Geller, Dayna Goldfine, and Po Bronson, *Something Ventured: Risk, Reward, and the Original Venture Capitalists*, video recording (Zeitgeist Films, 2011).

23. Wilson, *New Venturers*, 53.

24. Donald T. Valentine, "Atari," Sequoia, accessed Sept. 29, 2016, sequoiacap.com/company-story /atari-story.

25. Al Alcorn, Atari's engineering chief, recalls being asked by Bushnell to develop a home version of Pong as early as 1973. But this was just one among a stream of ideas flowing from Bushnell to the engineering department. See Allan Alcorn, "First-Hand: The Development of Pong: Early Days of Atari and the Video Game Industry," *Engineering and Technology History Wiki*, Jan. 12, 2015, ethw.org/First-Hand:The_Development_of_Pong:_Early_Days_of_Atari_and_the_Video _Game_Industry. For his part, Valentine recalled, "Only after we were persuaded that the company would be taken in the direction of a home product were we persuaded to invest." Steve L. Kent, *The Ultimate History of Video Games* (New York: Three Rivers Press, 2001).

26. The count of IPOs comes from a 1985 report by Morgan Stanley.

27. The venture-capital quotation is from Margaret O'Mara, *The Code: Silicon Valley and the Remaking of America* (New York: Penguin Press, 2019), 158. For the attrition among hedge funds, see Sebastian Mallaby, *More Money Than God: Hedge Funds and the Making of a New Elite* (New York: Penguin Press, 2010), 41.

28. Data from Venture Economics Inc.

29. O'Mara, *Code*, 168. Recalling 1975, Len Baker of Sutter Hill says, "There was a real question about whether there was a way to make a living in this business." Baker, interview by the author, Sept. 20, 2017.

30. Preliminary IPO prospectus for Atari, Al Alcorn Papers (M1758), Department of Special Collections and University Archives, Stanford University Libraries. See also Curt Vendel and Marty Goldberg, *Atari Inc.: Business Is Fun* (Carmel, N.Y.: Syzygy Press, 2012), 152.

31. Vendel and Goldberg, *Atari Inc.*, 155.

32. Valentine, author interview. The iconic Sears catalog reached most American homes, and fully 57 percent of households owned a Sears card. See Berlin, *Troublemakers*, 129.

33. Berlin, *Troublemakers*, 129.

34. The link between Valentine's mediation and the Sears buyer's visit was unclear to some Atari staff who have since described the Sears-Atari alliance without mentioning Valentine. But both Valentine and Gordon Crawford, the Capital Research investor with a large stake in Sears, recall conferring about brokering a connection between Sears and Atari. Crawford, author interview.

35. Vendel and Goldberg, *Atari Inc.*, 158.

36. Preliminary IPO prospectus for Atari, Alcorn Papers (M1758).

37. Scott Cohen, *Zap! The Rise and Fall of Atari* (Philadelphia: Xlibris, 1984), 50.

38. In 1976 there were 34 IPOs, raising a total of $234 million. In contrast, in 1969 there had been 1,026 IPOs, raising a total of $2.6 billion. Data from Morgan Stanley.

39. Wilson, *New Venturers*, 63.

40. In 1975, Valentine left Capital Group and ran Sequoia independently, though he continued to manage the fund investing on behalf of Capital employees. Crawford, author interview; Valentine, author interview.

41. Crawford, author interview. According to Berlin, Eastwood made the sandwich for Bushnell on the return flight to the West Coast. But Crawford, who was on the flight out east, is certain that he witnessed this episode. See Berlin, *Troublemakers*, 173. For his part, Valentine recalls, "That was the highlight of Nolan's trip. It was not an accident that he made Nolan a sandwich. He didn't make my sandwich. He made Nolan a sandwich."

42. Author's calculation based partly on information given in Wilson, *New Venturers*, 60. The return on the S&P 500 with dividends reinvested was 9.1 percent between June 1974 and June 1980.

43. The Qume CEO was Bob Schroeder. Baker, author interview. The boldness of West Coast venture capital helps to account for the region's strength relative to other apparently superior technology hubs. As of the mid-1970s, the Boston area dominated the minicomputer business, New York's IBM dominated the mainframe business, and Texas produced more microprocessors than California. But other regions lacked dense networks of venture capitalists and the practice of compensating people with equity. In the late 1970s, Boston received half as many VC dollars as Silicon Valley. See O'Mara, *Code*, 101, 111. Furthermore, Boston VCs were more risk averse. For example, Greylock, established in 1965, preferred to supply "developmental capital" to existing companies than to back startups. During its first twelve years of operation, the safer developmental investments drove most of the returns. Nicholas, *VC*, 163, 165–66.

44. Tom Perkins, *Valley Boy: The Education of Tom Perkins* (New York: Gotham Books, 2008), 45.

45. Perkins, *Valley Boy*, 47.

46. "Tom Perkins: Early Bay Area Venture Capitalists: Shaping the Economic and Business Landscape," interview by Sally Smith Hughes, 2009, Regional Oral History Office, Bancroft Library, University of California, Berkeley, 2010, 4, digitalassets.lib.berkeley.edu/roho/ucb/text/perkins_tom.pdf, 28.

47. The host at the breakfast was Sandy Robertson, a technology banker with whom both Perkins and Kleiner invested.

48. Sanford R. Robertson, "Sanford R. Robinson: Early Bay Area Venture Capitalists: Shaping the Economic and Business Landscape," interview by Sally Smith Hughes, Regional Oral History Office, Bancroft Library, University of California, Berkeley, 2011. See also Matt Marshall, "San Jose, Calif.–Area High-Tech Icon Dies at Age 80," *Knight-Ridder/Tribune Business News*, Nov. 25, 2003.

49. Perkins, *Valley Boy*, 103.

50. Perkins, "Tom Perkins: Early Bay Area Venture Capitalists," 31–32.

51. Perkins, "Tom Perkins: Early Bay Area Venture Capitalists," 33. Somewhat less colorfully, Kleiner concurred: "The other VCs would turn over the money to the entrepreneur and then just watch in the grandstand.... We weren't going to be checkbook investors." See Peter Meyer, "Eugene Kleiner: Engineer, Venture Capitalist, Founding Father of Silicon Valley," Office of Uni-

versity Relations, Polytechnic University, Brooklyn, Feb. 2006, engineering.nyu.edu/news/_doc/article_69/giantsofpoly-kleiner.pdf.

52. Perkins, *Valley Boy*, 101.
53. David A. Kaplan, *The Silicon Boys and Their Valley of Dreams* (New York: Perennial, 2000), 172.
54. Perkins, *Valley Boy*, 109–10.
55. Gaye I. Clemson, *Tandem Computers Unplugged: A People's History* (Campbell, Calif.: FastPencil, 2012), 19.
56. Treybig, interview by the author, April 2018.
57. Perkins, *Valley Boy*, 110–11.
58. The computer scientist was Bill Davidow. Treybig, interview by the author, April 2018.
59. The hardware engineer was Jim Katzman; the software engineer was Mike Green. Clemson, *Tandem Computers Unplugged*, 12.
60. Byers, interview by the author, May 16, 2018.
61. Perkins, *Valley Boy*, 110–11.
62. Treybig, author interview.
63. Perkins, "Tom Perkins: Early Bay Area Venture Capitalists," 39.
64. Around 1974–1975, Sutter Hill made no venture investments, preferring to buy undervalued public stocks. This proved to be a good bet, but it made life harder for startups such as Tandem. Bill Younger, interview by the author, May 16, 2018.
65. Perkins, *Valley Boy*, 112.
66. The only other venture investor who came into the deal was Pitch Johnson, the man who had rented Pontiacs with Bill Draper a decade and a half previously. But Johnson's bet on Tandem came to all of $50,000.
67. Although Tandem was not the only home run in the first Kleiner Perkins fund, the other one, Genentech, had not yet come good when KP raised its second fund in 1977. The Perkins confession is taken from Clemson, *Tandem Computers Unplugged*, 13.
68. Susan Benner, "Tandem Has a Fail-Safe Plan for Growth," *Inc.*, June 1, 1981.
69. Kaplan, *Silicon Boys*, 176.
70. David Arscott said of Swanson, "He could be like a puppy." Berlin, *Troublemakers*, 193. See also Perkins, "Tom Perkins: Early Bay Area Venture Capitalists," 43.
71. Swanson, interview by Sally Smith Hughes, Regional Oral History Office, University of California, Berkeley, 1996–1997, content.cdlib.org/view?docId=kt9c6006s1&&doc.view=entire_text.
72. Berlin, *Troublemakers*, 193.
73. Sally Smith Hughes, *Genentech: The Beginnings of Biotech* (Chicago: University of Chicago Press, 2011), 33–34.
74. Perkins, *Valley Boy*, 119.
75. Hughes, *Genentech*, 32.
76. Hughes, *Genentech*, 34.
77. Berlin, *Troublemakers*, 194–95.
78. Berlin, *Troublemakers*, 195.
79. A bronze statue, depicting the first meeting between Swanson and Boyer in a San Francisco tavern, now sits outside a research building on Genentech's campus.
80. Swanson, interview by Hughes.
81. Perkins, "Tom Perkins: Early Bay Area Venture Capitalists," 46.
82. Hughes, *Genentech*, 37.
83. Unbeknownst to anybody in the room, this was the same day that Jobs and Wozniak formed Apple.
84. Perkins, *Valley Boy*, 120.
85. Perkins, interview by Glenn E. Bugos, Regional Oral History Office, University of California, Berkeley, 2001, content.cdlib.org/view?docId=kt1p3010dc&brand=calisphere.
86. Edward J. Sylvester and Lynn C. Klotz, *The Gene Age: Genetic Engineering and the Next Industrial Revolution* (New York: Scribner, 1983), 87.
87. Perkins, Bancroft Library Oral History Collection, quoted in Berlin, *Troublemakers*, 200.
88. John F. Padgett and Walter W. Powell, *The Emergence of Organizations and Markets* (Princeton, N.J.: Princeton University Press, 2012), 419.
89. Other successful startups of the era were launched on terms as tough as Perkins offered. In November 1977, Michael Markkula invested $91,000 for 26 percent of Apple. See Walter Isaacson, *Steve Jobs* (New York: Simon & Schuster, 2015), 75.
90. Kleiner to Nathaniel I. Weiner, May 7, 1976, box 342652, folder "Genentech," Chiron Corporation, quoted in Hughes, *Genentech*, 41.

91. These shares are calculated from data in Genentech's public filings. "Form S-1 Registration Statement: Genentech, Inc.," Securities and Exchange Commission, Oct. 14, 1980.

92. Dave Goeddel, a Genentech scientist, recalls, "We understood that Genentech could only carry on if we won the race for synthetic human insulin, and it was motivating." Goeddel, interview by the author, June 11, 2018.

93. Perkins, "Tom Perkins: Early Bay Area Venture Capitalists," 53.

94. Dave Goeddel recalls an interchange between a staff researcher and Swanson. "One guy said, 'Bob, what if I just want to save my money and not buy the stock?' Swanson retorted, 'Well, you can save your money to go get your head examined.'" Goeddel, author interview.

95. The scientist was Richard Scheller. See Felda Hardymon and Tom Nicholas, "Kleiner-Perkins and Genentech: When Venture Capital Met Science" (Harvard Business School, Oct. 27, 2012), 6. See also Judith Michaelson, "Genentech Soars: $300 in Stock Turns Buyer into Millionaire," *Los Angeles Times*, Oct. 16, 1980.

96. Fred Middleton, Genentech's finance director, says of Swanson, "Bob and I both had a tremendous amount of respect for Tom Perkins as a highly visible promoter, marketer, strategist, and financier. . . . Bob felt that if you needed to climb mountains, and you needed to go out and establish a beachhead somewhere new, that Tom was the guy to lead the charge." Middleton, interview by Glenn E. Bugos, Regional Oral History Office, University of California, Berkeley, 2001, content.cdlib.org/view?docId=kt8k40159r&brand=calisphere&doc.view=entire_text.

97. Goeddel, author interview. See also Stephen Hall, *Invisible Frontiers: The Race to Synthesize a Human Gene* (Oxford: Oxford University Press, 1987), 244–45.

98. "I was happy to get the order. And happy to get it from Perkins, who was a big shot." Goeddel, author interview.

99. Perkins, Bancroft Library oral history, quoted in Berlin, *Troublemakers*, 263.

100. John March, "The Fascination of the New," *HBS Bulletin*, Oct. 1982, 55–62.

101. According to the partnership's internal accounts of 1984, the checks written in 1976 and 1977 generated a combined 236x. See Wilson, *New Venturers*, 70. Wilson's numbers show an investment of $200,000 in 1976, but this represents two investments, occurring in 1976 and 1977.

102. Author's calculations based on data presented in Wilson, *New Venturers*, 70.

CHAPTER FOUR: THE WHISPERING OF APPLE

1. Leslie Berlin, *Troublemakers: Silicon Valley's Coming of Age* (New York: Simon & Schuster, 2017), 213.

2. Robert Finkel and David Greising, *The Masters of Private Equity and Venture Capital: Management Lessons from the Pioneers of Private Investing* (New York: McGraw-Hill Education, 2009), 160.

3. Gordon Moore reacted similarly when an Intel employee suggested building a home computer. "What the heck would anyone want a computer for in his home?" Moore demanded. The only use case he could come up with was housewives storing recipes. Gordon Moore, "The Accidental Entrepreneur," *Engineering and Science* (Summer 1994): 3, calteches.library.caltech.edu /3777/1/Moore.pdf.

4. Berlin, *Troublemakers*, 230.

5. Walter Isaacson, *Steve Jobs* (New York: Simon & Schuster, 2015), 75.

6. Tom Perkins, "Tom Perkins: Early Bay Area Venture Capitalists: Shaping the Economic and Business Landscape," interview by Sally Smith Hughes, 2009, Regional Oral History Office, Bancroft Library, University of California, Berkeley, 2010, 61, digitalassets.lib.berkeley.edu /roho/ucb/text/perkins_tom.pdf.

7. Valentine's suitability as an Apple investor is underlined by his own descriptions of his investment approach. "We don't spend a lot of time wondering about where people went to school, how smart they are and all the rest of that. We're interested in their idea about the market they're after, the magnitude of the problem they're solving." Felda Hardymon, Tom Nicholas, and Liz Kind, "Don Valentine and Sequoia Capital," Harvard Business School Case Study, April 13, 2014, 49.

8. Isaacson, *Steve Jobs*, 57.

9. Jessica Livingston, *Founders at Work: Stories of Startups' Early Days* (Berkeley, Calif.: Apress, 2008), 44.

10. Brent Schlender and Rick Tetzeli, *Becoming Steve Jobs: The Evolution of a Reckless Upstart into a Visionary Leader* (New York: Crown Business, 2016), 46.

11. Isaacson, *Steve Jobs*, 76.

12. Mike Markkula, "Oral History of Armas Clifford (Mike) Markkula, Jr.," interview by John Hollar, Computer History Museum, May 1, 2012, 24, archive.computerhistory.org/resources/access /text/2012/08/102746385-05-01-acc.pdf. See also "Interview with Mike Markkula," *Silicon Genesis: Oral Histories of Semiconductor Industry Pioneers*, June 3, 2014, silicongenesis.stanford .edu/transcripts/markkula.htm.
13. "Apple Computer, Inc.: IPO Prospectus," Dec. 12, 1980, 25, www.swtpc.com/mholley/Apple /Apple_IPO.pdf.
14. Markkula, interview by the author, May 16, 2018.
15. Berlin, *Troublemakers*, 239.
16. Michael Phillips, interview by the author, Dec. 6, 2017. See also Michael Phillips, "Rock," *Pro Commerce* (blog), Aug. 3, 2005, phillips.blogs.com/goc/2005/08/rock.html. The future investor Michael Moritz, who met Rock around this time, captured his style: "He was quite old-fashioned, believing that television was the curse of modern society, that marijuana addled the mind, and that there had been no significant developments in literature or art for a couple of decades." Michael Moritz, *Return to the Little Kingdom: Steve Jobs, the Creation of Apple, and How It Changed the World* (New York: Overlook Press, 2009), 227.
17. Rock, interview by the author, Jan. 30, 2018.
18. Arthur Rock, "Arthur Rock: Early Bay Area Venture Capitalists: Shaping the Economic and Business Landscape," interview by Sally Smith Hughes, 2008, Regional Oral History Office, Bancroft Library, University of California, Berkeley, 2009, 56.
19. Peter Crisp, interview by the author, April 26, 2018; Smith, interview by the author, April 26, 2018.
20. Peter Crisp, "Oral History of Peter Crisp," interview by Marguerite Gong Hancock, Computer History Museum, Aug. 30, 2018, archive.computerhistory.org/resources/access/text/2019/04 /102717367-05-01-acc.pdf.
21. Smith, author interview.
22. Crisp, author interview.
23. "That investment was highly unusual for us. We did not at that time invest in raw startups." Smith, author interview. The relatively conservative East Coast VC culture was summed up by Paul Ferri, founder of the Boston-based Matrix: "We're not visionaries the way some people on the West Coast are. We don't stick our necks out." Karen Southwick, *The Kingmakers: Venture Capital and the Money Behind the Net* (New York: Wiley, 2001), 84. Equally, the Boston-based Greylock focused more on "developmental capital" than startups, as noted earlier.
24. Crisp, interview by Carole Kolker, National Venture Capital Association Oral History Project, Oct. 2008, 47, digitalassets.lib.berkeley.edu/roho/ucb/text/vcg-crisp.pdf.
25. Crisp, author interview.
26. As in most venture financings, it is hard to pin down precise numbers. The initial plan to invest $300,000 for 10 percent of Apple is recalled by Peter Crisp. See Crisp, Kolker interview. According to the IPO prospectus, dated December 31, 1997, Apple ultimately sold a total of 5,520,000 shares of common stock at $0.09 per share, for an aggregate amount of $517,500. "Apple Computer, Inc.: IPO Prospectus," Dec. 31, 1980, II-2. Having shared some of its allocation with Arthur Rock, Venrock took $288,000 of the total.
27. For this metaphor, I am indebted to Moritz, *Return to the Little Kingdom*, 223.
28. Moritz, *Return to the Little Kingdom*, 227.
29. Markkula, author interview. The size of Valentine's investment is not reported in the S-1. It is reported as $150,000 in Moritz, *Return to the Little Kingdom*, 227. Wilson reports the amount as $200,000. See Wilson, *New Venturers*, 64.
30. Momentum investing has sometimes been shown to work in public stock markets, because news about companies reaches investors gradually, causing stock prices to move in the same direction as the information is absorbed. But there is a far stronger rationale for momentum investing in Silicon Valley, where the buzz around companies can become an almost self-fulfilling prophecy.
31. This phone call, absent from other accounts of Apple's financing, was recalled by Kramlich and confirmed by Crisp. Crisp, author interview; Kramlich, interview by the author, Nov. 17, 2017.
32. Crisp, author interview.
33. Kramlich, author interview.
34. The story involving Montagu and Apple is based on an interview with Kramlich and emails from Peter Dicks, Montagu's partner at Abingworth. Kramlich, author interview; Dicks, emails to the author, Jan. 25, 2019.

35. Montagu's family had founded Samuel Montagu, a London merchant bank. His older brother, David, had become chairman, and as the younger brother, Anthony, had set up his own firm.

36. Anthony Hoberman, then an executive at the Ford Foundation, recalls Valentine consulting him about selling the Apple stake early, prior to the IPO. Having invested Ford's money in Sequoia as a limited partner, Hoberman was delighted that Valentine was showing appropriate risk adversity. Hoberman, interview by the author, Dec. 4, 2019; Hoberman, email to the author, Dec. 4, 2019. This contradicts Valentine's suggestion that the stake was sold when he was traveling and out of contact with the office. Valentine, interview by the author, April 7, 2018. The multiple realized on Apple was provided by Sequoia.

37. For Venrock, Apple was the power-law investment that transformed its performance from solid to outstanding during the 1970s. Tom Nicholas, *VC: An American History* (Cambridge, Mass.: Harvard University Press, 2019), 171–72.

38. Crisp, author interview.

39. Moritz, *Return to the Little Kingdom*, 230.

40. Moritz, *Return to the Little Kingdom*, 286.

41. Moritz, *Return to the Little Kingdom*, 276.

42. Hambrecht, interview by the author, Feb. 7, 2018.

43. Paul Gompers and Josh Lerner, "Money Chasing Deals? The Impact of Fund Inflows on Private Equity Valuations" (Jan. 1998), 6–7, ssrn.com/abstract=57964. In 1978, pension funds accounted for 15 percent of venture funding. By 1988, they had become the largest source of capital, accounting for 46 percent of the $3 billion of inflows. Paul Gompers, "The Rise and Fall of Venture Capital," *Business and Economic History* 23, no. 2 (Winter 1994): 13.

44. Cuts in the capital-gains tax rate might have encouraged taxable investors (rich individuals) to invest in venture partnerships or to be active as "angel" investors. (The effect is muddied by the lifting of the prudent-man rule and the influx of pension capital.) At the same time, capital-gains cuts might have boosted the supply of inventors willing to take the risk of devoting their time to a startup. On this point, Nicholas cites research by James Poterba. Nicholas, *VC*, 181.

45. Data from Venture Economics Inc.

46. William D. Bygrave and Jeffry A. Timmons, *Venture Capital at the Crossroads* (Boston: Harvard Business School Press, 1992), 149.

47. Wilson, *New Venturers*, 60.

48. Thomas K. Perkins, "Kleiner Perkins, Venture Capital, and the Chairmanship of Genentech, 1976–1995," interview by Glenn E. Bugos, 2001, Regional Oral History Office, Bancroft Library, University of California, Berkeley, 2002.

49. In 1984, New Enterprise Associates raised a $125 million fund. Udayan Gupta, ed., *Done Deals: Venture Capitalists Tell Their Stories* (Boston: Harvard Business School Press, 2000), 195.

50. As of the early 1980s, at least 150 graduate schools were offering courses or setting up research centers in the new science of launching startups. Wilson, *New Venturers*, 211.

CHAPTER FIVE: CISCO, 3COM, AND THE VALLEY ASCENDANT

1. The Merrill Lynch report appeared in 1978, just as capital began to flood into VC funds. See Margaret O'Mara, *The Code: Silicon Valley and the Remaking of America* (New York: Penguin Press, 2019), 177. It should be noted that Merrill Lynch's view appeared reasonable given that R&D spending by major public corporations dwarfed venture-capital investments by a factor of almost ten. Charles Newhall, "Financing Technical Change" (presentation to the OECD Committee for Scientific and Technological Policy, circa 1984), 6. Copy provided to the author by Dick Kramlich.

2. In 1987, Japan's chip makers had enjoyed a nineteen-percentage-point lead in production yield over U.S. rivals; in 1991 they still enjoyed a nine-point lead. (Jeffery T. Macher, David C. Mowery, and David A. Hodges, "Reversal of Fortune? The Recovery of the U.S. Semiconductor Industry," *California Management Review* [Fall 1998]: 116, table 2.) Sematech also helped U.S. manufacturers of chip-making equipment boost their share of the global market to 53 percent by 1993. (U.S. Congress, Office of Technology Assessment, *Contributions of DOE Weapons Labs and NIST to Semiconductor Technology, OTA-ITE-585* [Washington, D.C.: U.S. Government Printing Office, 1993], 67.) However, the main factor behind the comeback of the U.S. chip industry was its shift from memory chips to higher-margin microprocessors. This owed nothing to Sematech. Indeed, Intel decided on this shift before Sematech's formation, and the focus on novel chip design was also encouraged by semiconductor startups launched before Sematech got going, notably Cypress Semiconductor, Altera, and Micron. On the hard-to-measure cost-effectiveness of Sematech, see Douglas A. Irwin and Peter J. Klenow, "High-Tech R&D Subsi-

dies: Estimating the Effects of Sematech," in "Symposium on Growth and International Trade: Empirical Studies," special issue, *Journal of International Economics* 40, no. 3 (May 1996): 323–44, doi.org/10.1016/0022-1996(95)01408-X.

3. AnnaLee Saxenian, *Regional Advantage: Culture and Competition in Silicon Valley and Route 128* (Cambridge, Mass.: Harvard University Press, 1994).

4. By the same logic, clusters have deep pools of complementary companies: a router manufacturer seeking an esoteric microchip can find exactly the right sort of semiconductor design firm within a fifty-mile radius. See Enrico Moretti, *The New Geography of Jobs* (New York: Mariner Books, 2013), 126–27, 134.

5. Granovetter's 1973 article in *The American Journal of Sociology*, "The Strength of Weak Ties," is the seventh most cited social science paper ever, according to an analysis of Google Scholar by Elliott Green of LSE.

6. Larissa MacFarquhar, "The Deflationist: How Paul Krugman Found Politics," *New Yorker*, March 1, 2010.

7. Niall Ferguson, *The Square and the Tower: Networks, Hierarchies, and the Struggle for Global Power* (New York: Penguin Press, 2017), 15.

8. See Jonathan M. Barnett and Ted Sichelman, "The Case for Noncompetes," *University of Chicago Law Review* 86 (Jan. 2020). The paper points out that non-compete clauses are enforceable in California under some conditions and non-enforceable in Massachusetts under other conditions: thus, the contrast between the two states is less stark than is generally asserted. Further, California employers use other mechanisms to restrict employee mobility. These include nondisclosure agreements, patent infringement suits, and deferred compensation mechanisms. On the other side of the debate, see Matt Marx, Jasjit Singh, and Lee Fleming, "Regional Disadvantage? Non-Compete Agreements and Brain Drain" (July 21, 2010). Available at SSRN: ssrn.com/abstract=1654719 or dx.doi.org/10.2139/ssrn.1654719; and Evan Starr, "The Use, Abuse, and Enforceability of Non-compete and No-Poach Agreements," Feb. 2019 Issue Brief, Economic Innovation Group. Surveying the literature, Starr cites the telling example of Hawaii, which banned enforcement of non-competes for tech workers in 2015. The result was an increase in labor mobility within the state, with average job tenure falling by 11 percent, implying additional cross-pollination of ideas and more dynamic matching between tech-worker skills and emerging opportunities. A fair verdict would seem to be that nonenforcement of non-compete provisions is healthy for venture-driven trial-and-error startup ecosystems, but that it is not a decisive variable in determining success. Its power may lie principally in amplifying the company-formation efforts of VCs.

9. Of the many entrepreneurs profiled in this book, only one (Patrick Brown) had been a Stanford professor, although David Cheriton is mentioned in passing. Meanwhile, this book features multiple figures who worked at Stanford but who did not enjoy tenure, making the supposed distinction with MIT irrelevant. Examples include the founders of Cisco, Yahoo, and Google. If the argument for Stanford's pro-entrepreneurial porousness is not tied specifically to tenure, but rests on a vaguer contention that Stanford has a startup-friendly vibe, then there is a chicken-and-egg question. As Patrick Brown's story shows (see introduction), the presence of Sand Hill Road next to Stanford probably influenced the culture of academia at least as much as academia drove entrepreneurship.

10. Younger, interview by the author, May 16, 2018.

11. Building on the research of Granovetter and Saxenian, later analysis plots venture-capital connections within technology clusters. The chief insight from these network charts is that clusters are productive to the extent that the agents within them are actively linked to one another. The role played by venture capitalists in cultivating such links is illuminated in the study of life-science clusters by Woody Powell of Stanford and coauthors. See Walter W. Powell, Kelly A. Packalan, and Kjersten Bunker Whittington, "Organizational and Institutional Genesis: The Emergence of High-Tech Clusters in the Life Sciences," Queen's School of Business Research Paper no. 03-10. For more on the networking role of VCs, see Michel Ferrary, "Silicon Valley: A Cluster of Venture Capitalists?," *Paris Innovation Review* (blog), Oct. 26, 2017, parisinnovationreview.cn/en/2017/10/26/silicon-valley-a-cluster-of-venture-capitalists/. See also Mark Granovetter and Michel Ferrary, "The Role of Venture Capital Firms in Silicon Valley's Complex Innovation Network," *Economy and Society* 18, no. 2 (2009): 326–59.

12. Dennis Taylor, "Cradle of Venture Capital," *Silicon Valley Business Journal*, April 18, 1999, bizjournals.com/sanjose/stories/1999/04/19/focus1.html.

13. Richard A. Shaffer, "To Increase Profits, Venture Capital Firms Are Investing Earlier in Fledgling Concerns," *Wall Street Journal*, Oct. 31, 1983.

14. Joel Kotkin, "The Third Wave: U.S. Entrepreneurs Are Filling New Niches in the Semiconductor Industry," *Inc.*, Feb. 1984.

15. Marilyn Chase, "Venture Capitalists Rush in to Back Emerging High-Technology Firms," *Wall Street Journal*, March 18, 1981.

16. Chase, "Venture Capitalists Rush in to Back Emerging High-Technology Firms." Chase also quotes A. Robert Towbin of L. F. Rothschild, who described the continuous flow of picture-perfect investor-entrepreneur marriages as "a dreamland."

17. Jessica Livingston, *Founders at Work: Stories of Startups' Early Days* (Berkeley, Calif.: Apress, 2008), 284.

18. Len Baker, interview by the author, Sept. 20, 2017.

19. The technology manager was Gordon Bell, DEC's vice president of engineering. Quoted in Saxenian, *Regional Advantage*, 65.

20. Allen Michels, quoted in Saxenian, *Regional Advantage*, 65. Similarly, Rick Burnes of the Boston-based Charles River Ventures recalls, "When Apple was founded, it was a hope and a dream and a guy in jeans who had not graduated from college. Here in New England, that wasn't the way it was done. We wanted experience. We needed people who knew what they were talking about." Burnes, interview by the author, Oct. 11, 2017.

21. Cox, interview by the author, Oct. 12, 2017. Greylock's founder, Bill Elfers, had concluded early that "developmental capital," buyouts, and the public stock of unrecognized companies made for safer bets than "speculative new companies." Tom Nicholas, *VC: An American History* (Cambridge, Mass.: Harvard University Press, 2019), 163.

22. The 3Com story that follows was constructed from multiple sources and then verified in an email exchange with Metcalfe. Metcalfe, email to the author, April 2, 2019.

23. Robert Metcalfe, "Oral History of Robert Metcalfe," interview by Len Shustek, Computer History Museum, Nov. 29, 2006, archive.computerhistory.org/resources/text/Oral_History/Metcalfe _Robert_1/Metcalfe_Robert_1_2.oral_history.2006.7.102657995.pdf.

24. John W. Wilson, *The New Venturers: Inside the High-Stakes World of Venture Capital* (Reading, Mass.: Addison-Wesley, 1985), 177.

25. In another example of East Coasters failing to capitalize on an invention, the early networking firm Ungermann-Bass had spun out of a company called Zilog. Like Xerox, Zilog had East Coast DNA: it had been funded by the New York–based corporate development team at the oil company Exxon. Like Xerox, Zilog proved bad at getting products to market. Charlie Bass, interview by the author, June 12, 2018.

26. Metcalfe, Shustek interview.

27. Metcalfe, Shustek interview.

28. Metcalfe, Shustek interview.

29. Howard Charney, email to the author, March 19, 2019. See also Tom Richman, "Who's in Charge Here? Travel Tips Article," *Inc.*, June 1, 1989, www.inc.com/magazine/19890601/5674.html.

30. Bill Krause, interview by the author, May 15, 2018.

31. Krause says of Treybig, "He and Tom Perkins were the role model for a lot of us to follow. He inspired me to be willing to take the risk of joining Bob." Krause, author interview.

32. Thirty-eight years later, Krause joked that his wife still held him to her condition. Krause, author interview. Charney confirms that he attended the dinner. Charney, email to the author, March 19, 2019.

33. Krause recalls that he made the decision to leave HP at the start of January, almost a month before the financing negotiations were concluded. Krause, email to the author, March 11, 2019.

34. The investor at Fidelity Ventures was Tom Stephenson, who later gave up on the East Coast and joined Sequoia. Metcalfe, email to the author, April 2, 2019.

35. This quotation and the account that follows are taken mostly from the excellent account in Wilson, *New Venturers*, 178–79.

36. Wilson, *New Venturers*, 178–79. See also Metcalfe, Shustek interview.

37. Charney, interview by the author, July 18, 2018.

38. Wilson, *New Venturers*, 178–79.

39. Valentine said of the Wagon Wheel, "This was my graduate school." Valentine, interview by the author, April 7, 2018.

40. Krause, author interview. The aphorism about sharing secrets is attributed to Ed McCracken, former CEO of Silicon Graphics. See Chong-Moon Lee et al., eds., *The Silicon Valley Edge: A Habitat for Innovation and Entrepreneurship* (Stanford, Calif.: Stanford Business Books, 2000), 10.

41. Joe Kennedy, interview by the author, June 11, 2018.

42. Charles Bass, interview by James L. Pelkey, Computer History Museum, Aug. 16, 1994, archive .computerhistory.org/resources/access/text/2018/03/102738753-05-01-acc.pdf.

43. Bass, interview by Pelkey. Bass added, "I thought he was going to be in cardiac arrest right there." Doerr says he has no memory of this episode and that he has never been close to fainting in any meeting. Doerr, interview with the author, March 5, 2021.

44. Bass, interview by Pelkey.

45. Kennedy, author interview.

46. KP's decision to compensate Ungermann-Bass is vindicated by research showing the positive relationship between a venture capitalist's "network centrality" and returns. See Yael V. Hochberg, Alexander Ljungqvist, and Yang Lu, "Whom You Know Matters: Venture Capital Networks and Investment Performance," *Journal of Finance* 62, no. 1 (Feb. 2007). The authors note that the relationship is twice as strong in Silicon Valley as it is nationwide. In addition, Arthur Patterson, the Accel founder who appears in chapter 6, notes that reputation disciplined behavior in the venture industry in many other ways. Entrepreneurs shared their plans with VCs even in the absence of nondisclosure agreements. It was understood that VCs would honor confidentiality and would be punished by the industry if they failed to do so.

47. By 1997, U.S. companies controlled 50 percent of the semiconductor market, compared with Japanese companies' 29 percent. Jeffery T. Macher, David C. Mowery, and David A. Hodges, "Reversal of Fortune? The Recovery of the U.S. Semiconductor Industry," *California Management Review* (Fall 1998): 41.

48. The venture-backed disk-drive companies were a clearer success in terms of building Silicon Valley's industrial leadership than in terms of generating returns for investors: the public returns exceeded the private ones. Because VCs backed so many disk-drive makers, most inevitably failed. See Jerry Neumann, "Heat Death: Venture Capital in the 1980s," *Reaction Wheel* (blog), Jan. 8, 2015, reactionwheel.net/2015/01/80s-vc.html. See also Udayan Gupta, "Recent Venture Funds Perform Poorly as Unrealistic Expectations Wear Off," *Wall Street Journal*, Nov. 8, 1988; Jeff Moax, "When Your Investors Are Entrepreneurs," *Venture*, Oct. 1980; Clayton M. Christensen, "The Rigid Disk Drive Industry," *Business History Review* 67, no. 4 (Winter 1993): 542.

49. Saxenian cites a wealth of data demonstrating that Silicon Valley overtook Boston's Route 128 during the 1980s. See Saxenian, *Regional Advantage*, 106–8.

50. Joseph Nocera and Anne Faircloth, "Cooking with CISCO," *Fortune*, Dec. 25, 1995. On Bosack's robotic manner, one contemporary said, "Every topic you gave him, he wanted to kind of iterate through every piece of it to understand it all." See Edward Leonard, interview by Charles H. House, Computer History Museum, Sept. 11, 2015, 19. Leonard was the Valley lawyer who introduced Lerner and Bosack to Sequoia.

51. Kirk Lougheed, interview by the author, July 20, 2018. Lougheed was one of the first employees at Cisco. On Lerner's studies, see also "Women in Computing: The Management Option, Panel Discussion," Computer History Museum, YouTube, Aug. 30, 2016, youtube.com/watch?v=QmckAhX4U5w.

52. Dana Wechsler Linden, "Does Pink Make You Puke?," *Forbes*, Aug. 25, 1997.

53. "Nerds 2.0.1: A Brief History of the Internet, Part 3," PBS, 1998, archive.org/details/Nerds_2.0.1_-_A_Brief_History_of_the_Internet_-_Part3.

54. Linton Weeks, "Network of One," *Washington Post*, March 25, 1998.

55. "Nerds 2.0.1: A Brief History of the Internet, Part 3."

56. "Nerds 2.0.1: A Brief History of the Internet, Part 3." Bosack apparently shared Lerner's willingness to bend the rules. Lougheed recalls, "Len was somebody who thought the rules were for other people." Lougheed, author interview.

57. Private venture partnerships raised $1.4 billion in 1982, $3.4 billion in 1983, and $3.2 billion in 1984. *Venture Capital Journal*, Jan. 1986, 8.

58. Pete Carey, "A Start-Up's True Tale," *San Jose Mercury News*, Dec. 1, 2001, pdp10.nocrew.org/docs/cisco.html.

59. "Nerds 2.0.1: A Brief History of the Internet, Part 3."

60. Valentine, author interview.

61. The chief executive was Bill Graves. The military-linked Cisco customer was Ed Kozel, who was then working for SRI International. Kozel, interview by the author, July 19, 2018. Kozel later worked for Cisco.

62. Kozel, author interview.

63. Leonard, House interview, 19.

64. Bass, author interview.

65. Reflecting on Sequoia's Cisco deal years later, Bass marveled at the courage that it took. "I am not sure I would have made that investment," he admitted. "Don's approach was to surround the founders with adults. I did not have the vision to think in terms of those resources and that level of commitment." Bass, author interview.

66. John Morgridge and Don Valentine, "Cisco Oral History Panel Part One," interview by John Hollar, Computer History Museum, Nov. 19, 2014, 11.

67. David Bunnell and Adam Brate, *Making the Cisco Connection: The Story Behind the Real Internet Superpower* (New York: John Wiley & Sons, 2000), 11.

68. The banker was Thom Weisel, head of Montgomery Securities. Michael Moritz, *DTV* (self-published, 2020), 61.

69. Cisco sold 2,365,000 shares of its Series A Preferred Stock for $1 per share to three venture-capital funds managed by Sequoia and to Suez Technology Fund, co-managed by Sequoia. Another $135,000 was invested by two other Sequoia affiliates. See Cisco S-1 filing.

70. Valentine, author interview.

71. Leonard, author interview; John Bolger, interview by the author, July 23, 2018; John Morgridge, interview by the author, July 23, 2018.

72. Lougheed, author interview.

73. Lamond, interview by the author, May 17, 2018.

74. Valentine and Morgridge, Hollar interview, 8.

75. Nocera and Faircloth, "Cooking with Cisco."

76. Cisco's S-1 filing states that Morgridge received options to buy 745,812 shares of common stock, equivalent to 5.9 percent of the company. The S-1 also puts Morgridge's total ownership at 6.1 percent, presumably because he had purchased or been given equity in addition to equity options. His stake was larger than some Valley founders own at flotation. For example, T. J. Rodgers of Cypress Semiconductor owned only 3.1 percent of his company at the time of its 1986 flotation. See "Amendment No. 2 to Form S-1 Registration Statement: Cypress Semiconductor Corporation," Securities and Exchange Commission, May 30, 1986.

77. Morgridge, interview by Dayna Goldfine, Stanford University Libraries, Department of Special Collections and University Archives, July 17, 2009, purl.stanford.edu/ws284fg2355.

78. Lougheed, author interview. See also Robert Slater, *The Eye of the Storm: How John Chambers Steered Cisco Through the Technology Collapse* (New York: HarperBusiness, 2003), 81.

79. Recalling the manufacturing operation before Valentine's investment, Kirk Lougheed says, "I was the manufacturing department, putting together these machines by myself. Sandy brought in people to help me, but they had no manufacturing skills. I don't know where she found these people." Lougheed, author interview.

80. Slater, *Eye of the Storm*, 86.

81. Cisco sold almost $28 million worth of equipment in the year to July 1989, up from $1.5 million two years previously. Net revenues jumped from almost nothing to $4.2 million. Cisco S-1A, as filed to the SEC on Feb. 16, 1990, 6.

82. *Something Ventured*, directed by Dayna Goldfine and Daniel Geller (Miralan Productions, 2011).

83. Bolger, author interview.

84. Valentine, author interview.

85. Valentine and Morgridge, Hollar interview, 25.

86. Lerner, interview by Dayna Goldfine, June 21, 2010, purl.stanford.edu/mb678nw9491.

87. Laura Lambert, *The Internet: A Historical Encyclopedia* (Santa Barbara, Calif.: ABC-CLIO, 2005), 37.

88. Reflecting on the Valley of twenty-five years later, the venture investor Marc Andreessen observes, "So the myth in Silicon Valley is that the VC turns on the founder and boots him and brings in a CEO. The more common pattern that we see is the team in the company turns on the founder." Andreessen, interview by the author, May 14, 2019.

89. Christianne Corbett and Catherine Hill, "Solving the Equation: The Variables for Women in Engineering and Computing," AAUW (report), 2015, 9, files.eric.ed.gov/fulltext/ED580805.pdf.

90. Jeremy Quittner, "Sandy Lerner: The Investor Is Not Your Friend," *Inc.*, Feb. 27, 2013, www.inc.com/magazine/201303/how-i-got-started/sandy-lerner.html.

91. Leonard, House interview.

92. Cisco's S-1 filing reports that each founder had 1,781,786 shares, or 17.6 percent of the company. Two-thirds of these were subject to vesting, which happened monthly over four years, starting in December 1987. Because the founders left the company thirty-two months later, they stood to lose one-third of their options, or two-ninths of their total equity. But Cisco might have paid out on the unvested options as part of the undisclosed termination settlement.

93. The investor pressure on Severino was mitigated by the fact that both his backers had made money from his earlier startup, Interlan, and were friends with him. See James Pelkey, "Internetworking: LANs and WANs, 1985–1988," in *Entrepreneurial Capitalism and Innovation: A History of Computer Communications, 1968–1988* (website), 2007, historyofcomputercommunications .info/Book/12/12.27_Wellfleet.html. Russ Planitzer, Wellfleet's chairman, regrets not challenging Severino on his decision to accept a bespoke engineering project for one customer that sidetracked the company from pursuing its core market. Planitzer, interview by the author, April 30, 2020.
94. "15 Years, a Lifetime," *Network World*, March 26, 2001, 87. In another contrast between the coasts, Cisco seized market share by snapping up other startups, a risky and expensive strategy that Valentine backed wholeheartedly. "If I went to my board and said I want to buy this company for $150 million and I've got ten days to do it . . . they would have looked at me like I was crazy," Severino marveled.

CHAPTER SIX: PLANNERS AND IMPROVISERS

1. Frank Rose, "Mitch Kapor and the Lotus Factor," *Esquire*, Dec. 1984, 358, frankrose.com/Mitch _Kapor_and_the_Lotus_Factor.pdf.
2. The story that follows about GO is distilled from Kaplan's memoir. All facts and quotations come from Kaplan's account unless otherwise noted. See Jerry Kaplan, *Startup: A Silicon Valley Adventure* (repr., New York: Penguin Books, 1996).
3. The racehorse quotation comes from Kaplan. See John Swartz, "Tech's Star Capitalist," *San Francisco Chronicle*, Nov. 13, 1997. The rival VC quotation comes from Len Baker of Sutter Hill. Baker, interview by the author, Sept. 20, 2017.
4. David A. Kaplan, *The Silicon Boys and Their Valley of Dreams* (New York: Perennial, 2000), 188.
5. Doerr, interview with the author, March 5, 2021.
6. Doerr, author interview.
7. Kapor, interview by the author, June 21, 2018. Commenting on the GO episode, Doerr argued that startups require evangelical support and that this is not the same as hubris. Doerr, author interview.
8. G. Pascal Zachary, "Computer Glitch: Venture-Capital Star, Kleiner Perkins, Flops as a Maker of Laptops," *Wall Street Journal*, July 26, 1990.
9. Doerr touted these technologies at a speech to the National Venture Capital Association in 1990. See William Bygrave and Jeffry Timmons, *Venture Capital at the Crossroads* (Boston: Harvard Business School Press, 1992), 149. Quoted in Jerry Neumann, "Heat Death: Venture Capital in the 1980s," *Reaction Wheel* (blog), Jan. 8, 2015.
10. Don Gooding, interview by the author, June 12, 2018.
11. Don Gooding, an Accel analyst, recalls, "Jim was an enormously principled person in an industry not known for its principles. A lot of the backbone that I have now comes from emulating him." Gooding, author interview. See also Jim Swartz, "Oral History of Jim Swartz," interview by John Hollar, Computer History Museum, Oct. 11, 2013, 2, archive.computerhistory.org /resources/access/text/2015/05/102746860-05-01-acc.pdf.
12. The company was PictureTel. Brian Hinman, interview by the author, July 11, 2018.
13. Accel closed its Princeton office in 1997.
14. Accel Telecom Fund offering document, 1985, Jim Swartz personal files. I am grateful to Swartz for access to his papers and for multiple conversations.
15. One year George Gilder wowed Accel's guests by predicting that telephony would abandon its wired infrastructure in favor of cordless connections while TV would do the opposite, switching from wireless broadcast to internet cables. Swartz, interview by the author, Nov. 8, 2017.
16. Swartz, author interview.
17. In its first ten years, Accel had exited forty-five companies: seven had folded, twenty-four had achieved an IPO, and fourteen had merged. Jim Swartz presentation delivered at Carnegie Mellon University, Sept. 27, 1994, Swartz personal files.
18. Patterson, interview with author. I am grateful to Patterson for multiple conversations and introductions to fellow investors.
19. Patterson was an admirer of Bain Consulting, which propounded the view that by specializing and dominating a niche, businesses would accumulate intellectual property that would translate into superior profits.
20. The companies were PictureTel, Vivo, and Polycom. PictureTel and Polycom made 14x. I am grateful to Swartz and Accel for providing me with extensive performance data for Accel's first five funds.

21. In addition to its distinctive approach, Accel was strong in more typical ways. Entrepreneurs respected Patterson and Swartz and used them to help recruit key hires. John Little, the founder of Portal Software, the biggest single hit in Accel's first five funds, said of Patterson, "When we wanted to seal the deal with a key engineer, we would get him to talk to Arthur. People would get off the phone after talking to Arthur, and they would be convinced that this was the biggest thing that ever hit Silicon Valley. And then they would sign. Of course, we were competing to hire people who had lots of options. And if they mentioned the other options, Arthur knew how to sow a bit of doubt about those other options." Little, interview by the author, May 22, 2018.

22. Accel Telecom achieved an internal rate of return net of fees of 18.7 percent. The median venture fund launched in 1985 achieved an internal rate of return net of fees of 8 percent. Data on the first five Accel funds was provided by Jim Swartz. My understanding of industry-wide data owes much to Steven N. Kaplan of the University of Chicago. Following Kaplan's advice on rival VC data sets, I am using numbers from Burgiss, whose data are relatively free from distortions.

23. To be precise, 95 percent of Accel Telecom's returns came from the top five of the twenty-four companies in its portfolio.

24. Rick Adams, UUNET's founder, recalls, "Naming is really hard. The business plan had to go out at five o'clock, and literally it said 'New Co' in there. The protocol that the modem worked on was called UUCP NXTX. At one point that was the UU part. And there was a EUnet, Europe Unix Users Network. And we talked about the U.S. Unix Users Network—another UU. I would claim officially that UUNET is not an acronym and it doesn't mean anything. But there are lots of versions out there, some of them quoting me. People I didn't talk to have quoted me." Adams, interview by the author, June 12, 2018.

25. In 1983, an estimated 200 machines were connected to the internet. In 1989, the number was still only 159,000. See Mary Meeker and Chris DePuy, "The Internet Report," Morgan Stanley Research, Feb. 1996, 18. See also Janet Abbate, *Inventing the Internet* (Cambridge, Mass.: MIT Press, 2000), 186.

26. The loose association of computer scientists was the USENIX society, which brought together programmers who used Unix computers.

27. UUNET greatly simplified the process of connecting to the informal network of Unix computers, called Usenet. Before, you could only join Usenet if invited. With UUNET, any customer could send and receive email, access news feeds, and conduct batch file transfers.

28. For an account emphasizing the public-sector role in creating the internet, see Mariana Mazzucato, *The Entrepreneurial State: Debunking Public vs. Private Sector Myths* (New York: Anthem Press, 2013), 76.

29. For an example of the excitement about Gore's vision, see John Markoff, "Building the Electronic Superhighway," *New York Times*, Jan. 24, 1993.

30. The key figure in this process was Stephen S. Wolff, the program director for computer networking at the NSF. In November 1991, Wolff issued a plan to replace the NSFNET with competing commercial networks. From 1992 to 1995 the NSF worked with internet service providers to transfer internet infrastructure to private industry. On April 30, 1995, the NSFNET backbone was decommissioned, having been fully replaced by competing commercial providers. John Cassidy, *Dot.Con: The Greatest Story Ever Sold* (New York: HarperCollins, 2003), 22–23.

31. By 1992, UUNET had hooked up twenty-four hundred corporate subscribers. "Offering Memorandum UUNET Technologies, Inc.," Aug. 1992, 3.

32. Kapor, author interview.

33. O'Dell, interview by the author, June 2, 2018.

34. Kapor, author interview.

35. Mitch Kapor, "Oral History of Mitch Kapor," interview by Bill Aspray, Computer History Museum, Nov. 19, 2004, 12.

36. Kapor to Ben Rosen, reproduced in full in William A. Sahlman, "Lotus Development Corporation," Harvard Business School case study, 1985, 13–14.

37. Kapor, author interview.

38. Kapor had founded the Electronic Frontier Foundation, a nonprofit that advocated open access to the web. Its mission complemented UUNET's founding goal of connecting private users. In interviews with the author, both Kapor and Adams recognized the importance of nonprofit idealism in forging their business partnership.

39. Kapor initially lent money to UUNET, taking warrants that gave him a stake in UUNET's future expansion. He later made an equity investment of $200,000 that was finalized in November 1992.

40. Doerr, interview by the author, Sept. 13, 2018.

41. Kevin Compton, interview by the author, Feb. 12, 2019; Floyd Kvamme, interview by the author, Feb. 13, 2019.
42. The quotation is recalled by Joe Schoendorf, the Accel executive who took Kapor's call. Schoendorf, interview by the author, July 19, 2018.
43. McLean, interview by the author, July 12, 2018.
44. Kapor, email to Adams, Jan. 29, 1993.
45. McLean, author interview.
46. Kapor, email to Adams, Feb. 23, 1993.
47. Adams, author interview; Adams, email to Kapor, March 26, 1993.
48. Adams, email to Kapor, March 26, 1993.
49. Barris recalls, "I was so struck by the fact that Arthur Patterson came all the way to Dallas to meet me. That served as a guide to me, when I later joined the VC industry, as to the importance of building one's 'people network.'" Barris, email to the author, Jan. 3, 2021.
50. Barris, interviews by the author, May 30 and June 2, 2018.
51. Kapor, email to Adams, July 9, 1993.
52. Jarve, interview by the author, July 18, 2018.
53. The Series A round was signed October 4, 1993. UUNET raised $1.7 million (counting in Kapor's $200,000 investment from the previous November) at an $8.3 million post-money valuation.
54. Adams, author interview.
55. Barris, author interviews.
56. Adams, email to Kapor, Dec. 6, 1993. In the end, the three VCs invested an additional $294,000 each, with Kapor adding less. The valuation and price per share were lower than in the earlier financing.
57. John Markoff, "A Free and Simple Computer Link," *New York Times*, Dec. 8, 1993.
58. Peter Barris, Eulogy to John Sidgmore, 2004.
59. Barris also stressed the opportunity to sell use of the network to businesses by day and households by night, a trick that GE had figured out for its time-share services. Barris, author interviews.
60. By holding on to UUNET stock for longer, NEA earned $300 million. Barris, author interviews.
61. Adams, email to Kapor, May 26, 1995. Adams's wealth rose further as UUNET's stock appreciated.
62. Jared Sandberg, "The Rumpled Genius Behind Netscape," *Globe and Mail*, Aug. 14, 1995.
63. Jim Clark, *Netscape Time: The Making of the Billion-Dollar Start-Up That Took On Microsoft*, with Owen Edwards (New York: St. Martin's Griffin, 2000), 40–42. See also George Gilder, "The Coming Software Shift," *Forbes*, Aug. 28, 1995.
64. Clark, *Netscape Time*, 58.
65. In reality, Clark had been treated somewhat roughly, but not as roughly as he thought: T. J. Rodgers, the superstar founder of Cypress Semiconductor, had likewise owned only 3.1 percent of his company when it had gone public in 1986, because semiconductor companies require a huge amount of capital to get started.
66. Michael Lewis, *The New New Thing: A Silicon Valley Story* (New York: W. W. Norton, 2014), 39–41.
67. Clark, *Netscape Time*, 75–77.
68. Clark, *Netscape Time*, 7.
69. "Amendment No. 6 to Form S-1 Registration Statement: Netscape Communications Corporation," Securities and Exchange Commission, June 23, 1995, 48.
70. Doerr commented, "Metcalfe taught me about Metcalfe's law, and I could see that the value of a network would grow with the square of the number of users. So Netscape could be huge." He added, "These tsunami-like waves of innovation come about every thirteen years or so, each driven by a power law. The PC around 1980–81; the internet in 1994; mobility and cloud in 2007. The next is AI." Doerr, interview by the author, Sept. 13, 2018.
71. For a lucid analysis of the relationship between Metcalfe's law and Moore's law, see Bob Metcalfe, "Metcalfe's Law Recurses Down the Long Tail of Social Networks," VC Mike's Blog, Aug. 18, 2006, vcmike.wordpress.com/2006/08/18/metcalfe-social-networks.
72. Khosla, interview by the author, July 30, 2018. What was distinctive about Doerr and Khosla was not that they were ready to invest in a browser; by 1994, "it was very clear to all of us what was happening in the browser world," Jim Swartz of Accel commented. (Swartz, email to the author, May 11, 2020.) Rather, the distinctive thing about KP was that it was so enthusiastic about the compounding power-law effects that it was price insensitive.
73. The partner was Frank Caufield. See Kaplan, *Silicon Boys*, 243.

74. "Amendment No. 6 to Form S-1 Registration Statement: Netscape Communications Corporation," Securities and Exchange Commission, Aug. 8, 1995, 1.

CHAPTER SEVEN: BENCHMARK, SOFTBANK, AND "EVERYONE NEEDS $100 MILLION"

1. Gooding, interview by the author, June 12, 2018.
2. William H. Draper III, *The Startup Game: Inside the Partnership Between Venture Capitalists and Entrepreneurs* (New York: Palgrave Macmillan, 2011), 4–9.
3. Robert H. Reid, *Architects of the Web: 1,000 Days That Built the Future of Business* (New York: Wiley, 1997), 254.
4. Karen Angel, *Inside Yahoo! Reinvention and the Road Ahead* (New York: John Wiley & Sons, 2002), 18.
5. Brian McCullough, "On the 20th Anniversary—the History of Yahoo's Founding," *Internet History Podcast* (blog), March 1, 2015, www.internethistorypodcast.com/2015/03/on-the-20th -anniversary-the-history-of-yahoos-founding.
6. "David Filo & Jerry Yang," *Entrepreneur*, Oct. 9, 2008, www.entrepreneur.com/article/197564.
7. Valentine, interview by the author, April 7, 2018. Doug Leone of Sequoia remarked, "It's really funny, this 'publishing background is not particularly useful for technology investing.' Boy, when the internet hit, it became front and center. All of a sudden Mike was a domain expert. What did I know about it?" Leone, interview by the author, May 14, 2019. In his tribute to Valentine, Moritz emphasizes the pitfalls of hiring overexperienced venture partners. Michael Moritz, *DTV* (self-published, 2020), 40.
8. Moritz, interviews by the author, May 14 and Oct. 5, 2019, and May 21 and Nov. 23, 2020. See also Reid, *Architects of the Web*, 254–55.
9. Yang, interview by the author, Feb. 13, 2019.
10. Michael Krantz, "Click till You Drop," *Time*, June 24, 2001, content.time.com/time/magazine /article/0,9171,139582,00.html?iid=sr-link1.
11. Moritz and Yang also independently recalled joking about the fact that Sequoia's star investments had five-letter names: Atari, Apple, Cisco. Moritz, author interviews; Yang, email to the author, Dec. 18, 2019.
12. "As a journalist, I understood that two young founders who were good characters would make for rich magazine stories." Moritz, author interviews. As well as offering advice on public positioning, Moritz counseled Yang on other lessons from Apple: make sure that products are easy to use; don't be afraid to defy conventional wisdom. Yang, email to the author, Dec. 18, 2019.
13. Angel, *Inside Yahoo!*, 32.
14. Yahoo's spending on sales and marketing came to $815,000 in 1995, $15 million in 1996, and $44 million in 1997. Sales and marketing expenditures outpaced product development expenses by a wide margin; for example, in 1997 the ratio was almost four to one. See *Yahoo Annual Report*, 1997, 24.
15. *National Venture Capital Association 2010 Yearbook*, 20, fig. 2.02.
16. Son spoke about his early life in a speech at the SoftBank thirtieth anniversary shareholder meeting. See Masayoshi Son, "SoftBank's Next 30-Year Vision," SoftBank Group, June 25, 2010, group.softbank/en/philosophy/vision/next30.
17. Amy Virshup, "Yahoo! How Two Stanford Students Created the Little Search Engine That Could," *Rolling Stone*, Nov. 30, 1995.
18. Mayumi Negishi, "Ties to Saudi Prince Weigh on SoftBank Fund's Future," *Wall Street Journal*, Oct. 17, 2019.
19. Reid, *Architects of the Web*, 259.
20. According to Yahoo's SB-2 filing, the company raised $5 million in its Series B financing. Of this, $1 million came from Sequoia, $2 million came from SoftBank, and an undisclosed additional amount came from Ziff Davis, another of Son's vehicles. The valuation was $35 million pre-money, or $40 million post. For Yang's reaction, see Reid, *Architects of the Web*, 259.
21. By way of comparison, the Accel co-founder Arthur Patterson recalls that around the same time Accel attracted attention by leading a $110 million financing round. This was considered shockingly large, but the money was raised from multiple VC funds.
22. The average fund size when you took into account lesser VC firms was much lower. The National Venture Capital Association put it at $57 million in 1995. See National Venture Capital Association Yearbook 2010, 17, fig. 1.04.
23. In the mid-1990s a trio of Boston-based "growth funds" specialized in minority investments in the $15 million to $20 million range. These were TA Associates, founded in 1968; Summit Part-

ners, established in 1984; and Spectrum Equity, founded in 1994. In addition to the relatively small check size, the Boston growth investors were fundamentally different from Son in the types of companies they backed. They steered clear of unproven or loss-making companies, avoided outfits that were venture backed, and aspired to returns of 3x or 5x. In short, they were not power-law investors.

24. The following scene is reconstructed from interviews with Moritz and with Ron Fisher and Gary Rieschel, who attended the meeting as Son's lieutenants. Moritz, author interviews; Fisher, interview by the author, March 21, 2019; Rieschel, interview by the author, March 18, 2019.

25. Rieschel, author interview. See also Daisuke Wakabayashi and Anton Troianovsky, "Japan's Masayoshi Son Picks a Fight with U.S. Phone Giants," *Wall Street Journal*, Nov. 23, 2012. The *Journal*'s otherwise excellent article conflates Son's Series B and Series C investments.

26. Moritz reflected, "One thing I learned from that meeting was never, ever again to be bullied by an investor with a boatload of money. I only made that mistake once." (Moritz, email to the author, Oct. 29, 2020.) Sequoia's determination to avoid being muscled by Son contributed to its later decision to raise a series of large growth funds. Moritz, author interviews. Moritz's partner Doug Leone makes the same point: "Sequoia having a growth fund stops someone who says, 'Take my capital or I'll invest in your greatest competitor.'" Leone, author interview. See also Alfred Lee, "SoftBank Exerts More Control over Startups," *Information*, Oct. 1, 2018.

27. The gist of this conversation is reconstructed from Yang, interview by the author, Feb. 13, 2019, and Moritz, author interviews.

28. The money came in two tranches: nearly $64 million in March 1996, then another $42 million at the start of April. "Amendment No. 4 to Form SB-2 IPO Registration Statement: Yahoo! Inc.," Securities and Exchange Commission, April 11, 1996.

29. Yahoo had rejected Goldman's advice to price the IPO at $25 per share, opting for a far more cautious $13. The spike on the first day of trading vindicated Goldman's recommendation, although the spike also served Yahoo's purpose of garnering maximum media attention from the flotation.

30. Moritz, author interviews.

31. The investor was Brad Feld. Feld, interview by the author, March 14, 2019.

32. Rieschel, author interview. The atmosphere of the time was also recalled by Jerry Colonna. Colonna, interview by the author, April 4, 2019.

33. As noted previously, the earlier Boston-based growth funds pursued different types of deals. Son was the first to launch a growth fund that took follow-on stakes in high-flying venture-backed companies.

34. In several cases, Son's Japanese imitations were better run and more successful than their American parents. His skill at launching U.S. tech businesses in Japan helped him to talk his way into deals in California.

35. In early 2000, *Forbes* estimated Son's personal fortune at $19.4 billion, up from $4.6 billion in the spring of 1996, when he had placed his monster bet on Yahoo. A large chunk of the extra $15 billion in treasure could be chalked up to Son's move into U.S. technology investing.

36. Moritz, author interviews.

37. Moritz, author interviews.

38. Moritz, author interviews.

39. Moritz, author interviews.

40. Benchmark experimented with offices in London and Israel, but soon closed both operations.

41. The account of Benchmark and eBay owes much to the marvelous work of Randall Stross, who was granted extraordinary access to the partnership in its early years. See Randall E. Stross, *eBoys: The First Inside Account of Venture Capitalists at Work* (New York: Ballantine Books, 2001). I am also grateful to three of the four Benchmark founders—Dunlevie, Kagle, and Rachleff—for reading an early draft of my account and providing feedback.

42. In their first fund, the Benchmark partners kept 20 percent of the profits until their investors got their money back. Thereafter they kept 30 percent. In subsequent funds, they kept 30 percent of all profits. Rachleff, email to the author, Jan. 19, 2020.

43. Rachleff said, "With every successful technology company, if I described to you at the time of their founding what they were going to do, you would have said that's the stupidest idea I ever heard." Rachleff, interview by the author, Nov. 9, 2017.

44. Dunlevie, interview by the author, Feb. 10, 2017.

45. Rachleff held this view even though he later disagreed with it. He later believed that an outstanding board member can improve a 3x outcome, turning it into a 6x. But this is not enough

to significantly impact an early-stage venture fund. In contrast, a 20x outcome, which does impact the fund significantly, is likely to be a huge winner independent of the board member. However, being perceived as a great board member helps increase the likelihood that you have an opportunity to invest in other companies that may deliver a 20x return. Rachleff, email to the author, Jan. 19, 2020.

46. Dunlevie reflects, "You need to give advice in sympathetic terms. I often say, 'Look, I'm not telling you what to do. I'm just telling you what I think might be a better approach to the plan that you've put forward.' That's often ignored, and I bet half the time it's rightly ignored, and I think that's what makes it an interesting business." Dunlevie, author interview.

47. Dunlevie, author interview.

48. Stross, *eBoys*, 28.

49. Stross, *eBoys*, 21–22.

50. AnnaLee Saxenian, *Silicon Valley's New Immigrant Entrepreneurs* (San Francisco: Public Policy Institute of California, 1999).

51. Stross, *eBoys*, 26.

52. Dunlevie, author interview.

53. Stross, *eBoys*, 24.

54. Stross, *eBoys*, 27.

55. Alex Rosen, interview by the author, May 29, 2018.

56. Rachleff, author interview.

57. Stross, *eBoys*, 28.

58. Rachleff, author interview.

59. Laura Holson, "Defining the On-Line; Ebay's Meg Whitman Explores Management, Web Style," *New York Times*, May 10, 1999.

60. Stross, *eBoys*, 59.

61. Stross, *eBoys*, 60.

62. Stross, *eBoys*, 209–10.

63. The columnist was Christopher Byron of MSNBC.com. See Stross, *eBoys*, 211.

64. Sequoia's Yahoo bet would ultimately earn more than this, because the partnership held on to some of the stock into 1999. Meanwhile, another Kleiner Perkins bet, on Juniper Networks, would eclipse Benchmark's eBay return after Juniper soared following its April 1999 flotation.

65. Stross, *eBoys*, 213.

66. eBay's stock had split, so the face value of each share was lower.

67. This multiple would rise as more portfolio companies matured. As of January 2000, Benchmark's most mature fund racked up an astonishing 92x.

68. Son's habit of delegating operational details is emphasized by those who worked with him, including Jan Boyer, a SoftBank investing partner between 1999 and 2002. Boyer, interview by the author, March 7, 2020.

69. Between Alibaba's 2014 IPO and WeWork's failure to go public in 2019, Son was arguably the world's most influential technology investor.

70. The average VC deal had risen from $5.3 million in 1996 to $15 million in 1999. Stross, *eBoys*, 294–97.

71. Stross, *eBoys*, 296.

72. Stross, *eBoys*, 294–95.

73. Both bets, especially the one on Uber, nonetheless generated large profits. As of early 2020, Uber was on course to be the second most profitable deal in Benchmark's twenty-five-year history. (Dunlevie, email to the author, Feb. 4, 2020.) On WeWork, Benchmark reportedly generated a multiple of about 15x, having been able to sell some shares before the valuation collapsed.

CHAPTER EIGHT: MONEY FOR GOOGLE, KIND OF FOR NOTHING

1. Bechtolsheim, interview by the author, Nov. 30, 2018.

2. Little, interview by the author, May 22, 2018.

3. Little's company, Portal Software, sold a billing system for early internet service providers. It was the greatest hit in Accel's first five funds, generating a multiple of 293x for Accel and a profit of $1.7 billion. (Data from Accel.) Based on a back-of-the-envelope calculation, Little concluded that Bechtolsheim probably earned more from his Portal investment than from co-founding Sun. Little, author interview.

4. Richard Brandt, *The Google Guys: Inside the Brilliant Minds of Google Founders Larry Page and Sergey Brin*, 2nd ed. (New York: Portfolio/Penguin, 2011), 48.

5. David Vise and Mark Malseed, *The Google Story: Inside the Hottest Business, Media, and Technology Success of Our Time*, 2nd ed. (New York: Bantam Dell, 2008), 48.
6. Vise and Malseed, *Google Story*, 48.
7. Jacob Jolis, "Frugal After Google," *Stanford Daily*, April 16, 2010.
8. Bechtolsheim, author interview. In 2013, angel investors' habit of investing in startups without saying how much of the company they were buying found expression in an innovation called the SAFE note. This allowed angels to inject capital into startups while deferring the valuation until a later and more formal investment round.
9. Other early angel investors included Ross Perot. See Udayan Gupta, "Venture Capital Dims for Start-Ups, but Not to Worry," *Wall Street Journal*, Jan. 4, 1990, B2.
10. Conway raised a second, much larger angel fund in 1999, with capital of $150 million.
11. By some reckonings, angels provided more money to startups than venture capitalists did. See Andrew Wong, "Angel Finance: The Other Venture Capital," Graduate School of Business at the University of Chicago, Aug. 2001, ssrn.com/abstract=941228.
12. Ken Auletta, *Googled: The End of the World as We Know It*, 2nd ed. (New York: Penguin Books, 2010), 44.
13. Shriram, interview with the author, Dec. 2, 2020.
14. Shriram recalls that Google's valuation was $10 million and there were no "control mechanisms" in the term sheet. Shriram, author interview. The lack of control mechanisms was typical for angel investors, who usually did not go in for the safeguards used by venture capitalists to mitigate the risk in illiquid early-stage investments. See Wong, "Angel Finance," 2–3.
15. National Venture Capital Association Yearbook 2010, 20, fig. 2.02.
16. National Venture Capital Association Yearbook 2010, 9, fig. 1.0.
17. Two conspicuous hedge-fund traders who bet against tech stocks were Stanley Druckenmiller and Julian Robertson. In 1999, Druckenmiller flipped his position and joined the tech bandwagon.
18. John Cassidy, *Dot.Con: The Greatest Story Ever Sold* (New York: HarperCollins, 2002), 213.
19. Auletta, *Googled*, 48.
20. The student author of the Google business plan was Salar Kamangar. The business development executive was Omid Kordestani. Shriram, author interview.
21. The insider was the Netscape co-founder Jim Clark. John Heilemann, "The Networker," *New Yorker*, Aug. 11, 1997.
22. Heilemann, "Networker."
23. Heilemann, "Networker."
24. Heilemann, "Networker."
25. The description of the meeting between Doerr and the Googlers is taken primarily from John Doerr, *Measure What Matters* (New York: Portfolio/Penguin, 2017), 4–5. See also Auletta, *Googled*, 57–58, in iBook.
26. One Sequoia partner commented, "Doug built the relationships that allowed us to exist in the ecosystem."
27. Sameer Gandhi recalls being with Leone during the meeting. He says that afterward the pair discussed Google in the car. "We were both like, 'I have no idea what's there, but something's there. We need to get them to come in.'" Gandhi also recalls a discussion with Moritz in which he described Google as a "gold plated" search engine. Gandhi, interview by the author, May 17, 2019.
28. Moritz, author interviews.
29. Khosla, interview by the author, July 31, 2018.
30. The perception that brands would dominate the internet was summed up by the buoyant stock price of America Online, a portal that aggregated content and services. Moritz, author interviews.
31. Later, Moritz remarked that he had invested in Google at least partly "to help ensure that Yahoo was taken care of." Vise and Malseed, *Google Story*, 65.
32. Shriram, author interview.
33. Vise and Malseed, *Google Story*, 67.
34. Om Malik, "How Google Is That?," *Forbes*, Oct. 4, 1999, forbes.com/1999/10/04/feat.html#10cf995a1652.
35. Moritz recalled, "The understanding when we invested was that a CEO would, among others, be hired over time." Moritz, author interviews.
36. Steven Levy, *In the Plex: How Google Thinks, Works, and Shapes Our Lives* (New York: Simon & Schuster, 2011), 79–80.

37. The lieutenant was Dave Whorton. See John Heilemann, "Journey to the (Revolutionary, Evil-Hating, Cash-Crazy, and Possibly Self-Destructive) Center of Google," *GQ*, Feb. 14, 2005.
38. Vise and Malseed, *Google Story*, 106.
39. Heilemann, "Journey to the (Revolutionary, Evil-Hating, Cash-Crazy, and Possibly Self-Destructive) Center of Google."
40. This summary of venture performance is based on data provided by the data company Burgiss, with additional calculations performed by Steven N. Kaplan of the University of Chicago.
41. Leone, author interview.
42. Jim Swartz, "Oral History of Jim Swartz," interview by John Hollar, Computer History Museum, Oct. 11, 2013, archive.computerhistory.org/resources/access/text/2015/05/102746860-05-01-acc.pdf.
43. Alex Rosen, interview by the author, May 29, 2018.
44. Doerr, interview by the author, March 12, 2021.
45. Levy, *In the Plex*, 80.
46. Heilemann, "Journey to the (Revolutionary, Evil-Hating, Cash-Crazy, and Possibly Self-Destructive) Center of Google."
47. Heilemann, "Journey to the (Revolutionary, Evil-Hating, Cash-Crazy, and Possibly Self-Destructive) Center of Google."
48. Levy, *In the Plex*, 80.
49. Auletta, *Googled*, 64.
50. Doerr, interview with the author, March 5, 2021.
51. Auletta, *Googled*, 67.
52. "Schmidt April Fool Cars 1986 & 2008," May 16, 2008, YouTube, youtube.com/watch?v=cs9FjfSv6Ss.
53. Auletta, *Googled*, 67; Heilemann, "Journey to the (Revolutionary, Evil-Hating, Cash-Crazy, and Possibly Self-Destructive) Center of Google."
54. Auletta, *Googled*, 67. This reconstruction also draws on Schmidt, interview by the author, May 8, 2019.
55. Schmidt, author interview.
56. Moritz recalled that Schmidt's combination of managerial and deeply technical experience was the clincher, adding that Doerr deserves the credit for the hiring. Moritz, email to the author, Oct. 29, 2020. On another occasion, he recalled, "Eric had a professorial demeanor. That helped everything." Moritz, author interviews.
57. Around 2001 the angel backer David Cheriton joked that all he'd received from his Google investment was the "world's most expensive T-shirt." Levy, *In the Plex*, 79.
58. Schmidt, author interview.
59. Other sources notwithstanding, the Google S-1 filing shows that the senior managers and pre-IPO investors were due to retain 82.1 percent of the voting power after flotation. Brin and Page would control 15.8 percent each. See Google's Form S-1 Registration Statement, Aug. 18, 2004, 103.
60. Moritz also felt that the dual share structure contradicted the ideal that Google embodied: that information should be spread widely so that decisions could emerge from open debate rather than from entrenched bosses. Moritz, author interviews.
61. Those who claim that stock market investors under-appreciate future company profits are by definition arguing that overvaluation of stocks will not occur. Given the history of market bubbles, this claim is unconvincing.
62. Google IPO Prospectus, Aug. 18, 2004, www.sec.gov/Archives/edgar/data/1288776/000119312504143377/d424b4.htm. Again, it should be noted that public tech companies including Netflix, Amazon, Salesforce, and Tesla made similar pronouncements and were rewarded with buoyant share prices. There is little evidence that being unlisted is a reliable prerequisite for being farsighted. The advantages of being unlisted lie elsewhere: lower regulatory costs, clearer oversight of managers (provided that boards are vigilant), and a greater ability to surprise competitors with innovations that are developed under the radar.
63. Between 1999 and 2019, an average of only two IPOs per year were conducted as auctions. See data from Jay Ritter of the University of Florida, table 13, site.warrington.ufl.edu/ritter/files/IPOs2019Statistics.pdf. Following Google's Dutch auction, tech startups tended to opt for traditional IPOs: examples include Facebook, LinkedIn, and Twitter. Later, other sorts of IPOs were tried. Spotify and Slack chose direct listings, not auctions. The Benchmark partner Bill Gurley emerged as a champion of IPO reform, sponsoring a conference on the subject in October 2019. On Gurley's advocacy, see Shawn Tully, "Why Famed VC Bill Gurley Thinks IPOs Are

Such a Rip-Off," *Fortune*, June 16, 2020, fortune.com/2020/06/16/vc-bill-gurley-ipo-rip-off-venture-capital.

64. This was the Sequoia fund raised after the one that hit the jackpot with Google.

65. The VC partnerships that returned capital to limited partners included Accel and Kleiner Perkins, as well as Benchmark's European operation. In all, nearly $4 billion was returned to limited partners in the first half of 2002. Lisa Bransten, "A Slowing Environment, High Fees Prompt Return of Uninvested Capital," *Wall Street Journal*, July 1, 2002, wsj.com/articles/SB1025209176769923200.

66. Data from the National Venture Capital Association. As late as 2004, even an elite partnership such as Accel was still experiencing trouble. The Princeton and Harvard endowments cut it off. Yale and MIT declined to take their places. Jim Breyer, interview by the author, Feb. 9, 2019. Breyer was the managing partner of Accel at the time.

67. The entrepreneur was Sean Parker, of whom more in chapter 9. See Adam Fisher, *Valley of Genius: The Uncensored History of Silicon Valley* (New York: Hachette, 2018), 318.

68. These quotations are taken from Paul Graham, "How to Start a Startup," paulgraham.com (blog), March 2005, paulgraham.com/start.html.

69. Paul Graham, "The Venture Capital Squeeze," paulgraham.com (blog), Nov. 2005, paulgraham.com/vcsqueeze.html.

70. Graham elaborated, "Fairchild needed a lot of money to get started. They had to build actual factories. What does the first round of venture funding for a Web-based startup get spent on today? More money can't get software written faster; it isn't needed for facilities, because those can now be quite cheap; all money can really buy you is sales and marketing. A sales force is worth something, I'll admit. But marketing is increasingly irrelevant. On the Internet, anything genuinely good will spread by word of mouth." Paul Graham, "Hiring Is Obsolete," paulgraham.com (blog), May 2005, paulgraham.com/hiring.html.

71. Paul Graham, "A Unified Theory of VC Suckage," paulgraham.com (blog), March 2005, paulgraham.com/venturecapital.html.

72. Paul Graham, "Hiring Is Obsolete."

CHAPTER NINE: PETER THIEL, Y COMBINATOR, AND THE VALLEY'S YOUTH REVOLT

1. Valentine, interview by the author, April 7, 2018.

2. Botha, interviews by the author, May 14 and Sept. 24, 2019, and Nov. 4, 2020.

3. David Kirkpatrick, "With a Little Help from His Friends," *Vanity Fair*, Sept. 6, 2010.

4. Mylene Mangalindan, "Spam, or Not? Plaxo's Service Stirs Debate," *Wall Street Journal*, Feb. 27, 2004.

5. Steve Bertoni, "Sean Parker: Agent of Disruption," *Forbes*, Sept. 21, 2011.

6. Bertoni, "Sean Parker."

7. Kirkpatrick, "With a Little Help from His Friends."

8. Bertoni, "Sean Parker."

9. Bertoni, "Sean Parker."

10. David Kirkpatrick, *The Facebook Effect: The Inside Story of the Company That Is Connecting the World* (New York: Simon & Schuster, 2010), 48.

11. Earlier, Moritz had introduced Parker to Thiel and invited Thiel to invest in Plaxo. So Parker knew Thiel before being reintroduced by Hoffman. Moritz, email to the author, Oct. 29, 2020.

12. Pincus went on to found Zynga, the social-gaming company. Thiel's company, PayPal, had experimented with viral marketing techniques, and Thiel had made other social-networking investments, including in LinkedIn and a Facebook rival called Friendster.

13. Adam Fisher, *Valley of Genius: The Uncensored History of Silicon Valley* (New York: Twelve, 2018), 318.

14. This dialogue and the ensuing scene are based on Levchin's recollection. Levchin, interviews by the author, Sept. 18 and 20, 2017.

15. Moritz recalls that some Sequoia partners initially resisted diluting Sequoia's stake. Moritz, interview by the author, May 28, 2020.

16. Jeremy Stoppelman, interview by the author, Nov. 15, 2017.

17. Botha, author interviews.

18. Luke Nosek, interview by the author, May 12, 2019.

19. Levchin, author interviews.

20. This episode was recalled in detail by Levchin. Moritz did not remember the detail but endorsed the thrust of Levchin's account. Levchin, author interviews; Moritz, author interviews.

21. Thiel's friend David Sacks, who worked for Confinity, told *Fortune*, "Peter was never a nuts-and-bolts operations guy. But he had a knack for identifying all the big strategic issues and getting them right." See Roger Parloff, "Peter Thiel Disagrees with You," *Fortune*, Sept. 22, 2014.

22. "If you are an investor, you don't have a feel for the day-to-day inside the company. You don't know how the CEO is managing the VPs. So if the VPs declare they are at breaking point, you have to respect that." Moritz, author interviews.

23. The investor was Tim Hurd of Madison Dearborn.

24. Nosek, author interview.

25. Thiel's plan was described by numerous sources, including Luke Nosek, John Malloy, and Roelof Botha.

26. Malloy, interview by the author, Feb. 12, 2019.

27. Moritz, interviews by the author, Sept. 24, 2019, and May 21, 2020.

28. Moritz, interview by the author, May 28, 2020; Levchin, email to the author, June 7, 2020.

29. Roelof Botha recalled, "Honestly, Peter didn't really want to run a company. It wasn't his aspiration." Botha, author interviews.

30. Thiel expounded on entrepreneurship in a series of lectures delivered at Stanford in 2012. These later appeared as a book. See Peter Thiel, *Zero to One: Notes on Startups, or How to Build the Future*, with Blake Masters (London: Virgin Books, 2014).

31. Thiel, *Zero to One*, 34.

32. Roelof Botha reflected on Sequoia's experience with Zuckerberg: "Part of what I've realized in this business is that you need to modulate yourself. There's a class at Stanford around power dynamics, meaning when do you play high and when do you play low. I think the danger is that if you're a successful investor and you've made a lot of money, especially if you grew up in an era where capital was a source of power, you play high the whole time. And I don't think that's a recipe for success in this business." Botha, author interviews.

33. "When the press release came out, it was a surprise to us to find out that our CEO was gone. It didn't feel great." Botha, author interviews.

34. Jessica Guynn, "The Founders Fund Emerges as Venture 2.0," *San Francisco Chronicle*, Dec. 13, 2006.

35. Guynn, "Founders Fund Emerges as Venture 2.0."

36. Howery had planned to call the fund Clarium Ventures until Nosek counter-proposed the name Founders Fund. Nosek, author interview.

37. Nosek, author interview.

38. Of the first fund's $50 million, $35 million came from Thiel and Howery. There was only one institutional investor—a British one. Nosek, author interview.

39. Thiel, *Zero to One*, 83.

40. Lynnley Browning, "Venture Capitalists, Venturing Beyond Capital," *New York Times*, Oct. 15, 2000.

41. In the forty-five years between 1974 and 2019, even the premier venture firm, Sequoia, had just forty-two investments that returned 20x or better. Michael Moritz, *DTV* (self-published, 2020), 51.

42. Nosek also believed that a laissez-faire attitude to founders would attract the best founders to Thiel's venture fund. "The entrepreneurs that are really, really committed to running these companies know that they're the ones to do it and nobody else is able to do it. . . . It's weaker entrepreneurs that would self-select for a VC who might fire them." Nosek, author interview.

43. Trae Stephens, interview by the author, March 29, 2019. Stephens became a partner at Founders Fund in 2014.

44. The analogy with the diamond trade is taken from Browning, "Venture Capitalists."

45. "The hazards of imitative competition may partially explain why individuals with an Asperger's-like social ineptitude seem to be at an advantage in Silicon Valley today," Thiel wrote. Thiel, *Zero to One*, 40.

46. Thiel, *Zero to One*, 173.

47. Thiel, *Zero to One*, 34, 188.

48. Nosek, author interview.

49. Nosek, author interview.

50. Sebastian Mallaby, *More Money Than God: Hedge Funds and the Making of a New Elite* (New York: Penguin Press, 2010), 84–86.

51. Asked in 2019 whether Founders Fund would press the founder-friendly principle as far as not firing a clearly problematic leader such as Travis Kalanick of Uber, Trae Stephens replied that Founders Fund would not have removed Kalanick. Stephens, author interview.

52. Cyan Banister was a partner at Founders Fund from 2016 to 2020. Banister, interview with the author, May 16, 2019.

53. In one celebrated instance in 1992, Soros urged Druckenmiller to "go for the jugular"—to multiply the size of his notorious bet against the British currency tenfold, a move that precipitated Britain's ejection from the European exchange-rate mechanism. Mallaby, *More Money Than God*, 161.

54. In a $1 billion fund, Founders Fund might well bet half its cash on as few as five companies. Stephens, author interview.

55. Nosek, author interview.

56. Guynn, "Founders Fund Emerges as Venture 2.0."

57. Nosek, author interview.

58. Alex Konrad, "Move Over, Peter Thiel—How Brian Singerman Became Founders Fund's Top VC," *Forbes*, April 25, 2017.

59. The other potential investor was the aerospace giant Northrop Grumman. Konrad, "Move Over, Peter Thiel."

60. Thiel's first venture fund, raised in 2005, returned six times capital, net of fees. His second fund, from 2007, returned better than 8x. His third fund, from 2010, had returned 3.8x as of 2019. See Katie Roof, "Founders Fund, a Premier Venture Firm in Transition, Has Outsize Returns," *Wall Street Journal*, Feb. 26, 2019.

61. The official capacity of 305 Emerson is eighty-five people. Ohanian reports that about a hundred had crowded in to hear Graham. Alexis Ohanian, *Without Their Permission: The Story of Reddit and a Blueprint for How to Change the World* (New York: Grand Central Publishing, 2013), 47.

62. Christine Lagorio-Chafkin, *We Are the Nerds: The Birth and Tumultuous Life of Reddit, the Internet's Culture Laboratory* (New York: Hachette, 2018), 20.

63. Paul Graham, "Paul Graham on Doing Things Right by Accident," interview by Aaron Harris and Kat Manalac, *Startup School Radio, Y Combinator* (blog), Feb. 17, 2016, blog.ycombinator .com/paul-graham-startup-school-radio-interview/.

64. Ohanian, *Without Their Permission*, 47–54.

65. Lagorio-Chafkin, *We Are the Nerds*, 4.

66. Graham, "Paul Graham on Doing Things Right by Accident."

67. Livingston, interview by the author, June 6, 2019.

68. Graham, emails to the author.

69. Graham, emails to the author. Livingston recalled, "To a programmer like Paul the idea of standardizing everything about investing was smart and efficient. Instead of ad hoc investing, we processed people as a group." Livingston, author interview.

70. Before Y Combinator, there had been startup "incubators." The first was Idealab, based in Pasadena, California, and founded in 1996. It offered office space, administrative support, and other services to startups. See Laura M. Holson, "Hard Times in the Hatchery," *New York Times*, Oct. 30, 2000.

71. Ohanian, *Without Their Permission*, 138.

72. Ryan Singel, "Stars Rise at Startup Summer Camp," *Wired*, Sept. 13, 2005, wired.com/2005/09 /stars-rise-at-startup-summer-camp.

73. The speaker was Olin Shivers of Northeastern University. Lagorio-Chafkin, *We Are the Nerds*, 48.

74. Margaret Kane, "Say What? Young People Are Just Smarter," *CNET*, March 28, 2007, cnet.com /news/say-what-young-people-are-just-smarter.

75. Paul Graham, "Startup Investing Trends," paulgraham.com (blog), June 2013, paulgraham.com /invtrend.html.

76. Graham, "Startup Investing Trends." Graham also explored the displacement of corporate hierarchies by startup networks in Paul Graham, "The High-Res Society," paulgraham.com (blog), Dec. 2008, paulgraham.com/highres.html.

CHAPTER TEN: TO CHINA, AND STIR

1. Rieschel, interviews by the author, March 18 and Nov. 7, 2019.

2. Rieschel recalled a mentor in Japan advising him, "Gary-san, I have something very important to tell you. Don't try to be Japanese. We're better at it than you are." Rieschel, interviews by the author.

3. Data are from the FRED database maintained by the Federal Reserve Bank of St. Louis.

4. Rieschel, author interviews.

5. "The Valley of Money's Delight," *Economist*, March 27, 1997, economist.com/special-report/1997 /03/27/the-valley-of-moneys-delight.

6. In the five years starting in 2015, China-focused VCs raised a total of $216 billion and U.S. VCs raised $215 billion. Data on Chinese venture capital come from China's Zero2IPO Research Center. Data on U.S. venture capital come from the National Venture Capital Association.

7. Qiming's first three funds, raised between 2006 and 2011, generated 1.8x, 7.1x, and 3.4x net to investors. Total capital raised was $961 million. Total distributions net to investors were $4.1 billion. In health care, home runs included Gan & Lee, Venus, Zai, Tigermed, and CanSino.

8. In 2018, China boasted 206 unicorns, compared with 203 in the United States. Meanwhile, the *Forbes* Midas List featured several Chinese investors among the top ten: Neil Shen (1), JP Gan (5), Kathy Xu (6), and Hans Tung (7). See Peter Elstrom, "China's Venture Capital Boom Shows Signs of Turning into a Bust," *Bloomberg*, July 9, 2019, bloomberg.com/news/articles/2019-07 -09/china-s-venture-capital-boom-shows-signs-of-turning-into-a-bust.

9. Shen was ranked first in the Forbes Midas List in 2018, 2019, and 2020.

10. As of 2016, 17 percent of Chinese venture investors were women, compared with 10 percent in Silicon Valley. Shai Oster and Selina Wang, "How Women Won a Leading Role in China's Venture Capital Industry," *Bloomberg*, Sept. 19, 2016.

11. Chinese banks were generally unwilling to lend even to large private companies on the basis of their cash flows. Startups were way off their radar screens.

12. Before Lin, there were a handful of Asian venture investors, notably Ta-lin Hsu of H&Q Asia Pacific and Lip-Bu Tan of Walden International. These pioneers had been trained in the United States and financed mainland Chinese ventures in the early 1990s. But, much like General Doriot in New England in the 1950s and 1960s, they seized the lion's share of the equity in the projects they financed and refused to share profits with their own investment staff. And so, also like Doriot, they were soon eclipsed by rivals who were readier to spread the bounty.

13. Duncan Clark, *Alibaba: The House That Jack Ma Built* (New York: HarperCollins, 2016), 112.

14. Lin, interview by the author, Oct. 9, 2019. I am grateful to Lin for a marathon interview, lasting most of a day, as well as for numerous follow-up emails.

15. Lin, author interview.

16. Lin, author interview. See also Clark, *Alibaba*, 114.

17. Lin, author interview.

18. Lin, author interview.

19. Lin, author interview.

20. Son, interview by David Rubenstein, *The David Rubenstein Show*, Oct. 11, 2017.

21. Gary Rieschel, who at the time worked for Son at SoftBank, says the Beijing handshake sealed the Alibaba investment and specified terms: $20 million for 20 percent of the company. However, Lin recalls that Son's apparent commitment still needed to be translated into a firm deal, not least because Goldman held rights in Alibaba that effectively empowered it to veto a new injection of equity. Son therefore had to negotiate with Lin, and the Tokyo meeting set this process in motion. Lin's account is supported by Mark Schwartz and also by Ed Sun, who handled legal work associated with Goldman's private investments in Asia. Rieschel, author interview; Lin, author interview; Sun, interview with the author, July 29, 2020.

22. Lin, author interview.

23. Rieschel, author interviews.

24. In follow-up negotiations, Son tried to persuade Goldman to let him take a $40 million investment in Alibaba. As with Yahoo, when he saw a bet he liked, he wanted as much of it as possible. In the end, Goldman allowed Son to invest only $20 million but let him have a larger stake than had been envisaged: not 20 percent, but 30 percent. Lin, author interview. See also Clark, *Alibaba*, 127.

25. Son says that for three days in early 2000 he was richer even than Bill Gates. Son, Rubenstein interview.

26. The exact profit Son made on Alibaba is unclear, because his initial $20 million investment was supplemented by a promise to absorb losses at Alibaba's e-commerce arm. SoftBank insiders seem unsure how much that promise cost. However, the $58 billion payout makes it safe to say that this was the greatest venture bet ever.

27. Son's Alibaba coup did not protect him from another round of disgrace in 2019–2020, when huge and hasty bets made through his Vision Fund turned sour.

28. The claims of preferred stock holders come before those of common stock holders in bankruptcy, and preferred stock can confer protection against ownership dilution when the company raises more capital.

29. Shirley Lin of Goldman Sachs was among the western investors who pushed for the novel legal structure. She recalls, "I spent a lot of time with the lawyers to come up with a semi-legal structure which the GS investment committee would agree to, which was a high bar." Her bills with the law firms Davis Polk and Sullivan & Cromwell were "astronomical." Lin, author interview.

30. Sometimes the internet licenses were owned by Chinese citizens rather than a Chinese operating company. See Kaitlyn Johnson, "Variable Interest Entities: Alibaba's Regulatory Work-Around to China's Foreign Investment Restrictions," *Loyola University Chicago International Law Review* 12, no. 2 (2015): 249–66, lawecommons.luc.edu/cgi/viewcontent.cgi?article=1181&context=lucilr.

31. The ambiguity of China's position on the legal status of foreign-backed internet startups caused uncertainty for western investors into the early years of the twenty-first century.

32. China's early startup successes illustrate the point that it is often easier for developing economies to outsource legal institutions than to create them. This is an insight often stressed by Paul Romer, a Nobel laureate and former chief economist at the World Bank who has promoted the controversial idea of charter cities. See Sebastian Mallaby, "The Politically Incorrect Guide to Ending Poverty," *Atlantic*, July/Aug. 2010.

33. Of the atmosphere in Shanghai in 1999, the prominent entrepreneur Bo Shao remembered, "Nobody knew what the hell a stock option was. I struggled for several months thinking how to translate the concept." Shao, interview by the author, Feb. 14, 2019.

34. Wu, interview by the author, Nov. 12, 2019.

35. Wu, author interview.

36. Lau, interview by the author, July 31, 2019.

37. Looking back, Lin believes the partner might have been trying to warn her off an investment path that would do her career at Goldman no good. Lin, author interview.

38. Wu, author interview. Ed Sun, the Goldman Sachs lawyer responsible for the firm's private stakes in Asia, confirms that the investment committee in New York was willing to liquidate Lin's venture positions "for zero." Sun, author interview.

39. The Goldman Sachs sale of Alibaba stock was completed in two tranches, in December 2003 and March 2004. In a parallel incident, the U.S. venture group IDG off-loaded its Tencent stake to a South African publisher, Naspers, earning between 10x and 20x. Had it held on until 2020, it would have owned a large stake in the world's seventh-biggest company.

40. Xu, interview by the author, Nov. 8, 2019. See also Stephen Glain, "Rainmaker," *Forbes*, March 28, 2008.

41. Glain, "Rainmaker."

42. Xu moved from her audit company to an investment bank, and thence to a private-equity firm, Baring Private Equity Asia. Xu, author interview. See also Glain, "Rainmaker."

43. Xu, author interview.

44. In its early years, JD.com went by a variety of names, including 360buy.com.

45. Xu, author interview.

46. Xu, author interview.

47. Xu, author interview.

48. Shen, interviews by the author, June 20 and Nov. 10, 2019, and Nov. 6, 2020.

49. Where a western first name is used, it is presented before the family name. Where a Chinese first name is used, Chinese practice is followed and the first name is presented after the family name.

50. Leone, interview by the author, May 14, 2019.

51. Shen, author interviews.

52. Sequoia China's first fund was also slightly smaller than Qiming's, which weighed in at $192 million.

53. Glen Sun, who joined Sequoia China soon after its founding, was struck by the modesty of the office. He had previously worked at the U.S. private-equity firm General Atlantic. Sun, interview by the author, Nov. 10, 2019.

54. David Su, interview by the author, Nov. 8, 2019. Su was one of KP's China partners.

55. Kleiner Perkins went on to raise a second China fund in 2011. This one performed better than the first. Doerr, interview with the author, March 5, 2021.

56. Leone undertook the responsibility for overseeing the China business at first. Around 2008, he shifted focus to Sequoia's growth funds, and Moritz took the lead in overseeing China and India. Years later, Gary Rieschel credited Moritz and Leone with investing an unusually large amount of time in China, which made it possible to integrate Shen and his team. Rieschel, author interviews.

57. Moritz, author interviews.
58. Shen, author interviews.
59. The medical research company was Green Villa Holdings. See Amy Orr, "Carlyle Suing Rival over a Deal in China," *Wall Street Journal,* Dec. 10, 2008.
60. At the time of Zhang's departure, Sequoia China's public statement listed the deals he had led. Of these, the most prominent was Asia Media, but this had been forced to delist from the Tokyo Stock Exchange in September 2008 following allegations that the CEO had misappropriated funds. See Sequoia China press release, Jan. 25, 2009, it.sohu.com/20090125/n261946976.shtml. See also Lindsay Whipp, "Audit Problems Hit Asia Media," *Financial Times,* July 25, 2008.
61. The Sequoia China IPOs included a wealth manager and a fast-food chain. The fact that these ventures were less tech intensive than a normal Valley startup signaled that Moritz had allowed Shen to adapt to Chinese conditions. Shen, author interviews.
62. Data on capital raising come from Zero2IPO. Data on U.S. deals in China are from Thilo Hanemann et al., "Two-Way Street: 2019 Update US-China Direct Investment Trends," Rhodium Group, May 2019, wita.org/atp-research/china-us-fdi-trends/.
63. Shen, author interviews.
64. Sun, author interview.
65. On a hike in September 2019, Wang asked the author questions about his past books, but evidently knew most of the answers already.
66. Sun, author interview.
67. When at Ctrip, Shen had upped the company's valuation before finalizing a deal with the New York growth investor Tiger Global. The reason was that the end of the SARS epidemic had transformed the business outlook. Scott Shleifer, interview by the author, Sept. 16, 2019.
68. Kai-Fu Lee, *AI Superpowers: China, Silicon Valley, and the New World Order* (Boston: Houghton Mifflin Harcourt, 2018), 24.
69. Also in 2015, U.S. VCs completed some 350 deals in China. Hanemann et al., "Two-Way Street," 38. Data also found in Zero2IPO.
70. The 2015 *Forbes* Midas List ranked Steven Ji of Sequoia China twenty-second, mainly because of profits from Dianping. It ranked Kui Zhou of Sequoia China sixty-first.
71. China's venture industry continued to differ from the United States' in that it was more geographically dispersed, with centers in Beijing, Shanghai, and Hong Kong. However, given the revolution in transport and communications that had occurred since Silicon Valley's formative years, China's geographic spread was unsurprising. A "cluster" no longer had to be in one location.
72. Xu, author interview.
73. In the case of the earlier Didi-Kuaidi merger, VCs do not appear to have played a leading role. Instead, this was played by the investment banker Bao Fan and by Jean Liu of Goldman Sachs.
74. The author is grateful to Shen for sharing photos of this scene.
75. Shen, author interviews.
76. In January 2016, Meituan-Dianping raised capital at a pre-money valuation of $16.2 billion, a $5 billion markup on the combined valuation of the two companies at their prior financings.
77. By late 2020, Sequoia's original $12 million investment in what was Meituan was worth more than $5 billion, exceeding the gain on Sequoia's $12.5 million investment in Google.

CHAPTER ELEVEN: ACCEL, FACEBOOK, AND THE DECLINE OF KLEINER PERKINS

1. Efrusy, interviews by the author, June 7, 2018, and Aug. 18, 2020.
2. Efrusy, author interviews.
3. The two keen cyclists were Peter Fenton and Jim Goetz, both of whom would emerge as venture superstars over the next decade.
4. Accel internal records, access provided to the author by Jim Swartz.
5. Swartz, email to the author, Aug. 19, 2020.
6. Golden, interview with the author, July 25, 2018.
7. Golden, author interview.
8. Efrusy, author interviews. In 2005, eBay bought Skype for $2.6 billion.
9. Golden, author interview.
10. Here and in many places in my account, I am indebted to the masterful work of David Kirkpatrick, whose accuracy my own sources confirmed. See David Kirkpatrick, *The Facebook Effect* (New York: Simon & Schuster, 2010), 115.
11. Golden recalled, "Everyone came away from that process realizing that sometimes you have to shut out all the noise. Never mind the nature of the founders; just focus on the usage and adoption and seize on that." Golden, author interview.

12. Efrusy, author interviews.

13. Efrusy, author interviews.

14. Kirkpatrick, *Facebook Effect*, 116.

15. Fenton, interview by the author, May 14, 2019.

16. The young Accel colleague was Ping Li. Li, interview by the author, March 27, 2019.

17. The following encounter at the Facebook office draws heavily from Kirkpatrick, *Facebook Effect*.

18. Patterson recalls, "I was just able to reinforce Kevin's naturally good analytical judgement that this was a can't-miss project, and urge him to stay close to them for the weekend and get them to present on Monday to the partnership. He executed flawlessly." Patterson, email to the author, May 2, 2019.

19. Efrusy recalls, "Because of our prepared-mind exercise, Arthur was so bought in that when he saw Facebook that Friday evening he said immediately we have to do this one." Efrusy, author interviews. Equally, Jim Swartz comments, "People look at us and think Facebook just happened. But it didn't. It was the result of a prepared-mind exercise." Swartz, interview by the author, Nov. 8, 2017.

20. Kirkpatrick, *Facebook Effect*, 118.

21. Theresia Gouw, interview by the author, March 29, 2019.

22. Gouw, author interview.

23. Kirkpatrick, *Facebook Effect*, 120.

24. Efrusy, author interviews.

25. Gouw, author interview; Fenton, author interview; Jim Breyer, interview by the author, Feb. 9, 2019.

26. Breyer, author interview.

27. Kirkpatrick, *Facebook Effect*, 123.

28. Kirkpatrick, *Facebook Effect*, 123.

29. In 2008, Zuckerberg invited Graham to join Facebook's board.

30. Kirkpatrick, *Facebook Effect*, 146.

31. Kirkpatrick, *Facebook Effect*, 148.

32. Pui-Wing Tam and Shayndi Rayce, "A $9 Billion Jackpot for Facebook Investor," *Wall Street Journal*, Jan. 28, 2012.

33. John Heilemann, "The Networker," *New Yorker*, Aug. 11, 1997.

34. In an interview with the author, Doerr disputed this vigorously. (Doerr, interview with the author, March 5, 2021.) However, a 2017 slide tracking shifting perceptions of top VC partnerships over time, produced by the Brown University endowment, listed Kleiner Perkins as number one from 1980 to 2005 but left Kleiner off its top-eight list thereafter. (The Brown University slide is reproduced in the appendix.) In another typical indication, a 2013 Reuters article reports that Kleiner Perkins did not feature on an industry list of the top ten VC partnerships. The list was composed by researchers from Morgan Stanley and the 451 Group and was based on a study of successful venture exits. (See Sarah McBride and Nichola Groom, "How CleanTech Tarnished Kleiner and VC Star John Doerr," Reuters, Jan. 16, 2013.) The annual Midas List compiled by *Forbes* provides a third measure, although (like any venture ranking) it is backward looking. As reported in the text, in 2001, Kleiner's top partners, Vinod Khosla and John Doerr, came first and third, respectively. Each year from 2005 to 2009, Doerr was listed first or second on the Midas List. But in 2015 he came thirtieth, and only one other Kleiner partner (Mary Meeker) featured in the top fifty; two other KP partners, Beth Seidenberg and Ted Schlein, ranked ninety-first and ninety-ninth. The 2020 Midas List showed further attrition. Doerr came forty-fourth, and the only other Kleiner figure on the list was Mamoon Hamid, who came ninety-third.

35. A 2005 study suggests a correlation of nearly 0.7 between the returns of one venture-capital fund and that firm's next fund. See Steven N. Kaplan and Antoinette Schoar, "Private Equity Performance: Returns, Persistence, and Capital Flows," *Journal of Finance* 60, no. 4 (Aug. 2005): 1791–823. Another study has found that "a 10 percentage-point higher IPO rate among a VC firm's first ten investments—that is, one additional IPO—corresponded to a more than 1.6 percentage point higher IPO rate for all subsequent investments by that firm." See Ramana Nanda, Sampsa Samila, and Olav Sorenson, "The Persistent Effect of Initial Success: Evidence from Venture Capital" Harvard Business School Entrepreneurial Management working paper 17-065, July 25, 2018). As noted in the conclusion, both studies indicate that path dependency is not absolute. VC firms cannot rest on their laurels.

36. John Doerr, "Salvation (and Profit) in Greentech," TED2007, March 2007.

37. Doerr, "Salvation (and Profit) in Greentech."

38. While Kleiner bet on cleantech, Accel conducted a prepared-mind exercise and decided to avoid it.

39. Kleiner's 2006 fund eventually returned capital primarily thanks to two health-care investments, Arresto and Inspire Medical Systems, and two cybersecurity investments, Carbon Black and LifeLock. Data from John Doerr and Amanda Duckworth, March 14, 2021. The weighted (or "pooled") average gross return on the venture industry's 2006 vintage funds was about 2x, so by merely "returning capital," Kleiner's 2006 fund underperformed. Separately, Doerr stresses that only one KP fund has ever lost money; this was the fund hit by the Nasdaq crash of 2000. Doerr, author interview.

40. Kleiner reported that its 2010 vintage fund, KPCB XIV, was up 7x before subtracting fees, as of March 2021. However, Kleiner's reported results are "as if held," meaning that they include appreciation on shares even after these are distributed to limited partners.

41. Kleiner impressed upon the author that, as of Q1 2021, its total cleantech portfolio had generated $5.7 billion on investments of $1.9 billion before subtracting fees. Without further detail and disaggregation, which Kleiner declined to provide, this number is hard to evaluate. First, Kleiner's reported results are inflated to an unknown degree by the use of the nonstandard as-if-held convention (see previous note). Second, it's not clear which vintage the result should be compared to. Kleiner's 3x return compares favorably with the average of 2.8x gross for the industry's vintage 2008 funds but unfavorably with the average 3.6x gross return on the industry's 2010 vintage. Third, all benchmark data used here take Q3 2020 as the end point. Because Kleiner was reporting results as of late Q1 2021, the equity market's appreciation in the interim flatters the partnership's performance. Benchmark data are from Steven N. Kaplan of the University of Chicago.

42. As stated in note 34, above, the Midas List is backward looking. Hence Doerr could appear on the list despite having stepped down as a Kleiner investing partner.

43. The following account of Kleiner's internal culture draws on interviews with numerous partners, including Brook Byers, Frank Caufield, Kevin Compton, John Doerr, Vinod Khosla, Aileen Lee, Mary Meeker, Ted Schlein, and Trae Vassallo.

44. Frank Caufield, interview by the author, May 15, 2018.

45. Khosla recalls that Mackenzie was "a great check on everybody else because he always asked the hard questions." Khosla, author interview.

46. Aileen Lee, interview by the author, June 20, 2019; Trae Vassallo, interview by the author, June 24, 2019.

47. One former Kleiner partner recalls, "Bringing in very senior managers came with a risk. At that point in their career, these senior people are used to calling the shots. But on the board of a portfolio company, a VC is just one voice: you have to wield influence and not bark out commands. And not all operators make great investors. If you look at [Ray] Lane's track record as an investor, it was bad. He had no sense of how bullish to be on some companies. He didn't know when to double down."

48. "I don't think I saw anything in cleantech that was 10x different," Compton observed later. Compton, interview by the author, Feb. 12, 2019.

49. Doerr, author interview.

50. Paul A. Gompers and Sophie Q. Wang, "Diversity in Innovation" (working paper 17-067, Harvard Business School, 2017), hbs.edu/faculty/Publication%20Files/17-067_b5578676-e44c-40aa-a9d8-9e72c287afe8.pdf. The authors add that the proportion of women receiving science and engineering PhDs was at least three times higher than the proportion of women entering the venture industry: it increased from 30 percent to more than 40 percent between 1990 and 2012. Likewise, the proportion of women receiving MBAs increased from 35 percent to 47 percent over this period.

51. Lee, interview by the author, June 20, 2019.

52. Lee, author interview.

53. Lee, author interview.

54. Lee, author interview.

55. Lee, author interview.

56. Vassallo, interview by the author, June 25, 2019.

57. Vassallo, author interview.

58. Later, the Pao trial surfaced emails from Pao to Doerr. In one she wrote, "I have no problem with a Randy board seat at all. . . . I'm very happy with the outcome and have absolutely no issue

with it." See Nellie Bowles and Liz Gannes, "At Kleiner Perkins Trial, Randy Komisar Accuses Ellen Pao of 'Politicking,'" *Recode*, March 17, 2015, vox.com/2015/3/17/11560414/at-kleiner-perkins-trial-randy-komisar-accuses-ellen-pao-of.

59. "The old folks should invest time in the younger partners to cultivate them. They should not exploit the young folks to leverage their brands." Vassallo, author interview. Commenting on this point, Doerr described the question of whether senior partners should take board seats as "a judgment call." Doerr, author interview.
60. Ellen Pao, "This Is How Sexism Works in Silicon Valley," *New York*, Aug. 21, 2017, thecut.com/2017/08/ellen-pao-silicon-valley-sexism-reset-excerpt.html.
61. Deborah Gage, "Former Kleiner Partner Trae Vassallo Testifies of Unwanted Advances," *Wall Street Journal*, Feb. 25, 2015.
62. Pao's complaints are set out on October 16, 2013: s3.amazonaws.com/s3.documentcloud.org/documents/1672582/pao-complaint.pdf.
63. These details are taken from Vassallo's sworn testimony in the Pao trial. See Gage, "Former Kleiner Partner Trae Vassallo Testifies of Unwanted Advances."
64. Trae Vassallo et al., "Elephant in the Valley," www.elephantinthevalley.com.
65. Paul A. Gompers et al., "Gender Effects in Venture Capital," SSRN, May 2014, ssrn.com/abstract=2445497.
66. The four ex-Kleiner women running their own firms were Mary Meeker, Aileen Lee, Beth Seidenberg, and Trae Vassallo. The first three were also on the Midas List in 2018, 2019, and 2020, with Meeker ranked among the top ten VCs worldwide. Doerr invested his personal wealth with all these managers.
67. Commenting on this verdict, Doerr argued that a lack of formal management is typical and indeed healthy at venture partnerships and that he personally was not in charge of the partnership because leadership was collective. Doerr, author interview.
68. Accel's top seven winners after 2006 were CrowdStrike (Sameer Gandhi), Qualtrics (Ryan Sweeney), Slack (Andrew Braccia), Atlassian (Rich Wong), Flipkart (Subrata Mitra), Supercell (Kevin Comolli), and Tenable (John Locke and Ping Li). These seven included three startup and four growth investments across three geographies, the United States, Europe, and India.
69. Theresia Gouw became an Accel managing partner; Sonali De Rycker became co-lead of the London office.
70. Swartz, author interviews.
71. In 2015, in a confirmation that famous venture firms could not take their supremacy for granted, a study showed that just over half the top VC investments since 2000 had been done by new and emerging partnerships. Cambridge Associates, "Venture Capital Disrupts Itself: Breaking the Concentration Curse" (2015).

CHAPTER TWELVE: A RUSSIAN, A TIGER, AND THE RISE OF GROWTH EQUITY

1. Yuri Milner, interviews by the author, May 13 and July 27, 2019, and Nov. 24, 2020. See also Jessi Hempel, "Facebook's Friend in Russia," *Fortune*, Oct. 4, 2010, fortune.com/2010/10/04/facebooks-friend-in-russia/.
2. The partner was Alexander Tamas, later the founder of Vy Capital.
3. Milner, author interviews.
4. David Kirkpatrick, *The Facebook Effect: The Inside Story of the Company That Is Connecting the World* (New York: Simon & Schuster, 2010), 285.
5. Milner, author interviews.
6. Milner, author interviews.
7. Julia Boorstin, "Facebook Scores $200 Million Investment, $10 Billion Valuation," CNBC, May 26, 2009, cnbc.com/id/30945987.
8. Dan Primack, "Marc Andreessen Talks About That Time Facebook Almost Lost 80% of Its Value," *Fortune*, June 18, 2015, fortune.com/2015/06/18/marc-andreessen-talks-about-that-time-facebook-almost-lost-80-of-its-value.
9. Milner, author interviews.
10. Milner, author interviews.
11. Following his initial investment in Facebook, Milner had continued to accumulate stock from ex-employees and early investors, ending up with shares worth $800 million by the end of 2010. Milner, author interviews.
12. Milner's 2009 investment helped Facebook to delay going public until 2012. This three-year extension seems typical. In the 1990s the median age for a U.S. tech company going public was

seven and a half years; in the decade following the Facebook deal, the median age rose to ten and a half years. See data from Jay Ritter of the University of Florida, table 4a, site.warrington .ufl.edu/ritter/files/IPO-Statistics.pdf

13. Milner's hands-off style demanded a calm nerve. Stock market investors can be indifferent to governance because they hold liquid positions: they don't have to vote their shares, because they can easily sell them. In contrast, Milner was buying an illiquid position. Milner, author interviews.

14. In the 1980s, most but not all tech IPOs involved profitable companies. In 1999 only 14 percent were profitable. See Ritter data, table 4a.

15. See Sarah Lacy, "How We All Missed Web 2.0's 'Netscape Moment,'" *TechCrunch*, April 3, 2011, techcrunch.com/2011/04/03/how-we-all-missed-web-2-0s-netscape-moment.

16. Coleman, interviews by the author, June 18 and Sept. 17, 2019.

17. Shleifer, interviews by the author, Sept. 16 and 17, 2019. Shleifer's friend was Andrew Albert of Jacob Asset Management.

18. Peter Lynch, "Stalking the Tenbagger," in *One Up on Wall Street: How to Use What You Already Know to Make Money in the Market*, with John Rothchild (New York: Simon & Schuster, 1989), 95–106.

19. Coleman, author interviews.

20. Coleman investment letter, July 2003.

21. Shleifer, author interviews.

22. Shleifer, author interviews.

23. Coleman, author interviews.

24. Coleman recalls, "There was no good analogy for what they were trying to do." Likewise, Tiger missed an opportunity to invest early in the Chinese search engine Baidu, partly because Google's huge profitability had not yet been demonstrated in the United States. In the absence of a strong analogy, Tiger was leery of committing capital. Tiger was already taking enough risk by venturing into China, trusting in the unproven VIE structure, and moving from public markets into private equity. As Coleman says, "Institutionally, there is only so much risk an investment company is set up to take." Coleman, author interviews.

25. Shen, interview by the author, Nov. 6, 2020.

26. Shleifer, author interviews.

27. Coleman, author interviews.

28. Michael Wolff, "How Russian Tycoon Yuri Milner Bought His Way into Silicon Valley," *Wired*, Oct. 21, 2011.

29. Alexandra Wolfe, "Weekend Confidential: Yuri Milner," *Wall Street Journal*, Nov. 22, 2013, wsj .com/articles/weekend-confidential-yuri-milner-1385166742.

30. Starting in 2005, successive Tiger private investment partnerships backed DST. When DST was listed in London in 2010, Tiger owned two-fifths of it. By this point, the Tiger partner leading the relationship with Milner was Lee Fixel. Shleifer, author interviews; Fixel, interview by the author, Dec. 4, 2019.

31. Milner, interview by the author, May 13, 2019.

32. Sequoia had raised a growth fund at the peak of the bubble, in 1999. After the 2000 crash, its value was down to 0.3x the initial capital. The fund ultimately returned about 2x, but only because the Sequoia partners reinvested their shares of winning positions in the fund, essentially working for the outside investors for free until they made them whole. Leone, Moritz, and Botha, author interviews.

33. Over the course of several purchases, Tiger Global bought about 2 percent of Facebook before its IPO, at an average valuation of $20 billion.

34. Coleman, author interviews.

35. In August 2011, Milner led a round for the social network Twitter, coupling his purchase of $400 million of company-issued primary stock with a deal to buy a further $400 million from employees. In the two years since the Facebook transaction, Milner's deal structure had not changed. But the dollar numbers had doubled.

36. On the total amount of capital in tech investments, see Begum Erdogan et al., "Grow Fast or Die Slow: Why Unicorns Are Staying Private," McKinsey & Company, May 11, 2016. Other sources suggest that by 2018 nearly $120 billion was invested.

37. Aileen Lee, "Welcome to the Unicorn Club, 2015: Learning from Billion-Dollar Companies," *TechCrunch*, July 18, 2015, techcrunch.com/2015/07/18/welcome-to-the-unicorn-club-2015 -learning-from-billion-dollar-companies.

38. Yuri Milner, "Looking Beyond the Horizon" (MBA graduation speech, Wharton School of the University of Pennsylvania, Philadelphia, May 14, 2017).

39. In a later blog post, Horowitz listed no fewer than twenty-four long-lived technology firms whose founders had remained at the helm for years. See Ben Horowitz, "Why We Prefer Founding CEOs," Andreessen Horowitz, April 28, 2010, a16z.com/2010/04/28/why-we-prefer-founding-ceos.

40. An analysis of the top hundred venture-backed exits between 2009 and 2014 by CB Insights, a data provider, shows that Sequoia Capital portfolio companies accounted for twenty-two of the total. NEA and Accel Partners, respectively, participated in thirteen of the exits each. See "The Venture Capital Power Law—Analyzing the Largest 100 U.S. VC-Backed Tech Exits," CB Insights Research, March 8, 2014, cbinsights.com/research/venture-capital-power-law-exits.

41. Andreessen appeared on Charlie Rose on February 19, 2009.

42. The quotation is taken from Andreessen's blog. See Marc Andreessen, "The Truth About Venture Capitalists," *pmarca* (blog), June 8, 2007. In addition, academic survey work suggests that the most important VC skill is deal selection. See Paul A. Gompers et al., "How Do Venture Capitalists Make Decisions?," *Journal of Financial Economics* 135, no. 1 (Jan. 2020): 169–90.

43. Casado, interview by the author, Aug. 7, 2019.

44. Casado, author interview.

45. Horowitz, author interview.

46. Andreessen, author interview.

47. Horowitz, author interview.

48. Horowitz, author interview.

49. Horowitz, author interview.

50. Andreessen declares, "The founder-friendly thing is completely constructed from the outside. That's not from us. This was one of the big myths. We are pro-founder performance." Andreessen, author interview.

51. Horowitz had been a network engineer early in his career. He invested in Nicira partly because he was struck by how little the networking industry had been disrupted since then. Horowitz, author interview.

52. The Zynga investment was profitable. The Foursquare investment was a disappointment.

53. Dan Primack and Marc Andreessen, "Taking the Pulse of VC and Tech," June 18, 2015, in *The a16z Podcast*, produced by Andreessen Horowitz, youtu.be/_zbZ9ja19RU. Andreessen also cited Milner's cross-country comparisons and willingness to buy secondary shares as influential innovations. Andreessen, author interview.

54. Zoë Bernard, "Andreessen Horowitz Returns Slip, According to Internal Data," *Information*, Sept. 16, 2019, theinformation.com/articles/andreessen-horowitz-returns-slip-according-to-internal-data.

55. Bernard, "Andreessen Horowitz Returns Slip." The funds referred to here are Funds II and III, launched in 2010 and 2012, not the accompanying Annex or Parallel Funds launched in 2011 and 2012. Both funds had yet to mature fully, so this performance measure is not definitive.

56. Alex Konrad, "Andreessen Horowitz Is Blowing Up the Venture Capital Model (Again)," *Forbes*, April 30, 2019. Both founders admit to Konrad that their original marketing pitch was exaggerated. "Venture capital wasn't an industry in crisis," Andreessen says. "I went too far," Horowitz confesses. The non-entrepreneur who made general partner was Connie Chan.

57. Yael V. Hochberg, Alexander Ljungqvist, and Yang Lu, "Whom You Know Matters: Venture Capital Networks and Investment Performance," *Journal of Finance* 62, no. 1 (Feb. 2007): 253. In addition, evidence from a large survey of VCs suggests that only one in ten venture investments are in portfolio companies that had no preexisting link to a VC's network. See Gompers et al., "How Do Venture Capitalists Make Decisions?" Accel, Benchmark, and Founders Fund are examples of venture shops that launched with a claim to a novel approach, but whose success owed at least as much to the preexisting networks of the founding partners.

CHAPTER THIRTEEN: SEQUOIA'S STRENGTH IN NUMBERS

1. See Bruce Schoenfeld, "What Happened When Venture Capitalists Took Over the Golden State Warriors," *New York Times*, March 30, 2016. On data in basketball, see Ben Cohen, "The Golden State Warriors Have Revolutionized Basketball," *Wall Street Journal*, April 6, 2016; and Chris Smith, "Team of the Decade: Golden State Warriors' Value Up 1,000% Since 2009," *Forbes*, Dec. 23, 2019.

2. "Why Startups Are Leaving Silicon Valley," *Economist*, Aug. 20, 2018.

3. See Christopher Mims, "China Seeks Out Unlikely Ally: U.S. Tech Firms," *Wall Street Journal*, Sept. 21, 2015; and Gardiner Harris, "State Dinner for Xi Jinping Has High-Tech Flavor," *New York Times*, Sept. 25, 2015.

4. In 2009, there were fourteen hundred investors looking for deals in the United States. A decade later there were thirty-five hundred. Before 2009, fewer than five thousand startups were funded per year. By 2019, the rate was about ten thousand. See "NVCA 2020 Yearbook," National Venture Capital Association, March 2020, nvca.org/wp-content/uploads/2020/04 /NVCA-2020-Yearbook.pdf.

5. Sequoia had hired two women to make bioscience investments in the late 1980s and 1990s. They left later in the 1990s. After that, the next female investing partner at Sequoia in the United States was Jess Lee, hired in 2016. In 2017, a former analyst was promoted to partner. In 2018, two more women became investing partners. By 2020, women accounted for a bit over a fifth of the U.S. investing team. Sequoia's focus on supporting new investing partners, explained later in this chapter, helped women at the firm avoid the frustration experienced by their peers at Kleiner Perkins. The low point for Sequoia on gender came in 2016, when a partner named Michael Goguen was accused of horrific abuse by an exotic dancer. Goguen left the firm and later won the legal fight against his accuser.

6. On hiring preferences, Moritz was describing the approach of his mentor, Don Valentine, but it was his own approach, too. Michael Moritz, *DTV* (self-published, 2020), 40.

7. Alex Ferguson, *Leading: Learning from Life and My Years at Manchester United*, with Michael Moritz (London: Hodder & Stoughton, 2015), 377. The quotations are taken from the epilogue, which is by Moritz.

8. Calacanis, email to the author, Oct. 3, 2019. Likewise, an investor who spent some years at Sequoia but did not do well enough to stay made the same point to the author: "The secret of Sequoia is that they will work harder than you."

9. Ferguson, *Leading*, 353.

10. The senior partner was Pierre Lamond. Botha, interviews by the author, May 14 and Sept. 24, 2019, and Nov. 4, 2020.

11. Botha, author interviews.

12. Leone, author interviews.

13. Botha, author interviews. The muscular player was Jim Goetz.

14. "This is just one small example of going above & beyond the call of duty," the memo stated. Sequoia Capital, "WhatsApp Milestone Note," Feb. 19, 2014.

15. Formally, the shift occurred in 2009, but it had begun informally a year or so earlier. Goetz, author interview.

16. The problem of being reactive was all the more acute because founders tended to pitch to Sequoia late; they practiced their lines on less demanding audiences before performing on Broadway. The upshot was that Sequoia was not only reactive. It had to react to pitches under the pressure of short deadlines.

17. Speaking of Botha's efforts, Jim Goetz said, "The work he did on behavioral psychology was possibly the most important change we made within venture." Goetz, author interview.

18. The VC quoted here is CRV's George Zachary. The quotation is taken from the October 12, 2020, edition of the impressive podcast series *20VC*, produced by Harry Stebbings.

19. Botha, author interviews.

20. Botha also stressed the behavioral literature on "anchoring." In putting a value on a startup, Sequoia's partners sometimes were influenced by what other investors believed it might be worth, even when those other investors knew less than they did. In January 2015, for example, Sequoia passed on an opportunity to double down on the 3-D software platform Unity because it was anchoring on the value assigned to the firm in a recent acquisition offer. Seven months later, Sequoia acknowledged its error and invested. But by then Unity's valuation had almost doubled. Sequoia Capital, "Unity Milestone Note," Sept. 18, 2020.

21. Botha, author interviews.

22. Goetz, author interview.

23. Leone, author interviews.

24. Botha, author interviews.

25. Amira Yahyaoui, interview by the author, Nov. 11, 2020. Yahyaoui was a Sequoia-backed founder.

26. Despite his unspecified health issue, Moritz remained fit; on his sixty-fifth birthday, in 2019, he led a peloton of younger men on a celebratory cycle ride.

27. In a valedictory letter to the limited partners, Goetz invoked Sequoia's tradition of betting on youth. "That willingness to renew and reinvent—often by empowering the less experienced

among us—has been the foundation of our success." Michael J. de la Merced, "Sequoia Capital Reshuffles Leadership," *New York Times*, Jan. 31, 2017.

28. Reflecting on Sequoia's winning culture, a well-connected endowment investor observed, "Sequoia manages to have world-class titans that want to be on the A team. They are rich enough that they don't need to work another day. Any of them could leave and raise billions of dollars on their own. But they all want to stay on the A team."

29. Yang, author interview. For the Zingale quotation, see George Anders, "Inside Sequoia Capital: Silicon Valley's Innovation Factory," *Forbes*, March 26, 2014.

30. The partnership's board seats at Dropbox and Airbnb were occupied by Bryan Schreier and Alfred Lin, neither of whom had sourced the deals but both of whom were rising talents.

31. Leone's commitment to coaching recruits was reflected in his contempt for a common venture-capital nostrum: that you can't identify good recruits until years have passed and you can assess their track records. In Leone's estimation, only a distracted manager could hold such a view. Engaged managers know who is good at a much earlier stage because they are paying attention. "You don't have to wait until the final exam to find out if someone is a good student." Leone, author interviews.

32. Gandhi, interview by the author, May 17, 2019.

33. Y Combinator, "Jim Goetz and Jan Koum at Startup School SV 2014," YouTube, youtube.com/watch?v=8-pJa11YvCs.

34. Later, the idea of tracking app store downloads was embraced by all Valley VCs, and the information was sold by a third-party provider. But at the time of the WhatsApp investment, Sequoia had an edge from its proprietary tracker. Goetz, author interview.

35. Brad Stone, *The Upstarts: How Uber, Airbnb, and the Killer Companies of the New Silicon Valley Are Changing the World* (New York: Little, Brown, 2017), 89.

36. Graham recalls of Airbnb, "They might not have raised money at all but for the coincidence that Greg McAdoo, our contact at Sequoia, was one of a handful of VCs who understood the vacation rental business, having spent much of the previous two years investigating it." See Paul Graham, "Black Swan Farming," Sept. 2012, paulgraham.com/swan.html.

37. Sequoia Capital, "Dropbox Milestone Note," March 23, 2018.

38. Other Iranian Americans in tech included Ali and Hadi Partovi, software entrepreneurs and angel investors; Shervin Pishevar, a VC who backed Uber; and Omid Kordestani, an early executive at Google. For more than fifty other examples, see Ali Tamaseb, "Iranian-Americans in Silicon Valley Are Getting More Powerful," Medium, Aug. 28, 2017.

39. Anders, "Inside Sequoia Capital."

40. The scouts program also gave Sequoia a chance to test the investment acumen of potential hires, including Alfred Lin, Mike Vernal, and Jess Lee.

41. Stephen Armstrong, "The Untold Story of Stripe, the Secretive $20 Billion Startup Driving Apple, Amazon, and Facebook," *Wired*, Oct. 5, 2018.

42. In addition to its other virtues, the Collison plan involved targeting the service at coders—the people who actually built e-commerce sites. This community would understand why the Collison solution worked better than credit cards, which sounded reliable in theory but were clunky and costly to build into online platforms.

43. Graham, email to the author, May 31, 2021. The two YC founders were Harj and Kulveer Taggar.

44. Altman and Collison had stayed in touch, sharing ideas on software and startups. "We just hit it off. I didn't expect anything to come of it," Altman said later. Altman, interview by the author, Sept. 20, 2017.

45. Altman, author interview.

46. "Patrick was willing to let us have 4 percent for 30k. In a moment of greater generosity than I realized at the time, I said I'd split it with Sam." Graham, email to the author, Dec. 8, 2020.

47. Botha, author interviews.

48. John Collison, interview by the author, Sept. 21, 2019.

49. Patrick Collison, interview by the author, Sept. 19, 2017.

50. Other early investors in Stripe included Peter Thiel, a16z, Elon Musk, and General Catalyst, as well as Paul Graham and Sam Altman.

51. Data from Burgiss.

52. Proving it was not afraid of risk, Sequoia lost money on nearly half of these 155 venture bets.

53. Shahed Fakhari Larson, "Silicon Valley's Quiet Giant," *Brunswick Review*, Sept. 18, 2019, bruns wickgroup.com/sequoia-capital-doug-leone-silicon-valley-i11786.

54. Sequoia India raised a $400 million growth fund in 2006 and a $300 million early-stage fund in 2007.

55. Shailendra Singh, interview by the author, June 20, 2019.
56. Singh, author interview.
57. Shah, interview by the author, Nov. 4, 2020.
58. Manish Singh, "Sequoia Announces $1.35 Billion Venture and Growth Funds for India and Southeast Asia," *TechCrunch*, July 6, 2020, techcrunch.com/2020/07/06/sequoia-announces -1-35-billion-venture-and-growth-funds-for-india-and-southeast-asia.
59. Botha, author interviews; Leone, author interviews.
60. The first Moritz-Leone growth fund ended up at 2x. Confusingly, this fund was called Growth Fund III because Sequoia had experimented with one growth fund in the late 1980s under Don Valentine's leadership. That early fund performed well, generating 4.5x net to investors, but the average check size was $2 million, meaning that it was invested rather like a venture fund. Leone, author interviews.
61. In 2006, Sequoia hired Scott Carter and Alexander Harrison from Summit Partners. In 2007 it hired Pat Grady and Mickey Arabelovic. The fifth growth specialist was Chris Olsen of TCV. By 2015 all but Grady had left.
62. Pat Grady, interview by the author, Oct. 28, 2020.
63. The history of hedge funds is full of these innovative fusions. For example, in the 1980s figures such as Stanley Druckenmiller combined the company analysis of stock pickers with the chartist traditions of commodity investors.
64. Leone, author interviews.
65. Grady, author interview.
66. Grady, author interview.
67. Grady recalled, "When we started in the growth business [at Sequoia], a lot of the stuff that we did was driven by spreadsheets. When we invested in ServiceNow in 2009, I built the model in sixty minutes fiddling on my couch the minute before we made the final decision. It wasn't about the model. It was about the team, it was about the product, it was about the market." Grady, author interview.
68. The following account of Luddy's Valley tour comes mainly from Grady. Grady, email to the author, Nov. 11, 2020.
69. This point of law was not well understood partly because venture capitalists often have preferred stock conferring rights to block a sale of a company. Sequoia had bought secondary stock in ServiceNow and so did not have this advantage.
70. Leone, author interviews.
71. These results for Sequoia's growth funds are net of fees and carry. They can be compared to QQQ, the publicly traded fund that tracks the Nasdaq-100 index of tech stocks. QQQ returns for the period 2009 to 2021 were 21.5 percent per year. Returns from 2011 to 2021 were 20.3 percent per year.
72. Goetz, author interview.
73. Lizette Chapman, "'Psychological Torture': The Alleged Extortion of a Venture Capitalist," *Bloomberg*, March 14, 2020, bloomberg.com/news/features/2020-03-14/the-story-behind-the -alleged-extortion-of-michael-goguen?sref=C3NLmz0P.
74. Moritz, memo to the Stewards' Council, April 14, 2016.
75. Jeff Wang, email to the author, Nov. 3, 2020.
76. From inception in September 2009 through December 2020, the fund's compounded annual net return was 19 percent. From June 1, 2016, through December 2020, it was 34.5 percent. Over both periods, the MSCI World Index compounded annual growth rate was about 11.5 percent.
77. Moritz, author interviews.
78. Johnson, interview with the author, Sept. 24, 2019.
79. Johnson, author interview.
80. Johnson, author interview.
81. Johnson, author interview.
82. Leone, author interviews.
83. The figure refers to the return net of fees as of September 2020. It is based on the weighted average of fifty-three venture funds captured in the high-quality database maintained by Burgiss. The comparison is with the S&P 500 with dividends reinvested. The top 5 percent of funds outperformed the market index by twenty-three percentage points per year. Data from Steven N. Kaplan at the University of Chicago.
84. In the summer of 2019, Moritz put Wall Street on notice that its IPO fees might be insecure. He predicted that technology firms would soon arrange their own public listings, without

seeking the services of Wall Street. See Michael Moritz, "Investment Banks Are Losing Their Grip on IPOs," *Financial Times*, Aug. 18, 2019, ft.com/content/7985bb78-bdbf-11e9-9381 -78bab8a70848.

CHAPTER FOURTEEN: UNICORN POKER

1. John Carreyrou, *Bad Blood: Secrets and Lies in a Silicon Valley Startup* (New York: Knopf, 2018), 208–9.
2. For an example of the sea change in popular opinion toward venture-backed startups, see Erin Griffith, "The Ugly Unethical Underside of Silicon Valley," *Fortune*, Dec. 28, 2016. In the view of some especially insistent critics, the tech giants had banished private contemplation and autonomous thought. See Franklin Foer, *World Without Mind: The Existential Threat of Big Tech* (New York: Penguin Press, 2017).
3. Carreyrou, *Bad Blood*, 16.
4. William Alden, "How Zenefits Crashed Back Down to Earth," *BuzzFeed*, Feb. 18, 2016.
5. William Alden, "Startup Zenefits Under Scrutiny For Flouting Insurance Laws," BuzzFeed, Sept. 25, 2015.
6. Rolfe Winkler, "Zenefits Touts New Software in Turnaround Effort," *Wall Street Journal*, Oct. 18, 2016.
7. Wondery, "WeCrashed: The Rise and Fall of WeWork | Episode 1: In the Beginning There Was Adam," Jan. 30, 2020, YouTube, youtube.com/watch?v=pJSgJpcx1JE.
8. Dunlevie recalled, "We don't do real estate, but we did WeWork because we thought the entrepreneur was so special." Dunlevie, interviews by the author, May 15, 2019, and Oct. 12, 2020.
9. David Benoit, Maureen Farrell, and Eliot Brown, "WeWork Is a Mess for JPMorgan. Jamie Dimon Is Cleaning It Up," *Wall Street Journal*, Sept. 24, 2019.
10. Benoit, Farrell, and Brown, "WeWork Is a Mess for JPMorgan. Jamie Dimon Is Cleaning It Up."
11. Eric Platt et al., "WeWork Turmoil Puts Spotlight on JPMorgan Chase and Goldman Sachs," *Financial Times*, Sept. 24, 2019.
12. Dunlevie, author interviews.
13. By October 2015, nine of the ten most highly valued venture-backed private tech companies in the United States had instituted dual-class shares. See Alfred Lee, "Inside Private Tech Voting Structures," *Information*, Oct. 29, 2015.
14. JPMorgan owned a larger stake in WeWork than the other investment banks. Benchmark owned almost twice as many shares as JPMorgan. But with Neumann himself as the largest shareholder, Benchmark could not overrule him unless it got JPMorgan and the other banks on its side. After Neumann acquired super-voting stock, his position became impregnable. Ahead of the planned IPO, his voting rights were increased again, from ten votes per share to twenty.
15. Eliot Brown, "WeWork's CEO Makes Millions as Landlord to WeWork," *Wall Street Journal*, Jan. 16, 2019.
16. Rather than vetoing his self-dealing proposals, the board set up a process to vet them and, ultimately, approve them.
17. Brown, "WeWork's CEO Makes Millions as Landlord to WeWork."
18. Brown, "WeWork's CEO Makes Millions as Landlord to WeWork."
19. Nitasha Tiku, "WeWork Used These Documents to Convince Investors It's Worth Billions," *BuzzFeed*, Oct. 9, 2015.
20. WeWork hoped to attract additional customers by allowing them to use WeWork sites around the world when they traveled on business. However, this form of network effect was comparable to that of a global hotel chain with a loyalty program; it was not a tech-style network effect.
21. Maureen Farrell and Eliot Brown, "The Money Men Who Enabled Adam Neumann and the WeWork Debacle," *Wall Street Journal*, Dec. 14, 2019.
22. Farrell and Brown, "Money Men Who Enabled Adam Neumann and the WeWork Debacle."
23. Before the launch of the Vision Fund, the largest venture fund had been raised in 2015 by New Enterprise Associates.
24. Michael Moritz, email to Sequoia leaders, Sept. 17, 2017.
25. Steven Bertoni, "WeWork's $20 Billion Office Party: The Crazy Bet That Could Change How the World Does Business," *Forbes*, Oct. 24, 2017.
26. Bertoni, "WeWork's $20 Billion Office Party."
27. Amy Chozick, "Adam Neumann and the Art of Failing Up," *New York Times*, Nov. 2, 2019.
28. Farrell and Brown, "Money Men Who Enabled Adam Neumann and the WeWork Debacle."

29. The value of this downside protection soon became evident. In the spring of 2020, SoftBank's earnings report indicated that WeWork's value had collapsed from a peak of $47 billion to $2.9 billion.

30. Randall Stross, *eBoys: The First Inside Account of Venture Capitalists at Work* (New York: Ballantine Books, 2001), 233–34.

31. Stross, *eBoys*, 239.

32. Arthur also mentioned "customer groove in"—the tendency of customers to stick to a service once they had mastered it. See W. Brian Arthur, "Increasing Returns and the New World of Business," *Harvard Business Review*, July–Aug. 1996.

33. Of course, the 90 percent penetration meant that the San Francisco rep was chasing a small number of residual targets. But this disadvantage was swamped by the strong local network effect. Gurley, interview by the author, May 16, 2019.

34. Gurley, author interview.

35. Gurley, author interview. Gurley had also considered investing in a taxi marketplace called Cabulous.

36. Benchmark bought $11 million of primary stock, but it also paid $1 million for secondary stock sold by Garrett Camp, Kalanick's co-founder. The total was $12 million at a post-money valuation of $60 million. Gurley, author interview.

37. Gurley, author interview.

38. The friend was Mark Cuban. Gurley, author interview.

39. Gurley, author interview.

40. Michael Arrington, "SGN Founder's Rambling, Jetlagged, Semi-lucid, and Beautiful Email on Entrepreneurism," *TechCrunch*, Sept. 27, 2008.

41. Arrington, "SGN Founder's Rambling."

42. Kalanick thought a16z was offering $300 million on a "pre-money" basis. Benchmark had invested at a post-money valuation of $60 million. Comparing the post-money value after the Series A with the pre-money value in the Series B is the best way to gauge the multiple created by the company in the interim.

43. Pishevar, interview by the author, April 13, 2019.

44. Pishevar, author interview.

45. Pishevar, author interview.

46. Kalanick's friend was Michael Robertson; the two knew each other from a previous startup. See Brad Stone, *The Upstarts: How Uber, Airbnb, and the Killer Companies of the New Silicon Valley Are Changing the World* (New York: Little, Brown, 2017), 173–74.

47. Pishevar, author interview.

48. Mike Isaac, *Super Pumped: The Battle for Uber* (New York: W. W. Norton, 2019), 193.

49. Stone, *Upstarts*, 200–4.

50. Matthew Lynley, "Hailo Raises $30.6 Million, Looks to Digitize New York's Cabs," *Wall Street Journal*, Feb. 5, 2013.

51. Gurley, author interview.

52. Gurley, author interview.

53. Gurley, author interview.

54. Aswath Damodaran, "Uber Isn't Worth $17 Billion," *FiveThirtyEight*, June 18, 2014.

55. The angel investor was Rob Hayes. In addition, the angel investor Chris Sacca was told to stop attending board meetings as an observer.

56. Sarah Lacy, "The Horrific Trickle Down of Asshole Culture: Why I've Just Deleted Uber from my Phone," *Pando*, Oct. 22, 2014.

57. Ben Smith, "Uber Executive Suggests Digging Up Dirt on Journalists," *BuzzFeed*, Nov. 17, 2014.

58. Isaac, *Super Pumped*, 122–25.

59. The super-voting rights left Kalanick with about 16 percent of the votes. His co-founders, seed investors, a few employees, and the Series A and B investors excluding Benchmark controlled another 59 percent. See pie chart in Alfred Lee, "Uber Voting Change Proposal Could Face More Hurdles," *Information*, Oct. 2, 2017.

60. Bill Gurley, "Investors Beware: Today's $100M+ Late-Stage Private Rounds Are Very Different from an IPO," *Above the Crowd*, Feb. 25, 2015.

61. Although Gurley didn't cite the numbers, they supported his claim. In the decade leading up to 2015, valuations at all investment stages had risen: the median value in Series A, B, and C deals had roughly doubled. But the late-stage investment rounds were frothiest, as Gurley said; their median value had more than tripled. After Gurley warned of a bubble in 2015, the median val-

uation in Series D rounds or later fell in 2016 and 2017, confirming his sense that unicorns had been overvalued. Subsequently, in 2018 and 2019, late-stage valuations rose more dramatically than ever, reflecting Masayoshi Son's huge and reckless influence. The ratios given here are calculated from data provided to the author by the investment adviser Cambridge Associates.

62. For example, a marketplace company might highlight the total sum of payments flowing through its platform, failing to note that at least 80 percent of this cash went to the outside businesses that supplied the goods or services.

63. Ironically, Didi was a formidable rival because it was itself the product of a Valley-style merger, engineered by shareholders including SoftBank and Yuri Milner.

64. As well as enjoying liquidation preferences, late-stage investors might extract promises of free additional stock grants (so-called PIK dividends) or a guaranteed payout in the event of an IPO. Again, the effect was to reduce the risk they shouldered and encourage them to press for more ambition.

65. Bill Gurley, "On the Road to Recap: Why the Unicorn Financing Market Just Became Dangerous . . . for All Involved," *Above the Crowd*, April 21, 2016.

66. "Having billions more on the balance sheet just meant we were going to keep spending." Gurley, author interview.

67. Gurley, author interview.

68. Gurley, author interview.

69. According to Crunchbase, Didi raised money at a $23.5 billion pre-money valuation in June 2016 and again at a $33.6 billion pre-money valuation in September, after swallowing Uber China. Uber's 18 percent stake would have been worth something close to the $6 billion implied by the second number. Uber sold some of its stake in Didi in September 2020, when it was valued at $6.3 billion.

70. Unlike in the case of WeWork, where Benchmark got lucky with SoftBank's willingness to buy some of its stake, Gurley had not had the opportunity to sell a single share in Uber.

71. Sheelah Kolhatkar, "At Uber, a New C.E.O. Shifts Gears," *New Yorker*, March 30, 2018.

72. Gurley, author interview.

73. Mike Isaac, "How Uber Deceives the Authorities Worldwide," *New York Times*, March 3, 2017. Uber's general counsel had determined that Greyball could go ahead because there were no specific laws against ride hailing in Philadelphia, where the program was first used. However, when Greyball became publicly known, Uber discontinued its use and the Department of Justice opened a criminal probe.

74. Gurley, author interview.

75. Kolhatkar, "At Uber, A New C.E.O. Shifts Gears."

76. Isaac, *Super Pumped*, 279.

77. Isaac, *Super Pumped*, 290–91.

78. Jessica E. Lessin, Serena Saitto, and Amir Efrati, "At $45 Billion Price, SoftBank Talks Enflame Uber Tensions," *Information*, Aug. 4, 2017.

79. A spokesman for Kalanick denied the allegations in the suit, saying, "The lawsuit is completely without merit and riddled with lies and false allegations." Mike Isaac, "Uber Investor Sues Travis Kalanick for Fraud," *New York Times*, August 10, 2017.

80. *Benchmark Capital Partners VII, L.P., v. Travis Kalanick and Uber Technologies, Inc.* (2017), online .wsj.com/public/resources/documents/BenchmarkUberComplaint08102017.PDF.

81. Press reports portray Khosrowshahi and Goldman Sachs as the lead architects of this reshuffle. But the idea of eliminating super-voting powers had been developed by Benchmark's lawyers during the preparation for the Chicago ultimatum, before Khosrowshahi was recruited. See Isaac, *Super Pumped*, 289.

82. Alfred Lee, "Uber Voting Change Proposals Could Face More Hurdles," *Information*, Oct. 2, 2017.

83. Charles Duhigg, "How Venture Capitalists Are Deforming Capitalism," *New Yorker*, Nov. 30, 2020.

84. SoftBank itself provided $33.1 billion to the Vision Fund. Saudi Arabia provided $45 billion, Abu Dhabi $15 billion. A handful of tech companies invested a combined $5.5 billion, but $3.4 billion of that came in the form of debt-like preferred equity.

85. Michael Ewens and Joan Farre-Mensa, "The Deregulation of the Private Equity Markets and the Decline in IPOs," *Review of Financial Studies* 33, no. 12 (Dec. 2020): 5463–509.

86. Heather Somerville, "Toyota to Invest $500 Million in Uber for Self-Driving Cars," Reuters, Aug. 27, 2018.

87. Sam Nussey, "SoftBank's Son Admits Mistakes After Vision Fund's $8.9 Billion Loss," Reuters, Nov. 6, 2019.

88. Arash Massoudi and Kana Inagaki, "SoftBank Imposes New Standards to Rein In Start-Up Founders," *Financial Times*, Nov. 4, 2019.

89. The number covers venture-backed IPOs of U.S.-headquartered companies. The previous record had been set in 2019. It was $24 billion. In 2016 it was just $5 billion. Jay Ritter, "Initial Public Offerings," Feb. 1, 2020, table 4d (updated), site.warrington.ufl.edu/ritter/files/IPO-Statistics.pdf.

CONCLUSION: LUCK, SKILL, AND THE COMPETITION AMONG NATIONS

1. Tim Sullivan, "That Hit Song You Love Was a Total Fluke," *Harvard Business Review*, Nov. 1, 2013, hbr.org/2013/11/was-gangnam-style-a-fluke.

2. The venture fund in the ninety-fifth percentile generated a return that was 2.9x the "public-market equivalent," meaning the return from the S&P 500 with dividends reinvested. The seventy-fifth percentile returned 1.3x. The median fund returned 0.95x. These returns are net to limited partners. For a visual presentation, see the appendix. Data from Steven N. Kaplan of the University of Chicago.

3. For an excellent exploration of feedback loops in startup firms, see David Easley and Jon Kleinberg, *Networks, Crowds, and Markets: Reasoning About a Highly Connected World* (New York: Cambridge University Press, 2010), 549–50.

4. Ramana Nanda, Sampsa Samila, and Olav Sorenson, "The Persistent Effect of Initial Success: Evidence from Venture Capital" (working paper 24887, National Bureau of Economic Research, 2018), nber.org/papers/w24887.pdf.

5. Further, the NBER authors report that half of the 1.6 percentage point increase can be explained by factors other than path dependency. VC partnerships tend to specialize in particular technologies or industries and particular investment stages. If a sector or stage is profitable when the VC firm launches, it may remain profitable for some years, which explains part of the serial correlation in VC performance. This is distinct from the brand and deal-access advantages associated with path dependency. Paul A. Gompers et al., "How Do Venture Capitalists Make Decisions?," *Journal of Financial Economics* 135, no. 1 (Jan. 2020): 169–90.

6. The study looked at the top hundred deals each year between 1995 and 2012. In the average year, new and emerging venture partnerships captured half the value. Cambridge Associates, "Venture Capital Disrupts Itself: Breaking the Concentration Curse," 2015.

7. The value of venture-capital coaching is affirmed in Morten Sørensen, "How Smart Is Smart Money? A Two-Sided Matching Model of Venture Capital," *Journal of Finance* 62, no. 6 (Dec. 2007): 2725–62, and Yael V. Hochberg, Alexander Ljungqvist, and Yang Lu, "Whom You Know Matters: Venture Capital Networks and Investment Performance," *Journal of Finance* 62, no. 1 (Feb. 2007): 251–301. The value of venture-capital coaching is also affirmed, but only in the case of first-time founders or founders who had previously failed, in Paul Gompers et al., "Skill vs. Luck in Entrepreneurship and Venture Capital: Evidence from Serial Entrepreneurs" (working paper 12592, National Bureau of Economic Research, 2006), nber.org/papers/w12592.

8. Shai Bernstein, Xavier Giroud, and Richard R. Townsend, "The Impact of Venture Capital Monitoring," *Journal of Finance* 71, no. 4 (Aug. 2016): 1591–622.

9. These data refer to gross returns, before subtracting fees, and come from Sand Hill Econometrics. They are cited in Josh Lerner and Ramana Nanda, "Venture Capital's Role in Financing Innovation: What We Know and How Much We Still Need to Learn," *Journal of Economic Perspectives* 34, no. 3 (Summer 2020): 246, pubs.aeaweb.org/doi/pdfplus/10.1257/jep.34.3.237.

10. Cleantech investments both inside and outside the United States earned an annual gross return of just over 21 percent in 2014–2018. In contrast, the gross annual return for 2005–2009 was minus 1.2 percent. Data from Liqian Ma of Cambridge Associates.

11. Data from Sand Hill Econometrics confirms that these examples are representative. In 1992, first-round investors got an average of one-third of the equity. By 2017–2019, the share was a bit less than a fifth.

12. Despite venture capital's supposed unsuitability for green projects, a lot of smart money is betting on the opposite theory. Corporations and billionaire philanthropists have set up venture funds to take stakes in cleantech. They could have channeled money to green research in any form they chose, but they opted to borrow the venture-capital model. The most prominent example is Breakthrough Energy Ventures, launched by Bill Gates. John Doerr is among the board members.

13. Wolfe, interview with the author, Oct. 3, 2017.

14. Lux Capital reported that its returns were in the top quartile for VCs. They were boosted in particular by the spectacular sale of the medical robotics company Auris.

15. Between inception in 2000 and early 2018, Flagship Pioneering and its portfolio companies conducted more than fifty clinical trials for novel therapies and patented more than five hundred inventions. The firm reported that its internal rate of return on funds raised between 2007 and 2015 was 35 percent. See Hong Luo, Gary P. Pisano, Huafeng Yu, "Institutional Entrepreneurship: Flagship Pioneering," Harvard Business School case study, 9-718-484, April 26, 2018.

16. NVCA-Deloitte Human Capital Survey, 3rd ed., March 2021, fig. 1.

17. The data on women in the law are from the U.S. Census Bureau. See Jennifer Cheeseman Day, "More Than 1 in 3 Lawyers Are Women," U.S. Census Bureau, May 8, 2018, census.gov/library/stories/2018/05/women-lawyers.html. For women in medicine, see "Active Physicians by Sex and Specialty, 2017," Association of American Medical Colleges, aamc.org/data-reports/workforce/interactive-data/active-physicians-sex-and-specialty-2017. It should be said that women account for only 17 percent of senior positions in investment banking, a share virtually the same as in venture. For women in banking, see Julia Boorstin, "Survey: It's Still Tough to Be a Woman on Wall Street—but Men Don't Always Notice," CNBC, June 26, 2018, cnbc.com/2018/06/25/surveyon-wall-street-workplace-biases-persist---but-men-dont-see-t.html.

18. Pam Kostka, "More Women Became VC Partners Than Ever Before in 2019 but 65% of Venture Firms Still Have Zero Female Partners," Medium, Feb. 7, 2020, link.medium.com/RLcsLvmNxbb.

19. Will Gornall and Ilya A. Strebulaev, "Gender, Race, and Entrepreneurship: A Randomized Field Experiment on Venture Capitalists and Angels" (working paper, 2020), 1.

20. "The US VC Female Founders Dashboard," PitchBook, Feb. 28, 2019, pitchbook.com/news/articles/the-vc-female-founders-dashboard.

21. Asians make up 6 percent of the labor force according to a 2018 report by the U.S. Bureau of Labor Statistics. See "Labor Force Characteristics by Race and Ethnicity, 2018," BLS Reports, Oct. 2019. Data on percentage of Asian VCs is from NVCA-Deloitte, fig. 2.

22. NVCA-Deloitte Human Capital Survey, 3rd ed., March 2021, fig. 2. See also Richard Kerby, "Where Did You Go to School?," The Journal Blog, July 30, 2018. Funding for Black entrepreneurs refers to 2020 and comes from Crunchbase.

23. "Financial manager" is a term used by the Census Bureau to refer to workers who create "financial reports, direct investment activities, and develop plans for the long-term financial goals of their organization." There are 697,000 in the United States, with a median salary of $130,000 per year. See "Labor Force Statistics from the Current Population Survey," U.S. Bureau of Labor Statistics, last modified Jan. 22, 2020, bls.gov/cps/cpsaat11.htm.

24. Data on Hispanics in VC from NVCA-Deloitte, fig. 3. On Hispanics in the labor market, see U.S. Bureau of Labor Statistics, "Labor Force Statistics from the Current Population Survey."

25. Lisa Cook and Jan Gerson, "The Implications of U.S. Gender and Racial Disparities in Income and Wealth Inequality at Each Stage of the Innovation Process," Washington Center for Equitable Growth, July 24, 2019.

26. "Introducing the Talent x Opportunity Fund," Andreessen Horowitz, June 3, 2020, a16z.com/2020/06/03/talent-x-opportunity.

27. Paul A. Gompers and Sophie Calder-Wang, "Diversity in Innovation" (working paper 17-067, Harvard Business School, 2017), 67. Some accounts make VC elitism sound even more pronounced. On one reckoning, 40 percent of VCs attended either Harvard or Stanford, a verdict presumably reached by counting attendance at either graduate or undergraduate study. See Kerby, "Where Did You Go to School?"

28. Tim Sullivan, "Blitzscaling," Harvard Business Review, April 2016, hbr.org/2016/04/blitzscaling.

29. Eric Johnson, "'Venture Capital Money Kills More Businesses Than It Helps,' Says Basecamp CEO Jason Fried," Vox, Jan. 23, 2019.

30. Tim O'Reilly, "The Fundamental Problem with Silicon Valley's Favorite Growth Strategy," Quartz, Feb. 5, 2019. O'Reilly was echoing a criticism of VC that goes back at least to the 1990s. When John Doerr funded GO, the handheld computer venture that was a concept without a technology, his critics denounced the attitude of "go big or go home"; with less ambition and more patience, GO could perhaps have made it.

31. Erin Griffith, "More Start-Ups Have an Unfamiliar Message for Venture Capitalists: Get Lost," New York Times, Jan. 11, 2019.

32. Martin Kenney and John Zysman, "Unicorns, Cheshire Cats, and the New Dilemmas of Entrepreneurial Finance," Venture Capital: An International Journal of Entrepreneurial Finance 21, no. 1 (2019): 39.

33. O'Reilly, "The Fundamental Problem with Silicon Valley's Favorite Growth Strategy."

34. Manju Puri and Rebecca Zarutskie, "On the Life Cycle Dynamics of Venture-Capital- and Non-Venture-Capital-Financed Firms," *Journal of Finance* 67, no. 6 (Dec. 2012): 2248.
35. Lerner and Nanda, "Venture Capital's Role in Financing Innovation," 240.
36. On the causal link between venture investments and patent filings, see Samuel Kortum and Josh Lerner, "Assessing the Impact of Venture Capital on Innovation," *Rand Journal of Economics* 31, no 4 (2000): 674–92. On the quality of VC-funded patents, see Sabrina Howell et al., "Financial Distancing: How Venture Capital Follows the Economy Down and Curtails Innovation" (working paper 20-115, Harvard Business School, 2020), 4, ssrn.com/abstract=3594239. The authors note that VC-backed firms are disproportionately likely to have more original patents, more general patents, and patents more closely related to fundamental science.
37. Author calculation based on table 4 in Jay Ritter, "Initial Public Offerings: Updated Statistics," site.warrington.ufl.edu/ritter/files/IPO-Statistics.pdf. In addition, VC-backed companies accounted for a rising share of U.S. employment. In the period from 1981 to 1985, their share was between 2.7 and 2.8 percent. By 1996–2000, this had risen to between 4.2 and 6.8 percent. By 2001–2005, it had risen again, to between 5.3 and 7.3 percent. See Puri and Zarutskie, "On the Life Cycle Dynamics of Venture-Capital- and Non-Venture-Capital-Financed Firms," 2256. Further, data from Sand Hill Econometrics indicates that the value of VC-backed U.S. firms as a percentage of the value of U.S. public companies rose from 0.5 percent in 1992 to 6 percent at the start of 2000.
38. Between 1995 and 2018, intangible assets rose from 68 percent to 84 percent of the enterprise value of companies in the S&P 500. See Jason Thomas, *Global Insights: When the Future Arrives Early*, Carlyle Group, Sept. 2020, carlyle.com/sites/default/files/Global%20Insights_When%20The%20Future%20Arrives_Sept_2020.pdf.
39. Jonathan Haskel and Stian Westlake, *Capitalism Without Capital: The Rise of the Intangible Economy* (Princeton, N.J.: Princeton University Press, 2017), 68.
40. Counting U.S. venture partners with at least one startup board seat at the fifty largest firms, 69 percent were based in the Bay Area, while just 11 percent were based in New York, with another 11 percent in Boston. (Lerner and Nanda, "Venture Capital's Role in Financing Innovation.") Likewise, the Valley has generated seventeen of the twenty-two American companies ever to have attained a private valuation of more than $10 billion. (Kyle Stanford, "The Bay Area Still Holds the Keys to VC," PitchBook *Analyst Note*, Feb. 26, 2021.) For data on the regional distribution of VC fundraising, see appendix.
41. Joe Lonsdale, "California, Love It and Leave It," *Wall Street Journal*, Nov. 15, 2020.
42. William R. Kerr and Frederic Robert-Nicoud, "Tech Clusters," *Journal of Economic Perspectives* 34, no. 3 (Summer 2020): 57.
43. Data on VC in Europe from Gené Teare and Sophia Kunthara, "European Venture Report: VC Dollars Rise in 2019," *Crunchbase*, Jan. 14, 2020.
44. Lerner and Nanda, "Venture Capital's Role in Financing Innovation."
45. In addition, critics object that startups leverage taxpayer-backed fundamental science so the resulting bonanzas for founders raise questions about fairness. But governments support R&D precisely in the hope that the private sector will use it to drive economic progress. Given the contribution of venture capitalists to growth and innovation, they are generating future tax payments that offset the assistance they get from government research.
46. In 2018, a global assessment by Tsinghua University found that China led the world in AI research papers, AI patents, and AI venture-capital investments. Moreover, Chinese startups' push into AI was encouraged by the Chinese state. In July 2017, China's State Council issued the *New Generation Artificial Intelligence Development Plan*. "AI is . . . a major strategy to enhance national competitiveness and protect national security," it stated. Gregory C. Allen, "Understanding China's AI Strategy," Center for a New American Security, Feb. 6, 2019.
47. "Life Is Getting Harder for Foreign VCs in China," *Economist*, Jan. 9, 2020.
48. DJI's software development has been carried out partly in Palo Alto by a staff consisting mainly of U.S. citizens.
49. Allen, "Understanding China's AI Strategy."
50. Meg Murphy, "MIT-SenseTime Alliance Funds Projects from All Five Schools," *MIT News*, Aug. 24, 2018.
51. In 2015 the combined R&D budgets of the top four defense contractors were only 27 percent of Google's R&D spending. *Innovation and National Security: Keeping Our Edge*, Independent Task Force Reports (New York: Council on Foreign Relations, 2019), cfr.org/report/keeping-our-edge/pdf/TFR_Innovation_Strat egy.pdf.

52. Lance Noble, "Paying for Industrial Policy," GavekalDragonomics, Dec. 4, 2018. See also Josh Lerner, *Boulevard of Broken Dreams: Why Public Efforts to Boost Entrepreneurship and Venture Capital Have Failed—and What to Do About It* (repr., Princeton, N.J.: Princeton University Press, 2012), 32.

53. Lerner, *Boulevard of Broken Dreams,* 123, 155–57. I am also grateful to Fiona Darmon of the Israeli venture group JVP for explaining the Israeli venture scene. Darmon, interview by the author, April 17, 2017.

54. Lerner, *Boulevard of Broken Dreams,* 124.

55. Lerner, *Boulevard of Broken Dreams,* 123.

56. A 2010 survey of twenty-five countries found that small subsidies could help startups but larger amounts were associated with a diminution in their prospects. See James Brander, Qianqian Du, and Thomas F. Hellman, "The Effects of Government-Sponsored Venture Capital: International Evidence" (NBER Working Paper Series, working paper 16521). For further evidence from fourteen European countries, see Marco Da Rin, Giovanna Nicodano, and Alessandro Sembenelli, "Public Policy and the Creation of Active Capital Markets," *Journal of Public Economics* 80, no. 8–9 (2006): 1699–723.

57. In Canada in the 1990s, an attempt to subsidize venture investments by the "little guy" created slush funds for labor unions and their allies. (Lerner, *Boulevard of Broken Dreams,* 119–22.) In Australia, the government backed eleven startup incubators, only to find that the incubator managers siphoned off much of the money. (Ibid., 11.) On the failure of Germany's public venture fund WFG, see Noble, "Paying for Industrial Policy." In several other cases, the strings attached to venture subsidies—that they should be focused on "pre-commercial" projects or on struggling regions—have fatally complicated the already difficult job of picking winners.

58. Robert E. Hall and Susan E. Woodward, "The Burden of the Non-diversifiable Risk of Entrepreneurship," *American Economic Review* 100 (June 2010): 1163–94.

59. These details are taken from an online guide published by the VC partnership Index Ventures. See Index Ventures, "Rewarding Talent: The Guide to Stock Options."

60. Data from the Rhodium Group.

61. I owe this formulation to colleagues at the Council on Foreign Relations. See *Innovation and National Security.*

62. Data are from the OECD and refer to national (not just government) expenditure. OECD, "Gross Domestic Spending on R&D (Indicator)" (2021), doi:10.1787/d8b068b4-en.

63. "China's Rulers Want More Control of Big Tech," *Economist,* April 10, 2021.

64. Stephens, interview by the author, March 29, 2019.

Timeline

1946 The Rockefeller and Whitney families launch experiments with venture capital.

1946 Georges Doriot establishes American Research and Development, a publicly listed venture vehicle.

1957 Reid Dennis forms "the Group," a club of San Francisco brokers that backs technology startups.

1957 Arthur Rock finances the "Traitorous Eight," creating Fairchild Semiconductor and kick-starting the West Coast chip industry.

1958 The U.S. federal government begins to subsidize venture funds known as Small Business Investment Companies.

1961 Arthur Rock quits New York to establish the first successful equity-only, time-limited venture partnership, Davis & Rock.

1962 In a speech in San Francisco, Rock explains that venture portfolios need grand slams to "average out the goofs."

1968 Davis & Rock rewards its backers with a return of more than 22x, outperforming both Warren Buffett and the hedge-fund pioneer Alfred Winslow Jones.

1968 Rock finances Intel, helping two members of the Traitorous Eight repeat the defection of 1957.

1972 American Research and Development closes, signaling the triumph of Rock's West Coast venture model.

1972 Don Valentine, a veteran of Fairchild Semiconductor, establishes Sequoia Capital.

1972 Eugene Kleiner, a member of the Traitorous Eight, teams up with Hewlett-Packard executive Tom Perkins to found Kleiner Perkins.

1973 Sutter Hill pairs the inventor of the electronic printing wheel with a strong outside CEO, establishing the "Qume model."

1974 Valentine backs Atari, showing how a hands-on venture capitalist can turn a chaotic company into a winner.

1974 Kleiner Perkins "incubates" Tandem Computers in-house before spinning it out as a startup.

1976 Kleiner Perkins backs Genentech, building it into a success through the device of stage-by-stage financing.

1977 After multiple rejections, Apple secures financing, proving that a network of VCs is superior to a few individuals.

1977 Dick Kramlich and two East Coast partners establish New Enterprise Associates.

1980 Apple and Genentech stage dramatically successful IPOs, anticipating later tech euphoria.

1981 Bob Metcalfe strives to raise venture finance on the East Coast but ends up with West Coast backers, a testimony to the strength of Valley venture capitalists.

1983 Arthur Patterson and Jim Swartz found Accel Capital, the first VC fund to specialize in particular industries.

1983 Following favorable tax and regulatory reforms, U.S. venture funds report assets under management of $12 billion, quadruple the sum of six years earlier.

1987 Sequoia backs Cisco and overhauls its management, ultimately generating the partnership's first gain of $100 million from a single investment.

1993 After running on the fumes of John Doerr's charisma, GO fails without dampening Doerr's appetite for "go big or go home" moon shots.

1993 Israel creates the Yozma Group, a successful government program to promote venture capital.

1993 Accel, NEA, and Menlo Ventures back UUNET, turning the government-run internet into a mass medium.

1994 Kleiner Perkins backs Netscape, transforming the online experience.

1995 Michael Moritz of Sequoia backs Yahoo, emerging as the leader of his firm and later of the venture industry.

1996 Masayoshi Son of SoftBank invests $100 million in Yahoo, heralding the rise of "growth investing" and earning the enmity of Moritz.

1996 John Doerr backs Amazon, signaling his status as the Valley's top internet investor.

1997 Bob Kagle of Benchmark backs eBay, ultimately generating a profit of $5 billion and demonstrating the power of Benchmark's small-is-beautiful model.

1998 Sergey Brin and Larry Page raise $1 million without talking to VCs, heralding the rise of angel investing.

1999 Google dictates funding terms to Kleiner Perkins and Sequoia, demonstrating the leverage of software founders.

1999 Shirley Lin of Goldman Sachs finances Alibaba, equipping it with stock options that enable its take-off.

2000 New capital commitments to U.S. VC funds hit a peak of $104 billion.

2000 Masayoshi Son follows Goldman Sachs into Alibaba, ultimately making up for his vast losses in the U.S. tech bust.

2003 Tiger Global becomes the first hedge fund to raise a dedicated pool of capital for private tech investments.

2004 Google goes public using a dual-class share structure, preserving founder control and setting a precedent for later IPOs that disempower shareholders.

2004 Kleiner Perkins embarks on a troubled experiment with cleantech.

2005 Peter Thiel launches Founders Fund, differentiating himself from traditional VCs by deferring to founders.

2005 Paul Graham and Jessica Livingston establish Y Combinator, creating a new model for startup incubators.

2005 Kathy Xu founds Capital Today, the first successful Chinese-run but western-style VC firm.

2005 Accel finances Facebook, proving the power of teamwork within venture partnerships.

2005 Sequoia recruits Neil Shen and launches Sequoia China.

2009 Yuri Milner makes a growth investment in Facebook, offering tech founders a way of delaying IPOs.

2009 Marc Andreessen and Ben Horowitz form a venture partnership, quickly becoming industry leaders.

2010 Sequoia China backs Meituan, which later surpasses Google as the most profitable bet in Sequoia's history.

2010 Vinod Khosla finances Impossible Foods, heralding a new and more successful wave of cleantech investments.

2012 Ellen Pao sues Kleiner Perkins for discrimination.

2013 As big tech firms increasingly remain private, Aileen Lee coins the term "unicorn."

2017 Masayoshi Son launches his $99 billion Vision Fund.

2017 With Moritz comparing Son to North Korea's dictator, Sequoia responds with an $8 billion growth fund.

2017 China generates more venture returns than the United States.

2017 Building on its success with Palantir and SpaceX, Founders Fund backs a third defense contractor, Anduril.

2018 Benchmark and its allies oust Travis Kalanick, Uber's founder, demonstrating the limits to "founder friendliness."

2019 WeWork's failed IPO demonstrates the dangers of hands-off venture tourists who neglect corporate governance.

2020 The coronavirus pandemic turbocharges the value of VC-backed companies.

2021 China clamps down on its technology sector.

Index